1 MONTH OF
FREE
READING

at

www.ForgottenBooks.com

By purchasing this book you are eligible for one month membership to ForgottenBooks.com, giving you unlimited access to our entire collection of over 1,000,000 titles via our web site and mobile apps.

To claim your free month visit:

www.forgottenbooks.com/free1303520

ISBN 978-0-428-68712-0
PIBN 11303520

HISTORY

OF

A SUIT IN EQUITY,

AS PROSECUTED AND DEFENDED

IN THE

VIRGINIA STATE COURTS

AND IN THE

UNITED STATES CIRCUIT COURTS,

BY

ALEXANDER H. SANDS.

SECOND EDITION.

J. W. RANDOLPH & ENGLISH, Publishers,
RICHMOND, VIRGINIA.
1882.

Copyrighted, 1882.

J. W. Randolph & English.

PRINTED BY
WM. ELLIS JONES,
RICHMOND, VA.

BOUND BY
J. W. RANDOLPH & ENGLISH,
RICHMOND, VA.

TO

JOHN R. COOKE, ESQ.,

The following work is respectfully inscribed as an humble yet sincere tribute to his eminent talents and profound learning as a jurist, and his noble qualities as a man.

April, 1854.

PREFACE TO SECOND EDITION.

In this edition of the Suit in Equity, I have aimed to engraft upon the matter contained in the former whatever there was of value, affecting equity practice, in the United States Supreme Court Reports and in the Reports of the Supreme Court of Appeals of Virginia, published since the first edition.

The arrangement of the work, as originally published, has been preserved, with this exception, that much of the matter found in the Appendix of the first edition has been placed in the body of the present.

The first part of the treatise, embracing the first book, traces the history of a suit in equity from its beginning until the entry of the final decree and its execution. The discussion of Interlocutory matters, Issues out of Chancery, Proceedings before Commissioners, Injunctions, and Bills other than original bills will be found in the second book. In the Appendix, I have placed the Rules of Equity Practice in the United States Circuit Courts, and have treated of the Doctrine of Parties in those courts and of other matters deemed important.

The chapters on Evidence[1] in Equity, pp. 399–501, and on Demurrers, Pleas and Answers, pp. 161–382, have been much enlarged. There seemed to be need for this.

It did not enter into my plan, to attempt a complete discussion of Parties to Suits in Equity in the Virginia State Courts. On that subject, there are many pages, 189–223, for the matter of

---

[1] In this chapter, I have followed Prof. Minor's Summary of matters of which the courts take judicial notice, pp. 407, 408. Prof. M.'s accuracy is well known and I have adopted his work in this particular without fear of mistake.

which I am largely indebted to the 2nd volume of Mr. Robinson's Practice, printed in 1835. I have made such additions from the decisions in the Virginia Supreme Court Reports published since Mr. Robinson's work, as were deemed necessary, pp. 189–223, 749–752. I must not omit to refer the reader to the admirable chapter of Mr. Barton on this topic.

The discussion of the Doctrine of Parties in the United States Circuits Courts, pp. 727–743, is much more full, and this because there was no Virginia treatise devoted to that subject.

It may not be amiss just here to recommend to the younger members of the profession a careful study of the Rules of Practice adopted by the Supreme Court of the United States for the use of the Circuit Courts, pp. 713–726. They were doubtless prepared by able and skilful lawyers, and there are but few rules printed among them which do not disclose to the reader some important matter affecting equity practice, the rule either giving emphasis to a principle already inaugurated in the courts or modifying or repealing it.

For the younger members of the profession especially, I have prepared the matter found on pages 548–571. There they will see a friendly suit for the Sale of Infants' lands traced from the filing of the bill to the final decree, with forms of every step in the proceeding.

Throughout the work, the Code of 1860 is cited as the *Code*, or the *Code of Virginia*. The Code of 1873 is so cited. Perhaps the list of amendments to the Code of 1873, found on pages 745–749, may lighten the labors of many. It has been prepared with no little care and toil, and is believed to be accurate.

ALEXANDER H. SANDS.

RICHMOND, *May 8th, 1882.*

CONTENTS.

BOOK I.

BOOK II.

APPENDIX.

ERRATA.

P. 25, n., 12th line, *3 Mun.* omitted.

P. 45, n., 5th line, should be *" Childers v. Smith."*

P. 51, 21st line, should be " 1865–6."

Pp. 55, 56, n., corrected, pp. 754, 755.

P. 70, 24th line, *petition* should be *partition.*

P. 85, 11th line, *returnable* should be *colorable.*

P. 115, 26th line, *names* should be *parties.*

P. 115, sec. 78, amended. See p. 748, n.

P. 139, sec. 94, amended. See p. 715.

P. 140, sec. 99, amended. See p. 715.

P. 141, sec. 100, amended. See p. 716.

P. 201, 32nd line, *vendee* should be *vendor.*

P. 207, after *connection*, 2nd line from bottom, add the reference, *" Williams vs. Lord & Robinson*, 5th Va. L. J. 243.'

P. 212, 36th line, *bill* should be *deed.*

P. 233, last line, *4 Com.* should be *4 Cowen.*

P. 247, sec. 176; see in connection p. 301.

P. 248, 20th line, *centra proferentem* should be *contra proferentem.*

P. 297, at *appear*, 25th line, refer to p. 261, sec. 205.

P. 401, n. 26, add the reference *" Jones & als. v. Abraham & als.*, 5 Va. L. J., p. 444."

P. 416, 4th line from bottom, *Lilienfield* should be *Lilienfeld.*

P. 430, 6th line from bottom, 328 should be 323.

P. 435, 12th line of note, strike out *not*, in reference to *Borst v. Nalle.*

P. 528, last line, *Randolph* should be *Kinney.*

P. 534, 21st line, *Millers's* should be *Mills's.*

P. 556, 8th line of note, after " 598" add the reference ; " but see *Thompson & als. v. Brooke & als.*, cited *post*, 753n."

P. 595, last line, after " behalf" add clause requiring security for costs already incurred. See p. 456.

P. 643, as 16th line, " See *Adams v. Hubbard*, 25 Grat. 136."

P. 660, 20th line, *Houston* should be *Shriver.*

P. 687, sec. 616, corrected on p. 751, lines 23–25.

P. 696, 5th line, *Hill* should be *Hilb.*

P. 696, note 4, see pp. 758, 759.

PART I.

SUIT IN EQUITY.

BOOK I.

CHAPTER I.

*Of Commencement of Suit in Virginia State Courts:
and of the Rules and Proceedings in the Clerk's
Office in these Courts anterior to filing of Bill or
Information.*

1. In England, it is the practice always to institute suits in equity by first filing the bill or information: a bill, when the claim preferred is on behalf of a subject; an information, when exhibited on behalf of the crown. Here, the practice is somewhat different. Suits in equity are usually begun in the Virginia State courts, by placing with the clerk of the court, in which the suit is instituted, a memorandum setting forth the names of the parties complainant and defendant, and directing a summons[1] to issue, returnable within ninety days after its date, to some rule day, or to the first day of next term of the court. This memorandum, in an ordinary case, is as follows:

---

[1] Formerly the writ used was a *subpœna*. The Code of Virginia has substituted in place of the subpœna the writ of summons.—Chap. 170, sec. 5.

To the Clerk of the —— *Court for the City* (or *County*)
                    of —— :

A. B. and C. D.,   -   -   -   Plaintiffs,
      against
R. H. and J. W.,   -   -   -   Defendants.

Issue summons in chancery to —— rules, (*or,* to the first day of the next term of the court.)

                              G. M., p. q.[2]

2. Upon the filing of this memorandum, the clerk

---

[2] Other forms of *memoranda* are as follows:

Suit by an Infant or Married Woman.

To the clerk, &c.:

A. B., an infant under the age of twenty one years, by John R., his next friend, [or, Julia B., the wife of Robert B., who sues by John R., her next friend,]   -   -   Plt'ff,
      against
James L.,   -   -   Def't.

Issue summons, &c., (as before.)
                              G. M., p. q.

Suit by an Administrator or Executor.

To the clerk, &c. :

A. B., administrator of the goods and chattels of Charles C., [or, A. B., executor of the last will and testament of Charles C.,]   -   Plt'ff,
      against
James L.,   -   -   Def't.

Issue summons, &c., (as before.)
                              G. M., p. q.

Memorandum in Creditor's Suit.

To the clerk, &c. :

A. B., who sues on behalf of himself and such other of the creditors of James R., deceased, as shall come in and contribute to the costs of this suit,   -   -   Plt'ff,
      against
James G., administrator of the goods and chattels of James R., deceased, Def't.

Issue summons, &c., (as before.)
                              G. M., p. q.

issues a summons in conformity to its directions. This summons is as follows :[3]

The Commonwealth of Virginia,
      To the Sheriff of —— county, greeting:

You are hereby commanded to summon R. H. and J. W. to appear at the clerk's office of our circuit court of the city (*or* county) of ——, at the rules to be holden for the said court, on the first Monday, in —— next, to answer a bill in chancery, exhibited against them in the said court by A. B. and C. D. And have then there this writ.

Witness, J. E., clerk of our said court, at ——, the —— day of ——, 18—, and in the —— year of the Commonwealth.

                  J. E., *Clerk.*

3. The summons may be executed on or before the return day by delivering copies to each of the defeudants.[4] It may be served by an officer, or by another person. When served by an officer, his return thereon that "the within summons has been executed by delivering a copy of the same to each of the parties

---

[3] In England, if a defendant be a peer of the realm, or entitled to the privilege of peerage, he has a right, before a subpœna is issued against him, to be informed by letter from the Lord Chancellor of the bill having been filed; this letter is called a letter missive, and must be accompanied by a copy of the bill. Here there is no difference in the character of the process, whatever the office and position the defendant holds.

[4] The service of the summons against husband and wife on husband alone, is ordinarily a good service, the husband being bound to answer for both. *Ferguson* v. *Smith,* 2 John. Ch. Rep. 139; but where the plaintiff is seeking satisfaction out of the separate estate of wife, there should be separate service upon her. Being considered in such case a *feme sole* for other purposes, she is so for this purpose also. *Jones* v. *Harris,* 9 Ves. 497.

defendant" will suffice;[5] when served by another person, an affidavit of the service is required.[6]

4. If a defendant be not found at his usual place of abode, the summons may be executed by delivering a copy, and giving information of its purport to his wife, or to any white person found there, who is a member of his family, and above the age of sixteen years; or, if neither he nor his wife, nor any such white person be found there, the summons may be served by leaving a copy of the summons posted at the front door of his abode.[7]

5. The mode of service of summons upon a corporation is as follows:

" It shall be sufficient to serve any process against, or notice to a corporation, on its mayor, rector, president, or other chief officer, or in his absence from the county or corporation in which he resides, or in which is the principal office of the corporation, against or to which the process or notice is, if it be a city or town, on the president of the council or board of trustees, or in his absence, on the recorder, or any alderman or trustee; and if it be not a city or town, on the cashier or treasurer; and if there be none such, or he be absent, on a member of the board of directors, trustees or visitors. If the case be against a bank of circulation, and be in a county or corporation wherein the bank has a branch, service on the president or cashier of such branch bank shall be sufficient; and if the case be against some other corporation, whether incorporated by the laws of this State or any other State or country transacting business in this State, or any agent

---

[5] See Code of Virginia, chap. 170, sec. 2; chap. 49, sec. 27.

[6] Ibid., chap. 170, sec. 6, and chap. 167, sec. 1.   [7] Ibid., chap. 167, sec.1.

thereof, or any person declared by the laws of this State to be an agent of such corporation; and if there be no such agent in the county or corporation, publication of a copy of the process or notice, as an order is published under the eleventh section of this chapter, shall be sufficient. Service on any person under this section shall be in the county or corporation in which he resides; and the return shall show this, and state on whom and when the service was, otherwise the service shall not be valid."[8]

6. In the clerk's office of every circuit, county and corporation court, the rules are held on the first Monday in every month, except when a term of a circuit court, or a term of a county or corporation court, designated for the trial of civil cases in which juries are required, happens to commence on the first Monday in a month, or either of the two following days, or on the preceding Tuesday, Wednesday, Thursday, Friday or Saturday, in either of which events the rules which otherwise would have been held for said month on the first Monday are held on the last Monday in the preceding month; and when in any county or corporation the said courts commence on the Monday before the first Tuesday of any month, the rules are held on the Monday before the commencement of said courts. The rules may continue three days; but when in any case such continuance interferes with the term of the court for which the rules are held, they do not continue beyond the day preceding the commencement of the term of such court.[9] At the rules, all steps are taken necessary to mature the suit

---

[8] Code. chap. 170, sec. 7; Sess. Acts, 1872-'3, p. 220.

[9] Sess. Acts, 1871-'2, pp. 10, 11.

for the hearing of the court, and it not unfrequently happens that an end is put to a suit in the clerk's office before it has come under the eye of the court.

7. Thus, the plaintiff may dismiss his suit at the rules : or by his neglect he may incur a dismission, or the suit may abate at rules by operation of law : or the defendant may confess a decree in the clerk's office for so much principal and interest as the plaintiff may be willing to accept a decree for.[10]

8. A defendant may appear at the rules, at which the process against him is returnable, or if it be returnable in term, at the first rule day after the return day, and if the bill be not then filed, may give a rule for the plaintiff to file the same.   If the plaintiff fail to file his bill at the succeeding rule day, after a rule has been given him by a party defendant to file it, he will be non-suited.[11]

9. If the plaintiff suffer three months to elapse after the summons is returned executed as to any one or more of the defendants, without filing his bill, the clerk will enter his suit dismissed, although none of the defendants may have appeared.[12]

10. When a summons to answer a bill is against a defendant, whom the officer (receiving it) knows does not reside in his county or corporation, the officer, unless he find him therein before the return day, should return him a non-resident : and if the court has jurisdiction simply on the ground of such defendant's residence in the county or corporation, the suit will abate as to that defendant.[13]

---

[10] Code of Va , chap. 171, sec. 41.

[12] Ibid., chap. 171, sec. 6.

[11] Ibid., chap. 171, sec. 5.

[13] Ibid , chap. 171, sec. 7.

CHAPTER II.

Of the several kinds of Bills; of the matter and form of Bills, and of Informations.

SEVERAL KINDS OF BILLS.

11. The several kinds of bills have been usually considered as capable of being arranged under three general heads. *First.* Original bills, which relate to some matter not before litigated in the court by the same persons standing in the same interests. *Second.* Bills not original, which are either an addition to, or a continuance of, an original bill, or both. *Third.* Bills, which though occasioned by, or seeking the benefit of a former bill, or of a decision made upon it, or attempting to obtain a reversal of a decision, are not considered as a continuance of the former bill, but in the nature of original bills. And though this arrangement is not perhaps the most perfect, yet, as it is nearly just, and has been very generally adopted in argument, and in the books of reports and of practice, it will be convenient to treat of the different kinds of bills with reference to it.

12. *First.* A bill may pray relief against an injury suffered, or only seek the assistance of the court, to enable the plaintiff to defend himself against a possible future injury, or to support or defend a suit in a court of ordinary jurisdiction. Original bills

have, therefore, been divided into bills praying relief, and bills not praying relief. An original bill praying relief may be, 1. A bill praying the decree or order of the court touching some right claimed by the person exhibiting the bill, in opposition to some right claimed by the person against whom the bill is exhibited. 2. A bill of interpleader, where the person exhibiting the bill claims no right in opposition to the rights claimed by the person against whom the bill is exhibited, but prays the decree of the court touching the rights of those persons, for the safety of the person exhibiting the bill. 3. A bill praying the writ of certiorari[1] to remove a cause from an inferior court of equity. An original bill not praying relief may be, 1. A bill to perpetuate the testimony of witnesses. 2. A bill for discovery of facts resting within the knowledge of the person against whom the bill is exhibited, or of deeds, writings, or other things in his custody or power.

13. *Second.* A suit imperfect in its frame, or become so by accident before its end has been obtained, may, in many cases, be rendered perfect by a new bill, which is not considered as an original bill, but merely as an addition to, or a continuance of, the former bill, or both. A bill of this kind may be, 1. A supplemental bill, which is merely an addition to the original bill. 2. A bill of revivor, which is a continuance of the original bill, when by death some party to it has become incapable of prosecuting or defending a suit, or a female plaintiff has by mar-

---

[1] This bill is rarely if ever used in America, and is not of very frequent occurrence in England.

riage incapacited herself from suing alone.[2] 3. A bill both of revivor and supplement, which continues a suit upon an abatement, and supplies defects arisen from some event subsequent to the institution of the suit.

14. *Third.* Bills for the purposes of cross litigation of matters already depending before the court, of controverting, suspending, avoiding, or carrying into execution a judgment of the court, or of obtaining the benefit of a suit, which the plaintiff is not entitled to add to, or continue, for the purpose of supplying any defects in it, have been generally considered under the head of bills in the nature of original bills, though occasioned by, or seeking the benefit of, former bills; and may be, 1. A cross bill exhibited by the defeudant in a former bill against the plaintiff in the same bill, touching some matter in litigation in the first bill. 2. A bill of review to examine and reverse a decree made upon a former bill. 3. A bill in the nature of a bill of review, brought by the person not bound by the former decree. 4. A bill to impeach a decree upon the ground of fraud. 5. A bill to suspend the operation of a decree on special circumstances, or to avoid it on the ground of matter arisen subsequent to it. 6. A bill to carry a decree made in a former suit into execution. 7. A bill in the nature of a bill of revivor, to obtain the benefit of a

---

[2] Bills of revivor simply are very rare in Virginia. Suits are revived here by the writ of *scire facias*, when the party who dies, or, if a female who marries is a defendant; when the party who dies, or female marrying is a plaintiff, the person or persons for whom a *scire facias* might be sued out may, without notice or *scire facias*, move that the suit proceed in his or their name.—See Code of Virginia, chap. 173, sec. 4.

suit after abatement in certain cases which do n<
admit of a continuance of the original bill. 8. .
bill in the nature of a supplemental bill, to obtain tl
benefit of a suit, either after abatement in other cas<
which do not admit of a continuance of the origin:
bill, or after the suit is become defective withou
abatement in cases which do not admit of a suppl<
mental bill to supply that defect.₃

MATTER OF BILL.

15. Every bill should state the right, title or clai:
of the plaintiff with accuracy and clearness, an
should in like manner state the injury or grievan<
of which he complains, and the relief which he asl
of the court.₄

16. Every fact essential to the plaintiff's title :
maintain the bill and obtain the relief must be stat<
in the bill, otherwise the defect will be fatal; no fac
are properly in issue unless charged in the bill.₅ :
is certainly true, that the most liberal spirit whi<
always inclines courts of equity to get over form :
favor of substance, has often enabled them to g
over objections upon the ground of variance betwe<
the case stated and the case proved. *Carr*, J.
Zane's devisees v. *Zane*, 6 Mun. 416.₆ Yet while, :
Roane J. remarked in *Mayo* v. *Murchie*, 3 Mu
384, " a rigid and technical construction of bills
exploded," the good sense of pleading and tl
language of the books both require that every m

₃ The foregoing part of this chapter has, with some modifications, been tal
from the text of Lord Redesdale.

₄ Story's Eq. Plea. 284.   ₅ Ibid., 295; 4 Munf. 273; 5 Leigh 141

₆ See also *Taylor, adm'or of Holloway* v. *Bruce*, Gilm. 75.

terial allegation should be put in issue by the pleadings, so that the parties may be duly apprized of the essential enquiry, and may be enabled to collect testimony in order to meet it. *Kent*, C. J. in *James* v. *McKernon*, 6 John. R. 564; *Woodcock* v. *Bennet*, 1 Cow. 734; *Smith* v. *Smith*, &c., 4 John. Ch. R. 281. It will not therefore be allowed, even in equity, to recover upon a case proved, essentially differing from that alleged in the bill. *Green*, J. in *Anthony* v. *Leftwich*, 3 Ran. 263. Although the plaintiff should make out in evidence a good case, which under other circumstances would secure the interposition of the court, yet if it be not the case made by the bill, it will not do. *Carr*, Chancellor, in *Jackson's assignee* v. *Cutright*, &c., 5 Mun. 314. See *Brown* v. *Toell's adm'r*, 5 Ran. 543; *Thompson* v. *Jackson*, 3 Ran. 504; *Parker* v. *Carter & als.*, 4 Mun. 273; *Hunter's adm'rs*, &c. v. *Jett*, 4 Ran. 104; *Gibson* v. *Randolph*, 2 Mun. 310; *Sheppard's ex'or* v. *Starke*, 3 Mun. 29.

17. The bill must show sufficient matters of fact *per se* to maintain the case, and if it be defective in this the bill will be dismissed.[7] This rule has been carried to the extent, that if several persons join in filing a bill, and it appears that one of them has no interest, the bill will be open to demurrer, though it appear that all the other plaintiffs have an interest in the matter, and a right to institute a suit concerning it.[8] See *Harrison* v. *Hogg*, 2 Ves., Jr., 323; *Davoue*

---

[7] Mitf. Plea. 125.

[8] 1 Pr. Wms. 595; 1 Dan. Ch. Pr. 414, [322]. Now by statute in England, 15 and 16 Vict., chap. 86, sec. 49, this error may be rectified at the hearing. There should be a similar statute in Virginia.

v. *Fanning*, 4 John. Ch. R. 199; *Johnson* v. *Johnson*, 6 John. Ch. R. 163.

18. In all cases the bill must show that the parties defendant are in some way liable to the plaintiff's demand,[9] or that they have some interest in the subject of the suit;[10] and it must further show that there is such a privity between the parties defendant and the plaintiff as entitles him to sue them.[11]

19. Care should be taken not to attempt to embrace in the same bill too many objects. It is a rule of equity that two or more distinct subjects cannot be combined in one suit. An offence against this rule is termed multifariousness, and will render a bill liable to demurrer;[12] but it should be observed

---

[9] Mitf. Plea., 132. The extent of relief may depend materially upon the character in which the defendant is charged. *Shearman* v. *Christian*, &c., 6 Ran. 49. See *Bank of Virginia* v. *Craig*, 6 Leigh, 399.

[10] Ibid., 130.   [11] Ibid., 129; 1 Dan. Ch. Pr., 427.

[12] 1 Dan. Ch. Pr. 437; Becke v. Harris, &c., Hard. 337; Ward, &c. v. Duke of Northumberland, &c., 2 Anst. 469; Dilly v. Doig, 2 Ves., Jr., 486; Attorney Gen. v. Corp. of Camarthen, Cooper's Ch. Rep. 30; Whaley v. Dawson, 2 Sch. & Lef. 367; Saxton v. Davis, 18 Ves. 72; Stuart's heirs, &c. v. Coalter, 4 Rand. 74. These cases establish, that when the matter demanded against one defendant is separate, distinct and unconnected with the matter demanded against another defendant, and neither is at all interested in the defence to be made by the other, the bill asserting these several demands will be considered multifarious and demurrable for that cause; and though not demurred to, still it may be dismissed at the hearing. The objection, however, that a bill is multifarious, will have no influence upon a motion to dissolve an injunction. *Shirley* v. *Long*, &c., 6 Rand. 764. In *Ward* v. *Duke of Northumberland*, &c., 2 Anst. 469, the bill was against two executors, to recover from the two a demand against the decedent, and to recover from one of them a demand against him in his own right. To this bill the two defendants demurred separately, upon the ground that it blended two matters which had no other connection than that of one individual being a party in both; and against him the demands were perfectly distinct and unconnected. The demurrers were allowed.

that this rule will only apply where a plaintiff claims several matters of different natures by the same bill; where one general right only is claimed by the bill, though the defendants have separate and distinct interests, a demurrer will not hold.[13] A court of equity will not in one suit take cognizance of distinct and separate claims of different persons though standing in the same relative situation. When, for instance, an estate has been contracted to be sold in parcels to many different persons, a bill in the names of all of them to compel a specific performance would not be sustained. See *Birkley*, &c. v. *Presgrave*, 1 East 227. In *Harrison* v. *Hogg*, 2 Ves., Jr., 323, the bill was by two plaintiffs, who complained that the copyright of three works had been violated, and, according to their own showing, they were jointly interested in only one of the works. In the other two works one plaintiff was alone interested. A demurrer to the bill was allowed. It is a favorite object of equity to prevent a multiplicity of suits; and where several persons have a common interest arising out of the same transaction, although their interest, strictly speaking, is not joint, even the

---

In the case of *Stuart's heirs* v. *Coalter*, 4 Rand. 74, there were three co-terminous tenants claiming severally different parts of the land claimed by the plaintiff. It was not alleged that the whole controversy depended upon the establishment of one particular line; and if there had been any such allegation, the possession of one of the defendants might have given him a right, which the others would not have had. Neither defendant, therefore, could be regarded as at all interested in the defence made by the others.

Where the bill is against several defendants, the principle to be deduced from the cases is, that the bill must relate to matters of the same nature, and having a connection with each other, and in which all the defendants are more or less concerned. *Brinkerhoff*, &c., v. *Brown*, &c., 6 John. Ch. Rep. 157.

[13] Mitf. Plea. 147.

defendant may sometimes insist that they shall all
be made parties in the same suit, that he may be
only subjected to the trouble and expense of one litigation. *Eagar, &c.* v. *Price, &c.*, 2 Paige 333; *Robinson, &c.* v. *Smith, &c.*, 3 Paige 231; *Wendell* v.
Wendell, &c., 3 Paige 509.

It is a common case for creditors of a decedent to
unite in a bill against the personal representative for
an account of the assets; or for one or more creditors
to sue such representative on behalf of themselves
and of all other creditors. On the same principle
judgment creditors, whose liens are fixed by law, may
unite in a bill to remove impediments which have
been created by the fraud of their debtor, and which
equally affect all the creditors. They have one common object in view, which, in fact, governs the whole
case; and the subject in dispute may be said to be
joint as between the plaintiffs on the one hand and
the defendants on the other. 2 R. P. (old) 277.

In *Brinkerhoff, &c.* v. *Brown, &c.*, 6 John. Chan.
Rep. 139, there were four plaintiffs equally interested
in two judgments as to part of the amount of those
judgments, and the fifth plaintiff was entitled to the
surplus. In respect to these judgments it was clear
that the five plaintiffs were all properly united in one
suit. But it appeared that the fifth plaintiff had
obtained a judgment in which the other four plaintiffs had no interest. Here it was insisted was a case
of joint and several demands united in the same bill,
and the question was whether it could be permitted.
As the plaintiffs were seeking the aid of equity
against certain fraudulent acts affecting them all,

Chancellor *Kent* held that they had a right to unite in one bill. The gravamen of the bill was the fraud, and as Chief Baron *Macdonald* said, in *Ward*, &c. v. *Duke of Northumberland*, &c., 2 Anst. 477, there was one common interest among all the plaintiffs centering in that point. See *Reid*, &c. v. *Giffard & als.*, 1 Hopkins's Ch. Rep. 416; *Robinson* v. *Smith*, &c., 3 Paige 222; *Fellows*, &c. v. *Fellows*, &c., 4 Cowen 682; *Shields* v. *Thomas*, 18 How. 253.

20. A bill should not ' contain statements or charges which are scandalous or impertinent.[14] Scandal consists in the allegation of anything which is unbecoming the dignity of the court to hear, or is contrary to good manners, or which charges some person with a crime not necessary to be shown in the cause. Any unnecessary allegation bearing cruelly upon the moral character of an individual is scandalous.[15] Impertinences are described by Lord Chief Baron Gilbert to be ": where the records of the court are stuffed with long recitals, or with long digressions of matter of fact, which are altogether unnecessary, and totally immaterial to the matter in question.[16]

21. It is not a ground of demurrer that scandalous or impertinent matter is introduced in a bill; the parties defendant are only entitled to have the record purified by expunging such matter, and a reference to a commissioner for that purpose will be ordered.

22. Beside these requisites, it is further necessary

---

[14] 1 Dan. Ch. Pr. 452.   [15] Ibid., 452.

[16] Gilb. For. Rom. 209. The writer has seen but one case of scandal or impertinence in pleadings in Virginia. This occurred in an answer to a bill filed in the Court of Chancery at Richmond in a suit entitled " *Mason* v. *Mason & als.*"

in every bill to pray the court to grant the proper relief suited to the case as made by the bill; and if for any reason founded on the substance of the case, as stated in the bill, the Plaintiff is not entitled to the relief he prays, either in whole or in part, the parties defendant may demur.[17] It is usual to insert in every bill a prayer for general relief, and it seems that a special prayer is not absolutely necessary when this general prayer is inserted.[18]

23. There are other requisites appertaining to bills adapted to particular purposes. These will be seen on reference to the sections treating of such bills.

FORM OF BILLS.

24. Every bill should have a convenient form. Original bills praying relief being of more frequent use, and the several other kinds of bills so nearly resembling them in form, it is deemed proper here to set forth simply the form of original bills alone.

25. The form of an original bill praying relief usually consists of nine parts.[19] 1st. The address to the court. 2d. The names of the parties plaintiff. 3d. The statement of plaintiff's case, usually denominated the stating part of the bill. 4th. The charge of confederacy on the part of defendants with others to deprive the plaintiff of his right. 5th. The allegation that the defendants intend to set up a particular sort of defence, the reply to which the plaintiff

---

17 Mitf. Plea, 133 ; 1 Dan. Ch. Pr. 429.   18 See *post*, note to sec. 56.

19 This division into nine parts is not universally adopted by legal writers. Lube deems it illogical and incorrect; he makes only four. Adams, in his Treatise on Equity, makes the like number. Justice Story adopts the division in the text.

anticipates, by alleging certain facts which will defeat such defence; this is termed the charging part. 6th. The statement that the plaintiff has no remedy without the assistance of a court of equity, which is called the averment of jurisdiction. 7th. The interrogating part, in which the stating and charging parts are converted into interrogatories for the purpose of eliciting from the defendant a circumstantial discovery upon oath of the truth or falsehood of the matters stated and charged. 8th. The prayer for relief; and 9th. The prayer that process may issue.

In Virginia State Courts.—Some of these parts are rarely if ever used in Virginia. In bills prepared by eminent counsel the charging part is omitted altogether, while the purpose of the interrogating part is served by the general prayer that each of the defendants shall be required to answer the several statements of the bill as fully and particularly as if they were repeated, and the defendants specially interrogated in relation thereto.[20] The averment of jurisdiction is usually inserted. The charge of confederacy is not.

In United States Courts.—The rules of the Supreme Court of the United States, prescribed for the circuit courts of the United States, leave it optional with the party plaintiff to insert in his bill the confederacy clause; but expressly require that the prayer of the bill should ask the special relief to which the plaintiff supposes himself entitled, besides a prayer for general relief;[21] and further provide that the inter-

---

[20] See 1 John. Ch. Rep. 65.

[21] XXI. Rule of United States S. C.

rogating clause shall be inserted, the form of which is given in the 43d rule cited hereafter.

26. With these remarks upon the practice in this country, we proceed to lay before the reader the several purposes which these parts of the bill were intended to serve in England, and their forms as used there and here.

27. (1.) *Address of the Bill.*—In England every bill must be addressed to the person or persons who have the actual custody of the Great Seal at the time of its being filed, unless the person holding the seals is a party, or the seals are in the King's own hand, in which cases the bill must be addressed: " To the King's most excellent Majesty in his High Court of Chancery."[22]

28. In the United States Circuit Courts the address is as follows: " To the judges of the circuit court of the United States for the district of ———."[23]

29. In the Virginia State Courts, when suit is brought in a circuit (or county) court, the address is as follows: " To the Honorable J. C., Judge of the Circuit (or County) Court for the county of ———."

30. (2.) *Names of Plaintiffs.*—In England it is not only necessary that the names of the several complainants in a bill should be correctly stated, but the description and place of abode of each plaintiff must be set out.[24]

31. In the United States Circuit Courts it is requisite to state in the bill the names, residence and citizenship of the several parties plaintiff and defeu-

---

[22] 1 Dan. Ch. Pr. 462 (361-2); Mitf. Pl. 7.   [23] XX. Rule of United States S. C.
[24] 1 Dan. Ch. Pr. 463 (362).

dant.[25] The reason of this rule is obvious. Being courts whose jurisdiction, in most cases, is restricted to matters of controversy between citizens of different States, the citizenship should appear on the face of the bill.[26] See *Jackson* v. *Ashton*, 8 Pet. 148.

32. In the Virginia State Courts the names of the plaintiffs are usually inserted without a description of employment or place of abode. It is usual, however, whenever the bill is preferred by a next friend, or committee, or the like, to insert a description of the character in which the party plaintiff sues.

32 *a.* The bill must be in the names of those who have the cause of complaint, and not in the names of their agents. A suit cannot be maintained in the name of an attorney in fact. *Jones* v. *Hart's exo'rs*, 1 H. & M. 471.

33. In the English courts the manner of introducing the statement with the names of the plaintiffs is as follows: " Humbly complaining, sheweth unto your Lordship, your orator A. B., of the parish of ——, in the county of ——, *gentleman* (or *yeoman*), that," &c. In the United States Circuit Courts as follows: " A. B. of ——, and a citizen of the State of ——, brings this his bill against C. D. of ——, and a citizen of the State of ——, and E. F. of ——, and a citizen of the State of —— ; and thereupon your orator complains and says that," &c.[27] In the Virginia State Courts as follows · " Complaining, sheweth unto the court, your orator A. B., that," &c.[28]

---

[25] XX. Rule of United States S. C.

[26] Dodge v. Perkins, 4 Mason 435.   [27] XX. Rule United States S. C.

[28] It should be noted here that when a plaintiff sues on behalf of himself, and others of a class with himself, the fact is usually stated in this part of the

34. (3.) *Stating Part.*—This part of the bill contains the statement of the plaintiff's case. The statement should be clear, direct and positive as to all matters necessary to support the plaintiff's equity ; but where a matter essential to the determination of the plaintiff's claim is charged to rest within the knowledge of a defendant, or must of necessity be within his knowledge, and is consequently the subject of a part of the discovery sought by the bill, a precise allegation is not required.[29]

35. The statement should not be argumentative, nor should it contain long recitals from deeds or other instruments *in hæc verba*,[30] and as has been stated heretofore, the statement should not contain irrelevant or impertinent or scandalous matter.

---

bill, 1 Dan. Ch. Pr. 464. As in the case of a " Creditor's bill," which runs thus : " Complaining, sheweth unto your honor, your orator A. B., who sues on behalf of himself, and of such other, the creditors of C. D., deceased, who shall come in and seek relief by and contribute to the expense of this suit, that," &c. ; or, if the suit be by a next friend, say : " Complaining, sheweth unto the court, your orator J. M., an infant of tender years, who sues by R. B., his next friend, that," &c. ; or, " your oratrix, M. C., a married woman, the wife of D. C., who sues by R. B., her next friend," &c. There is a difference between suing as next friend of an infant and of a married woman. Any one may bring a bill as next friend of *an infant* without his consent; it is at the peril of him who brings it ; but no one can bring a bill in the name of a married woman as her next friend without her consent, and should such bill be brought upon her affidavit of the matter it will be dismissed. *Andrews* v. *Cradock*, Prec. in Ch. 376 ; *Randolph* v. *Dickerson*, 5 Paige 751. The husband may be the next friend of his wife in bringing a suit against another person. *Bein* v. *Heath*, 6 How. 240. A married woman cannot maintain a bill without some person being named as next friend. Such a bill will be demurrable. But the court will allow her in such case to amend her bill by inserting a proper and responsible person as her next friend. *Garlick* v. *Strong*, &c., 3 Paige 440.   [29] 1 Dan. Ch. Pr. (366.)

[30] *Hood* v. *Inman*, 4 John. Ch. Rep. 437. There are cases in which the plaintiff's case turns upon the construction of words in written instruments ; in such cases, it surely would not be deemed improper to spread on the face of

36. Although in bills in equity the same precision of statement that is required in pleadings at common law is not attainable, yet it is necessary that such a degree of certainty should be adopted as may give the defendant full information of the case which he is called upon to answer.[31]

37. Every fact necessary to the plaintiff's case should be set forth in the stating part of the bill; otherwise, he will not be permitted to offer or require any evidence of such fact.[32] A general charge or statement however of the matter of fact is sufficient, though it seems that a defect here cannot be cured by a subsequent interrogatory.[33]

38. In the English courts the stating part of the bill is kept distinct and separate from the confederating clause and the charging part. In the United States Circuit Courts a party plaintiff is at liberty to omit altogether the confederacy clause and the charging part of the bill, and in his narrative or stating part to state and avoid by counter averments—at his option—any matter or thing which he supposes will be insisted upon by the defendant by way of defence or excuse to the case made by the plaintiff for relief.[34] In the Virginia State Courts it is the practice to set forth the statement of the plaintiff's case in the stating part, and to merge in it the charge of con-

---

the bill the precise words of the instrument.—See Dan. Ch. Prac. (369). A plaintiff may state any matters of evidence in his bill which may be material in establishing the main charge, or in ascertaining the kind of relief proper to be administered. *Walworth*, Chancellor, in *Mechanics' Bank* v. *Levy*, &c., 3 Paige 608.

[31] 1 Dan. Ch. Pr. (373); Story's Eq. Pl., sec. 240 *et seq.*

[32] Story's Eq. Pl. sec. 28. See sec. 16 of this volume.

[33] *Parker* v. *Carter & als.*, 4 Munf. 273.   [34] XXI. Rule Supreme Court U. S.

federacy if deemed necessary, and any matter of offence or defence thought expedient by the plaintiff or his counsel.

39. The main point to be looked to is the fact, whether in the statement of his case in the bill the plaintiff has set forth every material averment necessary to support his right to the relief he asks.

40. The form of a statement in an English bill to foreclose a mortgage is as follows:

" That C. D., being seized to him and his heirs in fee simple or otherwise well entitled unto, the messuages, lands, tenements and hereditaments, hereinafter mentioned, applied to and requested your orator to advance and lend him the sum of £—— upon the security or mortgage of the said messuages, lands, hereditaments and premises; and your orator having agreed thereto, did accordingly advance and lend the same to the said C. D.; and thereupon for securing the repayment of the said £——, and interest for the same, an indenture (*recite mortgage securities.*) And your orator further sheweth, &c., that the said £——, or any part thereof, was not paid to your orator, or any other person on his account at the time limited and appointed in that behalf by the said last mentioned indenture, or at any other time, but default was made in the payment thereof, whereby the legal estate of the said messuages, lands, hereditaments and premises became vested in your orator; and your orator farther showeth, &c., that the whole of the principal sum of £—— is now due and owing to your orator, together with a large arrear of interest thereon; and your orator being desirous of being repaid the same, has frequently and in a friendly manner applied to and requested the said C. D. to come to a fair and just account with him for what is due and owing to him for principal and interest on his said mortgage security, of the —— day of ——, and to pay to your orator what shall be found due to him on taking such account; and your orator well hoped," &c.

41. This form of statement may be used in bills filed in the United States Circuit Courts and in the Virginia State Courts. The statement, however, is not usually so precise in bills filed in these courts.

42. (4.) *Charge of Confederacy.* This part of an English bill is as follows:

" But now so it is, may it please your Lordship that the said C. D., combining and confederating with divers other persons at present unknown to your orator (whose names when discovered your orator prays may be herein inserted with apt and proper matter and words to charge them as parties hereto), and in order to give some color to such refusal, sometimes pretends that he never had or received any such sum or sums of money of your orator as aforesaid, and that he never made and executed any such indenture as aforesaid, and that he goes out and pretends that there are many other mortgages, charges and eucumbrances affecting the said premises made and executed by him, or some person under whom he claims prior in point of time to that made by him to your orator. (Whereas," &c., *then follows the charging part hereafter cited.)*

43. In England this confederacy clause, though formerly used, is not necessary.[35] In this country, both in the United States Circuit Courts and in the Virginia State Courts, it is usually omitted.

44. (5.) *Charging Part.*—This part of an English bill is as follows :

---

[35] 1 Dan. Ch. Pr. 483 (375).

"Whereas your orator chargeth the truth to be that the said C. D. did receive of your orator the said sum of money, and that he did execute the indenture aforesaid. And your orator further charges, that if there are any mortgages, charges or encumbrances affecting the said mortgaged premises, or any part thereof, they are subsequent to your orator's said mortgage; and your orator farther charges, that the said mortgaged premises are a scanty security for the repayment of what is due for principal and interest upon the said mortgage ; all which actings, doings, and pretences of the said defendant are contrary to equity and good conscience, and tend to the manifest wrong and injury of your orator in the premises."

45. The practice which formerly prevailed in England, of inserting this clause, is said to have originated in order to obviate the necessity of setting forth by a special replication additional facts in avoidance of new matter introduced by the defendant's plea or answer.

46. It is not usual to insert this clause in bills drawn in this country. Whenever the plaintiff deems his bill not properly adapted to his case, he files an amended or supplemental bill adapted to the defence.[36]

47. (6.) *Averment of Jurisdiction.*—This part of an English bill runs thus : "In tender consideration whereof, and for as much as your orator is remediless in the premises by the strict rules of common law, and cannot have adequate relief except in a court of

---

[36] See *James* v. *McKennon*, 6 John. Ch. Rep. 564. Where the plaintiff after setting out his case in the bill stated what he understood was the pretension of the defendant, this was not such an allegation as constituted the answer responsive thereto evidence and thus threw the burden of disproving it upon the plaintiff. *Lea's ex'or* v. *Eidson*, 9 Grat. 277.

equity, where matters of this kind are properly cognizable and relievable." The form is the same when used here in the United States Circuit Courts and in the Virginia State Courts.

48. This clause, it is said, was originally intended for the purpose of giving the court jurisdiction. The making of it does not give the court jurisdiction when it has it not otherwise, and it has been settled that the omission of this averment will not deprive the plaintiff of relief.

49. The rules of the Supreme Court of the United States provide that it may be omitted in bills filed in the Circuit Courts of the United States.

50. In bills filed in the Virginia State Courts it is usually inserted, and immediately following, the names of the defendants are given thus: "Your orator prays that C. D., A. B. and R. M., in his own right and as executor as aforesaid of James B., deceased, may be made parties defendant to this bill, and required to answer, &c.[37]

---

[37] This might properly be called the "Prayer for Parties." It is important that it should be inserted in bills filed in the Virginia State Courts.

If among the defendants there be any one who fills several characters, and is a proper party in each character, care must be taken to make him a party in each. Where, for example, a devisee of the equity of redemption ought to be a party, although he be made a defendant in *the character of executor*, and answer as such, that will not suffice. He must be made a party, (called on to answer), as to his *individual* interest. *Mayo* v. *Tomkies*, 6 Mun. 520. In a bill brought by a residuary legatee against an executor, if the executor be administrator of one of the residuary legatees, he should be made a defendant as administrator of such legatee, as well as in his character of executor. *Sheppard's ex'or* v. *Starke*, &c., 29. And a decree cannot be made against a widow to restrain her from conveying her right of dower, if she be not made a defendant to the bill as widow, or in her own right, but merely as administratrix of the decedent and *guardian* of his children. *Pennington* v. *Hanby*, &c., 4 Munf. 144.

4

51. (7.) *Interrogating Part.*—The bill having shown the title of the persons complaining to relief, and that the court has jurisdiction for the purpose, prays that the parties defendant may answer all the matters contained in the former part of the bill, not only according to their positive knowledge of the facts stated, but also according to their remembrance, the information they have received, and the belief they are enabled to form on the subject.[38]

52. Experience having proved that the substance of the matters stated and charged in a bill may frequently be evaded by answering according to the letter only, sometimes there is added to the general requisition, that the defendants should answer the contents of the bill, a repetition by way of interrogatory, of the matters most essential to be answered; adding to the inquiry after each fact an inquiry of the several circumstances which may be attendant upon it, and the variations to which it may be subject, with a view to prevent evasion, and compel a full answer.[39] This is commonly called the interrogating part of the bill; and as it is used only to compel a full answer to the matters contained in the former part of the bill, it must be founded on those matters.[40]

53. The 40th rule of the Supreme Court prescribed, that in the United States Circuit Courts a defendant should not be bound to answer any statement or charge in the bill, unless specially and particularly interrogated thereto, or any interrogatory in the bill, except such as he was specially required to answer;

---

[38] Mitf. Plea. 51. [39] 1 Dan. Ch. Pr. 487; Mitf. Plea. 51.
[40] 1 Dan. Ch. Pr. 487.

but this rule has been repealed.[41] By another rule of
the same court, the interrogatories contained in the
interrogating part of the bill were required to be
divided as conveniently as may be from each other,
and numbered consecutively 1, 2, 3, &c., and the interrogatories which each defendant was required to
answer to be specified in a note at the foot of the bill
in the following form : " The defendant, A. B., is
required to answer the interrogatories numbered
respectively 1, 2, 3, &c. ;" and by another rule of the
same court, it was provided that instead of the words
of the bill *as used in the High Court of Chancery of
England*, preceding the interrogatory part, these shall
be used : " To the end therefore that the said defendants may, if they can, show why your orator should
not have the relief hereby prayed, and may upon
their several and respective corporal oaths, and
according to the best and utmost of their several and
respective knowledge, remembrance, information and
belief, full, true, direct, and perfect answer make to
such of the several interrogatories hereinafter numbered and set forth, as by the note hereunder written, they are respectively required to answer ; that is
to say—1. Whether, &c. ; 2. Whether," &c." See
the 93d rule which modifies the rule just cited.

54. It has been already stated that in the Virginia
State Courts the interrogatory clause is inserted,
though usually with not such particularity as in English bills.

55. The interrogatory clause in an English bill is
now like that contained in section 53. It formerly

---

[41] See XCIII. Rule.

ran as follows : "To the end therefore that the said
C. D. and his confederates when discovered may,
upon their several and respective oaths, according to
the best and utmost of their several and respective
knowledge, remembrance, information and belief, a
full, true, direct and perfect answer make to all and
singular the matters aforesaid, and that as fully as if
the same were here repeated, and they particularly
interrogated thereto; and more especially, that the
said defendant may, in manner aforesaid, answer and
set forth whether; (Here insert interrogatories to
probe the conscience of defendants.")

56. (8.) *Prayer for Relief.*—There is no doubt
that a prayer for general relief will, in most cases, be
sufficient to enable the plaintiff to obtain such a decree as his case entitles him to.[42] Injunctions ought
always to be prayed for specially.[43]. Under this general prayer, any relief may be granted which is suitable to the case, and consistent with the allegations
and proofs. *Cook*, &c. v. *Mancius*, &c., 5 John. Ch. R.
99 ; *Green*, J., in *Beverley* v. *Brooke*, &c., 2 Leigh 441.
In *Beall* v. *Silver*, 2 Ran. 401, the plaintiff was a
judgment creditor, and came into equity to subject
property fraudulently conveyed by his debtor, praying that so much of the property might be sold as
would satisfy *the amount of the judgment.* The property was held liable ; and then the creditor asked to
be allowed interest, though no interest had been recovered by the judgment. This claim of interest it
was considered might be allowed under the prayer
for general relief.

---

[42] The 21st rule of Supreme Court United States requires plaintiff to pray for
the special relief as well as for general relief.   [43] Eden on Injunctions 49.

It is indispensable however when relief is granted, which is not particularly prayed for, that it should be consistent with the case made by the bill. *Wilken, &c.* v. *Wilken,* 1 John. Ch. R. 117 ; *Franklin, &c.* v. *Osgood, &c.,* 14 John. Rep. 527 ; *English, &c.* v. *Foxall,* 2 Peters 595 ; *Colton, &c.* v. *Ross, &c.,* 2 Paige 396 ; *Sheppard's ex'or* v. *Starke & ux.* 3 Munf. 29.

But though the bill should contain neither a special nor general prayer for relief, yet if the defendants answer the allegations and submit themselves to the decree of the court on the merits, the defect as to the prayer will be disregarded by an *appellate* court. *Smith, &c.* v. *Smith, &c.,* 4 Ran. 95.

57. This part of an English bill is as follows :

SPECIAL RELIEF.

" And that it may be referred to one of the masters of this honorable court to take an account of what is due to your orator for principal and interest on his said mortgage security from the said defendant, and that the said defendant may be decreed to pay to your orator what shall be found due on such account, by a short day to be appointed by this honorable court in that behalf, together with your orator's costs ; and in default, that the said C. D., and all persons claiming under him, may be forever barred and foreclosed of, and from all right of redemption of, in, and to the said mortgaged premises, or any part thereof, and may deliver up to your orator all deeds, papers or writings in his custody or power, relating to or concerning the said mortgaged premises."

GENERAL RELIEF.

" And that your orator may have all such farther and other and general relief in the premises as the nature of his case may require, or to equity shall seem meet."

58. The prayer for general relief ought never to be omitted by the draftsman, because if the plaintiff should in his special prayer mistake the due relief, it may be given under the general prayer, if consistent with that which is actually prayed.[44]

59. 9. *Prayer for Process.*—The following is the prayer for process in an English bill: " May it please your Lordship to grant unto your orator his Majesty's most gracious writ of subpœna to be directed to the said W. B., thereby commanding him at a certain day, and under a certain pain therein inserted, personally to be and appear before your Lordship in this honorable court, then and there to answer the premises."

60. It will be observed that in this form the process is prayed to be directed to the party defendant. This is the practice in the United States Circuit Courts; but in the Virginia State Courts all process is directed to officers of the court. The prayer for process of subpœna in the United States Circuit Courts should contain the names of all the defendants named in the introductory part of the bill; and if any of them are known to be infants under age, or otherwise under guardianship, should state the fact. This is required by the 23d rule of Supreme Court. The prayer for process in United States Circuit Courts is as follows : "May it please

---

[44] Adams' Equity 566. If a bill contains no prayer either for specific or general relief, it is considered as a bill of discovery only. But see *Smith*, &c. v. *Smith*, &c., 4 Rand. 95, cited, sec. 56.

the honorable court to grant a writ of subpœna, directed to C. D., A. B. and R. M., in his own right and as executor as aforesaid of James B. deceased, and commanding them to appear and make answer unto this bill of complaint, and to perform and abide by such orders and decrees herein as to the court may seem required by the principles of equity and good conscience."

In the Virginia State courts the prayer for process is not unfrequently omitted altogether, and when inserted is usually drawn in terms such as these : "That proper process may be directed against the several defendants hereinbefore named;" and is often used in the bill before the prayer for general relief thus : "that proper process may be directed against the several defendants herein-before named, and that your orator may have all such farther and other and general relief as the nature of his case may require, or to equity may seem meet."

60 *a.* It is frequently laid down that none are defendants against whom process is not prayed. Coop. Eq. Pl. 16 ; *Brasher's ex'ors* v. *Van Cortlandt*, 2 John. Ch. R. 245. This seems to be founded upon what was said in *Fawkes* v. *Pratt*, 1 P. Wms. 593.⁴⁵ In Virginia, where the process issues, as matter of course upon the bill, and most frequently before the bill is

---

⁴⁵ In *Fawkes* v. *Pratt*, the defendant pleaded that the plaintiff was a bankrupt, and his assignees ought to be made parties. Upon this the plaintiff amended his bill and made allegations in the body thereof in relation to the assignees, but the prayer of process was only against the original defendants. The defendant put in the same plea to the amended bill, viz : that the assignees ought to be made defendants. Lord *Macclesfield* said, "the plaintiff may complain and tell stories of whom he pleases, but they only are defendants against whom process is prayed."

filed, the prayer in the bill for process is really formal;
" and it would be strange indeed if those only should
be regarded as defendants, against whom there is an
unnecessary prayer for process." 2 Rob. Pr. (old)
290. It may be admitted that every bill should
clearly designate some particular persons as defeudants, and that ordinarily the prayer for process
selects from the persons named in the bill those who
are made defendants. But this particular mode of
designation cannot be indispensable. It must be sufficient for the bill to state which of the persons named
in it are made defendants. *Ibid.*, 290. In *Elmendorf
& wife* v. *Delancey*, &c., 1 Hopkins's Ch. Rep. 555, no
persons were designated as defendants either by a
prayer of process against them, or by any statement
that they were impleaded as defendants. The bill
was adjudged bad on special demurrer assigning
this cause, but the complainants had leave to amend
on the usual terms.

61. Besides these several parts of bills, there are
other requisites necessary to be attended to in their
preparation; some equally applicable to every bill;
others alone proper in bills designed for special purposes.

62. Thus to every bill the signature of counsel
should be affixed;[46] to a bill of injunction, beside the

---

[46] This is specially required in bills filed in United States Circuit Courts, by
the 24th rule of United States Supreme Court. In the Virginia State Courts
the rules of practice which each equity court adopts for its own government
sometimes require the signature of counsel to bills; but the practice is very
loose in those courts, and in many instances the counsel does not affix his signature. In England, the rule is imperative that the signature of counsel must
be subscribed to every bill before it is filed (Mitf. Pl. 48), and if it be not, the
bill will be dismissed on the defendant's demurrer. 1 Dan. Ch. Pr. 409.

special prayer for the restraining order of the court or judge, an affidavit of the truth of the statements made in the bill should be annexed; and an affidavit is also required in bills of discovery and in other bills.

63. The reader will find, in subsequent chapters of this work, complete forms of bills as exhibited in the English courts, in the United States courts, and in the Virginia State courts, showing the several parts of the bill in juxta-position.

64. In *Ambler & als.* v. *Warwick & Co.*, 1 Leigh 195, the court permitted the case made out by the bill to be supplemented by the statements of one of the answers, and granted relief. The case, in this particular, can hardly be sustained on authority.

In *Brown* v. *Toell's adm'or*, 5 Rand. 543, the bill was filed to injoin a judgment at law, upon the ground that the complainant was entitled to credits, which had not been allowed, and a deposition was taken to prove the contract usurious. There being no allegation of usury in the bill, the testimony was considered irrelevant, and was disregarded.

In *Thompson* v. *Jackson*, 3 Rand. 504, the bill sought to rescind a contract because of a deficiency in the quantity of land sold. *Carr*, J. said, that the contract could not be rescinded on the ground of fraud, for no fraud or misrepresentation, no suppression of truth or suggestion of falsehood being charged in the bill, any evidence taken as to these points would be regarded as irrelevant.

In *Parker* v. *Carter & als.*, 4 Munf. 273, creditors filed a bill to subject certain slaves which their debtor had received from his father-in-law at the time of his marriage, insisting that the slaves had become the property of the debtor before the father-in-law made a deed conveying them for the benefit of his daughter and her children, it was *held*, that as the bill contained no charge, that the deed had not been duly delivered, the objection as to non-delivery could not be taken advantage of under the bill.

In *Hunter's adm'ors* v. *Jett*, 4 Rand. 104, there was an arrangement between a creditor and his principal debtor that the latter should have time upon giving collateral security; and the surety filed a bill asking information as to the details of the arrangement, and praying the benefit of the securities, which were the fruit of it. He did not by his bill deny his liability for the debt, but merely claimed the benefit of the collateral security, to enable him to pay it: *Held*, that the surety could not insist at the trial that the facts proved in the case amounted to a discharge; the surety if he had been ignorant of the precise character of the arrangement until he saw the answer, if he then intended to shift his ground and go for a discharge, should have insisted on it, and put it in issue by an amended or supplemental bill.

Where an executor has a claim against the estate of his testator, depending on a *quantum meruit* only, his proper remedy is by bill in equity against his co-executors and the legatees. Upon such a bill, what is a reasonable compensation will be determined and allowed out of the estate. *Baker* v. *Baker*, &c., 3 Munf. 222. In this case the executor failed to state his claim with reasonable certainty, by setting forth his own estimate of his services; the court did not dismiss the bill, but allowed him on motion to amend it.

Parker, J. said, in *James* v. *Bird's adm'or*, 8 Leigh 570, that the relief given by the decree of the Chancellor could not be granted under the prayer for general relief, and he would have reversed the decree on that ground; it was reversed on another. The case was this: Bird, with a view to hinder and defraud his creditors, conveyed his slaves to James, and took his bond for $8,000, as the price of them. He filed a bill to set the transaction aside, on the ground that it was not designed as a sale, but merely to save his property from sacrifice. Finding this ground untenable, he filed another bill, in which he gave a new character to the transaction, but the fraudulent intent still showed itself. He prayed to rescind the contract, to have the slaves restored, and *for general relief*. The Chancellor considered the sale good, and refused to set it aside, but under the prayer for general relief determined to decree relief to the complainant to the payment of the balance of his purchase money, and subjected the slaves to the payment thereof upon the supposed lien of the vendor. In the Court of Appeals the case went off on the point, that Bird having made the conveyance for the purpose of hindering and delaying, though most probably not of wholly evading the payment of his just debts, was not entitled to the aid of a court of equity; and the decree was therefore reversed. *Parker*, J. said, that he questioned whether the case made by the bill authorized a decree for the purchase money under the prayer for general relief. All the facts

charged by the bill are inconsistent with the idea of
a sale, or with a right to purchase money; and therefore to decree the latter, without an alternative
prayer or statement of facts justifying it, seemed to
him to be opposed to the current of English authorities, and, so far as the point had occurred, to our own.

In *Sheppard's ex'or* v. *Starke*, &c., 3 Munf. 29, the
bill was filed by one residuary legatee, claiming his
share of the estate. The bill contained a prayer for
general relief. This did not authorize a decree for a
share, to which the complainant was entitled as assignee of another legatee, or a portion which he
claimed as distributee of a third legatee.

If there be no averment or statement in the bill on
which to found a particular interrogatory, an exception to the answer for failing to respond to such interrogatory cannot be sustained. *Mechanics' Bank*
v. *Levy*, 3 Page 606. Nor will the interrogatory
avail at the hearing for the purpose of supplying a
defect in the bill. If evidence be relied on as to a
particular fact, and such evidence be objected to because the fact is not charged, the objection will not be
removed by an interrogatory calling for information
on the subject. *Parker* v. *Carter*, &c., 4 Munf. 273.

INFORMATIONS.

65. *Of their matter.* Informations, in every respect, follow the nature of bills, except in their style.
When they concern only the rights of the State, or of
those whose rights the State takes under its particular protection, they are generally exhibited in the

name of the Attorney General as the informant.[47] In the latter case always, and sometimes in the former, a relator is named, who, in reality, sustains and directs the suit. It may happen that this person has an interest in the matter in dispute, and bears the character of plaintiff as well as relator; in such event, the pleading is styled an "information and bill." The proceedings upon an information can only abate by the death or determination of interest of the defendant.

66. *Of their form.* The difference in form between an information and a bill consists merely in offering the subject-matter as the information of the officer in whose name it is exhibited, at the relation of the person who suggests the suit, in those cases where a relator is named, and in stating the acts of the defendant to be injurious to the State or to those whose rights the State thus endeavors to present. When the pleading is at the same time an information and bill, it is a compound of the forms used for each, when separately exhibited.

---

[47] In some cases other officers of the State and of the United States are necessary plaintiffs.

CHAPTER III.

Forms of Bills in suits for dower, for partition, and for lease or sale of lands of persons under disability in the Virginia State Courts.

DOWER.

Form of Bill for Dower in ordinary suit by Widow.

To the Honorable A. B., Judge of the —— court of the county of —— :

Complaining, showeth unto the court your complainant, Ellen F., that your complainant is the widow of John F., who recently departed this life intestate in this county; that the said John F. was, during the marriage between him and herself, seized of an estate of inheritance in real estate in this county, and in the counties of M. and N., which real estate is as follows, to wit* (here·briefly recite it) : *that the said J. F. died seized of the said real estate, and your complainant's dower therein has in no manner* been lawfully barred or relinquished[1]; that the following persons are the children and heirs at law of said J. F., to wit: Jane F., Susan F., Robert F., and Thomas F., the last named of whom is an infant under the age of twenty-one years; that your complainant is entitled to have her dower assigned *in the said real estate*, and she desires the same to be assigned to her.

---

[1] Code, chapter 110, section 1.

In tender consideration whereof, your complainant prays that the said Jane F., Susan F., Robert F., and Thomas F., may be made parties defendant to this bill; that the said adult defendants be required to answer the same on their corporal oaths; that a *guardian ad litem* be assigned the infant defendant, Thomas F., to defend his interests in this suit, and that the said *guardian ad litem* answer the said bill; that proper process issue; that your complainant's dower in the said real estate be assigned ánd set out and allotted to her by the decree of your honorable court; that all proper orders may be madé, and all proper inquiries be directed, and that all such other, farther ánd general relief may be afforded your complainant as the nature of her case may require, or to equity shall seem meet. And your complainant will ever pray, &c.

C. D. p. q.

Ellen F.

Form of Bill for Dower by Widow against an Alienee of her former Husband.

Follow last form to star*, then say: that the said John F., your complainant has been informed and believes, conveyed the said real estate to M. O., but in the deed of conveyance your complainant did not unite, and she avers that her dower in said real estate ·has in no manner been lawfully barred or relinquished; that your complainant is now entitled to dower therein, and she has demanded of the said M. O. her dower in the same, but the said M. O. refuses to assign and set out her said dower, alleging that she is not entitled to any dower in the said real estate.

Your complainant desires that her dower in the same may be assigned and allotted and set over to her in this suit.

In tender consideration whereof, your complainant prays that the said M. O. may be made a party defendant to this bill, and required to answer the several statements therein on his corporal oath ; that proper process issue ; that your complainant's dower in the said real estate be assigned and set out and allotted to her, &c. &c. (as in last form to conclusion.)

Form of Bill for Dower by Widow, and to set aside release made thereof for fraud and imposition.

[See 3 Dan. Ch. Pr. (edit. 1865), p. 1924, for form of such bill when presented in United States Circuit Courts. It may be readily adapted to a suit in the Virginia State Courts. The material allegations in such a bill, after averring the right of dower and demand of it, and refusal to assign, are, that the defendants pretend that the complainant had by some deed or other instrument of writing released and discharged her right of dower; that the pretended release or instrument was obtained by fraud and imposition upon the complainant, stating the manner of it ; that the complainant did not join with her husband, J. F., in any deed of conveyance of the real estate as the defendants pretend, and that she was not barred of her right of dower in the said real estate. The bill will then contain the usual prayer for process and for assignment of dower, and that the pretended release be declared void, and for general relief.]

PRACTICAL NOTES TO FORMS OF BILLS FOR DOWER.

See Code, chapter 110, 1 Lomax's Digest, title v., chapter 3, 4, pages 108–134, 4 Kent's Com. 64.

PARTIES TO SUIT BY WIDOW.—In a bill by a widow for dower in land sold in the lifetime of her husband, and coming to the present owner through several intermediate conveyances, the present owner is the only necessary party defendant. *Blair* v. *Thompson & als.*, 11 Grat. 441.

GROSS SUM IN LIEU OF DOWER.—There cannot be a decree for a specific sum, in lieu of dower, without the assent of all the parties. *Ibid.*, see note, p. 55, *post.*

EXTENT OF RECOVERY.—The Code, chapter 110, section 11, puts at rest the main question discussed in *Braxton* v. *Coleman*, 5 Call 433[2], and in *Tod* v. *Baylor*, 4 Leigh 498;[3] and also determines that the title to rents of dowable lands may be asserted after the widow's

---

[2] *Braxton* v. *Coleman*, 5 Call 433, is differently understood by Judge Lomax and by Mr. Robinson. The latter comments on it as distinguished from *Tod* v. *Baylor*, 4 Leigh 498 ; the former seems not to have found any difference in principle between the two cases. Judge Lomax extracts from *Braxton* v. *Coleman* the principle, that if the estate after being sold by the husband became deteriorated by inevitable accident in the possession of the purchaser, though he afterwards greatly improved it, the widow is not to be endowed of this improved value, nor yet of the value at the time of the husband's alienation, but of the deteriorated value to which it was reduced by the accident. The case was this : Braxton, after marriage, sold a mill with fifty acres of land attached to it. The mill was subsequently carried away by a freshet, as was another, which was afterwards built upon the same site. A third mill upon a more extensive plan was then built by the purchaser. On suit by the widow, it was held that she was entitled to dower only in the mill site, and the fifty acres of land, not in the new mill; and no regard seems to have had to the value of the mill standing at the time of the alienation.

[3] *Tod* v. *Baylor*, 4 Leigh 498, was this : The widow filed a bill against an alienee of the husband for dower in the land sold. The court held that she was entitled to rents and profits, not from the death of the husband, but from the date of the suing out of the subpœna in the cause, and that she was dowable of the lands, as of the value thereof, at the time of alienation, not at the time of assignment of dower : she was not entitled to any advantage from enhancement of the value, either by improvements made by the alienee, or from general rise in value, or from any cause whatever.

death by the widow's personal representative.[4]   The section reads thus: " Whether the proceeding of the widow be against one claiming under an alienation by the husband in his lifetime, or against his heirs or devisees, or their assigns, a recovery of dower in such real estate in kind shall be of a third of the estate as it is when the recovery is had. Against such heirs or devisees, or their assigns, the damages shall be for such time after the husband's death as they have withheld the dower, not exceeding five years before the suit is commenced. Against one claiming under such alienation by the husband, the damages shall be from the commencement of the suit against such claimant.   In either case they shall be to the time of the recovery. And if, after suit brought, the widow or the tenant die before such recovery of damages, the same may be recovered by her personal representative, or against his."   Here it is provided that the recovery of dower shall be " of a third of the *estate as it is when the recovery is had*," whether of a purchaser or of the heir.[5]   The account directed in *Tod* v. *Baylor* was " of the profits of the land from the suing out of the subpoena in the cause."[6]   So also in *Braxton* v. *Coleman*, the widow was decreed one-third of the profits from the commencement of the suit.   The 11th section of chapter 110 of the Code provides for the giving of damages *against the heir*, and " for such time after the husband's death, as the dower has been withheld, not exceeding five years before the suit is brought:" *against a purchaser from the husband*, damages are to be given from the commencement of the suit."

The Code, chapter 110, section 10, provides:

" A widow having a right of dower in any real estate may recover the said dower, and damages for its being withheld, by such remedy at law as would lie on behalf of a tenant for life having a right of entry; or by a bill in equity, where the case is such that a bill would now lie for such dower."

And section 12 provides:

---

[4] See *Lee* v. *Stuart*, 2 Leigh 33, and *Macauley* v. *Dismal Swamp Company*, 2 Rob. R. 507.

[5] Judge Kent had (4 Com. 64) rightly summed up the doctrine of the American cases, as this : that the widow takes her dower according to the value of the land at the time of the alienation, and not according to its subsequent increased or improved value as against a purchaser ; but when this recovery is sought out of the land descended to the heir, then it shall be according to the value at the time of the assignment.   Of course the statute cited in the text rules in the Virginia courts.

[6] See Lomax's remark on this entry, 1 Lom. Dig., p. 122, note *.

"The two preceding sections are subject to this qualification, that, on the application of one claiming under an alienation made by the husband in his lifetime, a court of equity may grant him relief from such recovery, on the terms of his paying to the widow, during her life, lawful interest from the commencement of her suit, on one-third of the value, at the husband's death, of the real estate so aliened, deducting the value of such permanent improvements then existing as may have been made (after the alienation) by the alienee or his assigns."

The rule laid down by this section mitigates the harshness of the enactment contained in the 11th section before cited,[7] so far as the purchaser is concerned. The right of the widow to claim as against the heir dower in one-third of the land in its improved condition, though the improvement be by his industry or at his charge, remains as it was before the statute. The widow was endowed according to the value at the time of the assignment as against the heir, whether the estate had deteriorated[8] or had improved, 1 Lomax's Digest, 123, 124; and so the rule is now. See note, p. 41, *ante*.

The Code, chapter 110, sections 13 and 14, provides:

13. No widow shall be precluded from her dower by reason of the real estate whereof she claims dower having been recovered from her husband, by a judgment rendered by default or collusion, if she would have been entitled to dower therein, had there been no such judgment. Nor shall any heir who was under the age of twenty-one years at the time dower was assigned to the widow, out of the lands of his ancestor, by his guardian, or by judgment by default or collusion against such guardian, be precluded from recovering the seizin of his ancestor from such widow, unless she show herself entitled to such dower.

14. Crops growing on the dower land of a widow at the time of her death may be bequeathed by her, and shall go to her personal representative in like manner as crops growing on any other land held for life.

Tod v. *Baylor*, 4 Leigh 498, was distinguished from *Macaulay's ex'or* v. *Dismal Swamp Land Co.*, 2 Rob. 530, in this, that in *Tod* v. *Baylor* the husband had conveyed in his lifetime the land to a purchaser, in *Macaulay* v. *Dismal Swamp Land Co.*, the husband, though he had mortgaged the property, died seized of the land: and while in *Tod* v. *Baylor* the court had given profits to the

---

[7] Page 41, *ante*.

[8] If the heir has voluntarily impaired the value, Lomax states that the widow should be recompensed in damages against him. 1 Lom. Dig. 124, citing 2 Bac. Abr. 369; Park on Dower, 257, 8.

widow only from the issuing of the subpœna, in the latter case the court decided to give a decree to the widow for her share of the profits from the date of the husband's death.

OF WHAT ENDOWED.—The Code, chapter 110, sections 1, 2 and 3, provides:

1. A widow shall be endowed of one-third of all the real estate whereof her husband or any other to his use was, at any time during the coverture, seized of an estate of inheritance, unless her right to such dower shall have been lawfully barred or relinquished.

2. When a husband, or any other to his use, shall have been entitled to a right of entry or action in any land, and his widow would be entitled to dower out of the same, if the husband or such other had recovered possession thereof, she shall be entitled to such dower although there shall have been no such recovery of possession.[9]

3. Where land is *bona fide* sold in the lifetime of the husband, to satisfy a lien or incumbrance thereon, created by deed in which the wife has united, or created before the marriage, or otherwise paramount to the wife, she shall have no right to be endowed in the said land. But if a surplus of the proceeds of sale remain after satisfying the said lien or incumbrance, she shall be entitled to dower in said surplus, and a court of equity having jurisdiction of the case may make such order as may seem to it proper to secure her right.[10]

When the husband is entitled to a reversion expectant on a term of years or other chattel interest, he is seized of the freehold, and his widow is dowable. 1 Inst. 32 a; 1 Lom. Dig. 100–1; 4 Kent's Com. 38. But a woman is not entitled to dower out of an estate in remainder or reversion, expectant on an estate of freehold, because the husband has no seizin. *Ibid.; Blow* v. *Maynard,* 2 Leigh 38; *Cocke's ex'or & als.* v. *Philips,* 12 Leigh 248. On a joint tenancy at common law dower did not attach, Coke on Lit. Bk. 1, chapter 5, section 45; but by the Code, chapter 116, section 18, "When any joint tenant shall die, whether the estate be real or personal, or whether partition could have been compelled or not, his part shall descend to his heirs, or pass by devise, or go to his personal representative, subject to debts, curtesy, *dower* or distribution, as if he had been a tenant in common. And if hereafter an

---

[9] This section changes the rule laid down in 1 Lom. Dig., pl. 24, page (79) 94.

[10] This section was reported by the revisors, without the last clause, so as to conform the law to the opinion of the majority of the judges in *Wilson* v. *Davisson,* 2 Rob. 398. The legislature added the last clause, which conforms to the opinion of the judge who dissented in that case.

estate of inheritance be conveyed or devised to a husband and his wife, one moiety of such estate shall, on the death of either, descend to his or her heirs, subject to debts, curtesy *or dower*, as the case may be." [11]

A woman is entitled to dower in an estate held in coparcenary, or in common, by her husband in fee. 1 Lom. Dig. 99.

Gilliam v. *Moore*, 4 Leigh 30, presented the question mooted in *Moore* v. *Gilliam*, 5 Munf. 346, whether, if a deed be made to the purchaser of land in fee simple, and, by deed of same date, the purchaser, without being joined by his wife, conveys the same land to trustees upon trust to secure the purchase money to the vendor, the widow of the purchaser is entitled to claim her dower, subject to the trust or paramount to it. The Court of Appeals held that she took her dower in the estate, *subject to the trust.* The authorities, say the court, leave no doubt on the point.[12] The conveyance of the land, and the re-conveyance in trust, being cotemporary and in fact and in law parts of one and the same transaction, Gilliam's seizin was merely transitory as well as instantaneous, and his widow was not entitled to dower against the trust. By the third section of chapter 110 of the Code (the present statute), the widow would be entitled to dower in the surplus remaining after satisfying the deed of trust. *Blair* v. *Thompson & als.*, 11 Grat. 441, differed from *Moore* v. *Gilliam*, 4 Leigh 30. In *Blair* v. *Thompson & als.*, Thompson bought land, and gave bonds, with Snapp as security, for the purchase money; and about eighteen months after the purchase, he executed a deed of trust upon the land and on personal property as a farther security: it was held that the widow of Thompson was entitled to dower in the land paramount to the deed of trust.[13] But where two persons

---

[11] See *Thornton* v. *Thornton*, 3 Rand. 179; *Norman's ex'ix* v. *Cunningham & wife*, 5 Grat. 63.

[12] Co. Lit. 31 b.; 1 Rop. on Prop. 370; 3 Bac. Abr. Dower, c. 2, p. 370; *Holbrook* v. *Finney*, 4 Mass. Rep. 566; *Clark* v. *Monroe*, 14 Id. 351; *Stow* v. *Tift*, 15 John. Rep. 458; *Childress* v. *Smith*, Gilm. 200. [See *May Curry* v. *Brien & als.*, 15 Pet. 21; 4 Kent Com. 38, 39.]

[13] The case arose before the statute abolishing the vendor's equitable lien, Code, ch. 119, § 1, and the position relied on to defeat the widow's claim to dower was, that the vendor's lien was superior to her right of dower. Allen, P., thus met this position: "It is said by Chancellor Kent (4 Kent's Com. 153), 'that the taking the note, bond or covenant is not of itself an act of waiver of the vendor's lien; for such instruments are only the ordinary evidence of debt. But taking a note, bill or bond, with distinct security, or taking distinct security exclusively by itself, either in the shape of real or personal property, from the vendee, or taking the responsibility of a third person, is evidence that the seller did not repose on the lien, but upon independent

purchased real estate jointly, and one of the terms of purchase was, that on receiving a conveyance from the vendor they should at the same time execute a mortgage of the property to secure payment of the purchase money, and the vendor made the conveyance to the purchasers, and owing to a difference between the vendor and purchasers as to the provisions to be inserted in the mortgage, the mortgage was not cotemporaneously executed, but was executed · ten months afterwards in fulfilment of the original contract of sale and purchase, the court *held* the rights of the mortgagee paramount in equity to the dower rights of the purchasers' wives, and upon the death of one of them his widow was dowable only of the equity of redemption of his moiety. *Wheatley's heirs* v. *Calhoun*, 12 Leigh 264.

That a widow would be entitled to dower in an equitable estate in fee simple[14] which her husband had acquired in his lifetime by a verbal contract, provided the contract be established by proof, and such as a court of equity would decree to be specifically performed, seemed to be a point conceded (though not decided) in *Rowton* v. *Rowton*, 1 H. & M. 92; but in *Wheatley's heirs* v. *Calhoun*, 12 Leigh 264[15] by articles between Calhoun and Wheatley they agreed, to make a joint purchase of land, and to divide the same between them by a specified time, Wheatley to pay the whole purchase money to the vendor, and Calhoun to pay to Wheatley his portion thereof in a certain time. After Calhoun had paid the greater part, but not the whole of the purchase money for his portion of the land to Wheatley, the agreement was rescinded, and the amount paid by Calhoun credited to him in another account—Calhoun never was in possession of the land. The court held that Calhoun had not such

---

security; and it discharges the lien.'" *Gilman* v. *Brown*, 1 Mason's R. 212; *Cole* v. *Scott*, 2 Wash. 141; *Brown* v. *Gilman*, 4 Wheat. 290. "So too (adds President Allen), the presumption that the vendor intended to rely on the implied equitable lien is repelled by the vendor's taking a mortgage on the property subsequent to the deed of conveyance to the vendee. *Little & al.* v. *Brown*, 2 Leigh 353. In such case the vendee becomes the owner without qualification at the time of the conveyance; he becomes beneficially seized to his own use; and the wife's title to dower attaches and cannot be divested by the subsequent incumbrance, unless she concurs therein." 11 Grat. 443–4.

[14] Act of 1785, chapter 62, section 1.

[15] The act of 1785 re-published, 1 R. C. 1819, chapter 99, section 31, [Code chapter 116, section 17.] This section, section 17, chapter 116 in the Code is as follows: "Where a person to whose use, or in trust for whose benefit another is seized of real estate, has such inheritance in the use or trust, as if it were a legal right, would entitle such person's husband or wife to curtesy or dower thereof, such husband or wife shall have curtesy or dower of the said estate."

an equity in the land as would entitle his widow to dower under the statute;[16] the contract between Calhoun and Wheatley being executory, and such as it was competent for them to rescind.

Though the right of the widow to dower in land purchased be subject to the vendor's lien for the purchase money, yet she is entitled to have the estate of her deceased husband either in the hands of the personal representatives or of the heirs first exhausted, before resort is had to her right of dower for the payment of the purchase money. *Warner* v. *Van Alstyne*, 3 Paige C. R. 513.

Where the mortgaged estate remains in possession of the mortgagor till his death, and the widow is entitled to dower in the equity of redemption; if neither the heir nor widow redeem, and the land is sold under the mortgage for more than the debt thereby secured, the excess is the value of the equity of redemption and the widow can only be endowed of one-third of that excess. *Coalter*, J. in *Heth* v. *Cocke and ux.*, 1 Rand. 347.

Daniel purchased a tract of land on which there was a deed of trust to secure a debt which the creditor might enforce by a sale of the land whenever he might direct, and D. retained the amount of the debt out of the purchase money for the purpose of paying it. D. died largely indebted, to a much greater amount than could be paid out of his personal estate: the court held that his widow's dower in the land was subject to the deed of trust, that the land was the primary fund for the payment of the debt secured by the trust deed, and that D.'s widow was not entitled to have it discharged out of his personal estate. *Daniel & als.* v. *Leitch*, 13 Grat. 195. In such case, if the trustee die or become unable to act, the widow might institute a suit in equity to have the land sold and the debt paid, and her dower assigned out of the residue of the purchase money. *Ibid.* Or the suit might have been instituted by the creditor, or the heirs, or any or either of them. *Ibid.*

Iage borrowed of the Richmond Building Fund Company on his shares in the company a sum of money upon the terms prescribed in their articles and by-laws, for the purpose of erecting a dwelling on land he owned. Iage and wife, by deed of trust, conveyed the land to secure the Company. Afterwards a written contract was made with a carpenter, Martin, to erect a dwelling on the land. The mechanics lien was by consent of Martin transferred to Boisseux, who undertook to advance the money for the building, and the contract was recorded. The cost of the building was $886 86. Of this sum Iage paid during the progress of the work $600. To make this payment of $600, it was known to the parties that Iage was to receive, and did receive of the Building Fund Company, in addition to the sum of $120 received before the execution of the trust deed, the farther sum of $461, which was paid to Boissieux,

---

[16] Code, chapter 116, section 17.

with the knowledge on his part that it was obtained from the Company. A suit was instituted by Bossieux, in which Iage and his wife, the Building Fund Company, and the trustees in the deed to secure the Company were parties. The Court of Appeals held that the suit by the assignee, Boisseux, could be maintained; that the Company was entitled to priority over the mechanic's lien for its advances made after the contract recorded, as well for its advances made before; that the wife's contingent right of dower, she having joined in the trust deed, was subject to the claim of the Company under the trust deed, but that it was paramount to the claim under the mechanic's lien; that the property should be decreed to be sold out and out, and first applied to the payment of the debt due the Company; and that proper provision should be made by the Circuit Court to compensate the wife's dower interest out of the surplus proceeds of sale, if any, before any part of it was paid to Boissieux, the assignee of the mechanic's lien.[17]

A widow is not endowed of partnership property as against the creditors of the firm. *Pierce* v. *Trigg*, 10 Leigh 406. See 1 Lom. Dig. 649. Where land is held as partnership property, and there is an agreement between the partners that on dissolution of the partnership the land shall be sold, it has been held that such an agreement converts the land into personalty. *Thornton* v. *Dixon*, 3 Bro. C. C. 199 by Belt, note. See *Wheatley's heirs* v. *Calhoun*, 12 Leigh 264, and *Pierce* v. *Trigg*, 10 Leigh 406. Judge Lomax deduces from the cases the following principle: that real estate purchased with the joint effects of a partnership will, as between the partners, be considered personal estate; and it has been inferred (he says) that real estate would with other joint property be primarily liable to the payment of the joint partnership debts, as

---

[17] The Court of Appeals also held, that before decreeing a sale of the house and lot the Circuit Court should have determined the priorities as between the Building Fund Company and the assignee of the mechanic's lien; and that it was error merely to decree a sale and direct the proceeds to be brought into court. *Iage* v. *Bossieux*, 15 Grat. 103. "It is a well settled rule, say the court, that where there are conflicting claims to priority of payment, out of the proceeds of land about to be sold to satisfy the liens upon it, the court, in order to prevent the danger of sacrificing the property by discouraging the creditors from bidding, as they probably might, if their right to satisfaction of their debts and the order in which they were to be paid out of the property, were previously ascertained, should declare the order of payment before it decrees the sale to be made. *Cole's adm'or* v. *McRae*, 6 Rand. 644; *Buchanan* v. *Clark*, &c., 10 Gratt. 164. It is, therefore, not sufficient that the court should direct the fund to be paid into court, and should declare the priorities afterwards. The purpose for which it is done requires that it should precede the sale."

between the representatives; and that if the heir or widow of a partner be entitled, their right can attach only to the surplus. 1 Lom. Dig. 649, citing 1 Rop. Prop., 2d edit., 346, and note. See *Brooke* v. *Washington*, 8 Grat. 248. Since 1808, when *Pitts* v. *Waugh*, 4 Mass. Rep. 424, was decided, the partnership law in regard to real estate has undergone great changes: By *Tucker, P.* in *Brooke* v. *Washington*, 8 Grat. 256, citing Collyer on Partnership, § 135, and notes.

A wife joining her husband in a lease for years, surviving her husband, is entitled to dower in the rent. *Herbert & als.* v. *Wren & als.*, 7 Cranch 370.

Equities of redemption are not in terms included with trust estates in the statute [Code, ch. 117, § 16; 1 R. C. ch. 99, § 31], yet the Court of Appeals of Virginia has construed that provision of the law as designed to place the rights of dower upon the same ground as the right to curtesy, and has, therefore, determined that a wife may, as against the heir, be endowed of the redemption of land mortgaged in fee. *Heth* v. *Cocke*, 1 Rand. 344.

A widow is dowable of land held by her husband in the Dismal Swamp, which is incapable of cultivation, and no otherwise productive or valuable than by selling or working the timber and making sale of the shingles into which it is converted; and she is entitled to an account of the profits thus made by the tenants from the land. *Macaulay* v. *Dismal Swamp Co.*, 2 Rob. R. 507, 528, 529; and though the land had been conveyed in trust, yet as the husband remained in possession during his life, the trustees making no sale under the trust deed until after his death, the husband was considered as having died seized of the land, subject to the deed of trust, and his widow was held entitled to dower in the land and to receive rents and profits from the husband's death in like manner as if the deed had not been made. *Ibid.* And the widow having died, her personal representative was entitled to recover the rents and profits up to her death. *Ibid.*

A widow may work mines already open upon land assigned to her for dower. 1 Lom. Dig. 106; 2 Rob. R. 525. She cannot open new mines (1 Lom. Dig. pp. 64, 97; 2 Rob. R. 525), but she may sink new shafts into the same veins of coal in which shafts have been sunk before (*Crouch* v. *Puryear*, &c., 1 Rand. 258), and she may sink a shaft into a seam lying below another already opened (*Ibid*),[18] and may open new pits or shafts for working the old veins of coals, for otherwise, the working the same mines would be impracticable. *Clavering* v. *Clavering*, 2 P. Wms. 388.

A woman is not dowable both of the land given in exchange and

---

[18] See *Coates* v. *Cheever*, 1 Cowen 460; *Findlay* v. *Smith*, &c., 6 Munf. 142; and 2 Rob. R. 525.

of the land taken in exchange, but she may have her election to be endowed of which she will. 1 Lom. Dig. 101.

The wife of a tenant in common acquires merely an inchoate right to dower in the land subject to the contingency of partition, incident to the estate, and by which her interest may be increased or diminished: if, therefore, partition be made of the land by the tenants in common, whether by deed or otherwise, the wife of one of the tenants in common will be dowable of such part only as is assigned to her husband by the partition. *Patter* v. *Wheaton*, 13 Mass. R. 504.

RELEASE OF DOWER.—Code, ch. 121, §§ 4 and 7; Session Acts 1869–70, p. 174. Must be 21 years of age. See *Thomas* v. *Gammell & ux.*, 6 Leigh 9.

WHAT WILL BAR DOWER.—Code, ch. 110, §§ 4, 5, as amended by Sess. Acts 1865–6, p. 166, provides as follows:

4. If any estate, real or personal, intended to be in lieu of dower shall be conveyed or devised for the jointure of the wife, such conveyance or devise shall bar her dower of the real estate or the residue thereof; and every such provision, by deed or will, shall be taken to be intended in lieu of dower, unless the contrary intention plainly appear in such deed or will, or in some other writing, signed by the party making the provision.

5. But if such conveyance or devise were before the marriage, without the assent in writing, or during the infancy of the feme, or if it were after marriage—in either case, the widow may, at her election, waive such jointure and demand her dower. Such election shall be made within one year after the death of the husband, or within one year after the admission of his will to probat where the provision is by will, and shall be made in any court of record in the county or corporation in which the husband resided at the time of his death, or in the clerk's office of which the instrument creating the jointure is recorded, or by a writing recorded in such court, or in the clerk's office thereof, upon such acknowledgment or proof as would authorize a writing to be admitted to record under chapter 121; and when she shall elect and receive her dower, the estate so conveyed or devised to her shall cease and determine.

Code, ch. 110, §§ 6 and 7, provides as follows:

6. If a widow be lawfully deprived of her jointure, or any part thereof, she shall be endowed of so much of the real estate whereof, but for said jointure, she would have been dowable, as is equal in value to that of which she was deprived.

7. If a wife of her own free will leave her husband, and live in adultery, she shall be barred of her dower, unless her husband be afterwards reconciled to her and suffer her to live with him.

The amendment to the 4th section of chapter 110 of the Code, made in the Session Acts 1865-'6, page 166, above cited, changes the rule laid down in *Higginbotham* v. *Cornwell*, 8 Gratt. 83. In that case the court held that a provision for a wife in the will shall not be construed as in lieu of dower, unless the will so declare in terms, or the conclusion from its provisions be as clear and satisfactory as if it was so expressed. The statute cited above requires that if a contrary intention do not appear plainly either in the deed or will of the party making provision for his wife, or in some other writing signed by the party making the provision, the courts shall hold such provision to be in lieu of dower.[19]

The question suggests itself whether if such provision be made by deed, this statute would be held by the courts as affecting the widow's right to dower in property acquired by the husband subsequent to the deed. If the statute shall be held to apply to such after acquired property, deeds making provision for a wife, at any stage of a man's fortune, should declare plainly the intention of the grantor, both as regards his then estate and his subsequently acquired estate. In *Craig's heirs* v. *Walthall and wife*, 14 Grat. 518, a case arising under the law as it stood in the Code before the amendment of 1866-'7, the testator devised all his land to his different children, giving the wife one of the parcels during her widowhood, which parcel had the improvements upon it. He also gave her his slaves for life, and all the rest of his property to enjoy and use for the best interests of his children; and the interest on the bonds due him to be used by her for the benefit of his children: The court held the will to be in lieu of dower.

In the case just cited, the widow was told that the provision in the will was in lieu of dower, and advised to renounce it. She declined to do so, and expressed herself satisfied with the provision. She took possession of the property, and held it for four years, until she married. The court decided that an election might be made by acts *in pais*, that she had elected to take under the will, and could not then claim her dower. 14 Grat. 525. The principles applicable to the case of a widow as to the necessity of electing between her right of dower and the provisions of the will are the same as those applicable to other persons; and if the widow's taking dower will clearly interfere with the provisions of the will, she must select. *Dixon* v. *McCue & als.*, 14 Grat. 540. The statute now requires to effect a waiver of the jointure and demand of dower, that the election shall be made in court, or in the clerk's office, or by a writing duly acknowledged or proved for record. Session Acts 1865-6, page 166, cited *supra*, p. 50.

---

[19] The amendment was probably suggested by the Act 3 and 4, Will. 4, chapter 105, section 9. See this statute cited, 1 Lea. Ca. in Equity (Amer. edit. 1852), page 247 (marg.)

Dower in the realty and the distributive share of the widow in the personalty are entirely different things, and in construing a marriage agreement, declaring that certain sums of money were " to be considered as in bar of and in full compensation for said E.'s dower," the court held that while the agreement barred E. of her dower in her husband's real estate, it did not deprive her of her distributive share of his personal estate. *Findley's ex'ors* v. *Findley*, 11 Grat. 434, 438. See *Colleton* v. *Garth*, 6 Sim. 19.

In *Healy & als.* v. *Rowan & als.*, 5 Grat. 430, the court cited with approbation the doctrine of *Tabb* v. *Archer*, &c., 3 H. and M. 399, that " marriage articles made between an infant feme and her intended husband, beneficial to her and her contemplated issue, are obligatory upon the parties, and will be enforced in a court of equity by a settlement in conformity therewith, on the application of the issue of the marriage ;" such a contract is thus distinguished from other contracts, voidable at the election of an infant party.[20]

The decision in *Healy* v. *Rowan*, 5 Grat. 430, was made in a case arising under the statute, 1 Revised Code, chapter 107, section 11, page 405, the language of which is as follows: " But if the said conveyance were before the marriage, and during the infancy of the feme, or, if it were after marriage, in either case the widow may, at her election, waive such jointure, and demand her dower." If in *Healy* v. *Rowan*, the infant feme had been a party to the marriage articles, they would have been held binding upon the wife ; but the marriage articles were there executed by the guardians of the feme and not by herself, and the court declared them to be of no obligatory force upon the infant feme, and that a deed of settlement made after the marriage, in conformity with these articles, had no greater effect, being merely void as to her for want of the privy examination required by law.

The election by the widow, if she mean to waive the jointure, and demand her dower, must be made under the terms of the statute, within a specified time. This statute was passed February 21st, 1866. This was not the rule before this statute. The provision in the Revised Code of 1819, ch. 104, § 26, requiring renunciation of the will by a certain time, related to personal property only. Tate's Dig. 293. See the cases as to making the election as the law stood prior to February 21st, 1866, so as to bar the widow's right of dower. Notes to *Streatfield* v. *Streatfield*, 1 Lea. Cas. Eq. (Amer. edit.), pp. 239 *et seq.* (marg.) ; *Blunt & als.* v. *Gee & als.*, 5 Call 481.

WHAT WIDOW ENTITLED TO BEFORE DOWER ASSIGNED.—Code, ch. 110, § 8, provides :

---

[20] Allen, P., would express no opinion on the point, it not being necessary to the decision of the case. 5 Grat. 432.

8. Until her dower is assigned, the widow shall be entitled to demand of the heirs or devisees one-third part of the issues and profits of the other real estate which was devised or descended to them, of which she is dowable; and in the mean time may hold, occupy and enjoy the mansion house and curtilage, without charge; and if deprived thereof may, on complaint of unlawful entry or detainer, recover the possession with damages for the time she was so deprived.

A widow may under this statute hold, occupy and enjoy the mansion house and curtilage without charge, until dower assigned; and until dower assigned is entitled to demand one-third of the rents, issues and profits of the other real estate. The language of the Code of 1819, 1 R. C., ch. 107, sec. 2, was as follows: "And till such dower shall be assigned, it shall be lawful for her to remain and continue in the mansion house and the messuage or plantation thereto belonging, without being chargeable to pay the heir any rent for the same; any law, usage or custom to the contrary in any wise notwithstanding." *Carr*, J., pronouncing opinion of the court, said that it was unnecessary in *Grayson & ux.* v. *Moncure*, 1 Leigh 451, to decide the general question whether the widow was entitled under that statute to all the rents, issues and profits of the mansion house and plantation thereto belonging until dower assigned; that the widow having obtained a decree against the infant heir, directing commissioners to assign dower which she might have had executed immediately, but did not for a year, during which she remained in the mansion house, and assented to the cultivation of the land by the agent of the heir, and after her dower assigned having received one-third of the rents of the messuage and plantation thereto belonging, accrued before dower assigned, and claimed no more at the time, she could not by a subsequent action recover the other two-thirds of the rents.

While the statute, 1 R. C. 1819, ch. 107, sec. 2, was in force, Joseph McReynolds, by his last will, devised that his wife Rebecca during her life should have the use and profits of all his real estate as a home and support for her during her life, and after her death to pass unencumbered in absolute fee to his son Isaac. The personal estate he gave in eight equal shares to his seven children and the children of a deceased son. The widow renounced the will. Her dower not having been assigned, she continued for some years to occupy the land herself or through her son Isaac. A bill was filed for the purpose of assigning her dower and making partition of the other two-thirds of the real estate, and seeking an account of the rents and profits thereof. The Circuit court directed an assignment of one-third of the real estate as dower, a partition of two-thirds of the real estate into eight parts among the eight children of the testator, or their heirs or vendees, and *an account of the rents and profits of the two-thirds from the time of the waiver and renunciation.* The Court of Appeals reversed the decree of the Circuit court in the last mentioned particular; held that the waiver and renunciation of the widow placed her in the same condition she would have occupied had there been no will; that she was entitled to occupy the mansion house and land thereto belonging without . rent until dower assigned, and that she might occupy the land herself or allow another to do it for her, and it was error to direct an account of the rents and profits whilst it was so held either by herself or by Isaac McReynolds with her permission. *McReynolds* v. *Counts & als.,* 9 Grat. 242. See also *Wiseley* v. *Findlay,* 3 Rand. 372.

How Dower Assigned.—Code, chapter 110, section 9, provides:

9. " Dower may be assigned as at common law; or upon the motion of the heirs or devisees, or any of them, the court in which the will of the husband is admitted to record, or administration of his estate is granted, may appoint commissioners, by whom the dower nay be assigned, and the assignment, when confirmed by the court, shall have the same effect as if made by the heir at common law. But nothing herein contained shall be construed to take away or affect the jurisdiction which courts of chancery now exercise over the subject of dower."

The widow is not entitled, as of right, to have the mansion house included in the dower assigned to her. *Devaughn* v. *Devaughn,* 19 Grat. 556.

At common law, the heir had the power of assigning dower without resorting to any court, and that power is not impaired by the statute. An assignment of dower by commissioners, under an order of court, at the instance of one of several coheirs, is binding on the widow, provided it be a full and just assignment; and it is binding also on the coheirs, though they be infants, provided the assignment is not excessive. *Moore & ux.* v. *Waller,* &c., 2 Rand. 418.

In *Fitzhugh & ux.* v. *Foote & als.,* 3 Call 13, there had been in 1780 an assignment of dower in lands and slaves by order of a county court by motion, and without a suit for the purpose. Some time after, the children of the testator filed their bill, complaining of the assignment of dower, and the Chancellor set aside the allotment of dower altogether in the slaves, the allotment being unequal and excessive, and ordered a new assignment. The Court of Appeals (in 1801) said, under all the circumstances of the case, a new division of the slaves, after such a length of time, for a small excess, ought not to have been ordered, especially as the whole of the dower slaves, with their increase, will belong to the appellees on the death of their mother. A reformation of that which was wrong ought to have been decreed, and a return or delivery of a part of the slaves, to the value of the excess, if that could be properly done; accounting also for profits, as usual in such cases; or, if that could not properly have been done, then a satisfaction in money, or in payment of interest for the amount of such excess, should have been directed."

In *Raper* v. *Saunders*, 21 Grat. 60, the testator directed first, that so long as his wife L. remained his widow, all his property, real and personal, should be kept together, and subject to the control of his executor, but the possession to remain with L. during her widowwood: second, if she married she was to take one-third of the estate, and the remainder to go into the possession of his executor; and if in his opinion it should at any time thereafter be for the interest of the testator's children to sell the entire estate, and lend the money for their benefit, the executor might sell the same in his discretion. The widow renounced the will, and dower was assigned to her by an order of court, to which the children were not parties. The executor and widow, she selling her dower interest, joined in selling and conveying the land, the executor acting under the power: The Court of Appeals held, that the executor had no authority to sell under the power during the widowhood of L.; that on a bill to set aside the sale filed by the children, the court might set the sale aside, so far as made by the executor, and confirm it, so far as made by the widow, and direct a new assignment of dower; and that though the bill did not pray that the sale should be set aside, yet as it made a proper case for such relief, it might be given under the prayer for general relief.

As already stated,[21] there cannot be a decree for a specific sum in lieu of dower without the assent of all the parties interested. *Blair* v. *Thompson & als.*, 11 Grat. 441; *White* v. *White & als.*, 16 Grat. 264; and where land in which there is a right of dower is sold in a suit in which the tenant in dower is a party, the other parties have a right to insist that instead of a sum in gross, one-third of the purchase money should be set apart, and the interest thereof paid annually to the tenant in dower during her life; *Wilson & als.* v. *Davisson*, 2 Rob. R. 384; *Herbert & als.* v. *Wren & als.*, 7 Cran. 380; the tenant in dower has the same right, *White* v. *White & als.*, 16 Grat. 264. But there are cases in which the dowress consenting, the dower may be commuted without the consent of the heirs.[22]

---

[21] Page 41, *ante*.

[22] The author has been furnished (with liberty to use it in this work) a note by *William Green, Esq.*, filed in the Chancery Court of Richmond in a suit by creditors of the decedent, the widow claiming her dower. The doctrines of this note are believed to be true:

" Upon a principle analogous to that acted upon and recognized in *Cole's*

PARTITION.

Form of a Bill for Partition.

To the Honorable A. B., Judge of the ———— Court
of the county of ———— :

Complaining showeth unto the court, your complainant, James J., that your complainant's father,
Thomas J., was in his lifetime seized and possessed
of certain real estate lying in the county of————
[here describe it], and being so seized and possessed
of the said real estate, sometime in the year 18—,
the said Thomas J. departed this life intestate, leaving your orator and Robert J., Emma J. and Samuel
J., his only children and heirs at law. The said

---

adm'r v. *McRae,* 6 Rand. 644; *Cralle* v. *Meem,* 8 Grat. 496; *Buchanan* v. *Clark,*
10 Grat. 164; *Iage* v. *Bossieux,* 15 Grat. 83; *Hovey* v. *Helms,* 20 Grat. 1; *Lipscomb* v. *Rogers, Ibid.* 658, it seems necessary that *before* a sale is made, the
dower of the widow should be set out, so that a purchaser may know what
part will pass at once into his possession, and what not, until her death, or
that a valid arrangement be made for dispensing with it. The latter seems
preferable for the creditors if it can be accomplished. In general, a gross sum
of money, by way of commutation for dower, is not allowable without the
consent of all parties concerned, *Herbert* v. *Wren,* 7 Cranch 370, 380, 81, 82;
Wilson v. *Davisson,* 2 Rob. R. 384, 402-3; *Blair* v. *Thompson,* 11 Grat. 441,
451, 452; and, in this case, it doubtless cannot be without the consent of the
dowress; but if she consents, it seems the court may bind all other parties to
the cause by its decree (though without their consent) that the land shall be
sold exempt from dower, and that she shall have in lieu thereof so much
of the sale money as shall be just compensation therefor, to be ascertained
and reported by a commissioner; the sale here being made for the satisfaction
of creditors, and being certain not to yield proceeds enough therefor. I do
not remember in our Virginia books any reported authority for this, but it has
certainly been so practiced in some cases in the Circuit courts, and I find reported authority for it elsewhere. *Cassamore* v. *Brooke,* 3 Bland 267; *McCormick* v. *Gibson,* 3 Bland 499, 502 n."

Emma and Samuel are infants under the age of twenty-one years.

And your orator farther states, that the said real estate is, as he believes, susceptible of partition among the parties thereto ; but if it be not, then your complainant desires the same to be sold, and the proceeds divided among the adult and the infant parties, according to their respective rights; the shares of the infants to be held as directed by the statute in such case made and provided. Should the property not be divisible in kind, your complainant believes, and here states, that the interests of those who are entitled to the said real estate, or its proceeds, will be promoted by a sale of the whole of said real estate, or by an allotment of part and sale of the residue.*

In tender consideration whereof, and forasmuch as your complainant is remediless in the premises save by the aid of a court of equity, where matters of this kind are alone and properly cognizable, your complainant prays that the said Robert J., Emma J., and Samuel J. may be made parties defendant to this bill, and required on their oaths to answer the same; that a proper *guardian ad litem* be assigned the infant defendants to defend their interests in this suit, who shall also answer this bill; that proper process issue; that the said real estate be divided between the several parties entitled thereto, and your complainant's portion thereof be allotted to him, and in case the said real estate cannot be partitioned and divided in kind, that the same be exposed to sale, and the proceeds of such sale be divided among the parties en-

titled thereto ; that all proper orders and decrees may
be made, and proper enquiries be directed, and that
all such other, farther and general relief may be
afforded your complainant as the nature of his case
may require, or to equity shall seem meet. And
your complainant will ever pray, &c.

JAMES, J.   X. X., p. q.

Form of Bill for Partition and Account.

Follow form on pp. 56, 57 to star *, then say :

Your complainant farther states, that the said
Robert J. has been enjoying the said property, the
whole of it, ever since the death of the said Thomas
J., and has been receiving the rents and profits
thereof, one-fourth of which rents and profits should
be paid to your complainant, and the other shares
thereof to the parties entitled thereto.

In tender consideration whereof, and forasmuch as
your complainant is remediless in the premises save
by the aid of a court of equity, where matters of this
kind are alone and properly cognizable, your complainant prays that the said Robert J., Emma J.,
and Samuel J. may be made parties defendant to
this bill, and required on their oaths to answer the
same; that a proper *guardian ad litem* be assigned to
the infant defendants to defend their interests in this
suit, who shall also answer this bill; that the said
real estate be divided between the several parties
entitled thereto, and your complainant's portion
thereof allotted to him, and in case the said real
estate cannot be partitioned and divided in kind,

that the same be exposed to sale, and the proceeds of such sale be divided among the parties entitled thereto; that an account be taken of the rents and profits of the said real estate from the death of the said Thomas J., and the said Robert J. be decreed and ordered to pay to your complainant his portion thereof; that proper process issue; that all proper orders and decrees may be made, and proper enquiries be directed, and that all such other, farther and general relief may be afforded your complainant as the nature of his case may require, or to equity shall seem meet. And your complainant will ever pray, &c.

JAMES, J. .   X. X., p. q.

Form of Bill for Partition when some of the Parties are unknown.[23]

To the Honorable A. B., Judge of the ———— Court of the county of ———— :

Complaining showeth unto the court, your complainant, James J., that your complainant's father, Thomas J., was in his lifetime seized and possessed of certain real estate lying in the county of [here describe it], and being so seized and possessed of the said real estate, sometime in the year 18—, the said Thomas J. departed this life intestate, leaving Robert J., Julian J., and Samuel J., his only children and heirs at law; the said Emma and Samuel are infants under the age of twenty-one years. The said

---

[23] Code, ch. 124, § 4; ch. 170, §§ 10, 11, 12, 13. Sess. Acts 1830–1, p. 99, ch. 31, §§ 1-6. Tate's Dig. 726–728.

Julian J., sometime after the death of the said Thomas J., removed to the State of Kentucky, and married Lucy R., and then removed to some other State, your complainant believes to Texas; and afterwards, as was reported, the said Julian J. departed this life, and his widow has also since died. Your complainant has heard, and believes that Julian left several children and heirs at law; the number and the names of whom are unknown to your complainant. The said children and heirs at law of said Julian J. would be entitled together to one-fifth of the said real estate.

And your orator farther states, that the said real estate is, as he believes, susceptible of partition among the parties thereto; but if it be not, then your complainant desires the same to be sold, and the proceeds divided among the adult and the infant parties according to their respective rights; the shares of the infants to be held as directed by the statute in such case made and provided. Should the property not be divisible in kind, your complainant believes and here states that the interests of those who are entitled to the said real estate or its proceeds will be promoted by a sale of the whole of said real estate, or by an allotment of part and sale of the residue. In tender consideration whereof, your complainant prays that the said Robert J., Emma J., Samuel J., and the unknown heirs at law of the said Julian J., deceased, may be made parties defendant to this bill, and required on their oaths to answer the same; that a proper *guardian ad litem* be assigned the infant defendants to defend their interests in this suit, who shall also answer this bill; that proper process issue; that an order of publication be made against the said unknown heirs at law of the said Julian J., deceased, and duly published; that the said real estate be divided between the several parties, &c., &c., (following form on p. 56, 57 to the end.)

Form of Bill of Partition by one Tenant in common against another.

See Willis's Equity Pleadings, 106.

[See Forms of Partition at Law before the Statute in Virginia giving equity complete jurisdiction, in 1 Rob. Forms 205, 206; also 3 Chit. Pl. 1390–1407.]

PRACTICAL NOTES TO BILLS FOR PARTITION.

Code, ch. 124, §§ 1–6, 1 Lom. Dig. 484–487 (marg.), 490–496 (marg.), 506–509 (marg.); Mitf. Pl. 119, 120, 122, 123; Story's Eq. Jur., §§ 646–658; 17 Ves. 545, 553, 554, *Agar* v. *Fairfax;* 2 Sch. & Lefr. 371, 372, *Whaley* v. *Dawson;* 1 Jac. & Walk., 473, *Miller* v. *Warmington;* 2 Ves., Jr., *Calmady* v. *Calmady;* 1 P. Wms. 446, 447, *Earl of Clarendon* v. *Hornby;* 6 Sim. R. 643, *Gaskell* v. *Gaskell;* 1 Younge & Col. 538, 2 Younge & Col. 586, *Storey* v. *Johnson;* 4 Barb. 228, *Haywood* v. *Johnson.*

As to partition between joint tenants, voluntary, see 1 Lom. Dig. 484 (marg.), by suit in equity, 1 Lom. Dig. 486 (marg.) *et seq.*

As to partition between coparceners, voluntary, see 1 Lom. Dig. 490–494 (marg.), by suit in equity, 1 Lom. Dig. 494, 495 (marg.).

As to partition between tenants in common, voluntary, see 1 Lom. Dig. 505 (marg.), by suit in equity, 506–509 (marg.).

At common law partition by joint tenants could be made only by deed, and by tenants in common only by livery without deed; and coparceners could make partition as well by parol without deed or livery as by deed.[24] Until the Statute, 31 Hen. VIII., ch. 1, only coparceners could be compelled to make partition; that Statute

---

[24] Litt., ? 250, and Coke's note.

authorized tenants in common and joint tenants to sue for partition. See this Statute as printed in Alln. on Partition, pp. 165, 166.

It is not necessary to state in the bill any peculiar ground of . equitable interference, Mitf. Pl. 120.

The present Statute of Virginia in regard to partition is as follows:

By Code, chap. 124,

Partition of Lands.

§ 1. Tenants in common, joint tenants and coparceners shall be compellable to make partition, and the court of equity of the county or corporation, wherein the estate or any part thereof may be, shall have jurisdiction in cases of partition, and in the exercise of such jurisdiction may take cognizance of all questions of law affecting the legal title that may arise in any proceeding.

§ 2. Any two or more of the parties, if they so elect, may have their shares laid off together, when partition can be conveniently made in that way.

§ 3. (As modified by Session Acts 1869–70, p. 548.) When partition cannot be conveniently made, the entire subject may be allotted to any party who will accept the same, and pay therefor to the other parties such sums of money as their interest therein may entitle them to ; or in any case now pending, or hereafter brought, in which partition cannot be conveniently made, if the interests of those who are entitled to the subject or its proceeds will be promoted by a sale of the entire subject, or allotment of part and sale of the residue, the court, notwithstanding any of those entitled may be an infant, insane person or married woman, may order such sale and allotment, and make distribution of the proceeds of sale according to the respective rights of those entitled, taking care, when there are creditors of any deceased person who was a tenant in common, joint tenant or coparcener, to have the proceeds of such deceased person's part applied according to the rights of such creditors. The court making an order for sale shall, when the dividend of a party exceeds the value of three hundred dollars, if such party be an infant or insane person, require security for the faithful application of the proceeds of his interest in like manner as if the sale were made under chapter 128.

§ 4. If the name or share of any person interested in the subject of the partition be unknown, so much as is known in relation thereto shall be stated in the bill.

§ 5. Any person who before the partition or sale was lessee of any of the lands divided or sold, shall hold the same of him to whom such land is allotted or sold, on the same terms on which by his lease he held it before the partition.

Partition of Slaves or other Chattels.

§ 6. When an equal division of slaves, goods or chattels cannot be made in kind among those entitled, a court of equity may direct the sale of the same and the distribution of the proceeds according to the rights of the parties.

By Code, chap. 123, sec. 15. Where any descendant of a person dying intestate as to his estate, or any part thereof, shall have received from such intestate in his lifetime, or under his will, any estate, real or personal, by way of advancement, and he or any descendant of his shall come into the partition and distribution of the estate with the other parceners and distributees, such advancement shall be brought into hotchpot with the whole estate, real and personal, descended or distributable, and thereupon such party shall be entitled to his proper portion of the estate, real and personal.

By Code, chap. 163, sec. 15. The clerk of the court wherein there is any partition of, or assignment of dower in land under any order, or any recovery of land under judgment or decree, shall transmit to the clerk of the court of each county or corporation, wherein such land is, a copy of such order, judgment or decree, and of such partition or assignment, and of the order confirming the same, and along therewith such description of the land as may appear in the papers of the cause. And the clerk of the court of such county or corporation shall record the same in his deed book, and index it in the name of the person who had the land before, and also in the name of the person who became entitled under such partition, assignment or recovery.

See also Code, chap. 104, sec. 30.

JURISDICTION IN EQUITY.

The claim to partition, before the statute, was in Virginia matter of right,[25] and not of discretion, when plaintiff showed a clear legal title. *Wisely* v. *Findlay & als.*, 3 Rand. 361; *Castleman, &c.* v. *Veitch, &c.*, 3 Rand. 598; *Stuart's heirs* v. *Coalter*, 4 Rand. 74. See note, p. 64 *post*.

Where the legal title was disputed or doubtful, it was the practice, before the Statute above cited, for the court of equity either to dismiss the bill, or retaining the bill, only to grant relief after the plaintiff had established his title at law, by ejectment or other legal remedy. *Straughan* v. *Wright*, 4 Rand. 493; *Stuart's heirs* v. *Coalter*, 4 Rand. 74.

By the present statute, courts of equity in Virginia "take cogni-

---

[25] By reason of the act, 31 Hen. VIII., chap. 1, as to joint tenants and tenants in common; at common law as to coparcerners. See Alln. Part. 55, 56. See also *Baring* v. *Nash*, 1 Ves. & B. 555, 556. *Parker* v. *Geriard*, Ambler R. 236, and Mr. Blunt's note.

zance of all questions of law affecting the legal title that may arise in any proceeding," Code, chap. 124, sec. 126.[26]

---

[26] This language is substantially the same with the concluding clause of the 4th section of this 124th chapter, as originally reported by the Revisors. The Revisors had said in that clause of that section : " But the court may decide upon the right or legal title of the plaintiff where it is disputed," and appended to the said section a note, in which they said, that while it was well settled that the right to have partition in equity is not discretionary with the court, but may be claimed *ex debito justitiæ*,.still it seems to be "an indispensable requisite to entitle the plaintiff to relief in such cases, that he shall have a clear legal title. If his title depends on difficult and doubtful questions of law, the decree is suspended until he establishes his title at law, not by writ of partition, but by ejectment or other legal remedy;" *Wisely* v. *Findlay*, 3 Rand. 370; *Stuart's heirs* v. *Coalter*, 4 Rand. 74; that they saw no reason for the restriction on the equity jurisdiction in Virginia, and proposed to abolish it. The Code, as enacted, removes the restriction.

In *Miller* v. *Warmington*, 1 Jac. & Walk. 473, Sir Thomas Plumer, M. R., said that it was essential to a partition in equity that the legal title should be before the court, and urged in support of his view, that if the equitable title only was there, the conveyances, if any were necessary, could not be made. This difficulty, in the English administration of relief in partition, does not embarrass us in Virginia. The Statute, Code, chap. 163, sec. 15 (copied from 1 R. C. 1819, p. 65, sec. 14), seems to dispense with conveyances, making the decree of the court decreeing partition take their place. And it has been the almost universal practice in Virginia not to decree mutual conveyances in cases of partition'. The Statute is as follows:—" § 15. The clerk of the court wherein there is any partition of, or assignment of dower in, land under any order, or any recovery of land under judgment or decree, shall transmit to the clerk of the court of each county or corporation, wherein such land is, a copy of such order, judgment or decree, and of such partition or assignment, and of the order confirming the same, and along therewith such description of the land as may appear in the papers of the cause. And the clerk of the court of such county or corporation shall record the same in his deed book, and index it in the name of the person who had the land before, and also in the name of the person who became entitled under such partition, assignment or recovery."— Under the terms of the New York Statute, which provided that all partitions made under and in virtue of the proceedings had in the court of chancery should be firm and effectual forever, and that the final decree of the court for, or upon the partition, &c., should be binding and conclusive, as if such partition, &c., had been made in a court of law ; Chancellor Kent held that it was unnecessary to decree mutual conveyances. ·His decree was: " That the said partition remain firm and effectual forever, and that the said parties respectively hold and enjoy in severalty the said portions of the premises set apart and allotted to them as aforesaid." *Young & ux.* v. *Cooper & als.*, 3 John. C. R. 295.

WHO MAY SUE FOR PARTITION, AND WHEN.

The doctrine of Lord Hardwicke, in *Cartwright* v. *Pulteney*, 2 Atk. 380, that in a partition between two joint tenants, or tenants in common, the plaintiff must show title in himself to a moiety, and not allege generally that he is in possession of a moiety; for, in this respect, equity was stricter than a partition at law, where seisin was sufficient, was based upon the position, that in chancery convey-. ances were directed, and not a partition only, and this made it dis- cretionary with the courts of equity whether they would grant a partition or not. When there were suspicious circumstances in the plaintiff's title, the court would leave him to his remedy at law. See 1 Sto. Eq. Jur. 605, 606.

If a testator devise to his widow, "her living" upon a tract of land during her life, and the same land to one of his sons in fee; a bill in equity lies for partition of the land *among the heirs of that son*, in the lifetime of his father's widow, and that too without making her a party; for the decree will be made subject to her right. *McClintock* v. *Mann*, 4 Munf. 328. This case differs from *Custis* v. *Snead*, 12 Grat. 260.

In *Currin & als.* v. *Spraull & als.*, 10 Grat. 145, the plaintiffs, before the Code, chap. 124, sec. 1, filed their bill in equity for partition. Their title was doubtful, but the Circuit Court (in the opinion certainly of three of the judges of the Court of Appeals, and perhaps in the opinion of all of them, exceeding its then jurisdiction,) decided at October term 1849 the question of legal title. From the decision of the Circuit Court an appeal was taken, and the appellate court in July, 1853, reversed the decree of the Circuit Court; but meanwhile the act, Code, ch. 124, sec. 1, having been enacted and in force, giving the Circuit Court as a court of equity jurisdiction in such a case, the Court of Appeals remanded the cause to the Circuit Court, with directions to allow the parties a reasonable time to prepare for trial, and then to decide the question of title between them, and that the general rules of practice, observed in courts of equity, should be observed in the case, for the purpose of ascertaining facts by a jury or otherwise, as might be proper; and that if the title should be adjudged to belong to the plaintiffs, they should have the partition and account of rents and profits prayed for if adjudged to the defendant, that the bill should be dismissed.

In *Otley* v. *McAlpine's heirs*, 2 Grat. 340, a tenant by the curtesy of land purchased the reversionary interest of one of the heirs; another interest was held by an infant heir, and another by an adult heir. The tenant by the curtesy sued in equity for partition the infant and the adult heir. The Circuit Court dismissed the bill, on the ground that the plaintiff was not at law entitled to demand partition of a reversion, and as in making partition equity follows the law, he was not entitled to partition in equity. The

Court of Appeals reversed the decision of the Circuit Court. Following *Agar* v. *Fairfax*, 17 Ves. R. 533, a case of partition decreed in equity in which no partition could have been maintained at law, the appellate court held that the Circuit Court, as a court of equity, should allow the plaintiff one-third of the land in severalty.

Ruffners v. *Lewis's ex'ors & als.*, 7 Leigh 720, was a bill in equity for partition, in which defendants, holding adversely to the plaintiffs, but holding so under the *bona fide* belief that they were the true owners, were treated as tenants in common with the plaintiffs; and the court also held that the defendants ought not to be charged with rents and profits where none had been made (provided the defendants appeared to have employed the property in good faith, with a view to make it profitable, but failed in doing so,) nor with speculative profits when the real profits were susceptible of being ascertained. The court also held that the defendants were not only fairly entitled to a credit for their expenses and actual services in the successful operation which terminated in discovering the salt water, which rendered the property of great value, but also for their expenses, labor and services in their unsuccessful experiments.

MODE OF PARTITION.

It is error to decree a partition of the land of an intestate subject to the widow's right of dower. She, and her husband, if she has married again, should be made parties, her dower first assigned, and a division made of the residue. *Custis* v. *Snead & als.*, 12 Grat. 260.

Where the same persons are entitled to lands derived from the father, and to lands derived from the mother, and some or all of the parties are infants, the court will not allow the lands to be blended in the division, unless it can be shown that the interest of the parties will be promoted thereby. *Custis* v. *Snead & als.*, 12 Grat. 260.

An interlocutory decree directed the commissioners to divide equally between the plaintiff and the defendant, who were infants, the tract of land of which A. B. died seized. Instead of doing so, the commissioners assigned to the appellee one-fifth of the tract, leaving the residue undivided; the Court of Appeals held that the commissioners in this respect had violated their duty, and that it was error in the Circuit Court to confirm their report. *Custis* v. *Snead & als.*, 12 Grat. 260.

As a general rule, prior to Code, chap. 124, sec. 2, the share of each parcener should have been assigned to him in severalty. And if from the condition of the subject or the parties it was proper to pursue a different course, the facts justifying a departure from the rule should, at least where infants are concerned, have been disclosed by the report, or otherwise appeared, to enable the court to judge whether or not their interest would be injuriously affected. *Custis* v. *Snead & als.*, 12 Grat. 260.

In decreeing a partition in favor of a plaintiff claiming by equitable title, the court ought to direct that the holders of the legal title shall convey the same to him in fee. *Christian's devisee* v. *Christians & als.*, 6 Munf. 534.

The plaintiff having acquired shares since the institution of the suit, may have a larger portion of the land allotted to him than he was entitled to at the time of instituting his suit. *Wisely* v. *Findlay & als.*, 3 Ran. 361.

In making partition in chancery, every part of the estate need not be divided, it will be sufficient if proportionate parts, according to the value of the estate, be allotted the respective owners, and sometimes recompense is made by a sum of money or rent for owelty of partition to those who have parts of less value than the rest. In *Clarendon* v. *Hornby*, 1 P. Wms. 446, a suit in equity, the defendant insisted on having one-third of a house and one-third of the park adjoining it assigned to him; that he was entitled to demand this at law on the writ of partition, and that it should be accorded him in equity. Lord Chancellor Parker said : " Care must be taken that the defendant shall have one-third part in the value of the estate.; but there is no color of reason that any part of the estate should be lessened in value, in order that the defendant should have one-third of it. Now if the defendant should have one-third of the house and park, this would very much lessen the value of both.[27] If there were three houses of different value to be divided amongst three, it would not be right to divide every house, for that would be to spoil every house. But some recompense is to be made, either by a sum of money or rent for owelty of partition to those who have the houses of less value. It is true, if there were but one house or mill, or advowson to be divided, then this entire thing must be divided in manner as the other side contend; secus, when there are other lands, which may make up the defendant's share. Therefore, since the plaintiff and his wife have two-thirds, I recommend it that the house and park be allowed to them, and that a liberal allowance out of the rest of the estate be made to the defendant in lieu of his share of the house and park."

Each part owner should have in severalty a part equal to his interest in the whole subject if practicable, having a due regard to

---

[27] See 4 Grat. 348, *Chinn* v. *Murray*, as to whether land designed as an advancement, when brought into hotchpot for a partition, should be valued as at the time of the advancement or at the death of the ancestor. See also *Edwards* v. *Freeman*, 2 P. Wms. 435; *Beckwith* v. *Butler*, 1 Wash. 224; *Hudson* v. *Hudson*, 3 Rand. 117; *Knight* v. *Yarbrough*, 4 Rand. 566; *Oyster* v. *Oyster*, S. & R. 422; *Osgood* v. *Breed*, 17 Mass. R. 356.

the interest of all concerned ; yet where owing to the limited extent
or nature of the property it cannot be equally divided without im-
pairing the value of all the portions, or some of them, the subject
may be divided into shares of unequal values, and the court will
correct the inequality by means of a charge of money on the more
valuable in favor of the less valuable portions or otherwise. *Cox*
v. *McMullin*, 14 Grat. 82.

Partition will be decreed between two classes only of part owners,
holding as tenants in common, without going into a partition among
those of the same class where the nature of the subject and the state
of title render the latter division inexpedient. *Cox* v. *McMullin*,
14 Grat. 82.

When the interest of both classes will be promoted, or where one
will be benefitted without injury to the other, the commissioners
may assign the parcels without putting the owners to the risk of an
allotment. *Cox* v. *McMullin*, 14 Grat. 82.

The principle observed in partition is, that if the thing divided
is given with due regard to the value of that thing *among the parties*, it is no objection that it is given, so as not to increase the *value
of other property* not the subject of partition. Alln. Part. 90 ;
Watson v. *Duke of Northumberland*, 11 Ves. 162.

The question is mooted in 1 Lom. Dig. 492–494 (marg.), whether
in Virginia a parol partition may still be made between coparceners.
Judge Lomax in his treatise indicates that, in his opinion, neither
the Statute, Code, chap. 143, sec. 1, nor the Statute, Code, chap.
116, sec. 1, embraces the case of partition between coparceners, and
that the law stood as it did before these statutes; *i. e.*, that coparcerners [not joint tenants or tenants in common] may make a parol
partition of lands. In *Coles & als.* v. *Whiting*, 2 Pat. & H. 197, the
court say : " Between parceners, deeds of partition, though the better practice, are not absolutely necessary ; they may mark and
establish the dividing line between them, and prove it by other
competent evidence ; and they will, from the time of marking and
establishing the line, be seized in severalty."

A tenant in common had been in possession and enjoyment of the
land for many years without any knowledge that others were entitled to it in common with himself. But upon discovering their
title, he immediately made it known to them, whereupon they filed
their bill against him for partition. The court considered it equitable that the defendant should account for the proportions of the
complainant in the rents which had been received by him, deducting disbursements he had made for securing the title ; and that all
the leases and agreements of lease he had made of the land should
be acquiesced in by the complainants ; and that for a part which he
had sold, he should pay the price received with interest from the
time of sale, the time of his receiving the price not appearing to be
different from the time of sale. The complainants would also have

been allowed interest on their proportions of the rents received by the defendant from the time of filing their bill; but by consent it was allowed from the beginning of the next year after the last receipt. *Carter's ex'or* v. *Carter & als.*, 5 Munf. 108.

In *Cooles* v. *Wooding*, 2 P. & H. 189, the coparceners executed deeds of partition, in which they say the line between them was "then run, made and established;" the deeds gave the courses and distances. A line of marked trees was run from one terminus to the other. It did not appear from the record at what time precisely this line was marked, or that the parties had the assistance of a surveyor in marking the line, or by whom the line was actually marked. The parties were certainly actually in possession without question from either side of the right of the other, according to the line of marked trees, and so remained from the time of the execution of the deeds for twenty years, less two days, when a writ of right was instituted by one of the coparceners against the grantee of the other coparcener. The contention was on the part of the plaintiff that the boundaries of the land as described in the deeds, and not as ascertained by the line of marked trees, were the measure of his right. The court held (following *Dogan* v. *Seekright*, 4 H. & M. 125) that in questions of boundary, natural landmarks, marked lines, and reputed boundaries, especially if known to and acquiesced in by the parties interested, should be preferred when in opposition to mere magnetic lines, which may be described by mistake in deeds and surveys, unless it shall appear clearly that the marked line was made by mistake, a mistake unknown to, and therefore not acquiesced in by the parties in interest—that between parceners, deeds of partition, though the better practice, were not absolutely necessary, and the coparceners having marked the dividing line between them (how long before the conveyances was not apparent, but certainly before them,) they were from the time of marking and establishing the line seized in severalty according to that line. The court distinguished the case from *Smith* v. *Davis*, 4 Grat. 50, in which there was a clear mistake, the commissioners there intending the dividing line to be straight, and the surveyor, without intending to do so, having run and marked a curved line.

Notwithstanding the parties had taken possession in severalty of the portions allotted to them by the report of commissioners, under an interlocutory decree for partition among parceners, the allotment under the report had been excepted to:—such possession was held not to be a conclusive partition· between the parties, so long as the case was pending, without any final decree upon the report and exceptions, which was for a period of more than twenty years, though some of the parceners had aliened their shares allotted, and expensive improvements had been made upon them, there being no evidence of any agreement between the parties subsequent to the allotment and the exceptions taken to it, that they would abide by the division as made, and that the exceptions had been abandoned. *Chinn* v. *Murray*, 4 Grat. 348.

The partition in *Chinn* v. *Murray*, 4 Grat. 348, was set aside, but allowance was decreed to be made for the permanent improvements so far as they added to the present value of the estate divided. 4 Grat. 406.

Two tenants in common, of full age, and laboring under no disability, made partition of land by deed according to an old survey. The parties enter into possession of the parts respectively, no fraud or misrepresentation averred; it was held that such division, however unequal, is binding on them and their assigns. *Jones's devisees* v. *Carter*, 4 H. & M. 184.

In *Bryan* v. *Stump*, 8 Grat. 241, a brother and sister, both of whom were married, owned a tract of land, having inherited the same from their father. The brother and his wife and the sister and her husband unite in a deed of partition of the land, and from thence the land is held in severalty by the parties respectively, and those claiming under them, from 1802 to 1843, at which last date the suit was instituted. The partition was held valid and binding on the parties, though no certificate of the privy examination of the wives was annexed to the deed.

OWELTY OF PARTITION.

Courts of equity are not restrained, as courts of law when they exercised the jurisdiction in partition were, to a mere petition or allotment of the lands or other real estate, between the parties, according to their respective interests in the same, and having a regard to the true value thereof; but a court of equity may, with a view to the more convenient and perfect partition or allotment of the premises, decree a pecuniary compensation to one of the parties for owelty of partition, so as to prevent any injustice or unavoidable inequality. 1 Lom. Dig. 506 (marg).

EFFECT OF PARTITION, &C.

See Allnat on Partition, 137–164; Code, chap. 124, sec. 5.

PARTITION OF PERSONALTY.

Code, chap. 124, sec. 6 cited, *ante*, p. 62. The jurisdiction was always in equity. See *Smith & als.* v. *Smith, &c.*, 4 Rand. 95. The Statute authorizes a sale for partition.

Tenants in common of personal estate cannot have partition at common law; and therefore a court of equity is the proper tribunal to decree a partition of it. *Smith et als.* v. *Smith, &c.*, 4 Rand. 95.

When in dividing slaves it cannot be conveniently done without separating infant children from their mothers, compensation may be made in money. *Fitzhugh et ux.* v. *Foote et al.*, 3 Call 13.

In a division of slaves among legatees, if those allotted to some of them be valued at more, and to others at less than their respective shares, and the commissioners making the division direct that each person whose allotment is too large shall pay a surplus without designating to whom ; it seems that such payments are to be made to the executor, and by him to the other legatees, so as to make the division equal, and he is accountable if he deliver the slaves allotted to any legatee without receiving the surplus payable from him or her. *Sheppard's ex'or* v. *Starke et ux.*, 3 Munf. 29. See note by reporter to this case, p. 29, 30.

Where the division of a testator's estate in pursuance of his will is not to be made at one and the same time, but at several periods, when any one or more of his children shall separate from the family, it is not necessary that all the legatees be made parties to each suit in chancery for a division, but only those entitled to participate in the division then in question. *Branch's adm'x* v. *Booker's adm'r*, 3 Munf. 43.

Where a joint owner of slaves, subject to division, sold one of them, it was held to be a partition *pro tanto*, and not a conversion to his own use. *Seay* v. *White*, 5 Dana 555.

SALE, &C., OF LANDS OF PERSONS UNDER DISABILITY.

Form of Bill for Sale of Lands of an infant by his Guardian.

To the Honorable E. W., Judge of the Circuit Court of the county of ———.

Complaining showeth unto your honor, your orator, A. B., guardian of C. D., an infant under 21 years of age, that the said C. D. is entitled to the fee simple estate in that certain tract or parcel of land lying in H—— county, adjoining the lands of E. F., &c., which is the only real estate, or interest in real estate, owned by said infant. The only personal property owned by said infant consists of [here describe it]. The said C. D. is over the age of four-

teen years. E. F., the father of the said infant,
would be his sole heir and distributee if he were
dead. Your orator states that a sale of the aforesaid tract of land would promote very much the
interests of the said infant for the following reasons [here state the facts which make the sale
proper]. Your orator farther states that the rights
of no person will be violated by a sale of the said
real estate. To the end therefore that justice may
be done, and forasmuch as your orator is remediless in the premises, save by the aid of a court of
equity where matters of this kind are alone and
properly cognizable, he prays that the infant C. D.
and the adult E. F. may be made parties defendant
to this suit, that a proper *guardian ad litem* may be
appointed to defend the rights of the said infant,
and that C. D. and the[28] said *guardian ad litem*, as
well *as the said* E. F., may be required to answer
the allegations contained in this bill on oath; that
the said tract of land may be sold, and the proceeds
of sale invested for the benefit of the said infant as
the court may direct; that all proper orders and
decrees may be made, and all proper accounts and
enquiries directed; and for such other, further and
general relief as the nature of the case may require,
or to equity shall seem meet. And your orator will
ever pray, &c.

A. B., *Guardian of C. D.*

S. L. & C., p. q.

---

[28] If infant be over 14 years of age, answer required of him under oath;
if under 14, no answer required.

—— County, to wit:

This day personally appeared before me the undersigned, a notary public for the county aforesaid, the above named A. B., guardian of C. D., plaintiff in the foregoing bill, and made oath that he believes the statements therein contained are true.

Given under my hand this —— day of ——————, 18——.

JAMES JONES, N. P.

Form of Bill by Guardian to make Lease of Infants' Lands.

To the Honorable A. B., Judge of the Circuit Court of the county of ——.

Complaining showeth unto the court, your orator, R. M., guardian of James C., an infant under the age of twenty-one years, that the said James C. is entitled to a fee simple estate in a tract of land lying in the said county, containing —— acres, lying on the Three Chopped Road, near the lines of L. D. and M. D., devised to the said James C. by his father, Robert C., by his last will and testament, duly admitted to probat in the Circuit Court of said county, an attested copy of which will is herewith filed, marked Exhibit A, and is prayed to be taken and considered as part of this bill; that by the said will the estate of the said James C. is charged with an annuity of $150 per annum in favor of his mother, Sarah C., during her natural life, and that in order to raise this annuity, and meanwhile to support and educate the said James C., it will be necessary either

10

to sell or lease the said land; the personal property owned by the said James C. consists of [here describe it], and is wholly insufficient for these purposes. Your orator states that the said land and the personal property before described is all the property in which the said James C. is interested. The said James C. is now over fourteen years of age, and his fortune justifies his liberal education, and he desires to be liberally educated, and in the opinion of your orator it will greatly promote his interests if the income of his property is expended in his education at the best schools in the State. This tract of land before mentioned is very valuable, and Robert R. has offered, if a lease of ten years be given him, to lease the same at the rental of $1,000 per year. Your orator believes that the letting of the said land for that time at that rent would promote the interests of the said James C., and that in such letting the interests of no other person would be damaged; and, if the said offer of R. R. is not accepted, that the said land should either be leased or sold to some other person or persons. If the said James C. should die under age, the following persons would be his heirs at law, George C. and Edmund C., two brothers of Robert C., the father of the said James C.

In tender consideration whereof, and forasmuch as your orator is remediless in the premises, your orator prays that the said James C., George C., and Edmund C., may be made parties defendants to this bill, and required on their corporal oaths to make answer to the several statements of this bill; that a *guardian ad litem* be appointed to the said James C., to defend his interests in this suit, who shall also answer the statements of this bill under oath; that proper process issue; that the said offer of lease by the said R. R. be accepted, and that a proper commissioner be appointed by the court, in conjunction with your orator, guardian as aforesaid, or that your orator be appointed such commissioner to execute a good and sufficient lease of the said land to the said R. R. for the said term of ten years at said rental per year; or if the court should not deem the same a sufficient rental for the said land, that the court decree that the said land be leased for ten years at public auction, or sold at public auction at such time and on such terms as to the court shall seem fit; that all proper orders and decrees may be made, and inquiries be directed, and that all such other, further and general relief may be afforded your orator as the nature of his case may require, or to equity shall seem meet. And your orator will ever pray, &c.

R. M., *Guardian of James C.*

S. & L., p. q.

Add affidavit as on page 73, *ante.*

PRACTICAL NOTES TO BILLS FOR THE LEASING AND SELLING OF LANDS OF PERSONS UNDER DISABILITY.

Code, chap. 128, Session Acts 1871–'2, pp. 96, 97. See also Session Acts 1872–'3, p. 178, amending and reënacting sec. 13, chap. 127 of Code.

See Appendix to this volume for full record in a suit for sale of lands of infants by court of equity.

No such power as that of a court of chancery to change the real estate of an infant into personal has ever been exercised in Virginia except under the particular provisions of the statute. Until the passing of these statutes (1 Rev. Code 1819, chap. 96, sec. 20 ; Ibid, chap. 108, sec. 16, 23,) no sale of an infant's real estate was ever made except under the authority of a private Act of Assembly ; and both of these statutes distinctly indicate the legislative understanding that the power asserted could only be exercised under legislative authority. *Tucker*, P. in *Pierce's adm'r, &c.* v. *Trigg's heirs*, 10 Leigh 406.

A court of equity will direct a sale of infant's real estate when it manifestly appears to be to their interest, and when the rights of others will not be violated thereby. *Garland, &c.* v. *Loving, &c.*, 1 Rand. 396, 400.

Equity has power to sell infants' lands unless the testator has expressly prohibited a sale. *Talley et al.* v. *Starke's adm'ix et als.*, 6 Grat. 339. In this case the testator said : " Believing that a division of my property at this time would be ruinous to the general interest of my wife and our children, my will and desire is that all my estate (after payment of my debts, as before provided for,) be kept together until my youngest child comes of age ; to be controlled and managed by my executors and my wife, with their best discretion, so as to make it productive of the greatest amount of profits for the support of my wife and children. It was held that the court might direct a sale of the real estate, it being for the benefit of the infant children, if those who were of age consented.

In *Cooper* v. *Hepburn & als.*, 15 Grat. 551, Hepburn devised real estate to M. during his natural life, and to his children, if he should have lawful issue; if not, then at his decease to H.'s grand children. At the death of Hepburn, M. was not married, but he afterwards married and had lawful children. The court held that upon the birth of the first child of M. the remainder was vested in that child, subject to open and let in the after-born children, as they severally came into being, and the remainder in favor of the grandchildren was defeated; and therefore the grandchildren were not necessary parties to a suit by the guardian of M.'s children for a sale of the real estate.

In *Cooper* v. *Hepburn & als.*, 15 Grat. 551, the guardian holding himself in his own right an estate for life, his bill was for the sale of the real estate held by himself for life, and by his children in remainder. The bill for the sale was authorized by the statute. And though the bill did not formally aver that the suit was brought by the plaintiff as guardian, yet as it stated that he was the guardian, and the whole frame of the bill was in pursuance of what was required to be set out in such a case, and the infants were made defendants, the omission of that formal averment did not vitiate the proceedings.

One of the infants in *Cooper* v. *Hepburn*, 15 Grat. 551, was over fourteen years of age when the bill was filed ; it was held to be irregular not to require her to file her answer, but the sale having been decreed, and it having been made more than six months after this decree,[29] and confirmed without objection, it was too late for the purchaser, eighteen months afterwards, to object to its irregularity. The court, if it deemed it necessary for the protection of the purchaser, might have directed the infant to file an answer after the objection was made.

The case is instructive on other points. The court decreed a sale, and directed the commissioners to sell at private sale, and he advertised for sealed proposals, which were to be opened at a certain day in the presence of the court. Proposals were put in, and the court accepted one of them, and forthwith confirmed the sale, and directed the party to execute it according to its terms. It was held by the court (two judges out of three) that the purchaser stood upon the same footing as any other purchaser at a judicial sale, and was not entitled to any other or further relief. *Robertson*, the dissenting judge, thought that when a sale is confirmed by the court at the same time that the bids were opened, and one of them accepted, the purchaser should be allowed a reasonable time after such confirmation within which to make objections to the title. *Cooper* v. *Hepburn & als.*, 15 Grat. 551.[30]

In *Faulkner & als.* v. *Davis & als.*, 18 Grat 651, the power of a court of chancery to sell infants' lands was much discussed. In that case the court, after the fullest argument, decided that courts of equity in Virginia have not authority under their general jurisdiction as guardians of infants to sell their real estate whenever it is for the advantage of the infants to do so; that the courts derived this power from the statutes, and that the statutes being remedial in their nature should be construed liberally. The court also held that by the statute, Session Acts 1852–'3, chap. 30, page 49 (Code, ch. 2, sec. 128), courts of equity had authority to sell land in which infants had an interest, whether in possession or remainder, vested or contingent, if the proper parties could be brought before the courts.

---

[29] Code, chap. 178, sec. 8.

[30] One may well query the doctrine announced in this case in the broad language in which it is put, "that when it appears to the appellate court that the order of a circuit court is based upon the evidence of facts not found in the record, the appellate court may reasonably and justly presume that the order was right, that it was in accordance with and justified by the facts." If the doctrine refers, as according to the facts stated by the reporter, it does refer to the case of a record incomplete in the circuit court for want of evidence which could there have been furnished, but was not, the language does not, in the view of the writer, state the law. Neither circuit courts nor appellate courts are permitted to decide causes by testimony outside the records of the causes they are trying.

The case was this : Two vacant lots in Richmond were conveyed in trust for Norton and his wife, and the survivor of them for life, and at the death of the survivor to be conveyed by the trustees to the children of Norton and wife, who should be living at the death of the survivor, and the descendants of such of the children as should be then dead leaving descendants; and upon the further trust, that if Norton should think it expedient to sell the lots, or any part of them, the trustees should permit him to do so, the proceeds of sale to be secured and held upon the same trusts. Norton died without selling the lots, leaving his wife and five children surviving him. A bill was filed by the widow of Norton against the children and trustees for a sale of the lots. The Court of Appeals held that the court of equity might decree a sale, and that the descendants of any child dying in the lifetime of the widow would be bound by the decree, the parties before the court representing any such descendants who may become entitled under the trusts of the deed. *Faulkner & als.* v. *Davis & als.*, 18 Grat. 651.

Although a bill is prepared with reference to the sale of the land of infants under the statute, yet all the facts having been stated in it, and all the proceedings having been regularly conducted, it is competent for the court to make a decree therein for the sale of the property, if upon the facts, upon any ground whatever, the court of chancery had authority to make such a decree. In the case just cited, the court held that the trust to sell continued after Norton's death, and that a court of equity might execute it. *Faulkner & als.* v. *Davis & als.*, 18 Grat. 651.

The doctrine of representation will frequently arise in the case of bills for the sales of infants' lands. See the doctrine discussed in *Faulkner & als.* v. *Davis & als.*, 18 Grat. 651, and *Baylor's lessee* v. *Dejarnette*, 13 Grat. 152.

By Session Acts 1872–'3, p. 178, it is enacted that 13th section of chap. 127 of the Code of 1860 should be amended and reënacted as follows :

Sec. 13. The circuit, county and corporation courts in chancery may hear and determine all matters between guardians and their wards, require settlement of the guardianship accounts, remove any guardian for neglect or breach of trust and appoint another in his stead, and make any order for the custody and tuition of an infant and the management and preservation of his estate; and when it shall be made to appear to the satisfaction of a circuit court in chancery that the proper maintenance and education, or other interests of an infant require that the proceeds of his real estate, beyond the annual income thereof, should be applied to the use of said infant, it shall be lawful for such court to make such orders from time to time as may be necessary to secure such application; and to the extent that such proceeds may be so applied, they shall be deemed and taken to be personal estate, but no further.

CHAPTER IV.

Forms of Bills of Discovery, and Bills of Injunction to Judgments at Law.

DISCOVERY.

Form of Bill of Discovery.

To the Honorable A. B., Judge of the ——— Court of the county of ——— :

Complaining show unto the court, your orators, A. M. and C. M.,[1] that by a certain instrument of assignment, dated the —— day of ———, made between J. D. of the City of Richmond of the first part, and your orators of the second part, the said J. D. bargained and sold, assigned, transferred and set over to your orators certain property, goods, choses in action, and securities for money therein, and in the schedules thereto, particularly mentioned, in trust for the benefit of his creditors, which instrument of assignment is herewith filed, marked exhibit A., and is hereby specially referred to, and prayed to be taken and considered as part hereof. And your orators further show, that at the time aforesaid, there was due and owing to said J. D. from one R. B., of the said city of Richmond, a defendant hereafter named, the full and just sum of $750, being the balance of an account between him the said R. B. and the said

---

[1] If in United States Circuit Courts, see secs, 28, 33.

J. D., the particulars of which account are set forth
in a schedule marked X., herewith filed as an exhibit, and to which your orators refer. And your
orators further show that they have repeatedly
applied to the said R. B. to pay them the aforesaid sum of $750, so justly due from him, with
which reasonable request he has refused to comply; and having so refused, your orators were
compelled to, and did commence an action at law
in the circuit court of the city of Richmond, for
obtaining payment thereof. And your orators
charge that the said R. B. hath pleaded in such
suit, and given notice of a set-off in the same, and
hath delivered a particular of such set-off, which,
down to the date of such assignment, corresponds
with the credit side of the account set forth in the
said schedule X., but that such defendant hath included in the said particular three several items, one
of $50, one of $48, and one of $36, being charges for
goods delivered in the course of the month of ——,
in the year ——, for which he claims credit in such
action.

Whereas your orators charge that the said R. B.
at the time of the delivery of each, and every of such
parcels of goods so charged for as aforesaid knew,
and was well apprised of the assignment to your
orators, or that he, the said J. D., had made some
assignment of all his property and effects for the
benefit of creditors.

And your orators have no means of proving such
knowledge or information on the part of the said R.
B. in the action at law aforesaid, and can only estab-

lish the same by means of a discovery from such defendant. And they are advised that they cannot safely proceed to the trial of such action without a discovery of the matters herein before stated from said defendant.

To the end therefore that justice be done, your orators pray that the said R. B. may be made a party defendant to this bill, and required on his corporal oath to answer and say whether or not when the parcels of goods for which said several items, viz: one of $50, one of $48, and one of $36, are charges, as having been delivered in ——, in the year 18——, for which the said R. B. claims credit in the said action at law were delivered, and the same were sold to the said J. D., he, the said R. B., knew of the assignment aforesaid to your orators by the said J. D; and further answer and say whether he did not know that the said J. D. had made an assignment of all his property and effects to your orators as trustees for the benefit of his creditors; and that said defendant may make a full and true discovery of all the matters aforesaid. And your orators will ever pray, &c. C. M., p. q.

Add affidavit, as on page 73.

Form of Bill of Discovery to aid in Defence of Action at Law.

To the Honorable A. B., Judge of the ——— Court of the county of ——— :

Complaining show unto the court your orators, C. D. and L. M., that one E. F. has instituted in the

11

circuit court of the .county of —————— his certain action of assumpsit against your orators, in which
action the said E. F. seeks to recover of your orators
the price of a certain horse alleged to have been sold
by the said E. F. to your orators, the price thereof in
the bill of particulars filed with the declaration in
said suit being alleged to be $200. Your orators
have filed in the said action two pleas: 1st, the plea
of non-assumpsit; and 2nd, a special plea to the
effect, that the said E. F. warranted the said horse
to be sound and free from defect. Your orators allege that the said E. F. made his bill of sale of the
said horse to your orators, in which bill of sale the
said E. F. covenanted to warrant, and did warrant,.
the said horse to be sound and free from defect. The
said bill of sale has been lost or destroyed, and your
orators are unable to produce the same on the trial of
the said action, and your orators are unable to establish the said covenant by other testimony than the
statement of the said E. F. And your orators further allege and charge that the truth of the matters
aforesaid would fully appear in case the said E. F.
would set forth the covenants contained in the said
bill of sale, and specially the covenant aforesaid warranting the said horse to be sound and free from
defect. Your orators can and will establish on the
trial of the said action by other evidence, that at the
time of the sale of the said horse to your orators by
the said plaintiff, the said horse was not sound and
free from defect, but on the contrary thereof was suffering then, and for a long time thereafter, from the
disease called the —————, and of that disease sub-

sequently died, and was, and continued at, and from the time of the sale, or shortly thereafter, until his death, wholly valueless to your orators.

Your orators are advised that they cannot safely defend themselves on the trial of said action without a discovery from the said E. F. touching said covenant in said bill of sale, and concerning the existence thereof, and forasmuch as your orators are remediless in the premises save by the aid of a court of equity, your orators pray that the said E. F. may be made a party defendant to this bill, and required to answer the same on his oath, that the said defendant may make a full and true discovery of all the matters aforesaid, and say whether or not at the time of selling the said horse to your orators, he, the said E. F., did not make a bill of sale of the said horse to them, and that the said E. F. disclose and say what were the covenants made by him in the said bill of sale according to the best of his knowledge, remembrance, information and belief. Your orators pray that proper process may issue. And they will ever pray, &c.

C. D.

S. L. & C. p. q.   L. M.

PRACTICAL NOTES TO BILLS FOR DISCOVERY ONLY.

Code of Virginia, chap. 176, secs. 39–41; *Gelston*, &c. v. *Hoyt*, 1 John. C. R. 543; *McIntyre & als.* v. *Mancius*, &c., 16 John. Rep. 597; *McFarland* v. *Hunter*, 8 Leigh; *Lyons* v. *Miller*, 6 Grat.; *Baker* v. *Morris*, 10 Leigh; *Vaughan & Co.* v. *Garland*, 11 Leigh.

BILL OF DISCOVERY BY DEFENDANT AT LAW.

The bill to compel a discovery from one who has brought an action at law ought to be filed as soon as the party discovers the necessity of appealing to the conscience of his adversary. He must not spin out litigation, take the chance of a jury, and, failing there, file his bill for a discovery. *Carr*, J., in *Faulkner's adm'x v. Harwood*, 6 Rand. 129. See also *Green*, J., in *Norris v. Hume*, 2 Leigh 336, *Mc Vickar*, &c. v. *Wolcott*, &c., 4 John. Rep. 510; *Barker* v. *Elkins*, &c., 1 John. C. R. 465.

Where the application is in due time, the effort is only a suspen- sion of the proceeding at law till the discovery is had : and then the case proceeds to judgment in the proper forum, and the facts are tried by a jury. *Carr*, J., in *Faulkner's adm'x* v. *Harwood*, 6 Rand. 129.

If instead of making the application in due time the party wait till judgment is rendered against him at law, and then apply to equity to enjoin the judgment and award a new trial, on the ground that a discovery is expected from the answer of the defen- dants, without showing any sufficient excuse for not filing the bill sooner, his application will be rejected. *Faulkner's adm'x* v. *Har- wood*, 6 Rand. 125.

It is not a sufficient allegation to entitle a party to a discovery that the defendants knew facts which ought to be disclosed, without the averment that the plaintiff is unable to prove them by other testimony. *Duvals* v. *Ross*, 2 Mun. 290.

See discussion by *Carr*, J., and *Tucker*, P., of pure bills of dis- covery, and of the weight to be attached to answers in such cases in . *McFarland* v. *Hunter*, 8 Leigh 492–497, 499–502.

In *McFarland v. Hunter*, 8 Leigh 503, *Tucker*, P., after examin- ing fully the doctrines of equity in relation to pure bills of dis- covery, and considering the statute authorizing parties to file inter- rogatories at law, sums up as follows : " I am, upon the whole, of opinion—1st. That neither party is entitled to introduce his own answers in evidence to the jury, though they have been drawn from him by interrogatories ; for the defendant to a bill of discovery can never introduce his answer to that bill as evidence on a trial at law. 2dly. That the plaintiff, after the answers to the interrogatories are filed, may waive introducing them to the jury. And 3rdly.. That if he does introduce them they have the effect only of a con- fession ; they must all go together to the jury, who must give them such weight as they think them entitled to, when placed in the scale of the countervailing testimony which the plaintiff is at liberty to give."

BILL OF DISCOVERY IN AID OF PLAINTIFF.

A bill of discovery may be filed not only to compel a party to . discover facts material to the defence of the complainant against a demand asserted in a court of law, but likewise to compel a party to discover facts material to sustain a demand of the complainant which he is unable to prove at law. 2 R. P. (old) 44. See form, p. 79, *ante*.

Where the bill was to recover slaves, who in a series of years had greatly increased, and were much scattered, and the plaintiffs averred that they could not without the aid of a discovery ascertain the names, sexes and residence of the slaves, so as to pursue their legal remedy, the Court of Appeals of Virginia has, in several cases, sustained the jurisdiction of a court of equity. *Gregory's adm'or v. Marks's adm'or*, 1 Rand. 355 ; *Rankin v. Bradford & als.*, 1 Leigh, 163. Without allegations of this kind, equity would not take jurisdiction. *Hardin's ex'ors v. Hardin*, 2 Leigh 572 ; *Duvals v. Ross*, 2 Munf. 291. Should the bill contain allegations which in this particular save it from demurrer, and they appear to be merely returnable, equity will not take jurisdiction. *Rankin v. Bradford*, &c., 1 Leigh 163 ; *Jones v. Bradshaw*, 16 Grat. 355 ; *Meys. v. Mayse*, 6 Rand. 658. See *Armstrong v. Huntons*, 1 Rob. R. 326.

When a party asserting a demand comes properly into equity for discovery, the court having possession of the subject will proceed to decide the cause without turning the party round to a court of law, notwithstanding relief might originally have been had at law if such discovery had not been necessary. *Chichester's ex'ors v. Vass's adm'or*, 1 Munf. 98 ; *Chinn v. Heale*, 1 Munf. 63 ; *Armstrong, &c. v. Gilchrist*, 3 John. Cas. 424 ; *Rathbone, &c. v. Warren*, 10 John. Rep. 587.

In *Baker v. Morris's adm'or*, 10th Leigh, 284, Morris having taken administration of his deceased wife's estate, and being unable to maintain an action at law on the bonds bequeathed to her by reason of the obligor being one of the executors of the obligee, exhibited a bill in equity against Baker, the obligor, to enforce payment of the debt due on the bonds. The suit was brought twenty-eight years[2] after the right to demand it accrued. The bill to rebut the presumption of satisfaction, arising from the lapse of time, called on the defendant to answer whether the debt had been paid or not. The defendant in his answer repelled the circumstances alleged in the bill to account for the delay in making and prosecuting the demand of the debt due on the bonds, and to rebut the presumption of satisfaction arising from the lapse of time ; he insisted that near thirty years having elapsed since the bonds came into the hands of his sister, then a feme sole (subsequently the wife of the plaintiff), and no demand having ever been made upon them, they ought to be presumed in law to be paid ; and he relied on this legal presumption as a full and sufficient defence to the plaintiff's claim ; but he made no answer to the interrogatory whether he had in fact paid

---

[2] It was before the statute, Code, chap. 149, sec. 5, making twenty years the limitation to actions on such bonds in Virginia. Before that statute the lapse of twenty years raised the presumption of payment only ; it was not an absolute bar to recovery of the debt, as now it is, when pleaded.

the debt or not. Exception was taken by the plaintiff to the sufficiency of the answer in that particular; and the circuit court sustained the exception, and ordered the defendant to put in a full
answer to the bill. This decision was unanimously sustained by a
court of three judges in the Court of Appeals. One of the two
remaining judges (Judge *Parker*) had decided the cause in the circuit court.

INJUNCTIONS TO JUDGMENTS.

Form of Bill of Injunction to Judgment at Law.

To the Honorable A. B., Judge of the ———— Court
of the county of ———— :

Complaining showeth unto the court, your orator,
James J., that George G., administrator of the
goods and chattels of Robert R., deceased, recovered
a judgment at law against your orator in the ————
court of ———— county, at the November term, 18—,
for $————, with interest on $————, part thereof
from the ———— day of ————, at the rate of seven per
centum per annum until paid, and the costs amounting to $————, an attested extract of which judg-
ment is herewith filed, marked exhibit A, and is
prayed to be taken and considered as part of this bill.
An execution of *fieri facias* has been issued upon the
said judgment, and is now in the hands of the sheriff
of this county, and is about to be levied on your
orator's property. Your orator states that the said
judgment is unjust, and ought never to have been
rendered against him. Your orator had a full and
complete defence to the action of the plaintiff in
which said judgment was had, and but for the fact
that the said plaintiff in the said action had lulled

your orator into security, and prevented by so doing, his defending the said action, the said judgment would not have been recovered against your orator. The facts are as follows : The said judgment was recovered on a note drawn by your orator on the —— day of ——, for the sum of $——, payable on the —— day of —— to the said Robert R. The said note' had long before the institution of said action been paid by your orator to the said Robert R. At the time of said payment, your orator was indebted to the said Robert R. by four several notes, amounting in the aggregate, principal and interest, to $1,260 50. Your orator paid the said sum to the said R. R., and took his receipt for the same, the said receipt specifying for what the money was paid, and showing that the amount of the said note on which said judgment was recovered was embraced therein. The three other notes were delivered to your orator by the said Robert R. at the time of signing the said note, and the fourth note was also demanded by your orator, but the said R. R. stated that it was lost or mislaid, and that when he found it it would be restored to your orator. The said receipt and the three notes delivered your orator are herewith filed, marked exhibits B. C. D. and E., and are prayed to be taken and received as parts of this bill. Shortly after the death of the said R. R. this note came into the possession of the said George G. as his administrator, and the said action was brought. Your orator, immediately on the institution of the said action, saw the said George G., administrator as aforesaid of said Robert R., deceased, and informed him of the facts, and exhibited to him the receipt and the notes, and the said George G., administrator as aforesaid, stated that he was fully satisfied that it was the same debt, and that it had been paid, and that your orator need not take any steps to defend the said action, that he would dismiss the same. Your orator relying on the promise of the said George G., administrator as aforesaid, to dismiss the said action, made no defence to the same, and the judgment was recovered without your orator's knowledge that the same would be asked for, and when he believed the said action had been dismissed. Your orator farther states that he had no knowledge of the rendition of the said judgment until the term of the court at which it was rendered had expired. Your orator alleges that the failure to dismiss the said action, after the promise before mentioned, was in fraud of your orator's just rights, and that the said judgment is unjust, inequitable and fraudulent, and should be set aside, and a new trial be granted your orator. In tender consideration whereof, and forasmuch as your orator is remediless in the premises save by the aid of a court of equity, where matters of this kind are alone and properly cognizable, your orator prays that the said George G., administrator as aforesaid of the said Robert R., deceased, may be made a party defendant to this bill, and required to answer the several statements thereof on his corporal oath, as fully and particularly as if the same were here again repeated, and he thereto specially interrogated; that the said defendant, his agents, attorneys, and all others, be injoined and restrained from proceeding to enforce the said judgment by issuing executions thereon, or otherwise; that specially the said sheriff of this county be injoined and restrained from levying the said execution of *fieri facias* now in his hands; that proper process issue, and all proper orders be made; that the said judgment be set aside, and a new trial of the said action at law be granted your orator, and that all such other, further and general relief may be afforded your orator as the nature of his case may require, or to equity shall seem meet. And your orator will ever pray, &c.

S. L. & C., p. q.   JAMES J.

County of ———, to wit:

This day personally appeared before me, the undersigned, a justice of the peace for the county aforesaid, James J., and made oath that he believes that the statements made in the foregoing bill are true.[3]

Given under my hand this —— day of ——, 18—.

SAMUEL SHIELD, J. P.

Form of Bill of injunction to Judgment on the ground of after discovered Evidence.

To the Honorable A. B., Judge of the —— Court of the county of ———.

Complaining, showeth unto the court your orator, James J., executor of the last will and testament of

---

[3] Code, chap. 171, sec. 40.   Code 1873, chap 167, sec. 41.

12

Merewether R., deceased, that one M. N. recently recovered in the —— court of —— county a judgment
against your orator, as executor as aforesaid of said
Merewether R., deceased, for the sum of $1,000, to
be discharged by the payment of $500, with interest
thereon at the rate of six per centum per annum
from the —— day of ———, until paid, and the
costs, amounting to $———; that the said judgment
was recovered on a bond executed by your orator's
testator, Merewether R., and one Alexander R., in
which bond the said Alexander R. was the principal
debtor, and your orator's testator was the surety.
Your orator further states, that when the action was
brought on the said bond against your orator, and
during the whole time the said action was pending,
the said Alexander R. was out of the country, and
though your orator made diligent enquiry for him,
he was unable to ascertain where the said Alexander
R. could be found, so as to communicate with him
about the said alleged claim. The judgment was recovered against your orator as such executor on the
—— day of ———. Your orator was wholly ignorant that any valid defence could be made to said
action until some time after the judgment had been
recovered, and after the term had expired at which
said judgment was recovered. After the recovery
of the said judgment, to wit: on the —— day of
———, Alexander R. returned to Virginia, and your
orator immediately communicated with him about
the said claim. Mr. Alexander R. informed your
orator that the said debt had been paid, and sent to
your orator a copy of the receipt, which had been

given him by the said M. N. when the debt was paid. Your orator herewith files the said copy, marking it Exhibit A, and the same is prayed to be taken and considered as a part of this bill. Your orator is confident that if a new trial be granted, the said M. N. will fail to obtain judgment for any sum against your orator as such executor. The said judgment is, as your orator verily believes, wholly unjust and inequitable, and should be set aside. In tender consideration whereof, and forasmuch as your orator is remediless in the premises save by the aid of a court of equity, where matters of this kind are alone and properly cognizable, to the end that justice be done, your orator prays that the said M. N. may be made a party defendant to this bill, and required on his corporal oath to make full answer to the several statements hereof as fully as if the same were here repeated, and he thereto specially interrogated; that the said M. N., his agents, attorneys, and all others, be injoined and restrained from enforcing the said judgment, from issuing executions thereon, and otherwise proceeding to collect the same; that the said judgment be set aside, and that a new trial of the said action be granted your orator; that proper process issue; that all proper orders and decrees may be made, and that all such other, farther and general relief may be afforded your orator as the nature of his case may require, or to equity shall seem meet. And your orator will ever pray, &c.   JAMES J , *Executor of*
    John M. P., p. q.   *Merewether R., deceased.*

Add affidavit as on page 89, *ante.*

Other forms of injunction bills will be given in future chapters of this treatise, and the reader will there find other practical notes on the subject of injunctions.

PRACTICAL NOTES.

Code of Virginia, chap. 179; Code 1873, chap. 175, pp. 1126–1129; Code 1873, chap. 56, § 13, p. 538; Rev. Repts., Code of 1849, pp. 326, 327; Code 1873, ch. 148, § 11.

Injunctions to Judgments at Law.

When a party comes into a court of equity to be relieved against proceedings at law, he must confess judgment at law, and rely on the court of equity for relief, though he may have grounds of defence at law distinct from the grounds of relief preferred to the court of equity. *Warwick & als.* v. *Norvell,* 1 Leigh 96.

In *Morgan* v. *Carson,* 7 Leigh 241, *Tucker,* P., said: "The plaintiff seeks here to arrest a judgment at law on a ground of defence, which might have availed him in a court of law, and which he neglected to make. Such an attempt cannot receive the countenance of this court. A long train of decisions, no longer necessary to be cited or reviewed, leaves us no room for hesitation in dismissing such a case from the equitable forum."

See *Turner* v. *Davis & als.,* 7 Leigh 227; *Haden* v. *Garden,* 7 Leigh 157; *Collins & als.* v. *Jones,* 6 Leigh 530; *Brown* v. *Swann,* 10 Peters 497; *Arthur* v. *Chavis,* 6 Rand. 142; *Faulkner's adm'x* v. *Harwood,* 6 Rand. 125; *Garland* v. *Rives,* 4 Rand. 316; *Oswald* v. *Tyler,* 4 Rand. 19; see also p. 338; *Collins & als.* v. *Jones,* 6 Leigh 530; *Vanlew* v. *Bohannon &c.,* 4 Rand. 537; *Norris* v. *Hume,* 2 Leigh 334; *Bierne* v. *Mann & als.,* 5 Leigh 364; *Donally* v. *Ginatt's adm'or,* 5 Leigh 359.

Where a cause has been once fully heard and decided in a court of common law, having competent jurisdiction of the case, a court of equity ought not to interfere, unless fraud [*Poindexter* v. *Waddy,* 6 Munf. 418] or surprise, [*Price's ex'or* v. *Fuqua's adm'or,* 4 Munf. 68], be suggested and proved, or some material adventitious circumstance had arisen which could not have been foreseen or guarded against. *Fenwick* v. *McMurdo & als.,* 2 Munf. 244. See *Tapp's admo'r* v. *Rankin,* 9 Leigh 478. Though in *Tarply's adm'or* v. *Dobyns,* 1 Wash. 185, and *Oswald* v. *Tyler &c.,* 4 Rand. 44, the plaintiff alleged surprise at law, the court of equity refused relief because the plaintiff might have had full redress by suffering a nonsuit.

In *Turner* v. *Davis*, 7 Leigh 227, a surety was compelled to satisfy the judgment of his principal against him, he failing to defend himself at law, and showing no good cause for the neglect.

Relief refused against judgment at law in *Turpin* v. *Thomas*, 2 H. & M. 139; *Maupin* v. *Whiting*, 1 Call. 224; *Barret* v. *Floyd*, 3 Call. 531; *Chapman* v. *Harrison*, 4 Rand. 336; *Morriss* v. *Ross*, 2 H. & M. 408; *Terrill* v. *Dick*, 1 Call. 546; *Brown* v. *Street*, 6 Rand. 1; *Kincaid* v. *Cunningham*, 2 Munf. 1; *Noland* v. *Cromwell*, 4 Munf. 155; *Syme* v. *Montague*, 4 H. & M. 180; *Threlkelds* v. *Campbell*, 2 Grat. 198; *Meem* v. *Rucker*, 10 Grat. 506.

Relief granted. *Poindexter* v. *Waddy*, 6 Munf. 418; *Lee* v. *Baird &c.*, 4 H. & M. 453; *West's ex'or* v. *Logwood*, 6 Munf. 491; *Hord* v. *Dishman*, 5 Call. 279; *Mayo* v. *Bentley*, 4 Call. 528; *Mason* v. *Nelson*, 11 Leigh 227.

Under special circumstances equity will relieve after a failure at law—such were found in *Talbert &c.* v. *Jenny & als.*, 6 Rand. 159; *Foushee* v. *Lea*, 4 Call. 279; *Price* v. *Fuqua*, 4 Munf. 68.

The decision in *Tomkies* v. *Downman*, 6 Munf. 557, in which relief was granted on the ground of "a general delusion on the subject of a point of law" can hardly be sustained on authority. Yet see *Lyon &c.* v. *Richmond & als.*, 2 John. Ch. R. 51; 14 Johns. R. (in error) 501, *S. C.*

Where the subject was peculiarly appropriate to the jurisdiction of a court of equity, as *trust* and *confidence*, and it was proper that the complainant should have a discovery from the defendant, the court of appeals relieved after a judgment at law, notwithstanding the plaintiff assigned no reason for not having defended himself at law, and though he did not aver in his bill that he needed the aid of the defendant's testimony. *Spencer & als.* v. *Wilson*, 4 Munf. 130. See *West's ex'or* v. *Logwood*, 6 Munf. 491.

If the defendant is taken sick on his way to the trial of his cause, and is thereby prevented from making an affidavit that the original deeds are lost, and for want of such affidavit the court refuses to receive copies of the deeds in evidence, the court of chancery will relieve against a verdict at law and a judgment obtained by the plaintiff. *Hord* v. *Dishman*, 5 Call. 279. See *Mead* v. *Merritt*, 2 Paige 402; *Mitchell* v. *Bunell*, 2 Paige 606; *Ld. Portarlington* v. *Soulby*, 3 Myl. & Keene 104, 15 Eng. Ch. Rep., p. 102.

The rule has been long established that a court of chancery will not entertain a bill for the purpose of allowing a defence which might have been made at law, unless some good reason be shown why that defence was not made in the court of law. This rule is founded on the principle that there should be an end of litigation; and that consequently when a matter has been once fairly investigated and decided in one *forum*, it should not again become the subject of controversy in another. It was intended as a shield for the party who had prevailed at law. But if he does not choose to avail himself of its benefit, if he voluntarily goes into the merits of the case, and in his answer admits facts, which if they had appeared in the court of law, would have there produced a different result, neither the rule, nor the principle of the rule, is violated by pronouncing a decree, justified by his own admissions. *Vanlew* v. *Bohannon &c.*, 4 Rand. 537.

Sometimes matter arising subsequent to the judgment at law makes its enforcement improper, and there equity will relieve. See *Royall's adm'ors* v. *Johnson & als.*, 1 Rand. 421; *Miller's ex'ors* v. *Rice & als.*, 1 Rand. 438; *Crawford* v. *Thurmond & als.*, 3 Leigh 85.

And any fact which clearly proves it to be against conscience to execute a judgment at law, and of which the injured party could not have availed himself in a court of law, will justify an application to a court of chancery. *Marine Ins. Co.* v. *Hodgson*, 4 Cranch 336. See *Royall's adm'or* v. *Royall's adm'or*, 5 Munf. 82; *Pendleton's adm'ors* v. *Stuart &c.*, 6 Munf. 377; *Pickett &c.* v. *Stewart &c.*, 1 Rand. 478.

Where a defendant is prevented from making a motion for a new trial, by one of the justices who tried the cause absenting himself from the court, an injunction should be granted to the judgment. *Knifong* v. *Hendricks*, 2 Grat. 212.

Who may Grant Injunctions.

Code 1873, chap. 175, §§ 5, 6, 7.
Where an injunction has been refused by a chancellor in open court, it is competent for a judge of the Court of Appeals, out of court, to award it. *Tollbridge* v. *Freebridge*, 1 Rand. 206.

An injunction refused by a judge of the Circuit Court is presented to a judge of the Court of Appeals, who also refuses it. It may be granted by another judge of the Court of Appeals. *Jaynes & als.* v. *Brock*, 10 Grat. 211.

A motion to reinstate an injunction on additional evidence, tendered by the complainant, is in the nature of an original application for an injunction, and on the refusal of the chancellor to reinstate, an application to a judge of the Court of Appeals, or to any of them, is proper. *Gilliam* v. *Allen*, 1 Rand. 414; *Webster* v. *Couch*, 6 Rand. 519.

Bond to be Required.

It is error in the chancellor to grant an injunction without requiring security, save in the cases of executors, administrators, and other fiduciaries. *Lomax* v. *Picot*, 2 Rand. 247; *Shearman* v. *Christian & als,* 1 Rand. 393.

The condition of the injunction bond is broken by a dissolution of the injunction *in part*, as well as by a *total* dissolution. *White* v. *Clay's ex'ors*, 7 Leigh 68.

To whom Order of Injunction Directed.

See Code 1873, ch. 175, § 4; Code of Virginia, chap. 179, § 4. *Randolph's ex'ors & als.* v. *Tucker &c.*, 10 Leigh 655; *Bickley* v. *Palmer*, 11 Grat. 625; *Muller &c.* v. *Bayly & al.*, 21 Grat. 531.

" § 4 of chap. 179, Code of Virginia, (chap. 175, § 4, Code 1873) applies only to a pure bill of injunction, and not to a bill seeking other relief, to which the injunction sought is merely ancillary. This was expressly decided in the case of *Winston & als.* v. *The Midlothian Coal Mining Company & als.*, 20 Grat. 686. See 2 Rob. old Pr. 249, and the cases there cited of *Hough* v. *Shreeve*, 4 Munf. 490; *Singleton* v. *Lewis &c.*, 6 Munf. 397; and *Pulliam* v. *Winston*, 5 Leigh 324." *Moncure, P.*, in *Muller &c.* v. *Bayly & al.*, 21 Grat. 531.

CHAPTER V.

Forms of other Bills in Virginia State Courts and in the United States Circuit Courts.

DIVORCE.

Bill for Divorce, a Vinculo Matrimonii and Injunction.

To the Honorable J. B. C., Judge of the Circuit Court for the county of Henrico.

Complaining, showeth unto the court your oratrix, Rebecca W., wife of A. W., who sues by L. L., her next friend, that she is now twenty-eight years old. At the age of fifteen she left her father's house (ran off, in common language,) with the said A. W., and was married to him, and since that time has been to him a constant, faithful and dutiful wife, and has borne him five children, to wit: Elizabeth, now 12 years old, Andrew, 10, Amelia, 7, Martha, 3, and George, not quite 1 year old.

Your oratrix's husband, on the other hand, has been negligent, excessively intemperate in drinking ardent spirits, and insufferably abusive and violent to her, frequently beating and choking her, until, to protect her person from violence and preserve her life, she has been compelled to fly from her residence, in the county of H., and seek refuge in the house of her father, B. F., in the city of Richmond where she now is, with her two youngest children. Your complainant's husband the said A. W. has not only treated her with cruelty but he has broken his marriage vows and has committed adultery with one Martha X. within the past few months. Indeed, he is reckless in his habits, and as your complainant has been informed and believes he is a habitual frequenter of bawdy houses in the city of Richmond. Your oratrix has a little home in the county of Henrico given to her by her father on her marriage.

. The said A. W. notwithstanding his brutality and his violations of his marriage vows, still pursues your oratrix at the residence of her father, infesting the house and while often using the most violent and threatening language to her, he insists on her returning to him with her children, and threatens, if she does not return, to take from her her infant children. In tender consideration whereof and forasmuch as your oratrix is remediless in the premises save in a court of equity she prays that the said A. W. may be made a defendant to this bill and required to answer the same upon his oath, that he may be enjoined and restrained from interfering with or in any manner molesting her and her children who are with her; that your oratrix may be divorced from him *a vinculo matrimonii* and that he may be compelled to deliver up her children to her and to surrender to her the tract of land in the county of Henrico given her by her father as a home, and that all such other, farther and general relief may be afforded your oratrix as the nature of her case may

13

require or to equity shall seem meet. And your oratrix will ever·pray, &c.

S. T., p. q.

Affidavit as on p. 89.

Injunction.—An injunction awarded to enjoin and
restrain the defendant A. W. from removing the infant children Martha W. and George W. from the
control and possession of their mother, R. W. until
the farther order of the court.

J. B. C., Judge, &c.

To the Clerk of the Circuit Court of H.

PRACTICAL NOTES.

What marriages void. Code 1873, ch. 105, sec. 1.

*When persons leave the State to evade the Virginia law prohibit-
ing marriages within certain degrees of relationship* : the marriage
governed by the same law, in all respects, as if solemnized in the
State. Code 1873, ch. 105, § 2.

Marriage under age of consent. If after such marriage the
parties separate during such non-age, and do not cohabit afterwards,
the marriage deemed void. Code 1873, ch. 105, § 3.

Suit to avoid or affirm a marriage. Code 1873, ch. 105, sec. 4, 5.

For what divorces decreed. From bond of matrimony, Code 1873,
ch. 105, sec. 6, from bed and board, Ibid. sec. 7.

*How, after divorce from bed and board for abandonment or deser-
tion, if five years elapse from the abandonment or desertion without
reconciliation, a divorce from the bond of matrimony may be had.*
Code 1873, ch. 105, sec. 15.

How decree for a divorce may be revoked. Ibid.

*How guilty party in case of a divorce a vinculo matrimonii may
be restrained from marrying again.* Code 1873, chap. 105, sec. 14.

How the prohibition may be revoked. Ibid.

*A person of the age of consent marrying one not of the age of con-
sent cannot sue to annul the marriage on that ground.* Code 1873,
ch. 105, sec. 4.

Grounds of divorce a mensa et toro. Cruelty, reasonable appre-
hension of bodily hurt, abandonment or desertion. Code 1873, ch.
105, sec. 7, [for how long not mentioned in the statute ; matter of
judicial discretion. *Bailey* vs. *Bailey,* 21 Grat. 48.]

Grounds of divorce a vinculo matrimonii. Wilful desertion or abandonment for five years, adultery and other grounds mentioned in Code 1873, ch 105, sec. 6.

Whether force or fraud, is ground of divorce, see 1 Min. Inst. 263. Frauds, certainly, if ground of divorce, are not those relating to fortune, &c, but *those relating to the identity of the person* and it is believed to those only. See *Ibid.*

Whether certain matters rendering a decree a vinculo possible in the lifetime of the parties e. g. want of reason, impotency, consanguinity or affinity, conviction of an infamous offence, pregnancy of the woman at time of the marriage, her notorious prostitution before the marriage without the knowledge of the husband can afterwards be asserted in impeachment of the marriage. 1 Min. Inst. 262, 263.

As to condoning the offence of adultery. See Code 1873, ch. 105, § 11, 1 Minor's Inst. 255 ; 1 Min. Inst. 257, *as to condoning offence of cruelty.*

What is desertion or abandonment. See *Latham* vs. *Latham,* 30 Grat. 307.

Unkind treatment not enough to secure a divorce. A husband may be rude and dictatorial in his speech to his wife, exacting in his demands, and sometimes unkind and negligent in the treatment of his wife even when she is sick and worn and weary in watching and nursing their sick child, yet these do not constitute legal ground for her leaving him so as to entitle her to a divorce. *Carr* vs. *Carr,* 22 Grat. 168.

A sufficient answer to charge of adultery that it was brought about by the other party's procurement or connivance, or that the person making the charge is also guilty. 1 Bl. Com. 441(*n*) 33 ; 2 Kent's Com. 100; 1 Min. Inst. 255 and cases cited.

Court may, during pendency of suit, in term or in vacation, decree sums for maintenance of woman or for carrying on the suit. Code, ch. 105, § 10.

Court may, in like manner, prevent husband from imposing any restraint on wife's personal liberty. Ibid.

Court may, in like manner, provide for custody and maintenance of the minor children. Ibid.

Court may, in like manner, preserve the estate of the man so that it may be forthcoming to meet any decree made in the suit. Ibid.

Court may, in like manner, compel the man to give security to abide the decree. Ibid.

Alimony. See discussions in *Purcell* vs. *Purcell,* 4 H. & M. 507 ; *Almond* vs. *Almond,* 4 Rand. 662; *Spencer* vs. *Ford,* 1 Rob. 684 ; *Bailey* vs. *Bailey,* 21 Grat. 52 ; *Latham* vs. *Latham,* 30 Grat. 307. Not given if wife, without sufficient reason, deserts her husband and refuses to live with him, *Harris* vs. *Harris,* 31 Grat. 13. See *Carr* vs. *Carr,* 22 Grat. 168. As to amount to be assigned, a matter of judicial not of arbitrary discretion. 1 Min. Inst. 283. General rule, *in respect to permanent alimony*, the wife entitled to a support corresponding to her husband's condition in life and his fortune and resources including his and her earnings or ability to earn money. 1 Min. Inst. 283.

In respect to temporary alimony, about one-fifth of the joint income as just defined: for *permanent alimony* from one-half to one-third, two-fifths being no uncommon proportion. *Ibid.* Alimony may be granted independently of any divorce or any application for one. See 1 Min. Inst. 282.

Evidence necessary to sustain the bill. See 1 Min. Inst. 256, Code 1873, ch. 105, §§ 9, 15.

What cruelty authorizes a divorce. Only that which tends to bodily harm, and thus renders cohabitation unsafe, or that involves danger to life, limb or health. *Latham* vs. *Latham*, 30 Grat. 307; *Carr* vs. *Carr*, 22 Grat. 173, 175.

Condonation applies to cruelty as well as to adultery. The rule as regards a condonation by the wife not so strict as that by a husband; forbearance in her may be a virtue. Condonation always conditional, so that if the offence is repeated the effect of the condonation is done away with. 1 Min. Inst. 257, and cases cited.

OTHER FORMS OF BILLS.

Bill by husband of legatee against an executor for payment of legacy.

[The form of this bill in the 1st edition of Suit in Equity, pp. 344, 345, is republished in Matthews's Forms, pp. 152, 153, and may now be safely used.]

Bill by next of kin for account.

[The form of this bill in the 1st edition of Suit in Equity, pp. 329, 330, is republished in Matthews's Forms, pp. 157–159, and may now be safely used.]

Bill in United States Circuit Court for the foreclosure of a mortgage.

[The form of this bill in the 1st edition of Suit in Equity, pp. 319, 321, is republished in Matthews's Forms, pp. 161, 162. The form as found in Matthews may be followed, with this modification. Instead of saying, at the conclusion, "*may it please the honorable court to grant a writ of subpœna directed to the Marshal of the district of —— and commanding, &c.*," say, "may it please your honors to grant unto your orator a writ of subpœna to be directed unto the said C. D., thereby commanding him, &c., &c.,. as on pp. 108, 109 of this volume.]

Bill of foreclosure in Virginia State Courts.

[The form of this bill in 1st edition of Suit in Equity, pp. 321, 322, is republished in Matthews's Forms, pp. 163, 164. It may now be safely used.]

Bill for specific performance by vendor against vendee.

[See post pp. 104–109 for form of bill in United States Circuit Courts. The form for Virginia State Courts in the 1st edition of Suit in Equity, pp. 322, 323, is republished in Matthews's Forms, pp. 164–166, and may be safely followed.]

Bill to enforce a lien of a judgment.

To the honorable R. M., Judge of the ——— Court of H. county:
Complaining showeth to the court your complainant, A. B., that he recovered a judgment for $600.00, with interest, &c., against C. D. in the ——— Court of ———, an extract of which judgment, marked Exhibit A, is herewith filed. Of this judgment, *though execution issued thereon,* no part has been paid; *the execution was returned " no effects"; and your complainant does not believe any part of it can be made from the personalty of the said C. D.*[1] The said C. D. owns a tract of land in this county containing sixty-eight acres, lying about ——— miles from the court-house on the Three-Chopped road. Your complainant avers and charges that the rents and profits of this land will not in five years satisfy your complainant's judgment, and that he is entitled to enforce the lien of the same by a sale of the said property. In tender consideration whereof your complainant prays that the said C. D. may be made a defendant to this bill and required to answer the same, that proper process issue, that all proper orders and decrees may be made and inquiries be directed, that if it shall appear that the said rents and profits of said real estate will not in five years satisfy your complainant's judgment that the said real estate be sold and the proceeds thereof be applied in satisfaction of your complainant's said judgment; that if such rents will so suffice the said land be rented out and the rents and profits be applied to the said judgment until the same is fully satisfied; and that all such other, further and general relief may be given your complainant as the

---

[1] The clauses in italics are not now necessary.

nature of his case may require or to equity shall seem meet.   And your complainant will ever pray, &c.

S., p. q.

Bill to enjoin the erection of a nuisance.

[The form of this bill in 1st edition of Suit in Equity, pp. 331–334, is republished in Matthews's Forms, pp. 171–175.   See *Miller* vs. *Trueheart*, 4 Leigh 569.]

Bill to perpetuate testimony.

[The form of this bill in 1st edition of Suit in Equity, pp. 142, 143, is republished in Matthews's Form, pp. 182, 183.]

Amended and supplemental bill.

To the Honorable Judge, &c.:

The amended and supplemental bill of your complainant, R. B., respectfully showeth to the court that he heretofore exhibited in this court his original bill of complaint against, &c. [setting forth original bill and proceedings, after which state the matter of amendment and supplemental matter, &c.]   To the end, therefore, that the said M. M. and L. L. may severally answer all and every the matters and things herein charged by way of amendment and supplement, and that they may discover and set forth, &c. (here add interrogatories.)   And that your complainant may have full and general relief in the premises, such as the nature of his case may require.   And your orator will ever pray, &c.

A. M., p. q.

Bill of Review.

[The form of this bill in 1st edition of Suit in Equity, pp. 343, 344 is copied in Matthews's Forms, pp. 187, 188.]

Bill of Interpleader.

[The form of this bill in 1st edition of Suit in Equity, pp. 345, 346 is copied in Matthews's Forms, pp. 188–190.

To the bill of interpleader there should be an affidavit, as follows:

County of ———, to wit: This day, personally appeared before

me, Alexander D., a justice of the peace in and for said county, J. R., the plaintiff in the annexed bill, and made oath that the statements made in the said bill so far as made upon his own knowledge are true, and so far as made upon knowledge or information derived from others he believes them to be true; and said J. R. farther made oath that there is no collusion between him and any one or more of the defendants in said bill or any other party thereto.

Given under my hand this —— day of ———.]

Cross Bill.

[The form of this bill in 1st edition of Suit in Equity, pp. 349, 350, is copied in Matthews's Forms, pp. 190–192.]

Bill impeaching a deed for fraud.

To the Honorable Judge of the Circuit Court of the county of H.:

Complaining showeth unto the court your complainant, R. R., that at the last term of this court he recovered a judgment against M. M. for the sum of $1,000 and his costs, amounting to $23. This judgment is yet due and unpaid. While the suit was pending on which such judgment was had, in anticipation that the judgment would be recovered, the said M. M., with the object and intent to prevent your complainant from realizing anything from the defendant's property, conveyed by deed dated the —— day of ———, to J. J. all his said property, consisting of (here describe it). Your complainant alleges and charges that no consideration whatever passed from the said J. J. to the said M. M. for the said deed; that the same was made to hinder, delay, and defraud your complainant; and he is entitled to have the said deed set aside and the property therein embraced subjected to the payment of your complainant's said judgment. In tender consideration whereof, &c. [The prayer of the bill should be to set aside the deed as fraudulent and void, to have the property embraced in it, or so much as is necessary to satisfy the complainant's claim, sold, and proceeds applied to complainant's claim and for general relief.]

J. M., p. q.

Creditors' bill against a decedent's estate.

[The bill contains statements of the decedent's death, and of the qualification of his personal representative, that complainants are creditors, and the amount of their claims; makes the personal representative and the heirs at law (or devisees) parties, prays for the settlement of accounts and taking proof of debts, for the sale

if necessary of the real property and the application of the proceeds of the property, real and personal, to the payment of the
debts according to the priorities, and for general relief. There
should be also a statement that proper counsel's fees will be asked
for in the progress of the suit. The names of the plaintiffs should
be stated as in the memorandum p. 2, *ante*.]

*Bill for Specific Performance in United States Circuit
Court of Virginia, by a Party residing in Virginia,
against Citizens of other States; Bill by Vendor
against Vendee.*

To the Honorable Judges of the Circuit Court of
the United States for the Eastern District of Virginia.

P. W., of the city of Richmond, and a citizen of
the State of Virginia, brings this, his bill against J.
B., of the city of Milwaukee, a citizen of the State of
Wisconsin, and John D., of the city of New York,
and a citizen of the State of New York.

And, thereupon, your orator complains, and says
that heretofore, to wit: on or about the 6th day of
June, 1861, at a sale made by W. V., trustee, Nathaniel C., William G. and your orator became the
purchasers of a tract of land containing five hun-.
dred acres, more or less, lying in the county of York,
Virginia; that a part of the purchase money thereof
having been paid, your orator, and the said Nathaniel C. and William G., were entitled, on the payment of the residue of said purchase money, to a
deed for said property from said trustee; that they
were put into possession of said property by said
trustee, and so remained in possession thereof until
and up to the time of the contract for sale of said
land to J. B., as hereinafter mentioned; that while
they were so in possession, and entitled to demand a

conveyance of said land, upon payment of the full purchase money thereof, your orator, and the said Nathaniel C. and William G., made a written contract of sale of the said land and the improvements thereon to the said I. B. on the following terms: that is to say, the price agreed on was $11 per acre for the five hundred acres, amounting altogether to $5,500. The terms as agreed on were $1,500 cash, and the balance in one, two and three years, with interest at 6 per cent. per annum from January 14th, 1871; said interest payable annually, the title to be made when the whole purchase money was paid. This contract was made on the 4th day of February, 1871, and the cash payment of $1,500 was made, and Mr. B. was put into possession of said tract of land. The name of the said tract of land is "Colton Hill." Since the cash payment by I. B., nothing has been paid, although two of the credit instalments have long since fallen due. While I. B. was in possession of this land, and the contract of sale to I. B. was in full force, William G. and Nathaniel C. transferred to your orator all their interest in the purchase of said land from the trustees aforesaid; and thereafter Wm. W., the trustee aforesaid, with the consent of the said Nathaniel C. and William G., who were parties to the deed, conveyed to your orator the said land called "Colton Hill," by which conveyance your orator became possessed of the legal fee simple title to said tract of land. The deed for the same is herewith filed, marked Exhibit B, and is prayed to be taken as part of this bill. Your orator has always been willing and ready to

14

transfer and convey by good and sufficient deed, with
general warranty and the usual covenants of title, to
the said B. the said land, when and as soon as the
full amount of the purchase money therefor was
paid, and to assure to him a good title therefor, and
in such deed the said William G. and Nathaniel C.
have also been willing to unite, and are now willing
to do so. They have furnished your orator with the
paper herewith filed, marked Exhibit "A," and
prayed to be taken as a part of this bill, in which
they state that they are now willing to fully carry
out and perform their contract of sale to said B.,
and to unite in the deed therefor with your orator.
The said B., although your orator has always been
ready to carry out said contract of sale and is now
ready to carry out and perform the same, has failed
to pay the credit instalments already due. and refuses to complete the said contract of sale.

One John D. claims to have some interest in the
said purchase of the said property by the said I. B.
What that interest is your orator is unable to say.
The contract of sale was made with I. B. The money paid for the cash instalment was paid by B.,
and the contract of sale was with B. If B. was
acting for J. D., that was a matter not disclosed either
to your orator or to W. G. or to N. C. Mr. J. D. is
made a party to this suit however, in order that his
interest, whatever it may be, may be fully protected.
Your orator has always been ready and willing to
perform this agreement, and proffers, on being paid
the remainder of his purchase money with interest,
to convey the said land to the purchaser thereof

with general warranty and the usual covenants of title. And your orator hoped that the said purchaser would have performed the said agreement on his part, as in justice and equity he ought to have done. To the end, therefore, that the said defendants may, if they can, show why your orator should not have the relief hereby prayed, and may upon their several and respective corporal oaths, and according to the utmost and best of their several and respective knowledge, remembrance, information and belief, full, true, and perfect answer make to such of the interrogatories hereinafter numbered and set forth as by the note hereunder written, they are respectively required to answer— that is to say,

1. Whether he, the said I. B., did or not contract to purchase the said land called "Colton Hill," containing five hundred acres, more or less, lying in Y. county, Virginia, at the rate of $11 per acre on the following terms, to wit: $1,500 cash, and the residue in instalments at one, two and three years, with interest at 6 per cent. per annum from January 14th, 1871, on the credit instalments, said interest payable annually.

2. Whether he, the said I. B., paid thereof $1,500, the cash instalment; and when, and to whom?

3. Whether any of the credit instalments of the purchase money of the said land have fallen due; and if any, when? and whether any part of the credit instalments have been paid by him, the said I. B., or by any person?

4. Whether the title was not to be retained to the

said land until the full purchase money thereof was paid?

5. Whether the said John D. has any interest in the said purchase of said land? and if so, what? and how he has acquired or holds such interest?

And your orator prays that the defendant I. B., or if the said J. D. shall be held to be the purchaser of the property, then that the said John D. may be compelled, by the decree of this honorable court, specifically to perform the said agreement of purchase, and to pay to your orator the remainder of the said purchase money, with interest on the same at the rate of 6 per cent. per annum from the said 14th January, 1871, your orator being willing, and hereby offering specially to perform the said agreement on his part, and on being paid the said purchase money and interest, to execute a proper conveyance of said land to said purchaser.

And your orator further prays, that in the event the said purchase money shall not be paid when decreed by this court to be paid, that the said land be directed to be sold by the proper officer of this court, or by a commissioner duly appointed by the court, and the net proceeds of sale thereof remaining, after satisfying the expenses of sale and costs of this suit, shall be applied to the payment of said unpaid purchase money and interest; and that your orator shall have such further and other and general relief in the premises as to your honors shall seem meet, and this case may require.

May it please your honors to grant unto your orator a writ of subpœna, to be directed to the said I. B.

and John D., thereby commanding them, and each of them, at a certain time, and under a certain penalty therein to be limited, personally to appear before this honorable court, and then and there full, true, direct and perfect answer make to all and singular the premises; and further, to stand to, perform and abide such further order, direction and decree therein as shall seem agreeable to equity and good conscience.

P. W.

A. M., *Of counsel
for plaintiff.*

Memo.—The defendant, I. B., is required to answer the several interrogatories, numbered 1, 2, 3, 4 and 5 respectively.

The defendant, John D., is required to answer the several interrogatories, numbered 1, 2, 3, 4 and 5 respectively.[2]

---

[2] See note 1, on page 103 *ante*; also, 40th and 93d rules Sup. Court.

CHAPTER VI.

*Of the filing of the Bill or Information, and of sub-
sequent Proceedings at Rules in the Virginia State
Courts.*

FILING OF BILL.

67. Without longer detaining the reader in the
consideration of the forms of bills in special cases,
our attention will now be given to the proceedings at
rules in the Virginia State Courts, subsequent to
those detailed in previous sections.[1]

68. If the plaintiff has not previously filed his
bill or information, he may do so at the next rules
after the summons has been issued, or at any subsequent rule day.[2] Care should be taken, however,
to file it at an early date, after the service of process
upon one or more of the defendants, otherwise the
suit may be dismissed on account of the failure to
file it; and so, too, when the defendant has appeared
and given a rule to file it, the plaintiff will, unless
he file his bill at the next rules, have his suit dismissed, and be required to pay the defendant his
costs, and five dollars damages.[3]

---

[1] §§ 1–10, pp. 1–6, *ante.*

[2] In injunction bills, and others requiring the action of the judge or court,
directing restraining process, the bill is uniformly filed before process issues.

[3] §§ 8, 9, *ante.*

DECREE NISI; RULE TO PLEAD.

69. If the summons has been executed on any defendant, he will be required to appear at the rules at which the process against him is returned executed, or when it is returnable to a term at the first rule day after it is so returned; and on his failure to appear, the plaintiff, if he has filed his bill, may have entered a *decree nisi* as to such defendant; when defendant has appeared, yet fails to plead, answer or demur to the bill when filed, the plaintiff should give him a rule to plead[4].

BILL TAKEN FOR CONFESSED.

70. At the next rules after the *decree nisi* has been entered, or a rule to plead given, if the defendant continue in default, the bill will be entered as taken for confessed as to him,[5] and the plaintiff may at the same rules, or at a succeeding rules, have the cause set for hearing as to such defendant.[6]

PLEA AND DEMURRER.

71. Usually the defendant either pleads, demurs to, or answers the bill at rules. If the defendant plead or demur, the plaintiff may have the plea or demurrer set down for argument; and should it be overruled, no other plea or demurrer will after-

---

[4] Code, chap. 171, sec. 42; Code, 1873, chap. 167, sec. 43. If the defendant wishes to plead to the jurisdiction, he should do so before a *decree nisi* or rule to plead, &c.; Code, 1873, chap. 167, sec. 20.

[5] Code, 1873, chap. 167, sec. 43. As to effect of confession, see *Cropper* v. *Burtons*, 5 Leigh 432.

[6] Code, chap. 171, sec. 40; Code, 1873, chap. 167, sec. 49.

wards be received, but there will be a rule on the defendant to answer the bill.' Or, in case of a plea, the plaintiff may take issue upon it, and the issue will be tried by a jury; if the plea be found false, the plaintiff will have the same advantages as if it had been so found by verdict at law.[8]

72. *Filing of Answer, Replication, &c.* The Virginia Statute provides that a defendant at any time before a final decree, may be allowed to file his answer; but a cause shall not be sent to the rules or continued, because an answer is filed in it, unless good cause be shown therefor;[9] yet after the suit has been set for hearing at the rules as to any defendant, it is the practice not to enter an answer as filed, unless directed to file it by an order of court; and the propriety of this practice has never been questioned In *Goddin* v. *Vaughn's ex'ix & als.*, 14 Grat. 115, it was contended that the answer of Mason having been filed in vacation, not at the rules nor in term time, was not a part of the record, but could only be regarded as an affidavit. The Court of Appeals said that while it was generally true that an answer can only be filed during the session of court or at the rules, yet by the statute an exception was made in cases of injunction.[10]

73. When the answer is filed, the plaintiff may

---

[7] Code, chap. 171, sec. 32; Code, 1873, chap. 167, sec. 33.   [8] Ibid, sec. 34.

[9] Code, chap. 171, sec. 34; Code of 1873, chap. 167, sec. 35.

[10] "The object of giving the Judge in vacation power to dissolve an injunction was to prevent delay, and this would be to some extent defeated if a party had to wait until the rule day or a session of the court before he could put in his answer and have the benefit of it on a motion to dissolve. *Lee J,.* in *Goddin* v. *Vaughan's ex'ix & als.*, 14 Grat. 130.

reply or except, or may have the cause set for hearing on the answer alone. If the answer is filed at rules, the plaintiff replying may have the cause set for hearing at the same rules at which the replication is filed."

74. If no replication is filed, and the cause come on to be heard on the bill and answer, without replication, the answer will be considered as true in all its parts. *Kennedy* v. *Baylor*, 1 Wash. 162.

When, too, the cause is heard by consent upon bill and answer, without being regularly set for hearing, the rule is the same as if it had been so set for hearing. *Jones* v. *Mason*, 5 Rand. 577. When a cause is set for hearing on the bill and answer, without replication, and when the cause is heard by consent on the bill and answer *without replication*, the facts which the answer states in relation to the controversy, whether responsive to the bill or not, will be taken to be true. *Findlay* v. *Smith &c.*, 6 Munf. 142. The only effect produced by the omission of a replication is, that the statements of the answer will be taken as true. *Pickett &c.* v. *Chilton*, 5 Munf. 483.

75. When the plaintiff files exceptions to the answer, they are set down for argument, and, if the exceptions be sustained, the defendant will be required to answer anew, and to the new answer, when filed, plaintiff may either reply or except as before.

---

11 Ibid, sec. 49. Formerly, special replications were in use. Their place is now supplied by an amendment of the bill whenever the plaintiff deems his bill not properly adapted to his case; and general replications are alone used in this country and in England. 2 Rob. Pr. (old) 315. *Kent*, C. J., in *James* v. *McKernon*, 6 John. Rep. 564; Mitf. Plead. 19, 255.

Should the defendant put in a second answer, which is adjudged insufficient, he may be examined upon interrogatories, and committed until he answers them.[12]

76. *When suit set for hearing by defendant, and defendant's right to have cause heard as to himself.* If four months elapse after the answer of a defendant is filed, without the cause being set for hearing by the plaintiff, and without exceptions being filed to the answer, the defendant may have the cause set for hearing as to himself,[13] and is, moreover, entitled to have the suit heard as to him, unless his interests be so connected with those of other defendants in the suit that it would be improper to decide upon their interests separately;[14] and, even though there be such connection of interests, such defendant may have an order upon the plaintiff to use due diligence to mature the cause for hearing as to the other defendants, and unless it be so matured within such time as the court may deem reasonable, such defendant will be entitled to a hearing or dismission of the suit as to him.[15]

77. *Infants or Insane Defendants.* Should there be an infant or insane defendant, a *guardian ad litem* may be appointed to defend his interest by the clerk at rules, whether the infant or insane defendant has been served with process or not; and the court may compel the person so appointed to act,

---

[12] Code, chap. 171, sec. 30; Code, 1873, ch. 167, sec. 37.

[13] Code, 1873, chap. 167, sec. 49.

[14] Ibid, sec. 51. See *Key* v. *Hord & als.,* 4 Munf. 485; *Cartigne* v. *Raymond &c.,* 4 Leigh 579.

[15] Code, 1873, ch. 167, sec. 51.

but he shall not be liable for costs, and shall be allowed his reasonable charges, which the party, on whose motion he was appointed, shall pay.[16]

78. *Absent or unknown defendants, &c.* Sometimes, if the ordinary process of summons was alone resorted to, the plaintiff would not be able to secure a hearing of his cause. To meet cases of this kind, the Virginia Statute provides, that on affidavit that a defendant is not a resident of this State, or that diligence has been used by or on behalf of the plaintiff to ascertain in what county or corporation he is, without effect, or that process, directed to the officer of the county or corporation in which he resides, or is, has been twice delivered to such officer more than ten days before the return day, and been returned without being executed, or that the defendant in a suit for a divorce from the bond of matrimony, is under sentence to confinement in the penitentiary, an order of publication may be entered against such defendant; and the statute farther provides, that in any suit in equity where the bill states that the names of any persons interested in the subject to be divided or disposed of, are unknown, and makes such persons defendants, by the general description of parties unknown, on affidavit of the fact that the said names are unknown, an order of publication may be entered against such

---

[16] Code, 1873, chap. 167, sec. 17. The *guardian ad litem* in Virginia usually files a formal answer, submitting the interests of the infant or insane defendant to the protection of the court. He may, however, if he deems it necessary, take the same mode of defence with other defendants, by plea or demurrer, or by an answer either contradicting or affirming the statements of bill.

unknown parties. It farther provides, that any order under this statute may be entered either in court or by the clerk of the court at any time in vacation; and that in a proceeding by petition there may be an order of publication in like manner as in a suit in equity."

79. This order of publication must state briefly the object of the suit, and require the defendants against whom it is entered, or the unknown parties, to appear within one month after the due publication thereof, and do what is necessary to protect their interests.[18]

80. The order should be published once a week, for four successive weeks, in such newspaper as the court may prescribe, or if none be so prescribed, as the clerk may direct, and should be posted by the clerk at the front door of the courthouse of the county or corporation wherein the court is held, on the first day of the next county or corporation court after it is entered.[19] See *Craig* v. *Sebrell*, 9 Grat. 131, and *Moore & als.* v. *Holt*, 10 Grat. 284.

81. When these requirements of the Virginia Statute are complied with, if the defendants against whom the order of publication has been entered, or the unknown parties, do not appear within one month after the publication is completed, the case may be tried or heard as to them, and the court may enter such decree or order upon such trial or hearing as may appear just.[20] When such publication is had,

---

[17] Code, 1873, chap. 166, § 10.   [18] Ibid, §14.   [19] Ibid.

[20] Ibid, sec. 15. When a trial is had under such circumstances, the Statute provides that the unknown party, or other defendant, who was not served

no other publication shall be thereafter required in
any proceeding in court or before a commissioner, or
for the purpose of taking depositions, unless specially
ordered by the court as to such defendants or unknown parties.[21]

The Virginia Statute farther provides, that personal service of a summons, *scire facias*, or notice,
may be made by any person not a party to, or otherwise interested in, the subject-matter in controversy,
on a non-resident defendant out of this State, which
service shall have the same effect, and no other, as
an order of publication duly posted and published
against him.[22]

PROCESS OF CONTEMPT.

82. It sometimes happens that a defendant neither
demurs nor pleads nor answers. When this is the
case, as we have seen, the plaintiff may have his bill
taken for confessed, and the cause set for hearing.
There are instances, however, in which the plaintiff
deems it proper to compel an answer from the defendant, and in such cases he may, in the Virginia State
Courts, either obtain an order to bring in the defendant to answer interrogatories, or he may resort to
the process of contempt.

---

with process, and did not appear in the case before the date of the decree or
order, or the representative of any such, may, within five years from that
date, if he be not served with a copy of such decree or order, more than a year
before the end of the said five years, and, if he be so served, then, within one
year from the time of such service, petition to have the cause reheard, and
may plead or answer, and have any injustice to the proceedings corrected.
Code, 1873, chap. 166, § 16.

[21] Code, 1873, ch. 166, § 15.   [22] Ibid,

83. The reader will see at a glance that there are difficulties connected with the third and fourth steps of the process of contempt, and for this reason it is preferable to pursue the other method pointed out by the statute; *i. e.*, bringing in the defendant to answer interrogatories.[23] This, as well as the process of contempt, may be resorted to even after the bill has been taken for confessed as to any defendant.[24]

84. If a defendant after process of contempt put in an answer, which is adjudged insufficient, the plaintiff may go on with the subsequent process of contempt, as if no answer had been filed.[25]

85. The process of contempt, originally in England, when directed against a person,[26] consisted of five steps:

1st. A writ of attachment directed to the sheriff of the defendant's county.

2nd. A writ of attachment with proclamations also directed to the sheriff of defendant's county.

3d. A writ of rebellion directed to commissioners appointed by the court, and directed to all the counties of England.

4th. An order that the sergeant-at-arms, as the immediate officer of the court, should effect the arrest; and

---

[23] Code, 1873, chap. 167, § 47.
[24] Code, 1873, chap. 167, sec. 47.　　　　　[25] Ibid, sec. 48.
[26] Not a corporation. In the case of a corporation, which cannot be attached, the first step in the process of contempt is by distringas, and the second by sequestration. There is this farther difference between the process of contempt against a private person, and that process against a corporation. In the case of a private person, the sequestration may be stayed on his entering his appearance—in the case of corporations, the sequestration cannot be stayed by entering their appearance.

5th. A writ of sequestration, issuable only on the return of *non est inventus*, by the sergeant-at-arms, or on a defendant in custody.

The question will naturally suggest itself to the reader how the third and fourth steps of this process may be taken in the Virginia State Courts. In the first edition of this work, comments and suggestions upon this subject were made, which are embodied in the note below.[27]

[27] In *Hook* v. *Ross*, 1 H. & M. 310, determined in 1807, these five steps were expressly recognized as then existent and in force in Virginia under the statutes of the State at that time.

There is no provision in our statutes expressly, or even by implication, re- voking, repealing, or altering any of the steps in the process as it was used at the time of the decision in *Hook* v. *Ross*.

The "process of contempt" is recognized as in existence in Virginia by the latest enactments affecting the subjects of this process (see Code of Virginia, chap. 167, sec. 48), yet a question presents itself in connection with the fourth of the steps, which, in the present state of our statutes, is somewhat difficult of solution, and may lead to an abandonment of this process altogether, unless the aid of the legislature be obtained to relieve the subject of this diffi- culty. Our law does not now recognize the existence of such an officer as the "sergeant-at-arms of the court of chancery." That office was abolished by the act found in 1 R. C., 1819, which authorized the "marshal" to exe- cute all the duties assigned theretofore to a sergeant-at-arms. In turn, the office of marshal of the courts of chancery was abolished by the act passed April 16, 1831 (Supp. Rev. C., chap. 107, sec. 70), and in the main, by that act, all the duties theretofore discharged by the marshals were confided to the sheriffs of the counties and the sergeants of the corporations. In the main we say, for we do not find that all the powers which the marshal exercised were given to the sheriffs or the sergeants. On the contrary, one essential ingre- dient for the due execution of the fourth step in the process of contempt, these officers lacked, and that is, the power to execute process in any county within the limits of the State. That this is essential—that the writ of seques- tration should not issue until a return of *non est inventus* by an officer, whose powers (at least *quoad* the process of sergeant-at-arms) were co-extensive with the limits of the State, is, we think, certain ; and this conclusion is based both upon the positive dictum of Judge Tucker in *Hook* v. *Ross*, and the manifest hardship which an opposite opinion would operate on parties whose property might be sequestrated without such a return. If this be true, what course

The forms of these processes in the Virginia State Courts are as follows:

I. ATTACHMENT.

.

The Commonwealth of Virginia,
To the Sheriff of ——— *county, greeting:*

We command you that you attach A. B., so that you have his body before our judge of the Circuit Court of ———, to answer as well of a certain contempt by him to us offered, as it is said, as to those things which to him shall be then and there objected; and further, to do and receive what our said court shall in that part consider. And this you shall in no wise omit. And have then there this writ.

---

should be taken to avoid the difficulty? Will the courts of Virginia specially appoint such an officer as that contemplated, and, indeed, required, for the due execution of this process; or will they abandon their right to enforce, in this form, obedience to their mandates? One or the other of these courses they must adopt; and in the absence of positive legislation on the subject, it would perhaps be better to pursue the former than to adopt one which would strip them to no little extent of the authority to compel obedience to their decrees. If this suggestion were acted on, then the difficulty might be removed by the appointment of the sheriff, as a special officer of the court, to execute the fourth step in this process, authorizing him as a special sergeant-at-arms, messenger, or by any other name, to serve the process in any county of the State. The return of *non est inventus* by such an officer, if the regularity of his appointment were not successfully attacked, would be a sufficient foundation on which to base the issue of a writ of sequestration. The subject, in the present state of our laws, to say the least, presents, in any point of view, an embarrassing question, and it would be well if the legislature passed an act authorizing our present sheriffs or sergeants to perform all the duties in connection with the process of contempt formerly discharged by a sergeant-at-arms. This would relieve the Virginia courts of every difficulty, and it seems to be demanded in order that these courts may compel a due and faithful compliance with their decrees, as well as require contumacious defendants to appear and answer bills in equity which may be exhibited against them.

Witness, J. E., clerk of our said court at the county of ———, this —— day of ———, and in the —— year of the Commonwealth of Virginia.

J. E., Clerk.

Endorse.—For not appearing to answer (or for not answering) the bill of complaint exhibited against him by C. D.

II. ATTACHMENT WITH PROCLAMATIONS.

The Commonwealth of Virginia,
  To the Sheriff of ——— *county, greeting:*

We command you, that in all and singular places in your bailiwick, where to you shall seem most expedient, you cause it publicly, on our part, to be proclaimed that H. O., under the penalty of his allegiance, before our judge of the Circuit Court of ——— in chancery, at the courthouse, on the first Monday in next month, personally do appear; and, .nevertheless, the said H. O., in the meantime, if you can find, you attach, so that you have his body before our judge of our said court, at the day aforesaid, to answer us as well of a certain contempt by him to us offered, as it is said, as upon those things which to him shall then and there be objected; and further to do and receive what our said court shall in that part consider. And this you shall in no wise omit. And have then and there this writ.

Witness, J. E., clerk of our said court, at the county of ———, this —— day of ———, and in the —— year of the Commonwealth of Virginia.

J. E., Clerk.

Endorse.—For not appearing to answer (or for not answering) the bill of complaint exhibited against him by C. D.

III. WRIT OF REBELLION.

The Commonwealth of Virginia,
To the Sheriff of —————— county, greeting:

Whereas, by public proclamation made in our behalf by the sheriff of ——————, in divers places, in that county, by virtue of our writ to him directed, C. P. hath been commanded, upon his allegiance, to appear before us in our Circuit Court of —————— county, at a certain day now past; yet he hath manifestly contemned our command, therefore we command you to attach, or cause the said C. P. to be attached, wheresoever he shall be found within our said Commonwealth, as a rebel and contemner of our said laws, so as you have him, or cause him to be before us in our said Circuit Court on the first day of the next term, to answer to us as well touching the said contempt, as also such matters as shall be then and there objected against him; and, further, to perform and abide such order as our said court shall make in this behalf, and hereof fail not. We hereby also strictly command all, and singular, mayors, sheriffs, bailiffs, constables, and other, our officers, and the good citizens of this Commonwealth, that they, by all proper means, diligently aid and assist you in all things in the execution of the premises. And have then and there this writ.

Witness, J. E., clerk of our said court at the county of ———, this —— day of ———, and in the —— year of the Commonwealth of Virginia.

J. E., *Clerk.*

Endorse.—For not appearing to answer (or for not answering) the bill of complaint exhibited against him by C. D.

IV. ORDER FOR SERGEANT-AT-ARMS.

A. B., ... Plaintiff,
vs.
C. D., ... Defendant.

Whereas the said defendant hath sat out all process of contempt to a commission of rebellion, for want of his answer to the plaintiff's bill, and it appearing by the certificate, on the commission of rebellion heretofore awarded, that the said defendant doth abscond himself, so that he cannot be taken, thereupon, it is therefore ordered upon the motion of ———, the plaintiff's counsel, that the Sergeant-at-Arms, attending this court, do apprehend the said defendant and bring him to the bar of the said court to answer the said contempt.

WRIT OF SEQUESTRATION.

The Commonwealth of Virginia,
To the Sheriff of ——— *county, greeting:*

Whereas in a suit now pending in the Circuit Court for the county of ———, between W. F., plaintiff, and J. F., defendant, process of contempt has been issued against the said J. F. for his contempt in refusing to file an answer to the bill in equity exhibited against him in the said court by the said W. F. Know ye, therefore, that we, in confidence of your prudence and fidelity, have given, and by these presents do give to you full authority and power to enter into all messuages, lands, tenements, and real estate of the said J. F. whatsoever, within the district of our said Circuit Court, and to take, select, receive and sequester into your hands not only all the rents and profits of his said messuages, lands, tenements and real estate, but also his goods, chattels and personal estate whatsoever within the district aforesaid; and, therefore, we command you that you do at certain proper and convenient days and hours go to and enter upon all the messuages, lands, tenements, and real estate of the said J. F., and that you do collect, take and get into your hands not only all the rents and profits of his said real estate, but also all his goods, chattels and personal estate, and detain and keep the same in sequestration in your hands until the said J. F. shall answer the said bill and do what our said court shall direct. And how you shall have executed this precept make known to the judge of our said court on the —— day of the next term. And have then and there this writ.

Witness, J. E., clerk of the said Circuit Court in the county of ——, this —— day of ——, and in the —— year of the Commonwealth of Virginia.

J. E., *Clerk.*

86. As was stated in a note on a former page, in the case of a corporation, which cannot be attached, the first step in the process of contempt is by distringas, and the second by sequestration.

The form of this writ, modelled after the English writ, may be as follows:

The Commonwealth of Virginia,
  To the Sheriff of the City of Richmond, greeting:

We command you to make a distress on the lands and tenements, goods and chattels of [here name the corporation] within your bailiwick, as that neither the said [naming the corporation], nor any other person or persons for them, may lay his or their hands thereon, until our court of the county of ———— shall make other order to the contrary; and, in the meantime, you are to answer to us for the said goods and chattels, and the rents and profits of the said lands, so that the said [naming the corporation] may be compelled to appear before us in our said ———— court of the county of ————, there to answer to us as well touching a contempt, &c. [as in the form of attachment], on page 121, to the end.

DEATH, MARRIAGE, OR LUNACY OF PARTIES, &C.

87. In the English courts, when a party dies, or a female party marries, a bill of revivor is necessary, to bring the personal representative, heirs and devisees of the deceased party in the one case, and the husband in the other, before the court. This also is the practice in the United States' Circuit Courts.

This course is not necessary in the Virginia State Courts. In either of the cases mentioned, if the party dying, or female party marrying, be a plaintiff, the personal representative, heirs and devisees of the deceased party, or the husband and wife, may move the court that the suit proceed in his or their name; and if no sufficient cause be shown against it, an order will be entered that the suit proceed according to such motion;[28] if, however, the party dying, or female party marrying be a defendant, then a writ of *scire facias*, the form of which will be given hereafter, is necessary, and after service of this writ upon the personal representative, or on the heirs or devisees (if necessary parties to the suit) (*a*) of the deceased party in the one case, or on the husband and wife in the other case, if no sufficient cause be shown against it, an order will be entered that the suit proceed, according to such *scire facias*, against the personal representative, heirs or devisees of the deceased party, or the husband and wife.[29]

88. And so, too, when a party becomes convict of felony, or insane, or the powers of a party, who is a personal representative or committee, cease, if such party be a plaintiff, the cause may be proceeded in on simple motion; if he be a defendant, then a *scire facias* may be issued, and the like proceedings had

---

[28] Code, 1873, chap. 169, sec. 4.   [29] Ibid.

(*a*) The heirs of Lewis were not necessary parties in *Ruffners* v. *Lewis's ex'ors & als.*, 7 Leigh 720. The case was this: A decree had ascertained the rights of the plaintiffs in respect to the land, and a partition made and a conveyance directed to be made to L. for the moiety sued for: L. died. It was held, that as the suit was then proceeded in for the rents and profits only, to which the executors of L. were entitled, it was proper to revive it in their names, and not in the names of the heirs of L.

as on a *scire facias* issued in the cases mentioned before.[30]

89. The writ of *scire facias* may be issued at any time, and made returnable to a day in court or to a rule day, and, when returnable to a rule day, the clerk will make the necessary order of revival in his rule book, if no sufficient cause be shown against it; the order to revive may be entered at rules, although the case is on the court docket.[31]

90. When, however, in any case the party whose powers cease is a defendant, the party plaintiff will not be allowed to proceed upon his previous bill against such defendant and his successor, unless an order that the suit proceed against the former party be entered at the first term after service of a *scire facias* for or against such successor.[32]

91. The practice in causes at rules in the United States Circuit Courts differs materially from the practice of the Virginia State Courts. The reader is referred to the next chapter of this treatise treating specially of this practice.

92. The following are forms of the several proceedings mentioned in this chapter, not already given in previous sections:

Form of Decree Nisi.

The summons awarded in this cause having been returned executed on the defendant C. D., and the bill of the plaintiff having been filed, and the said

---

[30] Ibid.   [31] Code, 1873, chap. 169, sec. 5.
[32] Ibid, sec. 6. See also § 7, § 8, § 9, chap. 169, Code 1873.

C. D. still failing to appear and plead, answer or demur to the said bill, on the motion of the plaintiff, it is ordered that it be entered of record that the said bill will be taken for confessed as to the said C. D. if the said C. D. shall continue in default.

Form of Rule to Plead.

The summons awarded in this cause having been returned executed on the defendant C. D., and the bill of the plaintiff-having been filed, and the said C. D. who has heretofore (*or* this day) appeared, yet failing to plead, answer or demur to the said bill, a rule is given to the said defendant to plead, answer or demur to the said bill at the next rules; and if the said C. D. shall then fail to plead, answer or demur to the said bill, the same will be taken for confessed as to him.

Form of rule taking bill for confessed, and setting cause for hearing.

The defendant, C. D., not yet having appeared and pleaded, answered or demurred to the plaintiff's bill, the same is taken for confessed as to the said defendant, *and the cause is set for hearing as to him; or,* the defendant, C. D., who has appeared to this suit, still failing to plead, answer or demur to the plaintiff's bill, the same is taken for confessed as to the said defendant, *and the cause is set for hearing as to him.*[33]

---

[33] The cause may be set for hearing at the same or at a succeeding rules. Code, 1873, chap. 167, sec. 49,

Form of Rule filing Plea or Demurrer.

The defendant, C. D., appeared and filed a plea (*or*, demurrer) to the plaintiff's bill,[34] and the said plea (*or*, demurrer) is set down for argument.

Issue taken on a Plea.

The defendant, C D., appeared and filed a plea to the plaintiff's bill, and the plaintiff took issue upon the statements made in the said plea, and it is ordered that the said issue be tried by a jury.

Answer filed, and General Replication and Cause set for hearing.

The defendant, C. D., appeared and filed his answer to the bill of the plaintiff, and the plaintiff thereupon replied generally to the said answer, and the cause is set for hearing as to the said defendant.

Answer filed.

The defendant, C. D., appeared and filed his answer to the bill of the plaintiff.[35]

Exceptions to Answer filed.

The plaintiffs this day filed exceptions to the de-

---

[34] If a demurrer, say: "And the plaintiff joined in the said demurrer."

[35] Regularly an answer should be signed and sworn to, but the signature and oath may be waived by the complainant, and the filing of a replication is evidence of such waiver. *Fulton Bank* v. *Beach & al.*, 6 Wend. 36.

A defendant prepares an answer, admitting the allegations of the plaintiff's bill, and it is certified as sworn to, but the person certifying, the affidavit does not style himself a justice of the peace, nor is it otherwise proved that he is a magistrate empowered to administer oaths; the defendant dies, and this paper so certified is filed in the clerk's office: *Held*, to be no answer of the party, nor evidence in the cause. *Sitlingtons* v. *Brown & als.*, 7 Leigh 271.

fendant's answer, and the said exceptions are set down for argument.

Cause set for hearing on Defendant's motion.

Four months having elapsed since the answer of C. D., a defendant in this cause, was filed, and the plaintiff herein not having set the cause for hearing as to such defendant, and not having filed exceptions thereto, on motion of the said defendant this cause is set for hearing as to him.

Guardian ad litem assigned Infant or Insane Defendant.

C. Y. is assigned *guardian ad litem* to the infant (*or,* insane) defendant, B. R., to defend his interests in this suit.

Order of Publication against Non-resident Defendants.

R. M., *plaintiff*, against L. C., D. R. and other *defendants.*

The object of this suit is [here state the object of suit], and affidavit having been made and filed that the defendants abovenamed are non-residents of this Commonwealth, the said defendants are notified to appear at the rules to be held in the clerk's office of this court on the first Monday in ———— next, and do what is necessary to protect their interests in this suit; and it is ordered that a copy of this order be published in the *Richmond Enquirer* (a newspaper published in the city of Richmond) once a week for four successive weeks, and that another copy thereof be posted at the front door of the courthouse of this county on the first day of the next County Court of this county.

Order of Publication against unknown Defendants.

R. M., *plaintiff*, against B. R. and others, made parties to the bill in this suit, as unknown parties, *defendants*.

The object of this suit is [here state object of suit], and affidavit having been made and filed that the names of the said parties to the bill in said suit made defendants as unknown parties, are unknown, the said unknown defendants are notified, &c. [the same as in the last form to the end.]

Order awarding Scire facias.

On motion of the plaintiff, a writ of *scire facias* is awarded against C. D., executor of the last will and testament of R. M., deceased, returnable to October rules.

Form of Scire facias against a Personal Representative.

The Commonwealth of Virginia,
　　　　To the ——— of ——— county, greeting:

Whereas in a certain suit in equity lately depending in the ——— court of ———, between J B. and N. C., plaintiffs, and R. W. and N. B., defendants, before any farther proceedings were had therein (*or*, before a final decree therein), the said N. B. departed this life intestate, and due administration of all and singular his goods and chattels, having, as we have been informed, been granted to R. X. by the ——— court of ——— county, and the said J. B. and N. C. having applied for a proper remedy in this behalf, and being willing that right and justice may be done, agreeably to the statutes of Virginia in such case made and provided, we command you that you make known, according to law, to the said R. X., administrator of all and singular the goods and chattels of the said N. B., deceased; that he be[36] before our said —— court of ——, in the ——, on the —— day of ——. next, to show if anything for himself he hath or can say why the said suit and the proceedings therein had should not stand and be revived against the said R. X., administrator as aforesaid, and be in all things in the same plight and condition as it was at the time of the decease of the said N. B.; and further, to do and receive what our said court shall in that part consider. And have then and there this writ.

Witness, J. R., clerk of our said court at ——, this —— day of ——, 18——, and in the —— year of the independence of the United States of America.

J. R., Clerk.

Form of Scire facias against Personal Representative and against Devisees, &c., of deceased Defendant.[37]

The Commonwealth of Virginia,
    To the —— of —— county, greeting:

Whereas in a certain suit in equity lately depending in the —— court of ——, between J. B. and N. C., plaintiffs, and R. B. and N. B., de-

---

[36] See note (a) on page 137.   [37] See Code 1873, chapter 169, sec. 4.

fendants, before a final decree was had therein, R. B., one of the defendants, departed this life, leaving, as we have been informed, the following children and sole heirs at law, to wit: John, Sallie and Bettie B., all of whom are over the age of twenty-one years; and as we have been further informed, due administration of all and singular the goods and chattels of the said R. B. has been granted by the ———— court of ———— county to M. N. and the said J. B., and N. C. having applied for a proper remedy in that behalf, and being willing that right and justice may be done agreeably to the statutes of Virginia, in such case made and provided, we command you that you make known according to law to the said John, Sallie and Bettie B., aforementioned children and heirs-at-law of the said R. B., deceased, and to the said M. N., administrator of the goods and chattels of the R. B., deceased, that they be before our said ———— court of ————, on the ——— day of ———— next, to show if anything for themselves they have or can say why the said suit and the proceedings therein had should not stand and be revived against them, and be in all things in the same plight and condition as it was at the time of the decease of the said R. B.; and farther, to do and receive what our said court shall in that part consider. And have then and there this writ.

Witness, J. R., clerk of our said court at ————, this ——— day of ————, 18——, and in the ——— year of the independence of the United States of America.

J. R., Clerk.

FORM OF CLERK'S DOCKET IN EQUITY

In this Docket d. n. means *decree nisi*, v. *versus*, o p. *order of publication*, rs. *rules*.

Plaintiff's Counsel.	Deft's Counsel.	Names of Parties.	January.	February.	March.	April.
J. W.	R. H.	L. M. vs. P. Q. & als.	(27th) Sum'ons to Feb. rules.	Summons ret'd ex'd on def't W. Bill filed. D. n. ag't W. New sum's vs. other def'ts.	Bill p. c. as to W. Sum'ons ret'd ex'd as to other deff'ants, and d. n. as to them.	Answer of def't P. Q. filed, and g. r. Bill taken for confessed as to def'ts R. H. and B. L.
G. M.	B. T.	X. Y. vs. A. B., C. D., & unknown defendants.	Bill filed, and sum'ons vs. A. B. to February rs. Affidavit of non-res'nce of C. D., &c., and O. P. vs. C.D., and unknown def'ts to Feb'y rules.	Sum's vs. A. B. returned; not time to execute, new sum'mons to April rules.	Ord. pub. vs. C. D. & unknown def't's filed. Affidavit of posting.	Set for hearing as to def'ts C. D. & unknown defendants.
L. B.	T. V.	G. M. vs. D. B., C. R and A. M.	Sum's v. def'ts to Febr'ary rs.	Def't C. R. appeared & gave rule to plaintiff to file bill. Sum'ons ret'd ex'd on D. B.	Bill filed. D. n. as to D. B. Rule on def't C. R. to plead. L. O. app'ted gu'an ad litem to inf'nt def'nt A. M. Answer of guardian ad litem filed, and general repl'n.	Answer of D. B. filed. C. R. failing to demur, plead or answer, and pl'tiffs wishing to compel an answer, attachment vs. C. R.
S. L. & C.	P. R.	M. T, vs. U. V., A. B. & als.			(23) Bill filed, and summons and inj'on to April rules.	New summons and inj'on to May rules.
R. B. H.	J. M. P.	L. N. vs. S. R.		(20) Summons vs. S. S. R. to April rules.	Continued.	Bill filed. Summons retur'd. No inhabit'nt, and it appearing that court has no jurisdiction in this suit, &c., bill dismissed. (See section 10 *ante*.)

CAUSES IN VIRGINIA STATE COURTS.

p. c. *pro confesso* (bill taken for confessed), and g. r. *general replication.*

May.	June.	July.	August.	Septe'ber.	October.	Nov'er.	Dece'ber.
Set for hearing as to defendant P. Q. on his answer, and as to other def'ts on bill taken for confessed as to them.							
Sum's vs. A. B. returned executed, & d. n.	Bill taken for confessed, and suit set for hearing as to A. B.						
C. R. brought in under attachment, and filing his answer, attachment discharged. G. r. as to answer of C. R.	Continued.	Continued.	Continued.	Four mos. having elapsed since D. B. filed his answer, on motion of D. B. suit set for hearing as to him.			
Summons returned executed on U. V., and d. n. against him. Sum'ons vs. other def'ts to July rs.	Plea of N. O filed. Rep'n and issue. A. B. app'd and filed a plea, which was, on motion of pl'tff, set down for argument.	Summons vs. J. K., L. M., X. X. N. P. & B. W. ret'ed ex'd. L. M. filed answer, to which pl'tff filed exceptions, and exceptions set down for argument. D. n. as to J. K., B. W. and X. X.	Bill p. c. & suit set for h'ing as to B. W. Disclaimer of J. K. filed, and cause set for hearing as to him. X. X.'s. An'r fi'd, and without repl'n cause set for hearing as to him.	Continued.	Continued.	Cause set for hearing as to N. P. on his motion.	

CLERK'S DOCKET—(Continued.)

Plaintiff's Counsel.	Deft's Counsel.	Names of Parties.	January.	February.	March.	April.
J. B.	M. N.	B. W. B., an infant by his next friend L. A. vs. R. W. & J. K.				
A. H. S.	J. H.	N. O. vs. X., Y. and Z.; [also M. B. and L.]		Summons vs. defendants to March rules.	Bill filed. Summons retu'd executed, and d. n. as to defendants X. Y. and Z.	Amend. and sup. bill vs. def'ts to original bill, and M. B. and L. Summons v. M. B. and L. to May rs., to answer original and amended bills. Suit set for hearing on original bill as to X Y. and Z. Summons v. X. Y. and Z. on amended and supple'tal bill to June rs.
L. L.	M. M.	N. N. vs. O. O. and P. P.	Sum'ns to Feb. rules.	Continued.	New summons to April rs.	Summons ret'd executed on O. O. New summons vs. P. P. to June rules.

CLERK'S DOCKET—(Continued.)

May.	June.	July.	August.	Septe'ber.	October.	Nov'er.	Dece'ber.
Bills filed, & summons to June rules.	Sum'ns ret'd executed on def't R. W.; not found as to J. K. D. n. as to R. W. New sum'ons vs. J. K. to July rules.	Bill p. c. and set for hearing as to R. W. New summons to October rs. vs. J. K.	Continued.	Continued.	New summons vs. J. K. to Dec. rs.	Cont'd.	Continued.
Continued.	Summons vs. M. B. and L. returned executed, & d. n.	Bill p. c. and cause set for hearing as to M. B. & L. New summons v. X., Y. & Z. to August rules.	Sums ret'd ex'ted on X. & Y., and d. n. as to them .Z. having died, *scire facias* against B. R/., ex'or of his last will, and S. S. & T. T., his devisees to Sept'r rules. (a)	*Sci. fa.* returned executed on B. R., S. S. & T. T., & suit revived ag't them, X. having married C. C. *Sci. fa.* v. C. C. & his wife to October rules. Bill p. c. as to Y., and cause set for he'ing as to him.	*Sci. fa.* returned executed on C. C. & wife, & suit revived ag't them.	Y. having become convict (or, lunatic), *sci. fa.* vs. O. O., his com'tee to Dec. rules.	*Sci. fa.* vs. O. O., comm'tee of Y., returned executed, and suit revived ag'st him.
Continued.	New sum'ons vs. P. P. Continued.		Three mos. having elapsed since service of summons on O. O., and bill not filed, suit dismissed				

(a) If *sci. fa.* be returnable to rules, instead of the words "*before our said ——— court of ——— in the ——— on the ——— day of ——— next,*" as found on page 132, say "*at the clerk's office of our ——— court of the ——— of ——— at the rules to be held for the said court on the first Monday in ——— next.*"

CHAPTER VII.

Of the filing of the bill or information, and of subsequent proceedings at Rules in the clerk's office, or at chambers, in the United States Circuit Courts.

FILING OF BILL.

93. The filing of the bill is the first step in a suit in equity in the United States Circuit Courts.[1] The court is always open for this purpose.[2] As soon as the bill is filed, the clerk issues the process of subpœna thereon, as of course, upon the application of the plaintiff, returnable into the clerk's office the next rule day, or the next rule day but one, at the election of the plaintiff, occurring after twenty days from the time of the issuing of the subpœna. At the bottom of the subpœna is placed a memorandum, that the defendant is to enter his appearance in the suit in the clerk's office on or before the day at which the writ is returnable, otherwise the bill may be taken *pro confesso*. When there are two or more defendants, a writ of subpœna may, at the election of the plaintiff, be sued out separately for each defendant, except in the case of husband and wife defendants, or a joint subpœna may be issued against all the defendants.[3]

---

[1] 11th rule United States Supreme Court.

[2] See 1st rule United States Supreme Court.

[3] 12th rule United States Supreme Court.

SERVICE OF PROCESS.

94. The service of all subpœnas is by delivery of a copy thereof by the officer serving the same to the defendant personally, or in case of a husband and wife to the husband personally, or by leaving a copy thereof at the dwelling house or usual abode of each defendant, with some free white person, who is a member or resident in the family.[4]

95. Whenever any subpœna is returned not executed as to any defendant, the plaintiff is entitled to another subpœna, *toties quoties*, against such defendant, if he shall require it, until due service is made.[5]

96. The service of all process in equity causes in these courts, whether mesne or final, is by the marshal of the district, or his deputy, or by some other person specially appointed by the court for that purpose, and not otherwise; in the latter case, the person serving the process must make affidavit thereof.[6]

97. Upon the return of the subpœna, as served and executed upon any defendant, the clerk enters the suit upon his docket as pending in the court, and states the time of the entry.[7]

APPEARANCE.

98. The appearance day of the defendant is the rule day to which the subpœna is made returnable; provided he has been served with the process twenty days before that day; otherwise his appearance day

---

[4] 13th rule United States Supreme Court.
[5] 14th rule United States Supreme Court.
[6] 15th rule United States Supreme Court.   See 2 Abb. U. S. Practice, 29 *n*.
[7] 16th rule United States Supreme Court.

will be the next rule day succeeding the rule day when the process is returnable. The appearance of the defendant, either personally or by his solicitor, will be entered in the order book on the day thereof by the clerk.[8]

BILL TAKEN FOR CONFESSED.

99. It is the duty of the defendant, unless the time be otherwise enlarged, for cause shown, by a judge of the court upon motion for that purpose, to file his plea, demurrer or answer to the bill in the clerk's office on the rule day next succeeding that of entering his appearance; in default thereof, the plaintiff may, at his election, enter an order (as of course) in the order book, that the bill be taken for confessed; and, thereupon, the cause will be proceeded in *ex parte*, and the matter of the bill may be decreed by the court at the next ensuing term thereof accordingly, if the same can be done without an answer, and is proper to be decreed; or the plaintiff, if he requires any discovery or answer to enable him to obtain a proper decree, will be entitled to process of attachment against the defendant, to compel an answer; and the defendant will not, when arrested upon such process, be discharged therefrom, unless upon filing his answer, or otherwise complying with such order as the court or a judge thereof may direct, as to pleading to, or fully answering the bill within a period to be fixed by the court or judge, and undertaking to speed the cause.[9]

---

[8] 17th rule United States Supreme Court.
[9] 18th rule United States Supreme Court.

100. When the bill is taken for confessed, the court may proceed to a decree at the next ensuing term thereof, and such decree will be deemed absolute, unless the court shall at the same term set aside the same, or enlarge the time for filing the answer, upon cause shown upon motion and affidavit of the defeudant. And no such motion will be granted, unless upon the payment of the costs of the plaintiff in the suit up to that time, or such part thereof as the court shall deem reasonable, and unless the defendant shall undertake to file his answer within such time as the court shall direct, and submit to such other terms as the court shall direct for the purpose of speeding the cause.[10]

AMENDMENTS OF BILLS.

101. The plaintiff is at liberty, as a matter of course, and without payment of costs, to amend his bill in any matters whatever, before any copy has been taken out of the clerk's office, and in any small matters afterwards, such as filling blanks, correcting errors of dates, misnomer of parties, misdescription of premises, clerical errors, and generally in matters of form. But if he amend in a material point, as he may do of course, after a copy has been so taken, before any answer or plea or demurrer to the bill, he is required to pay to the defendant the costs occasioned thereby, and without delay to furnish him a fair copy thereof, free of expense, with suitable references to the places where the same are to be inserted;

---

[10] 19th rule United States Supreme Court.

and if the amendments are numerous, he is required to furnish in like manner to the defendant a copy of the whole bill as amended, and if there be more than one defendant, a copy is to be furnished to each defendant affected thereby.[11]

102. After an answer or plea or demurrer is put in, and before replication, the plaintiff may, upon motion or petition, without notice, obtain an order from any judge of the court to amend his bill on or before the next succeeding rule day, upon payment of costs, or without payment of costs, as the court or a judge thereof may, in his discretion, direct; but after replication filed, the plaintiff will not be permitted to withdraw it and to amend his bill, except upon a special order of a judge of the court, upon motion or petition, after due notice to the other party, and upon proof by affidavit that the same is not made for the purpose of vexation or delay, or that the matter of the proposed amendment is material, and could not with reasonable diligence have been sooner introduced into the bill, and upon the plaintiff's submitting to such other terms as may be imposed by the judge for speeding the cause.[12]

103. If the plaintiff, so obtaining any order to amend his bill after answer, or plea, or demurrer, or after replication, do not file his amendments or amended bill, as the case may require, in the clerk's office, on or before the next succeeding rule day, he will be considered to have abandoned the same, and

---

[11] 28th rule United States Supreme Court.
[12] 29th rule United States Supreme Court.

the cause will proceed, as if no application for any amendment had been made.[13]

EXCEPTIONS TO BILL.

104. Usually, the defendant either pleads, demurs to, or answers the bill. If the bill contain unnecessary recitals of deeds, documents, &c., in *hæc verba*, or any other impertinent matter, or any scandalous matter not relevant to the suit, the defendant may file exceptions.[14] When exceptions are filed, the bill may be referred to the master by any judge of the court for impertinence or scandal, and if so found by him, the matter will be expunged at the expense of the plaintiff, and he will be required to pay to the defendant all his costs in the suit up to that time, unless the court or a judge thereof shall otherwise order. If the master report that the bill is not scandalous or impertinent, the plaintiff will be entitled to all costs occasioned by the reference.[15]

DEMURRER OR PLEA.

105. If the defendant demur or plead, the plaintiff may set down the demurrer or plea to be argued, or he may take issue on the plea. If upon an issue the facts stated in the plea be determined for the defendant, they will avail him, as far as in law and equity they ought to avail him.[16] If, upon the hearing, any demurrer or plea is overruled, the plaintiff will be entitled to his costs in the cause up to that

---

[13] 30th rule United States Supreme Court.
[14] See 26th rule United States Supreme Court.
[15] 26th rule United States Supreme Court.
[16] 33d rule United States Supreme Court.

period, unless the court shall be satisfied that the
defendant had good ground in point of law or fact to
interpose the same, and it was not interposed vexatiously or for delay; and upon the overruling of any
plea or demurrer, the defendant will be assigned to
answer the bill or so much thereof as is covered by
the plea or demurrer the next succeeding rule day,
or at such other period as consistently with justice
and the rights of the defendant the same can, in the
judgment of the court, be reasonably done; in default whereof, the bill will be taken against him for
confessed, and the matter thereof proceeded in, and
decreed accordingly." If, upon the hearing, any demurrer or plea is allowed, the defendant will be entitled to his costs; but the court may, in its discretion, upon motion of the plaintiff, allow him to
amend his bill upon such terms as it shall deem reasonable."

106. If the plaintiff do not reply to any plea, or
set down any plea or demurrer for argument, on the
rule day when the same is filed, or on the next succeeding rule day, he will be deemed to admit the
truth and sufficiency thereof, and his bill will be dismissed, as of course, unless a judge of the court shall
allow him further time for the purpose."

ANSWER SUGGESTING DEFECT OF BILL FOR WANT OF PARTIES.

107. If the defendant by his answer suggest that
the bill is defective for want of parties, the plaintiff

---

[17] 34th rule United States Supreme Court.
[18] 35th rule United States Supreme Court.
[19] 38th rule United States Supreme Court.

will be at liberty, within fourteen days after answer filed, to set down the cause for argument upon that objection only; and the purpose for which the same is so set down, shall be notified by an entry to be made in the clerk's order book in the form, or to the effect following (that is to say): "Set down upon the defendant's objection for want of parties;" and when the plaintiff shall not so set down his cause, but shall proceed therewith to a hearing, notwithstanding an objection for want of parties taken by the answer, he will not, at the hearing of the cause, if the defendant's objection shall then be allowed, be entitled, as of course, to an order for liberty to amend his bill by adding parties; but the court, if it thinks fit, will be at liberty to dismiss the bill.[20]

INJUNCTION PRAYED FOR TO STAY PROCEEDINGS AT LAW.

108. Whenever an injunction is asked for by the bill to stay proceedings at law, if the defendant do not enter his appearance and plead, demur, or answer the same within the time prescribed therefor by the rules of practice of the United States Supreme Court, the plaintiff will be entitled, as of course, upon motion without notice, to such injunction.[21]

WHEN SUPPLEMENTAL BILL FILED.

109. After leave is given the plaintiff to file a supplemental bill under the 57th rule of the United States Supreme Court—the leave being granted upon

---

[20] 52d rule United States Supreme Court.
[21] See 55th rule United States Supreme Court.

proper cause shown, and due notice to the other
party—if the supplemental bill be filed, the defendant should demur, plead, or answer thereto, on the
next succeeding rule day after it is filed in the clerk's
office, unless some other time is assigned by a judge
of the court.[22]

EXCEPTIONS TO ANSWER.

110. After answer filed on any rule day, the plaintiff is allowed until the next succeeding rule day to
file in the clerk's office exceptions thereto for insufficiency, and no longer, unless a longer time shall be
allowed for the purpose, upon cause shown to the
court or a judge thereof; and if no exception be filed
thereto within that period, the answer will be deemed
and taken to be sufficient.[23]

111. When the same solicitor is employed for two
or more defendants, and separate answers are filed,
or other proceedings had by two or more of the defendants separately, costs will not be allowed for such
separate answers or other proceedings, unless a master, upon reference to him, shall certify that such
separate answers and other proceedings were necessary or proper, and ought not to have been joined
together.[24]

112. When exceptions are filed to an answer for
insufficiency, within the period prescribed by these
rules, if the defendant shall not submit to the same,
and file an amended answer on the succeeding rule

[22] See 57th rule United States Supreme Court.
[23] 61st rule United States Supreme Court.
[24] 62nd rule United States Supreme Court.

day, the plaintiff is required forthwith to set them down for a hearing on the next succeeding rule day thereafter before a judge of the court; and to enter, as of course, in the order book an order for that purpose; if he do not so set down the exceptions for a hearing, they will be deemed abandoned, and the answer will be deemed sufficient; provided, however, that the court, or any judge thereof may, for good cause shown, enlarge the time for filing exceptions, or for answering the same in his discretion upon such terms as he may deem reasonable.[25]

113. If, at the hearing, the exceptions shall be allowed, the defendant will be bound to put in a full and complete answer to the bill on the next succeeding rule day; otherwise the plaintiff will, of course, be entitled to take the bill, so far as the matter of such exceptions is concerned, as confessed, or, at his election, he may have a writ of attachment to compel the defendant to make a better answer to the matter of the exceptions; and the defendant, when he is in custody upon such writ, will not be discharged therefrom but by an order of the court, or of a judge thereof, upon his putting in such answer, and complying with such other terms as the court or judge may direct.[26] If, upon argument, the plaintiff's exceptions to the answer shall be overruled, or the answer adjudged insufficient, the prevailing party will be entitled to all the costs occasioned thereby, unless otherwise directed by the court, or the judge thereof, at the hearing upon the exceptions.[27]

---

[25] 63d rule United States Supreme Court.
[26] 64th rule United States Supreme Court.
[27] 65th rule United States Supreme Court.

REPLICATION AND ISSUE.

114. Whenever the answer of the defendant is not excepted to, or is adjudged or deemed sufficient, the plaintiff must file the general replication thereto on or before the next succeeding rule day thereafter; and in all cases where the general replication is filed, the cause will be deemed, to all intents and purposes, at issue, without any rejoinder or other pleading on either side. If the plaintiff omit or refuse to file such replication within the prescribed period, the defendant will be entitled to an order, as of course, for a dismissal of the suit; and the suit will thereupon stand dismissed, unless the court, or a judge thereof, upon motion for cause shown, allow a replication to be filed *nunc pro tunc*, the plaintiff submitting to speed the cause, and to such other terms as may be directed.[28]

115. The complainant must reply to the answer of every defendant, when sufficient, without reference to the state of the cause or of the pleadings in regard to any other defendant. *Coleman* v. *Martin*, 8 Blatch. 291. When a demurrer interposed to the defendant's answer is overruled, and the plaintiff instead of relying upon its sufficiency files a replication, he thereby abandons the demurrer, and it ceases to be a part of the record. *Young* v. *Martin*, 8 Wall. 354.

GUARDIANS AD LITEM, &c.

116. *Guardians ad litem* to defend a suit may be appointed by the court, or by any judge thereof for

---

[28] 66th rule United States Supreme Court.

infants or other persons who are under guardianship, or otherwise incapable to sue for themselves; all infants and other persons so incapable, may sue by their guardians, if any, or by their *prochein ami*, subject, however, to such orders as the court may direct for the protection of infants and other persons.[29]

WHAT MAY BE DONE AT RULES OR AT CHAMBERS, &C.

117. The Circuit Courts of the United States, as courts of equity, are deemed always open for the purpose of filing bills, answers, and other pleadings, for issuing and returning mesne and final process and commissions, and for making and directing all interlocutory motions, orders, rules, and other proceedings, preparatory to the hearing of all causes upon their merits.[30] The clerk's office is required to be open, and the clerk to be in attendance therein, on the first Monday of every month, for the purpose of receiving, entering, entertaining and disposing of all motions, rules, orders, and other proceedings which are grantable of course, and applied for, or had by the parties or their solicitors in all causes pending in equity, in pursuance of the rules prescribed by the United States Supreme Court.[31]

118. Any judge of the Circuit Court, as well in vacation as in term, may at chambers, or on the rule days at the clerk's office, make and direct all such interlocutory orders, rules, and other proceedings,

---

[29] 87th rule United States Supreme Court. It is suggested in one case that the application for appointment of a *guardian ad litem* for an infant defendant must be made by petition. *Rhinelander* v. *Sanford*, 3 Day 279.

[30] 1st rule United States Supreme Court.

[31] 2d rule United States Supreme Court.

preparatory to the hearing of all causes upon their merits, in the same manner and with the same effect as the Circuit Court could make and direct the same in term, reasonable notice of the application therefor being first given to the adverse party, or his solicitor, to appear and show cause to the contrary at the next rule day thereafter, unless some other time is assigned by the judge for the hearing.[82]

119. All motions, rules, orders, and other proceedings made and directed at chambers, or on rule days at the clerk's office, whether special, or of course, are directed to be entered by the clerk in an order book, to be kept at the clerk's office, on the day when they are made and directed, which book is open at all office hours to the free inspection of the parties in any suit in equity and their solicitors. And, except in cases where personal or other notice is specially required or directed, such entry in the order book shall be deemed sufficient notice to the parties and their solicitors, without further service thereof, of all orders, rules, acts, notices, and other proceedings entered in such order book, touching any and all the matters in the suits, to and in which they are parties and solicitors. And notice to the solicitors will be deemed notice to the parties for whom they appear, and whom they represent, in all cases where personal notice on the parties is not otherwise specially required. Where the solicitors for all the parties in a suit reside in or near the same town or city, the judges of the Circuit Court may by rule abridge the time for notice of rules, orders, or other proceedings,

---

[82] 3d rule United States Supreme Court.

not requiring personal service on the parties, in their discretion.[33]

120. All motions and applications in the clerk's office for the issuing of mesne process and final process to enforce and execute decrees, for filing bills, answers, pleas, demurrers, and other pleadings; for making amendments to bills and answers; for taking bills *pro confesso;* for filing exceptions, and for other proceedings in the clerk's office, which do not, by the rules prescribed for the Circuit Courts by the United States Supreme Court, require any allowance or order of the Circuit Courts, or of any judge thereof, are deemed motions and applications, grantable, of course, by the clerk of the court. But the same may be suspended, or altered, or rescinded, by any judge of the court upon special cause shown.[34]

121. All motions for rules or orders, and other proceedings, which are not grantable of course, or without notice, will, unless a different time be assigned by a judge of the court, be made on a rule day, and entered in the order book, and shall be heard at the rule day next after that on which the motion is made. And if the adverse party, or his solicitor, shall not then appear, or shall not show good cause against the same, the motion may be heard by any judge of the court *ex parte*, and granted, as if not objected to, or refused, in his discretion.[35]

---

[33] 4th rule United States Supreme Court.
[34] 5th rule United States Supreme Court.
[35] 6th rule United States Supreme Court.

Form of Subpœna to answer Bill in United States Circuit Courts.[36].

{ SEAL OF COURT. } The President of the
United States of America,
To A. B. and L. M., greeting:

You are hereby commanded that you, and each of you, personally appear before the judges of the Circuit Court of the United States for the ——— district of Virginia, on the first Monday in ——— next[37], at the clerk's office of the said court, in the city of Richmond, to answer a bill of complaint in equity, exhibited against you in the said court by R. R., and to do further, and receive what the said court shall consider in that behalf; and this you are not to omit under the penalty of ——— each.

Witness the honorable M. R. Waite, Chief Justice of the Supreme Court of the United States, at the city of Richmond, on the ——— day of ———, in the year one thousand eight hundred and ———, and of the independence of the United States of America, the ———.

J. P., *Clerk.*

Memo:—The defendants are required to enter their appearance in the above cause in the clerk's office of this court on or before the first Monday of ——— next, or the bill will be taken *pro confesso* as to them.

J. P., *Clerk.*

---

[36] 12th rule United States Supreme Court. See p. 138, *ante.*

[37] Ibid.

Form of writ of Attachment in United States Circuit Courts.[38]

{ SEAL OF COURT. }
The President of the United States of America,
To the Marshal of the ———— District of ————, greeting:

You are hereby commanded that you attach A. B., if he may be found in your district, and bring him forthwith [*or*, on the —— day of ———, in the year 18——,] personally before the judges of the Circuit Court of the United States for the —— district of Virginia, held at the city of Richmond, at the court room of said court in the said district, to answer for certain contempts in not obeying our writ of subpœna to him directed, and on him duly served, commanding him to appear before the said Circuit Court on the —— day of ———, &c. [following terms of subpœna], to answer a bill of complaint exhibited against him in the said court by C. D.; and further, to perform and abide such order as our said court shall make in this behalf; and you are further commanded to detain him in your custody until he shall be discharged by the said court. And have you then there this writ.

Witness the honorable M. R. Waite, Chief Justice of the Supreme Court of the United States, at the city of Richmond, on the —— day of ———, 18——, and in the —— year of the independence of the United States of America. J. P., *Clerk.*

---

[38] See 7th rule United States Supreme Court. To compel an answer, under the 18th and 64th rules United States Supreme Court; to compel obedience in other cases, under 7th and 8th rules United States Supreme Court.

Form of writ of Sequestration in United States Circuit Courts.[39]

{ SEAL OF COURT. }

The President of the
United States of America,
To the Marshal of the
———— District of Virginia,[40] greeting:

Whereas A. B., complainant, exhibited his bill of complaint in our Circuit Court of the United States for the ———— district of Virginia, against C. D., defendant; and whereas the said C. D. being duly served with a writ, issuing out of our said court, commanding him, under the penalty therein mentioned, to appear to and answer the said bill, hath refused so to do; and thereupon a writ of attachment hath issued from our said court against the said C. D., directed to the said marshal; and whereas, on the said writ of attachment, the said marshal hath returned that the said C. D. could not be found; and whereas the said C. D. hath of late absconded, and so concealed himself, that the said marshal hath not been able to find him, as by the certificate of the said marshal appears: Know ye, therefore, that we, in confidence of your prudence and fidelity, have given, and by these presents do give, to you full power and authority to enter upon all the messuages, lands, tenements, and real estate whatsoever of the said C D.,

---

[39] See 7th rule United States Supreme Court.

[40] See 15th rule United States Supreme Court. See Dan. Ch. Pr. (Perk.) 1,064, 1,065; 1 Har. Chan. Prac. 255. The 15th rule United States Supreme Court seems to require that the writ shall be directed to the marshal and not to four sequestrators, according to the English practice.

and to collect, receive and sequester into your hands not only all the rents and profits of the messuages, lands, tenements and real estate, but also all his goods, chattels and personal estate whatsoever; and, therefore, we command you that you do, at certain proper and convenient days and hours, go to ánd enter úpon all the messuages, lands, tenements and real estate of the said C. D., and that you do collect, take and get into your hands, not only the rents and profits of all his said real estate, but also all his goods, chattels and personal estates, and detain and keep the same under sequestration in your hands until the said C. D. shall fully answer the complainant's bill, clear his contempt, and our said court make other order to the contrary.

Witness the honorable M. R. Waite, Chief Justice of the Supreme Court of the United States, at the City of Richmond, on the —— day of ————, in the year one thousand eight hundred and ————, and of the independence of the United States of America, the ————. J. P., *Clerk.*

Entry in Clerk's Order Book of filing the Bill.

This day came the plaintiff, B. C., and filed his bill against J. M. and N. O., and process of subpœna was awarded against the said J. M. and N. O. to appear and answer the exigency of the bill on the first Monday in —— next.

Entry of return of Process executed.

The process of subpœna awarded against the defendants, J. M. and N. O., returnable to this day, was returned executed; but the said process appearing not to have been executed twenty days before the return day, time is given to the said defendants until the first Monday in next month to enter their appearance.

Entry of Defendants' appearance.

This day appeared the defendant, J M., by his solicitor, W. J. L., and time is given him until the first Monday in next month to plead, demur, or answer to the plaintiff's bill.[41] And on this day also appeared the defendant, N. O., and filed a demurrer to the plaintiff's bill; and on the motion of the plaintiff the said demurrer is set down for argument.[42]

Entry taking Bill for confessed.

The defendant, J. M., still failing to plead, demur or answer to the plaintiff's bill, on the motion of the plaintiff the said bill is taken for confessed as to the said defendant.

Entry on filing Plea when Plaintiff replies, &c.

The defendant, R. R., this day appeared by his solicitor, M. M., and filed his plea to the bill of the plaintiff, and *the plaintiff took issue on the said plea* (or, *the plaintiff set down the said plea to be argued*).[43]

Entry on filing Plea, Plaintiff not replying, &c.

The defendant, R. R., this day appeared by his

---

[41] 18th rule United States Supreme Court, p. 140.
[42] 33d rule United States Supreme Court, p. 143.
[43] 33d rule United States Supreme Court, p. 143, *ante*.

solicitor, N. M., and filed his plea to the bill of the plaintiff, and time is given to the said plaintiff until the first Monday in next month to reply to the said plea, or set down the same for argument.

Entry dismissing Bill, Plaintiff not replying to Plea, &c.[44]

The plaintiff still failing to reply to the defendant's plea, filed at the last rules, and failing to set down the same for argument, it is ordered that the bill of the said plaintiff be dismissed.

Entry of filing Answer and Replication.

This day appeared the defendant, C. C., and filed his answer, and the plaintiff replied generally to the said answer.

Entry of filing Answer and Exceptions.

This day appeared the defendant, C. C., and filed his answer, and the plaintiff filed exceptions to the said answer,[45] and time is given to the said defendant until the first Monday in next month to file an amended answer.[46]

Entry if Defendant fails to file amended Answer after exceptions.[47]

The defendant having heretofore answered the bill of the plaintiff, and the plaintiff having filed exceptions thereto, and the defendant still failing to file an

---

[44] 38th rule United States Supreme Court, *ante*, p. 144.

[45] 61st rule United States Supreme Court, *ante*, p. 146. The plaintiff may file exceptions to answer the rule day succeeding that on which answer is filed.

[46] 63d rule United States Supreme Court, *ante*, pp. 146, 147.

[47] 63d rule United States Supreme Court, *ante*, p. 147.

amended answer, it is ordered that the said exceptions to the said answer be set down for hearing at the next rules before a judge of this court.

Entry on filing Answer, and Plaintiff asks leave to amend his Bill.[48]

This day appeared the defendant, C. C., and filed his answer, and the plaintiff not having replied to the said answer, moved for leave to amend his bill; and, thereupon, the judge of this court ordered that the plaintiff should have leave to amend his bill *on the payment by the said plaintiff to the defendant of his costs up to this time,*[49] provided such amended bill is filed on or before the first Monday in next month.

If replication has been filed, the leave to amend will not be granted, unless on the notice and the affidavit provided for in the 29th rule of the United States Supreme Court, *ante,* p. 142.

Entry when Bill amended after Answer filed.[50]

The plaintiff this day, in pursuance of leave granted him at the last rules, filed his amended bill against the defendant, C. M., and time is given the said C. M. until the next rules[51] to put in a new or supplemental answer to the said bill.

The Defendant failing to file Answer to amended Bill, same taken for confessed as to him.[52]

The defendant, C. M., not having put in a new or

---

[48] 29th rule United States Supreme Court, p. 142, *ante.*
[49] With or without costs, as the judge may, in his discretion, direct.
[50] 46th rule United States Supreme Court.
[51] The time may be enlarged. *Ibid.*
[52] 46th rule United States Supreme Court.

supplemental answer to the amended bill of the plaintiff, as required by the entry herein at the—— rules, it is ordered that the said amended bill be taken for confessed as to the said defendant.

Entry awarding injunction, Defendant not entering his appearance, &c.[53]

The plaintiff having heretofore filed his bill praying for an injunction to stay proceedings at law in the, &c. [here state it], and the process of subpœna in this cause, returnable to this day, having been executed on the said defendant twenty days before this day, and the said defendant still failing to appear and plead, demur or answer the said bill, it is ordered that an injunction be awarded to enjoin and restrain the said defendant from further proceeding, &c.

Entry filing Bill of Revivor and awarding Process.[54]

This day came the plaintiff, and Z. Z., one of the defendants in this suit, having departed this life, the said plaintiff filed his bill of revivor against M. M., executor of the last will and testament of the said Z. Z.; and process of subpœna on the said bill is awarded against the said M. M., executor as aforesaid, returnable to the first Monday in next month, requiring him to appear and show cause, if any he has, why this cause should not be revived.

Entry reviving Suit after Bill of Revivor filed, &c.

The process of subpœna awarded on the plaintiff's

---

[53] 55th rule United States Supreme Court, *ante*, p. 145.
[54] 56th rule United States Supreme Court.

bill of revivor against M. M., executor of the last will and testament of Z. Z., deceased, returnable to this day, having been returned executed on him, and it appearing that the said process was executed on the said M. M. fourteen days before this day, it is ordered that this suit stand revived against the said M. M., executor of the last will and testament of the said Z. Z., deceased.

Entry taking Bill for confessed after exceptions to Answer sustained, Defendant not answering.[55]

The exception of the plaintiff to the answer of J. J, heretofore filed, having been sustained by a judge of this court, and the defendant still failing[55] to file a full and complete answer to the said bill, it is ordered that the said bill be taken for confessed [or, *so far as the matter of such exception is concerned*].

Entry awarding an Attachment to compel an Answer.

The defendant, X. X., not having answered the bill of the plaintiff, although process has been duly served upon him more than twenty days before this day (*or*, the answer of the defendant, X. X., heretofore filed to the bill of the plaintiff having been excepted to by the plaintiff, and the said exception having been sustained, and the defendant still failing to file a full and complete answer to the bill of the plaintiff), on the motion of the said plaintiff, it is ordered that a writ of attachment be awarded against the said defendant to make answer (or, in the case of ex-

---

[55] That is, the rule day next succeeding the allowance of the exception. 64th rule United States Supreme Court, *ante*, p. 147.

ceptions sustained, *a better answer in the matter of exceptions*) to the bill of the plaintiff, returnable to the first Monday in next month.

— · —

CHAPTER VIII.

Of Defences to Suits in Equity, Demurrers, Pleas, Answers and Disclaimers.

122. As we have already seen, the appearance of the defendant is either voluntary or compulsory; voluntary, when the defendant comes in of his own accord before the writ has been served upon him, or after such service, and before process of contempt has been sued out against him; compulsory, when he is compelled to appear by the process of contempt, &c.

123. By the eighteenth rule of the Supreme Court of the United States, prescribing the mode of practice in the United States Circuit Courts, previously cited,[1] and by the statutes of Virginia governing the practice in the Virginia State Courts,[2] a party defendant appearing under compulsion, is debarred privileges which he would enjoy if his appearance were voluntary. In the United States Circuit Courts a defendant, arrested upon process of attachment, will not be discharged from arrest unless he file his answer, or otherwise comply with such order as the court or

---

[1] See page 140, *ante.*
[2] Code, 1873, chap. 167, ? 47.

a judge thereof may direct as to pleading to, or fully answering the bill within a period to be fixed by the court or judge, and undertake to speed the cause.[3] In the Virginia State Courts, no plea or demurrer will be received of a defendant who has been brought in by attachment against him, unless by order of court upon motion.[4]

124. When, however, the defendant's appearance is voluntary, he may adopt either of these several defences:[5]

1. By demurrer, which admitting the matters of fact alleged by the bill to be true, shows that, as they are therein set forth, they are insufficient for the plaintiff to proceed upon, or to oblige the defendant to answer.[6] 2. By plea, when the cause or some part of it may by denial or avoidance be stayed, or discharged by matter foreign to the record, by which it will be reduced to a single point.[7] 3. By answer, which controverting the case made by the plaintiff, confesses and avoids, or traverses and denies the several parts of the bill: or, admitting the case made by the bill, submits to the judgment of the court upon it, or upon a new case made by the answer, or both;[8] or, 4. By disclaimer, which at once terminates the suit, the defendant disclaiming all right in the matter sought by the bill. These several modes of

---

[3] 18th rule United States Supreme Court, p. 140, *ante.*

[4] Code, 1873, chap. 167, § 47.

[5] The case of exceptions to the bill for impertinence, &c., has been mentioned before. See § 104, *ante.*

[6] Mitf. Pl. 106, 108.   [7] Mitf. Pl. 219.

[8] Mitf. Pl. 106. Ch. Taylor in *Harris* vs. *Thomas*, 1 H. & M. 18; *Alderson* vs. *Biggars & als.*, 4 H. & M. 473.

defence, or any of them, may be used together, in the United States Circuit Courts if applied to separate and distinct parts of the bill;[9] in the Virginia State Courts they may be used together, though applied to the same parts of the bill.[10]

General nature of Demurrers.

125. Whenever any ground of defence is apparent upon the bill itself, either from the matter contained in it, or from defect in its frame, or in the case made by it, the proper mode of defence is by demurrer.[11]

The principal ends of a demurrer are, to avoid a discovery which may be prejudicial to the defendant, or to cover a defective title, or to prevent an unnecessary expense. If no one of these ends is obtained, there is little use in a demurrer.[11]

126. A demurrer is, in substance, an allegation by a defendant, which, admitting the matters of fact stated in the bill to be true, shows that as they are therein set forth, they are insufficient for the plaintiff

---

[9] See 32d rule United States Supreme Court.

[10] *Bassett's adm'or, &c. vs. Cunningham's adm'or*, 7 Leigh 402. In this case the Supreme Court of Appeals of Virginia decided that a defendant might demur and answer to the same matter in the bill. If the principle of the case be carried out to its legitimate extent, a defendant in the Virginia State Courts may plead and demur, or plead and answer, or demur and plead and answer to the same matter of a bill at the same time. The decision is based upon the statute of Virginia, declaring that in all actions at law the defendant may plead as many several matters, whether of law or fact, as he shall think necessary for his defence. (See the statute, Code 1873, chap. 167, § 24.) The court thought that this rule ought by analogy to be extended to the proceedings in courts of equity. Judge *Tucker* dissented from this opinion.

[11] Mitf. Pl. 107.

to proceed upon, or to oblige the defendant to answer;[12] or that for some reason apparent on the face of the bill, or because of the omission of some matter which ought to be contained in it, or for want of some circumstance which ought to be attendant thereon, the defendant ought not to be compelled to answer. It therefore demands judgment of the court whether the defendant shall be compelled to answer the plaintiff's bill, or that particular part of it to which the demurrer applies.[13] Thus a defendant may demur to a bill calling on him to answer any matter which may[14] subject him to fine, forfeiture, pains or penalties.[15]

127. A demurrer admits as true the matters of fact stated in the bill, or in that part thereof to which defendant demurs.[16] But while a demurrer confesses the matters stated in the bill to be true, the confession is confined to those matters, which are well pleaded, *i. e.*, to matters of fact:[17] it does not admit

---

[12] Prac. Reg. 162.   [13] Mitf. Pl. 108.

[14] 1 Dan. Chan. Prac. 590, Story's Eq. Pl., § 575.

[15] 1 Dan. Chan. Prac. 589. *Young* vs. *Scott*. 4 Rand. 416. But where the forfeiture or penalty is entirely in the power of the plaintiff, if in his bill he waives it, the defendant cannot demur, but must answer. *Ibid* 416, 419, 1 Dan. Chan. Prac. (Perk.) 589. See *Northwestern Bank* vs. *Nelson*, 1 Grat. 113, a case in which it was not in the power of the plaintiff to protect the defendant from penalties, &c. See Story's Eq. Pl., § 575.

[16] The rule mentioned in the text has been carried to this extent. A bill misstated a deed by alleging it to contain a proviso which it did not. On argument of a demurrer to this bill, Lord *Cottenham* refused to allow the defendant's counsel to refer to the deed itself, for the purpose of showing the incorrectness of the manner in which it was set out, although the bill contained a reference for "greater certainty as to its contents," &c,. to the deed, as being in the custody of the defendants. *Campbell* vs. *Mackay*, 1 M. & Craig 603, 613. See *Pryor* vs. *Adams*, I Call 391.

[17] *Ford* vs. *Peering*, 1 Ves. Jr. 72, 78. See note on p. 78, Sumner's edition, *Commercial Bank of Manchester* vs. *Buckner*, 20 How. 108.

matters of law, which are suggested in the bill or inferred from the facts stated; for, strictly speaking, arguments or inferences, or matters of law, ought not to be stated in pleading;[18] nor will the court have any regard to facts averred in a bill which has been demurred to, when they are contrary to any fact of which the court takes *judicial notice.*[19]

128. A demurrer may be to the whole bill, or to some part of it. It may be either to the relief prayed, or it may be to the discovery only, or to both, or to only a part of one or of both.[20] If it be to the whole relief, the English rule is, that it necessarily extended to the discovery.[21] Mr. Justice Story asserts that the American rule is different, and cites in support of his view *Laight* vs. *Morgan,* 2 Cain. Cas. in Err. 344; *Higginbotham* vs. *Burnet,* 5 John. Ch. 184; *Brownell* vs. *Curtis,* 10 Paige 210; *Livingston* vs. *Story,* 9 Peters 632, 658. In the last cited case, Mr. Justice Thompson said that it was an established and universal rule of pleading in chancery, that a defendant might meet a complainant's bill by several modes of defence; that he might demur, answer and plead to different parts of a bill; so that if a bill for discovery and relief contained proper matter for the one and not for the other, the defendant should answer the proper, and demur to the improper mat-

---

[18] 1 Dan. Ch. Pr. (Perkins) 567.

[19] 1 Dan. Chan. Prac. (Perkins) 568, 569.

[20] When the demurrer does not go to the whole bill, it should clearly express the particular part which it is designed to cover. *Jarvis* vs. *Palmer,* 11 Paige 650; *Clancy* vs. *Craine,* 2 Dev. Eq. 363; Sto. Eq. Pl., § 458, and notes.

[21] *Morris* vs. *Morgan,* 10 Sim. 341; *Price* vs. *James,* 2 Bro. Ch. 319; and other cases cited in Story's Eq. Pl., § 312, n.

ter, but that if he demurred to the whole bill, the demurrer must be overruled.[22]

129. Care should be taken that the demurrer is not too general; that is, that it do not cover, or is not applied to the whole bill, when it is good to a part only, for if not good to the full extent which it covers, but is so only to a part, it will be overruled.[23] And so the doctrine was formerly, that if a demurrer did not cover so much of the bill as it might by law have extended to, it was held to be bad;[24] but this has been changed, in England by the 36th of the Orders of the English Court of Chancery and in the United States Courts by the 36th rule of practice.[25]

Form of Demurrers.

130. Demurrers may be simply on the ground that there is no equity, or the particular defects and objections may be pointed out. The former will be sufficient when the bill is defective in substance. The latter is indispensable when the objection is to the defect of the bill in point of form.[26]

131. Demurrers, for want of form in the bill, will be sustained in the United States Circuit Courts; and

---

[22] But it was decided in *Mitchell* vs. *Green*, 10 Metc. 101, that if a bill of discovery also sought relief, which the court had no power to grant, the defendant might demur to the whole bill, and the demurrer would be sustained, unless the bill averred that a suit at law was pending, or was about to be brought, in which a discovery was material.

[23] Cooper's Eq. Pl. 112, 113; Mitf. Eq. Pl. by Jeremy 214, n. (i); Story's Eq. Pl., ? 443.

[24] *Dawson* vs. *Sadler*, 1 Sim. & Stu. 537, 542; 1 Cond. Eng. Ch. Rep. 277. In that case, the Vice Chancellor said he was disposed to give the defendants leave to amend their demurrers and answers, by making them general demurrers to the whole bill.

[25] Post, p. 172, section 139.   [26] Story's Eq. Pl,. ? 455.

it has never been questioned in the Virginia State Courts that demurrers for multifariousness, or for want of parties, or for want of jurisdiction as well as for want of equity, are proper.

132. The principle of a defence by demurrer is, that on the plaintiff's own showing his claim is bad. It is applicable to any defence which can be made out from the allegations in the bill, but the most ordinary grounds of demurrer are want of jurisdiction, want of equity, multifariousness, and want of parties.[27]

· 133. The frame of a demurrer is very simple, and after the formal commencement runs thus: " This defendant doth demur in law to the said bill, and for cause of demurrer showeth that it appears by the said bill, that," &c., stating in the regular form on what class of objection the defendant relies, or, if there be more than one ground of objection, stating each ground successively with the prefatory words; " and for further cause of demurrer showeth," &c.; and concluding with the words, " wherefore, and for divers other good causes of demurrer, appearing in the said bill, this defendant doth demur to the said bill, and prays the judgment of this honorable court whether he shall be compelled to make any other or further answer thereto; and he humbly prays to be hence dismissed with his reasonable costs in this behalf sustained."[28]

134. The assertion of a demurrer is, that the plaintiff has not, on his own showing, made out a case, and if that position can be established on any

---

ground, though not a ground of objection stated in the demurrer, it is good.[29]

135. It should specially be noticed, that a demurrer in the United States Circuit Courts should be accompanied by a certificate of counsel that, in his opinion, it is well founded in point of law, and supported by the affidavit of the defendant that it is not interposed for delay [30]

136. The following is the form of a general demurrer for want of equity:

In the Circuit Court of the county of ——:

> The demurrer of D. D., J. D. and S. K., three of the defendants to the bill of complaint of S. S., complainant:

These defendants, by protestation, not confessing or acknowledging all or any of the matters and things in the said complainant's bill contained to be true in such manner and form as the same are therein and thereby set forth and alleged, do demur to the said bill, and for cause of demurrer show that the said complainant has not by his said bill made · such a case as entitles him in a court of equity to any discovery from these defendants respectively, or any of them, or to any relief against them as to the matters contained in the said bill, or any of such matters; and that any discovery which can be made by

---

[29] Adams' Eq. 334. Some authorities are cited, to establish that when the demurrer is sustained on a ground different from that mentioned in the demurrer, costs will not be given. Mitf. 217, *Willesley* vs. *Willesley*, 4 M. & C. 554; 1 Dan. Chan. Prac. 539, 545.

[30] 31st rule United States Supreme Court.

these defendants, or any of them, touching the matters complained of in the said bill, or any of them, cannot be of any avail to the said complainant for any of the purposes for which a discovery is sought against these defendants by the said bill, nor entitle the said complainant to any relief in this court touching any of the matters therein complained of: wherefore, and for divers other good causes of demurrer appearing in the said bill, these defendants do demur thereto, and they pray the judgment of this honorable court whether they, or either of them, shall be compelled to make any further or other answer to the said bill; and they humbly pray to be hence dismissed with their reasonable costs in this behalf sustained."[a]

A. M., p. d.

137. The following is the form of a demurrer to so much of a bill as sought a discovery of title deeds, for want of proper affidavit:

In the Circuit Court of the county of ——— :

The demurrer, &c., (as in preceding form.)

These defendants, by protestation, not confessing or acknowledging, &c. (*as in preceding form to word alleged*), as to so much of the said bill as seeks a discovery of the marriage settlement of ———, the late father and mother of the said complainant, and of the title deeds and writings relating to the mes-

---

[a] If in the United States Circuit Courts, the demurrer should be entitled of the proper court, and an affidavit of the party and certificate of counsel be annexed to the demurrer, as required by the 31st rule United States Supreme Court. See § 139, post.

suages, lands and tenements in the said bill mentioned, and that the same may be delivered up to the said complainant, do demur in law, and for cause of demurrer show that no person or persons, by the ancient and approved rule of this honorable court, shall exhibit a bill of complaint in this honorable court against any other person or persons for a discovery of deeds and writings belonging to such complainant, and upon which, if in his possession, he might have remedy at law, and pray relief relating thereto, unless such complainant or complainants shall, at the time of exhibiting such bill, make affidavit that he, she or they, have not such deeds and writings so sought after in his, her, or their custody or power: wherefore, and for that, he, said complainant, hath not made affidavit of not having the deeds or writings in his custody or power so sought after by the said bill, these defendants do demur to such part of the bill as aforesaid, and humbly pray the judgment of this court whether they shall be compelled to make any farther or other answer to such part of the said bill as is so demurred to.[32]   A. M., p. d.

138. Care should be taken in framing a demurrer, that it be made to rely upon the facts stated in the bill, otherwise it will be what is called a *speaking demurrer*, and will be overruled.[33] In order to constitute a speaking demurrer, however, the fact or averment introduced must be one which is necessary to support the demurrer, and is not found in the bill.

---

[32] See note 31, at p. 169, *ante.*
[33] 1 Dan. Ch. Pr. (Perk.) 612, 613, *Brownsword* vs. *Edwards*, 2 Ves. 245.

The introduction of immaterial facts, or averments, or of arguments, is improper; but it is mere surplusage, and will not vitiate the demurrer.[34]

139. The special rules prescribed by the United States Supreme Court for the practice in United States Circuit Courts, in relation to demurrers and pleas, are as follows :

31. No demurrer or plea shall be allowed to be filed to any bill, unless upon a certificate of counsel that, in his opinion, it is well founded in point of law, and supported by the affidavit of the defendant that it is not interposed for delay: and, if a plea, that it is true in point of fact.

32. The defendant may, at any time before the bill is taken for confessed, or afterwards with the leave of the court, demur or plead to the whole bill, or to part of it, and he may demur to part, plead to part, and answer as to the residue; but in every case in which the bill specially charges fraud or combination, a plea to such part must be accompanied with an answer fortifying the plea, and explicitly denying the fraud and combination, and the facts on which the charge is founded.

33. The plaintiff may set down the demurrer or plea to be argued, or he may take issue on the plea. If upon an issue the facts stated in the plea be determined for the defendant, they shall avail him, as far as in law and equity they ought to avail him.

34. If, upon the hearing, any demurrer or plea is overruled, the plaintiff shall be entitled to his costs in the cause up to that period, unless the court shall be satisfied that the defendant had good ground, in point of law or fact, to interpose the same, and it

---

[34] 1 Dan. Ch. Pr. (Perk.) 613, *Cawthorn* vs. *Chalie,* 2 S. & S. 127; *Davies* vs. *Williams,* 1 Sim. 5.

was not interposed vexatiously or for delay. And
upon the overruling of any plea or demurrer, the
defendant shall be assigned to answer the bill, or so
much thereof as is covered by the plea or demurrer,
the next succeeding rule day, or at such other period
as, consistently with justice and the rights of the defendant, the same can, in the judgment of the court,
be reasonably done; in default whereof, the bill shall
be taken against him, *pro confesso*, and the matter
thereof proceeded in and decreed accordingly.

35. If, upon the hearing, any demurrer or plea
shall be allowed, the defendant shall be entitled to
his costs. But the court may, in its discretion, upon
motion of the plaintiff, allow him to amend his bill
upon such terms as it shall deem reasonable.

36. No demurrer or plea shall be held bad and
overruled upon argument, only because such demurrer or plea shall not cover so much of the bill as it
might by law have extended to.

37. No demurrer or plea shall be held bad and
overruled upon argument, only because the answer of
the defendant may extend to some part of the same
matter, as may be covered by such demurrer or plea.

38. If the plaintiff shall not reply to any plea, or
set down any plea or demurrer for argument, on the
rule day, when the same is filed, or on the next succeeding rule day, he shall be deemed to admit the
truth and sufficiency thereof, and his bill shall be dismissed, as of course, unless a judge of the court shall
allow him further time for the purpose.

140. As regards the Virginia State Courts, the provisions of the statute, Code 1873, cited in section 71,
on pages 111, 112, *ante*, need to be noticed.

Demurrers to Original Bills for relief.

141. The principal grounds of objection to the re-

lief sought by an original bill, which can appear on the bill itself, and may therefore be taken advantage of by demurrer, are these: 1. That the subject of the suit is not within the jurisdiction of a court of equity. 2. That the plaintiff is not entitled to sue by reason of some personal disability. 3. That the plaintiff has no interest in the subject, or no title to institute a suit concerning it.[35] 4. That the plaintiff has no right to call on the defendant concerning the subject of the suit. 5. That the defendant has not that interest in the subject which can make him liable to the claims of the plaintiff. 6. That for some reason, founded on the substance of the case, the plaintiff is not entitled to the relief he prays. To these may be added, 7. The deficiency of the bill to answer the purpose of complete justice, as, for instance, the want of proper parties. 8. The impropriety of confounding distinct subjects in the same bill, or of unnecessarily multiplying suits[36]; and 9. In the United States Circuit

---

[35] See *Morrison's ex'ors* vs. *Grubb*, 23 Grat. 342.

[36] Mitf. Pl. 110; 1 Dan. Ch. Pr. (Perkins) 581. A demurrer will lie for joining a plaintiff not interested, 2 R. P. 274; *Cuff* vs. *Platett*, 4 Russ. 242; 2 Cond. Eng. Ch. R. 651. The *King of Spain & als.* vs. *Machado & als.*, 4 Russ. 225; 2 Cond. Eng. Ch. R. 643 [but in *Clarkson & wife* v. *De Peyster, &c.*, 3 Paige 336, the wife was properly joined, though not interested in one part of the complainant's case]. In a bill by a creditor to enforce an assignment by the debtor for the payment of particular debts, the general creditors of the assignor should not be joined as plaintiffs. *Dias* vs. *Bouchaud*, 10 Paige 445.

And for making improper defendants. *Brinkerhoff, &c.* v. *Brown, &c.*, 6 John. Ch. R. 139 [though such demurrers should be cautiously allowed].

And for omitting proper parties. *Robinson, &c.* vs. *Smith, &c.*, 3 Paige 222 [on the question of omitting proper parties, see *Munford, &c.* vs. *Murray*, 6 John. Ch. R. 11; 2 R. P. 276; *Taylor's adm'or* vs. *Spindle*, 2 Grat. 45; *Harding* vs. *Handy*, 11 Wheat. 133; *Marshall* vs. *Beverley*, 5 Wheat. 313; *Conn, &c.* vs. *Penn*, 5 Wheat. 424].

And for asserting distinct rights. *Berkley, &c.* v. *Presgrave*, 1 East 227;

Courts, that the citizenship of the parties does not appear on the face of the bill.[37]

Demurrers to Original Bills for discovery.

142. The principal objections to a bill, which are causes of demurrer to a discovery, are these: 1. That the case made by the bill is not such in which a court of equity assumes a jurisdiction to compel discovery.[38] 2. That the plaintiff has no interest in the subject or not such an interest as will entitle him to call on the defendant for a discovery.[39] 3. That the

---

Harrison vs. *Hogg*, 2 Ves., Jr., 323 ; *Davoue* vs. *Fanning*, 4 John. Ch. R. 199; *Johnson* vs. *Johnson*, 6 John. Ch. R. 163 ; *Shirley* vs. *Long, &c.*, 6 Rand. 764 ; *Stuart's heirs, &c.* vs. *Coalter*, 4 Rand. 74; *Ward, &c.* v. *Duke of Northumberland, &c.*, 2 Anstr. 469 ; *Dilly* v. *Doig*, 2 Ves., Jr., 486 ; *Attorney General* vs. *Corp. of Carmarthen*, Cooper's Ch. R. 30 ; *Whaley* vs. *Dawson*, 2 Sch. & Lef. 367.

And for calling on defendant to answer any matter which may subject him to fine, forfeiture, pains or penalties. *Young* vs. *Scott, &c.*, 4 Rand. 416; *Northwestern Bank* vs. *Nelson*. 1 Grat. 113; 2 R. P. 43, 300. See note to section 126, on p 164, *ante*.

And to a bill for specific execution, if the agreement, as stated in the bill, appears to be a parol agreement only, and no sufficient grounds are alleged to take the case out of the statute. *Cozine* vs. *Graham, &c.*, 2 Paige 177.

And if the plaintiff from his own showing has a complete remedy at law, and sets up no particular title to the aid of the court. *Lynch* vs. *Willard*, 6 John. Ch. R. 342.

[Whether lapse of time can only be taken advantage of by plea or answer, see *McDowl* vs. *Charles*, 6 Johnson's Chancery Reports 132; *Livingston's ex'ors* vs. *Livingston*, 4 John. Ch. R. 299,] and 1 Dan. Ch. Pr. (Perkins) 584, 585, 586, and notes, and Story's Eq. Pl., § 503, and cases cited. Where there is no such positive limitation of time as comes within the Statute of Limitations, or the rules of the court which have been adopted by analogy to that statute, the question whether the court will interfere or not, depends upon whether from the facts of the case the court will infer acquiescence, or confirmation, or a release; such inference is an inference of fact, and not an inference of law, and cannot be raised on demurrer. *Cuthbert* vs. *Creasy*, Mad. & Geld. 189; Ld. *Raym.* 213, cited 1 Dan. Ch. Pr. (Perkins), p. 587.

[37] *Dodge* vs. *Perkins*, 4 Mason 435; Story's Eq. Pl., 492.

[38] Story's Eq. Pl., § 319, 321.   [39] Story's Eq. Pl., § 318.

defendant has no interest in the subject to entitle the plaintiff to institute a suit against him, even for the purpose of discovery.[40] 4. That although both plaintiff and defendant may have an interest in the subject, yet that there is not that privity of title between them which gives the plaintiff a right to the discovery required by his bill.[41] 5. That the discovery, if obtained, will not be material.[42] 6. That the situation of the defendant renders it improper for a court of equity to compel a discovery;[43] and 7. That the bill is a mere fishing bill.[44]

PRACTICAL NOTE TO SECTION 142.

1st. *That the case is not such as that a court of equity assumes jurisdiction to compel discovery.* Story's Eq. Pl., § 319, 321, 257 a, 322. Judge *Story* denies the doctrine, that if the bill is for discovery only, it is necessary to aver that the party cannot otherwise establish his defence at law. Story's Eq. Pl., § 319, n. 3; Hare on Dis. 1, 110; Mitf. Eq. Pl. by Jeremy 307: *Earl of Glengall* vs. *Frazer*, 2 Hare 99, 105; 24 Cond. Eng. Ch. R. 99; *Peck* vs. *Ashley*, 12 Metcalf 478. But if the bill is brought before any action, it is usual to aver in the bill that the discovery of the facts is necessary to enable the party to commence his suit right. *Moodelay* vs. *Morton*, 1 Bro. Ch. 470, 471. See Hare on Dis. 51, 110; see *Gregory* vs. *Marks*, 1 Rand. 355; *Rankin* vs. *Bradford*, 1 Leigh 163;

---

[40] Story's Eq. Pl., § 323.   [41] Story's Eq. Pl., § 324, § 571.

[42] Story's Eq. Pl., § 324 a.

[43] Story's Eq. Pl., § 325, and *Newkirk* vs. *Willet*, 2 Cain. Cas. in Err. 296; *Frietas* vs. *Don Santos*, 1 Y. & Jerv. 557.

[44] Mitf. Pl. 185; Story's Eq. Pl., 575, *et seq.* 599, 603. See note to section 141, *ante*, p. 173. The proper object of a demurrer is to prevent the necessity of a discovery, or to save the expense of a protracted litigation by settling the rights of the parties upon some dry point of law plainly arising upon the case made by the bill. *Walworth*, Ch., in *Western Ins. Co.* vs. *Eagle Fire Ins. Co.*, 1 Paige 284. See *Harris* vs. *Thomas*, 1 H. & M. 18; *Alderson* vs. *Biggars*, 4 H. & M. 473.

Harding's ex'or vs. *Hardin,* 2 Leigh 572; *Duvals* vs. *Ross,* 2 Munf. 291. See also *Meze* vs. *Mayse,* 6 Rand. 658 ; *Jones* vs. *Bradshaw,* 16 Grat. 355 ; *Webster* vs. *Couch,* 6 Rand. 519 ; *Hale & als.* vs. *Clarkson & als.,* 23 Grat. 42. As to the doctrine denied by Judge *Story, Duvals* vs. *Ross,* 2 Munf. 290, and *Bass* vs. *Bass,* 4 H. & M. 478, are sometimes cited as authorities for the position . he denies ; but see these cases. Sometimes, the time at which the bill is filed will prejudice the claim of the plaintiff. This seems to have been the ground of the decision in *Duvals* vs. *Ross,* 2 Munf. 290. The bill must be filed as soon as the party discovers the necessity of appealing to the conscience of the adversary. Equity will not suffer him to spin out litigation, take the chance of a jury, and, failing there, file his bill for a discovery. See *Faulkner's adm'x* vs. *Harwood,* 6 Rand. 129; *Norris* vs. *Hume,* 2 Leigh 336 ; *Baker* vs. *Morris,* 10 Leigh 284.

2nd. *That the plaintiff has no interest in the subject, or not such an interest as will entitle him to call on the defendant for a discovery.* 1 Dan. Ch. Prac. (Perkins) 323, 581; Story's Eq. Pl., § 318; Mitf. Eq. Pl. by Jeremy, 154–7, 187 ; *Morrison's ex'ors* vs. *Grubb,* 23 Grat. 342.

3d. *That the defendant has no interest in the subject to entitle the plaintiff to institute a suit against him, even for the purpose of discovery.* 1 Dan. Ch. Pr. (Perkins) 589, 596, 597, 598, 599, 134, 135; Story's Eq. Pl., § 323. A mere witness cannot be made a party defendant. *Wych* vs. *Meal,* 3 P. Wms. 310; but there is an exception to this rule : officers of a corporation may be made parties to a bill of discovery, for the purpose of enabling the defendant to obtain a knowledge of facts which could not be ascertained by the answer of the corporation, put in under their corporate seal, and without oath ;[45] *Vermilyia* vs. *Fulton Bank, &c.,* 1 Paige 37; and the reasons for the exception apply as well to the former as to the present officers of the corporation, when the knowledge of the facts, of which the discovery is sought, rests only with such officers, and especially when it relates to their own official acts. *Fulton Bank* vs. *Sharon Canal Company, &c.,* 1 Paige 219.

4th. *That although both plaintiff and defendant may have an interest in the subject, yet that there is not that privity of title between them which gives the plaintiff a right to the discovery required by his bill.* 1 Dan. Ch. Pr. (Perkins) 331, 605, 606, and notes ; Story's Eq. Pl., § 324, 571.

5th. *That the discovery if obtained will not be material.* Story's Eq. Pl., § 324 a; 1 Dan. Ch. Pr. (Perk.) 598.

6th. *That the situation of the defendant renders it improper for a court of equity to compel a discovery.* Story's Eq. Pl. 575, 599, 603; Mitf. Pl. 185; 1 Dan. Ch. Pr. (Perk.) 589, 596, 598, 599.

7th. *That the bill is a mere fishing bill.* Story's Eq. Pl. 325.

---

[45] 1 Dan. Ch. Pr. (Perk.) 135, note 3.

143. In the *Northwestern Bank* vs. *Nelson*, 1 Grat. 108, the court held, that where the bill seeks a discovery of matters which will expose the defendant to pains, penalties or punishment, or to a criminal prosecution, the defendant may demur;[46] and that it is not necessary that it should be made to appear that the defendant will be certainly exposed to peril by making the discovery sought; it is enough if it appear that, by answering the interrogatories of the bill, he will thereby be probably subjected to danger.[47]

144. A defendant does not forego any advantage as to the merits by not demurring; he may insist by answer on those matters which he might have insisted on by demurrer; and if he should even omit them in the answer, he may still avail himself of them in

---

[46] See ¿ 141, *ante*, p. 173, note.

[47] Note to ¿ 126. *U. S.* vs. *Saline Bank*, 1 Pet. R. 100; *Harrison* vs. *Southcote*, 1 Atk. 539. In *N. W. Bk.* vs. *Nelson*, 1 Grat. 108, the objection not appearing on the face of the bill, the demurrer was overruled, but the defendant was authorized to claim the same protection by plea or answer, and having made an answer claiming the protection, the answer was held sufficient. See Story's Eq. Pl., ¿¿ 575–598, ¿¿ 524, 525, and notes; 1 Dan. Ch. Pr. (Perkins) 589 *et seq.*, as to the cases embraced in this rule. It protects him from answering any question which may form a link in the chain to criminate him. Story's Eq. Pl., ¿ 577, 591; also from a discovery which may have a tendency to subject him to a penalty or forfeiture. Ibid, ¿ 579. [As to usury, see Code 1873, ch. 137, ¿¿ 9–12] But a defendant may by contract expressly preclude himself from the objection, so far as respects a penalty or forfeiture, but not so far as respects the discovery of a crime. Story's Eq. Pl., ¿ 589, 521, 577; *Green* vs. *Weaver*, 1 Sim. 404. A married woman may demur to a discovery which would subject her husband to a criminal prosecution. *Cartwright* vs. *Green*, 8 Ves. 405. The doctrine which formerly obtained that a demurrer would lie to any discovery which may tend to show the defendant to be guilty of any moral turpitude, *e. g.*, the birth of a child born out of wedlock, has been overturned, and it is now held that the defendant may be compelled to make a discovery of any act of moral turpitude, which does not amount to a public offence or an indictable crime. Hare on Discov. 142; *Chetwynd* vs. *Lindon*, 2 Ves. 451; Story's Eq. Pl., ¿ 595, 596.

argument at the final hearing of the cause.[48] *Benson, J.*, in *Leroy, &c.* v. *Veeder, &c.*, 1 Johns. Cas. 428. And at the hearing, though there be no demurrer, many objections which the defendant might have relied on by demurrer may be availed of. *Harris* vs. *Thomas*, 1 H. & M. 18; *Alderson* v. *Biggars, &c.*, 4 H. & M. 473; *Randolph's adm'x* vs. *Kinney, &c.*, 3 Rand. 398; *Stuart's heirs, &c.* vs. *Coalter*, 4 Rand. 78; *Hickman* vs. *Stout*, 2 Leigh 6. It was a question much discussed in *Ambler, &c.* vs. *Warwick & Co.*, 1 Leigh 211, whether if the bill did not show a cause for the jurisdiction of the court, and the defendant answered without demurring, and other matter subsequently appeared in the cause, showing that the case was of such a character as to give the court jurisdiction, the defendant could insist at the hearing on the objection to the jurisdiction appearing on the face of the bill. *Brooke, P.*, held that he might. The other judges decided to take jurisdiction in the case. *Green, J.*, said: "Upon the fair construction of the act (1 R. C. 1819, p. 214, § 86, and p. 256, § 52), I think it may be said that if the bill do not present a case for the jurisdiction of the court, and other matters appear in the progress of the cause, which supplies the defect, the defendant not having

---

[48] The remark in the text must not be construed as embracing the defence of the Statute of Limitations. It has been held, in several cases, that if the defendant wish to avail himself of the statute, and it be not pleaded in form, it should at least be insisted upon as a defence in the pleadings. *Hudsons vs. Hudson's adm'or, &c.*, 6 Munf. 352; *Hickman* vs. *Stout*, 2 Leigh 6. Where, however, slaves were the subject of controversy, a party, without pleading the Statute of Limitations, was permitted to show that a title had accrued in his favor by an actual adverse possession of them for more than five years. *Hudsons vs. Hudson's adm'or, &c.*, 6 Munf. 352.

demurred to the bill, cannot object to the jurisdiction at the hearing; as if the bill was for an account, without showing that the accounts were of such a character as to give jurisdiction, and that appeared from the answer and proof." The statute alluded to provided, that after answer filed, and no plea in abatement to the jurisdiction, no exception for want of jurisdiction should ever afterwards be made, nor should the court ever thereafter delay or refuse justice, or reverse the proceedings for want of jurisdiction, except in cases of controversy respecting lands lying without the jurisdiction of such court, and also of infants and femes covert. This statute was before the court for construction in *Pollard* vs. *Patterson's adm'or*, 3 H. & M. 67; and the unanimous opinion of the court was, that the statute meant to embrace those cases only, *in which the bill showed on its face proper matter for the jurisdiction of equity*, and the exception had to be taken by plea; and that the omission to plead gave equity no power to decree in favor of the plaintiff, if the case appeared upon the face of the bill to be a mere *legal* question.

The language of the present statute, Code 1873, ch. 167, sec. 20, is as follows: " *When the declaration or bill shows on its face proper matter for the jurisdiction of the court*, no exception, for want of such jurisdiction, shall be allowed, unless it be taken by plea in abatement, and the plea shall not be received after the defendant has demurred, pleaded in bar, or answered to the declaration or bill, nor after a rule to plead, or a conditional judgment or decree *nisi*."

See as to the construction of this statute, *Hudson*

vs. *Kline*, 9 Grat. 386, 387; *Beckley* vs. *Palmer & als.*, 11 Grat. 631, 632. See also *Green, &c.* vs. *Massie*, 21 Grat. 356.

Two exceptional cases are noted in Virginia by an accurate text-writer[49] to the rule, that a party by not demurring or pleading is held to have waived the objection to the jurisdiction. The general rule of equity is, that it will not entertain a bill for the purpose of allowing a man to make defence, which he might have made in the court of law, unless he shews some good reason why he did not avail himself of that defence in the court of law,[50] yet, if the party does not choose to avail himself of the benefit of this rule, if he voluntarily goes into the merits of the case, and in his answer admits facts, which had they appeared to the court of law would have there produced a different result, neither the rule, nor the principle on which it is founded, will, it is said, be violated by pronouncing a decree justified by his own admissions. Cabell, J. in *Van Lew* vs. *Bohannon, &c.*, 4 Rand. 540.

In *Brickhouse* vs. *Hunter, Banks & Co.*, 4 H. & M. 363, an injunction was granted to a judgment which was not liable to be examined in equity on any ground stated in the bill. The injunction might have been dissolved on motion; but instead of this, there was a reference by the parties of all matters in difference between them in the suit to certain arbitrators. The submission to reference was regarded as a waiver of the objection to the jurisdiction of

---

[49] 2 Rob. Pr. (old), p. 298.　　　[50] See pp. 92, 93, *ante.*

èquity; and a decree was entered pursuant to the award of the arbitrators.

145. The whole facts of a case appearing from the records of other ended causes, exhibited by the plaintiff with his bill, the court may pass upon it upon a demurrer to the bill without requiring the defendant to set out his defence in an answer.[51]

146. If a bill for relief in equity grounds its claim for relief on a parol agreement, made cotemporaneously with a written agreement, of which cotemporaneous agreement no legal proof can be furnished, it coming within the rule excluding parol evidence tending to vary or contradict the terms of a written agreement, the question may be rightly presented by demurrer, and the demurrer will be sustained,[52] and the application of the rule of evidence referred to, removing from under the case of the plaintiff the ground on which it rests, his case is incurably defective, and no amendment can help him: the bill should be dismissed.[53]

In *Towner* vs. *Lucas*, 13 Grat. 722, the bill was filed by one of three joint sureties for relief against a judgment recovered on a bond; the bill set out a parol promise of the obligee, made at the time the surety signed the bond, that he would not be required to pay any part of it, and that the obligee would give him a written indemnity to save him harmless. This was the sole ground on which relief was asked. The bill was demurred to. The court held, that as proof would be inadmissible to sustain the case made by

---

[51] *Young's adm'or* v. *McClung & als.*, 9 Grat. 336.

[52] *Towner* v. *Lucas's ex'or*, 13 Grat. 722, 725. [53] *Ibid.*

the bill, the demurrer should be sustained and the bill dismissed.

147. A demurrer cannot be good in part, and bad in part, but it may be good as to one of the defendants demurring, and bad as to others.[54]

148. On sustaining a demurrer, the plaintiff will be allowed in some cases to amend.[55] Even after the bill has been dismissed by order, the court has, in its discretion, permitted it to be set on foot again.[56]

149. A demurrer being frequently on matter of form, is not, in general, a bar to a new bill; but if the court on demurrer has clearly decided upon the merits of the question between the parties, the decision may be pleaded in another suit.[57]

150. After a demurrer to the whole bill has been overruled, a second demurrer to the same extent will not be permitted, for it would in effect be to rehear the case on the first demurrer; as, on argument of a demurrer, any cause of demurrer, though not shown in the demurrer as filed, may be alleged at the bar, and if good will support the demurrer.[58]

151. When a demurrer is overruled, a decree ought not to be pronounced against the defendant, but leave should be given him to file an answer.[59] If

---

[54] 1 Dan. Ch. Pr. (Perkins) 609; Story's Eq. Pl., § 445; *Mayor, &c. of London* vs. *Levy*, 8 Ves. 403.

[55] See 1 Dan. Ch. Pr. 624, 625.

[56] Lord *Coningsby* vs. Sir J. *Jekyll*, 2 P. Wms. 300, and other cases cited 1 Dan. Ch. Pr. (Perkins) 623.

[57] 1 Dan. Ch. Pr. (Perkins) 625, 626. See *N. W. Bank* vs. *Nelson*, 1 Grat. 108, 128.

[58] 1 Dan. Ch. Pr. (Perkins) 628; Mitf. Pl. 216.

[59] *Sutton* vs. *Gatewood & ux.*, 6 Munf. 398.

a defendant who is in default file a demurrer, which is overruled, he is not entitled to two months in which to file an answer.[60] But a defendant, though in default for want of an answer, ought to be permitted to file any proper answer at any time before a final decree; the trial of the cause, however, is not to be consequently delayed unless for good cause shown.[61]

Demurrers for multifariousness.

152. The following is the form of a demurrer for multifariousness, for joining in one bill distinct and independent matters:

In the Circuit Court of the county of ———:

"The demurrer of A. B. to the bill of complaint exhibited in this court by M. M. against himself and others.

This defendant by protestation, not confessing or acknowledging all or any of the matters and things in the said bill of complaint contained to be true, in manner and form as the same are therein set forth, doth demur thereto, and for cause of demurrer showeth, that it appears by the said bill that the same is exhibited against this defendant and J. H., J. C., T. S. and W. T., as co-defendants, for several and distinct matters and causes, in many whereof, as appears by the said bill, this defendant is not in any manner interested or concerned, by reason of which distinct matters the said plaintiff's said bill is drawn out to a con-

---

[60] *Reynolds* vs. *Bank of Virginia*, 6 Grat. 174.
[61] *Bowles* vs. *Woodson*, 6 Grat. 78.

siderable length, and this defendant is compelled to take a copy of the whole thereof, and by joining distinct matters together, which do not depend on each other in the said bill, the pleadings, orders and proceedings will, in the progress of the said suit, be intricate and prolix, and this defendant put to unnecessary charges in taking copies of the same, although several parts thereof no way relate to or concern him. Wherefore, and for divers other errors and imperfections, this defendant demands the judgment of this court whether he shall be compelled to make any further or other answer to the said bill, or any of the matters and things therein contained; and prays hence to be dismissed with his reasonable costs in this behalf sustained.

A. B.[62]

153. The following demurrer for multifariousness, to a bill for discovery, was sustained in *Shackell* vs. *Macaulay*, 2 Sim. & Stu. 79; 1 Cond. Eng. Ch. R. 355.

In the Circuit Court of the county of ———:

This defendant by protestation, &c., and for cause of demurrer showeth, that the said complainants have not in and by their said bill shown any right or title to the discovery or to the commission and injunction thereby sought; and for further cause of demurrer this defendant showeth, that the discovery and commission, by the said bill sought, relate to several distinct matters, by the said bill alleged to

---

[62] See § 135, *ante*, p. 168, as to demurrer in United States Circuit Courts.

have been pleaded by the said complainants to two several and distinct actions at law, in the said bill alleged to have been commenced by this defendant against the said complainants, and which two several actions appear by the said bill to relate to several and distinct matters, and to be founded on several and distinct causes of action, and such several and distinct matters so pleaded by the said complainants to the said two several actions ought not to have been joined together in one bill. Wherefore, and for other causes apparent, &c.

PRACTICAL NOTES TO DEMURRERS FOR MULTIFARIOUSNESS.

See section 19, *ante*, pp. 12–15, and notes. Story's Eq. Pl., §§ 271–286, 530–549, 610, 820.

By multifariousness in a bill is meant the improperly joining in one bill distinct and independent matters, and thereby confounding them: as for example, the uniting in one bill of several matters, perfectly distinct and unconnected against one defendant, or the demand of several matters of a distinct and independent nature against several defendants in the same bill. Story's Eq. Pl., § 271; Mitf. Pl. 181, 182.

It was said in *Gibbs* vs. *Clagett*, 2 Gill & J. 14, that the objection of multifariousness should be raised by a demurrer before answer, and that filing an answer and going into testimony was a waiver of the objection. See also *Ward* vs. *Cook*, 5 Madd. 122. To like effect is the ruling of *Nelson* vs. *Hill*, 5 How. 127, hereafter cited.

When one general right is claimed by the bill, though the defendants have separate and distinct rights, the demurrer will not be sustained. Mitf. Pl. 182. Where, however, the plaintiff claims several matters of different natures, the demurrer will be sustained. Ibid. *Dunn* vs. *Dunn*, 2 Sim. 329; *Maud* vs. *Acklem*, 2 Sim. 331.

In *Dunn* vs. *Dunn*, 2 Sim. 329, 2 Cond. Eng. Ch. 439, the infant heir and only son of an intestate joined with his sisters in a bill against their mother, the administratrix, for an account of the intestate's real and personal estates. A demurrer for multifariousness was sustained, the interests in the real and in the personal estate being distinct from each other.

24

The decisions are numerous, sustaining the rule as a general one, that a plaintiff is not to be permitted to demand by one bill several matters of different natures against several defendants. Were this allowed, it would tend to burthen each defendant with unnecessary costs, by swelling the pleadings with the state of the several claims of the other parties with which he has no connection. *Berke vs. Harris, &c.*, Hard. 337; *Ward, &c. vs. Duke of Northumberland, &c.*, 2 Anstr. 469; *Dilly vs. Doig*, 2 Ves., Jr., 486; *Att'y Gen. vs. Corporation of Carmathen*, Cooper's Ch. R. 30; *Whaley vs. Dawson*, 2 Sch. & Lef. 367; *Saxton vs. Davis*, 18 Ves. 72; *Stuart's heirs vs. Coalter*, 4 Rand. 74.

As to what constitutes multifariousness, it is impossible to lay down a general rule; every case must be governed by its own circumstances, and the court must exercise a sound discretion. *Gaines vs. Chew*, 2 How. 619; *Oliver vs. Piatt*, 3 How. 333.

A bill was filed against executors, denying their authority to act as such, and seeking to recover the property sold by them as such; the purchasers of the property were made co-defendants with the executors: *held*, that the bill was not multifarious. *Gaines vs. Chew*, 2 How. 619.

The objection of multifariousness cannot be taken by a party for the first time at the hearing of the cause; but the court itself may take the objection at any time. *Oliver vs. Piatt*, 3 How. 333. In the United States Circuit Courts the objection can be taken advantage of by a party, only by demurrer or exception to the pleading, and must be made before answer, and can be tested only by the structure of the bill itself. *Nelson vs. Hill*, 5 How. 127, 132.

Though the bill be not demurred to for *multifariousness*, the court may *sua sponte* raise the objection, and dismiss the bill at the hearing, but the court will not ordinarily do so. See *Chew vs. Bank of Baltimore*, 14 Md. 299.

The objection that a bill is multifarious will have no influence upon a motion to dissolve an injunction. *Shirley vs. Long, &c.*, 6 Rand. 764.

M. was the administrator of husband and wife, and it being doubtful whether the right to the fund was in the estate of the husband or the wife, he sued for it in both characters. A demurrer to the bill was overruled. *Brent vs. Washington*, 18 Grat. 526.

The statute requires the captain, or other officer of a vessel engaged in the oyster trade, to take out a license. A number of such captains or officers may unite in one bill to enjoin the sale of their vessels, and test the constitutionality of the act. *Johnson vs. Drummond*, 20 Grat. 419.

Legatees who had obtained a decree ascertaining the rights of all, on another bill sought satisfaction out of a common fund. It was held proper for all of them to unite in one suit, to get the benefit of the former decree, and that the bill was not multifarious. *Sheldon* vs. *Armistead*, 7 Grat. 264.

In *Hill & als.* vs. *Bowyer & als.*, 18 Grat. 364, it was held that the objection of multifariousness alone was not sufficient ground for reversing the decree. The court said: "If this objection had been raised in the case while it was in the Circuit Court it must have been sustained. But not having been raised there, an appellate court would not reverse the decree on that ground alone."

To determine whether a bill is multifarious, we must look to the stating part of the bill and not to the prayer alone; for if in his prayer for relief the complainant asks several things, to some of which he may be entitled, and to others not, the bill is not on that account multifarious; he will at the hearing be entitled to that specific relief only, which is consistent with the case made in the stating part of the bill. *Hammond* vs. *Michigan State Bank*, Walk. Ch. 214. See *Lewen* vs. *Stone*, 3 Ala. 485.

In *Segar & als.* vs. *Parrish & als.*, 20 Grat. 672, the case was this: A., B. and C. were the heirs of William Parrish, and also heirs of Mark Parrish; D. and E. were the heirs of Mark Parrish alone. They all appointed Segar their agent, to collect and sell land scrip due to William Parrish, and also land scrip due to Mark Parrish. The scrip was obtained and sold, but the agent did not pay over the proceeds. All the heirs, both of William and Mark Parrish, united in one suit for the recovery, and called for a discovery from the agent. The bill was held not to be demurrable either for multifariousness, or because the plaintiffs had a complete remedy at law.

In *Knye* vs. *Moore*, 1 Sim. & Stu. 61, 1 Cond. Eng. Ch. R. 32, a mother joined with her children as co-plaintiffs in a bill, the object of which was to establish two distinct claims arising under separate instruments; the mother claiming an annuity under one, and the mother and children claiming the benefit of a settlement under the other. It was held that the bill was not multifarious, upon the ground, that the whole case of the mother being properly the subject of one bill, the suit did not become multifarious, because all the plaintiffs were not interested to the same extent.

There is perhaps no rule established for the conducting of equity pleadings, with reference to which (whilst as a rule it is universally admitted) there has existed less of certainty and uniformity in application than has attended this relating to multifariousness. This effect, flowing perhaps inevitably from the variety of modes and degrees of right and interest entering into the transactions of life, seems to have led to a conclusion, rendering the rule almost as much an exception as a rule, and that conclusion is, that each case must be determined by its peculiar features. *Daniel, J.*, in *Shields* vs. *Thomas & als.*, 18 How. 259. See *Gaines* vs. *Chew*, 2 How. 619; *Oliver* vs. *Piatt*, 3 How. 333.

In *Shields* vs. *Thomas & als.*, 18 How. 259, several claimants of parts of an estate united in filing a bill; this, it was held, did not make the bill multifarious, the complainants all claiming under one and the same title.

Several different underwriters having claims to a return of moneys by them severally paid on account of loss, cannot unite in one bill. *Yeaton* vs. *Lenox*, 8 Peters 123.

There may be a demurrer for multifariousness, ordinarily so called, which is in fact a demurrer for misjoinder [of subjects]. The distinction between misjoinder and multifariousness was clearly exhibited in the case of *Ward* vs. *Duke of Northumberland*, 2 Ans. 469. In that case, the plaintiff had been tenant of a colliery under the preceding Duke of Northumberland, and continued also to be tenant under his son and successor, the then Duke, and he then filed a bill against the then Duke and Lord Beverley, who were the executors of their father, and seeking relief against them in respect to transactions, part of which took place in the lifetime of the former Duke, and part between the plaintiff and the then Duke after his father's decease. To this bill the defendants put in separate demurrers, and the forms of the two demurrers, which were very different, clearly illustrate the distinction between the two. The Duke could not say there was any portion of the bill with which he was not necessarily connected, because he was interested in one part of it as owner of the mine, and in the other as representing his father. But his defence was, that it was improper to join in one record a case against Lim as representative of his father, and a case against him arising out of transactions in which he was personally·concerned. The form of his demurrer was, that there was an improper joinder of the subject-matter of the suit. Lord Beverley's demurrer again was totally different; it was in the usual form of demurrer for multifariousness, and proceeded on the ground that, by including transactions which occurred between the plaintiff and the late Duke (with the latter of which only Lord Beverley could have any concern), the bill was drawn to an unnecessary length, and the demurring party exposed to improper and useless expense. Both demurrers were allowed.

DEMURRER FOR WANT OF PARTIES.

154. The following is the form of a demurrer for want of parties.

In the Circuit Court of the county of ———:

As in form on p. 183, to word "forth," then proceed: Do demur to the said bill, and for cause of demurrer show that it appears by the complainant's own showing that J. S., therein named, is a necessary party to the said bill, inasmuch as it is therein stated, &c. [here recite so much of the statements of the bill as show that J. S. should be made a party]; but yet the said complainant has not made the said J S. a party to the said bill. Wherefore, &c. (as on page 184 to the end).[63]

PRACTICAL NOTE.

A demurrer for want of necessary parties must show who are the proper parties, from the facts stated in the bill, not, indeed, by name, for that might be impossible, but in such a manner as to point out to the plaintiff the objection to his bill, and to enable him to amend by making proper parties.[64]

If it be not apparent on the face of the bill that necessary parties are omitted, the objection can be taken only by plea or answer. *Mitchell* vs *Lenox, &c.*, 2 Paige 280; *Robinson, &c.* vs. *Smith, &c.*, 3 Paige 222. The plea or answer must disclose facts showing that additional parties are necessary, and must show who the necessary parties are, and then the plaintiffs can have leave to amend their bill and make the proper parties. *Cook, &c.* vs. *Mancius, &c.*, 3 John. Ch. R. 427; *Milligan* vs. *Millidge, &c.*, 3 Cranch 220.

The defendants can demur only when it is apparent from the bill itself that there are other persons who ought to have been parties. *Robinson, &c.* vs. *Smith, &c.*, 3 Paige 222. If the demurrer be allowed, leave will be given the plaintiff to amend his bill on payment of costs, so as to bring out all proper parties before the court. *Mitchell* vs. *Lenox, &c.*, 2 Paige 280. See *Elliott's ex'ors* vs. *Dayton, &c.*, 3 Desau. 29.

Though no objection for want of parties be made by the pleadings, such objection may, notwithstanding, be generally taken at the hearing, if the ground of it appear on the face of the bill. In *Munford, &c.* vs. *Murray*, 6 John. Ch. R. 11, the objection did not prevail; but then the creditors, who it was said ought to be parties, had suffered twenty years to elapse without asserting their claims, and it was presumed that those claims had been satisfied or abandoned.

---

[63] See section 135, on page 168, as to demurrer in United States Circuit Courts.   [64] Mitf. Pl. 180.

When the objection for want of parties is made at the hearing, and the court is of opinion that the objection is well founded, it will not, because proper parties are wanting, dismiss the bill absolutely, but will give the plaintiff leave to amend his bill by adding proper parties on payment of the usual costs. *Green* vs. *Poole*, 4 Brown's Par. Cas. 122, Tomlin's edit., vol. 5, p. 504; Anon, 2 Atk. 15; *Jones* vs. *Jones*, 3 Atk. 111; *Colt* vs. *Lasnier*, 9 Cow. 334; *Allen & als.* vs. *Smith*, 1 Leigh 231.

Upon an appeal from a decree, if the appellate court shall be of opinion that the court below erred in proceeding to decree without having the proper parties brought before it, the decree will be reversed for this error, and the cause sent back, with liberty to the plaintiffs to amend their bill by making proper parties. *Harding* vs. *Handy*, 11 Wheat. 133; *Marshall* vs. *Beverley*, 5 Wheat. 313; *Conn., &c.* vs. *Penn.*, Id. 424. The appellate court will reverse for want of necessary parties, though the objection is not taken in the court below. *Taylor's adm'or & als.* vs. *Spindle*, 2 Grat. 45. But see the case of *Buck* vs. *Pennybacker's ex'or*, 4 Leigh 5, as to the reluctance of the appellate court to undo all that has been done, because of a failure to make certain persons defendants, who, strictly speaking, ought to have been made parties.

If it appear on the face of the record that proper parties to the suit are wanting, the decree will be reversed, unless the objection was expressly waived in the court below. *Sheppard's ex'or* vs. *Starke*, 3 Munf. 29.

In *Dickinson* vs. *Davis & als.*, 2 Leigh 401, when slaves were real estate, the heir at law of Richard Davis united with his sisters, distributees, together with himself, of Richard Davis, in a bill in equity for the slaves. The misjoinder was not objected to in the court below. There was a decree in favor of the plaintiffs. In the Court of Appeals the objection was insisted on. *Carr*, J., pronouncing the opinion of the court, said : I will not say what might have been the effect of this objection if properly pleaded, but in the present situation and stage of the cause I think it can have no other effect than this, that the court will consider the right, if there be any, as vested in Smithson [the heir], and bound by his acts or omissions. The court, however, reversed the decree on other grounds.

The proposition that a party may sometimes waive an objection as to the want of parties, is in no wise opposed to the maxim, that consent cannot give jurisdiction. The want of parties cannot be regarded (at least not in all cases) as a *sine qua non* of the jurisdiction of the court, without which no complete decree can be had. In many cases it may certainly be considered a privilege in favor of the defendant, rather than an ingredient of the jurisdiction of a court of equity, and such a privilege it is competent for him to relinquish. He may waive this privilege as he may waive any advantage that might be taken of error in the form of the proceedings, and rely altogether on the merits of his cause. Opinions of Judges *Roane* and *Fleming*, in *Mayo* vs. *Murchie*, 3 Munf. 400, 404, 409.

GENERAL RULE THAT ALL PERSONS INTERESTED MUST BE PARTIES. It is a general rule in equity that all persons materially interested in the subject-matter of the bill ought to be made parties to the suit, however numerous they may be. *Story*, J., in *West* vs. *Randall, &c.*, 2 Mason 190; *Carr*, J., in *Clark* vs. *Long*, 4 Rand. 452; *Wiser* vs. *Blachly, &c.*, 1 Johns. Ch. Rep. 437; *Colt* vs. *Lesnier*, 9 Cow. 329; *Bailey* vs. *Inglee, &c.*, 2 Paige 278; *Swan* vs. *Ligan, &c.*, 1 M'Cord's Ch. Rep. 231 The rule, however, is restricted to those who are interested in the property which is involved in the issue, and does not extend to persons who merely have an interest in the point or question litigated. In *Wendell* vs. *Van Rensselaer*, 1 Johns. Ch. Rep. 344, the testator had conveyed, with covenants of warranty, part of the lands owned by him, and had died seized of the other part; the defendants claimed the whole lands, as well that part which the testator had conveyed, as the other part of which he died seized ; the bill was by the testator's representatives for a discovery of the defendant's claim, and to be quieted in their right as representatives; and the objection was taken that the purchasers from the testator were not made parties. The objection was overruled, upon the ground that the purchasers had no interest in the estate of which the testator died seized, and which alone was the subject of the bill.

Many difficulties and delays must, of necessity, arise in suits in equity from the number of parties that are indispensable. But these delays and difficulties ought not to be unnecessarily increased. "On general principles," says Judge *Roane*, "it would seem that those who have, and those who want the entire subject of controversy, would be proper and *sufficient* parties. It is enough that all those should be parties, defendant to the suit, who possess all the rights in controversy in that suit, and therefore can enable the court of equity to make a complete decree upon the subject. It is not necessary that all those should be also parties, who will be necessary parties in *other* suits to which the decision of the suit in question may give rise, by reason of a warranty or otherwise. There is no need to essay the vain attempt to settle by *one* decision all other suits, and every consequential claim or injury which may grow out of the decision of the point in issue." *Mayo* vs. *Murchie*, 3 Munf. 401, 402.

The rule that all persons materially interested ought to be parties, was established, says Lord *Eldon*, for the convenient administration of justice, and must not be adhered to in cases to which, consistently with practical convenience, it is incapable of application. *Cockburn* vs. *Thompson*, 16 Ves. 326. See also *Clifton* vs. *Haig's ex'ors*, 4 Desau. 343.

CASES OF FRAUD. Where a suit is brought to set aside a conveyance upon the ground of a fraud practised by the grantee upon the grantor, and the grantor has died, if the conveyance be of real estate, it will be sufficient to file the bill in the name of the heirs or devisees of the grantor. *Livingston* vs. *Peru Iron Company*, 2 Paige 390. But if the conveyance was of personal estate, as well as real, then the administrator of the grantor must likewise be a party. In *Samuel* vs. *Marshall, &c.*, 3 Leigh 567, the conveyance was of the grantor's whole estate, both real and personal; and the bill was by the grantor's heirs and distributees. The conveyance was set aside *in toto.* But *held*, that though the plaintiffs were interested to set aside the deed, yet the defendant could not be decreed to surrender the personal estate to them; the personal representative of the decedent being no party to the suit. See also *Whelan* vs. *Whelan*, 3 Cow. 580; *Hansford. &c.* vs. *Elliott, &c.*, 9 Leigh 79.

Where a judgment creditor seeks to set aside an assignment or deed of trust made by his debtor, upon the ground that it is fraudulent and void, it has been *held* that he is at liberty to proceed against the fraudulent assignee or trustee, who is the holder of the legal estate in the property, without joining the *cestuis que trust*. *Rogers, &c.* vs. *Rogers, &c.*, 3 Paige 379. A distinction is taken between a bill of this kind and a bill to enforce a claim under the trust. On a bill by one *cestui que trust* against the trustee, the other *cestuis que trust* must generally be parties.

In *Tate* vs. *Liggat, &c.*, 2 Leigh 106, a creditor obtained a decree against his debtor, and sued out a *ca. sa.*, under which the debtor took the oath of insolvency; and then the creditor filed a bill to subject property which had been conveyed by his debtor in trust to secure a pretended debt. *Held*, that the marshal who levied the *ca. sa.*, and in whom the rights of the debtor vested by operation of law, upon the surrender of his effects as an insolvent debtor ought to be made a party. See also *Deas* vs. *Thorne, &c.*, 3 Johns. Rep. 543; *Movan & wife* vs. *Hays*, 1 Johns. Ch. Rep. 339; *Osgood* vs. *Franklin*, 2 Johns. Ch. Rep. 18; *Ward* vs. *Van Bokkelen, &c.*, 2 Paige 289; *De Wolf* vs. *Johnson*, 10 Wheat. 384.

BILL OF DISCOVERY. Officers of a corporation may be made parties to a bill of discovery, for the purpose of enabling the complainant to obtain a knowledge of facts which could not be ascertained by the answer of the corporation, put in under their corporate seal and without oath. *Vermilyea* vs. *Fulton Bank, &c.*, 1 Paige 37. This is an exception to the general rule, that a mere witness cannot be made a party defendant. See *Wych* vs. *Meal*, 3 P. Wms. 310. The reasons for the exception, which are given in the case just cited, apply as well to the former as to the present officers of the corporation, when the knowledge of the facts, of which the discovery is sought, rests only with such officers, and especially when it relates to their own official acts. *Fulton Bank* vs. *Sharon Canal Company, &c.*, 1 Paige 219.

REDEMPTION OF MORTGAGE. Where a mortgagee assigns the whole benefit of his security, he is not a necessary party to a bill for redemption, for he has no longer any interest in the subject. By Sir *John Leach*, Vice Chancellor, in *Norrish* vs. *Marshall, &c.* 5 Madd. Ch. Rep. 478, Am. edi. 290. In such case, the persons interested, by virtue of the assignment, must be made parties. *Hickock* vs. *Scribner*, 3 Johns. Cas. 311.

If, however, the mortgagee assigns only a part of the benefit of the security, his interest in the subject continues, and he is, generally speaking, a necessary party as well as the assignee. But even in this case he may be dispensed with if the amount as to which he made no assignment is acknowledged by him to have been paid. In *Norrish* vs. *Marshall, &c.*, above cited, the assignor was examined as a witness for the plaintiff, and swore that he had been fully paid, and had no longer any interest in the subject. Sir *John Leach* permitted the cause to be proceeded in without his being made a party.

Where the equity of redemption has been assigned, and the assignee of the mortgagor brings a bill to redeem, the mortgagor must sometimes be a party. In *Clark* vs. *Long*, 4 Rand. 451, the case was this. A debtor executed a deed of trust upon his land to secure a creditor, the debtor afterwards sold his equity of redemption, and his bargainee filed a bill to redeem, impeaching the consideration of the deed of trust, contesting the amount due under it, and calling for a settlement of these points. *Held*, that the debtor was interested in these questions, and he not being a party to the suit, the decree was reversed by an appellate court, and the cause sent back.

PURCHASER. When an attempt is made to subject land in the possession of a purchaser, with notice, to an equitable lien, the person under whom such purchaser claims, or his legal representative, ought to be parties to the suit. *Wilcox* vs. *Calloway*, 1 Wash. 38. If pending a suit to subject land in the hands of a purchaser to a judgment, the purchaser dies, his heirs are necessary parties. *Taylor's adm'or & als.* vs. *Spindle*, 2 Grat. 44.

In a suit by the claimant of an incumbrance against a vendee having notice, a person who joined the vendor in the deed for the purpose of relinquishing a collateral claim is not a necessary party. *Blair* vs. *Owls*, 1 Munf. 38.

VENDOR AND VENDEE. After judgment recovered by vendor against two joint vendees of land for a balance of the purchase

25

money, one of the vendees dies, and the other brings suit against the vendor for deficiency in the land, the representatives of the deceased vendee were held to be necessary parties. *Crawford & als.* vs. *McDaniel,* 1 Rob. R. 448.

In *Pennington* vs. *Hanby, &c.,* 4 Munf. 144, previously cited, p. 25 *n.,* it was held that a decree could not be made against a widow to restrain her from conveying her right of dower if she be not made a party defendant to the bill as widow, or in her own right, but merely as administratrix of the decedent and guardian of his children. But in *Kinney's ex'or* vs. *Harvey, &c.,* 2 Leigh 70, the defendant was charged in the bill as executrix and as devisee of a decedent. In the caption of her answer she professed to answer only as devisee, but in the body of her answer she, in fact, answered as devisee; it was held, that the answer placed her before the court in her character of devisee.

FORECLOSURE OF MORTGAGE. Where there has been no assignment by mortgagee or mortgagor, and both are alive, it will generally be sufficient to file the bill, to foreclose in the name of the mortgagee against the mortgagor. *Van Vechten, &c.* vs. *Terry, &c.,* 2 Johns. Ch. Rep. 197, is a strong case of this kind. A joint fund had been raised by above two hundred and fifty subscribers to purchase the property in *New York* known by the name of *Washington Hall.* The subscribers being too numerous to hold and manage the property as a copartnership, certain trustees were selected to whom the property was conveyed, and these trustees, in pursuance of a trust contained in the deed to them, mortgaged the premises. A bill to foreclose was brought by the mortgagees against the trustees, and a demurrer was filed because the stockholders were not made parties. The Chancellor thought it would be intolerably oppressive and burdensome to compel the plaintiffs to bring in all the *cestuis que trust.* It seemed to him that the trustees represented sufficiently all the interests concerned, and he overruled the demurrer.

Call vs. *Scott, &c.,* 4 Call 402, was a peculiar case. The endorser of a bill of exchange had a mortgage from the drawer for his security, and after the protest, and before payment, brought a suit against the mortgagor to foreclose the mortgage. The defence of usury was made. In regard to this defence the plaintiff stood on common ground with the defendant. If the bill were invalid, both plaintiff and defendant were discharged. The holder was entirely unrepresented. In this state of the matter it was considered erroneous for the court of chancery to proceed to decree upon the merits. Instead of pronouncing such decree, the court of appeals was of opinion that the court of chancery ought to have given leave to the plaintiff to amend his bill by making the holder a party, and if this were not done within a reasonable time that the bill ought to stand dismissed.

Where the mortgagor and mortgagee are both dead, if the mortgage be of slaves, or other personal property, and there has been no assignment, the bill to foreclose will be by the executor or administrator of the mortgagee against the executor or administrator of the mortgagor. *Harrison* vs. *Harrison, &c.*, 1 Call 419.

If the mortgage be of land, and the mortgagor has devised the equity of redemption in the mortgaged premises, the devisees must be made defendants to the bill to foreclose. Chancellor *Taylor* in *Graham's ex'or* vs. *Carter*, 2 H. & M. 6. A devisee must be made a party, notwithstanding the devise was upon certain conditions which the complainant alleges were never complied with; for whether the conditions were complied with or not, is a matter that cannot be investigated until the devisee is made a party. *Mayo* vs. *Tomkies*, 6 Munf. 520. In a suit against the devisees, the mortgagee is not obliged, before he can get hold of the mortgaged subject, to go into an account of the personal assets of the mortgagor; and hence there is no necessity to make the personal representative of the mortgagor a defendant, in order to obtain such account. Chancellor *Taylor* in *Patton* vs. *Page*, 4 H. & M. 449. But as the personal representative may have it in his power to show payment or satisfaction, he ought for this reason to be made a party. *Harrison* vs. *Harrison, &c.*, 1 Call 419.

Where the devisee has died, his heirs should be brought before the court. *Mayo* vs. *Tomkies*, 6 Munf. 520. If it appear that the devisee sold and conveyed the lands, and that the purchaser by his will authorized his executors to sell the same, the executors of such purchaser ought to be made parties. *S. C.* If there be several executors, all must be parties, and not merely that one who has attended to the making of the sales. *S. C.* So, too, if a purchaser from the executors be in possession of any part of the land, such purchaser should be made a party; and if there be more purchasers than one, all must be brought before the court, in order that they may be subjected to a ratable contribution. *S. C.*

All persons who are incumbrancers at the commencement of the suit must be made parties, or else their rights will not be affected by the decree and sale thereunder. In *Harris, &c.* vs. *Beach, &c.*, 3 Johns. Ch. Rep. 459, there had been a decree for the sale of the premises under the first mortgage, and a conveyance to the purchaser. But the second mortgagee was no party to the suit. On a bill by the executors of the second mortgagee, and by his heir and devisee against the purchaser, *held* that the plaintiffs were entitled to redeem notwithstanding the sale. See also *Ensworth* vs. *Lambert, &c.*, 4 Johns. Ch. Rep. 605; *McGown, &c.* vs. *Yerks, &c.*, 6 Johns. Ch. Rep. 450; and *Hallock* vs. *Smith, &c.*, 4 Johns. Ch. Rep. 649.

Where the mortgagee has made an absolute assignment of all his interest in the mortgage, and the assignee brings a bill to foreclose, there is no necessity for making the mortgagee a party, if there be nothing special and peculiar in the case. *Whitney* vs. *M'Kinney*, 7 Johns. Ch. Rep. 144; *Newman* vs. *Chapman*, 2 Rand. 93. It is otherwise where the assignment is not of the mortgagee's whole interest, as in *Hobart* vs. *Abbot*, 2 P. Wms. 643. There the sum of £350 was secured to the mortgagee, and he assigned to secure £300. On a bill by the assignee against the mortgagor, it was *held* that the representatives of the mortgagee ought to be parties, for they had a right to redeem.

DEEDS OF TRUST. Where the maker of a deed of trust conveys to trustees the whole of his estate, both real and personal, this passes equitable as well as legal estate, and the trustees are the proper persons to litigate any claim which the maker of the deed had to property of any kind. Thus in *Carter, &c.* vs. *Harris*, 4 Rand. 199, a deputy sheriff, who sold a slave under execution, purchased the slave under circumstances which rendered the sale invalid. After this the judgment debtor made a conveyance to trustees in the manner above mentioned. And they filed a bill claiming to redeem the property by paying the amount of the execution. It was objected that the judgment debtor was no party to the suit; and he alone, it was insisted, had a right to sue. But the objection was overruled.

In *Mitchell* vs. *Lenox & Taylor*, 2 Paige 280, the complainant had assigned all his property to trustees, in trust to pay certain debts due to the *United States* and to *H. Stevenson*, and to divide the surplus, or so much thereof as might be necessary, among such of the other creditors of the complainant as should come in under the assignment, and release him from the payment of their demands. Creditors having debts amounting to more than $44,000 came in under the assignment and complied with the condition thereof. Two of these creditors were afterwards paid by the complainant, who took from them an assignment of their debts. The bill of the complainant was against the surviving trustees, for an account of the trust property; and the defendants demurred, on the ground that the creditors who came in under the assignment should have been made parties. The demurrer was allowed, with liberty to the complainant to amend his bill, on payment of costs, so as to bring the proper parties before the court.

Where the conveyance is of *personal* estate as well as real, and the grantor has died, if a bill be brought by his heirs against the trustees for an account of the trust subject, the personal representative of the grantor must be made a party to the suit. *West* vs. *Randall, &c.*, 2 Mason 181.

RESULTING TRUSTS. Where the bill is by a grantee or his devisee against persons in possession of the lands granted, and from the showing in the bill it appears that the plaintiff is a mere nominal trustee, and that a particular individual is the *cestui que trust*, it is indispensable that such *cestui que trust* should be made a party. In *Malin vs. Malin, &c.*, 2 Johns. Ch. Rep. 238, the bill stated that a religious society was formed at *Jerusalem* in the county of *Ontario*, denominated "The Society of Universal Friends," of which *Jemima Wilkinson* was the founder and head; that for the support of herself and the poor of the society the said *Jemima* purchased certain lands and paid the purchase money, and as a rule of the society forbade any estate being vested in her, she nominated one of her followers to be her trustee, and the deed was taken in the name of that individual without any expression of the trust in the deed; that the grantee devised the lands to the plaintiff, but, owing to some alleged imperfection in the devise, the grantee's daughter and the husband of that daughter claimed the lands and had entered thereon. The husband and wife were made defendants; and the bill stated that the said *Jemima* was restrained by her profession and conscience from becoming a party to any suit or proceeding at law whatever. It was objected that she ought to have been made a party plaintiff, since, according to the shewing in the bill, she was the only person equitably entitled; and the objection was sustained. If it should be made to appear by affidavit or the report of a master, that she had religious scruples which could not be surmounted, the chancellor thought that perhaps she might be permitted to become plaintiff by her *prochein ami*. A person incompetent to protect himself, from age or weakness of mind, or from some religious delusion or fanaticism, ought, he said, to come under the protection of the court.

If a bill be brought by the *cestui que trust* against the grantee of the land, and such grantee die, the suit should be revived against the *heirs* or *devisees* of the grantee, and not merely against his executors. *Key's ex'ors vs. Lambert*, 1 H. & M. 330.

DISPOSITION OF ASSETS. A suit against legatees for a debt due from the testator should be against *all the legatees*, and the *executor* should likewise be a party. The necessity of making the executor a party can only be dispensed with, when it appears that the accounts of the executorship have been regularly settled, and the whole estate delivered over to the legatees. *Hooper vs. Royster*, 1 Munf. 119. See also *Beale's adm'or vs. Taylor's adm'or & als.*, 2 Grat. 532.

If a joint and several bond be executed by two obligors, and a suit be brought against the devisees of one of them, to subject to the payment of the debt the lands which such devisees hold, the court should not decree against them without having also the other obligor or his representatives before it; for the other obligor or his representatives may have paid the debt or a part thereof, and in such case their assistance is necessary to prevent the obligee from receiving payment a second time. *Foster & wife* vs. *Crenshaw's ex'ors,* 3 Munf. 514.

It has long been settled that if several pecuniary legacies be given to different persons, as £600 to A, £700 to B, and £700 to C, each legatee may sue for his own legacy, without making the others parties. *Haycock* vs. *Haycock,* 2 Cha. Cas. 124; *Brown* vs. *Ricketts &c.,* 3 Johns. Ch. Rep. 553. But where the fund out of which the legacies are to be paid proves deficient, and each legatee has to abate proportionably, then all whose legacies are to abate should be before the court. In *Jones* vs *Hobson,* 2 Rand. 505, the bill was filed against an executor and his sureties, to recover pecuniary legacies; and it appeared that other legacies were due besides those claimed by the plaintiffs, and the fund for which the sureties were responsible was not sufficient to pay all. All the legatees had a right to have the fund ratably distributed amongst them; and the court of appeals decided that all ought to be made parties.

In the case of *Brown* vs. *Ricketts &c.* above cited, the bill was filed by a single pecuniary legatee on behalf of himself and such other legatees of the testator as might choose to come in and contribute to the expense of the suit; and chancellor *Kent* seems to have considered it material that the bill should be so framed. See also *Fish* vs. *Howland, &c.,* 1 Paige 20; *Kettle & wife* vs. *Crary,* 1 Paige 417, *note* a; and *Manning* vs. *Thesiger, &c.,* 1 Sim. & Stu. 106. 1 Cond. Eng. Ch. Rep. 53.

When the bill is filed by a legatee who is entitled to priority of payment, he need not make the persons interested in the residuum of personal estate parties to the suit. The executor or administrator is in such cases the legal representative of the rights of the residuary legatees, and it is his duty to see them properly defended. *Pritchard* vs. *Hicks, &c.,* 1 Paige 270.

If the suit be not for a pecuniary legacy of certain amount, but for a share of a subject which is to be divided amongst several persons, the general rule is that all must be parties who are interested in the division of that subject. Accordingly it has been decided that in a suit brought by one of several *residuary* legatees against the executors to recover his share of the estate, all the residuary legatees should be made parties. *Richardson's ex'or* vs. *Hunt,* 2 Munf. 148; *Shobe's ex'ors* vs. *Carr,* 3 Munf. 19; *Sheppard's ex'or* vs. *Starke & wife,* 3 Munf. 29; *Davoue* vs. *Funning,* 4 Johns. Ch. Rep. 199. *Contra, Hallett, &c.* vs. *Hallett, &c.,* 2 Paige 15.

But where a testator by his will directed that when any one of his children should separate from the family, he should have his share of the estate, and a suit was brought by one of the children after the shares of others had been allotted to them, it was *held*

unnecessary to make all the children parties to the suit, but sufficient to make those parties who remained entitled to shares at the
time of instituting the suit.   A contrary rule, it was said, would
harass the persons interested, by a multiplicity of suits; for the
division could not be made for all the children at one and the same
time, and under the operation of the contrary rule *all* would be
made parties whenever any one separated from the family and
claimed his share. *Branch's adm'x* vs. *Booker's adm'r*, 3. Munf. 43.

Where a legatee has died without receiving his share of the
estate, a suit to recover the same must be in the name of his executor or administrator.   Generally speaking, a bill cannot be maintained in the names of persons suing as *children* of the legatee.
It was so adjudged, in a case in which the bill stated that the legatee had died intestate and no person had administered upon his
estate. *Moring* vs. *Lucas &c.*, 4 Call 577; *Hays's ex'or & others*
vs. *Hays & others*, 5 Munf. 418.   But where an intestate died
leaving eight children his distributees, and one of them died in his
infancy, it was *held* that the surviving distributees might recover
the whole amount due from the administratrix, including the share
of the infant distributee.   In this case it was considered that no
administration was necessary on the estate of the infant distributee, nor any security requisite for the plaintiffs' refunding what
they might receive on account of his share, because of the fact
that he died an infant and could not be supposed to owe any debts,
Myers & others vs. *Wade & others*, 6 Rand. 448.   See also *Sheppard's ex'or* vs. *Starke & wife*, 3 Munf. 29; and *Bradford* vs. *Fel-
der*, 2 M'Cord's Ch. Rep. 168.

Distributees of a decedent may maintain a bill in equity to assert their rights in the decedent's estate, but they cannot have
distribution thereof without having the executor or administrator
of the decedent before the court as a party to the cause.   *Hansford, &c.* vs. *Elliott, &c.*, 9 Leigh 79.   See *Samuel* vs. *Marshall
& als.*, 3 Leigh 567, cited *ante*, p. 192.

Legatees cannot sue an executor *de son tort* without setting up an
administrator *de bonis non* and making him a party.   Without doing
this, a recovery by the legatees would not protect the executor *de
son tort*.   He would be liable afterwards to the demand of an administrator *de bonis non*.   *Frazier, &c.* vs. *Frazier's ex'ors, &c.*,
2 Leigh 649.

Where two executors or administrators have qualified on a decedent's estate and acted jointly, a bill by the legatees or distributees
of such estate cannot be brought against one executor or administrator, but must be against both.   *Bregaw* vs. *Claw*, 4 Johns. Ch.
Rep. 116.   So if a testator devise *real* estate to be sold by his executors, and the proceeds divided into shares, and two of the executors qualify and sell the property, they must both be made defendants to a bill filed to recover a share of the proceeds.   *Findlay,*

ex'or, &c. vs. *Sheffey,* 1 Rand. 73. See also *Fabre & wife* vs. *Colden,* 1 Paige 166.

In *Findlay, ex'or, &c.* vs. *Sheffey,* a testator devised *real* estate to be sold, and the proceeds divided among certain persons who were specified. One of these persons assigned his interest, and the assignee filed a bill to recover the same. The only defendants were the executor and the assignor. It was held that the other devisees interested in the property ought likewise to have been made parties. See also *Fabre & wife* vs. *Colden,* 1 Paige 166.

Where a testator devises land to be sold, and directs the proceeds to be divided among his children, if the executor after selling the land should die without paying over the proceeds, a bill may be filed in the name of the children against the representative of the executor to recover the same. If the executor died before receiving the proceeds from the purchasers of the land, the bill may be filed in the name of the children against the purchasers. The administrator *de bonis non* of the testator need not be' made a party to the suit, because the proceeds of the land are not legal assets, and the administrator *de bonis non* would have nothing to do with the fund. *Graff & others* vs. *Castleman, &c.,* 5 Rand. 195.

Although after a judgment against an executor or administrator as such, and a return of *nulla bona,* an action at law may be brought suggesting a devastavit, yet the creditor is not confined to this remedy. If he does not know the state of the assets, nor the claims against the estate, he may file his bill in equity to have a discovery of these matters, and, on that discovery being made, may either proceed at law, or the court of equity may retain the cause and determine the dispute between the parties. *White, &c.* vs. *Banister's ex'ors,* 1 Wash. 166. In the suit in equity, the sureties of the executor or administrator, and other persons concerned in interest, may be made parties defendant, and decreed against. By *Taylor,* Ch., in *Clarke* vs. *Webb, &c.,* 2 H. & M. 8.

Although the assent of the executor to the bequest of a personal chattel will exempt the chattel at law from being taken under execution to satisfy a judgment against the executor, yet such assent can never defeat the right of a creditor to pursue in a court of equity the assets of a testator in the hands of the legatees, if necessary for the payment of the testator's debts. *Dunn* vs. *Amy & als.,* 1 Leigh 465; *Milligan* vs *Milledge, &c.,* 3 Cranch 228. The bill in such case should not be against the legatees alone. The correct way of proceeding is to file it against the executor as well as the legatees. *Frescott* vs. *Frescott & als.,* 1 McCord's Ch. Rep. 433. When the executor has died, his representatives should be made defendants. *Elliott's ex'ors* vs. *Drayton, &c.,* 3 Dis. 29. And whoever is then the personal representative of the first decedent should also be a defendant.

In such suit all the legatees must be made parties, that the charge may not fall upon one, but may be equally borne by the whole. *Burnley* vs. *Lambert*, 1 Wash. 308; *Waddy* vs. *Sherman, &c.,* Jeff. R. 5.

A will was dated in 1802. The testator died in 1815. One of the administrators *de bonis non* with the will annexed, conveyed his property in trust to indemnify his sureties on the administration bond. Creditors of the decedent brought a bill to subject to payment of their debts a fund, in the hands of a trustee, derived from the sale of the land conveyed to him in trust by the administrator to indemnify the sureties. The legatees not having been heard from from 1815 to 1827, the time of bringing the suit, were not deemed necessary parties. *Jones* vs. *Lackland*, 2 Grat. 81.

In a creditor's suit for the payment of his debt, the residuary legatee need not be made a party with the executor (*Peacock* vs. *Monk*, 1 Vez. 131), nor need he be made a party when the purpose is to obtain from the executor a sum of stock which had been sold by the deceased during his life. *Brown* vs. *Dowthwaite*, 1 Mad. 448; Story's Eq. Pl. 140, n. See Calv. Part. 20, 21, 172.

Legatees sued the personal representatives of a sheriff, of his deputy, and of his official sureties. There was a decree first against the representatives of the sheriff and of the deputy for the balance found due, and a *fieri facias* on this decree was returned *nulla bona testatoris*. It was held not to be necessary to direct accounts of administration by the representatives of the sheriff and deputy to ascertain whether they had committed a devastavit before proceeding to decree against the sheriff's sureties; and it was also held that it was not necessary, before decreeing against the sureties of the sheriff, to make the heirs of the sheriff and of his deputy parties to ascertain whether any real estate descended to them. *Dabney's adm'or & als.* vs. *Smith's legatees*, 5 Leigh 13.

In a suit by a judgment creditor to subject land in the hands of a *bona fide* purchaser from the vendee, pending the suit the purchaser dies. His heirs are necessary parties. *Taylor* vs. *Spindle*, 2 Grat. 44.

A judgment creditor, under the act 5 Geo. 2nd, ch. 7, sec. 4, might file a bill in equity against the executors and devisees to subject the real and personal estate to the payment of his debt. *Suckley* vs. *Rotchford*, 12 Grat. 60.

In a suit by residuary legatees against the executor for a distribution of the estate the specific legatees should be made parties, unless it satisfactorily appears that their legacies have been satisfied. *Nelson* vs. *Page*, 7 Grat. 160.

All the sureties of an executrix should be parties to a suit by legatees for distribution, or a sufficient reason should be shown for failing to make them parties before a decree is made against one of them. *Hutcherson* vs. *Pigg*, 8 Grat. 220. See *Taliaferro* vs.

26

Thornton, 6 Call. 21; Story's Eq. Jur., § 161, 162, 169; *Primrose* vs. *Bromley,* 1 Atk. R. 89.

One of two administrators who had taken no active part in the administration of the estate of an intestate died; his administrator was not a necessary party to a bill by the distributee against the other and active administrator for an account of his administration. *Wills* vs. *Dunn,* 5 Grat. 384. Nor was it necessary to make the personal representative of the widow of the intestate a party, she having received her third of the estate and having died, and the suit being by the only child of the intestate to recover his proportion of the estate from the administrator. *Ibid.*

In general, one distributee cannot maintain a suit to recover his distributive share of the estate without making the other distributees parties. *Sillings* vs. *Bumgardner,* 9 Grat. 273.

The widow is a necessary party to a suit for partition of land by the heirs. *Custis* vs. *Snead,* 12 Grat. 260. See p. 65 *ante.*

All persons having an interest, or color of interest, in the residuum of an estate must be parties to a suit in which the court is to decide upon the construction of the will affecting that residuum. *Osborne* vs. *Taylor,* 12 Grat. 17.

Tarr vs. *Ravenscroft,* 12 Grat. 642, was a bill by a residuary legatee against an administrator, with the will annexed, and his sureties, William Tarr and John Hendricks, the administrator being insolvent. Campbell Tarr, the son of William Tarr, had received assignments of a number of the legacies and claimed them as his own, but Hendricks insisted that they belonged to William Tarr, and were purchased at a large discount, the benefit of which he was entitled to share. Hendricks further insisted that Campbell Tarr should not be paid these legacies until William Tarr, or William Tarr and Campbell Tarr, should file a cross-bill against him and thus give him an opportunity to contest Campbell Tarr's right. If Campbell Tarr was not entitled to the legacies he was entitled to compensation for purchasing them up. The Court held that Campbell Tarr was a proper defendant to the original bill to have his right to the legacies settled.

When it is sought to charge the heirs of an intestate on the bond of their ancestor, his personal representative is a necessary party in order that the personal assets may be applied in their relief as far as they will go. *Beall* vs. *Taylor,* 2 Grat. 532. See Story's Eq. Pl., § 172. When the suit is by a creditor against an executor and legatees, if it appear that the executor has wasted the estate of his testator by delivering it over to the legatees, a decree may be rendered against him personally for the amount of the judgment at law. *Sampson* vs. *Payne's ex'or &c.,* 5 Munf. 176.

A creditor by bond specially binding the heirs of his debtor, brought a suit in the State Court, against the heirs to subject the lands descended to the debtor. It appeared that the lands had been previously sold under a decree of the United States Court to satisfy the debt of the ancestor to the United States as collector of customs. The purchasers under the decree of the United States Court, were held to be necessary parties to the suit. *King, adm'or, &c.*, vs. *Ashley*, 5 Leigh 408.

See *Ruffners* vs. *Lewis*, 7 Leigh, 720, cited *ante* p. 126, note.

A bill to marshal assets and for administration should be in behalf of all the creditors, and the heirs and devisees should be parties. *Stephenson* vs. *Taverners*, 9 Grat. 398.

When all the legatees, having obtained a decree in favour of all ascertaining their rights, may unite in one suit to enforce the former decree. *Sheldon* vs. *Armistead*, 7 Grat. 264.

PARTNERSHIP. See 2 Rob. Pr. (old) 128, 129, 130. Code 1873, ch. 141, § 13. 2 Lom. Dig. (old) 114.

In a suit for settling the accounts of a partnership, every partner should be made a party. *Waggoner* vs. *Gray's adm'ors*, 2 H. & M. 603. And if a creditor of a firm file a bill against the executor of a deceased partner and against the surviving partner, and the latter die pending the suit, it should be revived against his executor or administrator. *Carter's ex'or* vs. *Currie*, 5 Call 158.

See Calv. on Parties, 156, 260 *et seq.* 121, also Code 1873, ch. 114.

The creditor of a firm obtains judgment against the surviving partner, who dies and his personal assets are exhausted by creditors in paying other claims. The creditor files a bill against the administrators and heirs of the surviving partner and the representatives of the deceased partner. The bill seeks a decree for the sale of lands owned by the surviving partner and the firm; and when this fund is exhausted, seeks to charge the representatives of the deceased partner. The representatives of the deceased partner were rightly made parties. *Jackson* vs. *King's representatives*, 8 Leigh 689.

To a suit by a partnership creditor for payment of his debt, the heir as well as the executor of a deceased partner may be made a defendant with the surviving partner. Calv. on Parties 166. *Vulliamy* vs. *Noble*, 3 Mer. 619. *Ex parte Kendall*, 17 Ves. 526. See *Dabney* vs. *Preston's adm'or*, 25 Grat. 838.

SURETYSHIP. It becoming necessary to go into equity against a co-surety, though the surety might have maintained a suit at law against the principal alone, the suit in equity by the surety against the principal and the co-surety was sustained as to both, and the demurrer of the principal debtor to the surety's bill was overruled. *Trescot* vs. *Smyth, &c.*, 1 McCord's Ch. Rep. 301.

In a suit by a surety against the representatives of a co-surety to which the principal is not a party, there will be no decree for the plaintiff unless it appear that due diligence has been used against the principal, or that he is insolvent. *McCormack's adm'or* vs. *Obannon's ex'or & devisees*, 3 Munf. 484. See *Mc-Mahon* vs. *Fawcett, &c.*, 2 Ran. 531. If the principal had been a defendant in the suit, together with the co-surety, it would have been competent to the Court to decree in favor of the plaintiff against his co-surety as it could at the same time direct payment to that co-surety from the principal. *Lawson* vs. *Wright*, 1 Cox's Ch. Cas. 275.

In a bill by a surety, whose principal is dead, to compel his executor to pay the debt the creditor is a necessary party. *Stephenson* vs. *Taverners*, 9 Grat. 398.

Several persons endorsing negotiable paper in succession are not considered as joint sureties. See *Farmers Bank* vs. *Vanmeter*, 4 Rand. 554.

A guardian, having given bond with sureties, afterwards comes into court, without a rule upon him or order of court, and gives another bond with other sureties; the sureties on the first bond are discharged and are not necessary or proper parties to a bill by a ward against the guardian and his sureties for the settlement of his accounts. *Sayers* vs. *Cassell & als.*, 23 Grat. 525.

Suit by sureties of an executor against the purchasers of assets of the estate, the purchasers being participant with the executor in the devastavit, the sureties who were charged with the devastavit of their principal had a right to sue them, and they were proper parties. *Jones* vs. *Clark & als.*, 25 Grat. 642.

See *Hoffman* vs. *Shields*, 8 W. Va. 32.

ASSIGNMENTS. In *Burnett, &c.*, vs. *Harwell &c.*, 3 Leigh 95, it was said by *Tucker*, P., that if the assignees of the decree for which that action was brought, had sued in equity, their assignor would have been a necessary party. There is no doubt that according to the ancient practice of the English Court of Chancery, the assignor of a chose in action was a necessary party to a bill to recover the amount. 2 Rob. Pr. (old) 272. See *Cathcart* vs. *Lewis*, 1 Ves. Jr. 463, Mitf. Pl. 179. This subject was examined by Chancellor Walworth, in the case of *Ward* vs. *Van Bokhelm, &c.*, 2 Paige 289, and he came to the conclusion, that where there is an absolute assignment in writing, if there be nothing in the pleadings or proofs to induce the belief that the assignor has not parted with all his interests in the subject of the suit, it is an unnecessary and useless expense to make him a party. The true principle is doubtless as he states it.

In all cases where the assignment is absolute and unconditional, leaving no equitable interest whatever in the assignor, and the extent and validity of the assignment is not doubted or denied and there is no remaining liability in the assignor to be affected by •

the decree, it is not necessary to make the assignor a party. Story's Eq. Pl. 153, 8 Pet. 532. See *Brace* vs. *Harrington*, 2 Atk. 235. *Bromley* vs. *Holland*, 7 Ves. 14. See *Millar* vs. *Bear*, 3 Paige 467, 468. *Whitney* vs. *McKinney*, 7 John Ch. R. 144, and *Newman* vs. *Chapman*, 2 Rand 93. 2 Rob. Pr. (old) 272. In *James River and Kanawha Company* vs. *Littlejohn*, 18 Grat. 53, the court held that the assignor in such a case was not a necessary party. See *Fitch* vs. *Creighton*, 24 How. 159. *Gaines* vs. *Hennon*, Id. 553. Where a person had assigned a bond secured by a deed of trust upon land, the assignment being absolute, in a suit by the assignee against the vendee of the obligor to subject the land to satisfy the debt, the assignor was held not to be a necessary party. *Omohundro* vs. *Henson & als.*, 26 Grat. 511.

The mere possession of a writing by which a debt is acknowledged, without any written agreement from the person to whom that acknowledgment was made, is not sufficient to sustain a bill. In such case the person to whom the debt was originally due must be made a party to the suit. *Auditor, &c.*, vs. *Johnson's ex'ix*, 1 H. and M. 536. See *Corbin* vs. *Emerson*, 10 Leigh 663, 2 Rob. Pr. (old) 272.

In a suit against a corporation which has assigned all its stock and property to a successor, sometimes a creditor may prosecute his own claim against the corporation without convening all the creditors. Such a case was *Barksdale* vs. *Finney*, 14 Grat. 338. In that case it was also decided, that the creditors of H., to whom the successor of the corporation had contracted to pay an annual rent, were not necessary parties.

An assignee should be made a party to a suit, the object of which is to set aside a deed of trust under which he claims. *Tichenor* vs. *Allen*, 13 Grat. 15.

If a debtor, who has been discharged under the insolvent act, claim an interest in part of his property which has been sold by the sheriff, his scheduled creditors are necessary parties. *Tiffany* vs. *Kent*, 2 Grat. 231.

See *Cannon* vs. *Welford, Judge*, 22 Grat. 195; *Berger* vs. *Buckland & als.*, 28 Grat. 850.

H., a surviving partner, and the personal representative of P., the dead partner, in the firm of H. & P., brought suit against one D. to enforce a contract with the partnership. It appeared that H. had assigned all his interest in the firm to the firm for proper settlement of accounts and, after paying all he owed the partnership, the residue to C. H. became bankrupt. Held that for a decree against D. both the assignee in bankruptcy of H., and C., were necessary parties. *Dabney* vs. *Preston's adm'ors*, 25 Grat. 838.

In a suit by G., the assignee of two bonds given for the purchase-money of land, against the executors of the purchaser to subject

the land to the payment of the bonds, the executors answer and
say, that C. has sued them to establish a prior lien on the land, that
all the purchase-money has been paid, without notice of this prior
lien, except the two bonds held by G. and one held by S., and they
insist that they are entitled to have C.'s lien credited on the bonds
held by G. and S.; S. is a necessary party to the suit and no decree
should be made in the cause until he is made a party. And it
was held, also, that the objection might be taken at the hearing or
even in the appellate court. *Armentrout's ex'ors* vs. *Gibbons*, 25
Grat. 371.

In *Richardson* vs. *Davis*, 21 Grat. 706, S. assigned his life policy
to R. for the benefit of S.'s wife and her children; he afterwards
conveyed the same policy by deed to R. in trust for his wife and
her children by him, but if she died without children the principal
to be paid to S.'s children by his first wife. In a suit by the
widow of S., and her infant son against R., who had acted under
the deed, it was held that the children by the first wife were
necessary parties.

L. buys land of D. and T. and gives to each his bonds for his share
of the purchase money. Afterwards the contract is rescinded, but
before this is done D. assigns one of his bonds. On a bill to enjoin
a judgment recovered on this bond by the assignee, T. is not a
necessary party. *Drake* vs. *Lyons*, 9 Grat. 54.

It is a question constantly recurring in all courts of equity how
far one who is a party to the contract, but who has assigned his
interest, is a necessary party to a suit affecting the subject matter
of the contract. The rule is perfectly undeviating that no person
need be joined in a suit in equity, either as plaintiff or defendant,
upon the ground merely of having been a party to the contract if
he is no longer interested in the controversy. But there are some
cases where a party still remains liable to certain consequences
growing out of the contract and where the suit will have a bearing
upon such liability; and in such cases it becomes necessary to make
him a party to the suit. In all other cases the assignor of an interest in the contract is not a needful or proper party. Story's
Eq. Pl. (by Redfield) note (1) to § 153. See *Fitch* vs. *Creighton*, 24
How. 159; *Gaines* vs. *Hinnen*, *Id.* 553.

An objection to the joinder of an assignor with an assignee as
complainant in a bill comes too late on an appeal. *Livingston* vs.
Woodworth, 15 How. 546.

See *Willard* vs. *Tayloe*, 8 Wal. 557.

AWARD. Suit by next of kin to impeach an award. *Moore* vs.
Luckless's next of kin, 23 Grat. 160.

HUSBAND AND WIFE. A husband may sue the wife or the wife

the husband in equity, though at law neither can sue the other. See *Cannal* vs. *Buckle*, 2 P. Wms. 243, Mitf. Pl. 28, Story's Eq. Pl. 61, 62.

In suits by the wife for her separate property, she should sue as sole plaintiff by her next friend, and the husband be made a party defendant. Story's Eq. Pl. 63.

A *feme covert*, if her husband is banished or has abjured the realm or has been transported for felony, may maintain a suit in her own name as if she were a *feme sole*. Mitf. Pl. 28, Story's Eq. Pl. 61.

If the husband is an alien enemy, the wife domiciled in the realm, may sue alone. 1 Salk. 116, 1 Ld. Ray 147, 1 Aikens 174. So where the husband has deserted his wife in a foreign country, and she comes here and maintains herself as a *feme sole*. *Gregory* vs. *Paul*, 15 Mass. 31. See also note (4) to § 61, Story's Eq. Pl.

In a bill by a husband to restrain proceedings commenced at law against husband and wife, for the purpose of affecting her interests, she is a necessary party. *Booth* vs. *Albertson*, 2 Barb. Ch. 313.

A bill to recover a legacy or distributive share to which the wife is entitled should be filed in the names of husband and wife. *Schuyler* vs. *Hoyle*, 5 John. C. R. 210. And if the husband die pending the suit, it will be sufficient to suggest his death on the record, and then the cause will proceed in the name of the wife. *McDowl & wife* vs. *Charles*, 6 John. C. R. 132. Where the wife dies, living the husband, and then the husband dies without administering on the personal estate of the wife, Lord Hardwick held that the husband's representative was entitled to the wife's personal estate and might bring a bill to recover the same. *Elliot* vs. *Collier*, 3 Atk. 526, 1 Ves., Sen. 15; *Humphrey* vs. *Bullen*, 1 Atk. 458. Lord Hardwicke's decision is cited as authority by Chancellor Kent in *Stewart* vs. *Stewart*, 7 John. C. R. 244, and is referred to in *Chichester's ex'ix* vs. *Vass's adm'or*, 1 Munf. 115, and in *Templeman* vs. *Fauntleroy*, 3 Rand. 439. In the latter case, however, the judge who cited the decision went only so far as to intimate that the executor of the husband, who had not administered, might sue in equity for a debt from the guardian of the wife if it appeared that she married in her infancy, and there was no suggestion of her having contracted debts; "that being," in the language of the judge, "the only reason why a husband need in any case administer." See *Hendren* vs. *Colgin*, 4 Munf. 231, 234, 235.

The effect of the Statutes, Code 1873, ch. 119, § 10, and Sess. Acts 1874–5, chap. 359, pp. 442, 443, Sess. Acts 1876–7, p. 49, and Sess. Acts 1876–7, p. 333, and Sess. Acts 1877–8, p. 247, should be considered in this connection.

In *Tazewell & als.* vs. *Smith's adm'or*, 1 Rand. 313, a *feme covert* was entitled to the proceeds of land devised to be sold, and the wife died pending a suit brought by husband and wife in which they claimed to discharge the executor from the necessity of selling, and elected to take the land itself. In this state of affairs it seemed to the court that the heirs of the wife should be made parties. It was important to them to inquire whether the election had any operation in favor of the wife in restoring the land to its original character as land, and whether her rights therein had not descended to them. See *Pratt* vs. *Taliaferro*, 3 Leigh 419.

When the right of the wife, legal or equitable, appears against the husband, it is the duty of the court, *ex-officio*, to protect the wife from any injurious effects arising from the acts or admissions of the husband. And it is sufficient for the right of the wife to appear clearly in the record. It is not necessary that the point should be formally insisted on in the pleadings or proceedings in the cause. *Dandridge, &c.* vs. *Minge*, 4 Rand. 367. Even where the wife is a joint plaintiff with her husband she is not bound by any proceedings or admissions in the cause by the husband, if such proceedings or admissions affect her inheritance. A bill by husband and wife is regarded as the husband's suit only, and the wife is joined for conformity, to be bound only so far as in justice she ought to be bound. *Dandridge, &c.* vs. *Minge*, 4 Rand. 367; Story's Eq. Pl., § 61, 63.

See *Wake* vs. *Parker*, 2 Keen 59, 70, 73–75.

See Sess. Acts 1874–5, chap. 359, pp. 442, 443.

An action or suit may be maintained against the husband and wife jointly for any debt of the wife contracted before marriage; but the execution on any judgment or decree in such action or suit shall issue against, and such judgment or decree shall only bind, the estate and property of the wife which she shall own at the time of the marriage, or acquire subsequently thereto, and not that of the husband. Sess. Acts 1874–5. chap. 359, § 3, p. 443. See also Sess. Acts 1875–6, chap. 58, p. 49.

In a suit brought by a trustee of a married woman to assert and defend her rights, in which a full opportunity is afforded the *cestui que trust* to protect her rights, it is not necessary that she should be made a party. *Woodson, trustee* vs. *Perkins*, 5 Grat. 345.

M. was administrator of husband and wife, and it being doubtful whether the right to a fund was in the estate of the husband or of the wife, he sued for it, in equity, in both characters. The bill was held not to be demurrable for misjoinder of parties. *Brent* vs. *Washington's adm'or*, 18 Grat. 526.

When the husband is not within the country, so that process cannot be served upon him, the suit, if against the wife to charge her separate estate, may be carried on without him, with the leave and under the direction of the court. Mitf. Pl., 105; Story's Eq. Pl. 63.

When a surviving husband of one of the heirs is a proper plaintiff in suit for partition. *Persinger* vs. *Simmons & als.*, 25 Grat. 238.

Whether, in any case, a married woman may sue or be sued by a stranger merely in respect to her separate property, without her husband being a party, plaintiff or defendant, is a question discussed in 1 Fonb. Eq., B'k 1, ch. 2, § 6, and Story's Eq. Pl. 63, and notes.

DOWER. In a bill by a widow for dower in land sold in the lifetime of her husband and coming to the present owner through several intermediate conveyances, the present owner is the only necessary defendant. *Blair* vs. *Thompson & als.*, 11 Grat. 441.

The dower of a widow in the land of her husband is assigned to her, and upon bill filed the other two-thirds of the land are divided among ten of the twelve heirs (the other two refusing to bring their advancement into hotchpot); upon the death of the widow the heirs who refused to come into the first division may come into the division of the dower property, and one of the children who had refused to come into the first division having died after the death of the widow, the husband of such child was a proper party plaintiff for a division of the dower land. *Persinger & als.* vs. *Simmons & als.*, 25 Grat. 238.

IDIOTS AND LUNATICS. It is not necessary for the lunatic himself to be a party plaintiff with his committee to set aside an act done by him while under mental imbecility. Whether he be joined or omitted seems immaterial, according to the cases cited in *Ortly, &c.* vs. *Messere, &c.*, 7 John. C. R. 139; 2 Rob. Pr. (old) 273. See Code 1873, ch 82, § 48, p. 723. Story's Eq. Pl., 64, 65, 66, and § 70, n. 5. Mitf. Pl., 29.

See *Bolling* vs. *Turner*, 6 Rand. 584, and *Campbells* vs. *Brown's adm'or, &c.*, 1 Rob. R. 241.

Where no committee of a lunatic has been appointed, or where the committee appointed has been removed, or a committee has interests adverse to the lunatic, a suit may be brought in the name of the lunatic by his next friend, approved by the court. *Bird's committee* vs. *Bird*, 21 Grat. 712. See note (2) to § 64 Story's Eq. Pl. Idiots and lunatics defend a suit by their committees, who are by order of court appointed guardians *ad litem* for that purpose, as a matter of course, in ordinary circumstances. Mitf. Pl., 104. Story's Eq. Pl. 70. A person other than the committee may be appointed guardian *ad litem*. *Ibid.*

SPECIFIC PERFORMANCE. The vendee or his legal representative ought to be made a party to a suit brought by the vendor against a subsequent purchaser from the vendee to recover a

27

balance of purchase money, alleged to be due from the vendee. *Duval* vs. *Bibb*, 4 H. & M. 113.

Where the vendee has died without being able to recover the land sold him, and an action at law is brought against his administrator upon the bond given for the purchase money, the administrator and not the heir of the vendee, will be the proper plaintiff in a suit brought to enjoin the vendor from recovering the purchase money, if a discharge from the obligation to pay such purchase money is all that is sought. *Bullitt's ex'ors* vs. *Songster's adm'ors*, 3 Munf. 54. But if the representatives of the vendee claim compensation for a deficiency, credits for payments and a *conveyance*, and both vendor and vendee have died, the bill should be by *the heirs* as well as the administrator of the vendee against the administrator and heirs of the vendor, so that the court in allowing the compensation and credits, may decree a conveyance from the heirs of the vendor to the heirs of the vendee. In *Humphrey's adm'or* vs. *McClenachan's adm'or, &c.*, 1 Munf. 493, there was a failure to make the heirs of the vendee parties; and the court to get over the difficulty which this omission caused, was compelled to pronounce a decree somewhat anomalous. See also *Champion, &c.* vs. *Brown*, 6 John C. R. 410; 2 Rob. Pr. (old) 273–4.

If a bill is brought by a vendor to compel specific performance, the purchaser being dead, the personal representative is a necessary party, because the personal assets are primarily liable for the debt. *Townsend* vs. *Champerdown*, 9 Price 130. If the bill further seek to enforce the lien for the puchase money on the land itself, the heirs of the purchaser, if it is intestate estate, or the devisees, if it is devised, are necessary parties, *and the personal representative* also; for the heirs and devisees are entitled to relief over and to indemnity from the personal assets. *Smith* vs. *Hibbard*, 2 Dick. 730.

If the purchaser should die and specific performance be sought against the vendor, by the heirs of the purchaser, it is necessary to make the personal representative of the purchaser a party, for the heirs are entitled to have the contract primarily paid or discharged out of the personal assets. *Champion* vs. *Brown*, 6 John. C. R. 402.[65]

If the vendor should die, and his personal representative seek a specific performance against the purchaser, the heir or devisee of

---

[65] But where a mortagee brings a bill to foreclose the mortgage against the heir of the mortgagor, although the mortgage is primarily a debt charged upon the personal assets, yet it is not necessary to make the personal representative of the mortagor a party. Story's Eq. Pl. 175. If the heir would have the benefit of having the personal estate applied in exoneration of the real, he must enforce that right by filing a bill. *Duncombe* vs. *Hanstey*, cited 3 P. Wms. 333, Mr. Cox's note (A.)

the vendor should also be made a party to the bill. *Roberts* vs. *Marchant*, 1 Hare. 547; *Morgan* vs. *Morgan*, 2 Wheat. 297, 298. See *Mott* vs. *Carter's adm'or*, 26 Grat. 127.

It seems now to be established that where an assignee of the vendee sues for a title, the vendor need not be a party if he has parted with all his rights and there is written evidence of the fact. *Edgar* vs. *Donally*, &c., 2 Munf. 387; *Mayo* vs. *Murchie*, 3 Munf. 358; *Pennington* vs. *Hanly*, &c., 4 Munf. 140. This rule was acted on where the suit was not against the vendor, but against one to whom the vendor had conveyed by order of the vendee; the defendant being a purchaser with notice of the plaintiff's claim. *Lambert* vs. *Nanny*, 2 Munf. 196; 2 Rob. Pr. (old) 274.

In *Willard* vs. *Tayloe*, 8 Wal. 557, the purchaser of land had assigned a part interest in the contract to another, and afterwards brought a bill for specific performance in his own name alone. The court decided that the non-joinder of the assignee of the part interest in the contract, presented no obstacle to the decree sought in favour of the original party to the contract. See *Tasker* vs. *Small*, 3 M. & Craig. 69

In a bill for specific performance against a husband for the sale of an estate to the plaintiff, the wife is not a proper party merely because she claims the purchase money and has taken forcible possession of the title deeds and refuses to part with them. *Muston* vs. *Bradshaw*, 15 Sim. 192.

FOREIGN ATTACHMENT. Where there are two obligors, one of whom is in and the other out of the State, and a suit is brought against the absent defendant, the other obligor should be made a party. For if they be joint debtors the absent defendant is entitled to the aid of his co-obligor as well in the defence as in bearing the burden of the decree; and if the absent defendant be the surety of his co-obligor he will be entitled to a decree against that co-obligor. *Loop* vs. *Summers*, 3 Rand. 511. In a creditor's suit by foreign attachment or to marshal assets against heirs residing abroad, the lands having been sold under a decree at the suit of the heirs and the proceeds being in the hands of a commissioner, he should be a party to the creditor's suit as such commissioner, his being a party as administrator of the deceased debtor is not enough. *Carrington & als.* vs. *Didier, Norvell & Co.*, 8 Grat. 260. And if he is not made a party as commissioner and has in fact no knowledge of the object of the creditor's suit, and pays over the proceeds of sale to the heirs under the order of the court whose commissioner he was, he will not be affected by the *lis pendens* of the creditor's suit so as to be held liable to pay the money over again to the creditor. *Ibid.* A. and B. made their bond to C. and it was left in the hands of A. as the agent of C. A. forged an endorsement of it in C.'s name to D. E. sued C., a non-resident, and attached the money due by the bond and got a decree for its payment. D. sued B., one of the obligors, in C.'s name for his (D.'s) benefit. Thereupon B. sought to enjoin the suit. *Held* that E., the attaching creditor of C. or his representative, was a necessary party to B.'s suit. *Jameson* vs. *Deshields*, 3 Grat. 4.

PATENT FOR LAND. When the object of a bill is to prevent the issuing of a patent by the Register of the Land Office, the Register is a proper party in order to effectuate the relief that is to be decreed. *Lyne, &c.* vs. *Jackson, &c.*, 1 Rand. 119.

On a bill to set aside a patent on the ground that it was obtained with a knowledge of a prior entry, the patentee or his representative must be before the court; and if the patentee is assignee of the person who made the second entry with knowledge of the first, then both or their representatives are necessary parties. *Hagan, &c.* vs. *Wardens*, 3 Grat. 315.

If a person who makes an entry on land has knowledge of a previous entry and he assigns his entry to a third person who obtains a patent, the person making the entry, as well as the patentee or their representatives, must be made parties to a suit which seeks to set aside the patent. *Hagan* vs. *Warden*, 3 Grat. 301.

OFFICER NEGLECTING DUTY. The officer who returned the writ and bail bond ought, as well as the plaintiff at law, to be made a party defendant to a bill of injunction filed by the person returned as bail, who denies that he had executed the bond, for the officer is interested in the question in controversy and should be a party, that final and complete justice may be done. *Spottswood* vs. *Higginbotham*, 6 Munf. 313.

Justices who appoint a guardian and take insufficient security from him are not proper parties to a suit for the settlement of his guardian account, nor is the clerk taking such bond a proper party. *Austin* vs. *Richardson*, 1 Grat. 310.

FRAUD. A deed of trust purporting to indemnify one of the parties as to whom the deed is charged to be fraudulent as surety of the grantor for certain debts due to specified creditors, these creditors, as well as those creditors secured directly by the bill, are necessary parties. *Billups* vs. *Sears*, 5 Grat. 31.

To a bill to set aside fraudulent conveyances made by an insolvent debtor, the trustees and *cestuis que trust* in the deeds, the sheriffs of the counties in which the lands lie, and the execution creditors interested in the property should be parties. *Clough* vs. *Thompson*, 7 Grat. 26.

A bill is filed to subject lands to the satisfaction of a judgment after the death of the debtor, and charging fraud in certain conveyances by the debtor to his son. The son having conveyed some of the lands to third persons, all such persons must be made parties to the cause. *Henderson* vs. *Henderson*, 9 Grat. 394.

A defendant, in anticipation of a judgment in an action *ex delicto*, transferred bonds and conveyed his distributive interest in the personal and real estate of his father to avoid payment of the judgment; a bill was filed to subject the property to the judgment. To this bill it was held the obligors in the bonds should be defendants and the decree should go against them respectively for the amount due from each, if the same was still liable to satisfy the plaintiff's judgment. *Greers* vs. *Wright*, 6 Grat. 154.

VENDOR AND VENDEE. See pp. 193, 194, *ante*. L. buys land of D. and T. and gives to each his bonds for his share of the purchase money. The contract is afterwards rescinded; but before this is done D. assigns one of the bonds. On a bill to enjoin a judgment on this bond by the assignee, T. is not a necessary party. *Drake* vs. *Lyons*, 9 Grat. 54.

In a suit to recover a tract of land against a vendee on the ground that the vendor had previously agreed to convey the same land, in a certain event, to the plaintiff, the vendor or his legal representatives should be parties. *Lewis* vs. *Madisons*, 1 Munf. 303.

In a suit for the sale of infant's lands, a sale having been made and confirmed and a conveyance made to the purchaser, the purchaser must be brought before the court as a party before the court will inquire into the validity of the sale. *London* vs. *Echols*, 17 Grat. 15.

Suit to subject land to payment of purchase money; when prior lien-holders necessary parties. *Armentrout's ex'ors* vs. *Gibbons*, 25 Grat. 371. *McClintic* vs. *Wise's adm'ors*, 25 Grat. 448.

On a bill by the administrator of a vendor of land against a vendee who has not received a deed to subject the land to pay the purchase money, the heirs of the vendor should be made parties. *Mott* vs. *Carter's adm'or*, 26 Grat. 127.

See *Stimson* vs. *Thorn*, 25 Grat. 278—suit to rescind a contract of exchange of land.

TRUST DEEDS. See p. 196, *ante*. Story's Eq. Pl., §§ 207–217.

Though a deed of trust secures creditors in several classes, one or more may sue for the benefit of all, to have the trusts executed when the trustees refuse to act. *Reynolds* vs. *Bank of Virginia*, 6 Grat. 174.

One creditor, secured by a deed for the benefit of all the creditors, cannot maintain a bill for the account of the fund without making all the creditors who are preferred and all who are in the same class with himself, parties, either as plaintiffs or defendants.

Murphy vs. *Jackson*, 5 Jones Eq. 11. And it would seem that all the creditors should be made parties to the account as all are interested in the fund. Story's Eq. Pl. 219, *a*.

Upon a bill to set aside a deed of trust to secure a debt, an assignee of the debt is a necessary party; and the debtor and trustee in their answers stating that the debt has been assigned to a certain person, the plaintiff should be required to make him a party if, upon a rule for the purpose, it appears he is such assignee. *Tichenor* vs. *Allen*, 13 Grat. 15.

A deed of trust purported to indemnify one of the parties as to whom the deed was charged to be fraudulent as surety of the grantor for certain debts due to specified creditors, these creditors as well as those secured directly and whose debts were not assailed by the bill, were held to be necessary parties. *Billups* vs. *Sears*, 5 Grat. 31.

To a bill to set aside fraudulent conveyances made by an insolvent debtor, the trustees and *cestuis que trust* in the deeds, the sheriffs of the counties in which the lands lie, and the execution creditors interested in the property should be parties. *Clough* vs. *Thompson*, 7 Grat. 26.

In a bill to recover trust property sold by trustee and for an account, the trustee is a necessary party. *McDaniel* vs. *Baskervill*, 13 Grat. 228.

In *Jones* vs. *Tatum*, 19 Grat. 720, a purchaser at a judicial sale objected, after confirmation of the sale, that a trustee had not been made a party to the suit. The court refused to set aside the sale at the instance of the purchaser.

S. makes an assignment of a policy of insurance on his life to R. for the benefit of the wife of S. and her children. A few days afterwards he conveys the same policy to R. in trust for his wife and her children by him; but if she died without children, the principal to be paid to S.'s children by his first wife. The widow of S. and her infant son file a bill against R. claiming the insurance under the assignment. R. answers and says that he acted under the trust deed, and insists that the children of S. by his first wife are necessary parties. There is a decree on the merits against R. and he appeals. The children of S. by his first wife are necessary parties and the appellate court will reverse the decree for this error, without passing upon the merits. *Richardson* vs. *Davis*, 21 Grat. 706. See *Clark* vs. *Long*, 4 Rand. 452, *Collins* vs. *Lofftus & Co.*, 10 Leigh 5, and *Commonwealth* vs. *Ricks*, 1 Grat. 416.

When a creditor in a trust deed a necessary party. *Kendrick & als.* vs. *Whitney & als.*, 28 Grat. 646.

As to the frame of a suit by a *cestui que trust*, in respect of claims against strangers, as debtors, or liable to the trust, by reason of the misconduct of the trustees, or parties to whom the stranger is primarily liable, see *Lund* vs. *Blanchard*, 4 Hare, 28. Story's Eq. Pl. § 211, note.

Where there are several trustees who are implicated in a common breach of trust, for which the *cestui que trust* seeks relief in equity, it is laid down in a book of authority, that the *cestui que trust* may bring his suit against all of them, or against one of them separately, at his election. Story's Eq. Pl. 213, citing *Walker* vs. *Symonds*, 3 Swanst 75, and other cases. But this doctrine has been strongly denied. See *Munch* vs. *Cockerell*, 8 Sim. 219.

Scheduled creditors under a creditors' deed, who were not parties thereto have been held not necessary parties to a suit by a subsequent incumbrancer to have the moneys out of which it was intended to pay such creditors raised, the trustees being parties. *Powell* vs. *Wright*, 7 Beavan 444.

INSOLVENT DEBTOR. If a debtor who has been discharged under the insolvent act, claim an interest in part of his property, which has been sold by the sheriff, his scheduled creditors are necessary parties. *Tiffany* vs. *Kent*, 2 Grat. 231.

JUDGMENT DEBTOR. G. recovers a judgment against R. and upon a suggestion, obtains a judgment against S. Upon a bill by G. against S.'s executrix to have payment out of his estate, R. is not a necessary party. *Shands's ex'ix* vs. *Grove & als.*, 26 Grat. 652.

BANKING ASSOCIATIONS AND CORPORATIONS. When creditor of a corporation may prosecute his own claim alone. *Barksdale* vs. *Finney*, 14 Grat. 338.

A creditor of the corporation, B., presenting his claim against the successor of B. is not bound to make the creditors of H. (to whom the successor of B. has contracted to pay an annual rent) parties to the suit. *Barksdale* vs. *Finney*, 14 Grat. 338.

Holders of stock claiming to have equitable interests in the property of a corporation, (though not proper parties to a suit to annul such corporation, but for holding such equitable interests,) may be admitted as parties defendant in such a suit to protect their rights. *Wash., Alex. & Georgetown R. R. Co.*, vs. *Alex. & Wash. R. R. Co.*, 19 Grat. 592.

A testator gave money to trustees to establish a school, with power to them to fill vacancies in their body. Several vacancies occurring in the board are filled. The trustees may sue to recover the money; but the school having been incorporated after the suit was brought, the corporation should be made a party and the money should be decreed to be paid to it. *Kelly* vs. *Love*, 20 Grat. 124.

GUARDIAN AND WARD. A guardian is not authorized to file a bill in his own name to obtain possession of his ward's estate, but must file it in the name of the ward by his next friend. *Sillings & als.* vs. *Bumgardner, guardian*, 9 Grat. 273. In this case the plaintiff being interested as husband of one of the distributees of the estate, the court did not dismiss the suit but permitted the plaintiff to amend his bill by striking out the words "guardian of, &c.," (which the court said were mere *descriptio personæ* and did not change the personal character of the suit) and inserting the name of his wife as a co-plaintiff. *Ibid*, 276.

In a suit by a ward against the heirs of his guardian, the sheriff to whom his estate had been committed, his surviving surety and the administrator of his deceased surety, no service was made on a part of the heirs nor on the surviving surety, it was held that no decree could be rendered therein for want of proper parties brought before the court. *Bland* vs. *Wyatt*, 1 H. & M. 543.

A guardian having, when he was appointed, given a bond with sureties, afterwards, without a rule upon him or order of court requiring it, came into court and gave another bond with other sureties. The last bond was held valid and related back to his appointment as guardian and the sureties in the first bond were discharged and were held to be not necessary or proper parties to a bill by the ward against the guardian and his sureties for the settlement of his accounts. *Sayers* vs. *Cassell & als.*, 23 Grat. 525.

PERSONS OF A CLASS SUEING. The difficulty of bringing before the court all persons interested in the subject of a suit has also induced the court to depart from the general rule when the suit is on behalf of many in the same interest and all the persons interested cannot easily be discovered or ascertained, Thus a few creditors may sue on behalf of themselves and the other creditors of their deceased debtor for an account and application of his assets, real and personal, in payment of their demands. Mitf. Pl. 166. [If creditors decline to come in and assert their rights, they may be excluded the benefit of the decree and yet considered as bound by acts done under its authority. Mitf. Pl. 166.] So some of a number of creditors, parties to a trust deed for payment of debts, have been permittted to sue on behalf of themselves and the other creditors for execution of the trust (Mitf. Pl. 167): though in more classes than one, when the trustees refuse to act. *Reynolds* vs. *Bank of Virginia*, 6 Grat. 174. So a legatee is permitted to sue on behalf of himself and other legatees. Mitf. Pl. 167. And so for the application of personal estate amongst next of kin or among persons claiming under a general description as the relatives of a testator or other person, when it may be uncertain who are all the persons answering that description, a bill has been admitted by one claimant on behalf of himself and the other persons equally entitled. Mitf. Pl. 169. And the necessity of the case has induced the court frequently to depart from the general rule, when a strict adherence to it would probably amount to a denial of justice; and to allow a few persons to sue on behalf of great numbers having the same interest. Mitf. Pl. 169, 170.

See Story's Eq. Pl. 105, 106, 207, 207 *a*, 207 *b*.

Several captains of vessels were permitted to unite in one bill to enjoin the sale of their vessels engaged in the oyster trade, to test the constitutionality of the act. *Johnson* vs. *Drummond*, 20 Grat. 419.

PENDENTE LITE PURCHASERS. While a suit for specific execution of a contract against a purchaser was pending the purchaser conveyed the property in trust to secure a debt. The *cestuis que trust* were *pendente lite* purchasers and were not necessary parties to the suit. *Goddin* vs. *Vaughan*, 14 Grat. 102.

PERSONS DEFENDING NUMEROUS. The general rule is that the parties though numerous should all be made parties, but when the number of the parties interested amounts to a great practical inconvenience, or positive obstruction of justice, this excuses their being made, all of them, parties. Story's Eq. Pl. 95–96.

PERSON BEYOND THE JURISDICTION OF THE COURT. This ordinarily excuses his being made a party, and the court will proceed to a decree without him. Mitf. Pl. 164, 31., Story's Eq. Pl., § 78. But the rule is not universal. See Story's Eq. Pl. by Redfield, § 78. *Towle* vs. *Pierce*, 12 Metc. 329. *Vose* vs. *Philbrook*, 3 Story 335. See the doctrine discussed in Story's Eq. Pl., § 81–89.

PERSONS UNKNOWN. See Story's Eq. Pl. 90, 92, 93.

REMAINDERMEN. When not necessary parties. *Summers* vs. *Bean*, 13 Grat. 404. *Cooper* vs. *Hepburn*, 15 Grat. 551.

DOCTRINE OF REPRESENTATION. *Commonwealth* vs. *Levy & als.*, 23 Grat. 21. Calvert on Parties 19, *et seq. Baylor vs. Dejarnette*, 13 Grat. 152.

See as to protection afforded *cestuis que trust* by answer of trustee. *Johnston* vs. *Zane*, 11 Grat. 552.

DEBTOR TO DEBTOR. See Practical Note on the Doctrine of Parties in the United States Courts.

COLLUSION. Certain persons proper parties by reason of collusion. Calv. on Part. 157.

28

MISCELLANEOUS. As a general rule, the court will at any time before the hearing, grant leave to amend where the bill is defective as to parties, or in the mistake or omission of any fact or circumstance connected with the substance of the bill or not repugnant thereto. The amendment may be made by common order before answer or demurrer, and afterwards by leave of the court. *Holland & wife* vs. *Trotter*, 22 Grat. 136.

Mere interest in the question arising out of a collateral liability, does not make one a necessary party. *Austin* vs. *Richardson*, 1 Grat. 310.

In a suit brought by the trustee of a married woman to assert and defend her rights in which a full opportunity was afforded to the *cestui que trust* to protect her rights, it is not necessary that she should be made a party. *Woodson, trustee* vs. *Perkins*, 5 Grat. 345.

It is not necessary in a suit against a surviving obligor, to make parties the personal representatives of two deceased insolvent obligors. *Montague* vs. *Turpin*, 8 Grat. 453.

In a suit by the creditor of a tenant for life (with remainder in fee to his oldest son living at his death,) to subject the land, the life tenant represents the fee and it is not necessary to make a son born pending the suit a party. *Baylor* vs. *Dejarnette*, 13 Grat. 152. See *Faulkner* vs. *Davis*, 18 Grat. 651.

Pendente lite purchasers are not necessary parties. *Goddin* vs. *Vaughan*, 14 Grat. 102; *Price* vs. *Thrash*, 30 Grat. 515.

When in a suit in equity against a corporation to have it declared null, stockholders are not proper parties. *Wash. Alex. & G. R. R. Co.*, vs. *Alex. & Wash. R. R. Co.*, 19 Grat. 592. If the stockholders have equitable interests in the property, they may be admitted as party defendants to protect their interests. *Ibid.*

In the *Commonwealth of Virginia* vs. *Levy & als.*, 23 Grat. 21, Levy in his will gave property to the people of the United States in trust for the establishment of a school, and if the U. S. declined, then on the same trusts to the State of Virginia. The executors of L. instituted a suit in New York, asking for instructions in the administration. To that suit, the U. S. were parties. Held, that the decree in that suit was conclusive upon Virginia, though she was not a party to the suit.

In three actions of debt pending between the executors of W. L. as plaintiffs and N. G. M. as defendant, an agreement for submission to an award was made. The arbitrators intended to decide the case according to law, but had mistaken it and so had erred. The executors declined to oppose the confirmation of the award. The next of kin of W. L. filed their bill in equity to correct the error. Held that the court of equity had jurisdiction and that the next of kin might maintain the suit. *Moore* vs. *Luckess' next of kin*, 23 Grat. 160.

In a suit by T. against H. to rescind a contract for the exchange of land, it appeared that H. had been in possession of his land for twelve years and had paid all the purchase money; but D. from whom he purchased had died, and H. had brought a suit against D's. widow and heirs to have the title made to T. It was error to rescind the contract without having the widow and heirs of D. before the court. *Stimson* vs. *Thorn*, 25 Grat. 278.

To a bill by the administrators of a vendor of land retaining the title to subject it to satisfy a bond given for a part of the purchase money, the holder of another of these bonds assigned by the vendor in his lifetime is a necessary party. *McClintic* vs. *Wise's adm'ors*, 25 Grat. 448.

The sureties of an executor who have been sued to be held liable for his devastavit of the estate of his testator, may maintain a suit to subject the purchasers of the assets from E. who were participants with him in the commission of the *devastavit*, to pay the amount of the assets so purchased by them to the widow and legatee of the testator, in discharge *pro tanto* of their liabilities as the sureties of the executor. And in such case the sureties may and should unite in one suit all the purchasers whom they seek to make liable. *Jones's ex'ors* vs. *Clark & als.*, 25 Grat. 642.

H. and P. were partners, and they made a contract with D. in relation to a business to be conducted by D. After the death of P. his personal representatives and H. as surviving partner, filed their bill against D. to have an account and settlement of the business aforesaid. The bill showed that sometime previous to filing it, H. had assigned all his interest in the firm for proper settlement of accounts, and after paying his partners all he might owe them, the surplus, if any, was to be paid to C. It also appeared from the bill that H. had been declared a bankrupt. Both C. and the assignee in bankruptcy of H. were necessary parties, and a decree made in their absence, against D. will be reversed by the appellate court, though no objection was taken in the court below, for want of parties. *Dabney* vs. *Preston's adm'ors*, 25 Grat. 838.

A bill was filed by a residuary legatee, against an administrator with the will annexed and his sureties T. and H. The administrator was insolvent. C., the son of T., had received assignments of a number of the legacies and claimed them as his own. H. insisted that they belonged to T. and had been purchased at a large discount, the benefit of which he was entitled to share. H. insisted farther that C. should not be paid these legacies until T. or T. and C. should file a cross-bill against him, and thus give him an opportunity to contest C.'s right. It was held that C. was a proper party defendant to the original bill to have his right to the legacies settled; and T. and C. having filed a cross-bill against H. setting up C.'s right to the legacies, that H. could not object to it at the hearing, after having insisted on it; and, farther, that if C. were not entitled to the legacies he should be allowed compensation for purchasing them. *Tarr* vs. *Ravenscroft*, 12 Grat. 642. If one of two sureties of an insolvent administrator purchase up legacies for which the sureties are bound, at a discount, he can only charge his co-surety for his proportion of what he paid for the legacies, and of the expenses of purchasing them. *Ibid.*

A guardian of infants may maintain a suit for partition of real estate held jointly by the infants and adult parties. *Zirkle* vs. *McCue & als.*, 26 Grat. 517.

When the representatives of a deceased maker, and of a deceased endorser, though both die insolvent, should be made parties to a suit by the holder of a negotiable note to subject the estate of a deceased endorser to its payment. *Duerson's adm'or* vs. *Alsop & als.*, 27 Grat. 229.

When the Treasurer of the State is a proper party to suits by holders of insurance policies against the insurance company. *Universal Life Ins. Co.* vs. *Cogbill & als.*, 30 Grat. 72.

When the surviving husband of one of several heirs a proper party for a division of land. *Persinger & als.* vs. *Simmons & als.*, 25 Grat. 238.

155. The following is the form of a demurrer for want of parties in the United States Circuit Court:

Form of Demurrer for want of parties, in United States Circuit Court.

In the Circuit Court of the United States for the —————— Circuit and —————— District of —————— :

The demurrer of A. B. to the bill of complaint exhibited in this court by M. M. against the said A. B. and others:

This defendant, by protestation, not confessing or acknowledging all or any of the matters and things in the said bill of complaint contained to be true, in manner and form as the same are therein set forth, doth demur thereto, and for cause of demurrer showeth that it appears by the complainant's own showing that R. G. therein named is a necessary party to the said bill, inasmuch as it is therein stated, &c. [here recite so much of the statements of the bill as show that R. G. is a necessary party], but yet the said complainant has not made the said R. G. a party to the said bill. Wherefore, and for divers other errors and imperfections, this defendant demands the judgment of this court whether he shall be compelled to make any farther or other answer to the said bill or any of the matters and things therein contained; and prays hence to be dismissed with his reasonable costs in this behalf sustained.

A. B.

Eastern District of Virginia, sct.:

This day personally appeared before me the undersigned, a ——— ———, A. B. and made oath that the foregoing demurrer is not interposed for delay in the suit in which it is filed.

Given under my hand this ——— day of ———, in the year 18—

I, R. A., of counsel practicing in the United States Circuit Court for, &c., do certify that in my opinion the foregoing demurrer of A. B. is well founded in point of law.

R. A.

There will be furnished in the Appendix to this treatise a discussion of the Doctrine of Parties in the United States Circuit Courts.

NOTE ON MAKING IMPROPER PARTIES AND OMITTING PROPER OR NECESSARY PARTIES.

CONSEQUENCE OF MAKING IMPROPER PARTIES. *As plaintiffs:* See *Ouff* vs. *Platell*, 4 Russ. 242, 3 Cond. Eng. Ch. R. 651,

Makepeace vs. *Haythorne*, 4 Russ. 244, 3 Cond. Eng. Ch. R. 652. *The King of Spain* vs. *Michado & als.*, 4 Russ. 225, 3 Eng. Cond. R. 643, *Clarkson & wife* vs. *De Peyster, &c.*, 3 Paige 336. See also *Dickinson* vs. *Davis & als.*, 2 Leigh 401. *As defendants:* See *Brinkerhoff, &c.* vs. *Brown, &c.*, 6 John. C. R. 139, *Bailey* vs. *Inglee, &c.*, 2 Paige 278. See Story's Eq. Pl. §§ 509, 510, 237, 283, 541, 544.

Consequence of making improper parties as plaintiffs. In *Raffity* vs. *King*, Law Journal, Vol. 6 N. S. 93, 1 Keen 619, Lord Langdale said: "As to the objection of John Raffity being made a plaintiff, I am not satisfied it would, under any circumstances, be considered of such importance as to deprive the other plaintiffs of the relief they are entitled to. There have been cases in which the court with a view to special justice, has overcome the difficulty occasioned by a misjoinder of plaintiffs. In the case of *Morley* vs. *Hawke*, before Sir Wm. Grant (cited 2 Younge and Jer. 420) a tenant for life of a fund, at whose instigation and for whose benefit a breach of trust had been committed, was joined with the other plaintiffs to the bill. The defendant objected to any relief being granted in that state of the record; but the objection was overruled, and a decree was made against the defendants, and the offending tenant for life, who was one of the plaintiffs. * * * John Raffity does not appear to have had any interest whatever, and he is a mere formal party. And without determining the effect, if brought forward earlier, I think it is now too late. If the objection had been stated in the answer, the plaintiffs might have obtained leave to amend their bill, and might have made John Raffity a defendant instead of a plaintiff; for which there is the authority of *Aylevin* vs. *Bray*; and in such a case as this, where the objection is reserved to the last moment and even after the argument on the merits, I think it ought not to prevail." See *Dickinson* vs. *Davis & als.*, 2 Leigh 401. In *Dickinson* vs. *Davis & als.*, 2 Leigh 401, there was certainly *scintilla juris* in the daughters of the intestate sufficient to have supported the bill, if the objection had been taken at the proper time. See *Rhodes* vs. *Warburton*, 6 Sim. 717, in which legatees of a testator were joined with the executor as plaintiffs in suing for a debt of the estate and the bill was sustained. *Morley* vs. *Hawke*, 2 Younge and Jer. 420, cited by Lord Langdale as above, may well be questioned as authority. Though the judgment of an eminent judge, Sir Wm. Grant, it seems to be most clearly in conflict with the principles of equity pleading. Before holding the tenant for life as having instigated the breach of trust, and visiting its consequences upon her, she should certainly have had the privilege of replying to the charge, and this was denied her in the state of the pleadings. The plaintiffs should have been required to amend their bill, and make her a party defendant.

Consequence of making improper parties as defendants. The only result flowing from making as defendants improper parties is a dismission of the bill as to them, usually with costs. 2 Rob. Pr. (old) 275. If made after a suggestion by the co-defendants that they are proper parties and in consequence of such suggestion, raised either by demurrer or plea or answer, the costs should be visited upon the defendants making the suggestion: See Code 1873, chap. 167, §§ 22, 23, a statutory provision as to action at law.

CONSEQUENCE OF OMITTING PROPER PARTIES. The plaintiff's bill will not be dismissed, but leave will be given him to amend his bill by adding proper parties, on payment of costs. *Green* vs. *Poole*, 4 Bro. Par. Cas. 122, *Jones* vs. *Jones*, 3 Atk. 111, *Colt* vs. *Lasnier*, 9 Cow. 334.

The Court of Appeals will reverse a decree for the want of necessary parties although the objection was not taken in the court below. *Taylor's adm'or & als.* vs. *Spindle*, 2 Grat. 45. In *Jameson* vs. *Deshield*, 3 Grat. 4, the plaintiff had shown a right to relief against the defendant before the court, though he had omitted necessary parties. The Circuit Court dismissed his bill. The Court of Appeals reversed the decree and sent the cause back, with leave to make the necessary parties.

Demurrer to Part of the Bill or to a Part of the Relief.

In the Circuit Court of the United States for the ——— Circuit and ——— District of ——— :

The demurrer of A. B., defendant to a part of the [*or* to a part of the relief sought by the] bill in equity filed against him in this court by C. D., complainant.

This defendant, by protestation, not confessing or acknowledging all or any of the matters and things in the said complainant's bill to be true, in such manner and form as the same are therein set forth and alleged, as to so much and such part of the said bill as* seeks that this defendant may answer and set forth whether, &c., and whether, &c., and prays, &c. [if relief be prayed; or, if to a part of the relief alone, omit all after asterisk, saying instead, " prays that this defendant may," &c.], doth demur and for cause of demurrer showeth (here state the cause of demurrer). Wherefore, and for divers other errors and imperfections in the said bill, this defendant doth humbly pray the judgment of this honorable court whether he shall be compelled to make any answer to such part of the said bill as is so demurred to as aforesaid, and prays hence to be dismissed, &c., as in the form on p. 184, *ante.*

A. A. M., p. d.

Add certificate of counsel as on page 221, *ante,* and affidavit of party as on page 221, *ante.*

Demurrer to a bill for relief where the plaintiff has no interest in the subject or no title to institute a suit concerning it. [66]

In the Circuit Court of the county of ———— :

[As in form on p. 183 to word " forth," then proceed] doth demur thereto, and for cause of demurrer showeth that the said complainant hath not, as appears by his said bill, made out any title to the relief thereby prayed. Wherefore, &c., (as on p. 184 to the end).

---

[66] Mitf. Pl. 89, 125,

Demurrer for want of privity to a bill for relief by an unsatisfied legatee against a creditor of his testator.[67]

In the Circuit Court of the county of ———— :

[As in form on p. 183 to word "forth," then proceed:] doth demur thereto, and for cause of demurrer showeth that it appears by the said complainant's said bill that there is no privity between the said complainant and this defendant to enable the said complainant to call on this defendant for payment of any debt due to the estate of the said testator from this defendant. Wherefore, &c., (as on p. 184 to the end).

Demurrer to a bill brought for part of a matter only.

Proceed as in section 136, p. 168, to the word "*show*," then say: that the said complainant by his said bill, in order to split the cause and create a multiplicity of suits, seeks only to recover a part of an entire debt thereby stated to be due to him from these defendants; and in respect of other parts of the said debt has, as appears by his said bill, filed another bill of complaint in this honorable court against these defendants. Wherefore, &c., (as in section 136 to the end).

A. A. M., p. d.

If in the United States Circuit Court add affidavit of defendant and certificate of counsel as found on p. 221, *ante.*

---

[67] Mitf. Pl. 129, Willis's Pl. 456.

Demurrer to a bill of interpleader for want of the necessary affidavit.

Proceed as in section 136, p. 168, to the word "*show*," then say: that although the said complainant's said bill is on the face thereof a bill of interpleader and prays that these defendants and the other defendants thereto may interplead together concerning the matters therein mentioned, and may be restrained, by the order and injunction of this honorable court, from proceeding at law against the said complainant touching such matters, yet the said complainant has not annexed an affidavit to his said bill that he does not collude concerning such matters, or any of them, with these defendants and the other defendants thereto, or any or either of them, which affidavit ought, as these defendants are advised, according to the rules of this honorable court, to have been made by the said plaintiff and annexed to the said bill. Wherefore, &c., (as in section 136 to the end).

A. A. M., p. d.

If in United States Circuit Court, add affidavit of defendants and certificate of counsel as found on p. 221, *ante.*

Demurrer to a bill for discovery, in aid of a court which had of itself the power to compel the discovery .required.

Proceed as in section 136, p. 168, to the word "*show*," then say: that the said complainant has not in and by his said bill shewn such a case as calls for the interference of this honorable court, inasmuch as a discovery of the several matters in the said bill contained, could, if necessary, have been obtained in the court in the said bill mentioned, in aid whereof the discovery prayed by the said bill is sought to be enforced by this honorable court from these defendants.[68] Wherefore, &c., (as in section 136 to the end).

A. A. M., p. d.

If in United States Circuit Court, add affidavit of defendants and certificate of counsel as found on p. 221, *ante*.

Demurrer where the discovery would subject the defendant to pains, penalties and forfeitures.

Proceed as in general formula of demurrer p. — *post*, setting forth the cause of demurrer thus: that the said bill seeks to discover how this defendant came by the possession of the bonds therein mentioned, whether it was not by fraud, violence, contrivance or other means, and whether they were not the property of J. B. from whom in the said bill the said bonds are alleged to have been taken by this defendant and others; but this defendant is advised that any discovery of the manner in which such bonds came into this defendant's possession, would or might subject this defendant to fine or imprisonment, and the penalties of the several acts

---

[68] But let it be noticed, that a jurisdiction to compel discovery in equity, in aid of an action at law, is not taken away, simply because in the action at law the statutes now provide that discovery may be compelled.

of the General Assembly of Virginia, entitled &c.
Wherefore, &c., (as in general formula to the end).

J. M. P., p. d.

If in United States Circuit Court, add affidavit of
defendant and certificate of counsel as on p. 221.

*Demurrer to a bill for discovery, the defendant having
no interest in the subject.*[69]

Proceed as in general formula p. 229, and state
the cause of demurrer thus: that the said complainant has not in and by his said bill stated, charged or
shown that this defendant has, or pretends to have,
any right, title or interest in the matters and things
complained of by the said bill or any of them or any
right to call upon this defendant in a court of equity,
for a discovery of the said matters and things or
any of them. Wherefore, &c., (as in general formula, to the end).

J. M. P., p. d.

If in United States Circuit Court, add affidavit of
defendant and certificate of counsel, as on p. 221.

*Demurrer to bill for discovery, when there is no privity
of title between the plaintiff and defendant.*[70]

In the Circuit Court of the county of ———:

As in form on p. 183, to word "forth," then proceed: doth demur thereto and for cause of demur-

---

[69] Mitf. Pl. 185, 188. Story's Eq. Pl. ¿ 312.
[70] Mitf. Pl. 154.

rer showeth that the said complainant has not by his said bill, shown such privity of title, as entitles him in a court of equity, to the discovery from this defendant thereby sought. Wherefore &c., (as on p. 184 to the end).

General formula of demurrer.

In the ——— Court, of the ———.

The demurrer of A. B. defendant to the bill of complaint of C. D. complainant.

This defendant, by protestation, not confessing all or any of the matters and things in the said complainant's bill of complaint contained to be true in such manner and form as the same are therein set forth and alleged, doth demur to said bill, and for cause of demurrer sheweth that &c., [here set forth the cause of demurrer.] Wherefore and for divers other good causes of demurrer appearing in the said bill, the said defendant doth demur thereto, and humbly demands the judgment of this court, whether he shall be compelled to make any farther or other answer to the said bill; and prays to be hence dismissed, with his costs and charges in this behalf most wrongfully sustained.

JOHN G. WILLIAMS, p. d.

If in the United States Circuit Court, add certificate of counsel as follows:

Certificate of counsel.

I, J. G. W., of counsel practicing in the U. S. C. C.

for &c., do hereby certify, that in my opinion, the foregoing demurrer is well founded in point of law.

J. G. W.

And the following affidavit of the defendant:

Affidavit of defendant.

Eastern district of Virginia, sct :

Personally appeared before me this day, the undersigned, a commissioner, &c.; A. B. the defendant named in the foregoing demurrer, and made oath that the said demurrer is not interposed for delay in the suit in which it is to be filed.

Given under my hand, this ——— day of———, 18—.

R. R., comm'r, &c.

155a. The following is the form of a demurrer to a bill*for relief for misjoinder of parties:

Form of demurrer for relief for misjoinder of plaintiff, in Virginia State Courts.

In the Circuit Court of the county of ——— :

[As in form on p. 183 to word " forth," then proceed:] doth demur to the said bill, and for cause of demurrer showeth that it appears by the said bill, that the same is exhibited against this defendant, by Richard M., John B. and Charles C. as complainants, and the said Charles C. has no interest whatever in the matters complained of in the said bill,[71] and the said Charles C. has been improperly joined as one of the complainants in the said bill.[72] Wherefore &c., (as on p. 184 to the end).

Form of demurrer to bill for relief, for misjoinder of defendant, in the Virginia State Courts.

In the Circuit Court of the county of ———:

[As in form on p. 183 to word " forth," then proceed:] doth demur to the said bill, and for cause of demurrer sheweth that it appears by the said bill, that the same is exhibited against the said defendant Moses M. and óne Richard R. and the said defendant Moses M. has no interest whatever in the matters complained of in the said bill, and should not have been joined with the said Richard R. as one of the defendants therein. Wherefore &c., (as on p. 184 to the end).

See Story's Eq. Pl. § 232.

As to demurrers to bills of discovery for misjoinder of parties, see Story's Eq. Pl., §§ 569, 570, 571.

156. Demurrers to original bills have thus far been noticed. Many of the causes of demurrer applying to an original bill apply also to other bills; and distinct causes of demurrer are sometimes found

---

[71] The language used is probably broader than necessary. Though the plaintiff in a bill may have an interest in the subject, yet if he has not a proper title to institute a suit concerning it, a demurrer will hold. Mitf. Pl. 155. See *Edwards* vs. *Edwards*, 1 Jac. R. 335. See also Mitf. Pl. 156, 157.

[72] See *Makepeace* vs. *Haythorne*, 4 Russ. 244; *King of Spain* vs. *Michado*, 4 Russ. 225, 241; *Hunter* vs. *Richardson*, 6 Mad. 89; *Doyle* vs. *Muntz*, 5 Hare 514; Mitf. Pl. 160, 161; Story's Eq. Pl. 232.

in the pleader's not conforming in his draft to the
rules of practice specially applicable to bills other
than original bills. These causes of demurrer will
be noticed when such bills come under discussion in
this treatise.

157. The course of procedure on a demurrer depends on the plaintiff's opinion of its validity. If
he thinks, as the bill stands, the objection is good,
but that he can remove it by restating his case he
may submit to the demurrer and amend his bill. [73]
If he thinks the demurrer bad he may set it down
for argument.[74] If the demurrer is allowed on argument the suit is at an end, unless the demurrer is
confined to a part of the bill or the court give permission to the plaintiff to amend.[75] If the demur-

---

[73] If the plaintiff conceives that by amending his bill he can remove the
ground of demurrer he may do so before the demurrer is argued, on payment
of costs. Mitf. Pl. 215.

[74] Code (1873), chap. 167, § 33, Sess. Acts 1875-6, p. 209. It is stated that
there should not be a joinder to a demurrer in equity.

The reason for this is not perceived. Yet as our statute prescribes in
special terms that when a demurrer is taken the plaintiff may set it down for
argument, it is better to follow the statute So that in using the form found
on p. 129 the language in the note thereto may be omitted.

[75] See 2 Rob. Pr. (old) 302. Mr. Robinson says: " When the demurrer has
been argued upon the merits and the court is of opinion that the equity in
the case, though fully stated, will warrant no decree for the plaintiff, the bill
will be dismissed. *Lyon &c.* vs. *Tallmadge, &c.*, 1 John. Ch. R. 184. And
the defendant will have his costs. 1 R. C. 1819, p. 216, § 100, and p. 257,
§ 58. But if the defect of the bill be in not making proper parties, or in its
prayer for relief, or in the omission or mistake of some fact or circumstance
connected with the substance of the case but not forming the substance itself,
leave is usually granted to amend the bill. Kent, Ch., in *Lyon, &c.* vs. *Tallmadge, &c.*, 1 John. Ch. R. 188. Ordinarily it is considered premature, upon
a general demurrer, wholly to dismiss the bill, unless the complainant's case
is, from his own showing, radically such that no discovery or proof, properly
called for by or founded upon the allegations in the bill, can possibly make it
a proper subject of equitable jurisdiction. *LeRoy* vs. *Veeder, &c.*, 1 Johns.
Cas. 427; *Bleeker & wife*, vs. *Bingham & wife* 3 Paige, 246."

rer is overruled, in the English courts the defendant must make a fresh defence by answer, unless he obtain permission to avail himself of a plea.[76] In the United States Circuit Courts, after the overruling of a demurrer, the defendant is required to answer.[77] In the Virginia State Courts, after the overruling of a plea or demurrer, no other plea or demurrer will be received, but the defendant may, at the discretion of the court, be required to answer the bill forthwith, and in default thereof the bill may be taken for confessed and the matter thereof decreed, or the plaintiff may have an attachment against such defendant or an order for him to be brought in to answer interrogatories.[78]

157a. In general, if a demurrer would hold to a bill, the court, though the defendant answers, will not grant relief upon hearing the cause. There have been, however, cases in which the court has given relief upon hearing, though a demurrer to the relief would probably have been allowed. But the cases are rare.[79]

157 b. *Brief form of demurrer under Virginia statute.* In *Jones's ex'ors* vs. *Clark & als.*, 25 Grat. 642, the Court of Appeals held that under the stat-

---

[76] Adams's Equity 335, 336.

[77] 34th Rule U. S. Supreme Court.

[78] Sess. Acts 1875–6, p. 209. Prior to this statute, the practice of the Virginia State Courts was to enter a rule on the defendant to answer. See Code (1873), ch. 167, § 33.

[79] Mitf. Pl. 108, 3 P. Wms. 150, 12 Mod. 171. See *Underhill* vs. *Van Cortlandt*, 2 John. Ch. R. 339, *Grandin* vs. *Leroy*, 2 Paige's C. R. 509, *United States* vs. *Sturges*, 1 Paine's C. C. R. 526, and *Hawley* vs. *Cramer*, 4 Con. 717.

ute [Code 1873, chap. 167, sec. 31] the form therein prescribed was sufficient. "The defendant says that the bill is not sufficient in law."

157 *c.* The following form may be used:

Demurrer to a bill of discovery, the plaintiff showing no title to it.

Proceed as in section 136, p. 168 to the word "*show*" then say: that the said complainant has not in and by his said bill, shown such a case as calls for any discovery from this defendant as to the several matters in the said bill contained, or as to any of them. Wherefore &c., (as in section 136, to the end).

A. A. M., p. d.

PRACTICAL NOTE TO PRECEDING FORM.

When the attempt is to enforce a legal demand in equity, and the need of a discovery is the alleged ground of equity jurisdiction, and there is no averment in the bill, that the discovery is material and necessary, the bill is demurrable. *Childress & als.* vs. *Morris,* 23 Grat. 802.

II. PLEA.

General nature of pleas.

158. When an objection to a bill is not apparent on the bill itself, if the defendant means to avail himself of the objection he must show to the court the matter which creates it, either by answer or by plea.[80] A plea has been described as "a special

---

[80] In some cases the objection can be taken only by plea. Story's Eq. Pl. 721. In others it may be taken by plea or by answer, and in others, again,

answer showing, or relying upon one or more tnings as a cause why the suit should be either dismissed, delayed or barred."[81]

159. The proper defence by plea is such as reduces the cause, or some part of it, to a single point; and thence creates a bar to the suit, or to that part of it to which the plea applies.[82] It is not, however, necessary that it should consist of a single fact, for though a defence offered by way of plea consists of a great variety of circumstances, yet, if they all tend to one point, the plea may be good.[83] Thus a plea of title deduced from the person under whom the plaintiff claims may be a good plea, although consisting of a great variety of circumstances, for the title is a single point, to which the cause is reduced by plea.[84]

---

it may be taken only by answer. Story's Eq. Pl., § 647, See *Harris* vs. *Pollard*, 3 P. Wms. 348, Cooper's Eq. Pl. 302, as to defence to a bill of reviver by a person who is not entitled to revive; it seems that the defence must be taken by demurrer or by plea and not by answer; yet, if at the hearing it appears that the plaintiff has no title to revive, the bill will be dismissed.

[81] Mitf. Pl. 218, 219. Story's Eq. Pl. §§ 647, 649. *Roche* vs. *Morgell*, 2 Sch. & Lef. 725. Beames's Pl. 1, 11.

[82] Mitf. Pl. 219. See Beames's Pl. 10, 11. 2 Dan. Ch. Pr. (Perk.) 630.

[83] Dan. Ch. Pr. (Perk.) 631. Mitf. Pl. 296. Beames's Pl. 19. 14 Pet. 269.

[84] Mitf. Pl. 296, 297. *Whitbread* vs. *Brockhurst*, 1 Bro. Ch. 404, 415, *note* (9) by Belt.; S. C., 2 Ves. & B. 153, *note*. *Ritchie* vs. *Aylwin*, 15 Ves. 82. 14 Pet. 269. A defendant pleaded to an ejectment bill that he was seized in fee, and that there were no outstanding terms, nor mortgages, nor encumbrances, nor unexpired leases. The plea was held good. *Dawson* vs. *Pilling*, 16 Sim 203. See what is said by Lord Hardwicke in *Chapman* vs. *Turner*, 1 Atk. 54. See, also, *Lard* vs. *Sergeant*, 1 Edw. Ch. 164, and *Ashurst* vs. *Eyre*, 3 Atk. 341, and remark of Beames on last mentioned case. Beames's Pl. 19. In the *State of Rhode Island* vs. *The State of Massachusetts*, 14 Pet. 210, it was held that a plea was bad for duplicity which set up an accord and compromise and also lapse of time as defences. The case is an instructive one on the point of duplicity in pleading.

An allegation, if mere surplusage, will not prejudice a plea in equity by

160. The plea must be perfect in itself, so that if true in point of fact, there may be an end of that part of the cause to which it relates[85] If a creditor, anticipating that a release will be pleaded, charge in his bill that such release was obtained by misrepresentation, coercion and fraud, the defendant who pleads the release, must by his plea deny those charges in the bill which, if true, would avoid the release;[86] and these negative averments must not be involved and argumentative, but direct and issuable.[87]

161. In general, a plea relies upon matters not apparent upon the bill; and in most cases, it is a rule, that where a defendant insists upon matter by plea which is apparent upon the face of the bill, and might be taken advantage of by demurrer, the plea will not hold.[88]

162. Pleas which state matter not apparent upon the bill, are termed *affirmative pleas*, or pure pleas.[89] They usually proceed upon the ground that, admitting the case stated by the bill to be true, the matter suggested by the plea affords a sufficient reason, why the plaintiff should not have the relief he prays or

rendering it multifarious or double. *Claridge* vs. *Hoare*, 14 Ves. 59. Beames's Pl. 20.

[85] See 2 Rob. Pr. (old) 303.

[86] *Allen &c.*, vs. *Randolph, &c.*, 4 John. C. R. 693.

[87] Beames's Pl. 22. See sec. 181, *post.*

[88] Whether an objection to the jurisdiction which appears on the face of the bill can be taken advantage of by plea. See *Varick* vs. *Dodge*, 9 Paige C. R. 149; Cf. Code of Virginia (1873) ch. 167, § 20; See also § 144 of this volume; Beames's Pl. 7.

[89] Beames's Pl. 6.

the discovery he seeks; and when put in, the court in order to save expense to the parties, or to protect the defendant from a discovery he ought not to make, instantly decides upon the validity of the defence, taking the plea and the bill (so far as not contradicted by the plea) to be true.[90]

163. There are pleas, however, which, instead of introducing new facts, merely rely upon a denial of the truth of some matter stated in the bill upon which the plaintiff's right depends. Pleas of this sort are termed *negative pleas*.[91] It was at one time a matter of question how far a negative plea was good. In one case Lord Thurlow overruled the plea on the ground that it was a negative plea;[92] but this decision was afterwards doubted by the judge himself,[93] and since that time frequent instances have occurred in which negative pleas were allowed.[94] It is now well settled that such pleas are good.[95]

---

[90] Mitf. Pl. 295; Dan. Ch. Pr. (Perk.) 631. Of course affirmative pleas must be proved by the defendant. If his affirmative plea is entirely unsupported by the evidence, and at the hearing of the cause, he makes default, the complainant will be entitled to a decree against him in the same manner as if the several matters charged in the bill, had been confessed or admitted. *Dew, &c.* vs. *McMichael*, 2 Paige C. R. 345

[91] 2 Dan. Ch. Pr. (old) 98.

[92] *Newman* vs. *Wallis*, 2 Bro. C. C. 142.

[93] *Hall* vs. *Noyes*, 3 Bro. C. C. 488.

[94] 2 Dan. Ch. Pr. (old) 98, 99, Mitf. Pl. 230, 231, Beames's Pl. 123–128. Mr. Beames has given the reasoning upon which the doctrine is maintained. See what is said in Story's Eq. Pl., §§ 668, 669, and notes.

[95] *Faulder* vs. *Stuart*, 11 Ves. 302, *Shaw* vs. *Ching*, 11 Ves. 305, *Drew* vs. *Drew*, 2 Ves. & B. 159, 163, *Sanders* vs. *King*, 6 Mad. 61, S. C. 2 Sim. & Stu. 276, *Thring* vs. *Edgar*, 2 Sim. & Stu. 274, Mitf. Pl. 230, 233, 2 Dan. Ch. Pr. (old) 98, Story's Eq. Pl. 668.

164. There is another species of plea, often occurring in the books, which is not, strictly speaking,
either a plea affirming new matter or negativing the
plaintiff's title as alleged in the bill, but one which
re-asserts some facts stated in the bill and which the
bill seeks to impeach, and denies all the circumstances which the plaintiff relies upon as the ground
upon which he seeks to impeach the fact so set up.
Thus, where a bill is brought to impeach a decree on
the ground of fraud used in obtaining it, the decree
may be pleaded in bar of the suit, with averments
negativing the charges of fraud.[96]

165. Whatever the nature of the plea, whether
affirmative or negative or of the anomalous[97] character above alluded to, the matter pleaded must reduce
the issue between the plaintiff and the defendant to
a single point.[98] If a plea is double, _i. e._ tenders
more than one defence as the result of the facts
stated, it will be bad.[99] Although this is the general

---

[96] Dan. Ch. Pr. (old) 98, 99.   Beames's Pl. 3, 6.   Mitf. Pl. 230, 231.

[97] Mitford calls them _anomalous_ pleas—Mitf. Pl. 239.   Beames calls them
" incongruous "—Beames on Pl. 6.

[98] _Goodrich_ vs. _Pendleton_, 3 John. C. R. 384, _Milligan_ vs. _Milledge & wife_, 3
Cranch 220.

[99] 2 Dan. Ch. (old) 102; See Mitf. Pl. 295, 296; _The State of Rhode Island_
vs. _the State of Massachusetts_, 14 Pet. 210, 259. On duplicity in pleas, see
Beames's Pl. in Eq. 10–18, 27–32, 172–177, and the following cases: _Whit-
bread_ vs. _Brockhurst_, 1 Bro. Ch. 404; _Beachcroft_ vs. _Beachcroft_, cited 14 Ves.
63; _Wood_ vs. _Strickland_, 14 Ves. 66; _Didier_ vs. _Davison_, 10 Paige C. R. 515;
Nobkisson vs. _Hastings_, 4 Bro. Ch. 253; S. C. 2 Ves. Jr. 84; _Goodrich_ vs.
Pendleton, 3 John. Ch. 426; _Cooth_ vs. _Jackson_, 6 Ves. 12, 17; _Watkins_ vs.
Stone, 2 Sim. 49; _Cowne_ vs. _Douglass_, McC. & Younge, 321; _King_ vs. _Ray_,
11 Paige 239; _Corp. of London_ vs. _Corp. of Liverpool_, 3 Anst. 738; _Robertson_
vs. _Lubbock_, 4 Sim. 161; _Saltus_ vs. _Tobias_, 7 John. Ch. 214; _Bogardus_ vs.
Trinity Church, 4 Paige C. R. 178. " Every plea must rest the defence upon

rule there are cases in which it will be relaxed, where great inconvenience would result to the defendant from denying him this privilege,[100] but whenever a defendant desires to put in a double plea he must obtain an order for leave to do so.[101]

166. The rule, however, that a defendant cannot plead several matters must not be understood as precluding a defendant from putting in several pleas to different parts of the same bill; it merely prohibits his pleading a double defence to the whole bill, or to the same portion of it.[102]

166 a. Two pleas are sometimes allowed to the same matter in a bill.[103] Thus, a plea that the plaintiff is not heir, as asserted in the bill, and a plea of the statute of limitations have been allowed to be

---

a single point, which of itself creates a bar to the matter to which it is pleaded If it be multifarious, if for example it set up the statute of limitations, and allege that the plaintiff who sues as the personal representative, is not such representative, it will be condemned for mixing together this different and discordant matter." 2 Rob. Pr. (old) 303, citing *Goodrich* vs. *Pendleton*, 3 John. Ch. R. 384; *Milligan* vs. *Milledge & wife*, 3 Cranch. 220.

[100] 2 Dan. Ch. Pr. (old) 104; *Verchild* vs. *Paul*, 1 Keen's Ch. R. 87, 90; *Van Hook* vs. *Whitlock*, 3 Paige C. R. 409.

[101] 2 Dan. Ch. Pr. (old) 105. In *Kay* vs. *Marshall*, 1 Keen's Ch. R. 190, 197, Lord Langdale, M. R., on motion, gave the defendant, who was disputing the validity of a patent, leave to plead, *first*, that the invention was not useful and *secondly*, that it was not new.

[102] 2 Dan. Ch. Pr. (old) 105. In the Virginia State Courts it seems that under the ruling in *Basset's adm'or* vs. *Cunningham's adm'or*, 7 Leigh 402, a defendant in equity may plead several pleas to the same parts of the bill. See Code of Va. (1873), ch. 167, § 24.

Where the plaintiff seeks relief as to more than one subject the defendant may put in a plea to each subject. *Emmott* vs. *Mitchell*, 14 Sim. 432.

[103] Story's Eq. Pl. 657, *Gibson* vs. *Whitehead*, 4 Mad. 241, *Hardman* vs. *Ellames*, 5 Sim. 640, S. C. 2, *Mylne & Keen* 732, *Kay* vs. *Marshall*, 1 Keen 190, 197, *Saltus* vs. *Tobias*, 7 John. Ch. 214.

pleaded together.[104] Under the ruling in *Basset's adm'or, &c.* vs. *Cunningham's adm'or*, 7 Leigh 402, it can hardly be doubted that in the Virginia State Courts the defendant may plead two pleas to the same matter in a bill.

167. *When plea should be accompanied by an answer.* Sometimes it is necessary that a plea should be supported by an answer.[105] The occasion of this rule will explain when such support is necessary and to what extent it is required. It originated thus : It is a well established rule that whenever a bill, or part of a bill, the substantive case made by which may be met by a plea, brings forward facts which, if true, would destroy the effect of the plea, these facts must be negatived by proper averments in the plea ; otherwise they will be considered as admitted and the defendant will be thus deprived of his defence.[106] A plea, however, cannot be excepted to ; and as it is not necessary that an averment in a plea should do more than generally deny the fact in the bill, the plaintiff might, if no answer were required from the defendant in addition to his plea, be deprived of the indefeasible right which he has to examine the defendant upon oath as to all the matters of fact stated

---

[104] *Bampton* vs. *Birchall*, 4 Beavan 558.

[105] 2 Rob. Pr. (old) 299, 303.

[106] 2 Dan. Ch. Pr. (old) 112. To a bill alleging matters of evidence of the plaintiff's right as within the sole knowledge of the defendant which would enable the plaintiff to support his cause, as the plaintiff has a clear right to the discovery of such matters, the plea should be accompanied by an answer; for it would be against the principle entitling the plaintiff to such discovery if the defendant could, by merely denying in his plea the existence of the claim, deprive the plaintiff of the means of proving its validity. 2 Dan. Ch. Pr. (old) 113, and cases cited.

in the bill which are necessary to support his case.[107]
To obviate this result the rule has been adopted that
if there is any statement or charge in the bill which
affords an equitable circumstance in favor of the
plaintiff's case against the matter pleaded (such as
fraud or notice of title) that statement or charge
must be denied by way of answer as well as by averment in the plea.[108]

---

[107] Wigram on Disc. 21. The answer in such case is strictly matter in support of the plea and also proof, the discovery of which the plaintiff is entitled
to, notwithstanding the plea. The plea, without it, cannot correctly be said
to be a complete answer to the bill, for, though it repels the facts stated by
the plaintiff, it does not repel the right to a discovery of the facts from the
conscience of the defendant. Mitf. Pl. 239, 244. This explains the reason
why no answer need accompany a pure plea, for that being an averment of
matter *dehors* the bill, it is impossible that it can be required by any discovery
of those matters. It would not be responsive to the bill. Story's Eq. Pl.
§ 673, n. 1.

[108] 2 Dan. Ch. Pr. (old) 112. See *Haythorp* vs. *Hook*, 1 Gill & J. 270, *Smith*
vs. *Hunt*, 2 Rob. R. 206. It is competent for a defendant to plead to a bill
claiming as co-heiress to her deceased father, that the intestate was not seized
or possessed of any real estate whatever at the time of his decease, without
accompanying the plea with an answer. *Postgate* vs. *Barnes*, 9 Jur. N. S.
456, S. C. 11 W. R. 356. In *Sims* vs. *Lyle*, 4 Wash. C. C. R. 303, 304, Mr.
Justice Washington said: " A plea being nothing more than a special answer
to the bill, setting forth and relying upon some one fact, or a number of
facts, tending to one point, sufficient to bar, delay or dismiss the suit, it would
be a vice in the plea to cover any other parts of the bill than such as concern
the particular subject of the bar; its office being to reduce the cause or some
part of it to a single point and thus to prevent the expense and trouble of an
examination at large. It is true that all facts essential to render the plea a
complete defence to the bill so far as the plea extends must be averred in it or
it will be no defence at all. If the plea be to the whole of the bill it must
cover the whole; that is, it must cover the whole subject to which the plea
applies and which it professes to cover or it will be bad. As, if the bill respect the house and so many acres of land, and the plea, professing to cover
that charge, pleads only in bar as to the house. But if it cover the whole
subject and contains a full defence in relation to it there is no necessity, nor
would it be proper, to notice other parts of the bill not involved in the subject to which the plea applies. If the plea be only to a part of the bill the
rest of the bill ought to be answered, or else the court would consider the

167 a. The thirty-second rule of the United States Supreme Court requires that in every case in the United States Circuit Courts in which the bill specially charges fraud or combination a plea to such part must be accompanied by an answer fortifying the plea and explicitly denying the fraud and combination and the facts on which the charge is founded.

---

parts not embraced by the plea, or answered, as true. But there is no instance where the plea contains in itself a full defence to the bill that an answer is necessary, unless it is rendered so in order to negative some equitable ground stated in the bill for avoiding the effect of the anticipated bar ; as where fraud, combination, facts intended to avoid the force of the statute of frauds, or to bring the plaintiff within some of the exceptions to the act of limitations, as the one or the other of these defences may be expected. And in those and similar cases the defendant is bound, not only to deny those charges in his plea, but to support his plea by an answer, also denying them fully and clearly."

When, for example, a release is pleaded, the defendant denying the statements of the bill that it was obtained by misrepresentation, coercion and fraud, should accompany his plea by a full answer and discovery as to every equitable circumstance charged in the bill to avoid that release. So where the defendant relies on the statute of limitations and there are circumstances stated in the bill which, if true, would take the case out of the statute, a pure plea of the statute will be no bar unless the plea be accompanied by an answer meeting those circumstances particularly and precisely, and either denying them or destroying their force. *Goodrich* vs. *Pendleton*, 3 John. C. R. 384, *Kane* vs. *Bloodgood, &c.*, 7 John. C. R. 134, S. C., 8 Cowen 360. The rule, however, does not render it necessary for the defendant to deny positively in the answer matters of which it cannot be presumed he has any personal knowledge. It is sufficient for him to deny such matters according to his knowledge, information and belief. *Bolton* vs. *Gardner*, 3 Paige 273. See also *Kane* vs. *Bloodgood, &c.*, 7 John. Ch. 134, S. C., 8 Cowen 360.

When the plea of the statute of limitations is bad because it is not accompanied by an answer supporting it, and the court overrules the plea and orders the defendant to answer, liberty will be given him to insist on the benefit of the statute in his answer. *Goodrich* vs. *Pendleton*, 3 John. C. R. 394, *Saltus* vs. *Tobias, &c.*, 3 Paige 346. And, sometimes, when a plea is overruled for want of an answer to support it, the court will permit it to stand for an answer as far as it goes, with liberty to the complainant to except. *Orcutt* vs. *Orms*, 3 Paige 459, *Kirby, &c.* vs. *Taylor, &c.*, 6 John. C. R. 254.

168. In *Hartt* vs. *Corning*, 3 Paige C. R. 569, Chancellor Walworth said, that when it is unnecessary to support the plea by an answer the plea is not considered as evidence in behalf of the defendant as to any facts stated therein, and does not require the testimony of more than one witness to contradict it, even where it negatives a material averment in the bill.[109]

169. Mr. Hare[110] classifies the cases in which it is necessary to support a plea by an answer as follows: 1st. Those in which the plaintiff admits the existence of a legal bar and charges some equitable circumstances to deny its effect,[111] and 2nd. Those

---

[109] Sometimes it is in the power of a defendant to support his plea by the bill of the plaintiff and the documents filed with it. This was the case in *Lane's ex'ix* vs. *Ellzey*, 6 Rand. 661. The bill was to foreclose a mortgage which was given to secure the principal money, with interest, *and rent* of the mortgaged premises. This appeared by the bill and the deed and agreement filed with it. Issue was joined on the plea of usury but no depositions were taken on either side. The Court of Appeals of Virginia was of opinion that the bill and documents furnished such evidence in support of the plea that it must be taken as true, unless some explanation compatible with the pleadings had been adduced on the other side. No such explanation being given, the plea was sustained and the bill dismissed.

[110] Hare on Disc. 30.

[111] The limits to which the plea and answer extend respectively, in the first class of cases, are plainly marked—such as those of pleas put into bills brought to impeach a decree on the ground of fraud used in obtaining it, Mitf. Pl. 199, to set aside a release, Ibid. 213, or an award, Ibid. 211, or to open a stated account, Ibid. 211, or to avoid the effect of a judgment, Ibid. 208. In all these cases the bill admits the existence of a fact which if taken alone would be conclusive against the plaintiff, and then points out the particular circumstances upon which the plaintiff relies to overcome the anticipated bar; with regard to these the principles of equity require a discovery, and an answer in support of the plea is necessary. See 2 Dan. Ch. Pr. (old) 114, Hare on Disc. 33. Whether the bar is introduced by way of substantive averment or suggested as a pretence set up by the defendant the defendant should answer. *Roche* vs. *Morgill*, 2 Sch. & Lef. 721. If, how-

in which the plaintiff does not admit the existence of any legal bar, but states some circumstances which may be true and to which there may be a valid ground of plea, together with other circumstances which are inconsistent with the substantial validity of a plea.[112]

170. *When plea should be accompanied by an answer as to deeds, papers, &c., charged to be in defendant's possession.* When the bill states a case for the plaintiff and charges that the defendant has in his possession documents from which the matters aforesaid in the bill mentioned, or any of them, would appear, and the defendant pleads a pure affirmative plea not denying any part of the plaintiff's case, he will not be required to answer—indeed he ought not to answer as to the possession of the documents, because the documents being only charged in the bill to be of importance as proving the plaintiff's case, which the defendant by his plea does not controvert, the production of the documents would be unnecessary.[113]

---

ever, the plaintiff introduces the fact which constitutes the bar in the form of a pretence and meets it by a naked denial, without stating any circumstances to disprove it, the defendant may merely plead the fact without supporting his plea by an answer. Hare on Disc. 30.

[112] As a general rule, where no ostensible bar is admitted by the bill to exist, and yet the defendant would plead in bar to the bill, he must distinguish those facts which, if true, would not invalidate or disprove his plea and plead to the relief and discovery sought as to them, and then answer to the facts which, if true, would disprove or invalidate his plea; and also to those matters which are specially alleged as evidence of such facts. Hare on Disc. 34. See *Bayley* vs. *Adams*, 6 Ves. 598, *Whitchurch* vs. *Bevis*, 2 Bro. C. C. 559, *Morison* vs. *Turnour*, 18 Ves. 175, *Spunier* vs. *Fitzgerald*, 6 Ves. 548, *Evans* vs. *Harris*, 2 Ves. & B. 361, *Crow* vs. *Tyrell*, 2 Mad. 409, *Baillie* vs. *Sibbald*, 15 Ves. 185, *Roche* vs. *Morgell*, 2 Sch. & L. 721, *Jones* vs. *Davis*, 16 Ves. 262, *Salkeld* vs. *Science*, 2 Ves. 107.

[113] *MacGregor* vs. *East India Company*, 2 Sim. 452, Dan. Ch. Pr. (Perk.) 646.

171. Wherever the bill states or charges any facts which are inconsistent with the defendant's plea, or which would take the plaintiff's case out of the operation of it, and charges that the defendant has in his possession documents from which the mattters in the bill mentioned would appear, then it will be necessary to accompany the plea by a discovery of the documents in the defendant's possession.[114]

172. With respect to negative pleas, if a plaintiff indicates by his bill that he requires an answer as to documents alleged to be in the defendant's possession, in proof of his title, the defendant must make the discovery.[115] If the negative averments of the plea be as to matters not alleged to be the acts of the defendant, or if from the nature of the case he cannot be supposed to have any personal knowledge of the subject, it is sufficient for him to deny the facts charged upon his belief only.[116]

173. An answer in support of a plea is no part of the defence; the defence is the matter set up by the plea, the answer is that evidence which the plaintiff has a right to require and to use to invalidate the defence made by the plea.[117]

174. *Answer in aid of a plea.* There are cases in

---

[114] *Emerson* vs. *Harland*, 3 Sim. 499, *Hardman* vs. *Ellames*, 5 Sim. 240, S. C. 2 M. & K. 732, Dan. Ch. Pr. (Perk.) 646.

[115] Dan. Ch. Pr. (Perk.) 647; in order "to negative the negative plea." *Hardman* vs. *Ellames*, 2 M. & K. 744.

[116] *Bolton* vs. *Gardner*, 3 Paige 278, *Hartt* vs. *Corning*, 3 Paige 566, *Drew* vs. *Drew*, 2 V. & B. 159.

[117] Mitf. Pl. 199 (n) h, 241, Dan. Ch. Pr. (Perk.) 647, Story's Eq. Pl., § 671.

which a defendant may support his plea by an answer touching matters not charged in the bill. Thus, in the case of a plea of purchase for valuable consideration the defendant may deny notice in his answer as well as in his plea, because by so doing he does not put anything in issue which he would cover by his plea from being put in issue. He may also, by this means, put upon the record any fact which tends to corroborate his plea so as to enable him afterwards to prove it. An answer of this sort is termed an answer *in aid* or *in subsidium* of the plea.[118]

175. *When plea overruled by answer.* It was at one time quite important so to draw an answer as not to overrule the plea already put in by the defendant, but the learning on this subject has now become of little practical utility, either in the Virginia State Courts or in the United States Circuit Courts.[119] In the former the decision in *Bassett's adm'or, &c.* vs. *Cunningham's adm'or,* 7 Leigh 402, permitting a defendant in equity to demur and plead to the same matter in a bill is believed to extend the privilege to him to answer and plead to the same matter;[120] and in the latter, the United States Circuit Courts, the practice is now regulated by the 37th rule of the United States Supreme Court, which declares that " no demurrer or plea shall be held bad and over-

---

[118] Mitf. Pl 237, Beames's Pl. Eq. 77, Dan. Ch. Pr. (Perk.) 648, 649.

[119] And this is true also in the English Court of Chancery since the 37th Order of August, 1841, which is identically alike the 37th Rule of the United States Supreme Court mentioned in the text.

[120] Prof. Minor refers to Code of 1873, ch. 179, sec. 1, in connection with *Bassett's adm'or* vs. *Cunningham's adm'or,* 7 Leigh 402, 4 Min. Inst. 1169, 1170.

ruled upon argument, only because the answer of the defendant may extend to some part of the same matter as may be covered by such demurrer or plea." Reference, however, may be had, on this subject, to the cases cited in the note.[121]

176. *Pleas of matters arising after filing oj the bill.* As a matter of course where such matters operate a full discharge from the claim of the plaintiff asserted in the bill they may be pleaded. It is said that the bankruptcy of the plaintiff does not cause an abatement[122]; the suit, however, becomes defective.[123]

177. *The plea to be not only single, but to an issuable point.* The plea should not only reduce the cause to a single point but it should also be such a point as is issuable, and also such as is material to delay, dismiss or bar the bill; for if the issue tendered is immaterial it can never finally dispose of the cause.[124]

---

[121] *Fergusson* vs. *O'Harra*, Pet. C. C. 493, *Bolton* vs. *Gardner*, 3 Paige C. R. 273, *Lacraft* vs. *Dempey*, 4 Paige C. R. 124, *Bogardus* vs. *Trinity Church*, 4 Paige C. R. 178, *Bangs* vs. *Strong*, 10 Paige C. R. 11, *Summers* vs. *Murray*, 2 Edw. Ch. 205, *The Bank* vs. *Dugan*, 2 Bland 254, *Episcopal Church* vs. *LeRoy*, Riley Ch. 156, *Saddler* vs. *Glover*, 1 B. Monr. 53. When the statute of limitations was pleaded to a bill which did not require an answer to support the plea and there was an answer notwithstanding which overruled the plea, it was held that if the plea be good in substance, as to the whole or any part of the relief sought, the court would permit the plea to stand as a part of the answer, or would allow the defendants the full benefit of insisting upon the statute in their answer. *Sanger & wife* vs. *DeMeyer, &c.,* 2 Paige 577.

[122] *Lee* vs. *Lee*, 1 Hare 617, 621. See Beames's Pl. 294–9.

[123] Story's Eq. Pl. 329. As to remedying this and other defects mentioned in this section see subsequent sections of this work.

[124] Beames's Pl. Eq. 20, 21; *Morison* vs. *Turner*, 18 Ves. 175.

And a plea is bad if it raises by averment an issue not raised in the bill.[125]

178. All matters essential to bring the defence to a single point, should be stated on the face of the plea, so that the court may at once decide whether the defence made by the plea, is a bar to the case made by the bill, or to that part of it which the plea seeks to cover.[126] And the plea must cover effectually all it professes to answer whether it be the whole or only a part of the bill. Thus, where a defendant to avoid putting in an account, pleaded to all the relief and some of the discovery sought, and the plaintiff was entitled to some of the relief which the plea did not specifically meet, it was held that it covered too much and was overruled.[127]

179. *The plea should exclude intendments.* The plea should exclude intendments which would otherwise be made against the pleader,[128] for the rule in equity as at law is, *ambiguum placitum interpretari debet centra proferentem.*[129]

Therefore, if there is any charge in the bill which is an equitable circumstance in favour of the plaintiff's case against the matter pleaded, such as fraud or notice of title, the court will intend the matters so charged against the pleader, unless they are met by averments in the plea.[130]

---

[125] *Emmett* vs. *Mitchell,* 14 Sim. 432.

[126] Mitf. Pl. 222; Dan. Ch. Pr. (Perk.) 637.

[127] *Hewit* vs. *Hewit,* 8 Law T. N. S. 630, see sec. 160.

[128] Mitf. Pl. 222; Dan. Ch. Pr. (Perk.) 638. Story's Equity Pl. ₹ 665.

[129] Beames's Pl Eq. 26.

[130] Mitf. Pl. 241; Story's Eq. Pl. 684; Dan. Ch. Pr. (Perk.) 638; See *Hony* vs. *Hony,* 1 S. & S. 568. The rules stated in sections 178, 179 were laid down

180. Whenever fraud or collusion or any other matter is specifically charged in the bill, in such manner that if true, it would obviate the bar arising from the matter pleaded, it must be negatived by averment in the plea, as well as by answer in support of the plea.[181]

181. The plea should be direct and positive and not state matters by way of argument, inference and conclusion which have a tendency to create unnecessary prolixity and expense.[132] Thus where there was a charge of facts as constructive notice of the plaintiff's title in a bill and the defendant in his plea averred that to the best of his knowledge and belief, he had not any notice, either constructive or actual, the plea was bad; the defendant should have denied

---

by Daniell in the several editions of his work in illustration of the necessity of averments in pleas. The use of such averments in pleas may be briefly stated to be, to introduce facts not stated in the bill, to negative allegations in the bill calculated to overrule the plea, and to supply the want of a rejoinder (in the old practice.) Averments may be *affirmative*, such as those which are not suggested by any matter upon the face of the bill inconsistent with the matter pleaded, but which are necessary to render the matter pleaded a complete bar; or *negative*, contradicting any statement or charge in the bill which, if uncontradicted, would do away with the effect of the matter pleaded. Dan. Ch. Pr. (Perk.) 638, 639; Mitf. Pl. 122; *Bicknell* vs. *Gough,* 3 Atk. 558. Sometimes, both affirmative and negative averments occur in the same plea, as in pleading a purchase for valuable consideration, and denying notice.

If the matters charged in the bill are in substance fully and clearly denied, it ·may be sufficient to support the plea, although all the circumstances charged in the bill may not be precisely answered. Story's Eq. Pl 684.

[131] 2 Dan. Ch. Pr. 112; Dan. Ch. Pr. (Perk.) 639; *Hoare* vs. *Parker*, 1 Bro. C. C. 578; S. C. 1 Cox 224; *Devie* vs. *Chester*, Mitf. Pl. 223. note y. See *Fish* vs. *Miller*, 5 Paige R. 26; Story's Eq. Pl. 684.

[132] Beames's Pl. Eq. 21, 22; *Jerrard* vs. *Saunders*, 2 Ves. Jr. 187, S. C. 4 Bro. C. C. 322; *Boone* vs. *Chiles*, 10 Pet. 179, 210–13.

the facts charged in the bill, from which constructive notice was deducible and not have assumed to himself the province of the court, to whom it belongs to draw the conclusion.[133] He should also have denied the notice positively, fully and precisely, even though it were not charged on the other side.[134] But where the facts are not charged to be within the defendant's own knowledge, as if they occurred in the time of his testator or ancestor, there it will be sufficient to negative the averment according to his best knowledge and belief.[135]

Different grounds of pleas.

182. A plea may be either to the relief or to the discovery, or to both. If it is a good plea to the relief, it will be also good to the discovery; in the same manner that a demurrer which is valid as to the relief prayed is, as has been mentioned, good to the discovery sought by the bill.[136]

183. The usual arrangement of pleas in equity is, 1, to the jurisdiction of the court; 2, to the person of the plaintiff or defendant, and 3, in bar of the suit. This is the plan adopted by Lord Redesdale.[137] Mr. Beames adds a fourth, viz: pleas to the bill.[138]

---

[133] Ibid. *Galatian* vs. *Cunningham*, 8 Cowen 361; Story's Eq. Pl. 662, 805, 806.

[134] *Galatian* vs. *Cunningham*, 8 Cowen 361; Story's Eq. Pl. ¿ 697; *Boone* vs. *Chiles*, 10 Pet. 179, 210–13.

[135] *Bolton* vs. *Gardner*, 3 Paige 273; *Hartt* vs. *Corning*, 3 Paige 566; Story's Eq. Pl. 662, 664.

[136] Dan. Ch. Pr. (Perk.) 649.

[137] Mitf. Pl. 219.

[138] Beames's Pleas in Equity, 57.

Mr. Beames's arrangement is as follows: 1. Those pleas which are commonly called "pleas to the jurisdiction," which do not usually proceed the length of disputing the right of the plaintiff in the subject of the suit, or allege any disability on the part of the plaintiff to prosecute the suit, but simply assert that the court of chancery[139] is not the proper court to take cognizance of those rights. 2. Pleas to the person which do not dispute the validity of the rights which are made the subject of the suit, or deny that the court has jurisdiction over them; but they assert that the plaintiff is incapacitated to sue, or that the defendant is not the person who ought to be sued. 3. Pleas to the bill which do not dispute the validity of the right made the subject of the suit, or contend that the court has not generally jurisdiction over it, nor do they allege that the plaintiff is under any disability to sue, or that the defendant ought not to be sued; but they assert that the suit, as it appears on the record, is defective in not answering the purposes of complete justice, or ought not for some other reason to proceed. 4. Pleas in bar, distinguished from all other pleas in admitting the jurisdiction of the court and not disputing the ability of the plaintiff to sue and the liability of the

---

[139] In Virginia this language should be modified, for in suits in equity, as in suits at common law, the jurisdiction is controlled by the Statute, Code 1873, Ch. 165, §§ 1, 3, and it not unfrequently happens that one court of equity has jurisdiction where another has not. The language in the text might thus be changed so as to make it applicable to Virginia—"these pleas commonly called pleas to the jurisdiction, which simply assert that the subject matter of the bill is not within the jurisdiction of a court of equity, or is not within the jurisdiction of the court of equity in which the suit is brought."

defendant to be sued; and tacitly conceding that there are none of these objections to the suit which constitute the grounds of pleas to the bill, but alleging matter which, if true, destroys the claim made by the suit, and by showing that the right made the subject of the suit has no existence, or that it is vested in the defendant, put an end to all litigation concerning it.[401]

184. *Pleas to the jurisdiction.* The generality of cases in which a court of equity has no jurisdiction cannot easily be so disguised in a bill as to avoid demurrer, but there may be instances to the contrary, and in such cases a plea of the matter necessary to show that the court has no jurisdiction will hold.[141]

185. When the plea is filed in a court of general jurisdiction nothing shall be intended to be out of its jurisdiction which is not shown to be so.[142] It is requisite, therefore, in a plea to the jurisdiction in courts of general jurisdiction both to allege that the court has not jurisdiction and to show by what means it is deprived of it[143]; it is requisite, also, to show what court has jurisdiction, and if the plea omits these requisites it is bad in point of form.[144]

186. It is laid down in the English books that only one plea shall be admitted to the jurisdiction,[145]

---

[140] Beames's Pleas in Eq., 57, 65.

[141] Mitf. Pl. 222. See note 139 to § 183, *ante.*

[142] Mitf. Pl. 224, 1 Ves. 204, 2 Ves. 357.

[143] Mitf. Pl. 224, 2 Bro. C. C. 291–301, 1 Ves. Jr. 371.

[144] Mitf. Pl. 224, 1 Vern. 59, 1 Ves. 202, 1 Dick. 122. See *Hortons* vs. *Townes,* 6 Leigh 58.

[145] Dan. Ch. Pr. (Perk.) 653.

and it is supposed that this rule will certainly apply to cases in the Circuit Courts of the United States. Whether it will apply to pleadings in the Virginia State Courts will depend upon the construction of the statutes cited in the note.[146]

187. An English law-writer lays down the rule in reference to the objection to jurisdiction in these broad terms: "An objection on the ground of jurisdiction must be taken either by demurrer, or plea, before answer, otherwise the court will entertain the suit, although the defendant may object at the hearing, unless it is a case in which no circumstance whatever can give the court jurisdiction."[147] The reader is referred on this subject to previous pages of this work cited in the note.[148]

188. *Pleas to the person.* These are usually divided into such as regard the person of the plaintiff and such as regard the person of the defendant. *As to the person of the plaintiff*, the following: 1, Alienage; 2, Outlawry[149]; 3, Infancy; 4, Coverture; 5, Idiocy or Lunacy; 6, Bankruptcy or Insolvency; 7, Pleas that the plaintiff does not sustain the character he

---

[146] Code 1873, ch. 167, §§ 20, 24, 33. Section 33 of ch. 167 of the Code of 1873 enacts that "a plaintiff in equity may have any plea or demurrer set down for argument. If the same be overruled no other plea or demurrer shall afterwards be received, but there shall be a rule upon the defendant to answer the bill." This is sufficiently clear where the defendant files but one plea to the jurisdiction in the first instance; but suppose he offers two pleas to the jurisdiction at the same time, claiming to do so under sec. 24 of the same chapter, would the court permit the two pleas to be filed? The writer doubts as to the answer the court would give to the question.

[147] Dan. Ch. Pr. (Perk.) 579.

[148] Pp. 177–181.

[149] See Code 1873, ch. 201, § 28.

assumes. *As to the person of the defendant*, the pleas are more limited than those to the person of the plaintiff, for it seems to be a rule at law that persons disabled to sue cannot plead their own disabilities when they are themselves sued,[150] and this rule is equally applicable to proceedings in courts of equity in all cases in which the suit seeks to compel the performance of a duty by the party[151]; but the rule that a person under disabilities cannot plead his own disqualification will not extend to cases where the disqualification is only partial, *e. g.*, a woman sued as a *feme sole* may plead that she is covert[152] A defendant may also plead that he is not the person he is alleged to be, or does not sustain the character he is stated to bear—such as heir, executor, or administrator.[153] He may also show that he is not sole heir, executor or administrator.[154] He may plead that he has not that interest in the subject of the suit which can make him liable to the demands of the plaintiff.[155]

---

[150] Beames's Pleas in Eq 122.

[151] 1 Dan. Ch. Pr. (1846) 255. See *Turner* vs. *Robinson*, 1 S. & S. 3, as to pleading disabilities of defendant in proceedings *in rem*. "In such cases," as Daniell truly remarks, "the plea amounts to no more than a plea of want of interest in the subject matter of the bill." 2 Dan. Ch. Pr. (1846) 142.

[152] Beames's Pl. Eq. 130.   [153] Mitf. Pl. 191.

[154] Beames's Pl. Eq. 130. This plea, however, partakes more of the nature of a plea for want of parties than of a plea to the person. 2 Dan. Ch. Pr. (old) 143.

[155] Mitf. Pl. 191. A witness to a will was made a defendant to a bill brought by the heir at law, and the bill charged a pretence of interest by the defendant. A demurrer to the bill was overruled; but the court said that the defence of want of interest might be pleaded. *Plummer* vs. *May*, 1 Ves. 426. See *Cartwright* vs. *Hately*, 3 Bro. C. C. 239, S. C. 1 Ves. Jr. 293. A plea of want of interest in the defendant is proper only in cases in which the defendant cannot satisfy the suit by general disclaimer. Mitf. Pl. 191.

189. *Pleas to the bill.* The defendant may plead: 1. That there is another suit already pending for the same matter,[156] or 2. That the bill as framed is insufficient to answer the ends of complete justice. This objection generally arises from want of sufficient parties to the bill.[157]

190. The pleas of the pendency of another suit, of want of parties, and of splitting up or multiplying suits do not apply to a bill of discovery.[158] Perhaps the plea for multifariousness would lie to such a bill,[159] and perhaps, too, the objection that the parties are not the same in the suit in equity as in the suit at law, in aid of which the discovery is sought, may be pleaded[160]; and so if the defendant in the bill of discovery was not a party to the suit at law.[161] The plea that the value of the matter in controversy is beneath the dignity of the court would also seem to be a good ground of a plea to the discovery.[162]

191. *Pleas in Bar.* Whatever destroys the plaintiff's suit and disables him forever from recovering may be pleaded in bar.[163] Pleas in bar are usually arranged: 1, Pleas of Statutes; 2, Pleas of matters

---

[156] As to the mode of procedure on the plea mentioned in the text, see 2 Dan. Ch. Pr. (old) 144-150, Dan. Ch. Pr. (Perk.) 656-662.

[157] See 2 Dan. Ch. Pr. (1846) 150, 151, Dan. Ch. Pr. (Perk.) 662.

[158] Story's Eq. Pl., § 820, 610, Cooper's Eq. Pl. 208, 209, Beames's Pl. in Eq. 273, 274, Hare on Disc. 124-6, Mitf. Pl. 200, 280.

[159] Story's Eq. Pl., § 820.

[160] Story's Eq. Pl., § 820, 610. *Glynn* vs. *Soares*, 3 M. & K. 450, 469-472.

[161] Story's Eq. Pl., § 820 and cases cited.

[162] Story's Eq. Pl., § 820, 500, 502. Cooper's Eq. Pl. 193. *Smets* vs. *Williams*, 4 Paige 364.

[163] Beames's Pl. in Eq. 160.

of record or as of record in the court itself or in some other court, and 3, Pleas of matters *in pais*.[164]

192. *Pleas of Statutes.* Any statute, public or private, which may be a bar to the demands of the plaintiff may be pleaded with the averments necessary to bring the case of the defendant within the statute and to avoid any equity which may be set up against the bar of the statute,[165] *e. g.* the statute of limitations,[166] the statute against frauds and perjuries,[167] and the statute against usury,[168] &c.

193. A plea of a statute must be put in upon oath, for although the statute itself is matter of record, the averments necessary to bring the case within it are matters *in pais*, which must be supported by the oath of the party.[169]

194. *Pleas of matters of record or as of record.* Pleas which consist of matters recorded or as of re-

---

[164] Beames's Pl. Eq. 160. Cooper's Pl. 251. See Lord Redesdale's arrangement, Mitf. Pl. 192.

[165] Mitf. Pl. 274.

[166] The statute of limitations cannot be pleaded to a trust. Dan. Ch. Pr. (Perk.) 666 and cases cited. See *Norton* vs. *Turville*, 2 P. Wms. 144, and *Jones* vs. *Scott*, 1 R. & M. 255, *Burke* vs. *Jones*. 2 V. & B. 275, 2 Dan Ch. Pr. (1846) n. to p. 155. See *Tazewell* vs. *Whittle*, 13 Grat. 329, as to the measure of strictness required in relying on the statute in equity.

[167] Thus to a bill for specific performance, there being no agreement in writing. Mitf. Pl. 265, Dan. Ch. Pr. (Perk.) 681, Story's Eq. Pl. 671; or to a bill to enforce a parol variation of a written contract, *Jordan* vs. *Sawkins*, 1 Ves. Jr. 402, unless the variation amounts to a mere waiver of a term in the agreement. *Ibid.* As to party's admitting parol agreement by answer and yet insisting on benefit of statute, see Dan. Ch. Pr. (Perk.) 682, n. 1, Story's Eq. Pl. 763.

[168] *Lane* v. *Ellzey*, 4 H. & M. 504. S. C., 6 Rand. 661.

[169] Dan. Ch. Pr. (Perk.) 683. *Wall* vs. *Stubbs*, 2 Ves. & B. 354. 1 Smith's Ch. Pr. 232.

cord in the court itself, or some other court of equity, or in some court not a court of equity, may be pleaded in bar;[170] e. g. a decree or order of the court by which the rights of the parties may have been determined, or another bill for the same matter dismissed.[171]

195. It has been held that a decree against a mortgagor, and order of foreclosure enrolled, will not be a bar to a bill by intervening encumbrancers though the mortgagee had no notice of their encumbrances.[172]

196. A decree not in its nature final or afterward made so by order will not be a bar.[173] A decree of any court of equity in its nature final or made so by subsequent order may be pleaded in bar of the new suit.[174]

197. The plea proceeds upon the ground that the

---

[170] Dan. Ch. Pr. (Perk.) 683.

[171] Mitf. Pl. 237. And this even if the party bringing the new bill were an infant at the time of the former decree, for a former decree enrolled can only be altered upon a bill of review   Dan. Ch. Pr. (Perk.) 683. The dismission can only be pleaded in bar if the dismission was upon hearing or was not in terms directed to be without prejudice. Mitf. Pl. 194. *Perine* vs. *Dunn*, 4 John Ch. 142, Story's Eq. Pl. 793, and cases cited. Dan. Ch. Pr. (Perk.) n. 5, p. 683, 684. But it must be understood that discussion of the merits when the dismission was had is not necessary; if the dismissal had been merely for want of evidence, the decree would be a bar to another suit. *Jones* vs. *Nixon*, 1 Younge 359. *Quære*—whether a mere default at the hearing resulting in dismissal is sufficient. *Pickett* vs. *Loggan*, 14 Ves. 232.

[172] *Merrit* vs. *Westerne*, 2 Vern. 663. See Mitf. Pl. 194.

[173] Mitf. Pl. 194. *Senhouse* vs. *Earle*, 2 Ves. 450. See *Neafee* vs. *Neafee*, 7 John Ch. 1. Story's Eq. Pl. § 791.

[174] Mitf. Pl. 245. *Fitzgerald* v. *Fitzgerald*, 5 Bro. P. C. 567. *Jones* vs. *Nixon*, 1 Younge 359. *Ferguson* vs. *Miller*, 5 Ham. 460. *Hughes* vs. *Blake*, 6 Wheat 453.

same matter was in issue in the former suit, and as every plea that is set up as a bar must be *ad idem*,[175] the plea should set forth so much of the former bill and answer as will show that the same point was then in issue.[176]

198. Pleas of matters of record or as of record, other than pleas of decrees of courts of equity, are mentioned in the English books as embracing: 1, Fines; 2, Recoveries; and 3, Judgments at Law. The two first-named have no application in this country. As to the last-named, judgments at law, their force and effect as a bar to a suit in equity for the same matter, it is believed, is as great here as in England.

199. A judgment which has finally determined the rights of the parties may be pleaded in bar to a suit in equity [177]; and this, whether the judgment be of a court of competent jurisdiction in this or in any other country.[178] Of course the bar of the judgment may be avoided by showing fraud, mistake or surprise.[179]

---

[175] Lord Hardwicke in 2 Atk. 603.

[176] Dan. Ch. Pr. (Perk.) 685. *Child* vs. *Gibson*, 2 Atk. 603. *Bk. of Michigan* vs. *Williams*, Harring Ch. 219. *Cates* vs. *Loftus*, 4 Monroe 439.

[177] Dan. Ch. Pr. (Perk.) 687 and cases cited. *Hunt* vs. *Terril*, 7 J. J. Marsh. 68, 70. Story's Eq. Pl. 780–782.

[178] Dan. Ch. Pr. (Peck) 687. But the court must have full jurisdiction to determine the rights of the parties. *Gage* vs. *Bulkeley*, 3 Atk. 215.

[179] See *Williams* vs. *Lee*, 3 Atk. 223, *Samuda* vs. *Furtado*, 3 Bro. C. C. 70, 71· The following Virginia cases are cases in which fraud, surprise or accident was the ground of relief against a judgment at the instance of the plaintiff in equity: *King* vs. *Smith & als.*, 2 Leigh 157. *Poindexter* vs. *Waddy*, 6 Munf. 418. *Lee* vs. *Baird*, 4 H. & M. 453. *West's ex'or* vs. *Legwood*, 6 Munf. 491. *Hord* vs. *Dishman*, 5 Call. 279. *Mayo* vs. *Bentley*,

200. *Pleas in bar of matters in pais.* Pleas in bar,
of matters *in pais* only, are principally: 1, a stated
account; 2, a release; 3, an award; 4, an agreement; 5, a title founded either on adverse possession
or on a will or conveyance, or other instrument
affecting the rights of the parties; 6, a purchase for
valuable consideration without notice of the plaintiff's title.[180]

201. *Plea of a stated account.* A plea of a stated
account is a good bar to a bill for an account,[181] for
there is no rule more strictly adhered to in a court of
equity than this, that when a defendant sets forth a
stated account he shall not be compelled to go upon
a general one.[182]

202. In support of the plea it must be shown to
have been final.[183] The defendant who pleads a stated
account must show that it was in writing, and likewise the balance in writing, or at least set forth what

---

4 Call. 528. *Price's ex'or. vs. Fuqua's adm'or*, 4 Munf. 68. *Knifong vs. Hendricks*, 2 Grat. 212. *Foushee vs. Lea*, 4 Call. 285. *White vs. Washington*
5 Grat. 645. *Rust vs. Ware*, 6 Grat. 50. See pp. 92–94 of this work.

[180] There are other pleas of this character, *e. g.*, a plea of accord and satisfaction, and others of a kindred nature. *Brown vs. Perkins*, 1 Hare 564, 570.

[181] Mitf. Pl. 258. *Dawson vs. Dawson*, 1 Atk. 1. *Chappedelaine vs. Diche-
naux*, 4 Cranch 306. And *a fortiori*, says Mr. Justice Story, a plea of a
settled account. Story's Eq. Pl., § 798. Story's Eq. Jur., § 527.

[182] *Sumner vs. Thorp*, 2 Atk. 1, Cooper's Eq. Pl. 277, *Taylor vs. Haylen*,
2 Bro. C. C. 310, *Johnson vs. Curtis*, 3 Bro. C. C. 266, *Carmichael vs. Carmichael*, 2 Phil. 101, 1 Story's Eq. Jur. § 527.

[183] *Dawson vs. Dawson*, 1 Atk. 1. A *stated* account properly exists only
where the accounts have been examined and the balance admitted as the true
balance between the parties without having been paid. Story's Eq. Pl. 798.
When the balance thus admitted is paid the account is deemed a *settled* account. *Endo vs. Caleham*, 1 Young 306, *Capon vs. Miles*, 13 Price 767, *Weed
vs. Small*, 7 Paige 573, Story's Eq. Pl., § 798.

the balance was.[184]   Errors excepted in an account
will not prevent its being a stated account,[185] nor is it
necessary to a stated account that it should be signed
by the parties.[166]

203. A verbal statement of an account and a receipt in full given for the balance then agreed to be
due have been held bad as a plea in bar to a bill for
opening the account, if there have been mistakes in
the transactions.[187]

204. A general release of all demands, *not under
seal*, may be pleaded as a stated account.[881] Signature to the account is not necessary; it is enough if
the account has been delivered and acquiesced in for
a considerable length of time,[189] but the mere delivery
of an account will not constitute a stated account
without some evidence of acquiescence affording
sufficient legal presumption of the fact.[190]

205. A defendant pleading a stated account must,

---

[184] Dan. Ch. Pr. (Perk.) 690, Story's Eq. Pl. § 798, *Burk* vs. *Brown*, 2 Atk.
399, *Sewell* vs. *Bridge*, 1 Ves. 297.

[185] *Johnson* vs. *Curtis*, cited, 2 Bro. C. R. 310; 3 Bro. Ch. R. 266, and Mr.
Belt's notes.

[186] *Willis* vs. *Jernegan*, 2 Atk. 251, 252.

[187] Cooper's Eq. Pl. 277, 278, Mitf. Pl. 259, 260.   *Phelps* vs. *Sproule*, 1
Mylne & Keen, 231.

[188] 2 Dan. Ch. Pr. (1846) 189, For. Rom. 57.

[189] *Murray* vs. *Toland*, 3 John. Ch. 569, *Freeland* vs. *Heron*, 7 Cranch 147,
Consequa vs. *Fauning*, 3 John. Ch. R. 587, *Wilde* vs. *Jackson*, 4 Paige 481,
Willis vs. *Jarnegan*, 2 Atk. 252.

[190] *Irvine* vs. *Young*, 1 S. & S. 333.   It has been said that among merchants
it is looked upon as an allowance of an account current, if the merchant who
receives it does not object to it in a second or third post.   *Sherman* vs. *Sherman*, 2 Vern. 276.   See *Tickel* vs. *Short*, 2 Ves. 239.

whether fraud be charged or not, aver that the stated account is just and true to the best of his knowledge and belief.[191] There should be, also, an averment in the plea, when such is the fact, that the vouchers have been delivered up.[192]

206. Of course if specific errors or fraud be charged in the bill for the purpose of impeaching the account, they must be denied by averments in the plea as well as by answer in support of the plea.[193]

207. Fraud in the settlement of accounts is sufficient to open the whole account,[194] and this has been done after the expiration of twenty-three years, and when the party who was guilty of the fraud was dead.[195] Where errors or mistakes exist in the account, the party will be permitted to surcharge and falsify them.[196] The distinction between opening

---

[191] Dan. Ch. Pr. (Perk.) 691, Anon. 3 Atk. 70 ; and see *Hankey* vs. *Simpson*, 3 Atk. 303, *Daniel* vs. *Taggart*, 1 Gill & John. 311, *Schwarz* vs. *Wendell* Harring. Ch. 395, Mitf. Pl. 260, 4 Min. Inst. 1160.

[192] Mitf. Pl. 260, *Willis* vs. *Jernegan*, 2 Atk. 252.

[193] Mitf. Pl. 261, *Phelps* vs. *Sproule*, 1 M. & K. 231.

[194] *Vernon* vs. *Vawdry*, 2 Atk. 119 ; *Matthews* vs. *Wallwyn*, 4 Ves. 125 ; *Beaumont* vs. *Boultbee*, 5 Ves. 485, 7 Ves. 599 ; S. C. 11 Ves. 358 ; *Allfrey* vs. *Allfrey*, 1 Mac. & Gor. 87; 1 Story's Eq. Jur., § 523 ; Story's Eq. Pl. 801, 802 ; *Barrow* vs. *Rhinelander*, 1 John. Ch. 550 ; *Baker* vs. *Biddle*, 1 Bald. 394 ; *Bainbridge* vs. *Wilcocks*, 1 Bald. 536, 540. Even though there be a bond. *Gray* vs. *Washington*, Cook 321 ; and though the bill contains no direct averment of fraud, if it appear in the proofs ; *Farnam* vs. *Brooks*, 9 Pick. 212.

[195] See *Matthews* vs. *Wallwyn*, 4 Ves. 118 (note *b*) ; *Botifuer* vs. *Weyman*, 1 McCord Ch. 161 ; and cases cited in Dan. Ch. Pr. (Perk.) 692, n. 1.

[196] *Vernon* vs. *Vawdry*, 2 Atk. 119. The burden of showing errors is on him who receives an account without objection. *Chapedelaine* vs. *Dechenaux*, 4 Cran. 203 ; Dan. Ch. Pr. (Perk.) 692, n. 2. In the case of transactions between trustee and *cestui que trust*, or guardian and ward (*Brownell* vs. *Brownell*, 2 Bro. C. C. 62), or between solicitor and client (*Matthews* vs. *Wallwyn*, 4 Ves. 125), the court allows a greater latitude.

the whole account and allowing surcharge and falsification is important. In an account opened the whole of it may be unravelled, and the parties will not be bound by deductions agreed upon between them on taking the former account,[197] but when the party has liberty to surcharge and falsify, the *onus probandi* is always on him; for the court takes it as a stated account and establishes it, with the privilege of showing omissions which is called *surcharging*, and of showing wrong charges which is called *falsification*,[198] both, however, by proof on his side.[199]

208. When parties are at liberty to surcharge and falsify, they are not confined to mere errors of fact, they may take advantage of errors in law,[200] and when one party is allowed to surcharge and falsify the other may do so too.[201]

209. *Plea of release.* A defendant may plead a release in bar of the bill,[202] and this will apply to a bill praying that the release may be set aside.[203] To be an effectual bar to an account however, the release must be under seal; otherwise, it must be pleaded as a stated account only.[204] In the plea the english books say, and Mr. *Justice Story* repeats, on american authority, that the defendant must set

---

[197] *Osborne* vs. *Williams*, 18 Ves. 379, 382.

[198] 1 Story's Eq. Jur. 525.

[199] *Pit* vs. *Cholmondely*, 2 Ves. 566.

[200] *Roberts* vs. *Kuffin*, 2 Atk. 112.

[201] 1 Mad Eq. 144.

[202] Mitf. Pl. 261; *Brown* vs. *Swadlin*, 1 Atk. 294; *Roche* vs. *Morgill*, 2 Sch. & Lef. 721.

[203] Mitf. Pl. 261.

[204] Mtf. Pl. 261; Story's Eq. Pl., § 796.

out the consideration upon which it was made.[205]   If
the consideration of the release is impeached by the
bill, the plea should be assisted by averments covering the ground upon which the consideration is so
impeached.[206]

210. *Plea of award.*   An award may be pleaded
in bar to a bill which seeks to disturb the matter submitted to arbitration.[207]   It may likewise be pleaded
to a bill to set aside the award and open the account,[208] and it is not only a good defence to the
merits of the case, but likewise to the discovery
sought by the bill.[209]

211. A mere covenant or agreement to refer disputes to arbitrators cannot be pleaded in bar to a

---

[205] Mitf. Pl. 261; For. Rom. 57. See *Roche* vs. *Morgell.* 2 Sch & Lef. 728;
Story's Eq. Pl. 797; 1 Story's Eq. Jur. 523, 527; *Capon* vs. *Miles*, 13 Price
767; *Phelps* vs. *Sproule*, 1 Myl. & K. 231; *Parker* vs. *Alcock*, 1 Younge &
Jerv. 432; *Fish* vs. *Miller*, 5 Paige 26; *Allen* vs. *Randolph*, 4 John. Ch. 693;
Bolton vs. *Gardner*, 3 Paige 273.

[206] Mitf. Pl. 261; *Salkeld* vs. *Science*, 2 Ves. 107-8; Story's Eq. Pl. 796,
797; *Parke* vs. *Alcock*, 1 Younge & Jerv 432; *Fish* vs. *Miller*, 5 Paige 26;
Allen vs. *Randolph*, 4 John. Ch. 693; *Bolton* vs. *Gardner*, 3 Paige 273; *Peck*
vs. *Burgess*, Walk. Ch. 485.

[207] *Tillenson* vs. *Peat*, 3 Atk. 529; *Farrington* vs. *Chute*, 1 Vern. 72.

[208] Mitf. Pl. 260.

[209] Mitf. Pl. 260; *Tillenson* vs. *Peat*, 2 Atk. 529; Story's Eq. Pl., § 803.
See *Rowe* vs. *Wood*, 1 Jac. & W. 315; 2 Bligh P. C. 505, for a case in which
the agreement was entered into after the bill had been filed; and see 1 Dan.
Ch. Pr. (1846) 192. *Dryden* vs. *Robinson*, 2 S. & S. 529, was a case in which
the award was made under an agreement entered into after the bill was filed,
to refer the whole subject-matter of the suit to an arbitrator. It was held
that such an award might be pleaded to the bill; but all the parties to the
suit not being parties to the award, although the plaintiff was a party to it,
and the prayer of the bill being for the execution of trusts in a deed under
which some of the parties to the suit were interested, who were not parties to
the award, the plea of the award was ordered to stand for an answer with
liberty to except.

bill.[210]   If the bill impeach the award on the grounds
of fraud, corruption or mistake, these charges should
be denied by averments in the plea and by answer
in support of it and every other matter stated in the
bill as a ground for impeaching the award should be
so denied.[211]

212. *Plea of a final agreement.*   While a mere
covenant or agreement to refer disputes to arbitrators cannot be pleaded, the reason of the rule being
that such an agreement is merely executory, when
the agreement entered into between the parties is
final and settles the whole matter it may be pleaded
in bar to a bill.[212]   An agreement to put an end to a
suit must be final not only as between the parties to
the bill to which it is pleaded, but it must be final
as to all the parties compromised by it.[213]

213. *Plea of Title.*   A defendant's title paramount to the plaintiff's title may be pleaded,[214]
whether founded on long peaceable possession or on
a will or on a conveyance[215] or otherwise.

214. *Plea of length of time and adverse possession.*
Length of possession is a good subject of a plea.[216]
When from the statement in the bill there appears

---

[210] Dan. Ch. Pr. (Perk.) 694, n. 8, and 695, n. 1, 2, 3.

[211] Mitf. Pl. 261. As to duties of arbitrators, when they are made parties
to a bill charging them with corruption and partiality, see Dan. Ch. Pr.
(Perk.) 695, 298, 299.

[212] 2 Dan. Ch. Pr. (old) 193; Dan. Ch. Pr. (Perk.) 695.

[213] 2 Dan. Ch. Pr. (old) 194; Dan. Ch. Pr. (Perk.) 695. See *Wood vs.
Rowe*, 2 Bligh P. C. 595; and *Rowe vs. Wood*, 1 Jac. & W. 315.

[214] Prac. Reg. 328; Story's Eq. Pl., § 811.

[215] Dan. Ch. Pr. (Perk.) 696.

[216] Prac. Reg. 328; Dan. Ch. Pr. (Perk.) 696.

to have been a possession adverse to it of above twenty years without any allegation of disability the defendant may demur,[217] but when the title is not so stated, the defendant must plead the facts necessary to shew the existence of the adversary possession;[218] and a mere general allegation in the bill that there have been disabilities arising from infancy or coverture will not be sufficient to invalidate such a plea.[219]

215. After a great lapse of time courts of equity will raise a presumption of some legal or equitable extinguishment of the adverse title, if the circumstances of the case will enable them to support it.[220]

216. A bill was filed for the payment of a rent charge; the defendant pleaded twenty-six years possession of the premises without accounting for or paying over to the plaintiff any part of the rents and profits. The plea was allowed.[221]

216 a. The time at which the plea of the statute of limitations begins to run in a case of fraud or mistake will in equity be held to be from the time the discovery of the mistake or fraud first became

---

[217] *Cholmondely* vs. *Clinton*, 1 T. & R. 107; *Blewitt* vs. *Thomas*, 2 Ves. Jr. 669.

[218] Dan. Ch. Pr. (Perk.) 696, 697

[219] Story's Eq. Pl. 814, 815; *Blewitt* vs. *Thomas*, 2 Ves. Jr. 669, 671; Cooper's Eq. Pl. 288; Beames's Pl. Eq. 247, 248. See the plea in Beames's Pl. in Eq. 331–333. As to form of plea of adverse possession, when the possession is derivative, see Dan. Ch. Pr. (Perk.) 697; *Hardman* vs. *Ellames*, 2 M. & K. 732. See also *Jerrard* vs. *Sanders*, 2 Ves. Jr. 187.

[220] *Cholmondely* vs. *Clinton*, 2 Jac. & W. 163; *Blewitt* vs. *Thomas*, 2 Ves. Jr. 669, 671.

[221] *Baldwin* vs. *Peach*, 1 Younge & Col. 453.

known and not from the time the original transaction took place.[222]

217. *Plea of will.* A will may also be pleaded in bar to a bill brought on a ground of equity by an heir at law against a devisee, to turn the devisee out of possession.[223] But a will cannot be pleaded to a bill by an heir at law praying for production of documents, and an injunction to restrain the defendants from setting up legal impediments, in an action of ejectment commenced by him against them.[224]

218. *Plea of conveyance.* Upon a bill filed by an heir against the person claiming under a conveyance from the ancestor, the defendant may plead the conveyance in bar of the suit,[225] and when a bill was filed by persons claiming under a will to set aside a conveyance made by the testator on the ground of fraud, and the defendant pleaded a conveyance by the testator, before the date of his will, of the estate which the plaintiffs claimed, the plea was allowed.[226]

219. In all cases it is necessary, whether the title be derived from adverse possession, or from a will or conveyance, to show that it had a commencement anterior to that of the plaintiff's title as shown by the bill; a title posterior to the plaintiff's title will

---

[222] Story's Eq. Pl. 815 *a*, 754; *Brookshank* vs. *Smith*, 2 Younge & Col. 58. See Story's Eq. Pl. 8138 *a*, 14.

[223] Mitf. Pl. 263. See Story's Eq. Pl., § 812; Willis's Eq. Pl. 559; Anon. 3 Atk. 17.

[224] Dan. Ch. Pr. (Perk.) 6.

[225] Mitf. Pl. 263, 264.

[226] *Howe* vs. *Duppa*, 1 V. & B. 511, 513.

not avail unless it be in some way connected with it.[227]

220. *Purchase for valuable consideration without notice.* There are cases, however, in which a conveyance may be insisted upon, though posterior in point of date to the plaintiff's title. In such cases, it is necessary to the validity of the plea that the conveyance should have been for a valuable consideration, and that at the time it was perfected, the defendant, or the person to whom it was made, should not have had notice of the plaintiff's right.[228] A plea of this kind is called a 'plea of purchase for valuable consideration without notice,' and is founded on the principle, that when the defendant has an equal claim to the protection of a court of equity to defend his possession, as the plaintiff has to the assistance of the court to assert his right, the court will not interpose on either side.[229]

221. Pleas of this character abound in the books of reports. When we come to consider the form of such pleas, we shall place in the practical notes to the forms references to many of the cases in which such pleas were filed.[230]

222. *Pleas to bills of discovery.* The grounds of these pleas are—1. Pleas to the jurisdiction; 2. Pleas to the person; 3. Pleas to the bill, or frame of the bill; 4. Pleas in bar, properly so called.[231]

---

[227] *Hungate* vs. *Gascoigne*, 1 R. & M. 698; *Jackson* v. *Rowe*, 4 Russ. 514; 2 Dan. Ch. Pr. (old) 198.

[228] Either actual or constructive notice.

[229] Mitf. Pl. 274; Dan. Ch. Pr. (Perk) 698–703; Story's Eq. Pl. 805–810.

[230] § 243, *post.*

[231] See what is said in § 190, *ante.* Story's Eq. Pl. 817.

223. *Pleas to jurisdiction in bills of discovery.* These properly apply when the plaintiff's case is such as not to entitle him to a discovery in his favor, although it is differently and falsely stated in the bill.[232] Among the objections to such bills are these—that the subject of the suit is of a political nature; that another court is competent to give the discovery; that the tribunal, or the cause, is not such that the court will aid by a discovery;[233] and that the plaintiff has no title or interest in the suit.[234]

224. *Pleas to the person in bills of discovery.* These are either to the person of the plaintiff; that he has no right or title or ability to call on the defendant for the discovery, or to the person of the defendant; that the defendant is not liable or compellable to make the discovery.[235]

225. If a claim of interest is alleged by the bill against a person who has no interest in the subject matter, he cannot by demurrer protect himself from a discovery, he must either plead or disclaim.[236] The plea denying interest in such a case must be supported by an answer.[237]

---

[232] Mitf. Pl. 282.

[233] For example, if it be of a criminal nature. Beames's Pl. Eq. 252, 254.

[234] Story's Eq. Pl. 817; and cases cited. Mitf. Pl. 154, 231, 233, 282.

[235] Beames's Pl. Eq. 254, 255; Mitf. Pl. 228–230, 232, 233; Story's Eq. Pl. 818.

[236] Cooper's Eq. Pl. 294, 295; Story's Eq. Pl. 819.

[237] Cooper's Eq. Pl. 294, 295; Beames's Pl. Eq. 265. As to right of party denying the charge of interest to protect himself by answer from answering as to matter as to which he may afterwards be called upon in the character of a witness to answer, see Story's Eq. Pl. 819; Mitf. Pl. 188, 283, 284; Hare on Disc. 256–259.

226. *Pleas to the bill or to the frame of the bill of discovery.* The plea that another suit is pending, or that there is a want of parties, or that there is unnecessary splitting up and multiplying suits, it is said, does not apply to a bill of discovery.[238] Lord Redesdale states that a demurrer for multifariousness would hold to a bill of discovery for several distinct matters against several distinct defendants in one bill,[239] and Mr. Justice Story suggests that it is possible that a plea to a bill of discovery for multifariousness would hold, as also the plea that the parties are not the same in the suit in equity as in the suit at law, in aid of which the discovery is sought.[240]

227. *Pleas in bar to bills of discovery.* The pleas most usual are those which render it improper for a court of equity to compel the discovery sought, *e. g.*, 1, that the discovery may subject the defendant to pains or penalties or a criminal prosecution. 2, that it will subject him to a forfeiture or something in the nature of a forfeiture. 3, that it will betray the confidence reposed in him as counsel, attorney or arbitrator, and 4, that he is a purchaser for valuable consideration without notice of the plaintiff's title.[241]

---

[238] Mitf. Pl. 200, 280 ; Beames's Pl. Eq. 273, 274.

[239] Mitf. Pl 200, 201.

[240] Story's Eq. Pl. 820. See § 190, *ante*. *Glynn* vs. *Soares*, 3 M. & K. 450, 469–472. Whether when suit at law is brought by an agent in his own name, the defendant at law may bring a bill for a discovery against the principal in aid of his defence at law, see Story's Eq. Pl., n. 6, § 820, and §§ 569, 610, *note*; and cases cited.

[241] Mitf. Pl. 284. And it might be added, as *Judge Story* suggests, that it would also be a good plea in bar to a bill of discovery that the bill sought a discovery of the defendant's title, and not merely of the plaintiff's title, if the

228. *Pleas to amended bills.* Pleas to amended bills may be put in upon the same grounds as pleas to original bills; but if a defendant has answered the original bill his answer may be read to counterplead his plea to the amended bill, and if upon so

---

facts should be so disguised in the bill as not to be open to demurrer. Story's Eq. Pl. 824, n. 2. Whether a defendant to a bill seeking a discovery in aid of an action at law can plead in bar to the discovery, that which is merely matter of legal defence to the action at law, is a question upon which authorities are conflicting. See Story's Eq. Pl. 821, and notes; Mitf. Pl. 187; Hare on Discovery 34, 41, 46–62; Wigram Disc. 153, 156–162.

Lord Redesdale states that the pleas to bills of discovery are nearly the same with those which are mentioned as causes of demurrer to discovery. They may be 1, that the plaintiff's case is not such as entitles a court of equity to assume a jurisdiction to compel a discovery in his favour; 2, that the plaintiff has no interest in the subject, or no interest which entitles him to call on the defendant for a discovery; 3, that the defendant has no interest in the subject to entitle the plaintiff to institute a suit against him even for the purpose of discovery only; 4, that the situation of the defendant renders it improper for a court of equity to compel discovery. Mitf. Pl. 282.

Pleas to bills of discovery have been discussed under the several heads: 1, to the jurisdiction; 2, to the person; 3, to the bill or frame of the bill; and 4, pleas in bar, properly so called, to such bills:

1. *To the jurisdiction.* Such objections as, that the subject is of a political nature; that another court is competent to give the discovery; that the tribunal or cause is not of such a character as will aid the discovery, (as if the cause be before arbitrators, or be of a criminal nature, or the plaintiff has no title or interest in the suit.)

2. *To the person.* Either, *of the plaintiff,* that he has no right or title or ability to call on the defendant for the discovery, such as that the plaintiff is outlawed, or an alien, or bankrupt, &c., or that he has no title to the character he assumes; or, *of the defendant,* that he is not liable or compellable to make the discovery sought by the bill, [such as that he has no interest in the subject matter, or is a mere witness, or does not sustain the character in which he is sued, or that there is want of privity between him and the plaintiff to sustain the bill.]

3. *To the bill or frame of the bill.* [The pendency of another suit, want of parties, splitting up or multiplying suits, do not apply to a bill of discovery. Story's Eq. Pl, 820.] Judge Story, following Lord Redesdale, suggests that the plea that the bill is multifarious would probably be good. Story's Eq. Pl. 820, Mitf. Pl. 200, 201. And a plea for misjoinder of parties. Story's Eq. Pl. 820, *Glynn* vs. *Soares*, 3 M. & K. 450, 469–472. And a plea that

reading it, it should appear that the facts stated upon the answer to the original bill would operate to avoid the defence made by the plea to the amended bill, the plea would be overruled.[242]

229. Pleas to supplemental bills, to bills of revivor, to cross bills, to bills of review, and to bills in the nature of bills of review, will be treated of after the nature and character of those bills have been discussed.

Of the form of pleas.

230. A plea is preceded by a title in the following form: "The plea of A. B., a defendant, to the bill of complaint exhibited against him by X. Y.," &c., or, "The joint and several plea of A. D. and C. D., defendants, to the bill of complaint exhibited against them by X. Y.," &c. When accompanied by an answer, it is entitled thus: "The plea and answer," or, "The joint plea and answer," or, "The joint and several plea and answer."[243]

231. A plea, like a demurrer, is introduced by a protestation against the confession of the truth of any matter contained in the bill.[244] Its commence-

---

the defendant in the bill was not a party to the suit at law, in aid of which discovery is sought. Story's Eq. Pl., 820. And a plea that the matter in controversy is beneath the dignity of the court to hear. *Ibid.*

4. *Pleas in bar.* Such as, a plea of a former judgment, or of a former decree on the merits, or a plea of the statute of frauds, or a plea of the statute of limitations, or of release, or of a stated account, or of an award.

[242] Mitf. Pl. 299, *Hyliard* vs. *White*; Ib., *Noel* vs. *Ward*, 1 Madd. 322; *Hyldyard* vs. *Cressy*, 3 Atk. 303.

[243] When the plea of man and wife, the words "and several" are not inserted.

[244] Dan. Ch. Pr. (Perk.) 704.

ment is as follows: "This defendant (or, these
defendants,) by protestation not confessing or acknowledging all or any of the matters in the said
complainant's bill of complaint mentioned and
contained to be true in such manner and form as
the same are therein set forth and alleged for
plea," &c.

· 232. The extent of the plea, that is, whether it is
intended to cover the whole bill, or a part of it only,
and what part in particular is usually stated in the
next place, and this, as before observed, must be
clearly and distinctly shewn.[245] Thus in the form in
preceding section, after "plea" say: "To the whole
of the said bill [or, to so much and such part of the
said bill as prays, &c., or seeks a discovery from
this defendant, &c."][246]

233. The matter relied upon as an objection to
the suit or bill generally follows, accompanied by
such averments as are necessary to support it; and
it should be noticed that where a plea is of matter
which shews an imperfection in the frame of the
suit, it should point out in what that imperfection
consists.[247]

---

[245] 2 Dan. Ch. Pr. (old) 206.

[246] In the English courts when the plea is to the whole relief sought by the
bill, but it is necessary that the defendant should support his plea by an
answer as to the facts stated which may avoid the bar, the plea must not
extend to the whole bill, but should be in the form of a plea *to all the relief
and all the discovery sought by the bill except certain parts of the discovery*
(which are to be answered). 2 Dan. Ch. Pr. (old) 206. This is not necessary
in the United States Circuit Courts (36th, 37th rules U. S. Supreme Court), nor
is it necessary in the Virginia State Courts. See Sec. 166, and n. 102, and
Sec. 166 a.

[247] 2 Dan. Ch. Pr. (old) 207.

234. The conclusion of a plea is as follows: "Wherefore the defendant prays judgment of this honorable court whether he shall be compelled to make any farther or other answer to the said bill, and prays to be hence dismissed with his reasonable costs and charges in this behalf most wrongfully sustained." [248]

235. Pleas should be signed by counsel. In the United States Circuit Courts it is necessary to comply with the requisites set forth in a previous section. [249] In the Virginia State Courts the practice is usually regulated by special rules prescribed by the respective courts. Notice should be taken of the statute, Code, 1873, chapter 167, sections 20, 24, 33, 34, 41 and 47; and chapter 137, section 8.

235 a. *What pleas under oath.* In the United States Circuit Courts an affidavit is necessary to every plea. See sec. 236, p. 274.

In the Virginia State Courts the provisions of the Code, 1873, chap. 167, sec. 20, 31, require an affidavit to pleas to the jurisdiction; and in equity, as at law, if there is an allegation that any person made, endorsed, assigned, or accepted any writing, no proof of the handwriting will be required unless the fact be denied by an affidavit with the answer, plea, or other pleading which puts it in issue. Code 1873, ch. 167, sec. 39. And so when plaintiffs sue, or are sued as partners, and their names are set forth

---

, [248] When the plea is accompanied by an answer, the answer should follow the conclusion of the plea. 2 Dan. Ch. Pr. (old) 210.

[249] Sec. 139, pp. 171, 172.

in the bill, or where plaintiffs or defendants, sue or are sued as a corporation, it will not be necessary to prove the fact of the partnership or incorporation, unless with the pleading, which puts the matter in issue, there be an affidavit denying such partnership or incorporation.   Code 1873, ch. 167, sec. 40.

235 *b*. Lord Redesdale said, on the authority of the Practical Register, that pleas to the jurisdiction of the court,[250] or, in disability of the person of the plaintiff as well as pleas in bar of any matter of record, or of matters recorded, or as of record in the court itself, or any other court, may be put in without oath.   Mitf. Pl., p. 301.   Daniell regards this as too broad a statement of the rule, and suggests the following: "The best mode to be adopted by the practitioners for determining the question will be to consider how far the oath will be necessary in the event of the plea being considered valid, and issue being joined upon it to establish its truth by evidence upon oath at the hearing; and in all cases where such evidence upon oath would be required at the hearing, to let the plea be accompanied by the oath of the defendant."[251]

236. The following is a general formula of a plea in equity:

General Formula of Plea in Equity.

The plea of A. B. a defendant to the bill of complaint exhibited against him by X. Y. in the ——— court of ———.

---

[250] See § 235 *a* as to pleas to jurisdiction in Virginia State Courts.
[251] 2 Dan. Ch. Pr. (old) 211.

This defendant, by protestation, not confessing or acknowledging all or any part of the matters and things in said bill of complaint contained, to be true in manner and form as the same are therein set forth, for plea nevertheless to the said bill, doth plead and aver that &c., [here state substance of plea.[252]] Wherefore, this defendant prays judgment of this honorable court whether he shall be compelled to make any farther or other answer to the said bill and prays hence to be dismissed with his reasonable costs and charges in this behalf most wrongfully sustained.[253]

M. P., p. d.

Certificate of Counsel in United States Circuit Courts.

I, M. P., of counsel for the defendant above named, practicing in the United States Circuit Court for the ——— circuit and ——— district of ——— do hereby certify that in my opinion the foregoing plea is well founded in point of law.

M. P.

Affidavit to Plea in United States Circuit Courts.

Eastern District of Virginia, to-wit:

I, X. X., a commissioner of the Circuit Court of the United States for the Fourth Circuit and Eastern

---

[252] In matters of substance there must be the same strictness and exactness in pleas in equity as in pleas at law. Story's Eq. Pl. 658; Beames's Pl. Eq. 8, 9; Mitf. Pl. 294.

[253] This formal conclusion of the plea is deemed sufficient in all cases in which the plea is to the whole bill. See, however, Story's Eq. Pl., § 194, and Beames's Pl. in Eq. 46, 47.

District of Virginia, do hereby certify that A. B., the defendant named in above plea, personally appeared before me in the district aforesaid, and made oath that the said plea is not interposed for delay in the suit in which it is made, and that the said plea is true in point of fact.

Given under my hand this —— day of —— 18—.

X. X., comm'r, &c.

237. The following is the form of a plea to part of a bill:

Form of Plea to part of a Bill.

The plea of A. B. to the bill of complaint exhibited against him by C. D. in the —— court of ——.

This defendant, by protestation, not confessing or acknowledging all or any of the matters and things in the said complainant's bill contained, to be true in such manner and form as the same are therein set forth and alleged for plea to so much and such part of the said bill as prays, &c., (here state the part of the bill pleaded to and state the substance of the plea). Wherefore the defendant doth plead to so much of the said bill as is hereinbefore particularly mentioned and prays the judgment of this honorable court, whether he should be compelled to make any farther answer to so much of the said bill as is hereinbefore pleaded to.[254]   [After this, if

---

[254] If the plea is intended as a bar to any part of the bill, its conclusion should not be more extensive than the subject matter to which it relates. It should not conclude to all the relief prayed for when the matter pleaded can

proper, follows an answer to the part of the bill not pleaded to.]

238. The following is the form of a joint, or of a joint and several plea:

Form of Joint and of Joint and Several Plea.

The joint plea of James B. and Caroline his wife [or the joint and several plea of James B. and Robert B.] to a bill of complaint exhibited against them by A. Y. in the —— court of ——.

These defendants, &c., (as in other forms).

Pleas to the Jurisdiction.

239. The following are the forms of a plea to the jurisdiction:

Form of Plea to the Jurisdiction in the Virginia State Courts.

In the Circuit Court of the County of Henrico, March Rules, 187—.

James R. Ramos, ... Defendant.
    ads
William W. Williams,   .   . · Complainant.

The plea of James R. Ramos, defendant, to the bill of complaint exhibited against him and C. C. in this court by William W. Williams.

---

only bar a part of that relief. But the remedy for this defect is mild and liberal. The plea will be ordered to stand for so much of the bill as it properly covers and no more, and the defendant may be required to answer to the residue. *French, &c.* vs. *Shotwell,* 5 John C. R., 562; S. C. 20 John Rep. 668.

This defendant, for plea to the said bill, saith that he is now and was at the time of the institution of this suit, a resident of the county of Hanover, and not a resident of the county of Henrico, that his co-defendant, C. C., is now and was at the time of the institution of this suit, also a resident of the county of Hanover, and not a resident of the county of Henrico, and that they are the sole defendants in the said suit, and that said suit is brought to subject to the alleged judgment of the said plain- tiff certain land every part whereof lies in the county of Hanover, and not any part thereof in the county of Henrico.[255] Wherefore the defendant doth plead to the said bill and to the jurisdiction of the said court, and prays the judgment of the court whether he should be compelled to make any farther or other answer to the said bill, and prays to be hence dismissed with his reasonable costs and charges in this behalf most wrongfully sustained.

C. R., p. d.

Affidavit should be added to this plea. Code 1873, ch. 167, §§ 20, 38.

Plea to Jurisdiction in United States Circuit Courts.

[When the jurisdiction is founded on the citizenship of the

---

[255] See Code 1873, chap. 165, §§ 1, 2, 3. The writer is not fully satisfied as to the sufficiency of this plea. If the second section of chapter 165, which uses the word "action" alone [not "action or suit"] shall be held to apply to proceedings in equity, then the plea should (as similar pleas in actions at law) contain the averment that "the cause of suit did not arise, and no part thereof arose in the county of Henrico, but the cause of suit arose, and every part thereof arose in the county of Hanover, a county other than that in which the suit is brought." In every case in which the facts will justify the pleader in making this averment, he should make it.

parties in different States, if the bill makes the necessary averments of the citizenship of the plaintiff and that of the defendant,
so that upon the face of the bill the jurisdiction attaches, the
defendant, if he means to contest the alleged citizenship, must do
it by *a plea to the jurisdiction;* he is not at liberty to put the
citizenship in issue by a general answer. *Livingston* vs. *Story*,
11 Pet. 351, 393; *Dodge* vs. *Perkins*, 4 Mason, 435; Story's Eq.
Pl., § 721.

When the citizenship, in such case, is not distinctly alleged, the
bill will be dismissed on demurrer or by motion. Story's Eq. Pl.
§ 492.]

In the United States Circuit Court for the ———
    circuit and ——— district of Virginia.

James R., ...   Defendant.
    ads
Robert B., ...   Plaintiff.

This plea of James R., a defendant to the bill in
equity exhibited against him in the said court by
Robert B., plaintiff.

This defendant, by protestation, not confessing or
acknowledging all or any part of the matters and
things in said bill contained, to be true in manner
and form as the same are therein set forth for plea,
nevertheless to the said bill, doth plead and aver that
the said plaintiff, Robert B., *is not now and* was not
at the time of filing said bill, and instituting this
suit, a citizen of the State of Pennsylvania, as in the
said bill alleged, but the said Robert B. was, at the
time of filing said bill and instituting this suit, *and
is now* a citizen of the State of Virginia, and this
defendant was then *and is now* also a citizen of the
said State of Virginia. Wherefore this defendant
prays judgment of this honorable court whether he
shall be compelled to make any other or farther

answer to the said bill,. and prays hence to be dismissed with his reasonable costs and charges, in this behalf most wrongfully sustained.

J. M., p. d.

The words *in italics* may be omitted.

Add affidavit to plea, see p. 171, and certificate of counsel, see p. 171.

240. The following are forms of pleas to the person.

PLEAS TO THE PERSON.

Form of Plea of Infancy of Plaintiff.

(Commence as in general formula, sec. 236, p. 274, then proceed:) that the said complainant at the time of filing his said bill was and now is an infant under the age of twenty-one years, that is to say, of the age of ——— years or thereabout. (Conclude as in general formula.)

Form of Plea that Plaintiff is a married woman.

(Commence as in general formula, sec. 236, p. 274, then proceed:) that the said complainant at the time of filing her said bill was and now is under coverture of one James B. her husband, who is still living, and in every respect capable if necessary of instituting a suit in equity in her behalf. (Conclude as in general formula.)

Form of Plea of Bankruptcy of Plaintiff.

(Commence as in general formula, sec. 236, p. 274,

then proceed:) that the said complainant was on the —————— day of —————— in the year 18—, duly adjudged and declared a bankrupt by the district court of the United States for the eastern district of Virginia, and on the —————— day of —————— the said plaintiff did assign, transfer and convey unto —————— his assignee in bankruptcy, all &c., (here set forth terms of assignment,) and therefore, and as the right claimed by the said bill to the estates therein mentioned, and the rents and profits thereof appears by the said bill to have accrued, and if the same is just and well founded, did really accrue before the said complainant was adjudged and declared a bankrupt as aforesaid, and before his property was assigned and transferred as aforesaid to said —————— assignee in bankruptcy, this defendant is advised that the complainant's right and interest to, and in the said estate and the rents and profits thereof was, at the time of filing the said bill, and is now, vested in the said assignee in bankruptcy of the said complainant, all which this defendant doth aver to be true. Wherefore, &c., (conclude as in general formula.)

The form, as drawn, is believed to be sufficiently full and specific.

Judge Story says, however, (citing *Carleton* vs. *Leighton*, 3 Meriv. 667, and Beames's Pl. in Eq. [122, 123,]) that "it seems that in a plea in bankruptcy all the facts and circumstances, which are necessary to establish the sufficiency of the proceedings in bankruptcy, and to show the party to be lawfully declared a bankrupt, must be set forth." Story's Eq. Pl. § 726. This doctrine, however sustained by

English authorities, is not believed to be the law here. The reasoning of the Lord Chancellor in the case cited (see 3 Meriv. 667,) is not applicable to the bankrupt law in this country.

An adjudication of bankruptcy is conclusive, unless it be afterwards set aside by the court, whose officer has adjudged the petitioner a bankrupt.

A fuller form may be found in Curtis's Eq. Prec. 159–161.

Form of Plea that Plaintiff was not Heir to the Person under whom he claims as Heir.[256]

(Commence as in general formula, sec. 236, p. 274, then proceed:) that the plaintiff is not the heir of the said Robert B. in the said bill named, as the said plaintiff in his said bill has untruly alleged. Wherefore, &c., (conclude as in general formula pp. 274, 5.)

J. M. P., p. d.

Form of Plea that Plaintiff is an Alien Enemy.

(Commence as in general formula, sec. 236, p. 274, then proceed:) that the said plaintiff is alien born of foreign parents, and in foreign parts, that is to say, at Paris in the Republic of France and out of allegiance to the United States of America, and under allegiance to the said Republic of France, which is an enemy to the United States of America, of which the defendant is a citizen, and the said plaintiff also before and at the time of filing his said bill was and now is an enemy of the said

---

[256] See Beames on Pleas (edit. 1824) 127–132. Purely negative pleas are good. See Story's Eq. Pl., § 668.

United States of America, and entered into the limits of the said United States of America without the safe conduct of the President or other lawfully authorized authorities of the United States of America, and has not been made a citizen of the said United States of America by naturalization or otherwise. Wherefore, &c., (conclude as in general formula.)

See the form of a plea of Alien Enemy in Beames on Pleas, 335, 336. See *Albrecht* vs. *Seissman*, 2 Ves. & B., 323.

Plea that Plaintiff is not Administrator of the Person he claims to be Administrator of.

(Commence as in general formula, sec. 236, p. 274, then proceed:) that the said plaintiff is not nor ever has been administrator of the goods and chattels, rights and credits, which were of the said Robert J., deceased, in the said bill named as the said plaintiff in his said bill has untruly alleged. Wherefore, &c., (conclude as in general formula.)

J. M. P., p. d.

Plea that the Defendant is a married woman.

(Commence as in general formula, sec. 236, p. 274, then proceed:) that this defendant at the time of filing the aforesaid bill was, and now is, under coverture of one James R. her husband, who is still living, and capable of defending the suit in her behalf. (Conclude as in general formula.)

Plea that the Defendant was never Administrator.

(Commence as in general formula, sec. 236, p. 274, then proceed:) that he, the defendant, is not executor or administrator of the said B. in the bill mentioned, or the legal representative of the said B., which said representative or representatives ought to be made party or parties to the complainant's said bill, as this defendant is advised. All which matters and things this defendant avers to be true, and pleads the same to the said bill. Wherefore, &c., (conclude as in general formula.)

241. The following are forms of pleas to the bill.

PLEAS TO THE BILL.

Plea of a former suit depending for the same matters in bar to a bill for account.[257]

(Commence as in general formula, sec. 236, p. 274, then proceed:) for plea saith that the said complainants, together with R. C., since deceased, did at the rules held on the first Monday in June, 18—, exhibit in this honorable court their bill of complaint which was afterwards amended against J. S., now deceased, and this defendant and G. S., now deceased, thereby praying amongst other things that &c., (stating the prayer); and this defendant for plea saith that he put in his answer to the said amended bill, and which suit is now depending in this honorable court; and this defendant avers that the said bill now exhibited against this defendant by

---

[257] Van Hethuysen, 658.

the said complainants is for the same matters as the amended bill before exhibited by the said complainants against this defendant, and the said J. S. and the said G. S., now respectively deceased, to which this defendant has appeared and answered, and which suit is still depending and undetermined; wherefore this defendant doth plead the said former bill and answer to the said complainants' now bill, and humbly prays the judgment of this honorable court, whether he shall be compelled to make any farther or other answer thereto: and this defendant prays to be hence dismissed with his reasonable costs and charges in this behalf most wrongfully sustained.

Plea that another suit is depending in another court of competent jurisdiction as to part of the matters embraced in the Bill.

The plea of A. B., a defendant, to part of the bill of complaint exhibited against him by X. Y. in the ——— court of ——— county, and the answer of the said A. B. as to the residue of said bill.

This defendant by protestation not confessing or acknowledging all or any part of the matters and things in said bill of complaint contained to be true in manner and form as the same are therein set forth, for plea as to so much and such part of the said bill as prays a discovery from this defendant of, &c. (here recite discovery asked for), and to so much and such part of the said bill as prays relief against this defendant for, &c. (here recite the relief asked for, to which plea is filed),

that before the said complainant's said bill was filed
in this court, to-wit: on or about the —— day of
——, the said complainant commenced a suit in
the —— court of —— county against this defendant in respect to the said (here recite the matter
about which discovery and relief are asked and
objected to), and such suit is still depending in the
said court, which, as this defendant avers, is a court
of competent jurisdiction to afford the discovery and
relief aforesaid, which the said complainant seeks
by his said bill. Wherefore this defendant avers
and pleads the same to so much of the said bill as
is hereinbefore particularly mentioned, and prays
the judgment of this court whether he should be
compelled to make any farther answer to so much of
the said bill as is hereinbefore pleaded to. And not
waiving, but relying on his said plea for answer to
so much of the said bill as is not above pleaded to,
this defendant answers and says, &c.

Form of Plea of want of proper Parties.

(Commence as in general formula, sec. 236, p. 274,
then proceed:) that in the said bill the plaintiff
seeks to subject a certain tract of land lying in the
county of H. to the payment of his judgment
against this defendant; that by agreement, under
their hands and seals, made between this defendant
and the personal representative and heirs-at-law of
James J., on the —— day of ——, to which agreement the said plaintiff was a party, and signed and
sealed the same, it was covenanted and agreed that
any claim which the said plaintiff might have or

assert against this defendant or his property, either at law or in equity, by reason of the claim on which said judgment was recovered, should be satisfied jointly from the property of the said James J., or belonging to his estate, and from the property of this defendant; that the said James J. died several years ago possessed of, and entitled to, personal property, and also real estate, which should contribute to the payment of the claim of the plaintiff asserted in this suit, and Robert J., the personal representative of said James J., and Susan, Robert, and John J., heirs-at-law of the said James J., ought to be, but are not, made parties to the said bill. Wherefore, &c. (Conclude as in general formula.)

Form of Plea of want of proper Parties.[258]

(Commence as in general formula, p. 274, then proceed:) that no part of the sum of $2,000, for securing the repayment whereof the bond in the bill mentioned was executed, was paid to, or received by, the intestate of this defendant, the said H. E., but the whole was paid unto A. W. in the said bond and in the said bill also named and received by him for his sole use, and that the said H. E. was only a surety for the said A. W. in the said bond; and the said complainant afterwards accepted a composition for what he alleged to be due on the said bond from the said A. W., without the privity

---

[258] It is questioned in the law books whether a plea for want of proper parties is a plea in bar, or a plea in abatement. See Story's Eq. Pl., § 745, n. 1; Mitf. Pl. 220, 280, 281; Beames's Pl. in Eq. 149, 150; Willis's Chan. Pl. 572, 573. It is not a proper plea to a bill of discovery merely. Story's Eq. Pl., § 745.

or consent of the said H. E. in his lifetime, or of
this defendant since the death of the said H. E.,
which occurred on the —— day of ———;[259] that
the said A. W. died several years ago seized of real
estate, and also possessed of personal estate, and
left a will duly probated, whereby he devised a part
of his real estate to John B. and his heir-at-law,
William W., and the said devisee of part of his real
estate, to-wit: John B., and also the representative
of his personal estate, to-wit: James Johnson, and
the said William W. ought to be, but are not, made
parties to the said bill. Wherefore, &c. (Conclude
as in general formula.)

*Form of Plea to a Bill for Partition by a Mort-
gagee, who has been made a Party.*

(Commence as in general formula, p. 274, then
proceed:) that he is the mortgagee of the undivided
share of A. M. in the land and premises in the bill
mentioned under a mortgage made and executed on
the —— day of ——— by A. M., and that he, the
said defendant, has no other interest in the said
property than under the mortgage aforesaid; and in
this suit for partition by Laura C. against the said

---

[259] Is it necessary that a plea of this description should point out the proper
parties and name them? *Vide*, Beames on Pleas 158; *Meriwether* vs. *Mellish,*
13 Ves. 435; *Cockburn* vs. *Thompson,* 16 Ves. 325; *Fawkes* vs. *Pratt,* P. Wms.
592; Mitf. Pl. 280. A plea containing the averment thus: "And that the
said A. W. died several years ago, seized of considerable real estate, and also
possessed of a large personal estate, and that his heir-at-law, or the devisee of
his real estate, and also the representative of his personal estate ought to be,
but are not, made parties to the said bill," was held good by Lord *Hardwicke* in *Ashurst* vs. *Ayres,* 3 Atk. 117. See the plea in Willis's Eq. Pl. 571;
Curtis's Eq. Prec. 175, 176; and Dan. Ch. Pr. (Perk.).

A. M. and Robert C., the co-defendants of this defendant, this defendant should not have been impleaded. Therefore this defendant prays judgment, &c. (Conclude as in general formula.)

PRACTICAL NOTE.

A partition never affects the rights of third persons. *Agur* vs. *Fairfax*, 17 Ves. 544. Mortgagees and judgment creditors have no concern with it. *Watten* vs. *Copeland*, 7 John. Ch. Rep. 140. And if they are made parties to the suit it will be dismissed as to them. *Sibring* vs. *Mersercan. & als.*, 1 Hopk. Ch. R. 501. When the incumbrance is created upon the undivided share of one of the parties, and the estate is then divided, such incumbrance will continue a lien on the share set off to the party, whose undivided share was before bound. *Walworth*, Chancellor, in *Harwood* vs. *Kirby*, 1 Paige 471. *Quœre* as to the effect of the Statute of Virginia, in relation to Partition on the doctrines announced in this note.

242. The following are forms of pleas in bar.

PLEAS IN BAR.

Pleas of Statutes.

Form of Plea of Statute of Limitations.

(Commence as in general formula, p. 274, then proceed:) that if the complainant ever had any cause of action or suit against this defendant, for or concerning any of the matters in the said bill mentioned, which this defendant doth in no sort admit, such cause of action or suit did accrue or arise above ——— years next before the filing of the said bill, or before serving or suing out process against this defendant, to appear to and answer the said bill, nor did this defendant, at any time within ——— years next before the said bill was exhibited, or process served on, or issued out against this defendant, to appear to and answer the same, promise, or agree *to and with the said plaintiff or any other person in writing*,[260] to come to any account for, or to make satisfaction, or to pay any sum or sums of money for or by reason of the said matters charged in the said bill. Wherefore, &c., (conclude as in general formula.)

Form of Plea of Statute of Frauds.

(Commence as in general formula, p. 274, then proceed:) that neither this defendant, nor any person by him authorized, did ever sign any contract or agreement in writing, for making or executing any sale or conveyance to the complainant of the land and premises in the bill mentioned and described, or any interest thereof, or to any such effect, or any memorandum or note, in writing, of any such agreement. Wherefore, &c., (conclude as in general formula.)

Form of Plea of Usury.

(Commence as in general formula, p. 274, with the modification suggested in the subjoined practical note, then proceed:) that the claim of the said plaintiff against this defendant is founded upon a loan of money to this defendant by the said plaintiff, to-wit: the loan of the sum of $——; and for the said loan the said plaintiff required

---

[260] The words in italics are designed to call attention to the Statute Code 1873, ch. 146, § 10. They are not deemed necessary to the validity of the plea.

of this defendant that he should pay to him, the said plaintiff, interest thereon, at the rate of eight per centum per annum, contrary to the Statute of Virginia, in such case made and provided, and this defendant agreed to pay the said usurious interest of eight per centum per annum, and the said agreement to pay the usurious interest as aforesaid, entered into and formed a part of the said contract of lending, and thereby, and by virtue of the Statute of Virginia, in such case made and provided all the interest on the said sum of $——— became, and was, and is forfeited, and all the securities for the payment of the same, became, and were, and are void. Wherefore, &c. (Conclusion.)

PRACTICAL NOTE.

Under the present Statutes of Virginia, Sess. Acts 1874, pp. 134–5, in force June 1st, 1874, the interest only is forfeited in the case of usury. The plea, then, should in conformity with the general rule in equity practice, be to only so much of the bill as claims the interest and not to that part claiming the principal. But see Sec. 8, Sess. Acts 1874, p. 135. If the court should hold that a party violating the laws against usury, has no right to be heard in a court of equity, then, the plea would be a full plea in bar of the suit, and the conclusion of the plea should be as in the general formula, p. 274. But the court under the present statutes would hardly deprive a plaintiff of his right to the principal. See the Statute, Sess. Acts 1874, p. 134–5, sec. 5, cited below.[261]

Unless there be strong reasons against relying on the usury in an answer, it is suggested that instead of pleading it by a separate plea it would be better to embody the defence of usury in the answer.

---

[261] "§ 5, All contracts and assurances made directly or indirectly for the loan or forbearance of money or other thing at a greater rate of interest than is allowed by the preceding section, [i. e., 6 per cent. per annum,] shall be deemed to be for an illegal consideration *as to the excess beyond the principal amount so loaned or forborne.*"

242. The following are forms of pleas of matters of record or as of record.

PLEAS OF MATTERS OF RECORD OR AS OF RECORD.

Form of a Plea of Decree to part of case made by the Bill, and answer as to the residue.

The plea of J. B., executor of Alexander B. deceased, a defendant, to part of the bill of complaint exhibited against him by Robert M. N. and Jane M. his wife, in the —— court of ——, and the answer of the said J. B., executor of said Alexander B. deceased, to the residue of said bill.

This defendant, by protestation, not confessing or acknowledging all or any part of the matters and things in said bill of complaint to be true in manner and form as the same are therein set forth, as to so much of the said bill of the complainants as seeks to compel this defendant to admit assets of his late father, Alexander B., deceased, come to his hands, or to set forth an inventory of the personal estate of his father come to his hands, or that this defendant may thereout pay to the said complainants the sum of $ —— in the said complainant's bill mentioned, with interest on the same from the time of the testator's death, this defendant doth plead thereto, and for plea saith that in the year ——, Jane M., now the wife of Robert M. N., (the complainants aforesaid) who was then unmarried, exhibited her bill of complaint in the —— court of ——, against this defendant, praying that the legacy bequeathed her by the said testa-

tor might be paid, being the same legacy mentioned
in the said bill of complainants, and in the said suit
by the said Jane M,. this defendant filed his answer
to her said bill, submitting to the said court to say
what right and interest the said Jane M. was entitled to under the said testator's will, and 'the said
————— court of ——————— made its decree in said cause,
decreeing that the said Jane M. was entitled only to
$————, with interest from the ———— day of ————,
which decree was duly signed and enrolled,[262] and the
said decree remains of record in the said court
wholly unreversed, and the said sum of $————,
with interest as aforesaid, was fully paid to the said
Jane M. on the ———— day of ————, prior to her
intermarriage with the said complainant, Robert M.
N., and was accepted by her in full discharge of her
legacy aforesaid, and of all right and interest which
she had or could have in or to the personal estate of
the said testator, or any part thereof; all which
matters and things this defendant doth aver and
plead in bar to so much of the said complainants'
bill as is hereinbefore particularly mentioned, and
prays the judgment of this honorable court, whether
he should make any further answer to so much of
the said bill as is hereinbefore pleaded to. And the
said defendant, for answer to so much, &c., &c.

*Plea of former Suit for the same Matter being dis-
missed on hearing.*

(Commence as in general formula, page 274, then

---

[262] See as to entering and recording decrees the chapter on Decrees in this
treatise.

proceed:) that the said complainant heretofore, to-wit: on the ——— day of ——— exhibited his bill of complaint in the ——— court of ——— against this defendant, by which bill the said complainant sought to subject the land of this defendant, lying and being in the county of ———, containing ——— acres, being the same land mentioned in the bill to which this is a plea, to the judgment of the said complainant being the same judgment mentioned in the present bill of complaint, and the said complainant in his said former bill of complaint, alleged that the said judgment was a lien on the said land, as he has alleged in the present bill, and prayed for the identical relief against this defendant's said land that he has prayed for in his present bill; and to the said former bill this defendant filed his answer, denying that his said land was subject to the said judgment, and examinations of witnesses for the said complainant and for this defendant were had and taken, and said former bill of complaint with the said answer and the examinations of witnesses came to a hearing before the said ——— court of ———, and the said court, after full hearing thereof, on the ——— day of ———, 18—, dismissed the said former bill, and decreed and ordered that the said complainant should pay to this defendant his costs by him about his defence in that behalf expended; all which matters and things this defendant doth aver and plead in bar to the said present bill of complaint of the said complainant, wherefore this defendant prays judgment of this honorable court whether he shall be compelled to make any farther or other answer to the said bill, and prays hence to be dismissed with his reasonable costs and charges, in this behalf most wrongfully sustained.

R. M., p. q.

Form of Plea of Judgment finally determining the Rights of the Parties in Bar to a Suit in Equity.

(Commence as in general formula, page 274, then proceed:) that before the institution of their present bill of complaint against this defendant, to-wit: on the ——— day of ———, the said complainants instituted their action at law in the ——— court of ——— against R. M. and this defendant, by which said action at law the said complainants demanded and claimed of the said R. M. and this defendant the sum of $———, with interest thereon from the ——— day of ———, as debt due by the said R. M. and this defendant to the said complainant; and the said R. M. and this defendant pleaded to the said action three several pleas, to-wit: the plea that the right of action did not accrue to the said plaintiff within five years prior to the institution of said action; the plea that the debt therein mentioned had been fully paid by the said R. M. and this defendant; and the plea that the action of the said complainant was founded on an usurious consideration, in this, that the debt therein demanded was for the loan and forbearance of money to the said R. M. and this defendant at a greater rate of interest than six per centum per annum, and issue being joined on the said several pleas, the whole matter was submitted to a jury, who returned a verdict finding for the said R. M. and this defendant on all the pleas before mentioned, and the said ——— court of ——— gave judgment in favor of the said R. M. and this defendant, against the said complainant; and the debt set forth and declared in the said complainant's bill on which the attachment against this defendant's property issued is the same identical debt on which he instituted his action aforesaid, and on the trial of which judgment went against the said complainant as aforesaid, all which matters and things this defendant doth aver and plead in bar to the said bill of complaint of the said complainant. Wherefore, &c., (conclude as in general formula.)

243. The following are pleas in bar of matters in pais.

PLEAS IN BAR OF MATTERS IN PAIS.[268]

Form of a Plea of Stated Account.

(Commence as in general formula, page 274, then proceed:) that on the ——— day of ———, which was previous to the said bill of complaint being filed, the said complainant and this defendant did make up, state and settle an account in writing

---

[268] Pleas in bar of matters in pais must be upon oath of the defendant. Story's Eq. Pl. 696. The principal matters in pais which may be relied on by plea are, according to Lord Redesdale, a stated account, award, release, will or conveyance or some instrument controlling or affecting the rights of the parties, plea of any statute creating bar to the plaintiff's demand. Mitf. Pl. 258. Judge Story puts as such principal pleas, release, stated account, settled account, award, purchase for valuable consideration, plea of title in defendant. Story's Eq. Pl. 795.

of all sums of money which this defendant had before that time, by the order and direction and for the use of the said complainant received, and of all matters and things thereunto relating, or at any time before the said ———— day of ————, being or depending between the said complainant and this defendant, (and in respect whereof the said complainant's bill of complaint has been since filed;) and the said complainant, after a strict examination of the said account and every item and particular thereof, which this defendant avers, according to the best of his knowledge and belief, to be true and just,[264] did approve and allow the same, and actually received from this defendant the sum of $————, the balance of the said account, which by the said account appeared to be justly due to him from this defendant and the said complainant thereupon, and on the ———— day of ————, gave to this defendant a receipt or acquittance for the same under his hand in full of all demands, which said receipt or acquittance is in the words and figures following, that is to say (here copy the receipt) as by the said receipt or acquittance now in the possession of this defendant and ready to be produced to this honorable court will appear. Wherefore, &c., (conclude as in general formula.)

PRACTICAL NOTE.

To a bill charging error or fraud, it is necessary to meet those charges by averments in the body of the plea, and also to support the plea by an answer denying them. Mitf. Pl. 259, 260; Beames on Pl. 222–226; Story's Eq. Pl. § 802.

---

[264] Story's Eq. Pl. 802. Mitf. Pl. 259, 260.

Form of a Plea of Release.

(Commence as in general formula, page 274, then proceed:) that previously to the said complainant's bill being filed, to-wit: on the —— day of ——, the said complainant in consideration of the sum of \$——, then paid to him by this defendant,[265] by a certain writing under his hand and seal, ready to be produced to this honorable court, did release and forever quit claim this defendant (among other things) the several matters and things in the said complainant's bill mentioned and complained of, and an account of which is thereby sought against this defendant, and this defendant avers that the said release was freely and fairly given and executed by the said complainant, on the day the same bears date, and that the said complainant well knew the nature and effect thereof previously to executing the same; and that the sum of \$——, so paid by this defendant to the said complainant, was a full and fair equivalent for any demand which the said complainant could or might have against this defendant in respect to the several matters therein and in the said bill also mentioned. Wherefore this defendant pleads the said release in bar of the said complainant's bill, and prays judgment, &c., (conclude as in general formula).

---

[265] Story's Eq. Pl. 797. If the consideration is impeached by the bill, the plea must be assisted by averments, and also by an answer covering the grounds on which the consideration is impeached. Mitf. Pl. 261–3; Story's Eq. Pl. 797.

Another Form of Plea of Release.

(Commence as in general formula, p. 274, then proceed:) that before the said complainant's bill was filed, that is to say, on the —— day of —— the said complainant, by a certain writing under his hand and seal, in consideration of $—— by him the said defendant then and there paid [266] to the said complainant, released and forever quitted claim this defendant from the several matters and things in the said complainant's bill mentioned and complained of, and from all demands and suits whatsoever which the said complainant then had, or might thereafter have, in respect of the several dealings and transactions, matters and things in the said bill mentioned, or any of them, therefore this defendant pleads the said release in bar to the said complainant's said bill, and prays the judgment of this court whether he ought to be compelled to make any farther answer to the said bill; and this defendant not waiving his said plea but insisting thereon, for answer and in support of his said plea he denies that the said release was unduly obtained by this defendant from the said complainant, as in the said bill is suggested, or that the complainant was ignorant of the nature and effect of such release, or that the consideration paid by this defendant as aforesaid was at all inadequate to the just claims and demands of the said complainant against this defendant, in respect of the several dealings and trans-

---

[266] See note to preceding form.

actions in the said bill mentioned.   Wherefore, &c.,
(conclude as in general formula.)

PRACTICAL NOTE.

If fraud, surprise, imposition, inadequacy of consideration or any
other objection to the release be charged in a bill seeking to set it
aside, the plea, as it is called, must deny those charges by averments and must also specifically negative them by an answer.
Beames on Pleas 226. In such case the following form is suggested as a proper conclusion of the plea: "Therefore this defendant pleads the said release in bar to so much of the said plaintiff's
bill as is hereinbefore particularly mentioned, and humbly prays
the judgment of this honorable court, whether he ought to be
compelled to make any farther answer to so much of the said bill
as is before pleaded unto; and this defendant not waiving the said
plea, but insisting thereon for answer to the residue of the said
bill, and in support of his said plea saith, he denies that the said
release was unduly obtained by this defendant from the said plaintiff, or that the said plaintiff was ignorant of the nature and effect
of such release, or that the consideration paid by this defendant to
induce the said plaintiff to execute the same was at all inadequate
to the just claims and demands of the said plaintiff against this
defendant in respect of the several dealings and transactions in the
said bill mentioned, or any of them, and this defendant denies, &c.

PLEA OF RELEASE SUPPORTED BY AN ANSWER.

It is now firmly established that the plea itself, as well as the
answer, must contain averments negativing the facts and circumstances set up in the bill in avoidance of the bar or defence.
Otherwise the plea will not amount to a complete defence to the
bill, since the denial of these facts and circumstances is in truth
the only point in controversy. Story's Eq. Pl. 680, 796: Mitf. Eq.
Pl. 239–244, and note (g), 298, 299; *Hartt* vs. *Corning*, 3 Paige
566; *Bayley* vs. *Adams*, 6 Ves. 586, 2 Dan. Ch. Pr. (old) 112–128;
Foley vs. *Hill*, 3 M. & C. 475, 480, 481, 2 Ves. & Beam. 364,
6 Mad. 64, 2 Sim. & Stu. 279, Story's Eq. Pl. 671, note.

In order to justify an answer in support of the plea, there must
be some specific facts charged in the bill to which such an answer
is a proper response. When the bill charges no specific fact inconsistent with the plea, negativing and avoiding as it were that plea
by anticipation, but only alleges generally that the defendant holds
papers and writings, by which the truth of the matters charged, or
some of them, would appear (which matters if true would not affect
the validity of the plea, but leaves it in its full force), it is not

necessary nor proper to put in an answer in support of the plea. Story's Eq. Pl. 681. But where the bill even in general terms charges that the defendant has in his custody or power divers books, papers and writings, by which if produced the truth of the several matters aforesaid, or some of them, would appear, there cannot be pleaded a plea to the discovery without an answer in support of it negativing the existence of such books, papers and writings. See Story's Eq. Pl. 681a, and cases cited.

Whether Release after filing of the Bill can be pleaded.

In section 176, it was stated that as to such matters as arise after the filing of the bill, when they operate a full discharge from the claim of the plaintiff, they may be pleaded. Dan. Ch. Pr. (Perk.) 60. In *Turner & als.* vs. *Robinson & als.*, 1 S. & S. 3, Vice-Chancellor Sir John Leach held, that "as any matter which arises between the declaration and plea may be pleaded at law, so matters which arise between the bill and plea may be pleaded in equity." See *Tarleton* vs. *Hornby*, 1 Y. & C. 101; *Earl of Leicester* vs. *Perry* 1 Bro. C. C. 305; *Dryden* vs. *Robinson*, 2 S. & S. 529, referred to in n. 209, p. 263, *ante*. There is no conflict between *Turner* vs. *Robinson*, 1 S. & S. 3, and *Hayne* vs. *Hayne*, 3 Chan. 19, 2 Swanst. 472, 474, cited by Lord Redesdale, Mitf. Pl. 82. In *Hayne* vs. *Hayne*, the defendant, without pleading it, relied on a release. The plaintiff wished to impeach the release. The plaintiff was directed to file a bill for the purpose, the release not being in issue. The case does not decide that the defence could not be presented by a plea: and the subsequent cases of *Turner* vs. *Robinson*, 1 S. & S., and others cited above, seem to sustain the position that it could be so presented. Lord Redesdale lays it down, however, that a cross bill will be necessary; Mitf. Pl. 82, but bases his opinion on *Hayne* vs. *Hayne*, cited above.

Form of Plea of Award.

(Commence as in general formula, page 274, then proceed;) that disputes having arisen between the said complainant and this defendant concerning (here state subject of dispute), for the settling of all such disputes the said complainant and this defendant agreed to submit the same to the final judgment award and arbitration of A. R., and the said A. R. having taken upon himself the burden of said

award, after having at large heard, read and duly
weighed and considered all and singular the allegations, proofs and evidences brought before him did
on the ———— day of ———— make his final award
in writing under his hand and seal of and concerning the matters of dispute aforesaid, and did thereby
award and find (here state substance of award) as
by the said award reference being thereto had will
more fully appear; and this defendant avers that
the matters complained of in said complainant's bill
were embraced in said award, and that the said
award hath hitherto remained and still is unim-
peached and in full force and effect: and this defendant avers that he hath paid in full to the said
complainant the sum of money awarded him by
said award, and that the said award was made and
said payment was made previously to the said complainant's bill being filed in this honorable court.
Wherefore, &c., (conclude as in general formula.)

PRACTICAL NOTES.

An award may be pleaded to a bill to set aside the award and
open the account, to the discovery as well as relief. · Mitf. Pl. 260.
But if fraud or partiality be charged against the arbitrators, those
charges must not only be denied by way of averment in the plea,
but the plea must be supported by an answer, showing the arbitrators to have been incorrupt and impartial; and any other matter
stated in the bill as a ground for impeaching the award must be
denied in the same manner. Mitf. Pl. 261.

Although an award, duly made, will be a good plea in bar to a
bill for the matters concluded by it,[267] a covenant or agreement to
refer disputes to arbitration, as it cannot be made the subject of a
bill for specific performance (*Price* vs. *Williams*, cited 6 Ves. 818),
so neither can it be pleaded in bar to a bill brought in consequence

---

[267] See 2 Rob. Pr. (old) 194; *Smith, &c.* vs. *Smith, &c.*, 3 Rand. 95; *Smallwood* vs. *Mercer, &c.*, 1 Wash. 290.

of such differences. Dan. Ch. Pr. (Perk.) 694; *Wellington* vs. *Mackintosh*, 2 Atk. 570; *Contee* vs. *Dawson*, 2 Bland 264. See *Sherman* vs. *Beale*, 1 Wash. 11; *Pleasants* vs. *Pleasants*, *Ib.* 156; *Morris* vs. *Ross*, 2 H. & M. 171, 408. [*Halfhide* vs. *Fenning*, 2 Bro. C. C. 336, a case in which partners had agreed to submit all matters to arbitration and a plea to that effect was sustained, has been overruled. See *Mitchell* vs. *Harris*, 4 Bro. C. C. 311; *S. C.*, 2 Ves., Jr. 129, 136; *Street* vs. *Rigby*, 6 Ves. 815.] Lord *Redesdale's* remarks on this topic are specially worthy of notice: "It seems impossible to maintain that such a contract should be specifically performed, or bar a suit, unless the parties had first agreed upon the previous question, what were the matters in difference, and upon the powers to be given to the arbitrators, amongst which the same means of obtaining discovery upon oath, and production of books and papers, as can be given by a court of equity, might be essential to justice. The nomination of arbitrators also must be a subject on which the parties must previously agree; for if either party objected to the person nominated by the other, it would be unjust to compel him to submit to the decision of the person so objected to as a judge chosen by himself. It must also be determined that all the subjects of difference, whether ascertained or not, must be fit subjects for the determination of arbitrators, which if any of them involved important matter of law they might not be deemed to be." Mitf. Pl. 264, 265.

See the comments on *Rowe* vs. *Wood*, 1 Jack & W. 315; and on *Dryden* vs. *Robinson*, 2 S. & S. 529, in 2 Dan. Ch. Pr. (old) 192.

Awards were set aside in *Graham* vs. *Pence*, 6 Rand. 529; *Lee* vs. *Patillo*, 4 Leigh 362; *McCormick* vs. *Blackford*, 4 Grat. 133; *Jenkins* vs. *Liston*, 13 Grat. 535.

Form of a Plea of a Final Agreement in Bar of a Suit.

(Commence as in general formula, p. 274, and then proceed:) that on the ——— day of ———, the said plaintiff A. B., and this defendant C. D., entered into an agreement, which agreement was signed and sealed by both parties, and by the said agreement the said A. B. covenanted and agreed with this defendant to release and absolutely to relinquish all claims or rights of action or suit, whether legal or equitable, against this defendant and against any property or rights of property of his, the said defendant, in consideration of the sum of three hundred dollars then to be paid to the said plaintiff by the said defendant; and this defendant saith that thereafter, to-wit: on the ——— day of ———, he paid the said plaintiff the said sum of three hundred dollars, and thereby all rights of action or suit against this defendant or against his property or rights of property, if any the said plaintiff had, ceased and was absolutely released, relinquished and determined: and the said defendant farther saith that the right of action or suit asserted by the said plaintiff in the bill in this suit against this defendant and his property and rights of property accrued to the said plaintiff, if at all, long prior to the date of the said agreement and the payment of the said sum of three hundred dollars, and the same was thereby released, relinquished and discharged as aforesaid.   Wherefore, &c., (as in general formula to conclusion.)

Form of Plea of Adversary Possession, when the possession of the Defendant is derivative.

(Commence as in general formula, p. 274, and then proceed:) that on the ——— day of ———, by deed duly acknowledged and recorded in the clerk's office of the county court of Henrico, one John B. conveyed to this defendant, R. H., the tract of land in the bill mentioned, described as follows (here describe land): that at the time of said conveyance by the said John B. to this defendant of the said tract of land, the said John B. had been for more than twenty years in the open, notorious, continuous and exclusive adversary possession of the said tract of land, and was then, at date of said deed, in the open, notorious and exclusive adversary possession of the said land, and from the day of the date of the said deed until now (the said deed being dated more than —— years prior to the institution of this suit) this defendant has been in the open, notorious, continuous and exclusive adversary possession of the said land, and is now in such open, notorious and exclusive adversary possession of the said land, and by such adversary possession by the said John B. and this defendant, the said plaintiffs, if they or their ancestors ever had any right to the said property, such rights were absolutely barred and extinguished, and the said plaintiffs are not entitled to implead this defendant in this court in reference to the said tract of land or any part or share thereof. Wherefore, &c., (as in general formula to the end.)

Form of Plea of Forty Years' Possession without Account, &c., Blewitt vs. Thomas, 2 Ves. Jr., 669.

This defendant, by protestation, not confessing or acknowledging all or any of the matters or things in the complainant's bill of complaint contained to be true, in such manner and form as the same are therein and thereby alleged and set forth, as to all the relief prayed in and by the complainant's bill of complaint, and as to all the discovery thereby prayed, save and except so much thereof as prays this defendant may discover, whether he is not now in possession of lands, tenements, and heredita-

ments, in the complainant's bill mentioned, and of
the rents and profits thereof, and how long this defendant, and those under whom he claims title thereunto, have been in possession thereof, doth plead in
bar, and for plea saith, that he and his ancestors,
and those under whom he claims to be entitled to
the said estate, have been in the lawful and uninter-
rupted possession thereof to his and their own absolute use and benefit for forty years last past and
upwards, that is to say, from the year 18— down to
the present time, without having ever paid over or
accounted for all or any part of the rents and
profits thereof, and without having to the knowledge or belief of this defendant paid to, or accounted with, the complainants, or any person
or persons under whom they claim and derive
title to the said estate, in and by their bill of
complaint, for any sum or sums of money owing
to them or any of them, which had been lent
or advanced upon any mortgages or mortgage of the
said estate, or any part thereof, (if any such there
were) or for or in respect of any interest due or
claimed by them or any of them, if any such ever
hath arisen, or been claimed by them or any of
them during the whole of that period, nor hath this
defendant, nor to the belief of this defendant have
any of his ancestors or other persons, under whom
he claims to be entitled to the said estate, ever
acknowledged or admitted to the complainants or
either of them, or any persons or person under
whom they claim title by their bill of complaint,
that any money was due and owing to them or any

of them, for or in respect of any money lent by them or any of them to this defendant or his ancestors, or any persons or person whom he claims to be entitled to the said estate, if any money was lent, and, therefore, that it is to be presumed that such mortgage as is stated in the complainant's bill to bear date the —— day of 18—, and to have been made by T. M. in the said bill named, deceased, under whom this defendant claims title to the said estate, if such mortgage was made, hath been long since paid, satisfied and discharged: all which matters and things this defendant doth aver and plead in bar to so much and such parts of the complainant's said bill as aforesaid, and humbly demands the judgment of this honorable court, whether he ought to be compelled to make any farther or other answer thereto.

Form of Plea of Will to a Bill brought by an Heir-at-law against a Devisee.

(Commence as in general formula, p. 274, and then proceed:) that the plaintiff claims to be the heir-at-law of one John B., and to have inherited as such among other property a lot of land in the city of Richmond, fronting twenty feet on the south side of Grace street, between Fourth and Fifth streets, and running back one hundred and fifty feet to an alley; that the said John B. being of sound mind and disposing memory prior to his death, made a last will and testament, and the same has been duly admitted to probate in the Chancery Court of the city of Richmond; and this defendant farther says, that by the said will so probated as aforesaid, the said John B. devised the said lot of land on Grace street to this defendant. Wherefore, &c., (conclude as in general formula.)

Form of Plea to a Bill for Dower.

(Commence as in general formula, p. 274, then proceed:) that the said John H., mentioned in the said bill, or any other person to his use, was not at any time during the coverture of said Catharine with him seized of an estate of inheritance in the premises in the bill mentioned, or of any part thereof. And this defendant prays judgment, &c., (as in general formula to the end.)

Form of Plea of Jointure to Bill for Dower.

(Commence as in general formula, p. 274, then proceed:) that during the coverture of the said Catharine with the said John H., mentioned in the bill on the —— day of ——, the said John H. made and executed his last will and testament, whereby he devised that the said Catharine should receive an annual income of $500 during her life out of the estate of the said John H., and that she should have the full use of the mansion house and other houses of the said John H., where the said John H. did then live, together with the ground on which they stood, and the garden, stable, and stable-lot during the life of the said Catharine; and the said defendant saith that the said devise in the said will set forth was in lieu of the said Catharine's right of dower in the estate of the said John H., and the said Catharine did after the death of the said John·H., and before the commencement of this suit actually enter into and occupy the property so as aforesaid devised to her to-wit: the mansion house and other houses where the said John H. did live, and the stable and stable lot and garden, and hath ever since been in the possession and occupation thereof in lieu of her dower aforesaid. Wherefore this defendant prays judgment, &c., (as in general formula to the end.)

Form of Plea of purchase for valuable consideration without notice, followed by an Answer in support of the Plea.[268]

[Follow general formula, p. 274, to the words "for plea nevertheless," then proceed:] to so much of the said bill as seeks to subject the land in the bill mentioned to the judgment of the plaintiff recovered of the defendant R. M., doth plead thereto, and for plea saith, that A. B. previously to and on the ———— day of ————, was, or pretended to be seized in fee simple, and was in, or pretended to be in the actual possession of all the said land, in the said bill particularly mentioned and described, free from all incumbrances whatsoever; and this defendant, believing that the said A. B. was so seized and entitled, and that the said land was in fact free from all incumbrances, on the ———— day of ————, agreed with the said A. B. for the absolute purchase of the fee simple and inheritance thereof; whereupon a

---

[268] 1 Smith's Ch. Pr. 228. This plea is designed to conform to the rule laid down in *Portarlington* vs. *Soulby*, 6 Sim. 356.

deed was executed to the said defendant, by the said A. B. conveying said land to the said defendant, and the same was thereupon duly recorded; and this defendant doth aver, that the said sum of $———, the consideration money in the said deed mentioned, was actually paid by this defendant to the said A. B., and this defendant doth also aver, that at or before the time of the execution of the said deed by the said A. B. and this defendant, and of the payment of the said purchase money, he, this defendant, had no notice whatsoever of the claim of the said R. M. to the said land, or of the said plaintiff, that in anywise affected the said land, so purchased by this defendant as aforesaid, or any part thereof; and this defendant insists that he is a *bona fide* purchaser of the said land for a good and valuable consideration, and without any notice of the said claim of said R. M., or of said plaintiff; all which matters and things this defendant avers and pleads in bar to so much of the said complainant's bill as is hereinbefore particularly mentioned; and prays the judgment of this honorable court, whether he should make any further answer to so much of the said bill as is hereinbefore pleaded to; and this defendant, not waiving his said plea, but relying thereon, and for better supporting the same, for answer saith, that he had not at any time before, or at the time of purchasing the said land, or since, until the said complainant's bill was filed, any notice whatsoever either expressed or implied of the said claim of said R. M. to the said land or of the said plaintiff, or that the same or any other incumbrance whatsoever was charged upon or in any wise affected the said land so purchased or any part thereof. [Here may follow other statements in the answer. If, for example, particular instances of notice or circumstances of fraud are charged in the bill, they must be denied as specially as charged in the bill and not evasively, and this special and particular denial of notice or fraud must be by way of answer. See Beames on Pl. 247. Conclude as in other answers.]

PRACTICAL NOTES.

The general rule of equity is that no man shall proceed to get a legal title to lands to which another has a prior and superior equitable right if he knows of such superior equity, but that he shall desist so soon as he is informed thereof; and if he proceeds after such knowledge, his legal title will not avail him in a court of chancery. *Coalter*, J., in *Noland* vs. *Cromwell*, 4 Munf. 161. In that event, he will be postponed to him who has the prior and superior equitable right on the ground that the taking the legal estate after notice of such equitable right makes him a *mala fide* purchaser and amounts to a fraud. *Curtis* vs. *Jones*, 6 Munf. 42. He acts with a corrupt conscience when he purchases that which he knows justly belongs to another. *Bumgardner* vs. *Allen*, 6 Munf. 446. And he cannot stand on any higher ground in relation to his purchase than the person from whom he bought. *Fitzhugh* vs. *Jones*, 6 Munf. 83.

A purchaser will be affected with notice if it be received at any time before he is a complete purchaser. The deed must be executed and the whole amount of the purchase money paid. 2 Rob. Pr. (old) 27, and cases cited. The payment of part of the purchase money does not constitute any lien upon the land. By two judges in a court of three in *Doswell* vs. *Buchanan*, 3 Leigh. 365.

An unrecorded conveyance of a legal title is void as to a subsequent purchaser for valuable consideration without notice. See *Rootes* vs. *Holliday*, 6 Munf. 251.

A purchaser with notice may avail himself of the want of notice of *his* vendor; otherwise the vendor would not be protected in the full enjoyment of his property. *Lacy* vs. *Wilson*, 4 Munf. 313; *Curtis* vs. *Lunn*, 6 Munf. 42; *Boone* vs. *Chiles*, 10 Pet. 171; Jos. Tate's Dig. 167; 2 Rob. Pr. (old) 29.

A purchaser without notice will take a good title even when claiming through or under parties affected with notice. *Connecti-*

cut vs. *Bradish*, 14 Mass. 296; *Knox* vs. *Selleway*, 10 Maine 221; *Mallery* vs. *Stodder*, 6 Ala. 801; *Milluck* vs. *Peeples*, 3 Kelly 446, 1 Mat. Dig. 558. *Tompkins* vs. *Powell*, 6 Leigh 576; *Southall* vs. *McKeand*, 1 Wash. 336, 2 Rob. Pr. (old) 30.

If the purchaser has paid the whole purchase money and obtained his conveyance before notice, his conduct has been fair, and having equal though posterior equity he will be protected because he has the legal title also fairly acquired. He must, however, have obtained the legal title or must show that, though posterior in time he has the best right to call for it. *Tucker*, P. in *Mut. A. Soc.* vs. *Stone & als.*, 3 Leigh 235.

Notice to one of several joint purchasers is not notice to the rest; notice to a husband not notice to a wife, especially as she paid the consideration out of her separate estate. *Snyder* vs. *Spinable*, 7 Hill 427.

Another Plea of Purchase for valuable Consideration without notice.

[Commence as in general formula, p. 274, then proceed:] that he the said defendant at a public sale of the said land in the bill mentioned made by L. W., trustee, under a deed from R. H. to said L. W. to secure the payment of a sum of money to V. E. became the purchaser of the said land at the price of $625, and paid the said purchase money thereof to the said L. W., trustee, and the same was conveyed to him by the said L. W., trustee; that the deed conveying the said land to the said L. W., trustee, to secure the said V. E. a debt due to the said V. E. by the said R. H was dated and delivered the ———— day of ———— and was duly recorded in the clerk's office of the Chancery Court of the city of Richmond on the ———— day of ————; that when the said deed of trust was delivered to the said L. W., trustee, to secure the said debt to V. E., the said debt was justly due and owing to the said V. E. by the said R. H., and neither the said L. W., trustee, nor V. E. at the time the said R. H. conveyed the said land to the said L. W. or at the time the said trust deed was recorded in the clerk's office of the Chancery Court of the city of Richmond had any notice of the alleged purchase by the said C. R. of the said land from the said R. H., nor did the said L. W., trustee, and V. E., or either of them have any notice whatever that the said C. R. had or asserted any claim on the said land, or any interest therein until long after the deed of trust aforesaid was executed by the said R. H. to the said L. W., trustee, and until long after said deed of trust was admitted to record as aforesaid. Wherefore, &c.

244. The following are forms of pleas to bills of discovery.

PLEAS TO DISCOVERY ONLY.

Plea to the jurisdiction when the discovery is sought in aid of another court of competent jurisdiction.

[Follow general formula, p. 274, to the words "for plea nevertheless," then proceed:] to so much and such part of the said complainant's bill as seeks a discovery from this defendant of all, &c., &c. (here describe the discovery sought), this defendant doth plead thereto, and for plea saith that long before the said complainant's said bill was filed in this honorable court, and on or about the —— day of ——, the said complainant commenced a suit in the —— court of —— against this defendant in respect to the identical matters as to which such discovery is

40

sought in this suit from this defendant, and that such suit is still depending in the said court, which, as this defendant avers, is a court of competent jurisdiction to afford the discovery which the said complainant seeks by his said bill. Wherefore this defendant avers and pleads the same to the said complainant's bill, and prays the judgment of this honorable court whether it will hold plea upon and enforce this defendant to answer the said complainant's said bill, for the cause aforesaid.

Plea that the discovery sought by the bill, would betray the confidence reposed in the defendant as attorney.

[Follow general formula, p. 274, to the words "for plea nevertheless," then proceed:] to so much and such part of the said bill as seeks a discovery from this defendant of the title of W. W. another defendant in the said bill named, to all or any of the lands, tenements, or hereditaments, late of C. W. his late grandfather, deceased, in the said bill also named; this defendant doth plead thereto, and for plea saith, that he this, defendant, is duly admitted and sworn an attorney, duly licensed and practicing as such in the courts of Virginia, and has for several years past practiced, and now practices, as such; and this defendant was employed by C. W., deceased, the late father of the said other defendant, W. W., in the life-time of the said C. W., and since his decease hath also been employed in that capacity by the said other defendant J. W., the mother, and guardian of the said W. W. during his minority; and by the said W. W. since he attained his age of twenty-one years; and in that capacity only, or by means of such employment only, hath had the inspection and perusal of any of the title deeds of and belonging to the said estate, or any part or parts thereof for the use and service of his said clients, and therefore ought not, as this defendant is advised, to be compelled to discover the same. Wherefore this defendant doth plead the several matters aforesaid in bar to such discovery as aforesaid as is sought by the said bill and humbly prays the judgment of this honorable court whether he is bound to make any further or other answer thereto.

Plea that discovery will subject defendant to pains or penalties.

[Follow general formula to words "for plea nevertheless" then proceed:] to so much and such part of the said complainant's said bill as seeks to compel this defendant to set forth and discover whether &c., (here set forth the discovery sought) this defendant doth plead thereto, and for plea saith that to make the said discovery sought by the said bill would subject this defendant to the pains and penalties imposed by the laws and statutes of Virginia on those who, &c., (here set forth the tenor of the statute imposing the penalty); and this defendant's answer to the said complainant's bill, in case he should thereby admit, &c., might be received and read in evidence against him, this defendant in the proper court of Virginia, in any suit or prosecution to be there commenced against him, this defendant, for such offence. Wherefore this defendant doth

plead the several matters aforesaid, in bar to such
discovery as aforesaid as is sought by the said bill,
and humbly prays the judgment of this honorable
court, whether he is bound to make any further or
other answer thereto.

PRACTICAL NOTE.

An interesting case illustrating this topic is referred to by Prof.
Minor in his Institutes, vol. 4, part ii, p. 1165; the case of *U. S.*
vs. *McRae*, 4 Equity Cases Law Rep. 335, *et seq.*, in which the English courts, Sir W. Page Wood, v. c., decided that as an act of Congress of the United States denounced the forfeiture of all property
of persons concerned in the rebellion or holding any office or
agency under the Confederate States government, the plea of the
defendant was good both as a plea to the discovery and relief
sought: to the *discovery* because it would or might subject the
defendant to the confiscation of his property in the U. S.; to the
relief because in a bill of such a character, forfeiture must always
be waived before the bill can be filed, inasmuch as he who asks
equity must do equity.   Mitf. Pl. 226; 1 Dan. Ch. Pr. 354.

245. The following is the form of a plea to part of
the bill, followed by an answer as to the residue:

Plea to part of the Bill, and answer as to the residue.

The plea of R. L. and M. his wife, to part, and
their answer to the residue of the bill of complaint
of H. W. complainant.   These defendants, by protestation, not confessing or acknowledging all or any
of the matters and things in the complainant's said
bill of complaint to be true, in manner and form, as
the same are therein set forth and alleged, as to so
much of the said bill as seeks to controvert the value
of the several goods and things in the bill mentioned
to be bequeathed to the said defendant, M. L., by
U. G., deceased, in the bill named, in respect of which,

this defendant, R. L., hath recovered a verdict against the said complainant, and which seeks to controvert the right and title of these defendants, or either of them, to the same goods; and also to so much of the said bill as seeks to impeach the said verdict, which this defendant, R. L., hath obtained against the complainant, in respect of the same goods and effects, these defendants plead in bar; and for plea say, that before the intermarriage of these defendants, this defendant, M. L. (then M P. spinster), was possessed of, and legally, and well entitled to the said several goods and effects by virtue of the last will and testament of the said U. G., and that the complainant afterwards got the same into his custody and power. And these defendants having afterwards intermarried, and the said complainant refusing to redeliver the said goods and effects to this defendant, R. L., upon a demand by him made thereof, he, this defendant, R. L., brought his action at law against the said complainant, in order to obtain satisfaction for the same goods and effects; and in the ———— court of ————, declared against the said complainant in an action of trover and conversion of the same goods and effects, and laid his damages therein at three hundred dollars, to which declaration the said complainant pleaded not guilty. And the said cause came on to be heard, when and where, upon a full defence made by counsel on behalf of the now defendant, R. L., as of the said complainant, the jury impanelled and sworn to try the said issue, brought in a verdict in favor of this defendant, R. L., for $200 damages, besides costs of suit; which said ver-

dict is still in full force, and has not been impeached
or set aside by the said court where the said action
was tried; nor hath the said complainant (to the
knowledge or belief of these defendants) so much as
complained to the said court of the said verdict, or
attempted to obtain a new trial in the said action, by
reason that the said jury had found excessive damages, or the said verdict was given against evidence,
or to the dissatisfaction of the judge, before whom
the said action was tried. And this defendant, R. L.,
avers that the aforesaid demands of this defendant,
which are controverted by the said complainant's
now bill of complaint, and the demands of this
defendant, which were so as aforesaid ascertained
and established by the said verdict, are the same,
and not otherwise, or different. All which matters
and things these defendants are ready to verify,
maintain and prove, as this honorable court shall
direct, and do plead the same in bar of so much and
such parts of the said bill as are hereinbefore mentioned to be pleaded unto; and humbly pray the
judgment of this honorable court thereupon, and
whether they are liable, or shall be compelled to
make any further or other answer to so much of the
said bill as they have hereinbefore pleaded unto.
And these defendants insisting upon their said plea,
and in no wise waiving or departing from the same,
or the benefit thereof, by saving to themselves the
benefit of the said plea; and also saving and reserving to themselves all and all manner of advantage
and benefit of exception to the many insufficiencies,
errors and imperfections of the complainant's said

bill of complaint for answer thereunto, or to so much thereof as they are advised concerns them to make answer unto, they, these defendants, answer and say," &c.

PROCEEDINGS ON PLEAS.

246. *Plea to be set down or issue taken on it.*—A plaintiff in equity may have any plea or demurrer set down to be argued. And when the plea is supported by an answer, if the plea be objectionable it should be set down for argument before an exception is filed to the answer. Exceptions to the answer will have the effect of allowing the plea in the same manner as a replication to the plea would do. Mitf. Pl. 317; Story's Eq. Pl. 689. If the same be overruled no other plea or demurrer shall afterwards be received, but there shall be a rule upon the defendant to answer the bill. Code of 1873, ch. 167, sec. 33. A plaintiff in equity may take issue upon a plea and have such issue tried by a jury. If the plea be found false, he shall have the same advantages as if it had been so found by a verdict at law. *Ibid*, sec. 34.

247. *When dismission of cause if plea not set down nor issue taken.* The former statute was that "if the complainant shall not proceed to reply to or set for hearing any plea before the second court after filing the same, the bill might be dismissed with costs." 1 R. C. 1819, p. 215, § 99, and p. 257, § 57. This statute was not re-enacted in the Code of 1850. But its place is supplied by the provision found in that Code and in the Code of 1873, chap. 167, sec. 8, de-

claring among other things that "if the plaintiff"
"shall at any time fail to prosecute his suit, he shall
be non-suited and pay to the defendant besides his
costs, five dollars."[269]

248. *When plea on argument sustained.* The plaintiff, after the plea is sustained on argument, may still
take issue upon it. Mitf. Pl. 240; *Holmes, &c.*
vs. *Remsen, &c.*, 7 John. Ch. R. 286.

249. *When plea on argument overruled* The defendant, after the overruling of his plea on argument, will not be permitted to file another plea, but
must answer; and there should be a rule upon him
to answer. See Code 1873, ch. 167, sec. 33.

250. Where the statute of limitations is pleaded to
a bill which does not require an answer to support
the plea, and there is an answer notwithstanding,
which overrules the plea, if the plea be good in substance as to the whole or any part of the relief
sought, the court will permit the plea to stand as a

---

[269] The form of the entries may be as follows:

Form of Rule to reply to Plea.

The defendant, C. D., appeared and filed his plea to the plaintiff's bill, and,
on his motion, a rule is given to the plaintiff until the next rules to take issue
upon the said plea, or to set it down for argument.

Form of Entry at succeeding Rules if Plaintiff continue in default.

The defendant, C. D., at the last rules having given the plaintiff a rule to
take issue upon his the said C. D.'s plea, or to set it down for argument; and
the said plaintiff still failing to take issue upon the said plea, or to set it down
for argument, and herein failing to prosecute his suit, on the motion of the
said C. D. it is ordered that the said plaintiff be non-suited, and that he pay
the said defendant five dollars and his costs by him about his defence in this
behalf expended.

part of the answer, or will allow the defendants the full benefit of insisting upon the statute in their answer. *Souzer and wife* vs. *De Meyer, &c.*, 2 Paige 577. So where a plea of the statute is bad, because it is n t accompanied by an answer supporting it, and the court overrules the plea, and orders the defendant to answer, liberty will be given him to insist on the benefit of his statute in his answer. *Goodrich* vs. *Pendleton*, 3 Johns. Ch. Rep. 394; *Saltus* vs. *Tobias, &c.*, 3 Paige 346. Sometimes when a plea is overruled, the court will permit it to stand for an answer so far as it goes, with liberty to the complainant to except. *Orcutt* vs. *Orms*, 3 Paige 459; *Kirby and wife* vs. *Taylor, &c.*, 6 Johns. Ch. Rep. 254.

250*a*. Where a plea of the statute of limitations and the answer accompanying the same overruled, upon the ground that the answer contains such an acknowledgment of the debt as to defeat the operation of the statute, and the defendants are ordered to put in a full and perfect answer, if this decree be affirmed by an appellate court, and a motion be made to send back the cause with directions to allow the defendants to amend their answer so as to do away the effect of their admission, such motion will generally be denied. *Murray, &c.* vs. *Coster, &c.*, 20 Johns Rep. 604–610. If after these proceedings the defendant, instead of answering fully, puts in an answer giving in fact no discovery or response to the subject matter of the bill, but confined to the setting up of the statute as a bar, such answer may be excepted to. The defendant will not be permitted to bring the very same matter again into discussion,

41

but will be compelled to make discovery and answer
to the main charges in the bill. *Coster, &c.*, vs.
Murray, &c., 7 Johns. Ch. Rep. 167; S. C., on appeal,
4 Cow. 617.

251. *When issue taken upon it, and plea found
false.* If issue be taken upon the plea and the plea
be found false, as already seen, the same advantages
will accrue to the plaintiff as if it had been so found
by verdict at law. Code 1873, ch. 167, sec. 34.

252. If the defendant's affirmative plea is entirely
unsupported by evidence, and at the hearing of the
cause he makes default, the complainant will be entitled to a decree against him in the same manner as
if the several matters charged in the bill had been
confessed or admitted. *Dows, &c.* vs. *McMichael*, 2
Paige 345.

253. *When plea sustained by the proof.* If the
facts relied on by the plea are proved and the plea
is to the whole matter of the bill, a dismission of
the bill at the hearing is a matter of course. *Hughes*
vs. *Blake*, 1 Mason 515, 6 Wheat 472, *Dows* vs.
McMichael, 2 Paige 345, *Holmes* vs. *Remsen, &c.*, 7
John. Ch. Rep. 290.

254. Sometimes it is in the power of a defendant
to support his plea by the bill of the plaintiff and
the documents filed with it. This was the case in
Lane's ex'ix vs. *Ellzey*, 6 Rand. 661. The bill was
to foreclose a mortgage which was given to secure
the principal money, with interest, and rent of the
mortgaged premises. This appeared by the bill, and

the agreement filed with it. Issue was joined on the plea of usury, but no depositions were taken on either side. The Court of Appeals was of opinion that the bill and documents furnished such evidence in support of the plea˙that it ˙must be taken as true, unless some explanation compatible with the pleadings had been adduced on the other side. No such explanation being given the plea was sustained and the bill dismissed.

III. ANSWERS.

General nature of answers

254a. If a defendant cannot protect himself either by demurrer or plea from answering the plaintiff's bill and does not disclaim all right and interest in the subject of the suit, he must put in his answer, either to the whole bill or to such parts of it as are not covered by his demurrer or plea. Mitf. Pl. 289.[270] As we have already seen the defendant in the Virginia State courts may file his answer at any time before a final decree. *Bean* vs. *Simmons*, 9 Grat. 389. See *Preston, &c.* vs. *Heiskell*, 32 Grat. 48.

If a plea is overruled, the defendant may insist on the same matter by way of answer. Mitf. Pl. 306. But see *Townsend* vs. *Townsend*, 2 Paige 413, as to the necessity of obtaining special permission from the court to rely on the same matter in the answer when the plea has been overruled on the merits.

255. One of the offices of the answer is to furnish the result of an examination of the defendant upon

---

[270]A defendant is not bound to answer a cross bill until the other party has put in his answer to the original bill. *Long* vs.˙*Burton*, 2 Atk. 218.

the allegations of the bill. Mitf. Pl. 9, 301, 307.[271]

Besides this, the answer has generally another duty to perform, that of stating to the court the nature of the defence upon which the defendant means to rely; 2 Dan. Ch. Pr. (old) 238, in this respect fulfilling the duties of a plea or of a series of pleas either denying facts upon which the plaintiff's equity as stated in the bill arises, or confessing such facts and avoiding them by the introduction of some new matter from which contrary inferences may be drawn. 2 Dan. Ch. Pr. (old) 239.

256. It is of importance to the pleader, in preparing an answer, to bear in mind that besides answering the plaintiff's case as made by the bill, he has to state to the court in the answer all the circumstances of which the defendant intends to avail himself by way of defence; it being a well-established rule that a defendant is bound to apprize a plaintiff by his answer of the nature of the case he intends to set up, and that he cannot avail himself of any matter of defence which is not stated in his answer, even though it should appear in his evidence. 2 Dan. Ch. Pr. (old) 239.

257. It will be well also to remember that the plaintiff has a right even when the facts are uncontroverted, to have notice upon the record, in a pre-

---

[271]The plaintiff may require a discovery of facts material to the merits of his case and to enable him to obtain a decree, when he cannot otherwise prove the facts, or in aid of proof, and to avoid expense. Story's Eq. Pl. 319 n., 845, Mitf. Pl. 307. He is entitled also to a discovery of the matters necessary to substantiate the proceedings and to make them regular and effectual in a court of equity. Story's Eq. Pl. 845.

cise and unambiguous manner of the nature of the conclusions to be drawn from them. This, however, does not extend to conclusions in law.[272]

258. In drawing answers, as indeed in the preparation of all other pleadings, the draftsman should bear in mind that evidence as to matter not noticed in the pleadings will be of no avail.[273]

---

[272]Conclusions of fact are alone intended; it would be contrary to correct pleading to set out conclusions of law. Where a defendant stated upon his answer certain facts as evidence of a particular case which he represented to be the consequence of these facts and upon which he rested his defence, he was not permitted afterwards to make use of the same facts for the purpose of establishing a different defence from that to which by his answer he had drawn the plaintiff's attention, Dan. Ch. Pr., edi. 1871, pp. 712, 713, Dan. Ch. Pr. (old) 240; but a defendant may by his answer set up any number of defences as the consequences of the same facts. 2 Dan. Ch. Pr. (old) 241. He cannot, however, insist upon two defences inconsistent with each other, or which are the consequences of inconsistent facts. 2 Dan. Ch. Pr. (old) 241, *Jesus College* vs. *Gibbs*, 1 Y. & C. 145, *Leich & Bailey*, 6 Price 504.

[273]In *Knibb's ex'or* vs. *Dixon's ex'or*, 1 Rand. 249, the complainant alleged that a bill of sale executed by him was intended merely as a security for money to be paid by the defendant to the complainant's creditors; and on the part of the defendant the transfer of the property was relied upon as an absolute one. But the testimony of the defendant was not confined to this question. It went on to establish that the bill of sale was executed by the complainant with intent to defraud creditors, and thus to show that the complainant was not entitled to be relieved by a court of equity. This fraud of the complainant not being put in issue by anything in the pleadings, the evidence in relation thereto was excluded.

In *Sale* vs. *Dishman's ex'ors*, 3 Leigh 548, the bill was filed in February, 1819, against the executors of a deceased partner to recover a balance which was due under a contract with the partnership made in March, 1812. It appeared that the partnership was dissolved in April, 1812; that by the terms of the contract the money became due January 1, 1813, and that the death of the decedent took place in June, 1813. The surviving partner was insolvent when the bill was filed, but how long he had been insolvent did not appear. There had been no proceedings against him by the creditor; and his *laches*, it was insisted in the appellate court, would rebut the equity raised in his behalf against the deceased partner. But the defendants had made no charge of *laches* in the answer, or in any part of the pleadings. The Court of

259. While it is necessary in an answer to use such a degree of certainty as will inform the plaintiff of the nature of the case to be made against him, it is not requisite that the same degree of accuracy should be observed in an answer as is required in a bill. 2 Dan. Ch. Pr. (old) 244.

260. If the defence which can be made to a bill consists of a variety of circumstances, so that it is not proper to be offered by way of plea, or if it is doubtful whether a plea will hold, the defendant may set forth the whole by way of answer and pray the same benefit of so much as goes in bar as if it had been pleaded in bar. Mitf. Pl. 308. So, also, if the defendant can offer a matter of plea which would be a complete bar, but has no reason to protect himself from any discovery sought by the bill, and can offer circumstances which he conceives to be favorable to his case and which he could not offer together with a plea, he may set forth the whole matter in the same manner,[274] and at the hearing any such benefit can be relied on, 2 Dan. Ch. Pr. (old) 244, but only at the hearing. *Ibid.*

Appeals held that the question not being presented by the pleadings could not be examined.

See *Stanley* vs. *Robinson*, 1 Russ. & M. 527.

[274]Mitf. Pl. 308. Thus, if a purchaser for a valuable consideration, clear of all charges of fraud or notice, can offer additional circumstances in his favor, which he cannot set forth by way of plea, or of answer to support a plea, as the expending a considerable sum of money in improvements, with the knowledge of the plaintiff, it may be more prudent to set out the whole by way of answer than to rely on the single defence by way of plea, unless it is material to prevent disclosure of any circumstance attending his title. Mitf. Pl. 309.

Matter of answer.

261. *General rule that defendant answering must answer fully.* The defendant is required, upon his oath, to make a full, true, direct, perfect and sufficient answer, according to the best of his knowledge, recollection, information and belief, to all and singular the several matters and things alleged in the bill. 2 Dan. Ch. Pr. (old) 238, Story's Eq. Pl. 846. As to all matters and statements in the bill against which the defendant does not protect himself by plea or demurrer, the answer must be fully responsive. *Ibid.* Submitting to answer, the defendant must· answer fully. This is the general rule.[275]

262. But there are exceptions to the rule. Thus, a defendant, though he does not protect himself by plea or demurrer, is not, by submitting to answer, bound to answer matters purely scandalous, or immaterial[276] or irrelevant, Story's Eq. Pl. 846; nor is he bound to answer anything which may subject him to a penalty, forfeiture or punishment; *Ibid.* See *Brockway* vs. *Copp*, 3 Paige 544, 2 Rob. Pr. (old)

---

[275]*Methodist Church* vs. *Jaques, &c.*, 1 John. Ch. Rep. 65, *Cuyler* vs. *Bogert, &c.*, 3 Paige 186, 2 Rob. Pr. (old) 307. See a discussion of the subject whether a party can by answer protect himself from making a full answer to all the matters contained in the bill in Wigram on Discovery, Dan. Ch. Pr. (Perk.) 733, Story's Eq. Pl. 847 and notes. Bridgman in his Digest, p. 29, pl. 146, collects all the cases prior to 1824. Sir John Leach thought the rule that a defendant who submitted to answer should answer fully was so useful a rule that he declared he should always adhere to it. *Mazareddo* vs. *Maitland*, 3 Madd. 70. See *Bk. Utica* vs. *Messerau*, 7 Paige 518.

[276]A defendant was permitted by answer to refuse to make discovery on the ground of the immateriality of the fact of which the discovery was sought. *Kuypees* vs. *Ref. Dutch Church*, 6 Paige 570, *Davis* vs. *Mapes*, 2 Paige 105.

307; nor is he bound to answer what would involve a breach of professional confidence. Story's Eq. Pl. 846, *Stratford* vs. *Hogan,* 2 Ball & Beat. 164.

263. *Whether a bona fide purchaser for value, without notice, can answer relying upon his purchase and make no farther disclosure.* It was stated by Mr. Robinson in his work on Equity Practice in Virginia that such a purchaser constituted one of the exceptions to the rule that a defendant who answered must answer fully. This exception as stated by him will be found in the note below.[277] Mr. Justice Story de-

---

[277] "It has been determined that equity will not take from one who is a purchaser for valuable consideration, without notice, any advantage which the law gives him. And therefore where a purchaser by his answer sets up his defence, and denies notice, and all the circumstances mentioned in the bill from which notice may be inferred, equity will not compel him to go on to make a discovery as to those circumstances which destroy his title. *Jerrard* vs. *Saunders,* 2 Ves. Jun. 454; *Cuyler, &c.* vs. *Bogert, &c.,* 3 Paige 186; *Frost, &c.* vs. *Beekman,* 1 Johns. Ch. Rep. 300. Whoever rests his case on the fact of his being a *bona fide* purchaser must deny notice in the answer, though it be not charged in the bill, and deny it positively, not evasively. *Tompkins* vs. *Mitchell,* 2 Rand. 428; Carr, J. in *Downman, &c.* vs. *Rust, &c.,* 6 Rand. 591; *Denning, &c.* vs. *Smith, &c.,* 3 Johns. Ch. Rep. 345; *Galatian* vs. *Erwin, &c.,* 1 Hopkins's Ch. Rep. 55, 56, 57, 58. It must also appear with certainty, in the answer, that he was a complete purchaser before notice. *Hoover* vs. *Donally, &c.,* 3 H. & M. 316. He must both have received a conveyance and paid his purchase-money, before notice. Pendleton, president, in *Wixcox* vs. *Calloway,* 1 Wash. 41. See also *ante,* p. 27. Yet even in the case of a *bona fide* purchaser, although the defendant may by answer show himself such a purchaser, and may object to any discovery as to the other matters of the bill, he is not permitted to select such parts of those matters as he thinks proper to answer, and leave the others unanswered. Where the fact of the defendant's being a purchaser without notice is stated in the answer instead of being pleaded, the rules of pleading will be applied. The defendant having by answer objected to the discovery of particular matters in the bill, and then answered those matters in part, his objection will be considered overruled, and the complainants will be entitled to a discovery of every material fact stated in the bill. *Cuyler, &c.* vs. *Bogert, &c.,* 3 Paige 186." 2 Rob. Pr. (old) 307, 308. See also *Doswell* vs. *Buchanan,* 3 Leigh, 365, and, specially, *Donnell, & als.* vs. *King's heirs,* 7 Leigh, 393.

clares the rule now to be that sucn a purchaser, if he wishes protection from answering the allegations of the bill, must protect himself by plea. Story's Eq. Pl. 847; *Portarlington* vs, *Soulby*, 7 Sim. 28. This is not the law in the Virginia State courts. See *Donnell, &c.* vs. *King's Heirs*, 7 Leigh 393.

The Virginia doctrine sustains Mr. Robinson. In *Donnell & als.* vs. *King's Heirs*, 7 Leigh 393, it was held, that the defence of purchase for valuable consideration without notice might be made by answer as well as by plea.

264. *Practice in the United States Circuit Courts.* The thirty-ninth and forty-fourth rules of the United States Supreme Court, found in a subsequent section,[278] settle the practice on the question mentioned in section 263, so far as the United States Circuit Courts are concerned.

265 *Whether other exceptions to the general rule.* Whether a defendant who has submitted to answer can in any case other than those already mentioned protect himself without a plea or demurrer, from answering fully, is a question as to which courts are divided. In the Court of Exchequer it was held that where there would be a clear and irresistible objection to the plaintiff's claim unless a particular fact exist and the answer of the defendant contains a positive denial of that fact, the defendant is not bound to answer farther; as, for example, when the

---

[278]See sec. 299, *post.*

[279]See the case of *Hornby* vs. *Pemberton*, Mosley 58, referred to in section 272 *post.*

bill states a partnership to have existed between the plaintiff and defendant and alleges that on taking the account a balance would be due the plaintiff and calls for a settlement, if the defendant by his answer state the true nature of the agreement between him and the plaintiff, and deny the existence of the partnership, it has been held that no exception can be taken to the answer for not making any farther discovery. *Jacobs* vs. *Goodman*, 2 Cox's Ch. Cas. 282, *Randal* vs. *Head*, &c., Hard. 188, *Gweet* vs. *Young*, 1 Amb. 353, *Richardson* vs. *Hulbert*, &c., 1 Anst. 65.[279] In the Court of Chancery the opinions expressed at different times are various and discordant. In many cases it is laid down that if a defendant has a defence which will excuse him from a discovery as to the whole or any material part of the bill he must make such defence by demurrer or plea. In all the discussions it is conceded that there are exceptions to the general rule See *Dolder* vs. *Lord Huntingfield*, 11 Ves. 283, *Faulder* vs. *Stuart*, *id.* 296, *Shaw* vs. *Ching*, *id.* 303. Chancellor Kent, after reviewing the authorities, came to the conclusion that no inflexible rule existed on the subject; that the general rule existed, but how far that rule should be controlled, he said, must be determined by the reason and convenience of each case. *Philips*, &c. vs. *Prevost*, 4 John Ch. Rep. 205.

In *Northwestern Bank* vs. *Nelson*, 1 Grat. 130, a bill of discovery the question was considered. The court of appeals of Virginia held, that, notwithstanding the overruling of a demurrer to a bill, a defendant is at liberty to file any sufficient answer;

an answer to a bill of discovery is sufficient when it
shows that the defendant is protected from making
the discovery sought by the bill; and in that case
the averments in the defendant's answer[280] were such
as if true entitled him to the protection which he
claimed.

266. The defendant is required to answer the
whole of the statements and charges in the bill, and
all the interrogatories founded upon them, at least,
so far as they are necessary to enable the plaintiff to
have a complete decree against him; 2 Dan. Ch. Pr.
(old) 247. See *Agar* vs. *Regents' Canal Company*,
Coop. 215;[281] but a defendant is not bound to answer
an interrogatory unless it is founded upon the previous statements or charges of the bill; *Gerrard* vs.
Saunders, 2 Ves. Jr. 454, 458, Story's Eq. Pl. 36, 37;
though if he does answer it he will thereby put the
matter in issue. 1 Dan. Ch. Pr. (Perk.) 729.

267. The defendant must speak directly, without
evasion, meeting particularly and precisely the specific charges in the bill and giving the most correct
account he can give. What circumstances connected with the facts charged are material and proper to be disclosed must depend upon the nature of

---

[280] Which were that to answer the matters alleged in the bill would expose
the respondent to pains, penalties or punishment, or to a criminal prosecution
therefor.

[281] A principal end of an answer upon the oath of the defendants, is to supply proof of the matters necessary to support the case of the plaintiffs; and
it is therefore required of the defendants either to admit or deny all the facts
set forth in the bill with their attending circumstances, or to deny having any
knowledge or information on the subject, or any recollection of it, and also
to declare themselves unable to form any belief concerning it. Mitf. Pl. 44.

the case. The detail of attending circumstances is not to be so minute as to become burdensome and oppressive nor so general as to withhold any information material and proper. *Meth. Ch.* vs. *Jaques, &c.,* 1 John C. R. 65.

If a defendant be called on to answer whether a debt due by him be paid, and he evade the question, he can be compelled to give a categorical answer. *Kyle* vs. *Kyle,* 1 Grat. 526.

268. When it is said that a defendant who answers should answer fully, it must be understood only as to matters which are well pleaded, that is, to the facts stated and charged. To matters of law or inferences of law drawn from the facts he need not answer. 2 Dan. Ch. Pr. (old) 247.[282]

269. In general if a fact is charged which is in the defendant's own knowledge as if done by himself, he must answer positively and not to his remembrance or belief only,[283] 2 Dan. Ch. Pr. (old) 256;

---

[282] Where a defendant who was a trustee, or in the nature of one, stated upon his answer, in general terms, that he was a stranger to several matters and things in the bill mentioned, and that he could not set forth any other or further answer thereto, either as to knowledge, belief or otherwise, it appearing clearly that no benefit would result to the plaintiff from requiring an answer to each fact and interrogatory, the answer was considered sufficient. *Jones* vs. *Wiggins,* 2 Y. & J. 385; Story's Eq. Pl. 846.

[283] As to facts which have not happened within the defendant's knowledge, he must answer as to his information or belief, and not state information or hearsay merely, without giving his belief one way or the other. *Smith* vs. *Lasher, &c.,* 5 John. C. R. 247; *Cuyler, &c.* vs. *Bogert, &c,,* 3 Paige 186. But where the defendant in his answer stated that he had not any "knowledge or information" as to the truth or falsity of a particular matter, without stating his belief concerning the same, it was considered sufficient, for he was not to be supposed to have any belief one way or the other. *Morris, &c.* vs. *Parker,* 3 John C. R. 297. So where a defendant answered that he knew nothing as to certain matters except what was set forth in the bill, but

Woods vs. *Morrell, &c.*, 1 John C. R. 107; *Slater* vs.
Maxwell, 6 Wal. 268; but where there is room to
doubt whether a positive answer can be given, as if
the fact had occurred at a great distance of time, the
court may allow an admission or denial according to
the best of the defendant's knowledge and belief.
Sloan vs. *Little*, 3 Paige 103, *Hull* vs. *Wood*, 1 Paige
404, *Davis* vs. *Mapes, &c.*, 2 Paige 107. When one
charge embraces several particulars, the answer
should be in the disjunctive, denying each particular,
or admitting some and denying others according to
the fact. *Davis* vs. *Mapes, &c*, 2 Paige 108. If the
defendant has knowledge or information only as to
one of the facts charged, he may answer as to that
fact in the usual manner, and deny all knowledge or
information as to the residue of the matters stated
in the bill. *Utica Ins. Co.* vs. *Lynch, &c.*, 3 Paige
210.

270. A defendant when called upon[284] to answer as
to his knowledge, remembrance, information and
belief, cannot by merely saying, "that a matter may
be true for anything he knows to the contrary,"
avoid stating what is his recollection, information or
belief concerning it or stating that he has no recollection or information, or that he cannot form any
belief concerning it, either in these words or in
equivalent expressions; and where defendants have

---

that he believed they were true as stated in the bill, it was considered that it
would be of no benefit to require a farther answer. *Davis, &c.* vs. *Mapes, &c.*,
2 Paige 105.

[284] The edit. of Dan. Ch. Pr. by Perkins, p. 736, used the words, "if so
called upon." In the earlier editions these words are not used; 2 Dan. Ch.
Pr. (old) 256; nor are they used in the edition of 1871. See pp. 723, 724.

in their power the means of acquiring the information necessary to give the discovery called for, they are bound to make use of such means, whatever pains or trouble it may cost them.[285] 2 Dan. Ch. Pr. (old) 257; see Story's Eq. Pl. 855*a*, 855*b*.

271. To so much of the bill as is necessary or material for the defendant to answer, he must not merely answer the several charges literally but he must confess or deny the substance of each charge. Mitf. Pl. 309. And wherever there are particular precise charges, they must be answered particularly and precisely, and not in a general manner, though the general answer may amount to a full denial of the charges. *Ibid.* 2 Rob. Pr. (old) 310.

272. Although the defendant by his answer denies the title of the plaintiff, yet in many cases he must make a discovery prayed by the bill though not material to the plaintiff's title, and though the plaintiff,

---

[285] In *White* vs. *Williams*, 8 Ves. 193, 195, Lord *Eldon* said that the plaintiff has a right in a suit for an account to have by the answer, connecting itself with books and accounts referred to as part thereof, the fullest information the defendant can give him.

The rule is laid down in reference to the answers of corporations aggregate; that, before putting in their answers, it is their duty to cause every deed, paper and muniment in their possession or power, to be diligently examined, and to give in their answer all the information which results from such an examination. Mr. Daniell thinks this rule may be applied to all individuals who are required to answer at all. 2 Dan. Ch. Pr. (old) 257, 258, 262, 263, 264. *Attorney General* vs. *Bailiffs, &c.*, of East Redford, 2 M. & K. 35.

In *Kittredge* v. *Claremont B'k*, 1 Wood & Minot, 244, *Woodbury*, J., said: That the officers answering for the bank sued, if they are not the same persons who were in office at the time of the transaction inquired about, ought to go not only to the records, books and files for information, but to the former officers if living, and ascertain as near as may be the truth about which they are interrogated.

if he has no title, can have no benefit from the discovery. Mitf. Pl. 310. Thus, if a bill is filed
against an executor by a creditor of the testator,
the executor must admit assets or set forth an account, though he denies the debt. *Ibid.* But where
the defendant sets up a title in himself apparently
good, and which the plaintiff must remove to found
his own title, the defendant is not generally compelled to make any discovery not material to the
trial of the question of title. Mitf. Pl. 311.

In a bill by one partner against another for a discovery of partnership dealings, the defendant was called on to discover what
goods he had consigned to England to other persons. The defendant set forth that he had consigned several parcels of goods to
plaintiff, and submitted, upon certain facts which he also stated,
whether plaintiff had not determined the partnership. Exceptions
were taken to this answer and sustained, for should it be determined that the plaintiff was entitled to the discovery, and the
defendant in the mean time die, the plaintiff had no means of
coming at the knowledge of these consignments. *Hornby* vs. *Pemberton*, Moseley 58.[286]

273. The true tests ascertaining whether questions
in a bill are to be answered or not, are, 1st. Whether
the answer might lead to the crimination of the defendant, and 2nd. Whether the subjects are relevant
and may be material to the case of the complainant.
Mant vs. *Scott*, 3 Price 477.

273*a*. Answers should not contain impertinent[287]

---

[286] See, however, *Jacobs* vs. *Goodman*, 3 Bro. C. C. 487 n., and other cases
cited in Mitf. Pl. 312, 313, n. (*a.*)

[287] As to impertinence in answers see Mitf. Pl. (Jeremy) 313, n. 1, and the
following cases: *Wagstaff* vs. *Bryant*, 1 Russ & M. 28; *Hood* vs. *Inman*,
4 John. Ch. R. 437; *Woods* vs. *Morrell*, 1 John. Ch. R. 103; *Slack* vs. *Evans*,
7 Price 278; *The King* vs. *Teale*, 7 Price 278. An exception for impertinence
must be supported *in toto*, and if it include any passage which is not imperti-

or irrelevant[288] matter, Mitf. Pl. 313, 2 Dan. Ch. Pr.
(old) 295; or scandalous[289] matter, Ibid.   Such mat-

---

nent, it must fail altogether.   *Wagstaff* vs. *Bryan*, 1 Russ. & M. 30.

Daniell mentions a case in which a defendant answering a bill, which calls.
for an account of the quantities of ore, &c., dug in particular mines, put in a
schedule of 3,431 folios, setting forth all the particular items of each trades-
man's bill connected with the mines: it was held impertinent. *Norway*
vs. *Rowe*, 1 Mer. 347, 2 Dan. Ch. Pr. (old) 263.

[288] 2 Rob. Pr. (old) 310; *Woods* vs. *Morrill, &c.,* 1 John. Ch. R. 103.

[289] Such an instance occurred in *Mason* vs. *Mason,* 4 H. & M. 414. This.
answer is a curiosity in legal literature.   It here follows:

ANSWER.

" If Abraham Barnes Thompson Mason can address the hon. court under
the title of orator, the clumsy clown, James W. Wallace, can do so too. Well,
then, your orator asks the hon. court if Mrs. Elizabeth Mason (whose honesty
and integrity will sound high in heaven) (and on earth where she is known,)
is proverbial for too delicate a sense of justice and honor by which she has
injured her finances—nay, brought herself from a sufficiency to want, I ask
if she kept in her own possession the books keeping the accounts of the estate
of James Wallace and Thompson Mason, dec'd, how can the orator, A. B. T.
Mason, know that there is a balance due from the one estate to the other?
with what propriety can he accuse a character like Mrs. Mason's of embezzlement?   How indelicate to such refined feelings, as I presume the court to.
possess, will come such a charge against a father's widow.   Test their souls
by analysis; will not A. B. T. Mason be found all caput mortuum?   Mrs.
Mason's, like the diamond exposed to heat, no residuum?   Your orator is no
lawyer, but follows another trade; is a dull, plain man—a mere Tom Bowlin,
and often gives offence where he means respect.   Being clumsy and heavy in
words, he knows no laws but those of honest integrity, and has no guide but
justice.   It appears to him that if Mrs. Mason used the tobacco (but does not
believe she used one pipe full), that she, Mrs Mason, the adm'x, is propria
persona the responsible person.   The prayer of the orator, A. B. T. Mason,
even admitting the embezzlement, is a prayer to visit the sins of the parent
upon the child; i. e., if the descendants of James Wallace are made defendants agreeable to the wish of the orator, A. B. T. Mason.

The character of Thompson Mason, deceased, I revere.   He appears to me,
from the best of my memory, to have possessed too much soul; too much
native honesty for the world he lived in—a just remark to his honorable
manes.

To the best of my knowledge, my brother, Robt. Wallace, clothed me
generally, and gave me what pocket money I got.   From the most mature
reflection, I am fully satisfied that l am not indebted to the estate of Thompson Mason one cent.   The orator, A. B. T. Mason, in his prayer to the hon-

ter will be expunged.   Mitf. Pl. 313, 4 H. & M. 414.
If an answer goes out of the bill to state some mat-

---

court, says Thompson Mason retained tobacco as an indemnity against his disbursements (I am not disposed to believe the assertions of A. B. T. Mason);
but let us take his word for it, for I suppose that he knew not that such an
acknowledgment is equal to a receipt in full.   Let him then prove what T.
Mason's ex'or did with the tobacco.   *He says* Mrs. Mason used it; let him
then prove it; even then the orphan proves his reimbursements, Thompson
Mason dying with full indemnity in his hands.   The orator, A. B. T. Mason,
says Mrs. Mason detains the books of the estate   Without knowledge then
on the subject, he roundly asserts a great balance.   Pray unde derivatur
such information?   Does it come from Terra del Fuego, Labrador, Botany
bay; or comes it fresh from the rapacious mouth of the white bear of Missouri?   Mrs. Mason was compelled to sell her dower in a thousand or twelve
hundred acres of land, I believe, to S. T. Mason for the pitiful sum of £100,
to buy even a bed to lie on at the sale of Thompson Mason.   Does this smell
of embezzlement of tobacco? does it show she was full-handed, or poor indeed?   It is the opinion of J. W. Wallace, that if any fraud has been practised, it was not by the but too honest E. Mason, but by the orator, A. B. T.
Mason.   A long life of virtue, honesty and religion will fully exculpate Mrs.
Mason.   Let the orator, A. B. T. Mason, put his hand on his heart, if any
there be in his breast, and say, " I never did but fairly."   There was a paper
from your court, served on me, accusing me of contempt to the court.   I am
innocent of such charge.   I never said, acted or thought with any such design.   To be plain, I know no more of your court than I do of the hydrography
of the moon, and have as little design to insult the one as navigate the waters
of the other.

Articles in the Bill of A. B. T. Mason.

1. The orator says that J. Wallace died in 1776 having made a will.
Ans. Grant it, but I don't know the date of his death.
2. That T. Mason married the widow of J. Wallace in 1778.
Ans. Grant it, but I know not the date of the marriage.
3. E. Mason was ex'x. or adm'x. of J. Wallace.
Ans. I always heard and believe she acted for the estate of J. Wallace
before her marriage with T. Mason.
4. T. Mason made disbursements for the est. of J. Wallace.
Ans. Ignorant on my part.
5. Thompson Mason died possessed of tobacco bonds to indemnify himself
for disbursements made for J. Wallace's estate.
Ans. Ignorant on my part, but the orator A. B. T. Mason says he did.
Now court, hear me; what became of this tobacco?   Cannot you give to the
orator A. B. T. Mason an anti-tobacco dose to work him the orator upwards,

43

ter not material to the defendant's case, it will be deemed impertinent. Mitf. Pl. 313.

274. Sometimes, the defence of one defendant is helped by the defence of a co-defendant. A creditor of a testator filed a bill against the executor and a legatee. The latter relied on the Statute of Limitations in his answer. It was held that this was enough to protect the estate from a decree against the executor. *Tazewell* vs. *Whittle*, 13 Grat. 329.

275. *Cooth* vs. *Jackson*, 6 Ves. 37, 38, may be referred to in the preparation of an answer to a bill for the specific performance of a parol agreement. *Smith* vs. *Nicholas*, 8 Leigh 330, is an instructive case as to the manner of answering in cases of usury.[290]

---

to work him the orator downwards, and make him the orator disgorge hogsheads of tobacco from both ends.

6. The estate of J. Wallace divided among his children.

Ans. I got I believe as much as the other children in negro property.

COMMENT. T. Mason lived and died lagely in debt. Court, is it reasonable that he would sell his own produce and tobacco for the support of the children of J. Wallace and do it with a full conviction of an injury to his own children when he had the tobacco of J. Wallace's estate in his own hands kept up forsooth for indemnity—would he not sell for their use, their own tobacco?

Oh! Jonah, why didst thou swallow the whale?

FAUQUIER, TO WIT: 1807 *May* 1st.

This day Jas. W. Wallace appeared before me, a justice of the peace, and made oath that this answer is true to the best of his memory and judgment.

SIMON MORGAN."

Chancellor Taylor referred the answer to a commissioner or master in Chancery, to expunge the impertinent and scandalous matter. 4 H. & M. 414.

An answer may be referred for scandal on the motion of a defendant; yet the Lord Chancellor thought there might be a difference between a plaintiff and a defendant referring for impertinence. *Coffin* vs. *Cooper*, 6 Ves. 514.

[290] See the answer in that case in a future section. The answer should

276. If the defendant wishes to avail himself of the Statute of Limitations and it be not pleaded in form, it should at least be insisted upon as a defence in the pleadings. *Hudsons* vs. *Hudson's adm'or, &c.*, 6 Munf. 352; *Hickman* vs. *Stout*, 2 Leigh 6; *Dey* vs. *Dunham*, 2 John. Ch. R. 191.

277. Where the complainant by his bill sets up an agreement which would be invalid by the Statute of Frauds, unless it were in writing, and it does not appear by the bill whether there was a writing or not, if there were in fact no writing, and the defendant desires to have the benefit of the statute, it is most prudent for him to state the fact that there was no writing and insist in the pleadings upon the benefit of the defence arising under the statute. *Cozine* vs. *Graham, &c.*, 2 Paige 177. Though, perhaps this is not always necessary; for if the answer deny the agreement stated in the bill, the plaintiff, it would seem, must produce legal evidence of its existence, and this can only be done by producing a written agreement duly executed according to the statute, or by making out a case of part performance. *S. C. and Ontario Bk.* vs. *Root, &c.*, 3 Paige 481. In no case need the statute be formally pleaded. It is always sufficient for the defendant to rely on the statute in his answer. *Rowton* vs. *Rowton*, 1 H. & M. 92.

---

distinctly allege the facts constituting the usury, but it is not necessary to allege the facts with the formal strictness of a plea of usury at law. *Smith* v. *Nicholas*, 8 Leigh 330. When *Smith* vs. *Nicholas* was decided, usury forfeited the whole debt. Now the contract is declared to be for an illegal consideration as to the interest alone. See note 261 to Practical Note on Plea of Usury, p. 291, *ante*.

Where an injunction bill injoining a judgment upon a note obtained by fraud, charged only fraud in the procurement of the
note *by the payee*, and the assignment to the holder who had obtained a judgment thereon, but did not charge that the holder was
an endorsee without value, or that he had notice of the fraud, and
the defendant in his answer averred that he was a holder for value
without notice of the fraud, and stated the consideration which he
gave for the note, it was held that this statement of the answer
was not responsive to any allegation of the bill and must be
proved. *Vathir* vs. *Zane*, 6 Grat. 246.

278. *A defendant charged in two characters should
answer in both.* A bill charged a defendant both in
the capacity of surviving partner and of executor
de son tort; he was not permitted to answer only in
the one capacity, and excuse himself from answering
in the other on the ground that the plaintiff was not
entitled to claim such answer. By submitting to
answer, the court held that he rendered himself
liable not only as to the accounts of the estate so
received by him but also as to the partnership dealings. *Leigh* vs. *Burch*, 9 Jur. n., s. 1265.

279. *Effect of not noticing in the answer a statement
in the bill.* In *Coleman* vs. *Lynes ex'or*, 4 Ran. 454,
the court considered the effect of an omission to
notice in the answer a statement of the bill. The
court held, in that case, that the allegations not
noticed were not to be deemed to be admitted.
Some of the Virginia cases countenance the idea
that allegations made in the bill and not denied
in the answer are to be considered as admitted;
but these are cases in which the allegation in the
bill was that some fact did *not* exist or that something was *not* done, or cases (as in *Scott* vs. *Gibbon*,
5 Munf. 86) where the documents and circumstances

in the cause prove *prima facie* that the fact alleged
and not denied is true. Tnus in *Page's ex'or* vs.
Winston's adm'or, 2 Munf. 298, a bill of injunction
charged the plaintiff at law with "refusing to deliver certain escape warrants properly endorsed
when demanded"; the answer took no notice of this
most material allegation: the omission to do so was
held to be a tacit acknowledgment of its truth,[291] and
the court decreed accordingly. In *Edgar* vs. *Donelly
&c.*, 2 Munf. 387, the plaintiff called upon the defendant as assignee of a bond to say whether he had
notice of its consideration when he received the
money due thereon. In his answer the defendant
said that he had no such notice when he took the
assignment; the answer was not considered as admitting notice when he received the money. In
Scott vs. *Gibbon*, 5 Munf. 86, a deed exhibited with
the bill bore date before the marriage and recited
that a marriage was about to be had and solemnized;
the deed was not acknowledged until after the marriage. *Leigh* alleged in the argument, and it was not
denied by the counsel on the other side, that "the
fact of the deed under which the plaintiff claimed
being executed before the marriage, was distinctly
alleged in the bill and not denied or even noticed
in the answers and *was not in issue.*" The court's
ruling sustaining the deed declared that "it was conceded in the cause that the deed was executed prior
to the marriage," thus adopting the position *Leigh*
had taken.

---

[291] The court held that there was no need in such case for an exception to
the answer or any interlocutory order taking the bill for confessed in part.

280. *Discovery of documents and papers.* A defendant is not compelled by his answer to discover or to produce documents and papers which wholly and solely respect his own title or defence. As a matter of right, the plaintiff is not entitled to the discovery and production of any documents or papers called for by the bill except those which appertain to his own case or the title made by his bill. Story's Eq. Pl. 858.

281. But if the defendant does answer and refer to documents and papers in his answer, the question will then arise, is he bound to produce them for the inspection of the plaintiff upon motion. This question may arise under different aspects of the answer; 1, they may be referred to in the answer and not be admitted to be in the defendant's possession; or 2, they may be in part set forth or shortly stated in the answer as in the defendant's possession, and referred to in the answer for greater certainty when produced; or, according to the common form, "as will appear by the said documents and papers, to which, for greater certainty, the defendant craves leave to refer." In the first case, the court cannot order the production of the documents and papers unless they respect the plaintiff's title, and unless although stated not to be in the possession of the defendant they happen to be in the hands of some person over whom the defendant evidently has a control. In the second case, in one of the decisions it was held that the defendant by his mode of referring to the documents and papers had made them a part of his answer and although they solely respected the de-

fendant's title he was required to produce them, *Hardman* vs. *Ellames*, 2 Mylne & Keen 757, but this decision of *Hardman* vs. *Ellames*, though affirmed by Lord Cottenham in *Adams* vs. *Fisher*, 3 Mylne & Craig 526, 548, is greatly weakened if not over-turned by the more recent case of *Howard* vs. *Robinson*, 5 Jur. n., s. 136.[292]

282. In *Hardman* vs. *Ellames*, 2 Mylne & Keen 757, it was held, and this is understood to be the doctrine of all the cases, that the documents and papers if not referred to in the answer if they relate solely to the defendant's title will not be required to be produced though admitted to be in the defendant's possession; if, however, they relate to the plaintiff's title their production will be ordered.[293]

283. If a defendant be called on to set out a deed or other instrument he is bound to produce, he should do so or give some reason for not complying; he may, however, avoid this by admitting that he has the deed, &c., in his possession and offering to give the plaintiff a copy. When he sets out the paper *in haec verba* or by way of recital, it is best always to crave leave to refer to it; by doing so, he makes it a part of his answer and relieves himself from any charge in case it should be erroneously set out. Dan. Ch. Pr. (Perk.) 739, 368, 369.

---

[292] See *Swinburne* vs. *Nelson*, 15 Eng. Law and Eq. 572; Wigram on Disc. 153–161; Hare on Disc. pp. 183–244; Gresley on Evidence 25–37; Story's Eq. Pl. 859 and notes. See *Tyson* vs. *Tyson*, 14 Geo. 167.

[293] If defendants in a case seeking for the discovery of a correspondence, set forth extracts of letters, and swear that these are the only parts of the correspondence upon that subject, it is sufficient. *Campbell* vs. *French*, 1 Anst. 58.

Form of Answer.

284. Two or more persons may join in the same answer, and where their interests are the same and they appear by the same counsel, they ought to do so, unless some good reason exists for answering separately. 2 Dan. Ch. Pr. (old) 265; Dan. Ch. Pr. (Perk.) 742.[294] Where two defendants answer jointly and one speaks positively for himself, the other may in cases where he is not charged with anything upon his own knowledge, say that he has perused the answer and believes it to be true, 1 Har. Ch. 185; but, adds Harrison, it is otherwise where the defendants answer separately. *Ibid.* We have no decision in the Virginia State Courts adopting this rule. No reason ' is perceived why an answer of one defendant adopting *totidem verbis* the answer of another should not be deemed sufficient.

285. An answer is headed by the title: "The answer of C. D., defendant to the bill of complaint exhibited against him [*or*, and others] by A. B., in the ———— court of ————." If two or more defendants join in the same answer, it is entitled, "The joint and several answer, &c," unless it be the answer of a man and wife, in which case it is called

---

[294] The 62nd rule of the Supreme Court prescribes: "When the same solicitor is employed for two or more defendants and separate answers shall be filed, or other proceedings had by two or more defendants separately, costs shall not be allowed for such separate answers or other proceedings, unless a master, upon reference to him, shall certify that such separate answers and other proceedings were necessary or proper, and ought not to have been joined together.

"The joint answer of," &c.[295] The answer of an infant or other person answering by guardian, or of an idiot or lunatic, or a convict answering by his committee is so entitled. 2 Dan. Ch. Pr. (old) 266.[296]

286. When a defendant is sued in two characters it ought to appear that he answers in both.[297] The answer of two partners should regularly be in the name of both, but where one partner answered in the name of both and the plaintiff filed a general replication and took no steps to compel an answer from the other partner, the answer was deemed sufficient as the answer of the two partners. *Freelands* vs. *Royall & als.*, 2 H. & M. 575.

---

[295] Mr. Justice Story says that when a married woman answers separately from her husband by leave of court, she answers *by her next friend*. Story's Eq. Pl. 873. A wife cannot answer separately from her husband without the leave of the court. *Perine* vs. *Swann, &c.*, 1 John Ch. R. 24.

[296] The answer of an idiot or lunatic is expressed to be made by his committee or his guardian, or by the person appointed his guardian by the court to defend the suit. Mitf. Pl. 315. By the Code 1873, ch. 167, sec. 17, provision is made for the appointment of a *guardian ad litem* to an insane defendant, as well as of infant.

As to convict, the Code 1873, ch. 206, sec. 7, provides that the committee of the convict "may sue and be sued in respect to debts due to or by such convict and any other of the convict's estate, and shall have the privilege of an administrator, as to the right of retaining for his own debt."

See the 87th rule of the U. S. Supreme Court before cited, sec. 116, pp. 148, 149.

[297] 2 Rob. Pr. (old) 306. But in *Kinney's ex'ors, &c.* vs. *Harvey, &c.*, 2 Leigh 70, one of the defendants was made a party both as executrix and devisee; and in the caption to her answer she was merely styled executrix. The answer itself was, however, responsive to all the allegations of the bill and related to the real as well as the personal estate. And the court held that the defendant thereby placed herself before the court in the character of devisee as well as executrix.

The cases of *Pennington* vs. *Hanby*, 4 Munf. 144, and *Freelands* vs. *Royall & als.*, 2 H. & M. 575, may be consulted in connection with it, also *Leigh* vs. *Burch*, 9 Jur. u., s. 1265, cited in sec. 278 *ante*.

287. In a suit against several executors if the answer is designed to be a joint answer of them all, it should be so stated. The answer filed by one executor will not be considered the answer of his coexecutor, notwithstanding a statement in the record that the *defendants* appeared by counsel and filed *their* answer: and should a final decree be rendered for the plaintiff upon the answer of one executor, without its appearing that process has been served on the others, that decree will be reversed. *Chinn* vs. *Heale*, 1 Munf. 63.

288. Where the answer has been prepared for five defendants Daniell lays down the rule that it cannot be received as the answer of two only, nor as the answer of six, 2 Dan. Ch. Pr. (old) 267; *Harris* vs. *James*, 3 Bro. C. C. 399; *Cope* vs. *Parry*, 1 Mad. 83; but he adds that it seems the defendant may apply by motion to have it taken off the file and amended by striking out the names improperly introduced. 2 Dan. Ch. Pr. (old) 267. *Ibid.* (Perk.) 744; *Cooke* vs. *Westall*, 1 Mad. 265; *Thatcher* vs. *Lambert*, 5 Hare, 228.

289. An answer usually begins by a reservation to the defendant of all advantage which may be taken by exception to the bill,[298] a form which has probably been intended to prevent a conclusion that the defendant, having submitted to answer the bill, admitted everything which by his answer he did not expressly controvert, and especially such matters as

---

[298] In answers of infants this reservation is usually left out. Mitf. Pl. 314; 2 Dan. Ch. Pr. (old) 267.

he might have objected to by demurrer or plea. Mitf. Pl. 313, 314.

290. Next after this reservation follow the answers to the several matters contained in the bill, together with such additional matter as may be necessary for the defendant to show to the court, either to qualify or add to the case made by the bill, or to state a new case on his own behalf. Mitf. Pl. 314. After this, adds Lord Redesdale, there is a general denial of that combination which is usually charged in the bill, and it is the universal practice to add, by way of conclusion, a general traverse or denial of all the matters in the bill. *Ibid.* 314.[299]

291. In strict practice, an answer should be signed by the counsel and the defendant whose answer it is. This rule of the English practice, under the 90th rule of the United States Supreme Court cited in the note below,[300] obtains in the United States Circuit Courts. In the Virginia State courts, the strict practice is not always followed.

292. All answers, excepting those of corporations aggregate, which are put in under their common

---

[299] Omitted in the answers of infants, as well as the denial of combination. Mitf. Pl. 314. See as to effect of this general traverse by way of conclusion. *Storms* vs. *Storms*, 1 Edw. V. C. R. 358; Mitf. Pl. by Jeremy 314, *note.*

[300] The 90th Rule of Practice of United States Supreme Court is as follows: "In all cases where the rules prescribed by this court, or by the Circuit Court, do not apply, the practice of the Circuit Court shall be regulated by the present practice of the High Court of Chancery in England, so far as the same may reasonably be applied, consistently with the local circumstances and local convenience of the district where the court is held, not as positive rules, but as furnishing just analogies to regulate the practice."

seal, must be upon oath of the parties putting them in[301] unless they be such as by the law are allowed to make a solemn affirmation in lieu of an oath.[302]

It has been said that a discovery cannot be compelled in a suit against a corporation, except through the medium of their agents and officers by making them parties defendants; and where there is an injunction it would be desirable that an officer or other person acquainted with the facts in the answer should swear to it, for the injunction cannot be dissolved upon the general answer of the corporation where the seal alone is sworn to. See *Fulton Bank* vs. *Sharon Canal Co.*, 1 Paige 218, Mitf. Pl. by Jeremy, Amer. edit. 103 (marg.) n. 1.

293. Upon consent of the plaintiff, an answer may be put in without oath or affirmation;[303] and the filing of a replication is evidence of the waiver of the oath.[304] But the court will not permit the answer of a defendant represented to be in a state of incapacity to be received without oath and signature, though a mere trustee and without interest; the usual course in such case being for the court to appoint a guardian by whom the defendant may answer. *Wilson* vs. *Grace*, 14 Ves. 172.

293 a. A defendant put in an answer to part of the

---

[301] A defendant prepared an answer admitting the allegations of the plaintiff's bill, and it was certified as sworn to, but the person certifying the affidavit did not style himself in the certificate a justice of the peace, nor was it otherwise proved that he was a magistrate authorized to administer oaths. Defendant died, and this paper so certified was filed in the clerk's office. It was held to be no answer of the party, nor evidence in the cause. *Sitlingtons* vs. *Brown & als.*, 7 Leigh 271.

[302] Code, 1873, ch. 12, sec. 5.

The 91st Rule U. S. Supreme Court: " Whenever under these rules an oath is or may be required to be taken, the party may, if conscientiously scrupulous of taking an oath, in lieu thereof, make solemn affirmation to the truth of the facts stated by him."

[303] See 2 Dan. Ch. Pr. (old) 271.

[304] *Fulton Bank* vs. *Beach & als.*, 6 Wend. 36.

bill, it was held that he had thereby admitted the plaintiff's capacity to sue, and that he could not by demurrer to the part of the bill not answered raise the issue of the plaintiff's capacity to sue. *Gilbert* vs. *Lewis*, 9 Jur. n.. s. 187; s. c. 1 DeGex, J. & S. 38.

293 b. *Whether a defendant should answer the clause of combination in the bill.* Where there is is the general clause of combination only in the bill, the defendants need not answer it; but where a particular combination is charged in a bill, a particular answer must be given, and a general denial will not do. Coop. Eq. Pl. 314, 315; *White* vs. *Williams*, 8 Ves. 193; *Faulder* vs. *Stuart*, 11 Ves. 296; Bridg. Dig. 29.

293 c. In *Glyn* vs. *Caulfield*, 6 Eng. Law and Eq. Rep. 1, the subject is fully discussed as to how far a party may decline to produce documents on the ground that they are in the custody of another. A respondent admitted that certain books were in the custody of his copartners and himself, but replied that his copartners refused to permit him to make the extracts. This was not deemed a sufficient excuse "since he had not stated any contract between himself and his copartners, which prevented him from inspecting the books and making extracts from them without their permission." *Stuart* vs. *Lord Bute*, 12 Sim. 490. See Story's Eq. Pl. 852.

As to the doctrines concerning the production and discovery of documents, see Seton's Decrees in Eq., pp. 1040–1062; old edition 420, 421, 430, 23.

293 d. *What part of a bill a defendant should an-*

swer. The defendant is liable so far as the bill prays relief against him; his defence may therefore be applicable to that part of the case only. Wigram on Disc. 70. The rule formerly prevailed in the United States Circuit Courts that the defendant should answer only the interrogatories he was specially required to answer;[305] but this rule was afterwards abrogated.[306] There is no doubt that in equity a defendant is not bound to answer the plaintiff's bill further than it is necessary to enable the plaintiff to obtain a complete decree against himself; but it is not always easy to apply this rule in practice; to draw the line between what is material and what is immaterial for each defendant to answer is often a task of great difficulty and responsibility.[307]

294. It has been questioned whether a defendant could be deprived of the weight of his answer under oath by the plaintiff's waiving an answer under oath by the bill. It was held in *Holbrook* vs. *Black*, 18 Law Rep. 89, that he could not be. So it was held by the United States Supreme Court, in *Clements* vs. *Moore*, 6 Wall. 299, but the decision in that case is virtually overruled by the amendment to the 41st rule of practice as printed in the subjoined note.[308] The rule obtains in the Virginia State

---

[305] 40th Rule, see Sec. 299, *n.* 312, p. 356.

[306] At the December term 1850. See Sec. 299, *n.* 312 p. 356.

[307] See Hare on Disc. 161; Dan. Ch. Pr. (Perk.) 732; Story's Eq. Pl. 853 *c.*

[308] The 41st rule of equity practice as amended at the December term, 1871, (13 Wal. xi) reads as follows:

"If the complainant, in his bill, shall waive an answer under oath or shall only require an answer under oath, with regard to certain specified interogatories, the answer of the defendant, though under oath, except such part

·courts, that a plaintiff cannot by waiving the oath of the defendant deprive the answer of its usual weight as evidence;[309] but special provision is made by statute as to cases of usury. Code 1873, chap. 137, sec. 12. See *Belton* vs. *Apperson*, 26 Grat. 207.

294 *a.* *Whether a defendant is compelled to state his belief.* In *Brooks* vs. *Byam*, 1 Story, 296, 301, Mr. Justice Story considered the question whether a defendant was compelled in his answer to state his belief. His conclusions were, that the plaintiff has a right to require that the defendant should state in direct terms, or at least in unequivocal terms, either that he does believe or that he does not believe the matter inquired of, or that he cannot form any belief, or has not any belief concerning the matter, and according as the answer shall be the one way or the other, that he calls upon the plaintiff for proof thereof, or he admits it, or he waives any controversy about it. See 2 Dan. Ch. Pr. (old) 257, 402; *Potter* vs. *Potter*, 1 Ves. 274; *Cooth* vs. *Jackson*, 8 Ves. 37, 38; Story's Eq. Pl. 854, 855, 868*b*.

295. The answers of infants are put in by their *guardian ad litem.* It is error to enter a decree against infant defendants without assigning them a *guardian ad litem, Roberts* vs. *Stanton*, 2 Munf. 129;

---

thereof as shall be directly responsive to such interrogatories, shall not be evidence in his favor unless the cause be set down for hearing on bill and answer only; but may nevertheless be used as an affidavit, with the same effect as heretofore, on a motion to grant or dissolve an injunction, or on any other incidental motion in the cause; but this shall not prevent a defendant from becoming a witness in his own behalf under section 3 of the act of Congress of July 2d, 1864." See Rev. Stat. U. S., sec. 858.

[309] *Thornton* vs. *Gordon*, 2 Rob. R. 719.

and although the infancy does not appear in the original proceedings, yet if it be alleged in a petition for rehearing (the decree being interlocutory), a *guardian ad litem* must be appointed. *Ibid.* See Code, 1873, ch. 124, sec. 4.

295 *a*. In certain proceedings, *e. g.* for the sale, &c., of lands of persons under disability, the Virginia Statute provides that the answer of an infant, if over fourteen years of age, must be sworn to by himself, and the answer of the *guardian ad litem* must also be sworn to. Code, 1873, ch. 124, sec. 4.

296. A married woman generally answers with her husband, but sometimes she answers separately by order of court, in which event, if of full age, she answers usually by her next friend. See Story's Eq. Pl. 873; 1 Smith's Ch. Pr. 253, 254.

297. A married woman living separate from her husband, *Portman* vs. *Popham*, Tothill 75; *Jackson* vs. *Haworth*, 1 Sim. & S. 161, or disapproving the defence he wishes to make, *Ex parte* Halsam, 2 Atk. 50; 2 Eq. Ca. Ab. 66, may obtain an order for liberty to defend the suit separately, Mitf. Pl. 104, and her answer may be read against her; *Ibid.* 105. If the husband has upon leave answered separately, the wife may upon order afterwards file her separate answer. *Bray* vs. *Akers*, 15 Sim. 616. If the husband is the plaintiff in the suit, and makes his wife a defendant, he treats her as a *feme sole*, and she may answer separately without an order of court for the purpose. Mitf. Pl. 105. And, in such case, the wife puts in her answer in her own name as a

feme sole. Ex parte Strangeways, 3 Atk. 478. Where a marriage has clearly taken place only to defraud creditors, a *feme covert* may be made to answer as if she were *sole.* Coop. Eq. Pl. 325.

The wife becomes a substantial party to a suit only from the time of the order that she should answer separately. *Jackson* vs. *Haworth,* 1 S. & S. 161. If the husband answer separately, before there is an order that the wife should answer separately, his answer will be received; but if it be a case in which an order could not be obtained for the wife to answer separately, she must answer jointly, and then his answer if on file must be taken off, in order that she may join in it. *Garey* vs. *Whittingham,* 1 S. & S. 163.

The wife of an exile, or of one who has abjured the realm, may defend, as she may sue, alone, and if a husband is out of the jurisdiction of the court, though not an exile, or, if he cannot be found, his wife may be compelled to answer separately. Mitf. Pl. 105. So if her husband is an alien enemy. 2 Kent 151; Story's Eq. Pl. 71. If a married woman obstinately refuses to join in the defence of her husband, she may be compelled to make a separate defence, and for that purpose an order may be obtained that process may issue against her separately. Mitf. Pl. 105.

If a married woman be of unsound mind, she must, in a proceeding for the sale of lands of persons under disability, defend by *guardian ad litem.* See Code, 1873, ch. 124, sec. 4. In other cases reference may be had to Code, 1873, chap. 82, sec. 48,

45

49, 50 and 51; and chap. 124, sec. 9, 10, 11, 12; also to sec. 297 *a, post.*

297 *a. Whether a married woman under age should defend, or be defended separately from her husband; and how.* It is stated on the authority of 4 John. Ch. Rep. 379, *matter of Whitaker*, and cases there cited, and of *Roach* vs. *Garvan*, 1 Ves. Sr. 157, that it has never been the course and practice of the court to appoint a *guardian ad litem* to an infant *feme covert.* Smith in his Chancery Practice, vol. 1, pp. 253, 254, announces the doctrine that if a married woman, who is under age, answers separate from her husband, she must answer by guardian. The language of the seventeenth section, chapter 167 of the Code of 1873, previously cited,[310] seems broad enough to authorize the appointment of a *guardian ad litem* to an infant *feme covert.* See also Code, 1873, chap. 124, sec. 4–11. The act of March 14, 1878, Sess. Acts 1877-8, pp 247, 248, declares that "where the wife is a minor, having an estate in the hands of a guardian, it shall not be lawful for said guardian to pay or turn over her estate before she attains the age of twenty-one years, notwithstanding her marriage."[311] This seems to ne-

---

[310] Pp. 114, 115 *ante.*

[311] The entire statute is as follows : " Be it enacted by the General Assembly, That section 2 of an Act approved April 4th, 1877, entitled ' An act securing to married women, on conditions, all property acquired by them before or after marriage,' be amended and reënacted so as to read as follows:

§ 2. All real and personal estate hereafter acquired by any woman, whether by gift, grant, purchase, inheritance, devise or bequest, shall be and continue her sole and separate estate, subject to the provisions and limitations of the preceding section, although the marriage may have been solemnized previous to the passage of this act; and she may devise and bequeath

cessitate making the guardian of the *feme covert* a party to every suit in which the interests of the *feme covert* in property which he held, or was entitled to hold as guardian, were involved. It certainly would be a cumbrous proceeding in such a case to require an answer from the husband and his wife, an answer from her separately by her *guardian ad litem*, and also an answer from the regular guardian; and yet would any proceeding, less cumbrous than this, afford certain protection to the rights of the infant *feme covert?*

298. *A bill treated as an answer in the Virginia State Courts.* In *Kyle* vs. *Kyle*, 1 Grat. 526, after an interlocutory decree made injurious to the interests of a person not a party thereto (he being a non-resident), instead of availing himself of the statutory·provision for objecting to the decree, he filed a new bill against the parties to the original bill. This new bill was treated as an answer to the original bill, and as a cross·bill in that suit.

299. *Answers in the United States Circuit Courts.*

the same as if she were unmarried; and it shall not be liable to the debts and liabilities of her husband: provided, that nothing contained in this act shall be construed to deprive the husband of·courtesy in the wife's real estate, nor the wife of dower in her husband's estate: and provided further that the sole and separate estate created by any gift, grant, devise, or bequest, shall be held according to the terms and powers, and be subject to the provisions and limitations thereof, and to the provisions and limitations of this act, so far as they are (not) in conflict therewith; provided that nothing herein contained shall be so construed as to modify or alter section seven of chapter one hundred and twenty-three of the Code of eighteen hundred and seventy-three, except as hereinafter provided; that is to say, where the wife is a minor, having an estate in the·hands of a guardian, it shall not be lawful for said guardian to pay or turn over her estate before she attains the age of twenty-one years, notwithstanding her marriage."

In the preparation of answers in the United States
Circuit Courts, reference may be had to the thirty-
ninth, forty-fourth, forty-sixth, fifty-second, fifty-
third, fifty-fourth, fifty-fifth, fifty-ninth, sixtieth and
sixty-second rules of practice adopted by the United
States Supreme Court,[312] which here follow:

39. The rule, that if a defendant submits to answer he shall
answer fully to all the matters of the bill, shall no longer apply in
cases where he might, by plea, protect himself from such answer
and discovery. And the defendant shall be entitled in all cases by
answer to insist upon all matters of defence (not being matters of
abatement, or to the character of the parties or matters of form) in
bar of or to the merits of the bill, of which he may be entitled to
avail himself by a plea in bar; and in such answer he shall not be
compellable to answer any other matters than he would be compellable to answer and discover upon filing a plea in bar, and an
answer in support of such a plea, touching the matters set forth in
the bill to avoid or repel the bar or defence. Thus, for example,
a *bona fide* purchaser for a valuable consideration, without notice,
may set up that defence by way of answer instead of plea, and
shall be entitled to the same protection and shall not be compellable to make any further answer or discovery of his title than he
would be in any answer in support of such plea.

44. A defendant shall be at liberty, by answer, to decline
answering any interrogatory or part of an interrogatory, from
answering which he might have protected himself by demurrer;

---

[312] The 40th Rule was as follows: "A defendant shall not be bound to
answer any statement or charge in the bill, unless specially and particularly
interrogated thereto; and a defendant shall not be bound to answer any interrogatory in the bill except those interrogatories which such defendant is
required to answer; and where a defendant shall answer any statement or
charge in the bill, to which he is not interrogated, only by stating his ignorance of the matter so stated or charged, such answer shall be deemed impertinent."

This 40th Rule was abrogated by the rule sometimes called the 93d Rule,
made at the December term, 1850, in the words following: "*Ordered*, That
the fortieth Rule heretofore adopted and promulgated by this court as one
of the rules of practice in suits in equity in the Circuit Courts be and the
same is hereby repealed and annulled. And it shall not hereafter be necessary to interrogate a defendant specially and particularly upon any statement
in the bill unless the complainant desires to do so to obtain a discovery."

and he shall be at liberty so to decline notwithstanding he shall answer other parts of the bill, from which he might have protected himself by demurrer.

46. In every case where an amendment shall be made after answer filed, the defendant shall put in a new or supplemental answer, on or before the next succeeding rule day after that on which the amendment or amended bill is filed, unless the time therefor is enlarged or otherwise ordered by a Judge of the Court; and upon his default the like proceedings may be had as in case of an omission to put in an answer.

52. Where the defendant shall, by his answer, suggest that the bill is defective for want of parties, the plaintiff shall be at liberty, within fourteen days after answer filed, to set down the cause for argument upon that objection only; and the purpose for which the same is so set down shall be notified by an entry, to be made in the clerk's order book, in the form or to the effect following (that is to say): "Set down upon the defendant's objection for want of parties." And where the plaintiff shall not so set down his cause, but shall proceed therewith to a hearing, notwithstanding an objection for want of parties taken by the answer, he shall not, at the hearing of the cause, if the defendant's objection shall then be allowed, be entitled, as of course, to an order for liberty to amend his bill by adding parties. But the court, if it thinks fit, shall be at liberty to dismiss the bill.

53. If a defendant shall, at the hearing of a cause, object that a suit is defective for want of parties, not having by plea or answer taken the objection, and therein specified by name or description the parties to whom the objection applies, the court (if it shall think fit) shall be at liberty to make a decree saving the rights of the absent parties.

54. Where no account, payment, conveyance or other direct relief is sought against a party to a suit, not being an infant, the party, upon service of the subpœna upon him, need not appear and answer the bill, unless the plaintiff specially requires him so to do by the prayer of his bill; but he may appear and answer at his option; and if he does not appear and answer, he shall be bound by all the proceedings in the cause. If the plaintiff shall require him to appear and answer, he shall be entitled to the costs of all the proceedings against him unless the court shall otherwise direct.

55. Whenever an injunction is asked for by the bill to stay proceedings at law, if the defendant do not enter his appearance and plead, demur or answer to the same within the time prescribed therefor by these rules, the plaintiff shall be entitled as of course, upon motion without notice, to such injunction. But special injunctions shall be grantable only upon due notice to the other party by the court in term, or by a judge thereof in vacation, after a hearing, which may be *ex parte*, if the adverse party does not appear at the

time and place ordered. In every case where an injunction, either the common injunction or a special injunction, is awarded in vacation, it shall, unless previously dissolved by the judge granting the same, continue until the next term of the court, or until it is dissolved by some other order of the court.

59. Every defendant may swear to his answer before any justice or judge of any court of the United States, or before any commissioner appointed by any circuit court to take testimony or depositions, or before any master in chancery appointed by any circuit court, or before any judge of any court of a State or Territory.

60. After an answer is put in, it may be amended as, of course, in any matter of form, or by filling up a blank, or correcting a date or reference to a document or other small matters, and be resworn at any time before a replication is put in, or the cause is set down for a hearing upon bill and answer. But after replication, or such setting down for a hearing, it shall not be amended in any material matters as by adding new facts or defences, or qualifying or altering the original statements, except by special leave of the court, or of a judge thereof, upon motion and cause shown after due notice to the adverse party, supported if required by affidavit. And in every case where leave is so granted, the court, or the judge granting the same, may, in his discretion, require that the same be separately engrossed and added as a distinct amendment to the original answer, so as to be distinguishable therefrom.

62. When the same solicitor is employed for two or more defendants, and separate answers shall be filed, or other proceedings had by two or more of the defendants separately, costs shall not be allowed for such separate answers or other proceedings, unless a master, upon reference to him, shall certify that such separate answers and other proceedings were necessary or proper, and ought not to have been joined together.

300. Here follow the general formula of answers and forms of answers in special cases:

GENERAL FORMULA OF ANSWER.

[For convenience this formula is divided into five parts, denoted thus:—(1.) Commencement; (2.) Introduction; (3.) Substance; (4.) Conclusion; (5.) Affidavit.]

(1.) The answer of A. B., defendant, to the bill of complaint exhibited against him [or, against him and others] in the —— court of —— county by R. M.

(2.) This defendant, now and at all times hereafter, saving and reserving to himself all benefit and advantage of exception which can or may be had or taken to the many errors, uncertainties and insufficiencies in the said bill contained, for answer thereto, or to so much thereof as he is advised it is material or necessary for him to answer, this defendant answering saith, &c.

(3.) [Here follows the substance of the answer, varying of course with each case.]

(4.) [And this defendant denies all and all manner of unlawful combination and confederacy wherewith he is by the said bill charged; without this, that there is any other matter, cause or thing in the said complainants' said bill of complaint contained, material or necessary for this defendant to make answer unto, and not herein and hereby well and sufficiently answered, confessed, traversed and avoided, or denied, is true to the knowledge or belief of this defendant; all which matters and things this defendant is ready and willing to aver, maintain and prove, as this honorable court shall direct, and humbly prays to be hence dismissed with his reasonable costs and charges in this behalf most wrongfully sustained.]

The foregoing between brackets may be used, or, in lieu thereof, the following:

"And now, having fully answered the complainants' bill, and denying all unlawful combination and confederacy as therein charged [when combination charged],[313] this respondent prays hence to be dis-

---

[313] See Sec. 293 *b*, p. 249, when a particular combination is charged.

missed with his reasonable costs in this behalf expended, and he will ever pray," &c.

J. M. P., p. d.

(5.) County of ———, to-wit: This day personally appeared before me, the undersigned, a justice of the peace for the county aforesaid, A. B., and made oath that the statements made in the foregoing answer, so far as made of his own knowledge, are true, and, so far as made upon knowledge or information derived from others, he believes them to be true.

Given under my hand this —— of ———, 18 ——.

M. M., *J. P.*

Answer of Husband and Wife.

(1.) The joint answer of James M. and Eliza his wife, defendants to the bill, &c., (as before.)

Answer of two Defendants, not Husband and Wife.

(1.) The joint and several answer of James M. and Robert R., defendants, to the bill, &c., (as before.)

Answer of Personal Representative, and in his own right.

(1.) The answer of James M., as executor of the last will and testament [*or*, as administrator] of X. X., deceased, and in his own right to the bill, &c., (as before.)

Answer of Guardian ad litem, &c. [314]

(1.) The answer of M. M., *guardian ad litem* to the infant defendants, L. L. and X. X., and the an-

---

[314] See *Durrett* vs. *Davis*, 24 Grat. 302.

swer of the said infant defendants by their said *guardian ad litem* to the bill, &c., (as before.)

Answer where Christian Names of some of the Defendants misstated in the Bill.

(1.) The joint and several answer of L. M. and J. P. (in the bill called L. E. and M. P.), and Q. X., to a bill exhibited against them and others in the ―――― court of ―――― by J. W.

Form of Plea and Answer.

(1.) See section 245, *ante*, p. 316.

Form of Answer of Defendant to Bill to foreclose a Mortgage.

The answer of G M., &c., [as in General Formula p. 358.]

This defendant answers and says, that he believes the statements in the bill in reference to the execution of the mortgage therein mentioned are true. This defendant knows nothing as to the truth or falsity of the statements in the bill as to the execution of the will in the bill mentioned by A. W., senior, nor of its probat, nor of the plaintiff's claim as devisee and legatee thereunder, nor of his right as such to seek to enforce the forfeiture of the said mortgage; he neither admits nor denies the same, but calls for proof thereof, and of all the statements in the bill not specially admitted to be true in this answer. This defendant admits that the debt secured by the said mortgage has not been paid. This defendant further answering saith that there is no other charge or encumbrance affecting the said mortgaged premises. This respondent asks the court, if it shall hold that the plaintiff is entitled to demand

46

a foreclosure of the said mortgage, to allow this respondent a reasonable time for the redemption of the mortgaged premises. And now having fully answered, this defendant prays hence to be dismissed with his costs, &c.

J. G. W., p. d.   G. M.

[Add affidavit.]

Modern Form of Answer in England.

[The answer of a defendant in England must now be in the first person and divided into paragraphs numbered consecutively, each paragraph containing as nearly as may be a separate and distinct allegation. 15 and 16 Vict. c. 86, sec. 14, and orders 7 Aug. 1852, cited Dan. Ch. Pr. (Perk) 724, 725.]

In Chancery.

John Lee, ...	*Plaintiff.*
James Styles and Henry Jones, .	*Defendants.*

The answer of James Styles, one of the above-named defendants to the bill of complaint of the above named plaintiff.

In answer to the said bill, I, James Styles, say as follows:

1. I believe that the defendant, Henry Jones, does claim to have a charge upon the farm and premises comprised in the indenture of mortgage of the first of May, one thousand eight hundred and fifty, in the plaintiff's bill mentioned.

2. Such charge was created by an indenture dated the first of November, one thousand eight hundred and fifty, made between myself, of the one part, and the said defendant, Henry Jones, of the other part, whereby I granted and conveyed the said farm and premises, subject to the mortgage made by the said indenture of the first of May, one thousand eight hundred and fifty, unto the defendant, Henry Jones, for securing the sum of two thousand pounds and inter-

est at the rate of five pounds per centum per annum, and the amount due thereon is the said sum of two thousand pounds, with interest thereon from the date of such mortgage.

3. To the best of my knowledge, remembrance and belief, there is not any other mortgage, charge, or incumbrance affecting the aforesaid premises.

M. N.

(Name of counsel.)

Answer of infant defendant by guardian ad litem, and answer of guardian ad litem to a friendly bill for sale of infant's lands.

The answer of James M., an infant under the age of twenty one years, by R. H., his guardian ad litem assigned to defend him in this suit, and the answer of the said R. H., guardian ad litem to the said infant defendant, James M., to a bill in equity, exhibited against the said James M. and others in the ———— court of ———— county by Robert L.

For answer to the said bill the said infant defendant by his said guardian ad litem answers and says, that being of tender years he does not know what his true interests are in relation to the subject matter of the said bill, nor does he know whether the statements therein contained are true or not. He confides the protection of his interests to the care of the court. And the said guardian ad litem to the said infant defendant for answer to the said bill answers and says that he knows nothing as to the truth or falsity of the statements in the bill contained. He prays full protection for the said infant defendant. And now having fully answered, these defendants pray hence to be dismissed with their costs, &c.

James M., by R. R., his guardian ad litem;
and R. R., guardian ad litem to the said James M.

[Add affidavit.]

Answer of defendant to a bill to compel the payment of a legacy and to compel the executor to account for the testator's estate.

The answer of G H., executor of the last will and testament of R. M. deceased, to a bill in equity, exhibited against himself and others, in the chancery court of the city of Richmond, by John B.

This defendant, for answer to the said bill, answers and says, that it is true that R. M. departed this life leaving a will which has been duly admitted to probat in the ———— court of ————, a copy of which is filed with the bill, and that this respondent qualified as his executor in the said court. This defendant admits the statement in the bill that the plaintiff is a legatee of the testator and that he has made demand upon this defendant for his legacy. This defendant has funds enough in his hands to satisfy the said legacy, if there were no debts against the estate of his testator, but there are claims asserted against the estate which if carried to successful issue will absorb so much of the estate as to render it doubtful whether anything will be left for the payment of legacies. The suits on these claims are now pending in this court and in other courts. Among other claims, one J. J. J. asserts a claim for $10,000, for which he has instituted his action against this defendant as executor in the circuit court of Richmond city. This defendant does not object to having his executorial accounts settled in this suit; and submits himself to the protection of the court. Of course, in no event, will a decree go for the payment of the legacy to the plaintiff without requiring the execution of the usual refunding bond. And now, having fully answered, this defendant prays hence to be dismissed with his costs, &c.

G. H. ex'or of R. M.

X. X., p. d.
[Add affidavit.]

[A single legatee may, without uniting other legatees, sue, if the executor admits assets enough to pay the whole; if the executor does not admit assets to pay all the legatees, the court will require the other legatees to be united in the suit. See p. 198, *ante.*]

Answer to a bill of injunction.

The answer of George G., administrator of R. R., deceased, to a bill in equity exhibited against him in the ——— court of the county of ———, by M. M.

This respondent for answer to the said bill answers and says that the judgment mentioned in the bill was fairly obtained, and if the plaintiff had any defence to the action in which it was recovered it was his duty to have made it at law. This respondent denies the statement in the bill that this respondent informed the plaintiff that he need not take any steps to defend the said action, and that this defendant would dismiss the same. Neither of said statements is true. This respondent also denies that he stated to the plaintiff that he was fully satisfied that the debt had been paid. On the contrary, this respondent stated to the plaintiff that if he had any defence to the action he could make it, and the verdict and judgment, if rendered against this respondent, would be a full protection to him in his representative capacity. The failure of the plaintiff to make defence at law either was gross negligence on his part, or because he had no confidence in his ability to satisfy the court and jury that his defence was a just one. In either event, the judgment ought to stand: and this respondent asks tnat the injunction awarded the plaintiff be dissolved and his suit be dismissed. And now having fully answered, this respondent prays hence to be dismissed with his costs, &c.

G. G. adm'or of R. R.

L. L., p. d.
[Add affidavit.]

Answer to bill of injunction to judgment.

The answer of M. N. to a bill in equity exhibited against himself in the ———— court of the county of ————, by James J., executor of the last will and testament of Meriwether R., deceased.

This respondent for answer to the said bill answers and says that it is true he recovered judgment as stated in the bill on the bond therein mentioned. In the said bond Meriwether R. was surety and Alexander R. was principal. This respondent believes the said Alexander R. was out of the country during the time the action was pending. This respondent knows nothing as to the diligence the plaintiff alleges he used to discover where Alexander R. was, and this defendant neither admits nor denies the same: but calls for proof thereof. This respondent is surprised that the plaintiff did not learn where Alexander R. was, for it was a notorious fact that when he left Virginia his purpose was to settle in Liverpool, England, and this respondent believes that during his whole absence from this country he was carrying on the business of a merchant at that place, and had many correspondents in Virginia: and this respondent has been informed and believes that one of those correspondents, Samuel J., was the son of the said James J.

This respondent denies that the debt secured by the bond has been paid, or any part thereof. This respondent admits having given a receipt to the said Alexander R., and that the receipt marked Exhibit A is the paper given by this respondent to the said Alexander R.; but though the receipt was given, the money was not paid, and all of it is now justly due this respondent. The receipt was given with the full knowledge of Meriwether R., under these circumstances: Alexander R. was anxious to arrange the said debt, and proposed to assign to this respondent certain claims amounting to $——, which, when collected were to be in full discharge of the debt; these claims were, one of $—— against C. M., and another of $—— against X. X. These claims were assigned to this respondent. This respondent agreed to take the assignment of these claims, and if the money was realized from them the debt was to be discharged. Both the said Alexander R. and this respondent thought the said C. M. and X. X. were solvent. The bond not being at hand, this respondent gave the receipt to the said Alexander R.; the body of the receipt is in the handwriting of the said Meriwether R., and the said Meriwether R. was fully cognizant of the arrangement between the said Alexander R. and this respondent and approved of the same. Shortly after the receipt was given, Alexander R. left the country. This respondent made application to the said C. M. and X. X. for the moneys on the claims; neither of them paid anything; suits were at once brought against them by this respondent, and judgments recovered, and on those judgments executions of fi. fa. were promptly issued and these executions were returned 'no effects.' Nothing whatever has been received by this respondent on either of the said claims, although this respondent was unusually diligent in prosecuting the same. These being the facts, your respondent was entitled to be paid his debt, and an action at law was brought by this respondent on the bond and judgment recovered as stated in the bill.

Your respondent is justly and fairly entitled to the said judgment. The injunction awarded the plaintiff should be dissolved and the bill dismissed.

And now having fully answered, this respondent prays hence to be dismissed with his costs, &c.

M. N.

O. P., p. d.
[Add affidavit.]

*Form of answer of executor admitting legacy and suf-
ficient assets to pay, but denying the right of plaintiff to legacy until he reaches twenty-one years of age.*

The joint and several answers of E. W. and William W., executors of Thomas A., deceased, to a bill
of complaint exhibited against them by James W.,
an infant, who sues by John W., his father and next
friend, in the ——— court of ——— county.

These defendants, now and at all times hereafter,
reserving all manner of benefit and advantage to
themselves of exception to the many errors and in-
sufficiences in said bill contained, for answer thereunto, or unto so much or such parts thereof as these
defendants are advised is material for them to make
answer unto, they answer and say: They admit that
Thos. Adkins, in said bill named, did duly make and
execute such last will and testament in writing, of
such date and to such purpose and effect, as is in
said bill mentioned and set forth; and did thereby
bequeath to the complainant, James Willis, such
legacy of $800 in the words for that purpose men-
tioned in said bill or words to a like purport and
effect. They further admit that the said testator,
Thomas Adkins, did by such will appoint these defendants executors thereof, and that the said testator died on or about the 20th day of December, 1871,
without revoking or altering the said will. And
these defendants further admit that they, sometime
after, to-wit: about the month of January, 1872, duly
qualified as executors of said will in the circuit court
of ——— county, in which court said will was admitted to probat. They further admit that the said
complainant, James Willis, by his said father, did
several times since the said legacy of $800 became
payable apply to them to have the same paid or
secured for the benefit of said complainant, but
these defendants declined to do so because the said

complainant was, and still is, an infant under the age of twenty-one years, and these defendants could not, as they are advised and believe, be safe in making such payment, or in securing said legacy in any manner, for the benefit of said complainant until he arrive at 21 years of age, save by the order and direction, and under the sanction of a proper court of equity.

And these defendants further answering, say, that by virtue of the said will, they possessed themselves of the real and personal estate, goods, chattels and effects of the said testator, to a considerable amount; and they admit that assets are come to their hands sufficient to satisfy said complainant's legacy, and subject to the payment thereof, and they are willing and desirous, and do hereby offer to pay the same as this honorable court shall direct. And these defendants deny all unlawful combination in said bill charged, without that any other matter or thing material for them to make answer to, and not herein sufficiently answered, averred or denied, is true to the knowledge or belief of these defendants. All which matters and things these defendants are ready to aver and prove as this court shall direct, and pray to be hence dismissed with their reasonable costs and charges in this behalf most wrongfully sustained.

E. W., ex'or.,
W. W., ex'or.

S. L. & O., p. q.

[Add affidavit.]

Answer relying on laches. [In an answer relying on laches, reference may be had to *Coleman* vs. *Lyne*, 4 Rand. 458.]

*Answer to a bill charging usury on which injunction
was obtained.*[315]

The answer of J. P. to a bill in equity exhibited
against him and G. S. executor of N. M. deceased in
the ——— court of the county of ——— by J. H.
plaintiff.

This respondent, now and at all times saving and
reserving to himself the benefit of all exceptions
which might be taken to the allegations of the bill,
for answer thereto or to so much thereof as this respondent is advised is material to answer, answers
and says, that as to the bond in the bill mentioned,
the suit and judgment thereon, the enquiries made
of the neighbours in relation thereto, the absence of
the witnesses and their return and the application to
this respondent, he admits them to be true as set
forth by the plaintiff in his bill of complaint; but
this respondent has no recollection that he stated to
the plaintiff that the bond was given for the balance
of a store account and of this he calls for proof, if it
be considered as material; for this respondent was
not present when the bond was given; it was taken
by the said N. M. in his lifetime who held some
money of this respondent's, and, with his own, was
at liberty to lend it out; but whether he lent it to
the said George Swift or not as stated in the bill
this respondent cannot say as the said N. M. died
soon after taking the said bond and before this respondent saw him; for this respondent obtained the
said bond from his executor the other defendant:
This is all the knowledge this respondent has in relation to the said bond. It is true this respondent

---

[315] This form is, in great part, taken from *Chancellor Taylor's Journal of his
Law School*, p. 351. The bill to which it is an answer is drawn by Chancellor
Taylor. See the bill in Taylor's Journal 348–350.

claims a moiety of it, upon the information derived from his co-defendant; but as to the loan of four hundred dollars and the usury of one hundred dollars comprised in the said bond this respondent can not either admit or deny, and therefore calls for the proof of these facts; and having answered, so far as it concerns this respondent, and denying all fraud and combination charged upon him, by the bill, humbly submits himself to the decree of this honorable court, and prays to be hence dismissed with his reasonable costs in this behalf expended, &c.

W. H. R., p. d.

Add affidavit as on p. 360.

In *Hogshead* vs. *Baylor*, 16 Grat. 99, a case arising when the Statute was in force giving relief only to the extent of excess of interest when the usury was established by the admission of the lender, the defendants by filing interrogatories to the plaintiff sought to avail themselves of the defence of usury without going into equity where if they succeeded they would still be required to pay the principal and interest of the debt. It was·an action against the maker and endorsers of a negotiable note. The defendants pleaded jointly *nil debit* and usury. They filed two interrogatories to the plaintiff: 1. From whom did you get the note in suit? 2. If from defendant C. what did you pay him for it? The plaintiff answered the first interrogatory, "I received the note from C. who so far as I had any knowledge was the owner of it." He declined to answer the second interrogatory. The defendants moved to strike out the last part of the answer to the first interrogatory. *Held:* 1. The only object of the question was to ascertain the character in which C. endorsed the note; and the answer is therefore responsive to the question. If that was not the object it was immaterial. 2. The pleas being joint, defendants were not entitled to an answer to the second question to reduce the amount of recovery against C., *nor were they entitled to the answer whilst they relied on the defence of usury.*

Answer in Smith vs. *Nicholas, &c., 8 Leigh* 330, *relying on usury as a defence to the whole claim of the plaintiff.*

After the usual introduction, the respondent answered,—

Respondent had several times borrowed money on

interest, in the county of Augusta, and in the winter
of 1812 he applied to E. Stribling to know if he
could negotiate a loan for him, as their mutual
friend J. Kinney had frequently done, at a rate of
interest from 10 to 12 per cent. per annum. After
some time, Stribling informed him by letter, that he
could obtain the sum of 5,000 dollars at the rate of
10 per cent for one or two years. In a subsequent
letter, respondent was informed by Stribling that
the negotiation was completed, and that he had received the money, which should be paid at any time
to respondent's order; but, if convenient, to delay
drawing; he would himself bring the money over in
about 15 days. No intimation was given that a contract for stock was expected, or any scruple felt at
receiving usurious interest. On the contrary, being
informed that the money was received and ready to
be paid, without a word being said about a purchase of stock, respondent could only consider it as
a loan of money. Accordingly, Stribling and the
plaintiff came to respondent's house about the first
of July, when respondent was informed (for the first
time, as he believes) that it was wished he should
engage to pay bank stock and bank dividends too;
which he positively refused to do, as it would subject
him to pay a double premium for the money, inasmuch as the price of the stock might be greatly
above par, and the dividends would certainly be
above six per cent. It was then agreed that the
engagement should be for stock, with such an indorsement upon the bond (marked A and exhibited
with this answer) as was actually made thereon: the
plaintiff frequently declaring that all he wanted was
to be secure of the dividends, which he believed
would give him at least ten per cent. for his money,
which would satisfy him. Respondent always considered the indorsement upon the bond as making it
a money debt, but that the loan was to be concealed

under cover of a pretended sale of stock; with which view and no other, as respondent supposed, the bond was drawn up. The indorsement binds respondent to discharge the obligation by paying money, and not stock. The bond itself obliged him to pay, as interest on the loan, whatever dividend the bank might declare semi-annually, on the stock pretended to be sold: which dividends, as appears by an account rendered by Smith (marked B, and exhibited with this answer) amounted generally to ten per cent. and never to so little as six per cent. Here, then, was money advanced to be repaid in money, and more than legal interest paid for its use. If this bond was not originally to secure the payment of a sum of money, as respondent understood it was, there can be no question that when it became due, it was to be discharged by the payment of 5,000 dollars in money, and not 50 shares of bank stock, so that all which was paid above six per cent. interest, after the bond became due, was usurious. Thus things continued, respondent paying nearly double rate of interest, until July, 1816, when by an alteration of the original contract, the usury became still more enormous. For, by an agreement of the 12th of July, 1816, (marked C and exhibited with this answer) respondent bound himself in the penalty of 30,000 dollars, to transfer 150 shares in the bank of the United States (then about to be organized) by the 1st of January, 1818. At the time of executing this contract, to the best of respondent's recollection, the 5,000 dollars due on the original bond were considered as money to be converted into United States bank stock at 80 dollars per share, and respondent received so much more money as, including the 5,000 dollars at 80 dollars per share, amounted to 150 shares of the stock.

To complete the ruinous extortion of this contract, it was further modified on the 2nd of January, 1818,

(see exhibit marked D) so as to bind respondent to
pay Smith, on the 1st of July 1818, the market price
of said stock on that day, or 150 dollars per share,
and the dividends declared in the meanwhile, as the
plaintiff should prefer; he chose the latter alternative; and accordingly, on the 1st of July, 1818, a
settlement was made; respondent having paid, or
binding himself to pay, for the 12,000 dollars, which
was all he ever received from Smith, from July,
1812, when the loan was first contracted, till July,
1818, the enormous sum of 26,068 dollars 50 cents.
In February, 1819, respondent redeemed his paper
due to Smith, gave his note for 2,000 dollars at 60
days, which has since been paid, and an additional
note for 10,000 dollars, still held by Smith, which
was to have been paid in stock. As security for respondent's compliance with his engagement of July,
1816, to transfer stock, he executed a deed of trust
(marked E and exhibited with his answer). Respondent, having answered, prays that plaintiff's
bill may be dismissed, &c.

Affidavit as on p. 160.

AMENDING ANSWER.

301. In the Virginia State courts, after an answer
has been put in upon oath the court will not, for obvious reasons, readily suffer any alterations to be
made in it. Mitf. Pl. 324. A special application is
necessary for the purpose, 4 Madd. 27. The application will be narrowly and closely inspected and a
just and necessary case must be clearly made out.[316]

---

[316] See Story's Eq. Pl. 896. *Smith* vs. *Babcock*, 3 Sumner 583. "In matters of form, or mistakes of dates, in verbal inaccuracies, courts of equity are
very indulgent in allowing amendments. But when application is made to

2 Rob. Pr. (old) 316; Kent, chancellor, in *Brown* vs. *Cross*, 4 Johns Ch. Rep. 375; *Gouverneur, &c.* vs. *Elmendorf, &c.*, 4 Johns Ch. Rep. 357. See Dan. Ch. Pr. (Perk.) 718, note 6. But no precise or absolute rule exists on the subject. The question, says Lord Eldon, is always for the discretion of the court in the particular instance. *Wells* vs. *Wood*, 10 Ves. 401.

302. *Where amendment will operate in plaintiff's favour.* Where the object is to remove out of the plaintiff's way the effect of a denial, or to give him the benefit of an admission material to enable him to obtain a decree, the court is generally inclined to yield to the application. In such case, the only

---

amend an answer in material facts, or to change essentially the grounds taken in the original answer, courts of equity are exceedingly slow and reluctant in acceding to it. To support such applications they require very cogent circumstances, and such as repel the notion of any attempt of the party to evade the justice of the case, or to set up new and ingeniously contrived defences and subterfuges. Where the object is to let in new facts and defences wholly dependent upon parol evidence, the reluctance of the court is greatly increased; since it has a natural tendency to encourage carelessness and indifference in making answers and leaves much room open for the introduction of testimony manufactured for the occasion. But where the new facts, sought to be introduced, are written papers or documents, which have been omitted by accident or mistake, there the same reason does not apply in its full force; for such papers and documents cannot be made to speak a different language from that which originally belonged to them. The whole matter rests in the sound discretion of the court." *Opinion of the court in Smith* vs. *Babcock*, 3 *Sumn.* 583. To permit such amendments the party must not have been "guilty of gross negligence," and the mistakes ascertained and the new facts come to his knowledge since the original answer was put in and sworn to. "When the party relies upon new facts which have come to his knowledge since the answer was put in, or where it is manifest that he has been taken by surprise, or where the mistake or omission is manifestly a mere inadvertence or oversight, there is generally less reason to object to the amendment, than there is where the whole bearing of the facts and evidence must have been well known before the answer has been put in. *Ibid.*

ground for hesitation arises out of the consideration that the defendant may have been guilty of perjury, and that a prosecution for the defence may be required by the public interest. By permitting the amendment, it has been said, the court decides against the propriety of the prosecution. Lord Eldon, however, thought that the permission ought to have no influence upon the prosecution, either way, and notwithstanding this ground of objection, allowed an amendment in several instances. *Edwards* vs. *McLeary*, 2 Ves. & Beames 225; *Strange* vs. *Collins*, *id.* 163.

303. *Where matter of law is to be relied on.* In *Jackson's assignees* vs. *Cutright, &c.*, 5 Munf. 308, the defendant desired, by way of amendment, to rely upon the statute of frauds and the statute of limitations. He swore that he had from the beginning relied on the matters contained in his amendment; that he had instructed his attorney to use them for his defence, and they were omitted through the mistake of his counsel, who conceived that a defence under either statute could be made without specially relying on it. Here the matter to be used in the amendment was matter of law; and there was *no danger of perjury.* The necessity arose, too, from the *mistake of counsel.* It was considered a proper case to permit amendment.

In *White* vs. *Turner*, 2 Grat. 502, the defendant was allowed to amend his answer in order to rely on the statute of limitations in bar of the plaintiff's claim.

In *Roemer* vs. *Simon*, 5 Otto 220, an amendment of the answer was permitted to insert the names and residences of other persons having prior knowledge and use of the thing patented, the defendant on the face of his answer at the time of filing it notifying the plaintiff that when discovered such names would be inserted.

A distinction is made between the allowance of an amendment as to a matter of fact and as to a conclusion in law. Min. Inst. 1194, Coop. Eq. Pl. 337, Story's Eq. Pl. 896, 897. *Dolder* vs. *B'k England*, 10 Ves. 285; *Wells* vs. *Wood*, 10 Ves. 401.

304. *Where defendant would vary in his favour statements of facts.* Livesay vs. Wilson, 1 Ves. & Beames 149, was a case of a different kind. To a bill for specific execution the defendant had acknowledged in his answer, that he took possession of the purchased property subsequent to the contract, and he wished to amend upon affidavit stating that at the date of the contract he was in possession of part of the premises as tenant; that he took possession, under the contract, of only part of the purchased premises; and that not conceiving the fact material, he had through ignorance omitted to inform his solicitor of it.

Lord Eldon said the whole case might turn upon the fact sought to be introduced, and refused to grant the motion to amend, unless the defendant would say, on his oath, that when he swore to his original answer, he meant to swear to it. See also *Liggon* vs. *Smith*, 4 H. & M. 405; and *Winston* vs. *Campbell*, 4 H. & M. 477.

305. *Amendment of Answers in the United States circuit courts.* The 60th rule of the United States Supreme court prescribes that "after an answer is put in it may be amended as of course in any matter of form, or by filling up a blank, or correcting a date, or reference to a document or other small mat-

ter, and be re-sworn, at any time, before a replication is put in, or the cause is set down for a hearing upon bill and answer. But after replication, or such setting down for a hearing, it shall not be amended in any material matters, as by adding new facts or defences, or qualifying or altering the original statements, except by special leave of the court, or of a judge thereof, upon motion and cause shown after due notice to the adverse party, supported if required, by affidavit. And in every case where leave is so granted, the court, or the judge, granting the same, may, in his discretion, require that the same be separately engrossed and added as a distinct amendment to the original answer, so as to be distinguishable therefrom.[317]

306. *In what manner amendment is made.* According to the former practice in the English chancery, where there was a clear mistake in the answer, proper to be corrected, the answer was taken off the file and a new answer put in. But Lord Thurlow adopted a better course, not taking the answer off the file, but permitting a sort of supplemental answer to be filed. This course leaves the parties the effect of what had been sworn to before, with the explanation given by the supplemental answer,[318] *Dolder* vs. *Bank of England*, 10 Ves. 285. And the English courts of equity seem to regard it as the settled practice. *Jennings* vs. *Merton College*, 8 Ves.

---

[317] See *Roemer* vs. *Simon*, 5 Otto 220, cited on p. 376.

[318] See last section as to manner of making amendment in United States circuit courts.

79; *Ridley* vs. *Obee*, Wightw. 32. But see *White* vs. *Godbold*, 1 Madd. Ch. Rep. 268.

307. *Amendment of Answer at hearing of the cause.* Where it appears that the answer has not put in issue the facts necessary to a proper decision the court in order to remove the embarrassment, permits an amendment of the answer to be made hardly less freely than of the bill; but this is only with a view to save expense and where no injury can arise to other parties from the indulgence. Mitf. Pl. 327, 328. But on the rehearing of a decree an answer cannot be amended but by consent of parties. *Ibid* 327, 328· Where a fact of advantage to a defendant has happened subsequent to his answer, the proper way it seems to put it in issue is not to amend the answer, but if it appears to the court on the hearing that it may thus be of advantage, the court will order the cause to stand over until a new bill, in which the fact can be brought to a hearing with the original suit—such a bill seems to be in the nature of a plea *puis darrein continuance* at the common law. See Mitf. Pl. 329; Story's Eq. Pl. 903.[319]

IV. DISCLAIMER.

Matter and Form of Disclaimer.

308. A defendant may disclaim all right or title to the matter in demand by the plaintiff's bill or by

---

[319] The court will permit a supplemental answer to be put in where new matter in an account is discovered before the hearing, but after a replication is filed. Mitf. Pl. 329; Story's Eq. Pl 903.

any part of it. *Archbald* vs. *Borrold*, Cary R. 99; *Seton* vs. *Slade*, 7 Ves. 265.

309. A disclaimer cannot often be put in alone, for if the defendant has been made a party by mistake, having at the time no interest in the matter in question, yet as he may have had an interest which he may have parted with, the plaintiff may require an answer sufficient to ascertain whether that is the fact or not; Mitf. Pl. 318; and if the defendant has had an interest which he has parted with, an answer may also be necessary to enable the plaintiff to make the proper party, instead of the defendant disclaiming. *Ibid.* 319.

310. Though a disclaimer is in substance distinct from an answer, it generally adopts in most respects the formal parts of an answer, the words of course preceding and concluding an answer being used in a disclaimer.

In substance, it is simply an assertion that the defendant disclaims all right and title to the matter in demand. Mitf. Pl. 319. From the nature of the case, in some instances, this may perhaps be sufficient, *Ibid;* but the forms given in the books of practice are of an answer and disclaimer. Mitf. Pl. 319. [See Minor's Inst., Vol. 4, p. 1175.]

311. If a defendant disclaims, the court will in general dismiss the bill as against him with costs: but it has been said that if the plaintiff shows a probable cause for exhibiting the bill he may pray a decree against the defendant upon the ground of the disclaimer. Mitf. Pl. 319.

When there is a disclaimer in the record by a party whose name is struck out to sustain the jurisdiction of the court, it will be noticed by the court so far as to learn from it what his interest is. *Vattier* vs. *Hinde*, Pet. 272.

312. When the defendant disclaims the plaintiff ought not to reply. Mitf. Pl. 319. If a disclaimer and answer are inconsistent the matter will be taken most strongly against the defendant upon the disclaimer. *Ibid.* 320.

313. A defendant cannot by disclaiming deprive the complainant of the right of requiring a full answer from him, unless it is evident that the defendant ought not, after such disclaimer, to be retained as a party to the suit. *Glassington* vs. *Thwaites*, 2 Russ. 458.

314. A defendant after filing his disclaimer cannot get rid of its effect, upon a distinct application supported by affidavits establishing special ground. *Sidden* vs. *Lediard*, 1 Russ. & M. 111.

315. The following is the form of a disclaimer.

Form of Disclaimer.

The disclaimer of Andrew Jackson to a bill in equity exhibited against him and others in the —— court of —— county by James K.
This defendant for answer and disclaimer to the said bill says that he does not know or believe that he ever had or ever claimed or pretended to have any right, title or interest of, in or to the said estates

and premises in the said bill set forth or any part thereof: and this defendant doth disclaim all right, title and interest to or in the said estates and premises, and every part thereof; and prays to be dismissed with his costs, &c.

ANDREW JACKSON.

[Add affidavit.]

315*a*. Besides the several modes of defence treated of in this chapter it sometimes becomes necessary that a party defendant, fully to present his case before the court, should file a cross bill. In a subsequent chapter cross bills will be treated of.

CHAPTER IX.

Of the filing of demurrers, pleas, answers and disclaimers, and of the course of the plaintiff when such defences are made.

316. The subjects of this chapter have already been treated of in previous portions of this work. It is deemed proper, however, to devote further sections to their more particular consideration.

317. Either of the several defences set forth in the eighth chapter may, under the limitations there pointed out, be made in the United States circuit courts at any time before the bill is taken for confessed, or afterwards with the leave of the court, 32nd Rule U. S. Supreme court; and in the Virginia

state courts a defendant may file his answer at any time before a final decree.[1]

There are cases however in which the taking of one of these modes of defence precludes the party from subsequently taking another.

318. Thus, after a demurrer to the whole bill has been overruled, the defendant is not at liberty to put in a plea to the whole bill or to any part of it or to put in a demurrer of a less extensive nature without first obtaining the leave of the court; 2 Dan. Ch. Pr. (old) 94, 95.

319. So, too, after answering the bill though the party may in many cases insist at the hearing upon matter not merely of form which he might have relied upon by plea or demurrer, yet he will not be allowed to file a plea or demurrer. See sec. 144, pp. 177, 178, and sec. 157 *a.*, p. 233, *ante.*

320. In the United States circuit courts, as we have already seen, the practice is much stricter in regard to filing a demurrer or plea than in the Virginia state courts; in the former there being required the certificate of counsel that in his opinion it is well founded in point of law, and the affidavit of the defendant that it is not interposed for delay, and, if a plea, that it is true in point of fact.

321. The rule has been generally adopted in the Virginia state courts that all pleadings should be signed by the party filing them and by his counsel. And it is understood to be the rule in the United

---

[1] Code of Va., ch. 171, sec. 34 ; Code 1873, ch. 167, sec. 53.

States circuit courts that bills, demurrers, pleas and answers are to be signed by counsel. See Story's Eq. Pl. 47, 461, Mitf. Pl. 216, 217; also 24th rule of practice. And in the case of answers, when an oath is not required, generally there must be the signature of the defendant to the answer. Story's Eq. Pl. 875.

322. *What pleadings sworn to.* All answers, save those of corporations aggregate, should be sworn to.

Pleas of every kind in the United States circuit courts must be sworn to. 31st Rule of Practice U. S. Supreme court. The Virginia state courts follow the English practice in this respect, save where there are special statutes. Pleas to the jurisdiction should be sworn to; also pleas in abatement; also pleas of statutes (sec. 193); pleas as to handwriting (sec. 235*a*); partnership (sec 235*a*); and all pleas not specially excepted by the rule laid down in section 235*b*.

Demurrers are not sworn to. But, as we have seen, in the United States circuit courts beside the certificate of counsel that in their opinion they are well founded in point of law, they must be supported by the affidavit of the defendant that they are not interposed for delay. There may be a waiver of the oath to these several pleadings save in those cases in which the statutes imperatively require that they should be sworn to.

323. *Pleadings in Writing.* Demurrers, pleas, answers and disclaimers are committed to writing.

324. *Made at Rules or in Term Time.* These seve-

ral modes of defence may be made at the rules or in court in term time, both in the Virginia State courts and in the United States circuit courts.

325. *Cause set for hearing without replication.* When an answer is filed, the plaintiff in the Virginia State courts may, as we have seen, set the cause for hearing on the answer alone without replication, Code 1873, ch. 167, sec. 49; and this seems to be the rule in the United States Circuit courts. See 60th Rule U. S. Supreme court   The 66th rule of practice, cited sec. 114, p. 148, *ante*, seeming to make it imperative on the plaintiff to reply to the answer on pain of dismission of his suit, should be construed so as to make it consistent with the 60th rule which clearly indicates that the cause may be set for hearing on the bill and answer without replication.[2]   See 60th rule in section 305, pp. 377, 378, *ante*.

326. *What done if plaintiff fail to set demurrer or plea down for argument.* In the United States Circuit Courts, see section 106, page 144, *ante*.   In the Virginia State courts, see sec. 247, p. 319, *ante*.

---

[2] It is said to be irregular to go to a hearing without a replication, *Wash. R. R.* vs. *Bradleys,* 10 Wal. 299.   In that case the court used the language:

" The 66th Rule is explicit on the subject.   The replication is necessary to put the cause at issue.   If the plaintiff omit to file it within the time limited, the defendant is entitled as of course to an order for the dismissal of the suit unless the court or a judge thereof upon cause shown shall allow it to be filed *nunc pro tunc* upon such terms as it may be deemed proper to impose."   But the court was not considering a case set for hearing on bill and answer without replication.   See *Leeds* vs. *Mar. Ins. Co. of Alexandria,* 2 Wheat. 380.

327. *When demurrer or plea overruled, what done.*
In the United States Circuit Courts, "if upon the
the hearing, any demurrer or plea is overruled, the
plaintiff shall be entitled to his costs in the cause up
to that period, unless the court shall be satisfied that
the defendant had good ground in point of law or
fact to interpose the same, and it was not interposed
vexatiously or for delay. And upon the overruling
of any plea or demurrer, the defendant shall be assigned to answer the bill, or so much thereof as is
covered by the plea or demurrer, the next succeeding rule day, or at such period as, consistently with
justice and the rights of the defendant, the same
can, in the judgment of the court, be reasonably
done; in default whereof, the bill shall be taken
against him, pro confesso, and the matter thereof
proceeded in and decreed accordingly." *34th Rule
of Practice.* In the Virginia State courts, if a demurrer or plea be overruled, no other plea or demurrer will afterwards be received; and the subsequent proceedings will be as stated in Sec. 157, *ante.*

328. *When demurrer or plea sustained.* In the
United States Circuit Courts, "if upon the hearing
any demurrer or plea shall be allowed, the defendant shall be entitled to his costs; but the court may
in its discretion upon motion of the plaintiff allow
him to amend his bill upon such terms as it shall
deem reasonable." *35th Rule of Practice U. S. Supreme Court.* In the Virginia State courts, the
usual course is to permit the plaintiff in a proper
case to amend his bill after a demurrer has been
sustained. See note 75 to sec. 157, *ante.*

329. When a plea has upon argument been sustained, as we have already seen, the party plaintiff may take issue upon it. Sec. 248 *ante*. Mitf. Pl. 240. In the United States Circuit Courts, the plaintiff may take issue upon a plea; and if upon the issue, "the facts stated in the plea be determined for the defendant, they shall avail him as far as in law and equity they ought to avail him."[3] 33rd Rule of Practice. In *Kennedy* vs. *Creswell*, 11 Otto 641, the plea was found false; and the consequences followed mentioned in the note.[4] In the Virginia State courts, the plaintiff may take issue upon a plea and have such issue tried by a jury. Code 1873, ch. 167, sec. 34. If the plea be found false he shall have the same advantages as if it had been so found by verdict at law. Code 1873, ch. 167, sec. 34; see also sec. 252 *ante*.

---

[3] See sec. 253 *ante*.

[4] The case was this. A bill was filed by Creswell for himself and other creditors against Kennedy's executor and devisees. It alleged that Kennedy was indebted to plaintiff, that the personal assets were insufficient to pay the debts and that the executor was paying some of them in full and leaving others unsatisfied. It prayed for an account of the personal estate, the application thereof to the payment of the debt, and the discovery of the real estate whereof Kennedy died seized. The defendants (the executors and devisees) pleaded in bar that the executor had in his hands assets sufficient to pay Creswell's claim and all others. To this plea the plaintiff filed a replication. The proofs sustained the allegations of the bill, but showed those of the plea to be untrue. Held, 1. That Creswell was entitled to a decree as though the bill had been confessed or admitted. 2. That as by reason of the executor's admission of assets no discovery was required, a decree against him rendering him individually liable was proper. 3. That there is nothing in the local law of the District of Columbia or in the jurisdiction of the supreme court of said District, sitting as a probate court, inconsistent with these rulings.

REPLICATION TO ANSWERS.

330. The plaintiff, if he does not think proper to file exceptions, may reply to the answer, or he may set down the cause for hearing without replication. [5] The effect of setting the cause for hearing without replication has been before noticed. [6]

, The general replication is now only used. For raising new issues, or supplying a defect in the statement in the bill, [7] the special replication has become obsolete both in England and in this country. Mitf. Pl. 322, 2 Rob. Pr. (old) 315. The office of the

---

[5] See 60th Rule U. S. Sup. Court, pp. 377, 378, and sec. 74, p. 113, *ante.*

[6] Sec. 74, p. 113. See *Kennedy* vs. *Baylor*, 1 Wash. 162; *Jones* vs. *Mason*, 5 Rand. 577; *Findlay* vs. *Smith, &c.*, 6 Munf. 142; *Pickett* vs. *Chilton*, 5 Munf. 483.

In *Cocke & als.* vs. *Minor & als.,* 25 Grat. 246, the denials and allegations of the answers, though there was no replication to them, were held to be insufficient to defeat the plaintiff's claim. Though the plaintiff failed to reply generally or otherwise to the answers, this did not relieve the defendants, the trustee, Minor, and the assignee, Derrick, from the burden of showing the *bona fides* of the transaction between them and the right of Minor to transfer the trust bonds at the ruinous sacrifice disclosed by Derrick.

There are conflicting decisions on the question, whether an infant admits the statements of the answer by omitting to file a replication. See *Legard* vs. *Sheffield*, 2 Atk., 377; *Thornton* vs. *Nutton*, 3 P. Wms. 237, *note e*; *Wrottesley* vs. *Bradish*, 3 Plow. 237; Gres. Eq. Ev. 22, *note c.*

[7] See Mitf. Pl. 18. See 45th Rule of Practice by the United States Supreme Court. Perhaps it is, in the absence of an express rule on the subject, not strictly accurate to say that the special replication is altogether disused for every purpose. It is stated in *note e*, p. 322, in Mitf. Pleadings, by Jeremy, that " if a plaintiff is disposed to controvert a part of the case made by the defendant's answer, and to admit the rest, he may still put in a replication, so far special, that it is confined to the particular matter controverted, instead of being a general denial of the truth of the whole answer; and then the defendant is put only to proof of the matter replied to.''

special replication is supplied by the filing of an amended bill.[8]

331. Where by mistake a replication has not oeen filed, and yet witnesses have been examined, the court has permitted the replication to be filed *nunc pro tunc.* Mitf. Pl. 323.

A decree in the court below was made when there was no replication to the answer. After an appeal by the defendant from the decree was perfected, the court below, on the motion of the plaintiffs, made an order permitting them to file a replication *nunc pro tunc.* If it was a proper case for such an order, the court should have required the plaintiffs to pay the costs of the amendment and

---

[8] It frequently happens that a defendant by his plea or answer sets up a defence, which can only be avoided by showing new matter. If, for example, the defendant pleads the statute of limitations, and the plaintiffs rely upon some of the exceptions allowed by the statute, the matter thus relied on, to avoid the statute, must appear in some way by the pleadings. *Tucker,* J., in *Lewis's exor.* vs. *Bacon's legatee,* 3 H. & M 104; *Hudsons* vs. *Hudson's* admr., 6 Mun. 352; *Miller's heirs* vs. *McIntyre, &c.,* 6 Pet. 61. So if the answer set up a particular agreement in bar of the bill, and the complainants insist that the agreement was procured by fraud, it is necessary to allege the fact of fraud in procuring the agreement. *James* vs. *McKernon,* 6 John. R. 564. In all such cases the complainant would formerly reply specially, and the pleadings might go on as at law to a rebutter. But special replications are now out of use. If the plaintiff conceives, from any matter offered by the plea or answer, that his bill is not properly adapted to his case, he may ask leave to amend his bill, and suit it to the defence, or he may file a supplemental bill. Mitf. Pl. 19, 255, 322; *Kent,* C. J., in *James* vs. *McKernon,* 6 John. R. 564.

In *Vattier* vs. *Hinde,* 7 Pet. 252, 275, the plaintiff, without leave of court, filed a special replication, setting out a different title from that relied on in the bill. Although, according to the rules of practice then governing the United States Circuit Courts, a special replication might be filed by special leave of the court, it was held by the Supreme Court of the United States that the special leave not being obtained in the Circuit Court, the case fell under the general principles, rules and usages of the Court of Chancery of England, and that by these rules the plaintiffs were not allowed to file a special replication, but should have amended their bill. (Mitf. Pl. 356.) For this fault the decree was reversed, and the cause remanded, with directions to permit the plaintiffs to amend their bill. 7 Pet. 275.

should have allowed the defendant time to take testimony to meet the new phase of the case presented by the issue thus taken on the answer. *Dabney* vs. *Preston's adm'ors*, 25 Grat. 838.

An order was made in a cause 'that on motion of the plaintiffs, and by consent of parties, the cause came on to be heard upon the bill and exhibits and answer and exhibits, on consideration whereof the court takes time to consider.' In fact, a number of deeds and two records had been placed by the clerk among the papers by direction of the plaintiff's counsel (but had not been endorsed as filed), which were intended to rebut the defence set up by the answer. Before the case was decided, the plaintiff's counsel discovering the error in the order, moved the court to set it aside, that the cause might be brought on on replication to the answer and on the evidence. The entry was not an order but a mere statement and should be set aside and the cause be heard upon the pleadings, as they were intended to be, and all the evidence. *Harrison's ex'ors & als.* vs. *Price's ex'ors & als.*, 25 Grat. 553.

332. By replying generally to the answer, the plaintiff admits its sufficiency: and the court will not afterwards allow his replication to be withdrawn for the purpose of excepting to the answer without good cause shown. *Brown* vs. *Ricketts, &c.*, 2 John, Ch. R. 425. See *Hughes* vs. *Blake*, 6 Wheat. 453. Upon good cause shown the court or judge in the United States Circuit Courts may allow a replication to be filed *nunc pro tunc*, the plaintiff submitting to speed the cause and to such other terms as may be directed. 66th Rule of Practice.

It must appear that the answer is defective, and it must be shown when the defect was discovered, and why it was not discovered sooner. *Brown* vs. *Ricketts, &c.*, 2 John. Ch. R. 425.

333. A general replication denies every allegation in the answer of a defendant whether responsive or not to the bill. Therefore the defendant must prove his allegation of a decree in a former suit pleaded by way of estoppel. *Humes* vs. *Scruggs*, 4 Otto 22.

334. The following is the form of a general replication.[10]

Form of General Replication.

In the ———— court of ———— county:

The replication of A. B., complainant to the answer of C. D., defendant.

This repliant, saving and reserving unto himself all and all manner of advantage of exception to the manifold insufficiencies of the said answer, for replication thereunto saith, that he will aver and prove his said bill to be true, certain and sufficient in the law to be answered unto, and that the said answer of the said defendant is uncertain, untrue, and insufficient to be replied unto by this repliant. Without this, that any other matter or thing whatsoever in the said answer contained, material or effectual in the law, to be replied unto, confessed and avoided, traversed or denied, is true. All which matters and things this repliant is and will be ready to aver and prove, as this honorable court shall direct, and humbly prays as in and by his said bill he hath already prayed.

335. *What deemed a sufficient replication.* In *Clements* vs. *Moore,* 6 Wal. 299, a paper put in after the answer was filed, and after part of the testimony was taken, stating that the "plaintiff in the cause hereby joins issue with the defendants

---

[10] In the Virginia State Courts replications are put in *ore tenus.* In the United States Circuit Courts they should be put in writing; at least, this is the safer practice. See 66th Rule of Practice.

(naming them), and will hear the cause on bill, answer and proofs against the defendants," was deemed a sufficient replication.

336. *When replication ought to be filed.* If the plaintiff intends to except to the answer he ought to do so before filing a replication. Sec. 332, *ante.* *Brown* vs. *Ricketts, &c.,* 2 John. Ch. R. 425. As we have already seen,[11] in the United States Circuit Courts the plaintiff is allowed a certain period after the filing of the answer to file the replication. This period is understood to be two rule days after the filing of the answer.[12] In the Virginia State courts there is no obligation on the plaintiff to file a replication, but if four months elapse after the answer of a defendant is filed, without the cause being set for hearing by the plaintiff and without exceptions being filed to the answer, the defendant may have the cause set for hearing as to himself. Code 1873, ch. 167, sec. 49.[13]

337. The replication to the answer puts the par-

---

[11] Sections 110, 114, pp. 146, 148.

[12] When the answer is filed on any rule day, by the 61st Rule of Practice the plaintiff is allowed until the next succeeding rule day to file exceptions. See sec. 110, p. 146. If no exception is filed within that period the answer is taken as sufficient. *Ibid.* By the 66th Rule of Practice the plaintiff is required to file a general replication on or before the next succeeding rule day after the answer is not execepted to or is adjudged and deemed sufficient. See sec. 114, p. 148 *ante.* The period thus prescribed for filing a replication is two rule days after the filing of the answer.

[13] Suppose the answer is filed by special leave of court after the cause has been set for hearing, what time should be allowed the plaintiff to reply or except? There is no statute on the subject. By analogy, it would seem, that four months should be given the plaintiff before the defendant under such circumstances would be entitled to have the cause heard.

ties fully at issue. We have in this country no rejoinder to replications.

Exceptions to answers.

338. Exceptions to answers ought regularly to be filed before a replication,[14] but after replication the court will, upon good cause shown, allow the replication to be withdrawn and permit the plaintiff to file exceptions.[15]

339. *Scandal or impertinence.* If when the answer is filed the plaintiff finds that it contains scandalous or impertinent matter, or that it does not sufficiently answer the allegations of the bill, he should file exceptions to it. 2 Dan. Ch. Pr. (old) 295; Mitf. Pl. 313, 315, 316.

When exceptions for scandal or impertinence are well taken, the court will order the matter held to be scandalous or impertinent to be expunged, and will direct the defendant to pay all costs occasioned by such matter. 1 Newl. Ch. Pr. 152, 275. Sometimes the answer is referred to a commissioner to expunge the impertinent and scandalous matter. *Mason* vs. *Mason*, 4 H. & M. 414. See sec. 273a.

340. *Exceptions to answer for insufficiency.* Generally speaking, if the answer is deemed insufficient from omitting to notice any material allegation in

---

[14] *Coleman* vs. *Lyne*, 4 Rand. 454.

[15] See sec. 332, *ante.* If the rule laid down in *Clarke* vs. *Tinsley*, 4 Rand. 250, in reference to withdrawing replications shall be followed, it would make the pleader more cautious in withdrawing replications. There the replication had been entered and afterwards withdrawn. It was held to be error in the court to order an account, or render a decree, until a new issue was made up. And a deposition which had been taken while the replication was standing, it was held, could not be read after the replication was withdrawn.

the bill,[16] the plaintiff should except to it, and call for a better answer. If instead of excepting for insufficiency, the plaintiff should enter a general replication, he cannot insist at the hearing that those allegations of the bill which are not expressly denied by the answer are admitted to be true. Were he permitted to do this, he might surprise the defendant. By chancellor Taylor, in *Dangerfield* vs. *Claiborne, &c.*, 2 H. & M. 17; *Colman* vs. *Lyne's ex'or*, 4 Rand. 454, 2 Rob. Pr. (old) 313.

Where a defendant pleads or demurs to any part of the discovery sought by a bill and answers likewise, if the plaintiff takes exceptions to the answer before the plea or demurrer has been argued, he admits the plea or demurrer to be good; for unless he admits it to be good, it is impossible to determine whether the answer is sufficient or not. Mitf. Pl. 317. But if the plea or demurrer is only to the relief prayed by the bill, and not to any part of the discovery, the plaintiff may take exceptions to the answer before the plea or demurrer is argued. *Ibid.*

341. If the defendant by way of avoidance, set up a distinct matter which is not called for by the bill and the complainant wish to have the details of such new matter, he should amend his bill and state the matter by way of pretences and call upon the defendant to answer as to the particulars thereof. He cannot except upon the ground of insufficiency to that part of the answer which is not responsive to the bill, though if the fact stated be wholly immaterial, the answer may be objected to for impertinence. *Spencer* vs. *Van Duzen, &c.*, 1 Paige 555.

342. *In Virginia State courts what done when exceptions filed.* In the Virginia State courts the statute

---

[16] See sec. 279, *ante.*

provides that when the plaintiff files exceptions to an answer they shall be set down to be argued, Code 1873, ch. 167, sec. 36, and when exceptions to an answer have been sustained, if the defendant puts in a second answer which is adjudged insufficient, he may be examined upon interrogatories, and committed until he answers them. *Ibid*, sec. 37.

343. The mode of excepting to an answer is a matter of practice with the court and not the subject of appeal; and if it were otherwise, the exception being sustained and the defendant having filed another answer, there the subject of the exception properly ended. *Craig* vs. *Sebrell*, 9 Grat. 131.

344. If exceptions for insufficiency are set down to be argued, the court is simply to decide whether the answer is sufficient or not. Should the chancellor, without deciding whether the exceptions are good or bad, proceed to decree as upon a hearing, and send the cause to a commissioner for an account; upon an appeal from the final decree the appellate court will reverse the decree, set aside the proceedings subsequent to the exceptions, and send back the cause for the exceptions to be heard. *Clarke* vs. *Tinsley's adm'or*, 4 Rand. 252. When the exceptions to the answer are heard, if the answer is thought sufficient, the exceptions will of course be overruled, and the cause will be sent to the rules for further proceedings. The plaintiff may then reply, and evidence may be taken. *S. C.* If the answer is deemed insufficient, the exceptions will be sustained, and the defendant ordered to put in a better answer within a reasonable time; and the cause will be

sent to the rules to be matured for a hearing. *S. C.*
Should no additional answer be filed within the time
prescribed, the bill may be taken for confessed generally; for, in that case, the defendant has not
obeyed the subpœna, which was to *answer the bill*,
the insufficient answer being regarded as no answer.
Turner vs. *Turner*, 4 Ves. 619, note d; Carr, J., in
Coleman vs. *Lyne's ex'or*, 4 Rand. 456. See also
Weaver vs. *Livingston*, 1 Hopkins's Ch. Rep. 595;
and *Davis* vs. *Davis*, 2 Atk. 21.

345. But if the exceptions to an answer are not
well founded it is not ground to reverse a decree
that they were not set down to be argued, but the
case was heard and decided without passing upon
them. *Goddin* vs. *Vaughan*, 14 Grat. 102.

346. Where a defendant pleads or demurs to any
part of the discovery sought by a bill, and answers
likewise, if the plaintiff takes exceptions to the
answer before the plea or demurrer has been argued,
he admits the plea or demurrer to be good; for
unless he admits it to be good, it is impossible to
determine whether the answer is sufficient or not.
But if the plea or demurrer is only to the relief
prayed by the bill, and not to any part of the discovery, the plaintiff may take exceptions to the
answer before the plea or demurrer is argued. If a
plea or demurrer is accompanied by an answer to
any part of the bill, even a denial of combination
merely, and the plea or demurrer is overruled, the
plaintiff must except to the answer as insufficient.
But if a plea or demurrer is filed without any answer, and is overruled, the plaintiff need not take

exceptions, and the defendant must answer the whole bill, as if no defence had been made to it.   Mitf. Pl. 317.   See Story's Eq. Pl. 689; *Kuypers* vs. *Dutch Ref. Church*, 6 Paige, 570.

347. As to the rules governing the filing of exceptions to answers, and the proceedings thereon in the United States Circuit Courts, see the 61st, 62nd, 63rd, 64th and 65th rules of practice of the United States Supreme Court previously cited.   See sections 110–114, *ante*, pp. 146, 147.   In the Virginia State Courts reference may be had to sections 73, 75, *ante*, pp. 112, 113, and to the Code 1873, ch. 167, sections 36, 37.

348. The mode in which an exception to an answer should point out the omission excepted to is a matter discretionary with the court in which it is filed, and not a subject of appeal.   *Craig* vs. *Sebrell*, 9 Grat. 131.   See *Clarke* vs. *Tinsley*, 4 Rand. 250, before referred to.[17]

349. The following is the form of exceptions to an answer:

Form of Exceptions to an Answer.

In the ——— court of ——— county :

John B.,	*Plaintiff*,
against	
Mary R. and James L., administrator of R. R.,	*Defendants.*

Exceptions of the plaintiff to the answer of the

---

[17] Sec. 344.

defendant, James L., administrator of R. R., deceased.

The plaintiff excepts to the answer of the defendant, James L., administrator of R. R., deceased:

1. Because, in his said answer, the said defendant has not answered and set forth a true inventory of the goods and personal estate of R. R., which came to the hands of the said defendant, and how much thereof, and to whom, hath been sold and disposed of, and whether any part thereof, and to what value or amount now remains undisposed of, and what is · become thereof.

2. Because, in his said answer, the said defendant makes no response to the allegation of the bill, "that the intestate of the defendant, James L., administrator as aforesaid of R. R., admitted in a conversation had between the plaintiff and the said R. R. and Mary R., on the ———— day of ————, 18—, at which conversation the said James L. was present, that the debt demanded by your complainant was due to him from the said R. R. and Mary R., and though the bond for the same had been lost, they were as much bound for the money as if it had not been lost."

In all which particulars the said complainant excepts to the answer of the said defendant as evasive, imperfect and insufficient, and humbly prays that the said defendant may be compelled to put in a full and sufficient answer to the said bill.

GEORGE N., p. q.

350. *When exceptions sustained.* In the Virginia State courts, see section 75, pp. 113, 114, *ante.* As to the United States Circuit Courts, see section 113, p. 147, *ante.*

351. *Disclaimers.* This defence is of such rare

occurrence that nothing further need be said of it than what is contained in the eighth chapter of this work.

CHAPTER X.

Of evidence in courts of equity.

352. For a full discussion of evidence in courts of equity a separate treatise would be required. It is proposed, in this chapter, to treat briefly of such evidence.

353. *What, if any, general issue in equity.* At law there is what is known as the general issue. There is no general issue, strictly so called, in ordinary suits in equity in the case of natural persons. The doctrine concerning corporations aggregate, whose answers are put in under their common seal and not under oath, seems to create a precise and exact general issue in equity, in which the rules of evidence as to the *onus* of proof are identically the same as at law.[18]

In cases of divorce under the Virginia statute, Code 1873, chap. 105, §§ 8, 9, there is some resemblance to the general issue at law; and in cases of usury and in the proceeding devisavit vel non hereafter mentioned. Sections 376, 378.[19] In the United States Circuit Courts, when an answer under oath is waived, there is a resemblance to the general issue. See 41st Rule of Practice as amended Dec. term 1871.

---

[18] See section 355.

[19] If *Randolph* vs. *Randolph*, 6 Rand. 198, subsequently cited, section 382, be sustained, it furnishes an instance of the general issue as to the matters so alleged and answered.

354. *General rules of equity: exceptions.* Generally, the same rules of evidence prevail in equity as at law. The facts proved ought to be material to the decree sought for or resisted and should be established by legitimate evidence, Adams's Eq. 362, 363; the evidence should be confined to matters in issue, the case as proved must be substantially the same with that stated upon the record, 2 Dan. Ch. Pr. (old) 410, 419; and usually, as at law, the burden of proof rests upon the party asserting the affirmative.[20] But there are exceptions. Courts of equity act according to rules peculiar to themselves in adjusting the burden of proof in the case of parties holding fiduciary and confidential relations,[21] in acting upon circumstances as indicating fraud which courts of law would not deem satisfactory proofs[22] and in the weight which they give to an answer,

---

[20] 2 Dan. Ch. Pr. (old) 408. The reader will bear in mind, as some of the exceptions to the general rule that the affirmative must be proved, that where a *prima facie* right is proved or admitted by the pleadings, the burden of proof is always upon the person calling such right in question, *Eyre* vs. *Dolphin*, 2 Ball and B. 303; *Saunders* vs *Leslie*, *Ib.* 515; and that in all cases when the presumption of the law is in favor of a party, it will be incumbent on the other party to disprove it, though, in so doing, he may have to prove a negative. 1 Phil. on Ev. 197, 2 Dan. Ch. Pr. (old) 409. See future sections on the *onus probandi*.

[21] *Jones* vs. *Thomas*, 2 Y. and C. 498; *Lewes* vs. *Morgan*, 3 Y. and J. 230; 1 Sto Eq. Jur 309–314; *Gibson* vs. *Joyes*, 6 Ves. 268; 3 Green. Ev., ? 253. The principle ruling in such cases in equity courts is this, that he who bargains in matter of advantage with a person, placing confidence in him, is bound to show that a reasonable use has been made of that confidence. The rule applies to parents, guardians, trustees, attorneys, pastors, medical advisers, and all others standing in confidential relations with those with whom they treat:—the burden is on them to establish by proof affirmatively the perfect fairness, adequacy and equity of their respective claims.

[22] 1 Sto. Eq. Jur., ? 190–193; *Chesterfield* vs. *Janssen*, 1 Atk. 301, 352; *Fullager* vs. *Clark*, 18 Ves. 481, 483.

hereafter noticed. Other exceptions will appear as we proceed.

355. *The weight of an answer in equity as evidence for the defendant.* Where there are no special statutes to the contrary[23] the rule in equity is, that the plaintiff having called on the defendant to answer, particularly and upon oath, every material' allegation, well pleaded in the bill, and having thus appealed to the conscience of the defendant for the truth of what he has alleged, it results as a consequence, held to be reasonable and just, and the law of the forum in which the suit is,[24] that the answer of the defendant under oath, so far as it is responsive to the bill, is evidence in the cause in proof of the facts of which the bill seeks a disclosure; and, being so, is conclusive evidence in the defendant's favor, unless the plaintiff can overcome its force either by the testimony of two witnesses, or of one witness, corroborated by other facts and circumstances sufficient to give it a greater weight than the answer,[25] or by such circumstances as will without the testimony of any witness outweigh the answer.[26]

---

[23] There is an enactment in West Virginia, Code 1868, chap. 125, § 59, to the effect that a denial in an answer of a material allegation of the bill only puts the plaintiff upon proof of such allegation.

[24] See *Thornton* vs. *Gordon, &c.*, 2 Rob. R. 719.

[25] The doctrine of the text is supported by almost numberless authorities: *Taylor* vs. *Moore*, 2 Rand. 575, *Bennett* vs. *Maule's adm'or*, *Gilm.* 319, *Love* vs. *Braxton*, 5 Call 539, *Fant* vs. *Miller, &c*, 17 Grat. 189, *Shurtz* vs. *Johnson*, 28 Grat. 657, 658, *Hughes* vs. *Blake*, 6 Wheat 433, *Shultz* vs. *Hansborough*, 33 Grat. 581. The testimony of two witnesses to two distinct conversations, *i. e.* one witness to each of the conversations, was, in *Love* vs. *Braxton*, 5 Call 537, held insufficient to outweigh the answer.

[26] *Clarke's ex'or.* vs. *Van Riemsdyk*, 9 Cranch 153.

In the United States Circuit Courts, by the 41st Rule of Practice as amended December term, 1871: "If the complainant in his bill, shall waive an answer under oath, or shall only require an answer under oath with regard to certain specified interrogatories, the answer of the defendant, though under oath, except such part thereof as shall be directly responsive to such interrogatories, shall not be evidence in his favor, unless the cause be set down for hearing on bill and answer only; but may nevertheless be used as an affidavit, with the same effect as heretofore, on a motion to grant or dissolve an injunction, or on any other incidental motion in the cause; but this shall not prevent a defendant from becoming a witness in his own behalf under Section 3 of the Act of Congress of July 2nd, 1864." 13 Wal. xi.

356. *Effect of an answer of a corporation aggregate.* In the case of a corporation aggregate, its answer being put in under the common seal of the corporation, and not under oath, is not evidence for the defendant though responsive to the bill: it is considered merely as a denial of the allegations in the bill analogous to the general issue at law, so as to put the complainant to the proof of such allegations. *B. & O. R. R. Co.* vs. *City of Wheeling,* 13 Grat. 62; *Union B'k of Georgetown* vs. *Geary,* 5 Pet. R. 99.

But where the answer of a corporation aggregate was sworn to by its president, and explicitly denied a fact stated in the bill, the court held that something more than one witness was required to overcome the answer, though the president was not in office when the alleged transaction took place. *Carpenter* vs. *Prov. Wash. Ins. Co.,* 4 How. 185; see also *Bronson* vs. *La Crosse R. R. Co.,* 2 Wal. 283.

357. *Burden of proof.* Cases and authorities on the burden of proof other than those already mentioned will be found in the subjoined note.[27]

---

[27] The issue should be proved by the party who states an affirmative, not by the party who states a negative; the courts will disregard the *forms* of affirmation and negation, and ascertain strictly which is the party making a substantial affirmation though it may be negative in form; *Pow. Evi.* 167,

358. *What is to be proved.* In considering what is necessary to be proved, .the pleader will regard as

---

168, the issue must be proved by the party who states the affirmative in substance and not merely the affirmative in form. *Ibid. Mercer* vs. *Whall*, 5 Q. B. 447, *Amos* vs. *Hughes*, 1 M. & R. 464, *Mills* vs. *Barber*, 1 M. & W. 427, *Williams* vs. *East Ind. Co.*, 3 East 193, *Seward* vs. *Leggatt*, 7 C. & P. 613, *Ashby* vs. *Bates*, 15 M. & W. 589, *Doe* vs. *Whitehead*, 8 A. & E. 571, Patterson J. in *Whittaker* vs. *Edmunds*, 1 M. & R. 386, *Harvey* vs. *Towers*, 4 L. & Eq. Rep. 531, *Berry* vs. *Alderman*, 23 L. J. 36, C. P. In every case the *onus probandi* lies on the person who wishes to support his case by a particular fact which lies more peculiarly within his knowledge, or of which he is supposed to be cognizant. *R.* vs. *Burdett*, 4 B. & Ald. 140, *Hartley* vs. *Whart*, 11 A. & D. 934, *Marsh* vs. *Horne*, 5 B. & C. 322, *Nepean* vs. *Doe*, 2 Sm. Lea. Cas. 306. Where the issue is, whether a party be living or not, the party asserting the death must prove it. *Wilson* vs. *Hodges*, 2 East 312. Notice the Va. Stat. Code 1873, ch. 172, §§ 47, 48 as to presumption of death arising from seven years absence without being heard from. See *Leete* vs. *Gresh. L. Ins. Co.*, 7 Eng. L. & E. R. 578. 1 Green. Ev. § 74, §§ 366, 370, §§ 78, 79, 80, 81, and cases cited.

VIRGINIA CASES.

Assignee of a party holding a fiduciary relation. An assignee taking an assignment, at large discount, of a chose in action of an intestate from the administrator: the burden of proof is on the assignee to show the fairness of the administrator's action. *Fisher* vs. *Basset & als.*, 9 Leigh 119.

Acknowledgement of an assignor to affect his assignee. An assignor of a claim acknowledging it to have been paid before the assignment;—his acknowledgment must be proved to have been made *before he assigned,* and the *onus* is on the debtor. *Wilcox* vs. *Pearman*, 9 Leigh 144.

How will prevents statute of limitations. A creditor, relying upon a charge in a will to prevent the operation of the statute of limitations, must show that the testator died before his debt was barred. *Tazewell* vs. *Whittle*, 13 Grat. 329.

Endorsee of note required to prove that he was holder for value without notice of fraud. In *Vathir* vs. *Zane*, 6 Grat. 246, the bill did not charge that the holder of a note was an endorsee for value or that he had notice of a fraud, which its maker had proved was perpetrated by the payee in its procurement. In the answer the defendant endorsee averred that he was a holder for value of the note without notice of the fraud in its procurement, and stated the consideration he gave for the note. It was held that this statement of the answer was not responsive to any allegation of the bill and must be proved.

Party surcharging executor's account. The *onus probandi* is on a party surcharging and falsifying an executorial account which has been confirmed.

sufficiently established without proof all matters of
which the courts take judicial notice, and all admis-

Nimmo's ex'ors vs. *The Comwth.*, 4 H. & M. 57, *McCall* vs. *Peachy's ad'mor*,
3 Mun. 288.

*A purchaser seeking relief from judgment for purchase money must show the
title bad.* A purchaser taking possession of the estate purchased cannot obtain relief in equity against a judgment for the purchase money on the
ground that the title of the vendor was not clearly shown to be good:—the
onus is on him to show that it is bad. *Grantland* vs. *Wight*, 5 Mun. 295.

Defendant, in slander suit, required to prove a negative. The *onus probandi*,
under plea of justification in an action of slander, is on the party defendant
who had alleged "that the plaintiff's affidavit was false," though to establish
the falsity of the affidavit involved the proof of a negative. *Hinchman* vs.
Lawson, 5 Leigh 695.

Sanity presumed in writer of olograph will. In the case of an *olograph*
will, the *onus probandi* is on the party asserting that the testator was incapable
of making a will. *Temple, &c.* vs. *Temple*, 1 H. & M. 476.

To recover on a bond given for purchase, must show delivery or tender. G.
agreed to sell certain escape warrants to W. on his giving bond and good
security for the purchase money. W. executes bond with a blank for the
surety's name, to be filled up at a certain time and place, when the escape
warrants were to be assessed and delivered by G. If W. fail to give the surety,
G. cannot take advantage of the bond without proof of his assigning and
delivering the escape warrants, or tendering them within a reasonable time;
and the *onus probandi* lies on him in equity to show this. *Page, ex'or*, vs.
Winston's adm'r, 2 Mun. 298.

Check given, to show that it was a loan to payee, burden of proof on drawer.
A check given is *prima facie* for the payment of a debt, or for a loan or money
by the payee to the drawer; and though the drawer may repel the implication
and establish by evidence, if he can, that the check was a loan to the payee by
the drawer; such evidence, being in conflict with the apparent purport of
the transaction, ought to be very strong to repel the implication. *Terry* vs.
Ragsdale, 33 Grat. 342.

What creditor of a decedent attacking a voluntary conveyance must show.
A voluntary conveyance by one largely indebted is void as to his creditors,
but the property so conveyed cannot be subjected by a creditor (after the death
of the grantor) without showing that there are no assets in the hands of the
executor or administrator of the donor to satisfy the debt *Chamberlayne* vs.
Temple, 2 Rand. 384.

Purchase under trust deed. A party insisting on a sale by a trustee under a
trust deed must prove due advertisement. *Gibson's heirs* vs. *Jones & als*, 5
Leigh 370; *Norman* vs. *Hill & als.* 2 P. & H. 676.

sions by either side made by the forms of the pleadings or by positive agreement.

CASES IN UNITED STATES SUPREME COURT.

What United States must show, claiming priority. When the United States claim priority because the debtor has made an assignment of all his property, and the deed of assignment does not show that it includes all the debtor's property, the burden of proof is on the United States to show that it does include the whole. *United States vs. Howland,* 4 Wheat. 108.

What necessary to establish collateral heirship. To establish collateral heirship, it must be proved not only that the ancestor is dead but that he died without issue; the burden of proof, as to both facts, is on the claimant. *Chivac vs. Reinicker,* 2 Pet. 613; Starkie on Evidence, 1099; *Doe vs. Griffin,* 15 East. 293.

What claimant under marshal's deed must show. In the case of lands sold for non-payment of taxes, the marshal's deed is not even *prima facie* evidence that the prerequisites of the law have been complied with; the party claiming under it must show positively that they have been complied with. *Williams & als* vs. *Peyton's lessee,* 4 Wheat. 77.

When party relying on an outstanding title must show it. In many cases the burden of proof is on the party within whose knowledge and means of information the fact is. But this rule is not universal. In the case under consideration the plaintiff had shown *prima facie* a good title to recover. The defendant sets up no title in himself but seeks to maintain his possession as a mere intruder by setting up a title in a third person with whom he has no privity. In such a case it is incumbent on the party setting up the defence to establish the existence first of an outstanding title beyond controversy. *Greenleaf's lessee* vs. *Birth,* 6 Pet. 302.

Account current unobjected to for two years casts burden of proof on recipient to disprove it. An account current sent by a foreign merchant to a merchant in this country and not objected to for two years is deemed an account stated, and throws the burden of proof upon him who received and kept it without objection. *Freeland* vs. *Heron,* 7 Cranch 147.

Averment of non-citizenship must be proved by the party averring. If the record contains sufficient averments of citizenship to give the court jurisdiction, the defendant must traverse them by a proper plea to the jurisdiction; and the burden of proof is on him to disprove these averments. If he plead to the merits, the jurisdiction is admitted. *Sheppard* vs. *Graves,* 14 How. 505.

Trust must be shown by party claiming that an absolute deed is a trust. A deed being absolute on its face, the party who alleges it to be a trust must establish it by proof; and in the case under consideration the circumstances shown were sufficiently strong to repel every presumption against the trust drawn from

359. *Matters judicially noticed.* Prof. Minor, in his Institutes, Vol. 4, p. 997, thus classifies and

---

the absolute terms of the deed. *Prevost* vs. *Gratz*, 6 Wheat. 494. But see *Morris* vs. *Nixon's exor.*, 1 How. 118.

Party alleging a decree must prove it. See *Humes* vs. *Scruggs*, 4 Otto 22 cited in section 333, *ante.*

Equitable owner must show notice to the purchaser of his rights. The burden of proof rests on an equitable owner to show that a purchaser had notice of his rights in due time. *Calais Steamship Co.* vs. *Van Pelt's admr.*, 2 Black. 372.

Stockholder, when presumed to be. A person is presumed to be the owner of stock when his name appears on the books of the company as a stockholder; and when he is sued as such the burden of disproving that presumption is cast upon him. *Turnbull* vs. *Payson*, 5 Otto 418.

Against a collector of customs for violation of the law, see *Arthur* vs. *Unkart*, 6 Otto 118.

On suit against infringer of a patent: as to profits, alleged to come from some other source. *Elizabeth* vs. *Pavement Co,.* 7 Otto 126.

Against one violating tobacco tax law. Lilienthall's Tobacco vs. *United States*, 7 Otto 237.

A party seeking to reform an instrument, burden on him. *Howland* vs. *Blake*, 7 Otto 624.

A party underwriting who afterwards denies an insurable interest, must prove it. *Hooper* vs. *Robinson*, 8 Otto 528.

Burden of proof on party alleging an infringement of the patent, if the answer denies it. *Bates* vs. *Coe*, 8 Otto 31.

When a plaintiff's knowledge of the fraud and his neglect promptly to rescind the contract is relied on to defeat the action, the burden of proving such knowledge and the time when it was acquired rests upon the defendant. *Colby* vs. *Reed*, 9 Otto 560.

A servant of a company using defective machinery, after giving notice of the defects to the proper officer if he uses it afterwards, is not necessarily, or as a matter of law, guilty of contributory negligence. The company must show the want of due care to show contributory negligence. *Hough* vs. *Railway Co.*, 10 Otto 213.

Burden of proof on Insurance Company. An answer to the question whether "there was hereditary disease,' made by the applicant for insurance that there was "no hereditary taint to his knowledge." The company must prove first that there was hereditary disease, and then that it was known to the applicant when he answered the question. *Ins. Co.* vs. *Gridley*, 10 Otto 614.

What onus the assignee in bankruptcy is under who attacks a deed as void for giving preferences and as fraudulent within the meaning of the 35th section of the Bankrupt act of March 2nd, 1867. *Barber* vs. *Priest*, 13 Otto 293.

enumerates the matters of fact of which the courts take judicial notice:

1st. Public functionaries, public seals and acts of state, including
The existence and titles of sovereign powers throughout the civilized world,
The usual symbols of nationality and sovereignty, namely, the flag and seal,
Where nations are divided the newly formed State is not officially recognized by the judicial tribunals, until acknowledged by the political department of the government, which with us is for this purpose, the federal Executive. Until so recognized the existence and the flag and the seal of the new State must be proved as facts, and consequently must be alleged in pleading,
Public acts, decrees and judgments of foreign States, exemplified under their public seals,
2nd. The law of nations, seals of notaries and of admiralty courts and in general all facts commonly known and notorious, including
The Law of Nations,
The seal of a notary public, he being an officer recognized by the whole commercial world,
The seals of foreign admiralty and maritime courts, which are regarded as courts of the civilized world,
The general customs and usages of merchants and of trade,
The usual course of trade, as for example, between the West and New York,
Things which must have happened in the ordinary course of nature; as the period of gestation, physiological impossibilities of procreation, &c.,
Course of the almanac and of the heavenly bodies and the ordinary measurement of time,
Difference of time in different longitudes,
Ordinary public fasts and festivals,
Coincidence of days of the week with days of the month.
Meanings of words in the vernacular tongue but not the meaning of special phrases,
Customary abbreviations,
Meaning of familiar literary allusions,
Legal weights and measures and legal coin and currency; but not the extent of its depreciation,
Usual practice and course of conveyancing,
Matters of public history affecting the whole people,
Public matters affecting the government of the country as in its relations with foreign powers, &c.,
Whatever ought to be generally known within the limits of their jurisdiction, such as any process of art or science which has become a matter of common knowledge, as that by photography like-

nesses are taken, that certain processes produce certain results, &c.,

3rd. Political divisions, events and public officers of the country, including

The territorial extent of jurisdiction and sovereignty exercised by their government,

The local divisions of their country as into States, provinces, counties, cities, towns, parishes and the like, so far as political government is concerned or affected,

The relative positions of such local divisions; but not the precise boundaries, further than as described in public statutes,

The distance of county seats from the seat of government (Mendum's case, 6 Rand. 704),

The political constitution or frame of their own government,

The essential political agents and public officers conducting its regular administration,

The essential and regular political operations, powers and action of the government,

e. g. Accession of the chief executive,

His powers and privileges,

His signature,

Heads of departments, principal officers of State and the public seals,

Election or resignation of a Senator of the United States,

Appointment of a cabinet or foreign minister,

Marshalls and sheriffs, and the genuineness of their signatures, but not deputies, except as deputies may be recognized by statute, as in Virginia they are;

County officers generally,

Courts of general jurisdiction, their judges, seals, rules, and maxims and course of proceeding,

Justices of inferior courts, with their jurisdiction, &c., as justices of the peace, &c.,

Public proclamations of war and peace,

Days of special public fasts and thanksgiving,

Stated days of general political elections,

Sittings of the legislature and its established course of proceeding and the privileges of its members, but not the transactions stated in its journals,

Ports and waters of the United States, in which the tide ebbs and flows, and probably all navigable waters—in the United States courts,

Boundaries of the several States and of the several judicial districts of the United States—in the United States courts,

Laws and jurisprudence of the several States and Territories—in the United States courts,

Jurisdiction of the inferior courts whose judgments are revised.

1 Green. Ev., § 6; 1 Whart. Ev., § 287, *et seq*; *Id.*, § 317, *et seq.*

Courts do not take judicial notice of foreign law; and the laws of the several States are foreign to each other (though not foreign in the courts of the United States); and so, in the Virginia State courts such foreign laws must be stated and proved. See 4 Min. Inst. 994, 1 Green. Ev 486, *et seq.*

359a. The Virginia State courts take judicial notice of the public statute law of their own State and of the United States; 1 Min. Inst. 38. As to private statutes, although by act, Code 1873, chap. 172, § 1, they may be given in evidence without being specially pleaded, they must be given in evidence, *i. e.*, the courts do not take judicial notice of them. But where such private statutes appear to have been relied on in the lower court, the statute provides that the appellate court shall take judicial notice of them. Code 1873, chap. 172, § 1. *Legrand* vs. *Hamp. Sid. Col.*, 5 Munf. 324; *Somerville* vs. *Wimbish*, 7 Grat. 225.

The Virginia Statute provides that the courts shall take notice of the signature of any of the judges, or of the governor of the State, to any judicial or official document. Code 1873, chap. 172, § 3.

360. *Admissions.* Of admissions, as already noticed, some are by the forms of the pleadings, others by express agreement.

361. *Admissions in the forms of the pleadings by the plaintiff.* Thus, in courts of equity, the bill may be read as evidence for the defendant of any of the matters therein directly and positively averred [28]:

---

[28] Dan. Ch. Pr. (edi. 1871), p 838, 839.

and so a bill filed in another suit may be read in evidence by the defendant on proof that it was exhibited by the direction or with the privity of the party plaintiff in it.[29]

When there is an amended bill, it should generally be read, not the original. See Dan. Ch. Pr., edi. 1871, p. 889, *Hales* vs. *Pomfret*, Dan. Ex. R., 141; *Fitzgerald* vs. *O'Flaherty*, 1 Moll. 347; 3 Green. Ev. § 275, and *McGowen* vs. *Young*, 2 Stewart, 276. Where the amended bill has altered the effect of the answer, or rendered it obscure, the original bill may be read by the defendant to explain the answer. *Hales* vs. *Pomfret, ubi sup.*

362. *An infant plaintiff.* The statements in a bill filed in behalf of an infant plaintiff are more binding than admissions in the answer of an infant. Often, the court will make a decree without a reference to a master upon statements in such a bill, which, if they were in an infant's answer, would be referred to the master to inquire into. *Gres. Eq. Evid.* 9.

See *Goddin* vs. *Vaughan*, 14 Grat. 123; *Brown* vs. *Armistead*, 6 Rand. 594; *Gregory* vs. *Molesworth*, 3 Atk. R. 626; *Brook* vs. *Hertford*, 2 P. Wms. 578, as to the effect upon the rights of infants of the institution of proceedings in their behalf as plaintiffs.

363. *Failing to file a replication.* As we have already seen, sec. 74 *ante*, a plaintiff who fails to file a replication admits the statements in the answer. See as to omitting to file a replication by an infant, note 6, to sec. 330 *ante*.

364. *Admissions in the forms of the pleadings by the defendant.* Sometimes, the bill may be read by the plaintiff as evidence against the defendant of his

---

[29] 3 Green. Ev. 275.

admission of the truth of the matters therein alleged
and not noticed in the answer. The principle governing this class of cases is, that the defendant being
solemnly required to admit or deny the truth of the
allegations in the bill has by his silence admitted it.
But this, say the authorities, applies only to facts
either directly charged to be within the knowledge
of the defendant or which may fairly be presumed
to be so[30]; Dan. Ch. Pr. (Perk.) 834, note 3; for if
the matters alleged are not of either of these descrip-
tions the better opinion is, that the omission of the
defendant to notice them in his answer is merely
matter of exception on the part of the plaintiff, in
order to obtain a distinct admission or denial on the
particular point.[31] See *Cropper* vs. *Burtons*, 5 Leigh
426; *Coleman* vs. *Lyne*, 454; *Page's ex'or* vs. *Winston's adm'or*, 2 Munf. 298, and other cases cited in
section 279, *ante.*

365. *On motion to dissolve injunction.* On a motion
to dissolve an injunction before an answer, the allegations of the bill are taken to be true, *Peatross* vs.
McLaughlin, 6 Grat. 64; and on motion to dissolve
when an answer is filed, the motion coming on on
the bill and answer, the allegations of the bill not

---

[30] The exception mentioned in the text is recognized in many cases. The
rule of West Virginia, referred to in the next note, appears to the writer to
be much wiser.

[31] There are special statutes in some of the States abrogating the rule.
Thus in West Virginia, Code 1868, chap. 125, sec. 36, "Every material allegation of the bill not controverted by an answer, and every material allegation of new matter in the answer constituting a claim for affirmative relief,
not controverted by a reply shall, for the purpose of the suit, be taken as
true, and no proof thereof shall be required." See N. Y. Code of Procedure,
p. 337, sec. 168.

denied by the answer are taken to be true. *B. & O. R. R. Co.* vs. *City of Wheeling*, 13 Grat. 40.

366. When a motion to dissolve comes on to be heard on bill and answer. and the answer denies all the equity of the bill, the injunction is usually dissolved, of course. *Hoffman* vs. *Livingston*, 1 John Ch. 211, *Delaney* vs. *Hutchinson*, 2 Rand. 183, *North's ex'or* vs. *Perrow*, 4 Rand. 1, *Hogan* vs. *Duke & als.*, 20 Grat. 244. It is otherwise, however, if on the facts disclosed, the court sees good reason for retaining the injunction, Dan. Ch. Pr. (Perk.) 1788 *notes*, or if the plaintiff has adduced auxiliary evidence of his right, *Orr* vs. *Littlefield*, 1 *Wood* vs. *Minot*, 13.

"If the whole merits are satisfactorily denied by the answer, the injunction is ordinarily dissolved. But there are exceptions to the doctrine, and these, for the most part, are fairly resolvable into the principle of irreparable mischief; such as cases of asserted waste, or of asserted mismanagement in partnership concerns, or of asserted violation of copyrights, or of patent rights. In cases of this sort, the court will look into the whole circumstances, and will continue or dissolve the injunction in the exercise of a sound discretion." Story, J., in *Poor* vs. *Carleton*, 3 Sumn. 74.

See 41st Rule of Practice in United States Circuit Courts as amended December 1871, in sec. 355, *ante*.

367. *Effect of statements in the bill as against an infant defendant.* Even when the infant answers, his answer cannot be read to establish a fact which it is against his interest to admit. Dan. Ch. Pr. (Perk.) 164. It follows, as a matter of course, that the taking of the bill pro confesso as to an infant or the failure of his guardian ad litem to notice in the answer any statement of the bill will not be to his prejudice.

368. *Effect of a bill being taken pro confesso against
an adult defendant.* If the defendant neglects to appear and answer, as we have seen, the bill will be
taken pro confesso. Sections 70, 92 *ante.* The effect
of taking the bill pro confesso was considered in
Pullen vs. *Mullen*, 12 Leigh 434. It was charged in
the bill that a trustee sold, and Pullen the defendant
purchased, only the life estate of Mrs. Mullen. Pullen failed to answer and the bill was taken for confessed. The court held that by permitting the bill
to be taken for confessed the defendant admitted the
truth of this allegation, and the admission dispensed
with the enquiry whether it would have been competent to introduce parol evidence to prove a mistake
made in the deed of the trustee conveying the whole
estate instead of an estate for the life of Mrs. Mullen. In *Findley's ex'or, &c.,* vs. *Sheffey,* 1 Rand. 73,
there was a want of certainty in the allegation of
the bill, the bill simply alleging that the sale of the
property was "for $2,000 *as your orator is informed.*"
The bill being taken for confessed, a decree was
rendered on that allegation against an executor.
The decree was reversed, the Court of Appeals holding that an account of the sales of the property
should have been taken before a decree.

Chancellor Sanford, in *Williams* vs. *Corwin, &c.,* 1 Hopkins's Ch.
Rep. 471, laid down these rules: "When the allegations of the
bill are distinct and positive, and the bill is confessed, such allegations are taken as true without proof. Where the allegations of a
bill are indefinite or the demand of the complainant is in its nature uncertain, the certainty requisite to a proper decree must be
afforded by proofs." Chancellor Kent said in *Caines* vs. *Fisher,*
1 John. Ch. R. 110, that if a defendant would not answer he ought
to be concluded in the same manner that he is by a neglect to
plead to a declaration at law. Chancellor Taylor had before him

several cases in which he settled the practice in his court by analogy to the course at law. He said that at law if a defendant made default in any action of debt founded upon a writing for the payment of money, judgment might be entered, but if the writing were not filed the plaintiff would not be suffered to have execution. So, in equity, if a suit be brought to foreclose a mortgage, and the bill be taken for confessed, a decree of foreclosure and sale may be entered if the deed of mortgage referred to in the bill be filed, but not otherwise. Again, at law, if an action on the case is brought for money had and received, and there is a judgment by default and a writ of enquiry awarded, upon the execution of the writ of enquiry the plaintiff cannot recover more than he can prove, and if he is without proof he shall not have a verdict for more than a cent. And so in equity if a suit be brought for the settlement of accounts and the defendant make default, yet the plaintiff shall not have a decree without proof. 4 H. & M. 476, 2 Rob. Pr. (old) 324.

369. *Effect of taking bill pro confesso as to absent defendants.* It is said that under the statute, 5 Geo. 2, chap. 25, when the bill is taken pro confesso (against an absconding defendant) the decree accordingly follows without any proof to satisfy the court of the justice of the demand. See 2 Rob. Pr. (old) 326. This is not understood to be the law of Virginia In *Platt* vs. *Howland*, 10 Leigh 507, the court said that the plaintiff in a foreign attachment suit should prove himself in a legal manner to be a creditor of the absent defendant. Our attachment law requires that the "claim of the plaintiff be established" before decree is rendered for him. Code 1873, chap. 148, sec. 23. And, in other cases, there is nothing in the statute to sanction a decree against absent defendants without satisfactory proof. See Code 1873, chap. 166, sec. 15.

Platt vs. *Howland*, 10 Leigh, 507, does not in express terms overrule *Morrison* vs. *Campbell*, 2 Rand. 216. Possibly, the two cases may be reconciled. In *Morrison* vs. *Campbell*, 2 Rand., it was held that while strict legal proof was not necessary there should be enough to satisfy the court that under all the circumstances of the case the demand was just. The plantiff claimed title to lands under a sale made by executors, and if strict proof had been required of the due execution of the will giving authority to sell, the plaintiff would have failed for there were no such proof. There were however circumstances which justified the belief that the will was duly executed to pass lands and that the executors sold the lands in question in that suit to the plantiff. The right of the plantiff was held, as against absent defendants, to be sufficiently established.[32]

370. *Answer read against a guardian.* The answer of an infant by his guardian may be read against the guardian; 1 Dan. Ch. Pr. (old) 214; and in *Beasley* vs. *Magrath*, 2 Sch. & Lef. 34, the answer of an infant by his mother and guardian in another cause was read against the mother in her own capacity.

371. *Answer of infant arriving at age and not amending his answer.* Where the infant defendant on arriving at full age neither amended his answer by his guardian, *ad litem*, nor made a new answer, but prayed a hearing of the cause *de novo*, his answer was held to be evidence against him. *Hind*, 422.

372. *An infant after arriving at full age who unreasonably delays making a better defence.* Prof. Greenleaf states the rule to be, that if the infant unreasonably delays after attaining full age to apply for leave to make a better defence, he will be taken to have

---

[32] So establishing it against the absent defendants, the court went farther and said, that in establishing the demand against the absent defendants, it was also established against other defendants residing in the commonwealth, the latter having only this interest in the case that the decree should exempt them from any new litigation with the heirs, devisees or executors of a testator (who were the absent defendants) in another suit, and the decree in favour of the plaintiff in this suit was a bar to any new suit in their behalf.

confirmed his former answer by guardian, and it may be read against him. 3 Green. Ev. § 279.

373. *Admissions in answers of idiots.* The rule in regard to infants differs from that as laid down in the english books in reference to idiots and persons of permanently weak intellects or those who by reason of age or infirmity are reduced to a second infancy. The answer of the latter made by their guardian is admitted to be read against them. The reason of the difference is said to be this, that as the infant improves in reason and judgment he is to have a day to show cause when he comes of age, but the case of the others being hopeless and becoming worse and worse, they can have no day. *Loving* vs. *Caverley*, Prec. Ch. 229, 2 Dan. Ch. Pr. (old) 403, 1 Dan. Ch. Pr. (old) 249.

374. *Admissions in answer of a wife or husband.* The answer of a wife is not evidence against her husband, *The City B'k.*·vs. *Bangs*, 3 Paige 36, nor is the admission of a married woman answering jointly with her husband evidence against her.[33] But when the married woman answers separately, either with or without the order of the court, she stands exactly as another defendant. *Gres. Eq. Ev.* 28. In *Frank, &c.* vs. *Lilienfield & als.*, 33 Grat. 377, the court considered the effect of a husband's answer upon the interests of a wife holding separate estate and answering separately. It was contended on behalf of

---

[33] In one case where the husband answered jointly with the wife and died and the suit abating as to the husband was continued against the wife, the answer was held good against her. *Shelberry* vs. *Briggs*, 2 Vern. 249.

the wife that the answer of the husband being responsive to the bill was evidence for the wife. The court held that it was not, and that the case fell under the general rule that the answer of one defendant cannot be used as evidence either for or against a co-defendant. But the court farther held that her answer was admissible as evidence in her own behalf and against the complainants so far as its statements were responsive to the bill and based on facts within her own knowledge. See *Clark's ex'or* vs. *Van Riemsdyk*, 3 Cranch R 153, 160, 161.

375. *Effect of an answer on the trial of an issue.* On the trial of an issue out of chancery, the statements of the answer responsive to the bill must be taken as true, unless contradicted by two witnesses or by one witness and corroborating circumstances. *Powell, &c.* vs. *Manson*, 22 Grat. 177.[34]

376. *Effect of answer as evidence in cases of usury.* In cases of usury, under the present Virginia statute, Code 1873, chap. 137, sec. 9, the borrower may compel from the lender a discovery of the usury and the lender will recover only the principal money without interest and will be made to pay the costs of the suit. There is no statute now in Virginia forfeiting the whole debt. When there was such a statute, the provision that where the bill charged usury and re-

---

[34] Issues out of chancery will be fully treated of in the second part of this treatise. The reader is specially referred to the above cited case of *Powell, &c.* vs. *Manson*, 22 Grat. 177, as constituting in itself an institute on the subject of issues out of chancery. The case was decided in the Chancery Court of Richmond city and the decision of the Chancellor was unanimously affirmed by the Supreme Court of Appeals of Virginia.

quired no disclosure from the defendant an issue should be made up and tried at the bar of the court whether or no the transaction was usurious, and on the trial of such issue, neither the bill nor the answer should be given in evidence was important, for then, establishing the usury without the oath of the lender, by independent proof, the borrower was relieved from the payment of the whole debt;[35] but in the present condition of the statute, the relief given the borrower is, it seems, in every case the same.

The provision just alluded to is embodied in the 12th sec. chap. 137, Code 1873. It reads: "Upon a bill requiring no discovery of the defendant, but praying an injunction to prevent the sale of property conveyed to secure the repayment of a sum of money or other thing borrowed at usurious interest, the court shall cause an issue to be made and tried at its bar by a jury whether or no the transaction be usurious. On the trial of such issue, neither the bill nor the answer shall be given in evidence. If the jury find the transaction usurious then the same relief shall be given as if the party claiming under the conveyance had resorted to the court to make his claim available. But the court may grant new trials as in other cases."

377. *Effect of answer on motion for a receiver.* When the application for a receiver is made after the coming in of the answer and the equities of the bill upon which the appointment of a receiver is sought are fully denied by the defendant's answer under oath, and the evidence adduced in support of the bill does not overcome the denial of the answer,[36] the court will refuse to appoint a receiver. High on

---

[35] See *Smith* vs. *Nicholas, &c.*, 8 Leigh 330.

[36] The appointment, &c., of receivers is elaborately discussed by Baldwin, J. in *Beverley* vs. *Brooke & als.*, 4 Grat. 187.

See the second part of this treatise as to the appointment of receivers.

Receivers, § 24. And if a receiver has already been appointed, he will be discharged upon the coming in of the defendant's answer fully denying the equities of the bill. High on Receivers, § 24.

The case is likened to a motion to dissolve an injunction on the coming in of an answer denying all the equity of the bill; as to which see sec. 366, *ante*.

378. *Effect of answer as evidence in a proceeding devisavit vel non.* On an issue devisavit vel non the answer of the defendant under the statute[37] does not become, of necessity, evidence in the cause on the question as to the validity of the will. Where there is no appeal to the conscience of the defendant, where no discovery is sought from him as to facts within his particular knowledge, but he is called on to answer merely as a step or part of the proceeding through which it is necessary to pass before obtaining a trial before a jury; in such a case it would be unjust to make the answer evidence as to the validity of the will. In such a case the statements of the answer are entitled to no more weight than the allegations of the bill. In such a case the position of a party as defendant entitles him to no advantage. Cabell, J., in *Kincheloe* vs. *Kincheloe,* 11 Leigh 398. But where, as in *Kincheloe* vs. *Kincheloe,* there is an appeal made directly to the conscience of the defendant by various searching interrogatories which he is called on to answer specially, and being thus called on and required to give evidence which might have operated against him, on the principle of chancery

[37] See Code 1873, chap. 118, sec. 34, 1 R. C. 1819, p. 378, sec. 13; Sess. Acts 1838, p. 72, ch. 92, §§ 3, 4.

practice, he is entitled to its benefit when it operates in his favour. *Ibid.*[38]

In view of the rulings cited in this section and in the note thereto, the draftsman of a bill contesting a will, unless there be strong reasons for a different course, will content himself with averring in general terms, that the writing of which probat "has been received, is not the will of the decedent." Such a bill was sustained in *Malone's adm'or & als.* vs. *Hobbs & als.*, 1 Rob. R. 346.

379. *Who is plaintiff in the issue devisavit vel non.* In the issue devisavit vel non, the party sustaining the will is the plaintiff and is entitled to the opening and conclusion of the case before the jury; and the party contesting the will is the defendant. *Coalter's ex'ors* vs. *Bryan & als.*, 1 Grat. 18.

380. *Reading an answer in equity in support of the plaintiff's case.* The plaintiff who reads the answer in support of his case is not bound, as at law, to read the whole answer. When a plaintiff chooses to read a passage from a defendant's answer he reads all the circumstances stated in the passage, and if it contains a reference to any other passage that other passage must be read also, but only for the purpose

---

[38] "The answer to a bill for an issue devisavit vel non cannot be used as evidence for the respondent in respect to facts alleged in the bill and thereby urged against the validity of the will and denied by the answer except where the facts are suggested to be, or from their nature must be, within the special knowledge of the respondent, and as to them an appeal is made to his conscience and a discovery specially called for from him. When therefore the bill suggests invalidity of the will for want of testamentary incapacity of the decedent by reason of age, or defect of intellect, or other cause not produced by the immediate agency nor coming within the particular knowledge of the respondent the answer asserting the testamentary capacity and denying the existence of the suggested defect or cause is not evidence to the jury for the respondent to prove such capacity." By Stanard, J., in *Kincheloe* vs. *Kincheloe*, 11 Leigh 402.

of explaining, as far as explanation is necessary, the passage previously read. If in the passage thus referred to, new facts and circumstances are introduced in grammatical connection with that which must be read for the purpose of explaining the reference, the facts and circumstances so introduced are not to be considered as read.[39]

381. The rule yet prevails in Virginia that there is a difference between answers to bills for relief and answers to pure bills of discovery. In reference to the former, as already stated, portions of the answers may be read in evidence; as to the latter the whole is required to be read, if any part. In *Lyons* vs. *Miller*, 6 Grat. 427, it was held that when the answer is to a bill of discovery, the plaintiff coming into equity on the ground of discovery only, the whole answer should be read as at law; but, in that case, the court also held that though the answer is to be read, it is liable to be discredited, as the testimony of any other witness. *Ibid.* See *Fant* vs. *Miller*, 17 Grat. 187.

Reference may be had, in the United States courts, to the 72nd rule of practice printed in the note below.[40]

---

[39] By Lord Eldon in *Bartlett* vs. *Gillard*, 3 Russ. 157. See *Rude* vs. *Whitchurch*, 3 Sim. 562, *Ld. Ormund* vs. *Hutchinson*, B. & A. 47, 53, 16 Ves 94, *Nurse* vs. *Bunn*, 5 Sim. 225, 2 Dan. Ch. Pr. (old) 400, 3 Green. Ev. ¿ 281, Dan. Ch. Pr. (Perk.) 835, 836, *Davis* vs. *Spurling*, 1 R. & M. 64, *Miller* vs. *Gow*, 1 Y. & C. 59, *Cennoss* vs. *Hayward*, 1 Y. & C. 24. Where a plaintiff in reading a passage from a defendant's answer has been obliged to read an allegation which makes against his case, he will be permitted to read evidence to disprove such allegation. *Price* vs. *Lytton*, 3 Russ. 206.

[40] "Where a defendant in equity files a cross bill *for discovery only* against the plaintiff in the original bill, the defendant in the original bill shall first

382. *What are admissions in the answer dispensing with other proof.* If a defendant replies that "he believes," or, "has been informed and believes," it is a sufficient admission. *Potter* vs. *Potter*, 1 Ves. 274; *Hill* vs. *Binney*, 6 Ves. 738. But a statement in the answer that the defendant was informed that the fact was as stated in the bill without stating defendant's belief was held not to be an admission. 1 Phil Ev. (Cow. & Hill) 360 *n.*

A statement by the defendant in his answer that he does not admit any particular allegations of the bill to be true is not a denial, although it is sufficient to put the plaintiff upon proof of the fact at the hearing. *Randolph* vs. *Randolph*, 6 Rand. 198.

383. *Answer of one defendant as evidence against another.* The general rule is, that the answer of one defendant cannot be read against another. *Clark's ex'ors* vs. *Van Riemsdyk*, 9 Cr. 153; *Leeds* vs. *Marine Ins. Co.*, 2 Wheat 380; *Frank, &c.* vs. *Lillienfield & als.*, 33 Grat. 377. But where the right of the plaintiff, as against one defendant, is only prevented from being complete by some question between the plaintiff and a second defendant, the plaintiff is permitted to read the answer of the second defendant for the purpose of completing his claim against the first. *Green* vs. *Pledges*, 3 Hare 165. And where persons are interested as privies or as joint co-obligors in a bond, the declaration or answer of one has been ad-

---

answer thereto, before the original plaintiff shall be compellable to answer the cross-bill. The answer of the original plaintiff to such cross-bill may be read and used by the party filing the cross-bill, at the hearing, in the same manner and under the same restrictions as the answer, praying relief, may now be read and used." *72nd Rule U. S. Sup. Court.*

mitted against the other.[41] *Cross* vs. *Bedingfield*, 12 Sim. 35.

C., under whom the defendant claimed having stated in an answer in another case that a certain arrangement was made by the consent of the parties interested, the defendant is bound by this admission, unless he can clearly show that it was made under a mistake. *Tabb* vs. *Cabell*, 17 Grat. 160.

Baldwin, J., in *Pettit* vs. *Jennings & als.*, 2 Rob. 676, adverted to the general rule that the admission of one person cannot be given in evidence against another. In his opinion in that case the learned judge, as already stated, commented on the doctrine laid down by Greenleaf, Vol. 1, § 178. See his review of the cases of *Field, &c.* vs. *Holland*, 6 Cran. 8, 24, and *Clark's ex'ors* vs. *Van Riemsdyk*, 9 Cran. 153, 156 in 2 Rob. R. 681, 682. It is important to notice the time at which the admission is made. In the case of admissions by joint tenants or copartners the joint interest to be affected by the admission must be a subsisting one at the time of the admission. In the case of a derivative interest the derivative interest to be affected must be acquired subsequently to the admission; if at the time an assignor makes the admission sought to be established against his assignee the assignor "has parted from his interest, his admission is not legal evidence against him to whom it has passed." Upon this point the authorities are clear and numerous. 2 Rob. R. 679, 680. These principles govern as well an admission in the answer of one defendant in a pending suit offered as evidence against his co-defendant. 2 Rob. R. 680, 681.

384. When one defendant refers in his answer to the answer of his co-defendant, the answer of the latter may be read in evidence against the former. *Anon.* 1 P. Wms. 301. And where a defendant stated that his memory was impaired by age and referred to another person as having been his agent and as possessing a more perfect knowledge of the

---

[41] Prof. Greenleaf states that the general rule that the answer of one defendant cannot be read against his co-defendant does not apply where the latter claims through him whose answer is offered in evidence, nor to cases where they have a joint interest, either as partners or otherwise, in the transaction. 1 Green. Ev. § 178. This statement of Greenleaf is commented on by Baldwin, J., in *Pettit* vs. *Jennings, &c.*, 2 Rob. R. 681, 682.

matters inquired after than himself. the agent was made a party and his answer was allowed to be used against the principal. *Anon.* 1 P. Wms. 109.

385. *Admissions plenary or partial.* Admissions are either plenary, admitting all that is alleged, or partial or qualified, admitting only a part of the allegations or admitting them under conditions or restrictions. It is not always easy to determine to what extent an admission reaches when, instead of being plenary, it is partial or qualified.

386. *Admissions by agreement of the parties.* It often happens that it is advisable for each party to waive the necessity of proof and to admit certain facts insisted upon by the other, but insufficiently proved by the pleadings. A form of waiver suggested by Mr. Gresley in his work on Evidence in Equity is as follows:

"We the undersigned, respectively [counsel for] the plaintiff and defendant in this case, do hereby agree to admit upon the hearing thereof and otherwise as may be necessary, that the several letters mentioned and referred to in the schedule hereunder written were respectively signed by the persons whose signatures they and each of them bear respectively; and that the said letters were respectively sent to, and received by, the persons to whom each of them was addressed respectively; and that the same shall respectively be read at the hearing of, or otherwise in, this cause, as either party may be advised, in the same manner as if the same had been respectively regularly proved; and that we will produce and permit to be read at the hearing of or otherwise in this cause such of the original letters respectively as are admitted in the copies thereof now signed by us respectively, to be in our respective possessions.

A. B.
C. D."

387. *Objections to evidence waived by agreement of the parties.* And objections to evidence are often waived and the examinations allowed to stand for as much as they would be worth if the defect had not existed. See *Goldie* vs. *Shuttleworth*, 1 Camp. 70; *Mounsey* vs. *Burnham*, 1 Hare 15.

388. *Clients bound by admissions of attorneys.* Clients are bound by the admissions of the attorney whose name appears on the record. *Young* vs. *Wright*, 1 Camp. 141; *Gainsford* vs. *Grammar*, 2 Camp. 13; *Laing* vs. *Raine*, ⸗ B. & P. 85. See 4 Min. Ins. 171, 173, 177.

There was a suit for partition of real estate by W. against L. W. died and the suit was revived in the name of his widow and infant son. The counsel employed by W. was presumed in the absence of evidence to the contrary, to be continued as counsel in the cause; and a decree for the sale of the property, entered upon the consent of this counsel, was held a valid decree and the sale under it sustained. *Wilson, &c.* vs. *Smith*, 22 Grat. 494.

389. *Admissions may be without writing.* It is not indispensably necessary that the agreement to admit be written. In some cases, *e. g.* waiver of proof by subscribing witnesses, a parol agreement either of the party or of the attorney has been held sufficient. *Laing* vs. *Raine*, 2 B. & P. 85; *Marshall* vs. *Cliff*, 4 Camp. 133. But parol admissions should be received with great caution. 1 Green. Evi. § 200.

The parol admission of a party to a suit is always admissible in evidence against him, although it relates to the contents of a deed or other written instrument, and even though its contents be directly in issue in the cause. *Taylor* vs. *Peck*, 21 Grat. 11.

390. *Admissions in propositions of compromise.* Admissions in propositions of compromise are excluded.

54

Baird vs. *Rice*, 1 Call 18, *Williams* vs. *Price*, 5 Munf. 507.

There is mentioned in 1 Greenleaf on Evidence, § 192, the rule that "in order to exclude distinct admissions of fact it must appear either that they were expressly made without prejudice or at least that they were made under the faith of a pending treaty and into which the party might have been led by the confidence of a compromise taking place"; "if the admission be of a collateral or indifferent fact, capable of easy proof by other means and not connected with the merits of the cause, it is receivable though made under a pending treaty," citing *Waldridge* vs. *Kenison*, 1 Esp. 143. Prof. Greenleaf adds in a note:

"The American courts have gone farther and held that evidence of the admission of any independent fact is receivable though made during a treaty of compromise." *Mount* vs. *Bogart*, Anthon's Rep. 190; *Murray* vs. *Coster*, 4 Cow. 635.

391. *Extent of the admission.* The extent of the admission will be narrowly and closely inspected by the court. See *Mounsey* vs. *Burnham*, 1 Hare 15. Admissions of this sort are not to be extended by implication beyond what is expessed in the agreement. *Goldie* vs. *Shuttleworth*, 1 Camp. 70; *Fitzgerald* vs. *Flaherty*, 1 Moll. 350.

In *Mounsey* vs. *Burnham*, 1 Hare 15, the admission was, "that the paper writing marked I is the notice served on the defendant, and that the paper writing marked J is a true copy of the lease referred to in the notice marked I." It was contended that the admission could not be construed to mean that the exhibit was a copy of a deed which never existed, that the admission of the copy admitted the lease. But the court held, that the admission merely substituted the admitted copy for the original and placed it on no better footing than the original, and that the party was not discharged from his obligation to prove the lease by calling the attesting witness. See *Clarke's lessee* vs. *Courtney*, 5 Pet. 319.

392. *Admissions evading principles of the law not sanctioned.* Courts will not sanction any agreement for an admission by which any of the known princi-

ples of law are evaded, *e. g.*, a husband's agreement that his wife should testify against him, *Barker* vs. *Dixie*, Rep. temp. Hardwicke 264; admissions by infants, *Morrison* vs. *Arnold*, 19 Ves. 671; admissions evasive of the stamp laws, *Owen* vs. *Thomas*, 2 My. & K. 353, 357.

393. *Documentary evidence.* As to documentary evidence, the methods of compelling the production of documents, the right of plaintiffs to inspect documents referred to in the answer, the kind of documents privileged from production, the reader is referred to Gresley's Eq. Ev. 25, 118, 193, 344; Seton's Decrees in Eq. (Edit. 1862) 1040, 1062; Story's Eq. Pl. 852, and Sec. 293*c* and Sections 280–283 of this work, and the cases found in the subjoined note.[42]

IN THE VIRGINIA STATE COURTS.

[42] *Books.—Lewis* vs. *Norton*, 1 Wash. 76; *Kerr* vs. *Love*, 1 Wash. 172; *Brown* vs. *Brown*, 2 Wash. 151; *Baker* vs. *Preston*, Gil. 235; *Courtney* vs. *Com.*, 5 Ran. 666; *Downee* vs. *Moorman*, 2 Grat. 250; *Griffin* vs. *Macaulay*, 7 Grat. 476; *Shackelford's adm'or* vs. *Shackelford & als.*, 32 Grat. 481.

Deeds.—Turner vs. *Stip*, 1 Wash. 319; against a settled account neither a deed of indemnity nor anterior debits evidence, *Johnson's ex'ors* vs. *Johnson*, 4 Call. 38; deed of thirty years, with possession, *Roberts's widow & als.* vs. *Stanton*, 2 Munf. 129; and without thirty years' possession, *Caruthers & als.* vs. *Eldridge's ex'or & als.*, 12 Grat. 670; of marriage settlement, *Scott & als.* vs. *Gibbon & als.*, 5 Munf. 86; deed excluded not sufficient proof of possession, *Shanks & als.* vs. *Lancaster*, 5 Grat. 110; *Masters* vs. *Varner's ex'or*, 5 Grat. 168; *Wiley & als.* vs. *Givens*, 6 Grat. 277; *Walton* vs. *Hale*, 9 Grat. 194; *Hassler's lessee* vs. *King*, 9 Grat. 115; *Robinett* vs. *Preston's heirs*, 4 Grat. 141; *Jesse* vs. *Preston*, 5 Grat. 120; *Cales* vs. *Miller*, 8 Grat. 6; *Olinger* vs. *Shepherd*, 12 Grat. 462; *Fulton's ex'ors* vs. *Gracey*, 15 Grat. 314; *Harman* vs. *Oberdorfer & als.*, 33 Grat. 497.

Depositions in the Same or Other Causes (not admitted).—*Jones* vs. *Williams*, 1 Wash. 230; *Collins* vs. *Lowry & Co.*, 2 Wash. 75; *Ritchie & als.*

394. *Rule that the best and primary evidence must be produced.* The rule that the best and primary evi-

---

vs. *Lyne,* 1 Call. 487; *Blincoe* vs. *Berkeley,* 1 Call. 405; *Richardson* vs. *Duble & als.,* 33 Grat. 730.

Affidavits (in case of award, what can be introduced).—*Pleasants & als.* vs. *Ross,* 1 Wash. 156; (not received, in will); *Read* vs. *Payne,* 3 Call. 225; not received to prove foreign account, *Lewis* vs. *Bacon,* 3 H. & M. 89; when of a notary not competent, *Walker* vs. *Turner,* 2 Grat. 534.

Surveys (patent for land).—*Johnson* vs. *Brown,* 3 Call. 259; in writ of right, *Overton* vs. *Davisson,* 1 Grat. 211; field notes of surveyor, *Richardson* vs. *Carey & als.,* 2 Ran. 87; diagram, *Harrison* vs. *Middleton,* 11 Grat. 527; (caveat) *Clements* vs. *Kyles,* 13 Grat. 468; (trespass) *Callison* vs. *Hedrick,* 15 Grat. 244; Ridley's Map of Norfolk not evidence, *Harris's case,* 20 Grat. 833, *Cline's heirs* vs. *Catron,* 22 Grat. 378.

Accounts.—Vaughan, &c. vs. *Fields's ex'ors,* 6 Call. 12; *Pastern* vs. *Parker,* 3 Ran. 458; *Mertens* vs. *Nottebohms,* 4 Grat. 16; executor's account under oath, *Cavendish* vs. *Fleming,* 3 Munf. 198.

Receipts.—Governor, &c. vs. *Roach,* 9 Grat. 13; *Staten* vs. *Pittman,* 11 Grat. 99; *Taylor* vs. *Peck,* 21 Grat. 11.

Commissioner's Report.—Major vs. *Dudley,* Jef. 51; when not evidence, *Pugh* vs. *Russell,* 27 Grat. 789.

Letters.—Downer & Co. vs. *Morrison,* 2 Grat. 250; to construe when evidence of local usage not admissible, *Cross & als.* vs. *Cross,* 3 Grat. 262; postmark, evidence, 1 Pat. & H. 228; in case of divorce, *Bailey* vs. *Bailey,* 21 Grat. 43.

In the United States Courts.

The decisions as to the admission of documentary evidence in the United States Courts are very numerous. Reference may be had to Curtis's Index and to Myer's Index of the Supreme Court Reports, and to the following reports: 5 Cran. 22, 6 Cran. 338, 8 Wheat 326, 9 Pet. 663, 12 How. 130, 19 How. 334, 24 How. 179, 1 Bl. 209, Id. 595, 1 Wal. 637, 3 Wal. 636, 5 Wal. 785, 6 Wal. 773, 9 Wal. 248, 11 Wal. 395.

Account Books.—18 Wal. 342, *Id.* 516.

Other Books.—5 Wheat 420, 9 Wal. 619, 3 Pet. 12, 5 Otto 337, 7 Pet. 554, 20 Wal. 125, 14 How. 218 (Ure's Dictionary, in a patent case), 14 How. 218, (historical), 7 Pet. 554.

Deeds.—(Map referred to) 2 Bl. 499, 17 How. 609, 9 Pet. 663, 19 Wal. 619, recorded plat varying from the original, 18 How. 150, 10 Wal. 263, interlineation. 10 Wal. 26, lost, 6 Pet. 124, 9 Cranch 122, 24 How. 179; ancient, 2 How. 284, 17 How. 576, 4 Wheat 213; 10 Wal. 26, notary dead, copy in Louisiana, 20 How. 235, 24 How. 242, 1 Wal. 702; tax deed, 14 Pet. 322, 4 Wh. 77, 13 Wal. 506, 14 Wal. 306.

dence must be produced prevails in equity as at law. The law requires the best evidence of which the nature of the thing is capable. Pow. Ev. 36. The design of the rule is to prevent the introduction of any evidence which, from the nature of the case, supposes that better evidence is in the possession of the party. 1 Green. Ev. § 82.

Thus it is a rule, when a contract has been reduced to writing, that the writing, so long as it exists, is the best and only evidence of the terms of the contract. Oral evidence is admissible to explain, but not to contradict it. But if the writing be destroyed; or if it cannot be found after diligent search; or if an adverse party, in whose hands it is, refuse to produce it, after having received due notice, then it is considered fair and reasonable that any

---

Foreign Documents.—3 Dal. 39, 13 Pet. 209, 14 Hen. 400.

Judicial Records.—5 Otto 418; as to those not parties, 2 Pet. 613; tribunal not legally constituted, 24 How. 553; 24 How. 195; 16 Wal. 390, as to commencement of suit, 10 Wal 427; 9 Pet. 607, a suit still pending, 10 Pet. 400; vice admiralty court of Jamaica, 5 Cran. 335, of debt against administrator in one State not evidence against him in another, 18 How. 16;. 17 How. 609, 1 How. 290, 17 Pet. 144; between parties, 4 Wheat 213; between parties and privies only, 1 Wheat 6; 16 Wal. 560, 24 How. 195, 7 How. 627; against a stranger, 6 How. 550; 7 Cran. 565, 7 Cran. 308; 24 How. 188, 20 Wal. 137 judgment conclusive; two administrators in separate jurisdictions, 4 How. 467; 7 How. 220, 7 Cranch 408

Letters.—Compromise not admissible, 3 Otto. 527; 14 How. 575, 6 Wal. 788, 16 How. 14, 17 How. 183, 18 Wal. 342; to show on what account draft was drawn, 23 Wal. 471, 17 Wal. 630; partnership, 2 Wal. 160, 1 Bl. 533; market value of goods by letters of third parties abroad, 3 Wal. 145, 9 Pet. 607.

Private Writings.—5 How. 53; 8 Wheat 326, books of notary after his death; 13 Pet. 378, 9 Pet. 62, 3 Dal. 39, 1 Pet. 311, 1 Pet. 386, 4 Otto 593; entries in family Bible and in church register, 5 Pet. 570.

Public Documents.—4 How. 251; town plats, 2 Pet. 613, 7 Pet. 554; 15 Pet. 519, 5 Pet. 398, 3 Dal. 39, 16 Pet. 25; Journals of Cong. and State Legislatures, 16 Pet. 25; 16 Pet. 148, 16 Pet. 162, 15 Wal. 123, 4 Pet. 332, 5 Pet. 349.

Wills.—9 Pet. 174, on question of will; 19 How. 130, old will never proved; 10 Wheat 465, how far evidence in various States; 10 Wheat 465, Maryland law as to wills in ejectment.

competent witness who is acquainted with the terms of the contract should be allowed to give oral evidence of it. Pow. Ev. 37.

395. *Primary evidence, sometimes, in distinct sources.* There may be distinct sources of evidence, one of which may be oral and another contained in writing; in such case both will be primary and therefore either will be admissible. Thus, to prove payment, a written receipt may be produced, out it is not the only evidence; payment may be proved by oral evidence. Pow. Ev. 37.

But see as to the latter clause of this section Bart. L. P. 205, 206, and 1 Rob. Pr. (old) 305, and cases cited. See the cases: *Twyman* vs. *Knowles*, 22 L. J. 143, *Rex* vs. *Castle Morton*, 3 B. & Ald. 590; also, *Keen* vs. *Meade*, 3 Pet. 1.

396. *Primary and secondary evidence, written or oral.* Because evidence is in writing it is not necessarily primary as compared with oral evidence. Sometimes the latter is primary and the evidence in writing is only secondary. Thus, a deposition of a witness, though it is in writing, is only secondary evidence, and cannot be read if the witness himself may be had to testify.

397. *Attesting witnesses.* Where there are attesting witnesses they or some one of them must be called to prove the execution of the instrument. Pow. Ev. 306, *McDowell* vs. *Burwell's adm'or*, 4 Rand. 328. If all the witnesses be dead it is sufficient to prove the handwriting of any one. Stark. Ev. 643.

398. *Parol testimony to explain or vary written documents.* The rule as stated is, that parol evidence is admissible to explain a latent ambiguity in a written

instrument, and is inadmissible to explain a patent ambiguity.

399. *The rule equally applicable to law and equity courts.* It is admitted on all hands to be a general rule equally applicable to courts of law and equity, that parol evidence is inadmissible to contradict or substantially vary the legal import of a written agreement. *Stevens, &c.* vs. *Cooper, &c.*, 1 John. Ch. Rep. 429, Carr, J., in *Ratcliffe* vs. *Allison*, 3 Rand. 539. The foundation of this rule is in the general principles of evidence. When treaties are reduced to writing such writing is taken to express the ultimate sense of the parties. In the case of a contract respecting land, this general idea received additional weight from the circumstance that a party cannot, according to the statute of frauds, contract on that subject but in writing. *Eyre,* Ch. Baron, in *Davis* vs. *Symonds,* 1 Cox's Ch. Cas. 404, 405.

In the subjoined note[48] are collected the cases on

IN THE VIRGINIA STATE COURTS.

[48] Parol evidence has been admitted to prove an absolute deed a mortgage, *Ross* vs. *Norvell,* 1 Wash. 14; to prove the meaning of parties in marriage articles, *Flemings* vs. *Willis,* 2 Call 5; to prove that the consideration of a deed was marriage, *Epps* vs. *Randolph,* 2 Call 125; to show whether a contract was for paper money, *Com.* vs. *Beaumarchais,* 3 Call 122; in a question of boundaries, *Baker* vs. *Seekright,* 1 H. & M. 177, to prove declarations as to a particular boundary in a patent, made by a person who is dead and had peculiar means of knowing it, *Harriman,* vs. *Brown,* 8 Leigh 697; to explain a written agreement in a suit for specific performance, *Coutts* vs. *Craig,* 2 H. & M. 618; to show that a vendor did not have the land he agreed to sell, *Buster* vs. *Wallace,* 4 H. & M. 82; to show the declarations of a guardian that he did not intend to charge his ward for board, *Hooper* vs. *Royster,* 1 Mun. 119; to prove that a fi. fa. was levied, though no return was made upon it, *Bullet* vs. *Winston,* 1 Mun. 269; to set

this subject in the Virginia State Courts and in the
United States Courts.

---

aside a deed for mistake and fraud, *Jones* vs. *Robertson*, 2 Mun. 187, to prove
the acknowledgment of a person that he received of the plaintiff money for
the defendant, *Holliday* vs. *Littlepage*, 2 Mun. 316, (in an action of detinue),
to prove that a deed was executed to defraud creditors, *Stratton* vs. *Min-
nis*, 2 Mun. 329 ; to prove that notice was given the plaintiff that a
note was without consideration, *Norvell* vs. *Hudgins*, 4 Mun. 496; to
show that a clause of warranty should not be in a deed, *Bumgardner* vs.
Allen, 6 Mun. 439; to show other valuable consideration than that
mentioned in the deed, the deed expressing, beside "love and affection"
the consideration of "one dollar" "as much" (said the court) "a valuable consideration, as a million of dollars," *Harvey* vs. *Alexander*, 1 Ran. 219,
233; to prove the contents of a will which had been probated but afterwards
destroyed by the enemy, *Smith* vs. *Carter*, 3 Ran. 167; to impeach evidence
under seal on the ground of fraud, *Starke* vs. *Littlepage*, 4 Ran. 368 ; to prove
the declarations of a grantor as to his valuation in making a deed, *Land* vs.
Jeffries, 5 Ran. 211 ; to raise an implied trust the land being purchased and
paid for by one person and conveyance executed to another, *B'k U. S.* vs.
Carrington, 7 Leigh 566; to show that a scroll was put on a will as a seal,
Pollock vs. *Glassell*, 2 Grat. 439; to prove that a note was signed as principal
and not as agent, *Early* vs. *Wilkenson, &c.*, 9 Grat. 68; to establish that a
cellar was rented with a certain tenement, parol proof was admitted to show
that a tenement rented by M. from S. was the same that was rented by him
from P. and that the cellar was indispensable to M. for the business in which
he was engaged, *Crawford* vs. *Morris*, 5 Grat. 90; to prove that the clerk of
the drawee of a bill was authorized to refuse acceptance, *Steinback* vs. *B'k of
Virginia*, 11 Grat. 260; to prove the contents of a book (the after evidence
showing good reason why the book could not itself be produced), *Pidgeon* vs.
Williams's adm'ors, 21 Grat. 251; to show that a covenant was executed prior
to its date, *Jas. R. & K. Co.* vs. *Adams*, 17 Grat. 427; to prove the intention
of the parties to a lease there being in it a latent ambiguity, *Mid. Coal M.
Co.* vs. *Finney & als.*, 18 Grat. 304; to prove for whom the labor mentioned
in a note was performed, *Richmond, F. & P. R. R. Co.* vs. *Snead & Smith*,
19 Grat. 354; to explain a paper of doubtful meaning, *Walker* vs. *Christian*,
21 Grat. 291; to prove that in a contract for the sale of land it was designed
to be in gross, *Caldwell* vs. *Craig*, 21 Grat. 132; to prove the true understanding of parties in a bond "to be paid in the currency used in the common
business of the country at the date of the maturity," *Colbreath* vs. *Va. Por-
celain & E. Co.*, 22 Grat. 697; to prove that the bond executed July 18,
1863, was a Confederate contract, *Sexton* vs *Wendell's adm'r*, 23 Grat. 534;
to prove that a deputy sheriff aided his principal in defending a suit against

400. There has been some difficulty where parol evidence has been offered as a defence against a bill praying specific performance but the evidence has been received in many cases. It is admitted on the

the latter, *Crawford & als.* vs. *Turk*, 24 Grat. 176; to prove the consideration of a bond for payment "in funds current in the State of Virginia, being money borrowed," and the character of the contract, *Wrightman* vs. *Bowyer & als.*, 24 Grat. 433; to prove the subject of a previous suit, *Kelly* vs. *B'd Pub. Works*, 25 Grat. 755; to prove that the forfeiture of an insurance policy was waived, *McLean* vs. *Piedmont & A. L. Ins. Co.*, 29 Grat. 361; to prove the consideration of a deed, *Summers* vs. *Darne & als.*, 31 Grat. 791; to show that payments on bonds payable "in current money of Virginia" were not to be in Confederate money, *Stearns* vs. *Mason*, 24 Grat. 484; in relation to the person or object and subject referred to in a bequest, *Roy's ex'ors* vs. *Rowzie & als.*, 25 Grat. 599; to prove, in ejectment, that the calls for course and distance in a deed are mistaken and do not designate the true boundary of the land intended to be conveyed, *Elliott* vs. *Horton*, 28 Grat. 766; to prove that the obligee in a bond perfect on its face had notice that it was delivered to him on condition that other persons were to sign it in order to make it effectual as to those who did sign it it, *Nash* vs. *Fugate & als.*, 32 Grat. 595; to prove that a check was not given in payment of a debt due by the drawer to the party in whose favour it was drawn, *Terry* vs. *Ragsdale*, 33 Grat. 342. See *McMahon* vs. *Spangler*, 4 Ran. 51.

IN VIRGINIA STATE COURTS, INADMISSIBLE.—But parol evidence was not admitted in the following cases: Not admitted to explain an ambiguity, an "&c.," in a deed, *Gatewood* vs. *Burrus*, 3 Call. 194; not admitted to prove the contents of a permit not proved to have been lost, *Dawson* vs. *Graves*, 4 Call. 127; not admitted, in ejectment, to prove that a patent was irregularly obtained, *Wetherinton* vs. *McDonald*, 1 H. & M. 306; not admitted, in slander, to prove what plaintiff swore to in another suit, without producing a copy of the record of that trial. to show that the testimony given by the plaintiff was material to the matter in question, *Kirtley* vs. *Dock*, 3 H. & M. 388; not admitted to prove declarations of a testator to explain a bequest, *Fuller's ex'or* vs. *Fuller*, 3 Rand. 83; not admitted of receipts taken, unless it is shown that the receipts were lost or out of the power of the plaintiff, *Hamlin* vs. *Atkinson*, 6 Rand. 574, [the witness in *Hamlin* vs. *Atkinson* did not speak positively and with certainty as to the dates and amounts of the payments made, and Mr. Robinson thinks this was the ground of the decision. See his comments on this case in 1 Rob. Pr. (old) 305, 306; see also *Givens* vs. *Mann, &c.*, 6 Munf. 191; not admitted to prove that a decree of a court was entered without any order of the court by agreement of the counsel of the parties, *Benson's adm'or* vs *Stephenson*, 7 Leigh 107; not ad-

principle that equity is not bound to interpose by
specifically performing the contract, and therefore
though the subject and import of the written con-

---

mitted to prove the usage for the off-going tenant to have the way-going
crop, the written lease being for a fixed and definite period, *Harris* vs. *Carson*,
7 Leigh 632; not admitted to prove agreement made at the time of executing
a deed, *Siter & als.* vs. *McClanahan & als.*, 2 Grat. 280; not admitted to prove,
in an action for a devastavit by creditor against executor and sureties, that
the legatee paid was not the legatee of the testator but of a person of whom
the testator was executor, and had sufficient assets to pay the legacy but had
not done it; the fact of the legacy and that the executor's testator was the
executor should be proved by the will and the record of his qualification;
parol evidence was inadmissible for that purpose, *Millers* vs. *Catlett*, 10 Grat.
477; not admitted to prove an agreement for an unequal division of land by
two purchasers purchasing jointly and giving bond for purchase money,
Jarrett vs. *Johnson*, 11 Grat. 327; not admitted to incorporate into a written
contract an incident occurring contemporaneously therewith and inconsistent
with its terms, *Towner* vs. *Lucas's ex'or*, 13 Grat. 705; not admitted in behalf
of a surety to prove obligee's promise that he should not be required to pay
any part of the bond, *Towner* vs. *Lucas's ex'or*, 13 Grat. 705; not admitted to
prove that a scroll at the foot of a writing was intended as a seal, *Clegg*
vs. *Lemessurier*, 15 Grat. 108; not admitted to prove that a deed was
only in part execution of a contract of sale and that the remainder of
the property was to be conveyed at another day, *Broughton* vs. *Coffer*, 18
Grat. 184; not admitted to prove an agreement varying the liability of an
endorser, *Woodward & als.* vs. *Foster*, 18 Grat. 200; not admitted to show
the opinion of the testatrix in order to show that she acted under a mistake,
the Court being of opinion that to revoke a will the mistake must appear on
its face, *Skipwith* vs. *Cabell*, 19 Grat. 758; not admitted to prove that bonds
for purchase money, to secure which a deed of trust was given, were not to
be paid according to the terms of the bonds and the deed of trust, but were
to be paid only out of the profits of the property purchased, *Sangston & als.*
vs. *Gordon, &c.*, 22 Grat. 75; not admitted to prove that the maker of a note
made it as agent of the Confederate Government, *Ruckman* vs. *Lightner's
ex'ors*, 24 Grat. 19; not admitted to prove that a bond, perfect on its face,
was delivered to the obligee as an escrow to be valid on another person's
executing it, *Miller* vs. *Fletcher & als.*, 27 Grat. 403 [the case of *Miller* vs.
Fletcher differs from *Nash* vs. *Fugate*, 32 Grat. 595,* in this, that in the

---

* In *Nash* vs. *Fugate & als.*, 24 Grat. 202, the case went up to the Court
of Appeals without proof that the obligee had notice of the condition that
the bond should not be delivered until executed by other persons; in *Nash*
vs. *Fugate & als.*, 32 Grat. 595, that proof was supplied, and discharged
the sureties.

tract are clear, so that there is no necessity to resort
to other evidence for its construction, yet if the defendant can, independently of the writing, show any
circumstances of fraud, mistake or surprise, making

latter case the sureties signed and delivered the bond to the principal *obligor*
on condition that he should obtain additional sureties to execute it before he delivered it to *the obligee*, and the obligor delivered the bond to the
obligee without such additional sureties. The Court held, in that case, that
the bond, though apparently perfect and complete, might be avoided by parol
proof that the obligee, at the time he received it from the principal obligor,
had notice that other persons were to sign it in order to make the instrument
effectual as to those who did sign it]; not admitted to prove, in defence to a
note given for a certain lease and furniture, where the contract of lease gave
the lessor until the end of the lease to make certain repairs, that the repairs
were to be made in time for the approaching spring season, *Calhoun, &c.* vs.
Wilson, 27 Grat. 639 ; not admitted to sustain resulting trusts, *Borst* vs. *Nalle
& als.*, 28 Grat. 423 ; not admitted to show that one making an application
for an insurance, who had signed it, never read his application, *So. Mut. Ins.
Co.* vs. *Yates*, 28 Grat. 585 ; not admitted to prove that a bill of exchange
was received in full payment of a debt and that the drawer was not liable
on it, and that without this agreement the bill would not have been drawn,
Martin's ex'ix vs. *Lewis's ex'or*, 30 Grat. 672.

IN THE UNITED STATES COURTS. *Parol evidence has been admitted*
to prove a trust in Texas, the Statute of Frauds in Texas not embracing trusts of real estate, *Osterman* vs. *Baldwin*, 6 Wal. 116 ; to explain a letter of credit, *Bell* vs. *Bruen*, 1 How. 169 ; to apply a written
instrument to its subject, *Noonan* vs. *Lee*, 2 Bl. 499, and to apply a contract in writing to its proper subject matter, *Bradley* vs. *Wash., Alex. &
Georgetown S. P. Co.*, 13 Pet. 89 ; to rebut or explain an equitable interest
Henkle vs. *Wanzer*, 17 How. 353 ; to explain the description in a sheriff's
deed, *Atkinson* vs. *Cummins*, 9 How. 479 ; to show that a contract was a
substitute for a former one, *The Farmers B'k of Va.* vs. *Graves*, 12 How. 57 ;
to explain when the terms of an instrument are technical or equivocal, *Sal-
mon Falls Man. Co.* vs. *Goddard*, 14 How. 446 ; to prove that defendant
acknowledged indebtedness on notes, *McNiel* vs. *Holbrook*, 12 Pet. 84 ; to
explain a loan by a bank being a part of the res gestae, *Bank* vs. *Kennedy*,
17 Wal. 19 ; to explain the object of papers introduced collaterally in a trial,
Ibid, 17 Wal. 19 ; to show the understanding respecting a letter of credit,
Douglass vs. *Reynolds*, 7 Pet. 113 ; to show the notoriety and names of places,
Meredith vs. *Pickett*, 9 Wheat. 573 ; to show the terms of a contract in reference
to Confederate notes, *The Conf. note case*, 19 Wal 548 ; to show the happening of
a contingency under a contract, *Barreda & als.* vs. *Silsbee & als.*, 21 How. 146,

it inequitable to decree a specific performance, a court
of equity, having satisfactory information upon the
subject, will not interpose. Sir Thomas Plumer, V.
Ch. in *Clowes* vs. *Higginson*, 1 V. & B. 526; Carr, J.

170; to show that the drawing of a check was an official act of the cashier of a
bank, *Merch. B'k of Alex.* vs. *B'k of Columbia*, 5 Wh. 326; to identify the objects called for in a grant, *Blake* vs. *Doherty*, 5 Wheat 359; to prove consent
to the substitution of a new obligor in a bond, *Speake* vs. *U. States*, 9 Cr. 28;
to show what was litigated in a former suit, *Miles* vs. *Caldwell*, 2 Wal. 35;
to show the circumstances under which an endorsment was made, *Rey & als.*
vs. *Simpson*, 22 How. 341; to show an agreement as to the place when payment was to be demanded, *Brent's ex'or* vs. *B'k of the Metropolis*, 1 Pet. 89;
to show that a new contract had been made, *Emerson* vs. *Slater*, 22 How.
29; to prove payment, though written evidence of a payment exists, *Keene*
vs *Meade*, 3 Pet. 1; to prove ownership of goods mentioned in a bill of parcels, *Harris* vs. *Johnston*, 3 Cr. 311; to prove the existence of a deed of gift,
to show the nature of the possession which accompanied the deed, *Spiers* vs.
Willison, 4 Cr. 398; to prove proceedings before magistrate in case of insolvent debtors, *Turner* vs. *Fendall*, 1 Cr. 116; to explain a note payable to A.
B. "cashier," *Baldwin* vs. *B'k Newbury*, 1 Wal. 234; to prove that it was a
custom or usage of more than 20 years standing of all the banks in the District of Colmbia to demand payment and give notice to endorsers of negotiable paper on the fourth day of grace, *Rennie* vs. *B'k Columbia*, 9 Wheat
581; to prove the time of delivery of deed, *Mayburry* vs. *Brien*, 15 Pet. 21;
to show military occupation of land, *Morrow* vs. *Whitney*, 5 Otto 551; to
show the purpose of a trust the deed being made to the grantee as "trustee"
without saying for what or for whom, *Railroad Compauy* vs. *Durant*, 5 Otto
576; on parol collateral contract, *Phillips* vs. *Preston*, 5 How. 278; to explain that a note drawing interest at "one m. per centum" meant one mill
per centum, *U. S.* vs. *Hardyman*, 13 Pit. 176; to carry out the intention of
parties to a contract, *Bradley* vs. *Wash., Alex. & Georgetown S. P. Co.*, 13
Pet. 89; to prove representations referred to in a policy of insurance, though
property had passed into other hands, *Clark* vs. *Man. Ins. Co.*, 8 How. 235;
to show how an application for an insurance was made out, *Insurance Co.* vs.
Wilkerson, 13 Wal. 222; to prove the answer made by applicant for the insurance was not the answer as written by the agent of the company in the
application. *Insurance Co.* vs. *Mahone*, 21 Wal. 152; to explain answers in an
application for insurance, *New J. M. Life Ins. Co.* vs. *Baker*, 4 Otto 610,
affirming 13 Wal. 222, and 21 Wal. 152; to show that a contract was made
by one as an agent, *Ford* vs. *Williams*, 21 How. 287; to prove the validity of
the acts of an agent to bind the principal, *Mec. B'k Alex.* vs. *B'k Columbia*,
5 Wheat 326; to prove the usage of heads of departmemts in allowing pay

in *Mc Mahon* vs. *Spangler*, 4 Rand. 54; *Gillespie, &c.*
vs. *Moon*, 2 John. Ch. Rep. 585, and *Keisselbrack* vs.
Livingston, 4 John. Ch. Rep. 144. In these two last
cases the admissibility of parol evidence to show a

---

for extra services, *U. S.* vs. *Fillebrown*, 7 Pet. 28; to aid the description in a deed, *Derry* vs. *Oray*, 10 Wal. 263; to explain a latent
ambiguity in a contract, *Bradley* vs. *Wash'n, Alex. & Georgetown Steam
Packet Co.*, 13 Pet. 89; *Boardman* vs. *The Lessees of Read & Ford*, 6 Pet.
328; to explain a bill of lading in so far as it was a receipt, *The Lady
Franklin*, 8 Wal. 325; to show that a bill of sale was a mortgage, *Morgan's
assignee* vs. *Shinn*, 15 Wal. 105; to prove that an absolute deed was a mortgage, *Morris* vs. *Nixon's ex'or*, 1 How. 118, *Russell* vs. *Southard*, 12 How.
139, *Babcock* vs. *Wyman*, 19 How. 289; to prove the existence of a priva-
teer's commission, *The Estrella*, 4 Wheat 298; to prove that a bond which
on its face purported to have been delivered absolutely had been delivered in
violation of the condition upon which it had been signed by some of the
parties, *Pawling & als.* vs. *U. S.*, 4 Cran. 219 [but the case of *Pawling & als.*
vs. *U. S.*, 4 Cran. 219, is understood to be overruled by *Dair* vs. *U. S.*, 16
Wal. 1. See also *Nash* vs. *Fugate*, 24 Grat. 202, *Nash* vs. *Fugate*, 32 Grat.
595, and *Miller* vs. *Fletcher & als.*, 27 Grat. 403]; to show that the names of
persons appearing as payees on a bill of exchange were not payees in fact,
Pease vs. *Dwight*, 6 How. 190; to prove the usage of trade, though origina-
ting in a law or edict, *Livingston* vs. *Md. Ins. Co.*, 7 Cr. 506; to prove foreign
laws respecting trade not proved to have been in writing as public edicts, *Ib.*,
6 Cr. 274; to rebut other parol evidence in a question of boundaries, *Atkinson's lessee* vs. *Cummins*, 9 How. 479; to prove the acts of the Board of Commissioners of the Navy Hospital Fund, they not being required by act of
Congress to record their proceedings, *U. S.* vs. *Fillebrown*, 7 Pet. 28; to prove
aliunde the fund that certain debts must be paid from to render the guarantor
in a written promise of indemnity liable, *Mauran* vs. *Bullus*, 16 Pet. 528.

IN UNITED STATES COURTS, INADMISSIBLE. *Parol evidence was not
admitted*, in the absence of fraud, accident or mistake, to vary
the terms of a written contract, in equity, in *Forsyth* vs. *Kimball*,
1 Otto 291; ought not to be admitted when bearing on written papers,
without the production of the papers to ascertain to the Court whether
it trenches on the rule against varying by testimony, *Phil. & Wash'n Railroad Co.* vs. *Stimpson*, 14 Pet. 448; to vary the terms of a bond so as to treat
him who appears therein to be the principal debtor as a surety, *Sprigg* vs.
B'k Mt. Pleasant, 14 Pet. 201; to vary the terms of a bill of exchange,
Brown vs. *Wiley & als.*, 20 How. 442; to explain a letter which is plain,
Partridge vs. *The Ins. Co.*, 15 Wal. 573; to explain a bill of lading so far as
it is a bill of lading, and not a receipt, *The Lady Franklin*, 8 Wal. 325; to

mistake in a writing, and the jurisdiction of equity
to relieve against such mistake, are very fully examined.

---

prove that a conveyance should operate as an exchange of lands in Ohio,
Clark vs. *Graham*, 6 Wheat 577; to enlarge or change the legal estate of the
grantee against the plain words of the instrument, *Lessee of Smith & als.* vs.
McCann, 24 How. 398; to take a case out of the statute of limitations in
Louisiana, *Adger* vs. *Alston*, 15 Wal. 555; to show the intention of testator
in Louisiana, *Mackie & als.* vs. *Story*, 3 Otto 589; nor to show that he intended in a devise to his "children" to exclude his daughters, *Weatherhead's
lessee* vs. *Baskerville*, 11 How. 329; to show that an agent disclosed his principal, the agent having entered into a written contract in which he appears
as principal, *Nash* vs. *Towne*, 5 Wal. 689; (in an action of covenant of
seizure) to prove prior claims on land, *Pollard, &c.* vs. *Dwight*, 4 Cr. 421;
to change the terms of a contract, *Shankland* vs. *Corp. of Washington*, 5 Pet.
390; to show the understanding in issuing preferred stock, *Bailey* vs. *The
Railroad Co.*, 17 Wal. 96; as to the place of stowage under a bill of lading,
the bill of lading being a "clean" bill of lading, *i. e.*, silent as to place of
stowage, *The Delaware*, 14 Wal. 579; as to scope of a patent on application
for a re-issue, *Seymour* vs. *Osborne*, 11 Wal. 516; as to place of payment of
a note, *Specht* vs. *Howard*, 16 Wal. 564; to explain meaning of term "steam-
boat debts" used in a contract, *Moran* vs. *Prather*, 23 Wal. 492; to prove
that warrants were rejected by entry takers, *Polk's lessee* vs. *Wendell & als.*,
5 Wheat 293; to show that letter of credit was intended for persons other
than those addressed, *Grant* vs. *Naylor*, 4 Cranch 224; to show that a contract of insurance was actually made before the loss occurred, though the
policy of insurance was executed and delivered and paid for afterwards, *Ins.
Co.* vs. *Lyman*, 15 Wal. 664; to contradict the value as stated in a valued
policy, *Mar. Ins. Co. of Alex'a* vs. *Hodgson*, 6 Cr. 206; to prove that one set
of written instructions from Postmaster-General suspended another, *Dunlop
vs. Munroe*, 7 Cranch 242; to prove that a clause in a written contract providing for the forfeiture of a fixed sum if the work should not be completed
by a certain day was intended to liquidate the damages for such failure, *Van
Buren* vs. *Diggis*, 11 How. 461; while it is true that in some classes of cases
a contract between persons not parties to the suit may, when introduced, be
contradicted or varied by parol testimony, the principle has no application
in a contract concerning real estate which the statute requires to be in
writing to make it valid, *Still* vs. *Huidekopers*, 17 Wal. 384; not admissible
to vary or contradict a written contract made, at the time of making and
endorsing a promissory note, in relation thereto, *Brown* vs. *Spofford*, 5
Otto 474.

401. *Hearsay evidence is generally inadmissible.* Hearsay evidence is generally inadmissible. The ground for the rejection of hearsay evidence lies in the fundamental principle that evidence has no claim to credibility unless it is given on oath, and unless the party to be affected by it has an opportunity of cross-examining the witness. Pow. Evi. 70. See *Mima Queen* vs. *Hepburn*, 7 Cranch 296.

A witness is always stopped when he is about to state something which he knows not from the personal cognizance of his own senses, but merely from the accounts of another person. Pow. Evi. 70. *Penner* vs. *Cooper*, 2 Wash. 461. Mere declarations not upon oath are not evidence. Littledale, J. in *Spargo* vs. *Brown*, 9 B. & C. 935.

Among the rules of evidence, "none is more firmly fixed or rests on a more solid foundation than this, that hearsay evidence is in its very nature inadmissible." Carr, J. in *Gregory* vs. *Baugh*, 4 Rand. 615.

402. *Exceptions to rule as to hearsay evidence.* Sometimes hearsay evidence is admitted to show that a witness's testimony is confirmed by what he stated on a former occasion, *Holliday* vs. *Sweeting*, Buller's N. P. 294; see 2 Wash. Rep. 148. Sometimes, it is admitted as to what a witness since deceased testified to on a former trial of the cause between the same parties. *Caton, &c.* vs. *Lenox*, 5 Rand. 31[44] When a will is disputed on ground of fraud the declarations of the testator are admissible. *Doe d. Ellis* vs. *Hardy*, 1 M. & Rob. 825. And hearsay evidence is admissible when essentially connected with the *res gestae, Norwich Trans. Co.* vs. *Flint*, 13 Wal. 3; and a declaration made even at a month's

---

[44] The *substance* of his testimony may be proved on the second trial, it is not necessary to repeat his very words, *Caton, &c.* vs. *Lenox*, 5 Rand. 31.

interval, if there be connecting circumstances, may form part of the *res gestae*. *Rouch* vs. *Great Western Railway*, 1 Q. B. 57.

A witness was allowed to state the declaration and conduct of a deceased mother when questioned about her child's parentage, *Hargrave* vs. *Hargrave*, 2 C. & K. 701; see *Gaines* vs. *Rolfe*, 13 How. 472, and *Jewell's lessee* vs. *Jewell*, 1 How. 219; but the unsworn declarations of a mother that her son was illegitimate were rejected in *Stegall & als.* vs. *Stegall's adm'or & als.*, 2 Brock 256. In 6 East 188, *Avison* vs. *Lord Kinnaird*, a wife, on whose life an insurance had been effected on her representing herself in good health, afterwards made declarations totally different in regard to the state of her health. These declarations were admitted in evidence.

403. *Other exceptions to rule as to hearsay evidence.* Hearsay evidence is admissible on matters of public and general interest, in proof of ancient possession and on questions of pedigree. See 1 Rob. Pr. (old) 334.

Popular reputation or opinion, or the declarations of deceased witnesses if made *ante litem motam*, and without reasonable suspicion of undue partiality or collusion, are received as competent evidence *in matters of public or general interest*, Pow. Evi. 78, *Rex* vs. *Hardwicke*, 11 East. 578; but the declarations must be *ante litem motam*, *Bassett* vs. *Richards*, 10 B. & C., 657, and L'd Mansfield said, in 4 Camp. 417, that the "*lis mota* dated not from the commencement of the suit but from the time the question began to attract attention as a controversy."

As evidence of ancient possession, what is in fact hearsay testimony is admitted. Thus, ancient documents purporting to be a part of the transactions to which they relate, and not a mere narrative of them, are receivable in evidence that these transactions actually occurred, provided they be produced from the proper custody. Pow. Ev. 89, *Roe d. Brune* vs. *Rawlings*, 7 East. 279; it is sufficient if the custody, though not strictly proper, be one which may be reasonably and naturally explained. *Doe d. Neale* vs. *Sampter*, 8 Ad. & E. 154.

In questions of pedigree the statements of a deceased person who was connected by a blood marriage are admissible. Pow. Ev. 95. See *Claiborne* vs. *Parish*, 2 Wash. 146. Old family documents, genealogies, inscriptions on tombstones are received. *Davies* vs. *Lowndes*, 6 M. & G. 47, Gres. Eq. Evi. 319.

The court considered, in *Gregory* vs. *Baugh*, 4 Ran. 611, the cases in which and the principles upon which hearsay evidence, as to pedigree, was admitted. See *Claiborne* vs. *Parish*, 2 Wash. 146. See *Stegall & als.* vs. *Stegall's adm'or & als.*, 2 Brock 256; *Gaines* vs. *Rolfe*, 13 How. 472; *Chirac* vs. *Reinecker*, 2 Pet. 613.

If hearsay evidence be admitted and excepted to such a case should be stated on the record as to show that it comes within some of the exceptions to the rule; otherwise the general rule will be against the admission. *Claiborne* vs. *Parish*, 2 Wash. 146.

404. *Other exceptions to rule as to hearsay evidence.* Hearsay evidence was admitted on a question of boundaries in *Harriman* vs. *Brown*, 8 Leigh 697; and as to a survey in *Overton* vs. *Davisson*, 1 Grat. 211. And in *Smith* vs. *Chapman*, 10 Grat. 445, the declarations of chainmen were admitted. Other cases will be found in the subjoined note.[45]

---

[45] The following are

VIRGINIA CASES ON HEARSAY EVIDENCE:

Jenkins vs. *Tom*, 1 Wash. 123; hearsay evidence admitted to prove pedigree.

Charlton vs. *Unis*, 4 Grat. 58; not admitted to prove freedom.

Taliaferro vs. *Pryor*, 12 Grat. 277; not admitted to prove that the occupier of the land was the owner.

Unis vs. *Charlton*, 12 Grat. 484; not admitted to prove the character of a master.

James R. & K. Co. vs. *Littlejohn*, 18 Grat. 53; written opinion of attorney not admitted.

Davis & als. vs. *Franke*, 33 Grat. 414; a witness who had testified to the good character of a person was asked, on cross-examination, if " he had not heard a number of that person's neighbors testify, in two suits against him, that they were acquainted with his character for truth and veracity, that it was bad, and they would not believe him on oath." This question was properly excluded.

The following are

UNITED STATES COURT CASES ON HEARSAY EVIDENCE:

Venable vs. *B'k United States*, 2 Pet. 107; declarations of grantor after his

405. *Handwriting.*　In some cases proof of hand-writing is dispensed with.　See section 235*a*, p. 273 *ante.*　Handwriting is proved usually by a witness who has seen the person write or who has had correspondence with him; even seeing him write *once* is enough.　Green. Ev. § 577; 2 Esp. N. P. 500. *Rogers* vs. *Ritter*, 12 Wal. 322; *Redford's adm'or* vs. *Peggy*, 6 Rand. 316, 327.

In *Pepper* vs. *Barnett*, 22 Grat. 405, the witness stated that he had never seen Mrs. B. write but once, and then only to make her

---

conveyance, though not admissible to defeat the title of the grantee, were admitted to control the effect of the grantor's answer.

Jewell's lessee vs. *Jewell*, 1 How. 219; admitted to prove non-marriage.

Amer. Fire Co. vs. *United States*, 2 Pet. 358; agent's declarations admitted.

Barclay vs. *Hewitt's lessee*, 6 Pet. 498; agent's declarations, employed to lay out a town, admitted.

Phil. & Trenton R. R. Co. vs. *Simpson*, 14 Pet. 448; hearsay evidence admitted in a patent case.

Phil., Wil. & Balt. R. R. Co. vs. *Howard*, 13 How. 307; act of counsel treating paper as a deed of a corporation admitted to prove that the seal affixed to the deed was the seal of the corporation.

Gaines vs. *Relf*, 12 How. 472; letter from husband to wife admitted in a controversy *inter alios.*

Riggs vs. *Lindsay*, 7 Cran. 500; letter discredited by hearsay evidence of conversations of the letter-writer.

Turner vs. *Yates*, 16 How. 14; commercial correspondence, though between third persons, admitted as evidence of the nature of their transactions and the relations they sustained to each other.

Conn. Mut. Life Ins. Co. vs. *Schwenk*, 4 Otto 598; entry of age in Odd-Fellows' book, not proved to have been made on the representation of the party himself, was not admitted to show the age of the person.

Scott's lessee vs. *Ratliffe*, 5 Pet. 81; admitted to prove death.

Boardman vs. *Lessee of Reed & Ford*, 6 Pet. 328; admitted as to declarations of a deceased witness as to boundaries.

Ellicott vs. *Pearl*, 10 Pet. 412; hearsay evidence not admitted as to facts in a survey.

U. S. vs. *Wiggins*, 14 Pet. 334; hearsay evidence not admitted to prove the forging of similar papers.

Carver vs. *Jackson*, 4 Pet. 1; the acts of parent, a life tenant, not admitted against remaindermen.

signature, that he would not be able from his knowledge of her handwriting to distinguish it from that of others; but that he was of opinion from having compared the present signature with the one he had seen her make, and from other circumstances not disclosed by the witness, he was of opinion it was in her handwriting. This evidence was held admissible.

In *Cody* vs. *Conly & als.*, 27 Grat. 313, a witness stated that some thirteen years before C. dug a well for witness, that he gave several orders on witness for money and from witness's recollection of his handwriting, he thought the paper shown was his, that witness never saw C. write, but witness paid the orders and they were recognized by C. in the settlement. It was held, that this evidence was clearly admissible.

406. *Proving handwriting by a comparison of hands.* It is not allowable, so say the authorities, to prove handwriting by a comparison of hands. The rule was laid down by the United States Supreme Court in *Strother* vs. *Lucas*, 6 Pet. 763, that evidence by comparison of hands is not admissible when the witness has had no previous knowledge, but is called upon to testify merely from a comparison of hands. The court did not deem that it was departing from this rule when in *Rogers* vs. *Ritter*, 12 Wal. 320, it permitted witnesses to testify to the genuineness of a controverted signature when they had acquired a knowledge of the handwriting not by seeing the party write nor by correspondence with him but by one of the "many methods in which one person can become acquainted with the handwriting of another besides having seen him write or corresponded with him." [46]

---

[46] The witnesses in *Rogers* vs. *Ritter*, 12 Wal. 317, became acquainted with the handwriting in this way: One of them had been for eight years clerk in the recorder's office of San Francisco; another had resided in California for 14 years, had had charge of the Spanish archives in the office of the Surveyor General, and the third had been secretary, interpreter and custodian for over four years of the land commission of the United States, which sat in California. They all stated that they were familiar with the handwriting of

See *Sharp* vs. *Sharp & als.*, 2 Leigh 249; *Redford's adm'or* vs. *Peggy*, 6 Rand. 316; *Rout's adm'or* vs. *Kyle's adm'or*, 1 Leigh 216. In *Nuckols adm'or* vs. *Jones*, 8 Grat 267, the court disapprove of an attempt to circumvent and entrap a witness by exhibiting to her a forged paper—a fact, says the court, of itself justifying the rejection of the evidence—and in that case the court held that while a witness called to prove the handwriting of a paper offered for probat may be impeached by proof of what she has said about that paper at another time, yet neither her capacity to judge of the handwriting or her credit was to be impeached by what she may have said about some other paper.

In *Sharp* vs. *Sharp & als.*, 2 Leigh 249 the witness had never seen the decedent S. write, but having qualfied as his administrator (supposing that S. died without a will) he acquired a knowledge of S.'s handwriting from examination of his papers after his death and testified from his knowledge of the handwriting thus acquired that the will of S. found after witness's qualification as administrator was written wholly in S.'s hand: this was held to be competent evidence of the handwriting in a court of Probate.

In *Nuckols* vs. *Jones*, 8 Grat. 267, the deposition of a witness unable to attend the court, who testified to the handwriting of a testamentary paper which had been before shown to him but which was not before him when he gave his deposition, was admitted.

Sanchez, one of them had frequently seen it in his office and had often made certified copies of papers to which his signature was attached; another had examined the correspondence of Sanchez while justice of the peace with the governor and other papers to which his signature was attached and the third testified to his knowledge derived from seeing his signature to certain depositions filed in his office. One of the witnesses testified, "I have seen so many instruments and papers passing through my hands that these signatures (naming them) are like household implements with us." On this testimony the U. S. Supreme Court permitted the witnesses to testify to the genuineness of the handwriting.

407. *When testimony of witnesses must be taken.* If the case of the party plaintiff is not established by facts of which the court takes judicial notice, nor by the admission of the opposite party, either by his pleadings or by positive agreement, nor by documentary evidence, it will of course be necessary to take the testimony of witnesses ; and it is, therefore, proper to consider who are competent witnesses and the methods of taking their testimony.

408. *What witnesses are incompetent.* Persons deficient in understanding are incompetent witnesses. Pow. Ev. 17, 4 Min. Ins. 691, 692. The Virginia rule is, that no person is incompetent as a witness on account of his real or professed religious opinions. Perry's case, 3 Grat. 632. The rule at common law was different. See 1 Green. Ev. §§ 368, 371. See the rule as laid down in Powell on Evidence, 22. Husband and wife are incompetent as witnesses for or against each other, during the coverture or after its termination. Code 1873, chap. 172, sec. 22. The 21st section of chap. 172, Code 1873, provides that no witness shall be incompetent to testify because of interest. But by the 22d section of the same statute it was provided that "where one of the original parties to the contract or other transaction which is the subject of the investigation is dead, or insane, or incompetent to testify by reason of infancy or other legal cause, the other party shall not be admitted to testify in his own favor, or in favor of any other party having an interest adverse to that of the party so incapable of testifying, unless he shall be first called

to testify on behalf of such last-mentioned party; and when one of the parties is an executor, administrator, curator or committee, or other person representing a dead person, an insane person, or a convict in the penitentiary, the other party shall not be permitted to testify in his own favor unless the contract or other transaction in issue or subject of investigation was originally made or had with a person who is living and competent to testify, except as to such things as have been done since the powers of such fiduciary were assumed." This statute as amended in Sess. Acts 1876–7, ch. 256, will be found in a subsequent section.

The statutes of Virginia ruling in the Virginia State courts, were in review before the Court of Appeals in *Grigsby & als.* vs. *Simpson, assignee, &c.*, 28 Grat. 348, in which the court held that in an action on a bond by the assignee of a deceased obligee the obligors were incompetent witnesses to testify in their own behalf under the statute, Code 1873, ch. 172, sec. 22. The court reaffirmed the doctrines laid down in *Mason & als.* vs. *Wood*, 27 Grat. 783, in which it was said:

"The language of the statute seems to be explicit. Where one of the original parties to the contract * * * is dead, * * the other party shall not be admitted to testify in his own favour," &c. The legislature may have intended to limit the incompetency to testify to transactions between the living and deceased party, or to the acts and declarations of the deceased party, and not to have otherwise restricted his general competency as declared by the 21st section; but if so intended it is not so expressed. By the terms and express letter of the law, parties in such cases are declared to be incompetent to testify in their favour. There is no limitation of incompetency as to the subject matter of the testimony. It is general and unrestricted. They are declared to be incompetent to testify in the cause in their own favor. It might have been reasonable in the legislature to have restricted the incompetency to such matters as the other party, if not incapacitated, might be qualified to speak to, as acts and declarations imputed to him, or transactions in which he acted a part, and left untouched his incompetency as to other matters; and such restriction might comport with the spirit of the act; but the legislature has not so said, and the court is not disposed to extend the operation of the act beyond its terms and express provisions; and the incompetency of parties to testify in their own favor in such cases being declared by the act in express terms, they must be held incompetent to testify to any matter bearing upon the issues in the cause."

409. The provisions of the Virginia statute, Code 1873, chap. 172, sec. 21, 23 and 24, and of Sess. Acts 1876–7, chap. 256, p. 265, will rule in the courts of the United States held in Virginia save so far as modified by the statute, U. S. Rev. Stat. sec. 858.

By the United States Revised Statutes, sec. 858, p. 162, it is provided that, "In the courts of the United States, no witness shall be excluded in any action on account of color, or in any civil action because he is a party or interested in the issue tried : Provided, that in actions by or against executors, administrators or guardians, in which judgment may be rendered for or against them, neither party' shall be allowed to testify against the other as to any transaction with or statement by the testator, intestate or ward, unless called to testify thereto by the opposite party or required to testify thereto by the court. In all other respects the laws of the State in which the court is held shall be the rules of decision as to the competency of witnesses in the courts of the United States in trials at common law, and in equity and admiralty."

410. *What witnesses are competent.* The recent statutes, Code 1873, ch. 172, sec. 21, 22, Sess. Acts 1876–7, ch. 256, U. S. Rev. Stat., sec. 858, p. 162, have not rendered incompetent any witnesses who were competent before their passage. On the contrary these statutes have greatly enlarged the competency of witnesses.

In sec. 409 the reader will find the United States

statute. The Virginia statute, Code 1873, chap. 172, sections 21, 23 and 24, is as follows:

Sec. 21. No witness shall be incompetent to testify because of interest; and in all actions, suits or other proceedings of a civil nature, at law or in equity, before any court, or before a justice of the peace, commissioner, or other person having authority by law, or by consent of parties to hear evidence, the parties thereto, and those on whose behalf such action, suit or proceeding is prosecuted or defended, shall, if otherwise competent to testify, and subject to the rules of evidence and of practice applicable to other witnesses, be competent to give evidence on their own behalf, and shall be competent and compellable to attend and give evidence on behalf of any other party to such action, suit or proceeding except as hereafter provided; but in any case at law, the court may, for good cause shown, require any party to attend in person and testify ore tenus, or exclude his deposition upon his failure to attend.

Sec. 23. If any party required by another to testify on his behalf shall refuse to testify, it shall be lawful for the court, officer or person before whom the proceeding is pending, to dismiss the action, suit or other proceeding of the party so refusing, as to the whole or any part thereof, or to strike out and disregard the plea, answer or other defence of such party, or any part thereof, as justice may require.

Sec. 24. A party called to testify for another, having an adverse interest, may be examined by such other party according to the rules applicable to cross-examination.

Sec. 22 of chap. 172, of the Virginia Statute as it is found in the Code of 1873, p. 1109, is printed in section 408 *ante.* The 22d section of the Virginia statute was amended in Session Acts 1876–7, chap. 256, pp. 265, 266, and now reads as follows:

Sec. 22. Nothing in the preceding section shall be construed to alter the rules of law now in force, in respect to the competency of husband and wife as witnesses for or against each other during the coverture, or after its termination, nor in respect to attesting witnesses to wills, deeds, or other instruments; and where one of the original parties to the contract, or other transaction, which is the subject of the investigation, is dead, or insane, or incompetent to testify by reason of infamy or any other legal cause, the other party shall not be admitted to testify in his own favor, or in favor of any other party having an interest adverse to that of the party so incapable of testifying, unless he shall be first called to testify on behalf of such last mentioned party, or unless some person having an interest adverse to that of the party so incapable of testifying shall have previously testified to some fact occurring before such inability accrued : or unless the contract or other transaction which is the subject of the investigation, was made or had with the agent of the party so incapable of testifying, who is alive and competent to testify ; or unless, in the case of partners or other joint contractors, when the person who has become incapable of testifying was not the only partner or other only joint contractor with whom such contract or other transaction was personally made or had ; and when one of the parties is an executor, administrator, curator or committee or other person representing a dead person, an insane person, or a convict in the penitentiary, the other party shall not be permitted to testify in his own favor, unless such contract or other transaction was originally made or had with a person who is living and competent to testify, except as to such things as have been done since the powers of such fiduciary were assumed, and except, also, when some other party in interest has previously testified ; or unless some person having an interest adverse to the party so incapable of testifying, shall have previously testified as aforesaid : provided however, that no witness who would have been competent to testify as the law stood before the passage of this and the preceding section shall be rendered incompetent hereby.

411. Because of the exceptions mentioned before, sec. 410, it becomes neceesary to consider the doctrines in force, prior to the recent statutes, in regard to the competency of witnesses. These doctrines rule in all the cases embraced in the exceptions.

The law concerning the incompetency of witnesses on account of interest, as it stood prior to the statutes, Code 1873, chap. 172, §§ 21, 24, Sess. Acts 1876–7, chap. 256, and United States Rev. Statutes, § 858.

412. The law rejected the testimony of persons whose interest was directly involved in the matter in issue. 1 Green. Evi. § 327.

The interest of a witness which disqualifies him must be in the result not in the question merely. *Masters* vs. *Varner*, 5 Grat. 168, 1 Green. Ev. § 389, *Barnett* vs. *Watson, &c.*, 1 Wash. 372, *Baring* vs. *Reeder*, 1 H. & M. 154, *Richardson* vs. *Carey & als.*, 2 Rand. 87: it must be direct and legal, 1 Green. Ev. § 386, and a certain interest in the event of the cause, *Taylor* vs. *Beck*, 3 Rand. 314, *Braxton* vs. *Hilyard*, 2 Munf. 49; it must be real and not merely a supposed interest, 1 Green. Ev. § 387; because a witness believes he is interested he is not therefore incompetent, 1 Rob. Pr. (old) 327, 328, (correcting the *syllabus* of *Richardson* vs. *Hunt*, in 2 Munf. 148); it must not be merely an honorary obligation, 1 Green. Ev. § 388. The true test of the disqualifying interest is, that the witness will either gain or lose by the direct legal operation and effect of the judgment, or that the record will be legal evidence for or against him in some other action, *Richardson* vs. *Carey & als.*, 2 Rand. 87, 1 Green. Ev. § 300. The magnitude and degree of the interest is not regarded, *Ibid.* 371; the disqualifying interest may be proved by the witness himself or by evidence aliunde, 1 Green. Ev. § 423. There is, sometimes, an interest arising from liability over in the event the suit is determined against the party for whom he testifies, 1 Green. Ev. § 393. Thus, in the case of an agent or servant, he is disqualified as a witness for his principal in a suit against the principal, on account of the neglect of the agent or servant, 1 Green. Ev. § 394; and so a co-contractor is incompetent as a witness, *Ibid.* § 395. But a notary is a competent witness to prove his own acts in presenting a note for payment, &c., though liable to the plaintiff for negligence if he had not presented it. *Cookendorfer* vs. *Preston*, 4 How. 317, and in *Hammen* vs. *Minnick*, 32 Grat. 249, it was held that a deputy sheriff who levied an execution on property was a competent witness for his principal to prove that he had levied other executions which previously came to his hands on the same property and the whole proceeds thereof were consumed in the payment of these executions and that the debtor had no other property. Even an implied warranty disqualifies, 1 Green. Ev. § 398; but this implied warranty in the case of sales by sheriffs, executors, administrators and other trustees is understood to extend no further than this, that they do not know of any infirmity in their title to sell in such capacity; and, therefore, they are in general competent witnesses. *Ibid.*

Liability to costs disqualifies a witness, 1 Green. Ev. §§ 401, 402, and title to restitution, *Ibid.* 403. In the note subjoined[47] will be

---

[47] The following are cases in the United States Courts other than those already cited:

Phillips vs. *Preston*, 5 How. 278. Two endorsers of a negotiable note confound other cases ruled in the United States Courts and in the Virginia State Courts concerning the incompetency of witnesses on the ground of interest.

---

tract that they will divide the loss between them; the payee is a competent witness to prove this contract.

Taber vs. *Perrott*, 9 Cr. 39. A, the sole owner of a bill of exchange endorses it in blank and delivers it to B to deliver to C for collection, and when collected to place the amount to the credit of A and B in account; C collects the amount but refuses to place it to the credit of A and B, and they settle their account with C and pay him the balance: In a suit afterwards instituted by A against C for the amount received upon the bill of exchange, B is a competent witness for A.

Davis vs. *Brown*, 5 Otto 423 (explaining and qualifying *B'k U. S.* vs. *Dunn*, 6 Pet. 51): an endorser of a promissory note, still held by the party to whom the endorsement was made, is a competent witness to prove an agreement in writing made with its holder at the time of his endorsement that he should not be held liable thereon.

Scott vs. *Lloyd*, 12 Pet. 145. The grantor of a rent charge who had devested himself of all interest in the land and who was released from all liability to costs, not being a party on the record, is a competent witness to prove usury.

Patton vs. *Taylor*, 7 How. 133. A naked trustee, having no interest in the trust fund, is a competent witness in a suit concerning that fund.

Evans vs. *Hettich*, 7 Wheat. 453. A person sued for an infringement of a patent is a competent witness for another person sued for infringing the same patent.

Evans vs. *Eaton*, 7 Wheat. 356. A person who has used the improvement claimed by the patentee, is a competent witness for one sued for violating the patent.

Tayloe vs. *Riggs*, 1 Pet. 591. The affidavit of a party is competent evidence of a loss of a paper; not conclusive, but to be weighed in connection with the circumstances.

In prize causes,—The Aune, 3 Wheat. 435; *Taylor* vs. *U. S.*, 3 How. 197; *U. S.* vs. *Murphy*, 16 Pet. 203.

Saltmarsh vs. *Tuthill*, 13 How. 229. A party to a bill of exchange is incompetent to prove any fact, which taken in connection with other facts, cuts off a part of the nominal amount of the bill.

U. S. vs. *Leffler*, 11 Pet. 86. The rule that a party to an instrument shall not be heard as a witness to impeach it, is confined to negotiable instruments.

Smyth vs. *Strader*, 4 How. 404. A party to a negotiable note cannot impeach it by his testimony; *a fortiori*, if he be also a party to the record.

B'k of the Metro. vs. *Jones*, 8 Pet. 12. In an action by an endorsee of a note against an accommodation endorser the maker is not a competent witness to prove that the endorsee informed the endorser he would incur no re-

413. The law also excluded parties and made them incapable of testifying in their own behalf and relieved them from testifying in behalf of their adversary ; and the rule extended to all the actual and

---

sponsibility by putting his name on the note. This was substantially the case of *B'k of U. S.* vs. *Dunn*, 6 Pet 51, and that case is modified by *Davis* vs. *Brown*, 5 Otto 423, cited *supra*.

Stein vs. *Bowman*, 13 Pet. 209. A curator, party to the record, is not a competent witness, even if his liability to costs were set aside.

Bridges & als. vs. *Armour & als,.* 5 How. 91. A party upon the record, although divested of all interest in the event of the suit, is not a competent witness in a cause. (It was a common law suit).

Riddle vs. *Moss*, 7 Cr. 206. The principal obligor in a bond is not a competent witness for the surety, in an action upon the bond; the principal being liable to the surety for costs in case the judgment should be against him.

VIRGINIA CASES.

Murray vs. *Carrott*, 3 Call 573. An agent purchasing a bill of exchange and endorsing it to his principal is a competent witness to prove the loss of the bill.

Wilson vs. *Alexander*, 9 Leigh 459. Deputy sheriff taking an indemnifying bond incompetent as a witness on behalf of the obligors in an action on the bond. *Accord, Carrington* vs. *Anderson*, 5 Munf. 32.

Blair vs. *Owles*, 1 Munf. 38. A purchasing agent competent to prove that his principal had notice of an incumbrance notwithstanding the agent had joined in a conveyance of the property to the principal free from the claim of any person whatsoever.

Gilliam vs. *Clay*, 3 Leigh 590. The obligee and assignor of a bond not a competent witness for the obligor in any controversy between the obligor and assignee to prove that the bond was founded on a usurious transaction between the assignee and obligor. *Accord, Wise* vs. *Lamb*, 9 Grat. 294.

Beverley vs. *Brooke*, 2 Leigh 425. A debtor in two mortgages is not a competent witness in behalf of the second mortgagee to prove usury in the first mortgage.

Kevan vs. *Branch*, 1 Grat: 274. A grantor in a deed of trust is a competent witness for the claimant under the deed to prove that the property levied on by an officer under an execution against him is the same conveyed in the deed. *Accord, Patterson* vs. *Ford*, 2 Grat. 18.

Jones vs. *Raine*, 4 Rand. 386. A principal obligor in a bond cannot be a witness for his surety jointly bound with him, because he is liable to the latter for the entire recovery against him including all subsequent costs.

real parties to the suit, whether they were named on the record as such or not. *Rex* vs. *Woburn*, 10 East. 395. A plaintiff or defendant liable as such for the costs which might be recovered by his adversary could not be admitted as a witness for his co-plaintiffs or co-defendants. *The King* vs. *Governor, &c., of St. Mary Magdalen, &c.*, 3 East. 7. The rule went farther in the case of co-plaintiffs. " The better opinion," says Prof. Greenleaf, " is that one of several co-plaintiffs who voluntarily comes forward as a witness for the adverse party is not admissible without the consent of his co-plaintiffs." 1 Green. Ev. § 354.

Caldwell vs. *McCartney*, 2 Grat. 187. A guarantor without consideration of a bond a competent witness for the obligors to prove usury.

Fraser vs. *Bevill*, 11 Grat. 9. When a co-administrator is a competent witness for a contingent legatee against a legatee for life who is also an administrator.

Dickinson vs. *Dickinson*, 2 Grat. 493. The widow of a testator a competent witness in a controversy between the legatees as to that part of the estate in which she is but remotely interested.

Hudgin vs. *Hudgin*, 6 Grat. 320. A creditor having been paid by a sale of land under a decree against the executor, and the devisees having recovered the land from the purchaser, the creditor is a competent witness for the purchaser against the devisees to prove the amount and justice of his debt.

Ford vs. *Nichols*, 3 Grat. 84. A drawer of a bill for whose accommodation it has been accepted is not a competent witness for the acceptors in an action thereon by the holder against them.

Steptoe vs. *Read*, 19 Grat. 1. In an action upon a joint or joint and several contract against two defendants, one of them is not a competent witness for the other to prove that the witness was the only party to the contract and is alone bound by it.

Eacho vs. *Cosby*, 26 Grat. 112. A trustee who is not named as a party plaintiff in an amended and supplemental bill, though named in the original bill, is not liable for costs and is a competent witness to prove what passed between the grantor and himself as to the preparation of the deed.

Shannon vs. *McMullen*, 25 Grat. 211. When sheriff a doubtful witness to sustain a bill brought by a surety against a creditor to be relieved on the ground that the creditor had authorized the sheriff to release the property levied on under an execution.

Where the suit was ended as to one, either by default or *nolle: prosequi*, or by verdict, as he had no direct interest in its event as to the others, if not otherwise disqualified he was a competent witness for them, his own fate being at all events certain. 1 Green. Ev. §§ 355, 360, 363. But in *Taylor* vs. *Beck*, 3 Rand. 316, which was a joint action upon a contract against several defendants, it was held that though one of them acknowledged the action it did not make him a competent witness for the other defendants; his acknowledgment of the action could only be received and entered as an interlocutory judgment, dependent on the final judgment to be entered in the case.

To the rule excluding parties there were other exceptions, even at law. Thus, when the oath *in litem* of the party was admitted after it had been proved that the party against whom it was offered had been guilty of some fraud or other tortious or unwarrantable act of intermeddling with the complainant's goods.[48] *Herman* vs. *Drinkwater*, 1 Greenl. 27. And when, on general grounds of public policy it was deemed essential to the purposes of justice, 1 Green. Ev. § 348; this latter is confined to cases where from its nature no other evidence is attainable. *U. S.* vs. *Murphy*, 16 Pet. 203.

414. *Balancing of interest.* When the witness. was equally interested on both sides he might testify. 1 Green. Ev. § 420. A preponderance of interest on the one side disqualifies the witness. *Ibid.*

In *Brown's adm'or* vs. *Johnson*, 13 Grat. 644, it was contended that the witness was competent on the ground that though interested in favour of the party offering him, his interest was equal or greater the other way. But the court rejected his testimony, because his interest in the latter case was not as direct and immediate as in the former. Judge Lee, in this case, collects the English cases upon the point.

In *Sitlingtons* vs. *Brown*, 7 Leigh 271, the debtor mortgaged the same land, by successive deeds, to two several creditors, and the second was duly recorded, but the first was not; the land was sold

---

[48] Where a ship master had received a trunk of goods and rifled its contents, the plaintiff after establishing the delivery of the trunk, was admitted as a. witness in his own behalf to prove the contents of the trunk. *Herman* vs. *Drinkwater*, 1 Greenl. 27. As to the question whether such evidence was admissible against a baillee in an action for negligence; see in support of it, *Clarke* vs. *Spence*, 10 Wall's R. 335, in denial of it, *Snow* vs. *East R. R. Co.*, 12 Metcalf 44.

under the provisions of the second deed, and the creditor in that deed became the purchaser: on a bill by first mortgagee against the mortgagor and second mortgagee charging the second mortgagee with notice of the prior unrecorded mortgage and praying that the land be resold to satisfy the plaintiff's debt, it was held that neither the mortgagor nor his wife was a competent witness for plaintiff to prove that the second mortgagee had notice of the plaintiffs prior mortgage.

415. In the equity courts the rule as to examining parties to the record was much more liberal than at law. A plaintiff might obtain an order as of course to examine a defendant, and a defendant a co-defendant, as a witness, on affidavit that he was a material witness and was not interested on the side of the applicant in the matter to which it was proposed to examine him and was not interested adversely to the rights of his co-defendants; the order being made subject to all just exceptions.[49] Green. Evi. § 361; 2 Dan. Ch. Pr. (old) 450, 452. Dan. Ch. Pr. (Perk.) 884-6, *notes.*

416. The rule permitting a defendant to be thus examined applied as well to a defendant who had by his answer submitted to a decree and had therefore ceased to have an interest, and to one who though having an interest had it in respect only of a part of the matters in issue. See Adams's Eq. 364, 2 Dan. Ch. Pr. (old) 450, 454. *Bradley* vs. *Root,* 5 Paige 633. Dan. Ch. Pr. (Perk.) 886, notes.

417. A party plaintiff was incompetent as a witness for his co-plaintiffs. If a co-plaintiff desired his

[49] Whenever a defendant was thus examined as a witness he was subject to a cross-examination by the other defendants, and his evidence could not be used in his own favor. *Benson* vs. *LeRoy,* 1 Page 122.

evidence and the defendant would not consent to the examination, the party must move to strike out his name as plaintiff on payment of the costs already incurred and make him a defendant by amendment. Adams's Eq. 365. The plaintiff's next friend was incompetent. To obtain his testimony his name was struck out and another next friend substitued on giving security for the costs already incurred. 2 Dan. Ch. Pr. (old) 449.

See *Burwell & als.* vs. *Corbin*, 1 Rand. 131, as to a party made next friend without his knowledge or consent being a competent witness.

418. *Whether a plaintiff by examining a defendant as a witness released him.* Before the statute 6 and 7 Vict. c. 85, Lord Denman's act, making persons interested competent witnesses and before the statute 14 and 15 Vict c. 99, the "Law of Evidence Amendment Act," making *parties to the record* competent and compellable to give evidence, it was held in the English courts that the examination of a defendant by the plaintiff as a witness ordinarily operated as an equitable release to him so far as regarded the matters to which he was interrogated; and no decree could be had against such defendant except as to matters wholly distinct from those to which he was examined. *Weymouth* vs. *Boyce*, 1 Ves. 417; *Nightingale* vs. *Dodd*, Amb. 583; *Thompson* vs. *Harrison*, 1 Cox C. C. 344; *Meadbury* vs. *Isdall*, 9 Mod. 448. The rule was followed in many of the American courts: in New York, *Benson* vs. *LeRoy*, 1 Paige 122; in Maryland, *Hayward* vs. *Carroll*, 4 H. & J. 518; in North Carolina, *Lewis* vs. *Owen*, 1 Ired. Eq. 93.

We have no Virginia decision on this point; and it is now contended that the rule is virtually abrogated by the new statutes in Virginia making a party compellable to give evidence for his adversary under penalty, if he refuses, of striking out his defence, or dismissing his suit, &c. See sec. 410 *ante*.

419. A defendant might sometimes examine the plaintiff, even before the recent statutes, and a co-plaintiff might generally be examined as a witness for the defendant, by consent, *Walker* vs. *Wingfield*, 15 Ves. 178, but leave will not be granted for a defendant to examine a co-plaintiff as a witness against another defendant for the purpose of sustaining the bill against him. *Echfield* vs. *Dekay*, 6 Paige 565, 3 Green. Ev. § 317. See *Ross* vs. *Carter*, 4 H. & M. 488

420. *Co-defendants as witnesses.* Co-defendants may be witnesses for each other; the testimony of a co-defendant may be had, in all cases in which he is either a merely nominal defendant, or has no beneficial interest, or his interest or liability is extinguished by release, or is balanced, or where the plaintiff cannot adduce some material evidence against him, or where no decree is sought, or none can be properly had against him. *Piddock* vs. *Brown*, 3 P. Wms. 288, *Franklyn* vs. *Colquhoun*, 16 Ves. 218, *Dixon* vs. *Parker*, 2 Ves. 219, 3 Green. Ev. § 318, n. 2.

421. *Husband and Wife.* Husband and wife are incompetent as witnesses for each other. See sec. 408 *ante*. *Johnston, &c.* vs. *Slater & als.*, 11 Grat.

320, *Wm. & M. College* vs. *Powell & als.*, 12 Ib. 372, *Steptoe* vs. *Read, &c.*, 19 Ib. 1, 12, *Murphy & als.* vs. *Carter*, 23 Grat. 477, 488, *Hord's adm'or* vs. *Colbert & als.*, 28 Grat. 49, 55, *Nelson* vs *Bowman & als.*, 29 Grat. 782, *Warwick* vs. *Warwick & als.*, 31 Grat. 70.

421a. *Restoring competency of witnesses.* A witness disqualified on the ground of interest might have his competency as a witness restored. There are various ways of restoring the competency of such witnesses. The most usual is by a release. See *Richardson* vs. *Carey & als.*, 2 Rand. 87, *Jones* vs. *Raine*, 4 Rand. 386, *Mandeville* vs. *Perry*, 6 Call 78, *Murray* vs. *Carret*, 3 Call 323. The competency of a witness is not always restored by a release of the matter in controversy. *Rowt* vs. *Kyle, Gilm.* 202, *Reynolds* vs. *Stephenson*, 11 Leigh 369, *Cogbills* vs. *Cogbills*, 2 H. & M. 467, *Scott* vs. *Lloyd*, 12 Pet. 145, *Downey* vs. *Hicks*, 14 How. 240.

The objection to a witness's competency may be waived by implication as where a party adopts an interested witness by examining him, *Rogers* vs. *Dibble*, 3 Paige 241: and where a plaintiff who knew of the objection to the competency of a witness at the time of his examination, proceeded, without first making objection to his competency, to cross examine the witness as to all the issues in the cause, it was held that this was a waiver of all objection to the witness's competency and that the objection could not afterwards be made. *Hord's adm'or* vs. *Colbert & als.*, 28 Grat. 49. But when the objection to the competency of a party as a witness is written at the commencement of the deposition the objection is not waived by the cross examination. *Statham & als* vs. *Ferguson's adm'or & als.*, 25 Grat. 28.

A partner who has been released is a competent witness, *LeRoy* vs. *Johnson*, 2 Pet. 186; and so a co-obligor in a bond who has been released, *U. S.* vs. *Leffler*, 11 Pet. 186. A witness may be rendered competent in certain cases by the covenant of the creditor not to sue him, *Waggener* vs. *Dyer*, 11 Leigh 384. Sometimes the competency of the witness is restored by striking off the name of the witness as an endorser, 1 Green. Ev. § 430, or in the case of a bail or surety for another by the substitution of another surety, *Ibid.* So a witness's competency is restored by his discharge as a bankrupt. *Ibid.* See *Reynolds* vs. *Callaway*, 31 Grat. 436. And a witness has been made competent to testify for a corporation by the transfer of his stock therein, 1 Green. Ev. § 430, and by assignment of his interest his competency is sometimes restored, *Toby* vs. *Leonards*, 2 Wal. 423, *Parrish* vs. *Parrish*, 11 Leigh 626.

422. *Exceptions to the rule.* A remote, contingent and uncertain interest did not disqualify a witness. Thus a paid legatee of a specific sum was a competent witness, 1 Green. Ev. § 408. A party entitled to a reward from the government upon conviction of the offender or to a restoration as owner of property stolen is a competent witness. *Ibid.* § 412. A party whose name has been forged is a competent witness. *Ibid.* § 414. In certain cases, agents, carriers, factors and other servants are admitted to prove the making of contracts, receipt or payment of money, receipt or delivery of goods and other acts done in the scope of their employment. *Ibid.* § 416. And so, in some cases, though not in all, a witness originally competent to testify is not disqualified by reason of any interest subsequently acquired in the event of the suit. See *Bent* vs. *Baker*, 3 T. R. 27.[50] And in *Goodtitle* vs. *Welford*, 1 Doug. 139, it was held that when an interested witness did all in his power to divest himself of his interest by offering to surrender or release it which the surrenderee or lessee, even though a stranger, refused to accept, the rule of exclusion no longer applied and the witness was decided to be admissible.

---

[50] The case of *Winship* vs. *Bank U. S.*, 5 Pet. 529, 552, should be referred to.

423. *Incompetency as to certain matters.* The rules disqualifying a witness as to matters disclosed to him as a solicitor or attorney or proctor or counsellor or scrivener or conveyancer of course apply to such matters only. See Gres. Eq. Ev. 378, 380, 11 Wheat. 280; *Parker* vs. *Carter*, 4 Munf. 273; *Lyle* vs. *Higginbotham*, 10 Leigh 75. The right to withhold the answer in such cases is the privilege not of the witness but of the client. Gres. Eq. Ev. 378. It was at one time decided that a party who had signed a deed or other writing would not be admitted to invalidate it by his testimony either by proving fraud or other defect. The rule was afterwards restricted so as to forbid such testimony only in the case of negotiable securities. This latter doctrine though sanctioned by some of the cases, Mr. Gresley states has been overturned in the English courts. See Gres. Eq. Ev. 385, 386 and cases cited. In the *B'k U. S.* vs. *Dunn*, 6 Pet. 51; *B'k Metropolis* vs. *Jones*, 8 Pet. 12; *Henderson* vs. *Anderson*, 3 How. 73; *U. S.* vs. *Leffler*, 11 Pet. 86; *Saltmarsh* vs. *Tuthill*, 13 How. 229 and other cases the rule has been applied by the United States courts to negotiable securities: and in an early case before the Virginia Court of Appeals, *Claiborne* vs. *Parish*, 2 Wash. 148, the court held that the testimony of a witness tending to fix fraud upon himself ought not to be regarded and the jury should be so instructed. But in *Clay* vs. *Williams*, 2 Munf. 105, the judges were not agreed on the question whether the evidence of a person employed by both parties as an attorney or scrivener to write a bond for a fraudulent purpose should be admitted to prove

the fraud. *Harrison* vs. *Middleton*, 11 Grat. 527, seems to remove the doubt suggested by *Clay* vs. *Williams*. In *Harrison* vs. *Middleton*, 11 Grat. 527, a subscribing witness was introduced to prove that a deed was misread to the defendant.

424. *Whether competent as a witness for one purpose only.* In *Steptoe* vs. *Read*, 19 Grat. 1, it was held that if a witness is competent at all he may be examined upon any matter upon the record; his competency depends on his interest in the event of the cause and not on the particular question to which the party calling him might choose to examine him. See the cases cited 19 Grat. 13. Mr. Barton supposes that this rule is now changed. Bart. L. P. 196. He cites *Field* vs. *Brown*, 24 Grat. 74, in support of his position.

Competency of witnesses under statutes Code 1873, *chap.* 172, *sec.* 21–24, *Sess. Acts* 1876–7, *ch.* 256, *and U. S. Rev. Stat.* § 858.

425. The doctrines of the preceding sections 412–24, are now controlled and modified by the recent acts. See the Stat. Code 1873, chap. 172 and Sess. Acts 1876–7, chap. 256 in section 410 *ante*, and the statute in U. S. Rev. Stat. § 858 in sec. 409, *ante*.

426. *U. S. Rev. Stat.* § 858. The statute of Congress, U. S. Rev. Stat. § 858 has come in review in the cases found in the subjoined note.[51]

---

[51] *Green* vs. *U. States*, 9 Wal. 655. The statutes of Congress declaring that there shall be no exclusion of any witness in civil actions "because he is a

427. *The Virginia Statutes.*   The recent Statutes of Virginia, Code 1873, chap. 172, §§ 21–24, have come into review in the cases found in the subjoined note.[51]

party to or interested in the issue tried" apply to civil actions in which the United States are a party as well as to those between private parties.

Cornett vs. *Williams*, 20 Wal. 226.   A common law cause, in which it was declared that the testimony of a witness under the statutes might be given by deposition.

Lucas vs. *Brooks*, 18 Wal. 436.   The act of Congress does not give capacity to a wife to testify in favour of her husband.

Texas vs. *Chiles*, 21 Wal. 488.   The intention of the act of Congress is to put the parties to a suit (except those named in the proviso to the enactment) on a footing of equality with other witnesses, *i. e.*, all are admissible to testify for themselves and all compellable to testify for others.

U. S. vs. *Clark*, 6 Otto 37.   A case concerning the construction of sec. 1079 of the Rev. Statutes, in which the court held that the petitioner was a competent witness to prove the contents of a package of government money taken from his official safe by robbers.

Potter vs. *National Bank*, 12 Otto 163.   An action against an executor in his representative capacity.   A, who was interested in the issue but not a party thereto, was introduced as a witness by the plaintiff and permitted to testify to statements of the testator touching the subject matter in controversy. The witness was compent and the evidence admissible.

[52] *Field* vs. *Brown*, 24 Grat. 74.   The plaintiff in a cause is not a competent witness under the statutes to prove the acts and declarations of a deceased person under whom the defendants claim.   See notice of this case in *Ellis* vs. *Harris*, 32 Grat. 691, and Bart. Law Pr. 195 and note 1.

Martz vs. *Martz*, 25 Grat. 361.   One party is not incompetent to testify merely because another party is incompetent on account of insanity or the relation of husband and wife or for any other legal cause unless he was a party to the transaction or the contract which is the subject of investigation. See Bart. Law Pr. 195.

Mason vs. *Wood*, 27 Grat. 783.   After the death of one of the obligors in a bond given for the price of a jack sold with a warranty of soundness, the surviving obligors are incompetent to testify as to conversations had with them long after the sale relating to the alleged breach of warranty ; though these conversations occurred after the death of the deceased obligor, and though the surviving obligors were offered as witnesses to rebut and countervail the testimony of witnesses as to conversations with them.

Grigsby vs. *Simpson*, 28 Grat. 348.   Obligors in a bond sued by assignee of a deceased obligee are not competent to testify in their own behalf.

Morris vs. *Grubb*, 30 Grat. 286.   The only proof of the execution of cer. tain bonds purporting to be executed by C and D and assigned to B was an

428. *Whether trustee, executor or other fiduciary liable for costs a competent witness.* The Statute, Code 1873, chap. 172, § 19, enacts among other provisions

---

acknowledgment by C to an agent of B made after the assignment to him, and the proof as to the payments was of payments made by D to B *in the lifetime of C*, held that B was not a competent withess under the Statute to testify in his own behalf.

Parent vs. *Spitler*, 30 Grat. 819. A and B commissioners sell land to C who executes his bonds for the deferred payments with D and E as his sureties, and subsequently sells the land to F. A being dead, D, E, and F, are incompetent witnesses to prove the payment of the bonds by C to A.

Burkholder vs. *Ludlam*, 30 Grat. 255. When a party to a suit is examined as a witness and testifies about transactions the other party to which is dead, if he does not testify in his own favor or in favor of any other party having an interest adverse to the party who is dead, or those claiming under him, but against his own interest and the interest of those having an interest adverse to the dead party, he is not incompetent.

Reynolds vs. *Callaway*, 31 Grat. 436. T. having been released from the payment by his discharge in bankruptcy was a competent witness at common law for the defendant to prove payment of the debt; and the recent statutes were only designed to remove incompetency in certain cases, not to create it in any. The court refers specially to the effect of Sess. Acts 1876-7 ch. 256.

Ellis vs. *Harris*, 32 Grat. 684. An action by E. against H.'s executor to recover damages for injury to his land by the overflowing and sobbing of his land lying on a stream on which H. had built a dam in 1848, the overflowing it was claimed was the effect of the dam. H. who built the dam being dead, the plaintiff E. was not a competent witness to prove anything occurring in the lifetime of H.

Carter vs. *Hale*, 32 Grat. 115. An action on a bond by the obligee against the surviving sureties and the representative of one deceased, the plea was payment, which consisted of notes given by one surety to the obligee. The surety was an incompetent witness.

Terry vs. *Ragsdale*, 33 Grat. 342. In an action against a surviving partner upon a transaction in which the deceased partner was the acting party, the plaintiff introduced the defendant as a witness. The defendant so introduced becomes a competent witness in the cause; but this does not render the plaintiff a competent witness.

Simmons vs. *Simmons*, 33 Grat. 451. A witness who was not a party to the contract or transaction which is the subject of investigation is not disqualified on account of *interest only;* although one of the original parties to such contract or transaction be dead, insane or incompetent to testify by reason of infamy, or any other legal cause, and for that reason the *other party* is rendered incompetent to testify.

that "no trustee, executor or other fiduciary shall be incompetent as a witness in any case by reason only of his being a party thereto, or of his being liable to costs in respect thereof; but if liable to costs he shall not be competent, unless some person undertake to pay the same." This statute was passed before the recent statutes extending competency of witnesses. Whether these statutes have repealed the above provision awaits judicial decision.

By Code 1873, chap. 118, § 21, "No person shall, on account of his being an executor of a will, be incompetent as a witness for or against the will."

429. *Mode of taking evidence in equity.* The mode of taking evidence in equity differs from that adopted in common law courts. At law it is taken viva voce and publicly: in equity, it is chiefly written and, in the English practice, it is secret.[53]

430. *Viva voce* testimony is sometimes allowed in equity causes in the United States Circuit Courts. By the 78th rule of practice, provision is made for "the examination of witnesses *viva voce* when produced in open court, if the court shall in its discretion deem it advisable."

431. The usual course however in equity causes in the United States Circuit Courts, is to take the testimony in writing.

432. The 67th rule of practice prescribes:

"After the cause is at issue commissions to take testimony may

---

[53] As to cases in the English courts, in which *viva voce* testimony admitted, see Gres. Eq. Evidence (edition 1837) 126, 128, 380; 2 Dan. Ch. Pr. (old) 436, 593, 848.

be taken out in vacation as well as in term, jointly by both parties or severally by either party, upon interrogatories filed by the party taking out the same, in the clerk's office, ten days' notice thereof being given to the adverse party to file cross interrogatories before the issuing of the commission; and if no cross interrogatories are filed at the expiration of the time, the commission may issue *ex parte.* In all cases the commissioner or commissioners shall be named by the court or by a judge thereof." See amendment to this last clause in section 463 post.

433. It was also prescribed by the 67th rule before cited that if the "parties shall so agree the testimony may be taken upon oral interrogatories by the parties or their agents without filing any written interrogatories;" but this provision has been substituted by the one hereafter noted in section 463.

434. Testimony may also be taken in the United States Circuit Courts after the cause is at issue, according to the provisions of the Act of Congress. The Revised Statutes of the United States provide—

By Sec. 862. The mode of proof in causes of equity and of admirality and maratime jurisdiction shall be according to rules now or hereafter prescribed by the Supreme Court, except as herein specially provided.

By Sec. 863. The testimony of any witness may be taken in any civil cause depending in a district or circuit court by depositions *de bene esse* when the witness lives at a greater distance from the place of trial than one hundred miles, or is bound on a voyage to sea, or is about to go out of the United States, or out of the district in which the case is to be tried, and to a greater distance than one hundred miles from the place of trial, before the time of trial, or when he is ancient or infirm.

The deposition may be taken before any judge of any court of the United States, or any commissioner of a Circuit court, or any clerk of a District court or Circuit court, or any chancellor, justice, or judge of a Supreme or Superior court, mayor or chief magistrate of a city, judge of a county court or court of common pleas of any of the United States, or any notary public, not being of counsel or attorney to either of the parties, nor interested in the event of the cause. Reasonable notice must first be given in writing by the party or his attorney proposing to take

such deposition, to the opposite party or his attorney of record, as either may be nearest, which notice shall state the
name of the witness and the time and place of the taking of his
deposition; and in all cases in rem, the person having the agency
or possession of the property at the time of seizure shall be
deemed the adverse party, until a claim shall have been put in;
and whenever, by reason of the absence from the district and want
of an attorney of record or other reason, the giving of the notice
herein required shall be impracticable, it shall be lawful to take
such depositions as there shall be urgent necessity for taking, upon
such notice as any judge authorized to hold courts in such circuit
or district shall think reasonable and direct.

Any person may be compelled to appear, and depose as provided
by this section, in the same manner as witnesses may be compelled
to appear and testify in court.

By section 864. Every person deposing as provided in the preceding section, shall be cautioned and sworn to testify the whole
truth, and carefully examined. His testimony shall be reduced to
writing by the magistrate taking the deposition, or by himself in
the magistrate's presence, and by no other person, and shall, after
it has been reduced to writing, be subscribed by the deponent.

By section 865. Every deposition taken under the two preceding
sections shall be retained by the magistrate taking it, until he delivers it with his own hand into the court for which it is taken; or
it shall, together with a certificate of the reasons as aforesaid of
taking it and of the notice, if any, given to the adverse party, be
by him sealed up and directed to such court and remain under his
seal until opened in court. But unless it appears to the satisfaction of the court that the witness is then dead, or gone out of the
United States, or to a greater distance than one hundred miles
from the place where the court is sitting, or that, by reason of age,
sickness, bodily infirmity, or imprisonment, he is unable to travel
and appear at court, such deposition shall not be used in the cause.

By Sec. 866. In any case where it is necessary, in order to prevent a failure or delay of justice, any of the courts of the United
States may grant a dedimus potestatem to take depositions according to common usage; and any circuit court, upon application to it
as a court of equity, may, according to the usages of chancery,
direct depositions to be taken in perpetuam rei memoriam, if they
relate to any matters that may be cognizable in any court of the
United States. And the provisions of sections eight hundred and
sixty-three, eight hundred and sixty-four, and eight hundred and
sixty-five, shall not apply to any deposition to be taken under the
authority of this section.

By Sec. 867. Any court of the United States may, in its discretion admit in evidence in any cause before it any deposition taken
in perpetuam rei memoriam, which would be so admissible in a

·court of the State wherein such cause is pending, according to the laws thereof.

435. The 70th rule of the United States Supreme Court prescribes :

"After any bill filed, and before the defendant hath answered the same, upon affidavit made that any of the plaintiff's witnesses are aged or infirm, or going out of the country, or that any one of them is a single witness to a material fact, the clerk of the court shall as of course, upon the application of the plaintiff, issue a commission to such commissioner or commissioners as a judge of the court may direct to take the examination of such witness or witnesses *de bene esse* upon giving due notice to the adverse party of the time and place of taking his testimony." [54]

436. *Three months allowed to take testimony in the United States courts.* In the United States Circuit courts, by the 69th rule of practice of the United States Supreme Court, "three months and no more are allowed for the taking of testimony after the cause is at issue, unless the court or a judge thereof shall, upon special cause shown by either party, enlarge the time; and no testimony taken after such period will be allowed to be read in evidence at the hearing. Immediately upon the return of the commissions and depositions containing the testimony, into the clerk's office, publication thereof may be ordered in the clerk's office by any · judge of the court, upon due notice to the parties, or it may be enlarged, as he may deem reasonable under all the circumstances. But by the consent of the parties, publication of the testimony may at any time pass in the clerk's office, such consent being in writing, and a copy thereof entered in the order book, or endorsed upon the deposition or testimony."

---

[54] See the rule in the English courts to the same effect in 2 Dan. Ch. Pr. (old) 541.

437. *In the Virginia State courts.* Testimony in equity causes in the Virginia State courts is usually taken by depositions, the witnesses are examined orally by the officer taking the deposition and their testimony is reduced to writing. The deposition is usually signed by the witness. It is not essential to the validity of the deposition that it should be signed. *Barnett* vs. *Watson*, 1 Wash. 372.

438. A commission or dedimus protestatem was formerly necessary in the Virginia State courts though the deposition was to be taken in the State. The act of March 7th, 1826, declared that "from the filing of the bill until the final hearing of any case, either party may without any order of court, obtain general commissions, and take depositions to be read therein," Sup. to Rev. Code, p. 132; and the act provided for "Special commissions to take the deposition of any party in a suit, if the same may lawfully be taken, saving all just exceptions to the reading of such deposition, and saving to the court the right to quash such special commission for good cause shown." Ibid. The present statute, Code 1873, ch. 172, sec. 34 is as follows:

"In any pending case[55] the deposition of a witness, whether a party to the suit or not, may, without any commission, be taken in

---

[55] This language designed to condense and embody the provisions of the prior statutes, 1 R. C. 1819, p. 300, ch. 83, sec. 2; p. 522, ch. 132; Sess. Acts 1822-3, p. 40, c. 39; 1825-6, p. 16. sec. 5; 1826-7, p. 19, ch. 20, sec. 1, and 1833-4, p. 75, ch. 62, sec. 2, is certainly as broad as the language of the act of March 7th, 1826, "from the filing of the bill until the final hearing of any case." It authorizes (it seems to the writer) the taking of depositions in chief from the time of the institution of the suit, certainly from the time of the filing of the bill, even before the parties are at issue.

this State by a justice or notary public, or by a commissioner in chancery; and if certified under his hand may be received without proof of the signature to such certificate. When a deposition appears to be of a party, all exceptions may be made to the reading of it which could have been made if it were taken under a special commission, but the taking of such deposition shall not deprive the party taking it of any relief he would otherwise be entitled to against the deponent." When the witness resides out of the State, or is out of it, in the service thereof, or of the United States, a commission to take the deposition is necessary. The mode of obtaining the commission is prescribed by the statute, Code 1873, ch. 182, sec. 35.

439. *Notice of taking depositions.* Reasonable notice should be given to the adverse party of the time and place of taking every deposition, and the deposition may be read, if returned before the hearing of the cause in equity, or though after an interlocutory decree, if it be as to a matter not thereby adjudged, and be returned before a final decree. Code 1873, ch. 172, sec. 36. *Fant* vs. *Miller,* 17 Grat. 187.

440. *Reasonable notice.* What is reasonable notice depends on circumstances.[56] Where a notice was left with the wife of the party at his dwelling-house, when it was known to the adverse party that he was absent on a journey to another State, and where it appeared also that the notice might previously have been given to the party himself, and that the taking of the deposition might have been postponed, as it respected the trial of the cause, till his return, it was held that the notice was insufficient and the deposition was rejected. *Coleman* vs. *Moody,* 4 H. & M. 1.

---

[56] A notice given at 8 P. M. of the taking of the deposition on the next day between 8 and 9 A. M. was held sufficient under the circumstances of the case in *McGinnis* vs. *Washington Hall Association,* 12 Grat. 602.

A notice was given by plaintiff to defendant for taking the depositions of several witnesses at a specified place in Missouri on six successive days between certain hours of each day. Considering the distance of the place appointed for taking the depositions, and the uncertainty of the precise time at which the party would be enabled to have things in readiness for taking them, the notice was held sufficiently definite. *Kincheloe* vs. *Kincheloe*, 11 Leigh 393.

441. A notice to take the depositions was held insufficient because it did not appear that notice of the place at which they were to be taken was given; and though the magistrates met on the day appointed by the notice they could not go on with the depositions at any future day without an adjournment to such day. *Hunter* vs. *Fulcher*, 5th Rand. 126. Notice was given that a deposition would be taken on the 8th of August, and that if not taken in one day the commissioners would adjourn from *day to day* until finished. The commissioners met on the 8th and adjourned from day to day until the 12th. From the 12th they adjourned to the 19th, on which day the deposition was taken. It was decided that the deposition was not taken agreeably to notice. *Buddicum* vs. *Kerk*, 3 Cr. 297 ; *Chaney* vs. *Saunders*, 3 Munf. 51.

442. *Deposition after an appeal.* In the Virginia State courts, in any case wherein there has been a decree or order from or to which an appeal, writ of error or supersedeas has been or might be allowed, a deposition may be taken for any party to such case, or for or against his or her husband, personal repre-

sentatives, heirs or devisees, in like manner, and by
such persons, as is prescribed for pending cases; and
it may be read in any future trial that may be
directed, if the same could properly be read had
there been no such decree or order. Code 1873, ch.
172, sec. 39.

443. *When, after interlocutory decree, new evidence
may be introduced.* There is no rule of practice or of
law which precludes the party from taking new evidence upon a question of fact passed upon by an interlocutory decree, even before a re-hearing is obtained. *Staples, J.*, in *Summers* vs. *Darne & als.*, 31
Grat. 805. The introduction of such evidence depends on the sound discretion of the court and all
the circumstances of the particular case. *Dunbar's
ex'or* vs. *Woodcock's ex'or*, 10 Leigh 628; *Moore* vs.
Hilton, 12 Leigh 1. See also *Alexander* vs. *Morris &
als.*, 3 Call. 89, in which a deposition taken after an
appeal from an interlocutory decree in chancery was
read upon the hearing of the appeal.

444. *Who authorized to take depositions in Virginia
State Courts.* The officers authorized to take depositions in the State are justices, notaries public, and
commissioners in chancery. Beyond the State, if in
the United States, a commissioner appointed by the
Governor of Virginia, or any justice or notary public
of the State wherein the witnesses may be, is authorized to take the depositions on a commission.
Outside the United States, the commission should be
directed to such commissioner or commissioners as
may be agreed upon by the parties or appointed by

the court, or if there be none such, to any American minister, plenipotentiary, charge d'affaires, consul-general, vice-consul, or commercial agent appointed by the Government of the United States, or to the mayor or other chief magistrate of any city, town or corporation in such county, or any notary public therein. Code 1873, ch. 172, sections 34, 35.

445. Any person or persons to whom a commission is so directed, may administer an oath to the witness, and take and certify the deposition with his official seal annexed; and if he have none, then the genuineness of his signature shall be authenticated by some officer of the same State or country, under his official seal, unless the deposition is taken by a justice out of this State but in the United States, in which case his certificate shall be received without any seal annexed or other authentication of his signature. Code 1873, ch. 172, sec. 35.

How witnesses summoned and compelled to attend, production of documents, &c.

446. *In the United States Courts.* The United States Revised Statutes prescribe—

By Sec. 868. When a commission is issued by any court of the United States for taking the testimony of a witness named therein at any place within any district or Territory, the clerk of any court of the United States for such district or Territory shall, on application of either party to the suit, or of his agent, issue a subpœna for such witness, commanding him to appear and testify before the commissioner named in the commission, at a time and place stated in the subpœna; and if any witness, after being duly served with such subpœna, refuses or neglects to appear, or, after appearing, refuses to testify, not being privileged from giving testimony, and such refusal or neglect is proven to the satisfaction of any judge of the court whose clerk issues such subpœna, such judge may proceed to enforce obedience to the process, or punish the disobedience, as any court of the United States may proceed in case of disobedience to process of subpœna to testify issued by such court.

By Sec. 869. When either party in such suit applies to any judge of a United States Court in such district or Territory for a subpœna commanding a witness, therein to be named, to appear and testify before said commissioner, at the time and place to be stated in the subpœna, and to bring with him and produce to such commissioner any paper or writing or written instrument or book or other document, supposed to be in the possession or power of such witness, and to be described in the subpœna, such judge, on being satisfied by the affidavit of the person applying, or otherwise, that there is reason to believe that such paper, writing, written instrument, book, or other document is in the possession or power of the witness, and that the same, if produced, would be competent and material evidence for the party applying therefor, may order the clerk of said court to issue such subpœna accordingly. And if the witness, after being served with such subpœna, fails to produce to the commissioner, at the time and place stated in the subpœna, any such paper, writing, written instrument, book, or other document, being in his possession or power, and described in the subpœna, and such failure is proved to the satisfaction of said judge, he may proceed to enforce obedience to said process of subpœna, or punish the disobedience in like manner as any court of the United States may proceed in case of disobedience to like process issued by such court. When any such paper, writing, written instrument, book, or other document is produced to such commissioner, he shall, at the cost of the party requiring the same, cause to be made a correct copy thereof, or of so much thereof as shall be required by either of the parties.

By Sec. 870. No witness shall be required, under the provisions of either of the two preceding sections, to attend at any place out of the county where he resides, nor more than forty miles from the place of his residence, to give his deposition; nor shall any witness be deemed guilty of contempt for disobeying any subpœna directed to him by virtue of either of the said sections, unless his fee for going to, returning from, and one day's attendance at, the place of examination, are paid or tendered to him at the time of the service of the subpœna.

By Sec. 871. When a commission to take the testimony of any witness found within the District of Columbia, to be used in a suit depending in any state or territorial or foreign court, is issued from such court, or a notice to the same effect is given according to its rules of practice, and such commission or notice is produced to a justice of the supreme court of said District, and due proof is made to him that the testimony of such witness is material to the party desiring the same, the said justice shall issue a summons to the witness, requiring him to appear before the commissioners named in the commission or notice, to testify in such suit, at a time and at a place within said District therein specified.

By Sec. 872.   When it satisfactorily appears by affidavit to any justice of the Supreme Court of the District of Columbia, or to any commissioner for taking depositions appointed by said court—

First. That any person within said District is a material witness for either party in a suit pending in any State or territorial or foreign court.

Second. That no commission nor notice to take the testimony of such witness has been issued or given; and

Third. That, according to the practice of the court in which the suit is pending, the deposition of a witness taken without the presence and consent of both parties will be received on the trial or hearing thereof, such officer shall issue his summons, requiring the witness to appear before him at a place within the District, at some reasonable time, to be stated therein, to testify in such suit.

By Sec. 873.   Testimony obtained under the two preceding sections shall be taken down in writing by the officer before whom the witness appears, and shall be certified and transmitted by him to the court in which the suit is pending, in such manner as the practice of that court may require.   If any person refuses or neglects to appear at the time and place mentioned in the summons, or, on his appearance, refuses to testify, he shall be liable to the same penalties as would be incurred for a like offense on the trial of a suit.

By Sec. 874.   Every witness appearing and testifying under the said provisions relating to the District of Columbia shall be entitled to receive for each day's attendance, from the party at whose instance he is summoned, the fees now provided by law for each day he shall give attendance.

By Sec. 875.   When any commission or letter rogatory, issued to take the testimony of any witness in a foreign country, in any suit in which the United States are parties or have an interest, is executed by the court or the commissioner to whom it is directed, it shall be returned by such court or commissioner to the minister or consul of the United States nearest the place where it is executed. On receiving the same, the said minister or consul shall indorse thereon a certificate, when and where the same was received, and that the said deposition is in the same condition as when he received it; and he shall thereupon transmit the said letter or commission, so executed and certified, by mail, to the clerk of the court from which the same issued, in the manner in which his official dispatches are transmitted to the Government.   And the testimony of witnesses so taken and returned shall be read as evidence on the trial of the suit in which it was taken, without objection as to the method of returning the same. [See §§ 4071–4074.]

By Sec. 876. Subpœnas for witnesses who are required to attend a court of the United States, in any district, may run into any other district: *Provided,* That in civil causes the witnesses living out of the district in which the court is held do not live at a greater distance than one hundred miles from the place of holding the same.

447. *In the Virginia State Courts.* The Code of 1873, chap. 172, sec. 26, prescribes that a summons may be issued, directed as other process, commanding the officer to summon any person to attend on the day and at the place that such attendance is desired to give evidence before a court, arbitrators, umpire, justice, notary public, or any commissioner appointed by a court. The summons may be issued, if the attendance be desired at a court, by the clerk thereof, and in the other cases by any person before whom, or a clerk of a court of a county or corporation in which the attendance is desired, or if it be desired before a justice, by such or any other justice. It shall express on whose behalf, and in what case, or about what matter the witness is to attend. This section shall be deemed to authorize a summons to compel attendance before commissioners or other persons appointed by authority of another State; but only in case they be citizens of this State, and the summons requires the attendance of a witness at a place not out of his county.

448. When it appears by affidavit that a writing or document in the possession of a person not a party to the matter in controversy is material and proper to be produced before a court, or any person ap-

pointed by it or acting under its process or authority, such court or a judge thereof in vacation may order the clerk of said court to issue a *subpœna duces tecum* to compel such production at a time and place to be specified in the order." Code 1873, chap. 172, sec. 27.

449. If any person, after being served with such summons, fail to attend to give evidence, or to produce such writing or document, according to the summons, the court whose clerk issued the summons, or a commissioner in chancery who had issued such summons, or if it was not issued by a clerk, or a commissioner in chancery, a court of the county or corporation in which the attendance is desired, on a special report thereof by the person or persons before whom there was the failure to attend, on proof that there was paid to him (if it was required by endorsement on the process), a reasonable time before he was required to attend, the allowance of one day's attendance, and his mileage and tolls, shall, after service of a notice to or rule upon him to show cause against it (if no sufficient cause be shown against it), fine him not exceeding twenty dollars, to the use of the party for whom he was summoned, and may proceed by attachment to compel him to attend and give his evidence at such time and place as such court or commissioner may deem fit. The witness shall, moreover, be liable to any party grieved for damages. See Code 1873, chap. 172, sec. 28.

450. If any person, after being served with such

summons, shall attend, and yet refuse to be sworn, or to give evidence, or to produce any writing or document required, he may, by order of the court whose clerk issued said summons, or of the person before whom he was summoned to attend, be committed to jail, there to remain until he shall, in custody of the jailor, give such evidence or produce such writing or document. Code 1873, chap. 172, sec. 29.

451. Any person before whom a witness is to be examined may administer an oath to such witness. Code 1873, chap. 172, sec. 30.

452. *When objection of incompetency should be made.* Objection to the incompetency of the witness must be expressly made; and the objection should be raised in sufficient time to enable the adverse party to remove it by a release or otherwise, or to supply the want of the testimony by other witnesses. *Mohawk Bank* vs. *Atwater*, 2 Paige 60; *Town* vs. *Needham*, 3 Paige 552.

453. When the objection is made before the justice, notary or commissioner, it should be noted by him at·the time it is made; and the examination may then proceed. The party making the objection may then cross-examine the witness, without losing his right to have the deposition excluded on the ground of incompetency. *Rogers* vs. *Dibble*, 3 Paige 238; *Perigal* vs. *Nicholson, &c.*, Wightweck 64; *Moorhouse* vs. *DePasson*, Coop. Ch. Rep. 300; S. C. 19 Ves. 433, 2 Rob. Pr. (old) p. 337.

454. Prof. Minor lays down the rule that the witness's incompetency should be objected to before he is examined in chief, if the ground of incompetency be then known, 4 Min. Ins. 695, and if the adversary is ignorant of the objection and it is brought to light in the course of the trial the witness's testimony will then be stricken out and the jury instructed wholly to disregard it. *Ibid.*

The objection for incompetency cannot be made for the first time in the Court of Appeals. *Simmons* vs. *Simmons*, 33 Grat. 460. See also *Fant* vs. *Miller, &c.*, 17 Grat. 187, *Beverly* vs. *Brooke, als.*, 2 Leigh 425, *Hord's adm'r* vs. *Colbert & als.*, 28 Grat. 49, 54, 55, 56, *Statham & als.* vs. *Ferguson's adm'or*, 25 Grat. 28, 38, *Baxter* vs. *Moore*, 5 Leigh 219.

455. *Objection for irregularity in taking deposition.* If there be any irregularity in taking the deposition, the objection to the deposition for such irregularity should be made in the court of chancery, by exception. And then the opposite party will have an opportunity of taking it over again, or removing the objection by proof. If no exception be taken, and the deposition be read at the hearing in the court of chancery, it cannot be objected to in the appellate court on account of any irregularity in taking it. Were this allowed it might have the effect of a surprise on the party relying upon the deposition. In *Dickinson* vs. *Davis and others*, 2 Leigh 401, before answer filed, leave was given to take a deposition *in chief*, whereas, as the law stood at that time, the court should only have awarded a commission to take the deposition *de bene esse*. No affidavit appeared in the record showing even that those grounds existed which authorized the commission *de bene esse*.

Nor did the record contain any certificate of the magistrates that the deponent was sworn. If these objections had been taken in the court of chancery by exception they would unquestionably have been fatal, unless the plaintiffs could have removed them by evidence. But the deposition having been read without any exception, the Court of Appeals was of opinion that the objection could not be looked into by the appellate court. See also opinion of *Lyons*, Pr., in *Rowton* vs. *Rowton*, 1 H. & M. 110, and of Roane, J., in S. C. 102, 2 Rob. Pr. (old) 337.

456. *Manner in which witness should depose.* Witnesses, says Lord Coke, ought to come to depose untaught and without instructions. 4 Inst. 279. Lord Hardwicke suppressed a deposition because the attorney for the party, before it was taken, had written down the whole of it in the exact form in which it was taken. Although it appeared that the witness had told the attorney the facts and circumstances mentioned in it, yet Lord Hardwicke thought it would be of dangerous tendency to permit the deposition to be read; for the attorney had methodized and worded it, and it was therefore no more than an affidavit. In a deposition he considered it material to state the evidence as given by the witness. Amb. 252. With a view of effectually excluding the mischief which would arise if the attorney or counsel were allowed to settle the deposition with the witness, it has been determined that a witness shall not in any case go before the justices, notary or commissioner with a prepared deposition. Whenever such a proceeding has been disclosed, the court has always

thought it right, without attending to the particular circumstances, to suppress the deposition. *Shaw* vs. *Lindsey*, 15 Ves. 380.

457. *Witness may be interviewed before examination.* Parties or their counsel may orally or by writing, previous to the examination of a witness, direct his attention to the facts in regard to which it is intended to examine him; and he may refresh his memory in regard to such facts by examining books or papers, and make memoranda from them or otherwise, especially of dates and amounts, and use such memoranda for the purpose of refreshing his memory at the time of giving his evidence. *Fant* vs. *Miller*, 17 Grat. 187.

458. *Interrogatories ought to be plain and pertinent.* The witness is to be free to answer the sifting interrogatories that are framed. *Underhill* vs. *Van Cortlandt*, 2 John. Ch. R. 346. And these interrogatories ought to be simple and plain, pertinent to the matter in question, and in no sort captious, leading or directory. 4 Inst. 279, 2 Rob. Pr. (old) 336.

459. *Who may not ask leading questions.* On an examination in chief a witness must not be asked leading questions. Pow. on Evi. 376. This general rule is, however, subject to this exception, that if it appear that the witness is hostile to the party calling him, or his evidence cannot be extracted by general questions as to his knowledge of material facts, the party may be permitted to put a leading question to the witness point blank as to such material fact and

require him to answer in the affirmative or negative. *Ibid.*

460. *Who may ask leading questions.* On cross-examination a witness may be asked leading questions. Pow. on Ev. 381. And when a witness is manifestly reluctant and hostile to the interest of the party calling him he may be asked leading questions. See *Moody* vs. *Rowell*, 17 Pick. 498, Green. Ev. § 435.

The evidence of a witness given in answer to leading questions, ought not on that ground to be suppressed, otherwise than by an order of the court made before the hearing of the cause, on motion or petition for that purpose, and founded on an exception endorsed upon the deposition within a reasonable time from the return thereof, and founded, moreover, upon an objection taken at the time of the examination of the witness, if the party seeking to exclude the evidence, his agent or attorney was then present. *McCandlish, adm'r, &c.* vs. *Edloe & als.*, 3 Grat. 334.

461. *Who may interrogate* The justices or persons before whom the deposition is taken are not bound to permit any one to examine the witness except a party to the suit, or the counsel or agent of a party. *Roane*, J. in *Rowton* vs. *Rowton*, 1 H. & M. 102; 2 Rob. Pr. (old) 336.

462. *Discrediting a witness.* Where the object of testimony offered is to impeach a witness by proof of statements previously made inconsistent with his testimony on the trial; or to discredit him, by proof of an attempt to fabricate testimony; the foundation for such impeaching or discrediting testimony must be first laid by an examination of the witness sought to be impeached, with reference to such in-

61

consistent statements or improper conduct, and these
rules are as applicable where a plaintiff is the witness sought to be impeached as in other cases. *Davis
& als.* vs. *Franke,* 33 Grat. 413.

A witness called to prove the handwriting of a
paper offered for probat may be impeached by proof
of what she has said about that paper at another
time; but neither her capacity to judge of the handwriting nor her credit is to be impeached by what she
may have said about some other paper. *Nuckols's
adm'or* vs. *Jones,* 8 Grat. 267.

On the trial of an action of slander a defendant was permitted
to discredit the testimony of two witnesses against him by evidence
of particular acts of hostility of these witnesses against him.
Rixey vs. *Bayse,* 4 Leigh 330.

In *Charlton* vs. *Unis,* 4 Grat. 58, it was held that though the
previous statements of a witness whether oral or written might be
introduced for the purpose of impeaching his credibility, yet that it
cannot be expected that a witness should come prepared to prove
the truth of every collateral statement he may have made on
another occasion; and where a question is put to a witness which is
collateral or irrelevant to the issue, his answer cannot be contradicted by the party who asked the question, but it is conclusive
against him. See 16 Grat. 556, 1 Green. Ev. § 449.

463. The 67th rule of practice cited in section 432
ante has been amended as follows:

December Term, 1854. Ordered that the 67th rule governing
equity practice be so amended as to allow the presiding judge of
any court exercising jurisdiction, either in term time or in vacation,
to vest in the clerk of the said court general power to name commissioners to take testimony in like manner that the court or judge
thereof can now do by the said 67th rule.

December Term, 1861. Ordered that the last paragraph in the
67th rule in equity [57] be repealed, and the rule be amended as follows:

Either party may give notice to the other that he desires the

---

[57] The paragraph of 67th rule cited in section 433 ante.

evidence to be adduced in the cause to be taken orally, and thereupon all the witnesses to be examined shall be examined before one of the examiners of the court, or before an examiner to be specially appointed by the court, the examiner to be furnished with a copy of the bill and answer, if any; and such examination shall take place in the presence of the parties or their agents, by their counsel or solicitors, and the witnesses shall be subject to crossexamination and re-examination, and which shall be conducted as near as may be in the mode now used in common law courts. The depositions taken upon such oral examination shall be taken down in writing by the examiner in the form of narrative, unless he determines the examination shall be by question and answer in special instances; and when completed, shall be read over to the witness and signed by him in the presence of the parties or counsel, or such of them as may attend; provided, if the witness shall refuse to sign the said deposition, then the examiner shall sign the same; and the examiner may, upon all examinations, state any special matters to the court as he shall think fit; and any question or questions which may be objected to shall be noted by the examiner upon the deposition, but he shall not have power to decide on the competency, materiality, or relevancy of the questions; and the court shall have power to deal with the costs of incompetent, immaterial, or irrelevent depositions, or parts of them, as may be just.

The compulsory attendance of witnesses. In case of refusal of witnesses to attend, to be sworn, or to answer any question put by the examiner, or by counsel or solicitor, the same practice shall be adopted as is now practiced with respect to witnesses to be produced on examination before an examiner of said court on written interrogatories.

Notice shall be given by the respective counsel or solicitors, to the opposite counsel or solicitors or parties, of the time and place of the examination, for such reasonable time as the examiner may fix by order in each cause.

When the examination of witnesses before the examiner is concluded, the original deposition, authenticated by the signature of the examiner, shall be transmitted by him to the clerk of the court, to be there filed of record in the same mode as prescribed in the thirtieth section of act of Congress, September 24, 1789.

Testimony may be taken on commission in the usual way by written interrogatories and cross interrogatories, on motion to the court in term time, or to a judge in vacation, for special reasons satisfactory to the court or judge.

December Term, 1869. Where the evidence to be adduced in a cause is to be taken orally, as provided in the order passed at the December term, 1861, amending the 67th General Rule, the court may, on motion of either party, assign a time within which the complainant shall take his evidence in support of the bill, and a time thereafter within which the defendant shall take his evidence in defense, and a time thereafter within which the complainant shall take his evidence in reply; and no further evidence shall be taken in the cause unless by agreement of the parties, or by leave of court first obtained on motion for cause shown.

463a. Forms of depositions in the United States Circuit Courts. The usual course pursued is the one prescribed by the sixty-seventh rule of practice. In conformity with that rule, after the cause is at issue, a commission is obtained from the clerk of the court by both parties jointly, or severally by either, upon interrogatories filed in the clerk's office and ten days' notice thereof given to the adverse party to file cross interrogatories before the issuing of the commission. The frame of the interrogatories depends of course upon the facts sought to be elicited by the testimony:

Interrogatories.

In the United States Circuit Court for the ——— Circuit and ——— District of ———.

A. B., a citizen, &c., complainant, ⎫
      vs.   ⎬ In equity.
R. M. and N. O. citizens, &c., defendants. ⎭

Interrogatories propounded by the complainant for the examination of X. X. and L. L., witnesses to be produced, sworn and examined in this cause in behalf of the complainant.

1st Interrogatory. Do you know the parties in this suit, or any or either of them, and how long have you known them or any or which of them? Declare the truth of the matters in this interrogatory inquired after according to the best of your knowledge, remembrance and belief?

2nd Interrogatory. Whether or no, &c., (as the case may be)? Declare the truth of the several matters by this interrogatory inquired after according to the best of your knowledge, remembrance and belief?

Last Interrogatory.[58] Do you know or can you set forth any other matter or thing which may be a benefit or advantage to the parties at issue in this cause or either of them or that may be material to the subject of this your examination on the matters in question in this cause? If yea, set forth the same fully and at large in your answer.

S. L. & C. Counsel for A. B.

Upon taking out a separate commission, the notice to the adverse party is as follows:

Notice.

To R. M. and N. O.:

Take notice that in the suit in equity depending in the Circuit Court of the United States for the ——— Circuit and ——— District of ———, wherein I am complainant and you are defendants, I have, in conformity with the 67th Rule of the Supreme Court of the United States prescribed for the use of the Circuit Courts of the United States, filed interrogatories to be propounded to X. X. and L. L., witnesses in my behalf, and that on the ——— day of ——— I shall apply at the clerk's office of the said court for a commission to take the depositions of said witnesses as the rule aforesaid prescribes; and, meanwhile, you can appear in the clerk's office of the said court and file cross interrogatories to be propounded to the said witnesses if you think fit.

Yours respectfully,

A. B.

If cross interrogatories be filed the clerk should enclose with the commission both the interrogatories in chief and the cross interrogatories to the officer who is to take the deposition. If no cross interrogatories be filed, the commission will issue *ex parte.* The commissioner or commissioners are to be named by the court or by a judge thereof; or by the clerk

---

[58] The form of the last interrogatory is prescribed by the 71st Rule of Practice of the Supreme Court.

when so authorized.[59]   The following is the form of the commission in either case.

Commission.

The President of the United States of America, To ——————[60]
    Greeting:

Know ye that in confidence of your prudence and fidelity and by these presents, you [or, any two or more of you] are invested with full power and authority to examine X. X. and L. L. on their corporal oath as witnesses in a suit depending in the Circuit Court of the United States for the —— Circuit and —— District of ——, wherein A. B. is complainant and R. M. and N. O. are defendants, on the part of the complainant upon the interrogatories annexed to this commission; and therefore you are hereby commanded that you [or any two or more of you] at certain days and places to be appointed by you for that purpose, do cause the said X. X. and L. L. to come before you, and then and there examine them on oath [upon the said interrogatories] and that you take such examination and reduce the same to writing and return the same annexed to this writ, certified, under your seal, [or under the seals of two or more of you] unto the said Circuit Court before the judges thereof with all convenient speed.

Witness—R. B. T., Chief Justice of the Supreme Court of the United States in the said court this —— day of —— in the year of our Lord ——, and of our independence the ——.

                                        P. M., Clerk.

In pursuance of this commission, the depositions are taken and returned to the clerk certified and sealed as the commission directs.

The following form of depositions will comply with the requirements of the 67th rule of practice.

---

[59] See 67th Rule U. S. Supreme Court, sections 432, 433 and amendments found in sec. 463.

[60] Commissioner or commissioners named by the court or a judge thereof, or by the clerk when the clerk has been authorized in pursuance of the amendment of the 67th rule made December term 1854. See sec. 463 *ante*.

Form of depositions under 67th rule of United States Supreme Court. .

The depositions of X. X. and L. L. duly taken before us, D. D. and E. E., two of the commissioners duly appointed in pursuance of the commission and notice hereto annexed, on the ———— day of ———— in the year ————, between the hours of 6 o'clock A. M. and 5 o'clock P. M. of that day, at the office of ———— in the city of ————, State of ————, to be read in evidence in behalf of A. B. plaintiff in a certain suit in equity depending in the Circuit Court of the United States for the ———— Circuit and ———— District of ————, wherein the said A. B. is complainant and R. M. and N. O. are defendants; the interrogatories and cross interrogatories propounded to the said witnesses, being the same enclosed and directed with the aforementioned commission to us the commissioners aforesaid.

X. X., one of the said witnesses being duly cautioned and sworn to testify the whole truth and carefully examined,[61] deposeth and saith as follows:

In answer to the several interrogatories in chief:

To *the first interrogatory in chief*, the witness says, &c., (here use the language of the witness).

To *the second interrogatory in chief*, the witness says, &c., (as before). [And so on to the end of the interrogatories in chief.]

And in answer to the several cross interrogatories, the witness says:

To *the first cross interrogatory*, the witness says that, &c., [using the language of the witness].

To *the second cross interrogatory*, the witness says that, &c., [as before and so on to the end].

And further the said witness saith not.

X. X.[62]

The witness L. L. not being yet examined the taking of these depositions is adjourned and continued until to-morrow at the same place and between the same hours.

D. D., Commissioner.
E. E., Commissioner.

———— 18—

Office of ————, between the hours of 6 A. M. and 5 P. M.

The witness L. L., being duly cautioned and sworn to testify the

---

[61] See Rev. Stat. U. S. sec. 864; p. 466 of this treatise.

[62] The deposition is to be signed by the witness. See Rev. Stat. U. S., sec. 864; p. 466 of this treatise.

whole truth and carefully examined deposeth and saith as follows:
In answer to the several interrogatories in chief:
[As in former deposition of X. X. to the end.]

State of ————,
County of ————, to wit:

We, D. D. and E. E., two of the commissioners to whom the annexed commission was directed in the suit in equity of A. B., plaintiff,
against R. M. and N. O., defendants, depending in the United
States Circuit Court for the ——— Circuit and ——— District of
————, do hereby certify that the foregoing depositions of X. X. and
L. L. were reduced to writing by the said D. D. one of us [or by the
said witnesses] in our presence and signed by the said X. X. and L. L.
and that the several proceedings therein mentioned were duly had
and taken before us at the times and place mentioned therein, and
we do further certify that we are not of counsel or attorneys for
either of the parties to the said suit, nor are we interested in the
event thereof.
Witness our hands and seals [of office] this ——— day of
————, 18—.

D. D., Commissioner, [Seal.]
E. E., Commissioner, [Seal.]

Oral Interrogatories.

The depositions by oral interrogatories under the
sixty-seventh rule of practice, has been substituted
by the oral examination mentioned in section 463,
pp. 482, 483, *ante*.

464. The following is the

FORM OF DEPOSITIONS IN THE VIRGINIA STATE COURTS.

When Taken in the State of Virginia.

Notice.

To R. M. and N. O.:
Take notice that on the ——— day of ——— at the office of J.
O. S. in the city of R———, between the hours of 9 o'clock A. M.

and 6 o'clock P. M. of that day, I shall proceed to take the depositions of X. X. and L. L. to be read in evidence in my behalf in the suit in equity depending in the ———— Court of ———— county, in which I am plaintiff and you are defendants; and, if from any cause the taking of the said depositions be not commenced on that day; or if commenced, if they be not completed on that day, the taking of the said depositions will be adjourned and continued from time to time at the same place and between the same hours until they are completed.

Respectfully,   A. B.

Affidavit of Service.

County of ————, to-wit:

This day personally appeared before me, the undersigned, a justice of the peace for the county aforesaid, Q. Q. and made oath that he did on this day deliver true copies of the above notice to R. M. and to N. O.

Given under my hand this ———— day of ————, 18—.

Q. Q., j. p.

Caption of Depositions, &c.

The depositions of X. X. and L. L., taken before me, W. H. S., a notary public for the city of R————, pursuant to notice hereto annexed, at the office of J. O. S. in the city of R———— on the ———— day of ————, 18—, between the hours of 9 o'clock A. M. and 6 o'clock P. M., to be read in evidence in behalf of the plaintiff in a certain suit depending in the ———— Court of ———— county, wherein A. B. is plaintiff and R. M. and N. O. are defendants.

Present: A. J. J., Counsel for Plaintiff;
B. M. M., Counsel for Defendants.

X. X., being duly sworn, deposeth and saith as follows:

1st question by A. J. J., counsel for plaintiff. State, &c.?

Answer. I am not.

2d question by same. Were you present at a conversation which occurred between the plaintiff A. B. and the defendants R. M. and N. O. about the ———— day of ————: if you were, state what occurred at that time and what was the agreement, if any, between the parties?

Answer. I was present; and [proceed to give the answer of the witness in his own words.]

3d question. (as before, &c. to the end of the examination in chief.)

Cross-examined.

1st cross-question by B. M. M. counsel for defendants. [Record the questions and answers as before to the end of cross-examination.]

Re-examination.

1st question by plaintiff's counsel on re-examination. [Record questions and answers as before.]

And further this deponent saith not.

X. X.

L. L. being offered as a witness in behalf of the plaintiff, the defendant by counsel objected to his being examined as such and required that he should be sworn on his voir dire: and thereupon the said L. L. being sworn on his voir dire, answered as follows:

Question 1st propounded on the voir dire to the witness L. L. by B. M. M. counsel for defendants. Are you or not the husband of one Jane L. and is she or not interested in the event of this suit?

Answer. I am her husband. I was not aware that she had any interest in this cause.

2d question by same. Did she or not prior to her marriage to you, convey by deed (which is now exhibited to you marked N. and is to be annexed to this question) the property embraced in this suit to the plaintiff A. B. warranting with general warranty the title to the same; and is she or not directly interested in the result of the suit?

Answer. A paper purporting to be such a deed is handed me by yourself. It bears date so long ago, and the acknowledgment is so distant that if acknowledged or executed by my wife it must have been when she was under full age; and I presume her covenant of warranty, if she made it, is not binding upon her.

The plaintiff asked no questions on the voir dire, and the witness thereupon signed the same.

L. L.

And the defendants thereupon repeated their objections to the competency of the witness; and protested against his testifying in this cause.

And the witness, L. L., being then duly sworn in chief, deposes and says as follows: [But before the first question was propounded the counsel for the defendant objected again to the competency of the witness, because he is the husband of one Jane L., who is directly interested in the result of this suit; and he desires his objection to be here noted.]

1st question by A. J. J. counsel for plaintiff. State, if you know, &c.

Answer. [Record it in the witness's words.]

2d question by same. Did you not hear the defendants state that, &c.

Exception. The defendant's counsel excepts to this question as a leading question.

Answer. [Record the answer of witness.]

3d question by same. [Record question and answers and so on as in the deposition of X. X. to the end of examination in chief.]

Cross-examination.

And the defendants, by counsel, before proceeding to cross-examine the witness, renews his objection to the competency of the witness; and not waiving but expressly relying on his said objection now cross-examines the witness.

1st cross-question by counsel for defendants. [Record questions and answers as in X. X.'s deposition.]

And further this deponent saith not.   L. L.

Certificate of notary at conclusion of deposition.

State of Virginia, City of Richmond, to-wit:

I, W. H. S., a notary public for the City of Richmond in the State of Virginia do hereby certify that the foregoing depositions of X. X. and L. L., were duly taken, sworn to and subscribed before me at the place and time mentioned therein and in the caption thereto, pursuant to the annexed notice. In witness whereof, I have hereto set my hand and official notarial seal on this ———— day of ———— 18— at the City of Richmond aforesaid.

W. H. S., n. p.

[Notarial Seal.]

Time employed in taking these depositions, 8 hours.

W. H. S.

Depositions taken outside the State to be used in the Virginia State Courts.

Commission.

The Commonwealth of Virginia to George B. M, a commissioner of deeds &c. for the State of Virginia residing in the City and State of New York, Greeting:

Know ye, that trusting to your fidelity and provident circumspection in diligently examining X. X. and L. L. witnesses in behalf of A. B. in a suit depending in our Circuit Court for the county of ———, wherein the said A. B. is plaintiff and R. M. and N. O. are defendants, we request and empower you that on such day and at such place as you shall appoint, you call and cause to come the witnesses aforesaid before you and them diligently examine on the Holy Evangelists of Almighty God and their examination into the said court distinctly and plainly, without delay, you send and certify enclosed, returning also this commission. ' Witness P. M. clerk of our said court at the courthouse of said county of ——— on the ——— day of ——— 18—, and in the ——— year of the Independence of the United States of America.

P. M., Clerk.

Notice.

To R. M. and N. O.:
Take notice that on the ——— day of ——— at the office of W. S. R., number — on Broadway, City of New York, between the hours of 9.o'clock A. M. and 6 o'clock P. M. (as in the notice on pp. 488, 489, to the end). Resp'y,

A. B.

Affidavit of service. As on p. 489 *ante.*

Caption of Depositions.

Depositions of X. X. and L. L. witnesses taken before me J. A. B. a commissioner of deeds, &c., for the State of Virginia in and for the City of New York in the State of New York on the ——— day of ——— and the other days hereinafter mentioned by virtue of the annexed commission and in pursuance of the annexed notice, at the office of W. L. R. number ———, Broadway, in the said City and State of New York, between the hours of 9 o'clock A. M. and 6 o'clock P. M. to be read in evidence in behalf of the plaintiff in a certain suit in equity depending in the ——— court of ——— county, State of Virginia, in which A. B. is plaintiff and R. M. and N. O. are defendants.

Present: R. R. counsel for plaintiff, P. O. counsel for defendants.

X. X. the witness, being first duly sworn, deposeth and saith as follows:

Question 1 by plaintiff's counsel. (State it).
Answer. [Record the answer in witness's words.]
Question 2. (As before on pp. 490, 491 to the end.)
And further this deponent saith not.

X. X.

L. L. the witness, being first duly sworn, deposeth and saith as follows:

[Questions and answers recorded as in X. X.'s deposition.]

And further this deponent saith not.

L. L.

Certificate.

State of New York,
  City of New York, *ss*:

I, George B. M., a commissioner of deeds, &c., for the State of Virginia in and for the City of New York in the State of New York do hereby certify that the witnesses whose depositions are as above were duly sworn by me at the times and place mentioned in the said depositions and that the said depositions were duly taken, reduced to writing, and signed by the witnesses respectively before me at the place and times therein mentioned pursuant to the annexed notice and commission. In witness whereof, I have hereunto set my hand and affixed my official seal at ――― aforesaid this ―― day ――― 18―.

Geo. B. M.,

[Official Seal.]   Commissioner of deeds for Virginia.

PRACTICAL NOTES.

Depositions taken in the State of Virginia, without any commission, before any justice, notary or commissioner in chancery. Outside the State, a commission necessary.

Reasonable notice to the adverse party must be given.

How commission obtained, see sec. 438, p. 469, and sec. 444, p. 471 *ante.*

Exceptions to any questions or answers should be noted at the time when made. Each witness to sign his deposition at its conclusion; but see section 437. Adjournments from day to day if so stated in the notice; or from time to time if so stated in the notice; the adjournments to be noted by the officer as well as the recommencements of taking the depositions. If adjournment by consent of the parties, the fact to be noted.

Any papers or writings referred to by witnesses or copies thereof to be annexed to the depositions and referred to by such marks or designations as to identify them.

If the officer or person who takes a deposition beyond the State has no official seal (unless he take the deposition as a justice of the peace in which case it is not required) the genuineness of his signature should be authenticated by some officer of the same State or country under his official seal.

When the depositions have been duly certified the officer taking

them should seal them up securely, and direct them to the clerk of
the court where the suit is pending and transmit them by mail or
otherwise:—endorsing the package as follows:

A. B.;   Plt'ff. ⎫ To the Clerk of the ——— Court of the
    vs.   ⎬ County of ———.
R. M. & N. O., Def'ts. ⎭

The depositions thus sealed and endorsed may be placed in an
outer envelope and sent to the care of any person interested in
their preservation. The depositions, unless carried to the clerk by
the officer taking them, are to be sent to him sealed up; and the
clerk endorses the fact that they were so returned to him.

A witness ought not to write his deposition or his answer beforehand; nor ought they to be written for him beforehand by counsel
or any other person; but he ought to answer the questions orally
or from memory as they are propounded to him. *Fant* vs. *Miller*,
&c., 17 Grat. 187. See section 456.

465. *Demurrer to interrogatories.* The treatises on
the practice in the English equity courts speak of a
demurrer to interrogatories *i. e.* a tender of reasons
by a witness for not answering any question propounded to him, 2 Dan. Ch. Pr. (old) 328, Seton on
Decrees 1061, 1235; and it is said that such demurrers
are set down to be argued as demurrers to a bill.
Seton on Decrees 1235.

While resembling demurrers, these exceptions are not strictly
such. The witness by demurring admits nothing; and he should
state in his demurrer why he objects to answering. By demurring,
he raises the question for adjudication whether he should be compelled to answer.. He may object in this way to answering because to do so would subject him to pains and penalties, and for
any other sufficient reason.

466. *Inspection in aid of proof.* Courts often order
that an infant be produced in court for satisfactory
proof of his existence, age and discretion; or, that
an original document or book be produced to be
satisfied of its genuineness and integrity, or of its

age and precise state and character, Gres. Eq. Ev. 451 ; and where the subject is immovable, the court will order the party in possession to permit an inspection by witnesses. *Kynaston* vs. *E. Ind. Co.*, 3 Swanst. 249; and, in patent causes, often the machine or instrument itself or an accurate working model is directed to be brought into court for inspection at the hearing. 3 Green. Ev. § 329.

467. *Farther evidence.* Courts sometimes require farther evidence to be produced, *Hood* vs. *Pimm*, 4 Sim. 101, 6 Cond. Eng. Ch. R. 58 ; and, sometimes, this farther evidence is introduced by the examination of witnesses viva voce at the hearing, See 3 Green. Ev §§ 330, 331; and, upon special order, the court permits the parties to read at the hearing any answers, depositions, or other proceedings, taken in another cause, and this without requiring a foundation first to be laid, by proving the bill and answer in the cause in which the depositions or other subsequent proceedings were taken. 3 Green. Ev. § 341.

It is sufficient if the point or matter in issue were the same in both causes and the party against whom the evidence is offered, or those under whom he claims, had full power to cross-examine the witnesses; it is not necessary that the parties in both causes should be identically the same. See *Roberts* vs. *Anderson*, 3 John. Ch. R. 371, 376; *Harrington* vs. *Harrington*, 2 How. 701.

468. *Depositions in a cross cause.* The English authorities say, that it is requisite that the witnesses be examined before publication in the original cause. has passed, otherwise the depositions are liable to be suppressed, *Pascall* vs. *Scott*, 12 Sim. 550; but if the

point in issue in both causes is the same and the
depositions in the cross cause were taken before either
party had examined witnesses in the original cause,
they may be read in the latter cause. *Wilford* vs.
Beasley, 3 Atk. 501, 2 Dan. Ch. Pr. (Perk.) 1658, and in
a case before Chancellor Kent, *Underhill* vs. *Van Cortlandt*, 2 John. Ch. R. 339, the judge, while permitting
depositions taken in the original cause to be read in a
cross cause, permitted only such facts to be read as
were pertinent to the issue in the original cause. The
writer is not aware that these rules prevail in the
Virginia State Courts. Whether they would govern
the practice in the United States Courts depends
upon the effect given to the 90th rule of practice of
the Supreme Court.

469 *Suppressing depositions.* Sometimes, it is expedient to move to suppress depositions or parts of
them before the cause comes on to be heard; thus
labor and expense are saved which would otherwise
be incurred in preparing the cause for a hearing,
Gres. Eq. Ev. 147; and where special exceptions
have been taken to parts of. the depositions or to
particular questions and answers, the rule is as stated
in section 476 post.

470. Scandalous matter may be thus suppressed.
Gres. Eq. Ev. 147. There may be latent objections
to the depositions which may be brought to the notice
of the court on affidavits, and when the objection appears on the face of the depositions it may be better
to have the point determined before the hearing, on
application to the court to suppress them. *Ibid.*

471. It has been questioned whether depositions would be referred to a master for impertinence alone. Lord Eldon refused, alleging the risk of expunging matter which might eventually prove to be material. Gres. Eq. Ev. 149.

472. The strict rules of the English courts leading to the suppression of depositions are set forth in Mr. Gresley's work on Equity Evidence, 1st Am. edit. pp. 149, 150; edit. 1848, pp. 220, 221.

473. *Refusal to suppress for irregularity.* A witness was examined inadvertently two days after the publication had passed and the other party cross-examined him; the court would not suppress his evidence. *Hammond* vs. ———, 1 Dick. 50. Where a witness died before cross-examination, the cross-interrogatories which were about to have been put to him not going to any point to which he had been examined in chief nor to his credit, the court refused to suppress his deposition. *O'Callaghan* vs. *Murphy*, 2 Sch. & Lef. 158.

474. The refusal of a witness (not a party) to be cross-examined is no reason for suppressing his deposition, but the adverse party must at the time enforce such right of cross-examination as he has, *Courtenay* vs *Hoskins*, 2 Russ. 253. But if the witness should secrete himself to avoid a cross-examination, there the court would, or at least might, suppress the direct examination. *Flowerday* vs. *Collett*, 1 Dick. R. 288. If a party to the cause refuse to testify, the rule laid down in sec. 410, p. 448 *ante*, will govern

475. It is by no means certain that where the direct examination has been completed and the other side is deprived by the death of the witness or by other inevitable accident, of the opportunity to cross-examine, that the direct examination will be suppressed. Mr. Justice Story in *Gass* vs. *Stinson*, 3 Sumn. 98, said, that the general doctrine so far from being established in that manner appeared strongly the other way. He cited *Arundel* vs. *Arundel*, 1 Chan. R. 90; *O'Callaghan* vs. *Murphy*, 2 Sch. & Lef. 158, and *Nolan* vs. *Shannon*, 1 Molloy 157, in which last case the Lord Chancellor held, that the direct examination of a witness might be read at the hearing, when a cross-examination had been prevented by his illness and death.

476. In *Copeland* vs. *Stanton*, 1 Ves 415, the defendant examined a witness after publication and on discovering the irregularity he obtained an order to re-examine the witness. The witness died before the re-examination. Lord Parker, C. ordered that the defendant might make use of the depositions sworn to by the witness, his re-examination having been prevented by the act of God.

477. *Exceptions to depositions.* Objections to the depositions in the United States Courts and the Virginia State Courts are usually taken by exceptions stating the reasons of the objections. These should be made always before the hearing of the cause; and in certain cases, unless taken at once, the benefit of taking them is considered as waived. See cases cited in sections 454, 455 ante. And the excep-

tions must, after they are taken, be brought to the notice of the court for the purpose of obtaining its judgment thereon; if not, an appellate court will not consider them. *Fant* vs. *Miller, &c.*, 17 Grat. 187.

478. *Re-examination of witnesses.* The examination of the witness should be completed, as much as possible, *uno actu*, and whenever it can be accomplished, no opportunity should be afforded, after the deposition is once completed, of tampering with him and inducing him to retract or contradict or explain away what he has stated in his first examination upon a second; but notwithstanding the unwillingness of the courts of equity to allow a second examination of the same witness, there are cases in which, if justice requires a second examination, an order will be made to permit it. Dan. Ch. Pr. (Perk) 970. See *Willan* vs. *Willan*, 19 Ves. 590; *Rowley* vs. *Adams*, 1 M. & K. 545; *Whitaker* vs. *Wright*, 3 Hare 412; *England* vs. *Downs*, 6 Beav. 281; *Remsen* vs. *Remsen*, 2 John. Ch. R. 501. The order of the court to permit the re-examination of the witness is necessary: the re-examination is against the ordinary practice of the court and is only granted under peculiar circumstances See *Phillips* vs. *Thompson*, 1 John. Ch. R. 140; *Beach* vs. *Fulton Bank*, 3 Wend. 573.[63]

---

[63] Re-examination permitted because depositions were suppressed for the interrogatories being leading, or for irregularity, or where it was discovered that a proper release to make the witness competent at the time he gave his deposition had not been executed. *Wood* vs. *Mann*, 2 Sumn. 316: see *Spence* vs. *Allen*, Prec. in Ch. 493, 1 Eq. Ca. Abr. 232; *Healey* vs. *Jagger*, 3 Sim. 494; *Shaw* vs. *Lindley*, 15 Ves. 380; *Atty. Gen.* vs. *Nethercote*, 9 Sim. 311. A witness incompetent by reason of interest may be re-examined after his competency is restored. *Haddix* vs. *Haddix*, 5 Litt. (Ky.)

479. Where the reason of the rule for re-examination of the witness only by leave of the court did not apply, e. g. a witness who had been examined to prove certain exhibits at the hearing called to prove other exhibits before the master, it was held that he could do so without a special order for re-examination. *Courtenay* vs. *Hoskins*, 2 Russ. 253.

NOTE TO SEC. 443, P. 471.

The language of Judge Staples in *Summers* vs. *Darne & als.*, 31 Grat. 805 as cited in section 443 may need modification. In *Richardson* vs. *Duble & als.*, 33 Grat. 730, the statute Code 1873, chap. 172, sec. 36, which declares that "in a suit in equity, a deposition may be read if returned before the hearing of the cause, or though after an interlocutory decree, if it be as to a matter not thereby adjudged, and be returned before a final decree" was before the court for its interpretation. The court held that under this statute, when there has been an interlocutory decree, a deposition taken thereafter cannot be read as to any matter thereby adjudicated, unless indeed as the foundation for a motion or petition to rehear the cause; that if no interlocutory decree has been rendered or though one has been rendered a deposition taken and returned before a final hearing as to any matter not adjudicated may be read; but the right is not an absolute one. Judge Staples, pronouncing the opinion of the court, said, that "in *Summers* vs. *Darne*, 31 Grat. 791, a petition for a rehearing was filed, founded upon depositions previously taken. It was objected that the depositions could

---

202. See other cases in which the court refused to permit a re-examination, *Noel* vs. *Fitzgerald*, 1 Hogan 135; *Gray* vs. *Murray*, 4 John. Ch. R. 412; *Hallock* vs. *Smith*, 4 John. Ch. R. 649; *Sterry* vs. *Arden*, 1 John. Ch. R. 62; *Newman* vs. *Kendall*, 2 A. K. M. 236. A re-examination was permitted to prove before the master some fact omitted to be proved upon the original deposition: whether the permission should have been accompanied by the direction that the witness should not be examined upon any points with respect to which he had been previously examined is a matter upon which there is difference of opinion; for such direction, see *Browning* vs. *Barton*, 2 Dick. 508; cited as *Browning* vs. *Barker*, in 1 Bro. C. C. 388; against such direction, see *Vaughn* vs. *Lloyd*, 1 Cox 312; Dan. Ch. Pr. (Perk.) 1181. Sir Lancelot Shadwell, Vice Ch., in *Hood* vs. *Pimm*, 4 Sim. 101, 6 Eng. Cond. Ch., collects many of the cases in which a re-examination was permitted. See also 3 Green. Evi. § 346 and note.

not be read; but this court held that there is no rule of law prohibiting a party from taking his depositions even after an interlocutory decree, *merely as a foundation for a motion or petition to re-hear the decree.* The depositions, of course, were only admitted in view and in connection with such petition showing a proper case for a rehearing."

CHAPTER XI.

Of Decrees.

480. It is the practice in England when the cause is set down for hearing for the plaintiff to give notice to the adverse party of the day appointed for the hearing. This is done by a writ called a *subpœna to hear judgment*, Dan. Ch. Pr. (Perk.) 985. This practice is substituted here by the entry of the cause upon the court docket, which is called at every term of the court. Code 1873, ch. 173, § 2.

481. The mode of hearing causes in equity is similar to that adopted in the courts of common law.[64]

[64] The hearing should be had at the first term succeeding the maturing of the cause. Code 1873, ch. 173, § 2. If the court refuse to try any cause or continue it without good cause shown, the party asking for a trial may have his application spread upon the record with a statement of the facts relative thereto. Code 1873, ch. 173, § 3. The former statute provided that upon such statement, it shall be lawful for the Court of Appeals on the application of the party injured to award a mandamus and compel a trial of the cause upon the proofs as they existed at the time when it was erroneously continued or the trial was improperly refused. Supp. Rev. Code, p. 133, sec. 14. This statute came under review in exparte Richardson, 3 Leigh 343; and the court there held that the statute authorized a mandamus to compel the courts of chancery to hear causes at the first term at which they were prepared for hearing when no special cause appeared for the refusal of the court to hear them, but the statute did not authorize a mandamus to compel the hearing of a cause which the court of chancery, in its discretion, for reasons satisfactory to it, thought proper to continue.

The party plaintiff, on the main hearing, or, in case of a motion, the party making the motion, usually opens the argument, to this there is a reply by the opposite party, and then the argument is closed by the former. For the convenience of the court, arguments in equity causes are usually in writing instead of being spoken ; but there is no positive rule on the subject.

482. *Causes to be heard together with others touching the same matters.* Where there are several suits in the same court between different parties claiming the same property they should generally be heard together to avoid decrees that may clash with each other. So, in the case of a cross-bill. as a general rule, both causes should be heard together that one decree may settle the whole dispute. But in this matter the court has a discretionary power which may be exercised as circumstances shall require for the attainment of justice; and when the plaintiff on a cross-bill has produced delay in preparing his suit for a hearing, that will be just cause for proceeding to hear the original bill. On an appeal from the decree pronounced on the original bill, if it be objected in the appellate court that the suit ought to have been suspended, and the papers in the two causes are not before the appellate court, that court will presume that the court below exercised its discretion properly. *McConnico* vs. *Moseley,* 4 Call 390.

483. *Suit to be properly matured.* In a suit against several defendants, if a decree be pronounced against one before the others have answered or been served

with process or had an order of publication executed against them, an appellate court will frequently reverse the decree for this cause, although it may think that defendant liable to the plaintiff. *Purcell* vs. *Mad dux*, 3 Munf. 79.

In *Bland* vs. *Wyatt*, 1 H. & M. 543, the bill was to recover money from a guardian. It was filed against the sheriff to whom the guardian's estate was committed, the heirs of the guardian, a surviving surety in the guardian's bond, and the administrator of a deceased surety. The cause was heard when some of the heirs and the surviving surety had not been served with process; and upon such hearing a decree was rendered against the administrator of the deceased surety, and the bill dismissed as to the other defendants. It was decided that there was error in proceeding to a hearing of the cause before all the defendants had been properly proceeded against and in prematurely dismissing the bill as to some of the defendants.

And in a suit against several defendants, if the plaintiff have it set for hearing as to some before it is ready as to others, and at the hearing the bill be dismissed as to all such a dismission will in many cases be error for which the decree may be reversed. In *Henderson, &c.* vs. *Anderson's ex'ix*, 4 Munf. 435, a suit against an executrix and her children, three of the children answered. There was nothing to show that the cause was ready as to the executrix and the other children. The plaintiff had the cause set for hearing as *to the defendants who had answered*. The chancellor dismissed the bill against all the defendants. The appellate court reversed the decree of the chancellor and remanded the cause to be proceeded in *against all the defendants*. In *Key* vs. *Hord, &c.*, 4 Munf. 485, the case was set for hearing on the plaintiff's motion and when it came on to be heard the chancellor dismissed the bill. On appeal, the court held that, as the case then appeared, the plaintiff had a claim against some of the defendants; but as to those defendants the cause had not been matured for a hearing. The decree was reversed and the cause remanded for the purpose of having the same matured as to those parties and to be otherwise legally proceeded in. In *Boyd, &c.* vs. *Hamilton's heirs*, 6 Munf. 462, the plaintiff claimed that he was entitled jointly with one defendant as co-devisee to land held by another defendant; and before the defendant who was jointly interested with the plaintiff had been brought before the court, the bill was dismissed as to that defendant against whom the claim was made. The court of appeals determined that this was erroneous, because the decree would not be binding on the defendant, who was a co-devisee with the plaintiff, until that defendant was before the court

Yet where a bill was brought by a legatee against the executor and the other legatees, for the purpose of surcharging the executor's account, and the cause was set down for hearing as to the executor *by direction of the plaintiff*, before the process against the legatees had been served, and upon its being heard on the merits the bill was dismissed, it was held that the plaintiff could not object in an appellate court that the decree of the chancellor was premature. *Wyllie, &c.* vs. *Venable's ex'or*, 4 Munf. 369, *Jackson's assignees* vs. *Outright, &c.*, 5 Munf. 308.

In *Robinson's ex'ors* vs. *Day*, 5 Grat. 55, the cause was ready for a decision as to the substantial parties at a regular term of the court. At a following intermediate term, the plaintiff amends his bill to make a formal party, who comes in and files his answer at the same term, and consents that the cause may come on to be heard. The court may hear the cause at the intermediate term, though it is objected to by the substantial defendant, as to whom it was ready at the preceding regular term.

484 After the cause is heard, the court proceeds to adjudicate the rights of the parties, and this adjudication is called its decree or order.

A distinction has been drawn in the books between decrees, strictly so called, and interlocutory orders, the latter having reference to proceedings prior to the full hearing of the cause upon the merits, the former containing the adjudication of the court after all preliminary matters have been adjusted and a full hearing is had.

Though accounts are directed the decree is still properly termed a decree, because the right of the plaintiff to call upon the defendant to account, which is often disputed, is determined by it; but a preliminary direction at the hearing for an inquiry only is not properly a decree, but a decretal order. *Horwood* vs. *Schmedes*, 12 Ves. 315.

485. Decrees have been defined as the sentence or order of the court pronounced on hearing and understanding all the points in issue and determining the right of the parties to the suit according to equity and good conscience. 2 Dan. Ch. Pr. (old) 631.

486. *Decrees interlocutory and final.* Decrees are either interlocutory or final. An interlocutory decree is when the consideration of the particular question to be determined, or of further. directions generally, is reserved until the final hearing. 2 Dan Ch. Pr. (old) 631. A decree is final when it fully decides and disposes of the whole merits of the case and reserves no farther question or directions for the future judgment of the court so that it will not be necessary to bring the cause again before the court for another decision. *Hol. Int. Eq.* 310.

It is not absolutely necessary to the finality of a decree that it should make such a disposition of every matter in the cause as that it may at once be removed from the docket. A decree disposing of the whole subject, deciding all matters in controversy, ascertaining the rights of all parties and awarding the costs though it appoint a commissioner to sell part of the subject and account for and pay the proceeds to the parties, with liberty for them to apply to the court to add other or substitute new commissioners, or for a partition of the subject to be sold in kind, is a final decree. *Harvey* vs. *Branson*, 1 Leigh 108.

In *Thorntons* vs. *Fitzhugh*, 4 Leigh 209, Judge Carr said, "Where anything is reserved by the court for future adjudication, in order to settle the matters in controversy, the decree is interlocutory; but where, upon the hearing, all these matters are settled by the decree, such decree is final, though much may remain to be done, before it can be completely carried into execution, and though to effectuate such execution, the cause is retained, and leave given the parties to apply for the future aid of the court." See *Sheppard's ex'or* vs. *Starke, &c.*, 3 Munf. 29, *Royall* vs. *Johnson*, 1 Rand. 427, cases in which decrees were held final. In *Thorntons* vs. *Fitzhugh*, 4 Leigh 209, there was difference of opinion as to the finality of the decree; two of the judges, Carr and Brooke, holding it to be final, and Tucker P. held it to be interlocutory.

In *Cocke* vs. *Gilpin*, 1 Rob. R. 20, Judge Baldwin investigated the subject very fully and after adverting to the prior cases before the Court of Appeals, held the decree to be interlocutory. The criterion he applied is this: When the further action of the court *in the cause* (contrasting it with the action of the court *beyond* the cause) is necessary to give completely the relief contemplated by the court there the decree is interlocutory. 1 Rob. R. p. 29, 36.

Allen J. and Cabell P. concurred with Baldwin. Judge Brooke dissented.

See *Young* vs. *Skipwith*, 2 Wash. 300. *Grymes* vs. *Pendleton*, 1 Call 54, *McCall* vs. *Peachy*, 1 Call 55, *Bowyer* vs. *Lewis*, 1 H. & M. 553, *Templeman* vs. *Steptoe*, 1 Munf. 339, *Aldridge, &c.* vs. *Giles*, 3 H. & M. 136, *Mackey* vs. *Bell*, 2 Mun. 523. *Goodwin* vs. *Miller*, 2 Munf. 42, *Hill's ex'or* vs. *Fox's adm'or*, 10 Leigh 587, *Fairfax* vs. *Muse's ex'ors*, 2 H. & M. 558, *Ellzey* vs. *Lane's ex'ix*, 2 H. & M. 592, *Allen* vs. *Belches*, 2 H. & M. 595, in all of which cases the decree was held interlocutory. See 1 Rob. R. 35, 36.

Other cases on the subject of final and interlocutory decrees in the Virginia State Courts and in the United States Circuit Courts will be found in the subjoined note.[65]

---

[65] Cases on interlocutory and final decrees in the

VIRGINIA STATE COURTS:

When final. *Thorntons* vs. *Fitzhugh*, 4 Leigh 209; *Davenport* vs. *Mason*, 2 Wash. 200 (a decree dissolving an injunction and decreeing complainant to pay costs); *Harvey* vs. *Branson*, 1 Leigh 108; *Vanmeter* vs. *Vanmeter*, 3 Grat. 142, and *Tennant's heirs* vs. *Pattons*, 6 Leigh 196 (decrees disposing of the whole cause and leaving nothing to be done); *Ruff* vs. *Starke*, 3 Grat. 129 (decree settling all matters in dispute omitting to decree upon a claim set up in the bill which after circumstances rendered unimportant); *Fleming & als.* vs. *Bolling & als.*, 8 Grat. 292; *Rogers* vs. *Strother & als.*, 27 Grat. 417; *Nelson* vs. *Jennings & als.*, 2 P. & H. 369.

Decree final as to manumission but not as to profits, *Paup, adm'or* vs. *Mingo*, 4 Leigh 163.

When interlocutory. *Fairfax* vs. *Muse*, 2 H. & M. 557, and *Allen* vs. *Belches*, 2 H. & M. 595 (decrees foreclosing equity of redemption and appointing commissioners to make sale); *Aldridge & als.* vs. *Gi'es*, 3 H. & M. 136 (decree directing that unless defendants answer the bill before a certain day, the tract of land mentioned in the bill should be surveyed and part allotted to the complainant and that the defendant should execute to the complainant a legal conveyance of such part and pay the costs of suit); *Templeman* vs. *Steptoe*, 1 Munf. 339 (a decree dismissing so much of a bill as claimed one of two separate subjects in controversy, and as to the other determined also the rights of the parties, but directed an account to be taken not final as to parties retained in court); *Mackey* vs. *Bell*, 2 Munf. 523 (seems to be directly antagonistic to *Thorntons* vs. *Fitzhugh*, 4 Leigh 209); *Chapman* vs. *Armistead*, 4 Munf. 382; *Hill's ex'or* vs. *Fox's adm'or*, 10 Leigh 587; *Dunbar's ex'ors* vs. *Woodcock's ex'ors*, 10 Leigh 629; *Young* vs. *Skipwith*, 2 Wash. 300; *Ambrouse's heirs* vs. *Keller*, 22 Grat. 769; *Smith & als.* vs. *Blackwell & als.*, 31 Grat. 291; *Cocke* vs. *Gilpin*, 1 Rob. 20; *Goodwin* vs. *Miller*, 2 Munf. 42 (a decree directing an executor for payment of debts to sell the lands of his testator and report his proceedings); *Fretwell* vs. *Wayt & als.*, 1 Ran. 415.

487. It rarely happens that a first decree can be final and conclude the cause. Thus, if any matter is strongly controverted, the court is so sensible of the deficiency of trial by written evidence that it will usually direct the matter to be tried by a jury. This

---

Whether interlocutory or final. Alexander vs. *Coleman & wife,* 6 Munf. 328.

Final as to some parties, interlocutory as to others. Royall's adm'ors vs. *Johnson & als.,* 1 Rand, 421.

A decree not partly final and partly interlocutory, in the same cause, for and against the same parties who remain in court. *Ryan's adm'or* vs. *McLeod & als.,* 32 Grat. 367.

Cases on interlocutory and final decrees in

UNITED STATES COURTS:

The decrees were declared in the following cases :

Interlocutory. Young vs. *Grundy,* 6 Cran. 51 (decree dissolving an injunction); *Lee* vs. *Kelly,* 15 Pet. 213 ; *Young* vs. *Smith,* 15 Pet. 287 ; *Brown* vs. *Swann,* 9 Pet. 1 ; *Bernard* vs. *Gibson,* 7 How. 650 ; *Pulliam* vs. *Christian,* 6 How. 209 ; *Perkins* vs. *Fourniquet,* 6 How. 206 ; *The Palmyra,* 10 Wheat. 502 ; *Chace* vs. *Vasquez,* 11 Wheat. 429 ; *Ayres* vs. *Carver,* 17 How. 591 (dismissing a cross bill. See 5 Otto 225); *Beebe & als.* vs. *Russell,* 19 How. 283 ; *U. S.* vs. *Fossatt,* 21 How. 445 ; *Hamilton* vs. *Stainthorp,* 2 Wal. 106 ; *Moore* vs. *Robbins,* 18 Wal. 588 ; *Railroad Co.* vs. *Swasey,* 23 Wal. 405 ; *Butterfield* vs. *Usher,* 1 Otto 246 ; and *Green* vs. *Fisk,* 13 Otto 518.

The decrees were declared in the following cases :

Final. Ray vs. *Law,* 3 Cran. 179, (a decree for a sale under a mortgage); *Forgay* vs. *Conrad,* 6 How. 201, (see *Thomson* vs. *Dean,* 7 Wal. 346); *West* vs. *Smith,* 8 How. 402; *Wabash & Erie Canal* vs. *Beers,* 1 Black 54; *Milwaukie & M. R. R. Co., &c.* vs. *Soutter,* 2 Wal. 440; *Bronsen* vs. *R. R. Co.,* 2 Black 524; *Withenbury* vs. *U. S.,* 5 Wal. 819; *Sampson* vs. *Welsh,* 24 How. 207; *French* vs. *Shoemaker,* 12 Wal. 86; *Stovall* vs. *Banks,* 10 Wal. 583; *Crosby* vs. *Buchanan,* 23 Wal. 420; *Railroad Co.* vs. *Bradley,* 7 Wal. 575; *Sage* vs. *Railroad Co.,* 6 Otto 712; and *Hinckley* vs. *Gilliam & als.,* 4 Otto 467. See Exparte *Railroad Co.,* 5 Otto 221.

Final decree defined. Beebe & als. vs. *Russell,* 19 How. 283, and *Thomson* vs. *Dean,* 7 Wal. 342. [In the last-named case the following cases are cited: *Whiting* vs. *B'k U. S.,* 13 Pet. 6; *Michaud* vs. *Girod,* 4 How. 505; *Orchard* vs. *Hughes,* 1 Wal. 657; *Milwaukie & M. R. R. Co.* vs. *Soutter,* 2 Wal. 440; *Withenbury* vs. *U. S.,* 5 Wal. 819.]

Final decrees cannot be made separately against one of several defendants upon a joint charge against all, *Frow* vs. *De la Vega,* 15 Wal. 552.

is called in the books, directing an issue out of chancery.

See sec. 375 *ante.* In contests concerning the validity of a will it is imperative on the court to direct an issue. Code 1873, ch. 118, § 34; in other cases, it is in the discretion of the court whether to direct an issue or not. See *Smith, &c.* vs. *Carll, &c.,* 5 John. Ch. R. 118. This discretion however is to be a sound discretion; and if in its exercise the court makes a mistake it is just ground of appeal, 9 Grat. 302. And when on the state of the proofs at the time an issue is directed, the bill should be dismissed, it is error to direct the issue; and although the issue is found in favor of the plaintiff the bill should notwithstanding be dismissed at the hearing. *Smith's adm'or* vs. *Betty & als.,* 11 Grat. 752 : See *Pryor* vs. *Adams,* 1 Call 382; *Wise* vs. *Lamb,* 9 Grat. 294; *Collins* vs. *Jones,* 6 Leigh 530.

In no case ought an issue to be ordered merely to enable a party to obtain evidence to make out his case. Daniel, J. in *Smith* vs. *Betty,* 11 Grat. 761. See *Grigsby* vs. *Weaver,* 5 Leigh 197; *Reed* vs. *Cline,* 9 Grat. 136; *Stannard* vs. *Graves,* 2 Call 369; *Dale* vs *Roosevelt,* 6 John. Ch. R. 255

Where an important fact is left doubtful by the testimony the court ought to direct an issue. *Marshall* vs. *Thompson,* 2 Munf. 412; *Bullock* vs. *Gordon,* 4 Munf. 450; *Nelson* vs. *Armstrong,* 5 Grat. 354.

488. In many cases, certain preliminary enquiries are necessary; and these are usually made by one of the Masters or Commissioners of the court. Thus, in all cases relating to the distribution of the estate of a decedent, or where there is a fund distributable among persons of several classes or of the same class, or where other accounts should be first settled, the court sends the cause to a Master or Commissioner.

What is carried on before the master is carried on before the court, of which the master's office is a part. *Erskine* vs. *Garthshire,* 18 Ves. 114.

489. Beside the decrees mentioned in the foregoing sections, the English books treat of *decrees nisi* or

conditional decrees. These are prepared by the party seeking them, and being entered up in the absence of the defendant (though he has been served with a subpœna to hear judgment) and without the action of the court, the plaintiff is not entitled to have such decrees made absolute until the defendant is served with a subpœna for that purpose and fails to appear at the time specified therein and show cause against them. 2 Dan. Ch. Pr. (old) 645, 650.

This practice does not prevail in the Virginia State Courts. The decrees nisi entered at the rules, sec. 69 *ante*, are totally unlike them. Nor is there any likeness between the decrees mentioned in section 489 and the privileges accorded an infant to shew cause against a decree after attaining full age, Code 1873, ch. 174, sec. 10, nor that given an absent or unknown defendant by Code 1873, ch. 166, sec. 16.

490. *Decrees between co-defendants.* Decrees may be made in equity causes in favor of one defendant against another defendant; but the practice appears to be limited to cases in which the plaintiff is entitled to a decree against some one of the defendants, *Holland* vs. *Goodwin*, 3 Leigh 522, and the practice should not be extended further. Ibid.

In the following cases there were *decrees made between co-defendants*:

McNiel, &c. vs. *Baird*, 6 Munf. 316, *Cocke* vs. *Harrison, &c.*, 3 Rand. 494, *Templeman* vs. *Fauntleroy*, 3 Rand. 484, *Mundy* vs. *Vawter & als.*, 3 Grat. 518, *Barger* vs. *Buckland*, 28 Grat. 850, and *Moorman* vs. *Smoot & als.*, 28 Grat. 80.

In the following cases the court refused to make a decree between the co-defendants:

Toole vs. *Stephen*, 4 Leigh 581, *Yerby* vs. *Grigsby*, 9 Leigh 387, *Allen, &c.* vs. *Morgan's adm'or & als.*, 8 Grat. 60, *Blair* vs. *Thompson & als.*, 11 Grat. 441, *Ould, &c.* vs. *Myers*, 23 Grat. 383, and *Law's ex'ors* vs. *Sutherland & als.*, 5 Grat. 357.

491. English writers make the following divisions

in the form of decrees: 1. The date and title; 2. The recitals; 3. The ordering part; to which may be added, 4. The declaratory part, which when made use of usually precedes the ordering part.

492. *Date and title.* The decree commences in the English courts with a recital of the day of the month and year when it was pronounced and the names of the several parties in the cause. 2 Dan. Ch. Pr. (old) 654.

493. *Recitals.* Formerly in the English courts decrees contained long recitals of the pleadings in the cause introduced by the words, " This cause coming on the —— instant and also on this present day to be heard and debated before the Right Honorable, &c., in the presence of counsel learned on both sides, the substance of the plaintiff's bill appeared to be, &c. (then followed a recital of its material parts), therefore that the defendants, &c., (reciting the prayer) and to be relieved in the scope of the plaintiff's bill; whereto the counsel for the defendants alleged that they by their answer, &c. (then followed the defences set up in the answer), Whereupon, &c." This preliminary statement in decrees has been greatly abbreviated in the English courts. See Dan. Ch. Pr. (Perk.) edit. 1865, p 1022.

494. By the 86th rule of practice of the United States Supreme Court governing the practice in United States Courts. it is provided that "in drawing up decrees and orders neither the bill nor answer, nor other pleadings, nor any part thereof, nor the report of any master, nor any other prior proceeding,

shall be recited or stated in the decree or order; but the decree and order shall begin, in substance as follows: 'This cause came on to be heard (or to be further heard, as the case may be) at this term, and was argued by counsel; and thereupon, upon consideration thereof, it was ordered, adjudged and decreed as follows, viz: [Here insert the decree or order.]' "

In the Virginia State Courts, the first decree recites the manner in which the cause has been matured. Subsequent decrees simply recite that the cause came "on to be heard on the papers formerly read" and on any papers or pleading filed or had since the former hearing, stating what the new pleadings, if any, are.[66]

495. *Ordering part.* The ordering or mandatory part of the decree contains the specific directions of the court upon the matter before it. These obviously depend upon the nature of the case before the court.

496. *Declaratory part.* The ordering part of the

---

[66] Thus in a cause where there is the answer of one defendant with replication, and the bill is taken for confessed as to the other, the recital would be:

"This cause came on this day to be heard on the bill taken for confessed and set for hearing as to the defendant C. D. and on the answer of the defendant E. F. with general replication thereto by the plaintiff, exhibits and examinations of witnesses, and was argued by counsel; on consideration whereof, the court doth adjudge, order and decree, &c.''

Or, in case of non-resident or unknown defendants as to whom order of publication has been made:

"This cause in which the plaintiff appears to have proceeded in the mode prescribed by law against the non-resident defendants A. M. and B. L. (or, against the unknown heirs at law of G. P.) came on this day to be heard, &c.''

Or, when cause has been heard before:

"This cause came on this day to be further heard on the papers formerly read and on, &c (if new bills and answers, replications, depositions, &c., specify them) and was argued by counsel. On consideration whereof, &c.''

decree is sometimes prefaced by a declaration of the rights of the parties. 2 Dan. Ch. Pr. (old) 668.

497. *Entering decrees.* In the English courts, the minutes of the decree are taken down by the registrar, and are often read over by him in the presence of the parties concerned or of their counsel and solicitors. 2 Dan. Ch. Pr. (old) 668. Subsequently the decree is drawn up by the registrar and is passed and entered up. Until this last step is taken, the decree is only inchoate: nor even after this is it strictly a record of the court, until it is "enrolled." 2 Dan. Ch. Pr. (old) 674. The manner of enrolling, according to the later orders, is as follows: The solicitor of the person enrolling the decree draws up the form of the decree for enrolment, reciting therein no part of the statements or allegations contained in any bill, answer, petition, affidavit, or report, but stating the filing of the bill or petition, or service of the notice of motion, the names of the parties thereto, together with the prayer of the bill or petition, or notice of motion, the filing of the several answers and other pleadings or proceedings and reports, whether confirmed or not, and the short purport or effect of any decree or order made, had, put in or taken before the date of the decree or order enrolled and leading thereto. This decree so drawn up is called the Docket of Enrolment. The clerk of Records and Writs certifies to the correctness of the Docket of Enrolment. This docket is then signed by the judge; if the decree be pronounced by the Lord Chancellor or one of the Vice-Chancellors it may be presented at once to the Lord Chancellor for

his signature; but if it be the decree of the Master of the Rolls that judge first signs it and after that the ·Lord Chancellor. Dan. Ch. Pr. (Perk.) edit. 1865, pp. 1034, 1035. The docket having been signed by the Lord Chancellor, the day and year when it was signed must be written at the foot of the docket, near the signature of the Lord Chancellor, after which the Record and Writ clerk enrolling the decree engrosses an exact copy thereof upon parchment rolls and carefully examines it with the docket, which, together with the parchment rolls, is carried into the record room of the Record and Writ clerks' office and deposited with the record keeper for safe custody. The enrolment is then complete, and a decree thus enrolled is pleadable, and cannot be reversed but by appeal to the House of Lords, or by bill of review. Dan. Ch. Pr. (Perk). edit. 1865, pp. 1035, 1036. .

498. In the United States Circuit Courts the decrees after being signed by the judge are entered of record by the clerk in the order book of the court. In the Virginia State Courts, the clerk enters in the order book all decrees or orders which the court pronounces. These are read in the hearing of the court and the entries are signed at the foot of each day's proceedings by the judge during the term ; or if the court be composed of more than one judge or justice by the presiding judge or justice. Code 1873, chap. 157, sec. 5.

.   The expiration of the term at which a final decree is pronounced, is, according to the Virginia practice, an enrolment of the decree. See *Erwin* vs. *Vint*, 6 Munf. 267.

499. *When and how decrees may be corrected.* In the Virginia State Courts, although the decree be final in its character, it is within the control of the court during the term at which it has been pronounced or entered, and during that term it may be set aside or altered, or amended, in such form and manner as the court shall deem fit; but after the term has closed, the court has no further power over decrees final in their character and such decrees can then only be altered on a bill of review or by an appeal to a higher court, unless such decrees come within the operation of the statute, Code 1873, chap. 177.

This statute is as follows:

Sec. 1. For any clerical error, or error in fact for which a judgment or decree may be reversed or corrected on writ of error *coram nobis*, the same may be reversed or corrected, on motion after reasonable notice, by the court, or if the judgment or decree be in a circuit court, by the judge thereof in vacation.

Sec. 2. A judgment on confession shall be equal to a release of errors.

Sec. 3. No judgment or decree shall be stayed or reversed for the appearance of either party, being under the age of twenty-one years, by attorney, if the verdict (where there is one), or the judgment or decree, be for him and not to his prejudice; or for want of warrant of attorney; or for the want of a *similiter*, or any misjoining of issue; or for any informality in the entry of the judgment or decree by the clerk, or for the omission of the name of any juror, or because it may not appear that the verdict was rendered by the number of jurors required by law, or for any defect, imperfection, or omission in the pleadings, which could not be regarded on demurrer, or for any other defect, imperfection or omission, which might have been taken advantage of on a demurrer, or answer, but was not so taken advantage of.

Sec. 4. No decree shall be reversed for want of a replication to the answer, where the defendant has taken depositions as if there had been a replication; nor shall a decree be reversed at the instance of a party who has taken depositions, for an informality in the proceedings, when it appears that there was a full and fair hearing upon the merits, and that substantial justice has been done.

Sec. 5. The court in which there is a judgment by default, or a decree on a bill taken for confessed, or the judge of said court in the vacation thereof, may, on motion, reverse such judgment or decree for any error for which an appellate court might reverse it, if the following section was not enacted, and give such judgment or decree as ought to be given. And the court in which is rendered a judgment or decree, in a cause wherein there is a declaration or pleading, or in the record of the judgment or decree, any mistake, miscalculation or misrecital of any name, sum, quantity or time, when the same is right in any part of the record or proceedings, or when there is any verdict, report of a commissioner, bond or other writing, whereby such judgment or decree may be safely amended; or in which a judgment is rendered on a forthcoming bond for a sum larger than by the execution or warrant of distress appears to be proper, or on a verdict in an action for more damages than are mentioned in the declaration; or in the vacation of the court in which any such judgment or decree is rendered, the judge thereof may, on the motion of any party, amend such judgment or decree according to the truth and justice of the case; or in any such case the party obtaining such judgment or decree may, in the same court, at any future term, by an entry of record, or in the vacation by a writing signed by him, attested by the clerk, and filed among the papers of the cause, release a part of the amount of his judgment or decree; and such release shall have the effect of an amendment, and make the judgment or decree operate only for what is not released. Every motion under this chapter shall be after reasonable notice to the opposite party, his agent or attorney, in fact or at law, and shall be within five years from the date of the judgment or decree.

Sec. 6. No appeal, writ of error or *supersedeas* shall be allowed by an appellate court or judge for any matter for which a judgment or decree is liable to be reversed or amended, on motion as aforesaid, by the court which rendered it, or the judge thereof, until such motion be made and overruled in whole or in part. And when an appellate court hears a case wherein an appeal, writ of error or *supersedeas* has been allowed, if it appear that, either before or since the same was allowed, the judgment or decree has been so amended, the appellate court shall affirm the judgment or decree, unless there be other error; and if it appear that the amendment ought to be, and has not been made, the appellate court may make such amendment, and affirm in like manner the judgment or decree, unless there be other error.

500. *In the United States Circuit Courts.* The 85th rule of practice provides, that, " clerical mistakes in

decrees, or decretal orders, or errors arising from any accidental slip or omission, may, at any time before an actual enrolment thereof, be corrected by order of the court or a judge thereof, upon petition, without the form or expense of a rehearing."

501. All decrees in the courts of the United States are deemed to be enrolled at the term at which they were passed. *Dexter* vs. *Arnold*, 5 Mas. C. C. R. 303. After the expiration of the term at which they are enrolled, these decrees, if final, are to stand without alteration or amendment, if an appeal thereon lies to the Supreme Court. See 88th rule United States Supreme Court. Such decree can only be set aside or amended upon proceeding by a bill of review or by an appeal to the Supreme Court. Ibid. But if no appeal lies, there is relief as provided for by the 88th rule cited in the next section.

502. The 88th rule of practice, is as follows: "Every petition for a rehearing shall contain the special matter or cause on which such rehearing is applied for, shall be signed by counsel, and the facts therein stated, if not apparent on the record, shall be verified by the oath of the party, or by some other person. No rehearing shall be granted after the term at which the final decree of the court shall have been entered and recorded, if, an appeal lies to the Supreme Court. But if no appeal lies, the petition may be admitted at any time before the end of the next term of the Court in the discretion of the Court."

A bill in the nature of a bill of review lies before enrolment of the decree; a bill of review after enrolment; and, in our practice, a decree is deemed to be enrolled at the close of the term when it was made. *Whiting* vs. *B'k U. S.* 13 Pet. 6.

503. *When right of rehearing by infant defendants and by absent or unknown defendants.* By Code of 1873, ch. 174, sec. 10 :

"It shall not be necessary to insert in any decree or order a provision allowing an infant to show cause against it within a certain time after he attains the age of twenty-one years. But in any case in which, but for this section, such provision would have been proper, the infant may within six months after attaining the age of twenty-one years, show such cause in like manner as if the decree or order contained such provision. This right of an infant shall not be affected by the seventh section."[67]

And by Code 1873, ch. 166, sec. 16 :

"Any unknown party or other defendant who was not served with process, and did not appear in the case before the date of such judgment, decree or order, or the representative of any such, may within five years from that date, if he be not served with a copy of such judgment, decree or order, more than a year before the end of the said five years, and if he be so served, then within one year from the time of such service, petition to have the case reheard, and may plead or answer, and have any injustice in .the proceedings corrected." [68]

---

[67] The seventh section (chap. 174) is as follows : "A court of equity, in a suit in which it is proper to decree or order the execution of any deed or writing, may appoint a commissioner to execute the same; and the execution thereof shall be as valid to pass, release or extinguish the right, title and interest of the party in whose behalf it is executed, as if such party had been at the time capable in law of executing the same, and had executed it."

[68] It is proper to note, in connection with the provisions contained in section 503, the language of the 11th sec., chap. 174, of the Code of 1873. That section provides that "If a sale of property be made under a decree or order of a court, after six months from the date thereof, and such sale be confirmed, though such decree or order be afterwards reversed or set aside, the title of the purchaser at such sale shall not be affected thereby ; but there may be restitution of the proceeds of sale to those entitled."

504. The following are forms of decrees in the
UNITED STATES CIRCUIT COURTS:

General formula.

As in section 494 ante, p. 511.

Decree for account.

The court doth order and decree that it be referred to Mr. E.,
one of the Masters of this Court, to take a mutual account of all
dealings and transactions between the plaintiff and the defendant,
to the better clearing of which account the parties are to produce
&c., (*books, documents, &c., &c, &c.,*) as the said Master shall
direct, who, in taking of the said account, is to make unto the
parties all just allowances, and is to ascertain what, upon
the balance of the said account shall appear to be due
from either party to the other. And it is further ordered
that the injunction formerly granted in this cause for stay of the
defendant's proceedings at law be in the mean time continued, and
the defendant's judgment is to stand a security for payment of
what, if anything, shall appear to be coming to him on the balance
of the said account; and the court doth reserve the consideration
of the costs of this suit, and of all further directions, until after
the said Master shall have made his report, when either side is to
be at liberty to apply, &c.

Order granting an injunction in case of copyright.

This court doth order that an injunction be awarded to restrain
the defendant, his servants, agents, or workmen, from printing,
publishing, selling, or otherwise disposing of the book in the bill
mentioned to have been published by the defendant, until the said
defendant shall fully answer the plaintiff's bill, or this court make
other order to the contrary.

*Decree for perpetual injunction restraining infringement of copy-
right.*

It is ordered, &c., that the injunction formerly granted in this cause for stay of the defendants, their servants, agents, or work-men, from printing, publishing, or vending a book, comedy, or farce called "Love a-la-mode," or any part thereof, be made perpetual. And the plaintiff waiving the account prayed by the bill, the court doth not think fit to direct any account. And it is further ordered that the defendants do pay to the plaintiff his costs of this suit, to be taxed, &c.

Decree for perpetual injunction restraining infringement of copyright and for payment of profits.

Upon the coming in of the Master's report, and on motion of the complainant's counsel, it is ordered and decreed by the court that the said report be confirmed and established, and that the said defendant B. and his agents and servants be perpetually enjoined from making, using, or vending to others to be used, any one or more locks substantially the same in mode of operation as the lock described in the letters patent in the said bill of complaint mentioned.

And the court doth further order and decree that the said defendant B. do forthwith pay unto the said complainant, Allen, the sum of eleven thousand seven hundred dollars, being the amount of profit found by the said Master's report to have been received by the said B. and his copartner S., mentioned in the said bill of complaint, from the sale of locks substantially the same in mode of operation as the lock described in the said letters patent, in violation of the exclusive right of the complainant, secured to him by the letters patent aforesaid. And the court doth further order and decree that the said defendant B. do pay to the said complainant Allen the costs of this suit to be taxed, &c.

505. The following are forms of decrees in the VIRGINIA STATE COURTS.

General Formulas.

Introduction of decree in a friendly suit; guardian ad litem assigned infant defendants in court, answers filed, &c.

This day came the plaintiff and filed his bill and R. R. is assigned guardian ad litem to the infant defendants L. L. and B. B. to defend their interests in this suit, and the said R. R. as such guardian ad litem filed the answer of the said infant defendants and his own answer to the bill of the plaintiffs, and J. J. and M. M. filed their answers, to which several answers the plaintiff by counsel replied generally, and the cause was docketed by consent, and coming on to be heard by like consent on the bill, answers, replications and exhibits filed, was argued by counsel. On consideration whereof, the court doth adjudge, order and decree, &c.

Introduction to decree in a case in which there are absent and unknown defendants, and in which a guardian ad litem has been assigned infant defendants at rules.

This cause, in which the plaintiffs have proceeded against the said M. P. in the mode prescribed by law against absent defendants, and as to the unknown heirs-at-law and distributees of X. Y., deceased, in the mode prescribed by law against unknown defendants, came on this day to be heard on the bill, the answers of the home defendants and of the infant defendants by their guardian ad litem, R. N., assigned to defend them in this suit, and on the answer of the said guardian ad litem to said infant defendants, general replications to the said answers, exhibits and examinations of witnesses, and was argued by counsel. On consideration whereof, the court doth adjudge, order and decree, &c.

Introduction to decree in which bill has been taken for confessed, as to part of the defendants, answers of the remainder, depositions, &c.

This cause came on this day to be heard on the bill taken for confessed as to the defendants, B. M. and J. W. on whom process has been duly served, they still failing to appear and plead, answer or demur to the said bill; on the answers of the defendants, L. W. and K. M., with general replications thereto, on the exhibits and examinations of witnesses, and was argued by counsel. On consideration whereof, the court doth adjudge, order and decree, &c.   •

Revival of suit against personal representatives of one of the defendants, against the real representatives of another, and decree.

The *scire facias* awarded against R. G., administrator *de bonis*

non with the will annexed of the defendant C. K. deceased, returnable to this term, having been returned executed on the said
R. G., administrator as aforesaid, and the said R. G. failing to show
any cause why this suit should not be revived against him in his
character aforesaid, it is ordered that the same be revived and
henceforth be conducted against the said R. G. as administrator *de
bonis non* with the will annexed of the said C. K., deceased; and
it further appearing that the *scire facias* awarded at the last term
against L. B., D. W. and N. O., children and heirs-at-law of the defendant R. M., deceased, returnable to this term, has been duly executed on the said L. B., D. W. and N. O., and they failing to show
any cause why this suit should not be revived and prosecuted
against them, as such children and heirs-at-law of the said R. M.,
deceased, it is ordered that the same be revived and henceforth be
conducted against the said L. B., D. W. and N. O. as defendants in
this suit; and thereupon the cause coming on to be heard, &c. was
argued by counsel. On consideration whereof, the court doth adjudge, order and decree, &c.

Usual conclusion of decree directing an account, &c.

And the said commissioner is directed to examine, state and settle the said several accounts, and make the several inquiries hereinbefore directed, and make report thereof to the court, together
with any matters specially stated deemed pertinent by himself or
which may be required by any of the parties to be so stated.

*Clause in decrees authorizing publication in lieu of personal ser-
vice.* (Code 1873, chap. 171, sec. 5.) Notice of the time and
place of taking the aforesaid accounts shall be published once a
week for four successive weeks in the Richmond ———, and this
notice shall be deemed sufficient as to all the parties interested in
lieu of personal service upon them, [except J. P. and W. D. H.
who shall have personal service.[69]]

Decree directing a sale of lands.

After usual introduction say : On consideration whereof the court
doth adjudge, order and decree that A. B., who is hereby appointed

---

[69] Exception in the discretion of the court.

66

a special commissioner for the purpose, do expose to sale at public auction, to the highest bidder, on the premises, the tract of land in the proceedings mentioned, after first advertising the time, place and terms of sale for —— days in some newspaper published in the city of Richmond and posting handbills of the sale in two or more public places in this county, upon the following terms: one-fourth of the purchase money to be paid in cash and the residue in two equal credit instalments at six and twelve months from the day of sale, the credit instalments carrying interest from the day of sale and the purchaser giving his bonds [or, negotiable notes] for the credit instalments, the title to the property to be retained until the full purchase money is paid and a conveyance directed by the court. And the said Commissioner A. B. is directed to report his proceedings hereunder to the court. But the said A. B. shall not receive any money from the purchaser at such sale or under this decree until he shall enter into bond, with sufficient security, in the clerk's office of this court, payable to the Commonwealth of Virginia, in the penalty of $—— and conditioned for the faithful discharge of his duties as such commissioner.

Decree confirming a report of sale.

This cause came on this day to be farther heard on the papers formerly read and on the report of A. B., the commissioner appointed by the decree entered herein on the —— day of ——, of the sale made by him of the tract of land called Glenmore in the proceedings mentioned, in obedience to said decree, to which report there is no exception, and was argued by counsel. On consideration whereof the court doth approve and confirm the said report and the said sale.

Clause in decree directing deed to purchaser.[70]

And the court doth further adjudge, order and decree that when and as soon as Robert M. shall have paid in full the two bonds to the said A. B. commissioner given for the credit instalments of his purchase, the said commissioner A. B. shall convey

---

[70] Until a sale is confirmed it is improper to direct a deed to be made to the purchaser.

by good and sufficient deed, with special warranty, unto the said Robert M. the property purchased by him as aforesaid, as follows: [Here describe fully the land sold.]

When commissioner reports funds in hand the cash proceeds of sale and bonds for future instalments of purchase-money, decree in reference thereto.

After decree confirming sale, say: And it appearing to the court from the said report that there are now in the hands of the said A. B. commissioner the sum of $———, the cash proceeds of sale, and the two bonds of the purchaser, Robert M., payable respectively at six and twelve months from their date, dated the ——— day of ———, the court doth adjudge, order and decree that the said commissioner A. B. do deposit the said sum of $——— in one of the banks in the city of ——— to the credit of the court in this cause and file a certificate of such deposit in the papers; and upon the said commissioner depositing the said sum in the said bank the following persons are authorized to check on attested extracts of this decree on the said ——— bank for the following sums, to-wit: Minor B. for $———, John R. B. for $———, Samuel S. for $———, and Alexander H. for $———. And the said commissioner is directed to collect the bonds of the said Robert M. for the credit instalments and deposit the amounts of his collections (deducting therefrom a commission of ——— per centum to himself for making such collections), as they are respectively made, in the said ——— bank to the credit of the court in this cause, and file certificates of such deposit in the papers; and when the first credit instalment is paid and deposited as aforesaid it is further adjudged, ordered and decreed that the following persons check on the said ——— bank on attested extracts of this decree for the following sums, to-wit: X. X. for $——— and Y. Y. for $———; and when the second credit instalment is paid and deposited as aforesaid it is adjudged, ordered and decreed that the following persons check on the said ——— bank, on attested extracts of this decree, for the following sums, viz: L. L. for $———, and B. B. for $———, and J. J. for $———.

DECREES FOR ACCOUNTS.

[The Court of Appeals of Virginia discountenance the practice of directing orders of account unnecessarily. In *Allen & als.* vs. *Smith*, 1 Leigh 252, the court said it was wrong to put the defendants to the trouble of rendering an account of rents and profits till it was ascertained that the plaintiff had a right to demand it. In *Cocke* vs. *Harrison, &c.*, 3 Rand. 494, the practice of ordering accounts of administration when a decree de bonis testatoris would be enough was discouraged.

When an order for account is proper it must be founded upon the pleadings and proofs. It should not be more extensive than the allegata and probata of the parties. Kent, Ch., in *Consequa* vs. *Fanning*, 3 John. Ch. R. 595.

When, to enable the plaintiffs to receive out of a particular fund, the rights of other persons must also be adjusted, the order must be so framed as to provide for the different persons interested in the fund, e. g. a decree for an account on a creditor's bill against a decedent's estate. See *Kinney's ex'ors* vs. *Harvey, &c.*, 2 Leigh 70. In a suit against an executor for distribution there may be a settlement of accounts between the testator and another person of whom the defendant is also executor. *Carter's ex'ors* vs. *Cutting, &c.*, 5 Munf. 223; and in such a suit a private account of the executor with his testator may be adjusted, although not specifically put in issue. *Ibid.*]

Decree for settlement of accounts.

This cause came on, &c. (as in preceding formula.) On consideration whereof, the court doth adjudge, order and decree that the defendant do render an account of the partnership transactions of the firm of A. B. & Co. in the bill mentioned (or an account of his dealings as, &c., in the bill mentioned,) before one of the commissioners of this court, who is directed to examine, state and settle the same, and make report thereof, with any matters specially stated, deemed pertinent by himself, or which may be required by any of the parties to be so stated.

Decree for settlement of administration and guardianship accounts of an intestate, also for settlement of administration account of intestate's estate, unless administrator will admit assets.

This cause in which the plaintiffs appear to have proceeded against the defendant, R. C. M., who is out of this Commonwealth, in the manner prescribed by law against absent defendants, and he still failing to appear and answer, came on this day to be heard on the order of publication as to said absent defendant, which has been duly published and posted as required by law, on the bill, which has been taken for confessed as to all the defendants, except M. T., the intestate of the defendant, P. S. J., on the answer of the said M. T., filed in his lifetime, with general replication thereto, and the exhibits filed, and was argued by counsel. On consideration whereof, the court doth adjudge, order and decree that the defendant, P. S. J., administrator of M. T., deceased, who was administrator *de bonis non*, with the will annexed, of S. W., deceased, and guardian of Sarah R. W., do render an account of the transactions of the said M. T. as administrator as aforesaid, and also an account of the transactions of the said M. T. as guardian as aforesaid, before one of the commissioners of this court; in rendering which accounts the said defendant is required to produce before the said commissioner, all necessary papers and vouchers in his possession or under his control, relating to the transactions of the said M. T., as administrator and guardian as aforesaid, in order to enable the said commississioner to state the said accounts, and the said commissioner is directed, in taking the said accounts, to regard as *prima facie* correct, but liable to be surcharged and falsified by the plaintiffs, any settled accounts of the said administrator and guardian, made under orders of a court of competent jurisdiction and returned to and ordered to be recorded by such court. And unless the defendant, P. S. J., administrator of M. T., deceased, shall admit assets of his intestate in his hands sufficient to satisfy any balances which may appear against his said intestate's estate, upon the settlement of the accounts above directed, then the court doth further adjudge, order and decree, that the said defendant render before the said commissioner an account of his own administration of the estate of the said M. T., deceased.

All which accounts the said commissioner will examine, state and settle, and report to the court, with any matter specially stated deemed pertinent by himself, or which may be required by any of the parties to be so stated.[n]

Decree overruling some exceptions to report of commissioner, sustaining others, and directing payment of balances found due.

This cause came on this day to be again heard on the papers

---

[n] If publication in lieu of personal service is directed, follow formula, p. 521, *ante*.

formerly read, and the report of commissioner W., made in pursuance of the interlocutory decree entered herein on the —————— day of ——————, and upon the exceptions of the plaintiffs and the defendant, P. S. J., administrator of M. T., deceased, returned with the said report, and also upon the exceptions of the said defendant this day filed, and the examination of witnesses and exhibits filed since the former hearing, and was argued by counsel. On consideration whereof the court doth overrule all the exceptions of the plaintiffs to the said report, and doth also overrule all the exceptions of the said defendant, P. S. J., administrator as aforesaid, except so far as one of the said exceptions of the said defendant refers to and embraces the first item in special statement F, made by the commissioner at the instance of the said defendant, to-wit: the item of $99 in said special statement, dated —————— day of ——————, for provisions furnished, as to which item and the interest thereon the court is of opinion that the same should have been allowed as a credit to the estate of the said M. T., deceased, and that the balance of $——————, reported by the commissioner as due to the plaintiffs, should be reduced by the said sum of ninety-nine dollars and the interest thereon, amounting to five dollars and ninety-five cents, leaving the sum of $—————— due the plaintiffs on the —————— day of ——————, for which, in the opinion of the court, they are entitled to a decree, and the court confirming the said report in all other respects; and it appearing therefrom by the special statement E, made by the commissioner at the instance of the said defendant P. S. J., administrator as aforesaid, that he has assets of his intestate in his hands sufficient to satisfy this decree, the court doth adjudge, order and decree that the defendant, P. S. J., administrator of M. T., deceased, do pay to the plaintiffs the said sum of $——————, with interest thereon, to be computed after the rate of six per centum per annum, from the —————— day of —————— until paid, and their costs by them about their suit in this behalf expended.

Decree for settlement of executorial or administration accounts.

This cause came on this day to be heard upon the bill, answer, replication and exhibits, and was argued by counsel, on consideration whereof the court doth adjudge, order and decree that the defendant,

N. A., do render an account of his administration of the estate of his intestate, W. F., (or an account of his executorial transactions as executor of the last will and testament of his testator, W. F., deceased) before one of the commissioners of this court, who is directed to examine, state and settle the same, and report the same to the court, with any matters specially stated deemed pertinent by himself, or which may be required by any of the parties to be so stated.

Decree for distribution of estate after return of commissioner's report made under next preceeding decretal order.

This cause came on this day to be farther heard on the papers formerly read, and the report of the commissioner made in pursuance of the order of the ——— day of ———, and was argued by counsel; on consideration whereof the court doth adjudge, order and decree that the defendant, F. F., executor of X. X., deceased, do pay to the plaintiff, P. F., the sum of $———, with interest at the rate of six per centum per annum from the ——— day of ——— until paid; to R. F., executor of N. F., deceased, the sum of $.———, with interest at the rate of six per centum per annum from the ——— day of ——— until paid. But the said P. F. and R. F., executor of N. F., deceased, are not to have the benefit of this decree until they shall respectively enter into bond, with sufficient security, in the clerk's office of this court in a penalty equal to double the sums decreed to them respectively, payable to the defendant, F. F., executor of .X. X., deceased, conditioned to refund a due proportion of any debts or demands which may hereafter appear against the estate of the said X. X., deceased, and of the costs attending the recovery of such debts or demands.

Decree for account, with special direction.

The court doth adjudge, order and decree that in the settlement of accounts, between the plaintiff and defendant, the defendant shall be charged with the sum of $626.——— borrowed by him from, &c., &c.; with interest at the rate of ——— per centum per annum, and the plaintiff is to be charged with, &c., &c.; and the court doth further adjudge, order and decree that the cause be referred to one of the commissioners of this court to state and take an account of all, &c., in stating which the charges before mentioned are to be made; and the parties, both plaintiff and defendant, are directed to produce, &c., all deeds or books and writings in their custody or power relating to the matters directed to be enquired of and are to submit to an examination upon all such matters before the said commissioner; and the said commissioner is directed to report the said account to the court, together with any matters specially stated deemed pertinent by himself or required by any party to be so stated.

Practical notes to decrees for account.

On reference to take and state an account the court may direct the parties to be examined on oath by the commissioner, 2 Rob. Pr. (old) 361, also to produce all books, papers and writings in their power. Ibid. In *Hart* vs. *Ten Eyck, &c.,* 2 John. Ch. Rep. 513, Chancellor Kent said, such orders were usually general in their terms, and it was for the party to object when any question was put that would lead to a violation of the restrictions imposed on such examinations.

When a party is examined before a commissioner, the rule obtained that the examination was in the nature of a supplemental bill of discovery, and the answers of the party examined, so far as responsive to the questions put, were evidence in his favor on the same principle, that the answer of a defendant to the bill is evidence against the complainant. 2 Rob. Pr. (old) 365, 366 and cases cited. Is this rule modified by the recent statutes of Virginia compelling parties to testify for the opposite party?

The persons authorized to take accounts are in the United States Courts their Masters in chancery and in the Virginia State Courts their Commissioners. On the manner of procedure before them, the notice to be given, the manner of making objection before them and exceptions to their reports, reference may be had to the Code 1873, ch. 171, §§ 4–10, and to the 73–84 rules of practice of U. S. Supreme Court.

In a creditor's suit the statute of limitations ceases to run against all debts from time of a decree for account. *Ewing's adm'or & als.* vs. *Ferguson's adm'or & als.,* 33 Grat. 548.

Accounts generally: Party applying for an account, though plaintiff, decreed against. *Hill* vs. *Sutherland,* 1 Wash. 128; *Fitzgerald* vs. *Jones,* 1 Munf. 150; *Braxton* vs. *Gregory,* Wythe's R. 73; *Todd* vs. *Bowyer,* 1 Munf. 447; Carr, J., in *Randolph* vs. *Randolph,* 3 Rand. 398.

After decree for an account, though no report, plaintiff not permitted to dismiss his bill. *Lashley* vs. *Hogg*, 11 Ves. 602.

Equity jurisdiction maintained: Hunter vs. *Spottswood*, 1 Wash. 145; *Bland* vs. *Wyatts*, 1 H. & M. 542; *Hickman* vs. *Stout*, 2 Leigh 6; *Sturtevant* vs. *Goode*, 5 Leigh 83.

Equity jurisdiction refused: Randolph vs. *Randolph*, 2 Call 537; *Smith* vs. *Marx*, 2 Rand. 449; *Poage* vs. *Wilson*, 2 Leigh 490; *Bassett* vs. *Cunningham*; 7 Leigh 402.

In *Eustace* vs. *Gaskins*, 1 Wash. 188, it was said that the value and profits of land being in the nature of damages should be ascertained by a jury, not by commissioners; but, afterwards, in *Roberts's widow* vs. *Stanton*, 2 Munf. 129, it was held not to be error for the court of equity to direct commissioners instead of a jury to state and report an account of the profits of land.

It is a general rule that when a party claims to charge another by virtue of an account rendered he must take that account altogether and not garble or falsify the same, unless he can surcharge and falsify it either by showing errors in calculation or by showing from other testimony that it is incorrect: *Freeland, &c.* vs. *Cocke's representatives*, 3 Munf. 352; See *Waggoner* vs. *Gray's adm'ors*, 2 H. & M. 603; but this rule is altered in cases in which the party keeping the account holds some trust or confidence for the faithful execution of which he is required to keep an accurate account. See *Robertson & als.* vs. *Archer's adm'or*, 5 Rand. 319.

It is not sufficient in an account to charge balances of other accounts as rendered and agreed—the accounts alleged to have been agreed must be produced, if in existence, and proven as alleged, unless there be proof of the defendant's acknowledgement of the justice of such accounts or of his promise of payment. *Lewis's ex'or* vs. *Bacon's legatees & als.*, 3 H. & M. 89. In this case a creditor kept an account current with his debtor and also an interest account, in which he charged interest on the several payments to the same period and charged in the *account current* the balance appearing in the *interest* account. A balance being then struck and a new account opened, in which interest was charged on that balance, thus consisting of principal and interest, *held* to be compound interest and not allowable.

An acknowledgement by *feme covert* is not sufficient to establish an account against her husband, though it be for articles furnished her before her marriage. *Sheppard's ex'or* vs. *Starke & wife*, 3 Munf. 29.

An injunction is granted to a judgment, and an account directed between the parties, credit ought not to be given to the plaintiff at law by the commissioner for certain items not exhibited to the jury, nor mentioned in the answer, and which are prior to the commencement of the suit. *Lipscomb's adm'or* vs. *Littlepage's adm'or*, 1 H. & M. 454. Account directed after a purchaser at fraudulent sale refuses obedience to order of court requiring delivery of slave. See *McNew* vs. *Smith*, 5 Grat. 84.

The attorney in a cause is not a competent commissioner to take an account ordered in it. *Brown's adm'or* vs. *Brown & als.*, 29 Grat. 697.

To make an account rendered an "account stated" there must either be an actual statement or adjustment of the account by the parties by going over the items together and striking the balance or an admission by one party of the correctness of the balance struck by the other, or an admission in some other way of the correctness of the account. *Robertson & als.* vs. *Wright & als.*, 17 Grat. 534.

Impeaching a settled account, in matters not alleged in the bill, by proceeding before the commissioner. *Shugart's adm'or* vs. *Thompson*, 10 Leigh 434. See *Corbin* vs. *Mills's ex'ors & als.*, 19 Grat. 465, cited post.

Decree confirming account reversed for error on its face, though no exceptions filed. *Walker* vs. *Walke*, 2 Wash. 195. See *Cookus* vs. *Peyton*, 1 Grat. 431.

A debtor transferred bonds and conveyed his distributive interest in his father's real and personal estate to avoid the payment of his debt; upon a bill to subject it there should be an account of what the father died possessed of. *Greer* vs. *Wright*, 6 Grat. 154.

It appearing from the evidence (though not shown in the pleadings) that certain transactions sought to be settled in equity arose out of a partnership for gambling, the accounts should be recommitted and an inquiry directed into the consideration on which the claims of the parties are founded. *Watson* vs. *Fletcher*, 7 Grat. 1.

On a bill by creditors to set aside as fraudulent the trust deed of a debtor for payment of his debts, though the deed is sustained, the plaintiffs are entitled to an account. *Marks* vs. *Hill*, 15 Grat. 400; *Penn* vs. *Spencer*, 17 Grat. 85.

In the absence of any proof to the contrary, a commissioner who is directed to take an account of the trust fund and the trust debts, in stating the accounts of the debts, should take the amount of the debts as stated in the deed. *French* vs. *Townes*, 10 Grat. 513.

Laches for nine years after dissolution of a partnership and after death of the other partner, under the circumstances, did not deprive plaintiff of right to an account. *Marsteller* vs. *Weaver*, 1 Grat. 391. But see Code, ch. 146, sec. 8.

When real estate of testator necessary for payment of debts; not improper to direct an account of rents and profits from his death, and by whom received. *McCandlish* vs. *Edloe*, 3 Grat. 315.

A defendant unsuccessful at law in his defence to a suit on an indemnifying bond, relying upon fraud in a deed, comes into equity on the ground of after-discovered evidence, and establishes the fraud as to some of the debts secured; equity jurisdiction being established, the court will not direct a new trial at law, but will retain the cause and allow the deed to be impeached:—it was a proper case for an account of the trust subject, and a disposition of its proceeds among the parties according to their respective rights. *Billups* vs. *Sears*, 5 Grat. 31.

Executor and administrator.

In *Burwell's ex'or* vs. *Anderson's adm'or, &c.*, 3 Leigh 348, the Court of Appeals prepared a formula exhibiting the manner in which accounts of executors and administrators should be settled. See this form in Sands's Forms, pp. 185-188.

A decree against an executor or administrator for a balance due on his administration account ought not to be "that he pay the same out of the estate of his decedent in his hands to be administered" but as his own proper debt. *Sheppard's ex'or* vs. *Starke & als.*, 3 Munf. 29. See *Moore* vs. *Ferguson & als.*, 2 Munf. 421; *Barr* vs. *Barr's adm'ors*, 2 H. & M. 26.

But it is error to make a personal decree against an administrator without an account or admission of assets in his hands sufficient to satisfy the decree. *Wills's adm'or* vs. *Dunn's adm'or*, 5 Grat. 384.

It is error to render a personal decree against administrators upon a claim against their testator without having first ordered an account of their testator's estate. *Lincoln* vs. *Stern*, 23 Grat. 816.

The court cannot decree a distribution in favor of persons not parties to the suit. *Sheppard's ex'or* vs. *Starke & ux*, 3 Munf. 29.

In a suit for distribution though there is a decree for the plaintiff, yet if the administrator has been in no default he shall have costs. *Eidson* vs. *Fountaine's adm'or & al.*, 9 Grat. 286.

The account of an executor having been settled by commissioners appointed by the court before which the will was proved, is not of course to be referred again to a commissioner, on a bill to surcharge and falsify; but some evidence should be exhibited to that effect, or something improper in the account should be disclosed in the answer; otherwise such order of account should not be made, but the bill should be dismissed. *Wyllie et ux.* vs. *Venable's ex'or*, 4 Munf. 369.

When the answer of a defendant executor asserts a right affirmatively in opposition to the plaintiff's demand, the defendant is as much bound to establish its assertions by indifferent testimony as the plaintiff is to sustain his bill. It would be monstrous indeed if an executor, when called on to account, were permitted *to swear himself into a part of his testator's estate*. *Beckwith* vs. *Butler & als.*, 1 Wash. 225.

An executor's account rendered on oath is *prima facie* evidence of the sums received by him for the estate of his testator, and of the times when received. *Cavendish* vs. *Fleming*, 3 Munf. 198.

An executor is not to be charged with the debts due to the estate of his testator, *at the time when they became due*, but only at the time when he actually received them, excepting such debts as are lost by his negligence or improper conduct. *Cavendish* vs. *Fleming*, 3 Munf. 198. He is, save when debts are thus lost, only chargeable with interest on his actual receipts. *Ibid.*

An executor or administrator may, with propriety, be credited for deductions made by him from accounts left by his testator or intestate, for collection; it appearing that his course might have produced benefit to the estate, the court not perceiving that he could have had any interest in making the deductions. *McCall* vs. *Peachy's adm'or*, 3 Munf. 288.

An executor or administrator is not chargeable specifically with tobacco received by him, and not disbursed on account of his testator's estate, but only with the price actually received for the tobacco, where that can be ascertained; and where not, with the then current value thereof. *Ibid.*

Where an *ex parte* settlement of an administration account has taken place before commissioners appointed by the court in which the executor or administrator qualified; if the legatees afterwards bring a suit in chancery for a new examination and settlement of such account, the *vouchers* in support thereof, if they be not ostensible, should be presumed to have existed, and the *onus probandi* thrown on the adverse party. *Ibid.*

In such case, if the vouchers or official copies of them be produced, the plaintiffs may nevertheless controvert the articles intended to be justified by them. *Ibid.*

An article ought to be allowed on the oath of the defendant, if it be of such a nature that the expense probably must have been incurred, or that, perhaps, a voucher for it could not have been procured; for example, mourning for the widow, midwife's fees, services performed by a negro carpenter, and the like. *Ibid.*

When a commissioner is stating accounts between executors and the estate of their testator, if one of them who had for collection the evidences of debt due the estate, which might have been collected by him, be dead, his representative cannot object to his estate's being charged with those debts unless the means be furnished the devisees of charging the surviving executor therewith; *Carter's ex'or* vs. *Cutting et ux.*, 5 Munf. 223, and in such case each executor's private account with testator and with his co-executor, and all accounts that are necessary to make a just settlement of the matters in controversy ought to be taken if requested, though not specifically put in issue in the cause. *Ibid.*

To make an executor answerable for paper money, at the scale of the day on which he received it, is in general wrong; but, if he hath charged himself so, and pointed out no other mode of adjusting it, he shall be bound by his own act. *Granberry's ex'or* vs. *Granberrys*, 1 Wash. 246.

Where an executor claims a sum of money advanced to him by his testator, in his lifetime, as a gift, and not a loan; this claim will not be allowed on the executor's oath, and slight circumstances; especially (as in this case) when the name of the executor is present to the testator's mind while making his will and the object of his bounty. *Ruth et al.* vs. *Owens*, 2 Rand. 507.

An administrator is entitled to credit in his account as of the date of division of estate for moneys expended in permanent improvements on the real estate of the heirs. *Jackson's adm'or* vs. *Jackson's heirs*, 1 Grat. 143.,

To ascertain the amount of credit in this case the cost of improvements subject to deduction for decay from the time of erection to date of the division would be the proper measure. *Ibid.*

The rule that where a party relies on account furnished by the other party, he is bound to take it altogether and admit the debits as well as the credits, unless he can surcharge and falsify it by proofs, is not applicable to an executor's account (not rendered before commissioners appointed for the settlement of the same); this was so held because the executor was under a moral and equitable, and indeed a legal obligation to furnish those to whom he was accountable the means of charging him to the full extent of his liabilities.[72] *Robertson & als.* vs. *Archer, adm'or*, 5 Rand. 319.

The rule that administration accounts, audited *ex parte* by commissioners appointed by the proper court, returned to the court and recorded, are to be taken as *prima facie* correct, liable to be surcharged and falsified on proof adduced by any party interested, rests not on the ground that such audited accounts stand on the same footing as stated accounts between parties, but mainly on the long established practice of the country, and on the supposed integrity of the tribunal provided by law for the adjustment thereof: therefore such audited accounts are only to be corrected in the particulars in which they are proved to be erroneous, unless corruption in the tribunal itself be established; and though great and numerous errors appear, or even though the executor or administrator appear to have taken an unfair advantage, does not return to the court, or exhibit to the auditors an inventory or appraisement of the estate, yet the audited accounts are to be taken as *prima facie* evidence, to be corrected so far as surcharged and falsified by proof. *Newton et ux.* vs. *Poole*, 12 Leigh 112. In *Street's heirs* vs. *Street*, 11 Leigh, 498, after an administration account had been

---

[72] See *White* vs. *Lady Lincoln*, 8 Ves. 363.

audited by the commissioners of a county court, the vouchers were required to be produced.

Upon a bill to surcharge and falsify an executor's account, audited by commissioners of county court, and approved and recorded, though plaintiff is held to specification of items of surcharge and falsification, yet it is always competent for him to show that the account is erroneous upon its face, and (without controverting the items) to show that they have been so arranged as to produce results injurious to him. *Garrett, ex'or, &c.* vs. *Carr & wife, &c.*, 3 Leigh 407.

The court will not, however, decree an account upon a general allegation that accounts so settled are erroneous; the accounts should be impeached on specific grounds of surcharge and falsification. *Corbin & als.* vs. *Mills's ex'ors & als.*, 19 Grat. 438.

When an account has been ordered upon a proper bill, if additional objections are discovered in the progress of the cause, the plaintiff may raise the objections before the commissioner by proper specifications in writing and the defendant may meet the objections by an affidavit, to which affidavit the same weight would be given as to an answer if the matter had been alleged in the bill. Joynes, J., in *Corbin & als.* vs *Millers's ex'ors & als.*, 19 Grat. 465.

Executor sells a slave belonging to his testator's estate, the sale not being necessary for the payment of debts, and he re-purchases the slave and thereupon holds him as his own. The slave is the property of the estate, and the executor shall account for his annual hires, with interest thereon, though he was not in fact hired out by the executor. *Rosser, ex'or of Wood* vs. *Depriest et als.*, 5 Grat. 6.

An executor takes bonds for purchases made at a sale by himself of testator's personal estate, and it does not appear when these bonds were paid off. He will be charged with the principal of the bonds in the year when they fell due, but with interest only from the end of the year. *Ibid.*

An administrator having failed to render an account of crops, rents and hires which came to his hands, proof of the estimated net annual value may be resorted to for the purpose of charging him. *Wills's adm'or* vs. *Dunn's adm'or*, 5 Grat. 384.

Bonds taken by an administrator not necessary for the reimbursement or indemnity of decedent's estate, will be turned over to the administrator de bonis non as unadministered assets. *Clarke* vs. *Wells's adm'or*, 6 Grat. 475.

An executor having the management of both real and personal estate, and making disbursements in the administration of the estate, and also for the support of the family; in the settlement of his accounts he is to be credited in his administration account with his disbursements as executor, and in his account of the real estate, with his disbursements for the family. *Hobson* vs. *Yancey et als.*, 2 Grat. 73.

Executors not keeping their accounts properly are to be held to a rigid accountability, yet this is not of itself sufficient to deprive them of their commissions. *Kee's ex'or* vs. *Kee's creditor*, 2 Grat. 116.

An administrator or executor is not bound to sue for the recovery of a debt due the estate where it is apparent the debtor is not able to pay it. *Mitchell's adm'or* vs. *Trotter & wife*, 7 Grat. 136.

An executor is not chargeable with interest on a legacy, payable to an infant, before a guardian has been appointed, and he has received notice of such appointment. *Cavendish* vs. *Fleming*, 3 Munf. 198. See also *Dilliard* vs. *Tomlinson et als.*, 1 Munf. 183.

An executor or administrator is chargeable with interest in all cases where he has received it, and also where paper money or specie remained in his hands more than a reasonable time (which in this case was said to be six months) without being applied to the purposes of the estate. *McCall* vs. *Peachy's adm'or*, 3 Munf. 288.

If an executor think that lending on interest the money in his hands would be dangerous, or find a difficulty in procuring borrowers, he ought to apply to the chancellor for his direction, or pay the money into court. *Granberry's ex'or* vs. *Granberrys*, 1 Wash. 246.

The propriety or impropriety of charging an executor with interest must always depend on the particular circumstances in each case. The general rule adopted in *Granberry* vs. *Granberry* is not deemed inflexible, and there may be strong cases in which to prevent gross injustice it may bend. Such a case was that of *Fitzgerald* vs. *Jones*, 1 Munf. 150. And it seems unreasonable that where a very large sum has been received in the last month of one year and paid away again in the first month of the succeeding year, or vice versa, to burden the executor on the one hand, or the estate on the other, with a full year's interest on such sum. See opinion of Tucker, president, in *Burwell's ex'ors* vs. *Anderson, adm'or*, 3 Leigh 364. See *Wood's ex'or* vs. *Garnett*, 6 Leigh 272.

Interest is not usually allowed upon conjectural and unliquidated hires. *Baird* vs. *Bland*, 5 Munf. 492. For until they are ascertained the party is in no default for not paying. *Shields, adm'or*, vs. *Anderson*, 3 Leigh 729. If, however, an executor has hired out the slaves, and has actually received the hires, then he will be chargeable with interest on the money so received as upon money received by him in ordinary cases. *Quarles's ex'or* vs. *Quarles*, 2 Munf. 321. In the case of *Cross's curatrix* vs. *Cross's legatees*, 4 Grat. 257, it was held by the Court of Appeals that although there may be circumstances which may exempt an executor from being charged with interest on balances in his hands, yet in general an ex-

ecutor is chargeable with interest on such balances; and where, in an
ex parte settlement by commissioners of an executor's accounts, the
commissioners improperly omit an interest account, and charge the
executor with interest, that is cause for surcharging and falsifying
the account. *Burwell's ex'ors* vs. *Anderson, adm'or, &c.,* 3
Leigh 348.

It is error to direct the account of the executor to be closed and
the account settled on the principles of ordinary debtor and creditor, before the debts outstanding have been ascertained to be due
from the estate. *Boyd* vs. *Boyd,* 3 Grat. 109.

When an executor has a claim against the estate of his testator
depending on the *quantum meruit* only, he may exhibit his bill in
equity against his co-executors and the legatees to have such claim
established and fixed at a certain sum, and in it he ought to state
with reasonable certainty his own estimate of his services; if he
does not, his bill ought not to be dismissed but he should be required to amend it. *Baker* vs. *Baker & als.,* 3 Munf. 222.

It is error to decree against the sureties of an executor for the
balance of an account composed of rents received from real estate
as well as receipts from the personalty, without its first appearing
that the disbursements on account of the real estate and the expenses of the family had absorbed all receipts from the real estate,
so that it might be evident that the balance was from the personal
estate. *Hobson* vs. *Yancey,* 2 Grat. 72.

The sureties of an administrator of a surety of an administrator
are not entitled to have a re-settlement of the administration accounts of this last mentioned administrator upon his intestate's
estate, settled in a creditors' and distributees' suit, when the sureties
were not parties. *Cookus* vs. *Peyton,* 1 Grat. 431.

An executor or administrator is properly chargeable with all
the decedent's personalty which either did or by due diligence
might have come to his hands. *Burnley* vs. *Duke,* 1 Rand. 113;
Wills vs. *Dunn,* 5 Grat. 385; *Lacy* vs. *Stamper,* 27 Grat. 47, even
though he got it from another State, *Andrews* vs. *Avory,* 14 Grat.
240; and when the will authorizes the personal representative to
sell real estate or receive the rents and profits thereof, he is also
responsible for that. See Code 1873, ch. 126, §§ 6–13, ch. 127, § 2.
He is liable for the proceeds of sales of the property, unless he
shows that loss occurred without any default on his part. 4 Min.
Inst. 1229.

As to responsibility of sheriff to whom an estate committed and
of his sureties, see *Cocke* vs. *Harrison,* 3 Rand. 494; *Dabney's
adm'or & als.* vs. *Smith & als.,* 5 Leigh 13; *Douglass's ex'or* vs.
Stumps & als., 5 Leigh 392; *Mosby's adm'or & als.* vs. *Mosby's
adm'or,* 9 Grat. 584, 601; *Hutcheson, sh'ff.,* vs. *Priddy,* 12 Grat. 85.

Debts collected by executor charged to him as at the time of collection. *Cavendish* vs. *Fleming,* 3 Munf. 198; *Quarles* vs. *Quarles,*

2 Munf. 321. Such debts as he loses by negligence, &c. charged as at the time they ought to have been received. Code 1873, ch. 128, sec. 7.

Credits to a personal representative are, (when he settles his accounts in time) a commission for his services, Code 1873, ch. 126, § 25; funeral expenses and charges of administration, lawyers' fees, clerk hire under special circumstances, *Lindsey* vs. *Howerton*, 2 H. & M. 9; *Hipkins* vs. *Bernard*, 4 Munf. 83; and this in preference to claims of creditors, *Nimmo's ex'or* vs. *Com.*, 4 H. & M. 57. All debts properly paid to be allowed, *Cookus* vs. *Peyton*, 1 Grat. 431; *Morris* vs. *Morris*, 4 Grat. 293; *Williams* vs. *Williams*, 11 Grat. 95. Debts due himself barred by statute of limitations not allowed though acknowledged by his co-executor, *Sieg* vs. *Acord*, 21 Grat. 369; demand for nursing the decedent in his last illness by the executor (who was a son-in-law of decedent) denied, *Williams* vs. *Stonestreet*, 3 Rand. 559; no credit allowed him for debts paid by him when he knows that they were for illegal consideration or barred by lapse of time, or otherwise could not be recovered. See Code 1873, ch. 128, § 7.

Interest on executors' and administrators' accounts.

Cases: *Jones* vs. *Williams*, 2 Call 105; *Fitzgerald* vs. *Jones*, 1 Munf. 150; *Burwell* vs. *Anderson*, 3 Leigh 364; *Handly* vs. *Snodgrass*, 9 Leigh 484; *Street* vs. *Street*, 11 Leigh 498; *Newton* vs. *Poole*, 12 Leigh 112; *Kee* vs. *Kee*, 2 Grat. 116; *Corbin* vs. *Mills*, 19 Grat. 458; *Jackson* vs. *Jackson*, 1 Grat. 143. [No interest in certain cases on estimated or conjectural rents, hires and profits, *Whitehouse* vs. *Hines*, 1 Munf. 557; *Dillard* vs. *Tomlinson*, 1 M. 183; *Baird* vs. *Bland*, 5 M. 240; *Payne* vs. *Graves*, 5 Leigh 561; *Roper* vs. *Wren*, 6 Leigh 38; but interest allowed upon estimated or conjectural profits, whether actually received or not, if it was the fiduciary's duty to have received them. *Cross* vs. *Cross*, 4 Grat. 265; *Rosser* vs. *Depriest*, 5 Grat. 6.]

When the debts are paid, or there has been time to pay them, and the executor has only legacies and distributive shares to deal with, the reason of the indulgence to the executor is at an end and he is thenceforward treated and settled with upon the footing of an ordinary debtor and creditor. 4 Min. Inst. 1238.

Interest runs, and is not affected by the absence abroad of the creditor, nor even by the non-existence of the person entitled to the money, nor as is presumed by his hostile alienage. 4 Min. Inst. 1239 and cases cited, *Burwell* vs. *Anderson*, 3 Leigh 438; *Anderson* vs. *Burwell*, 6 Grat. 405; *Bourne* vs. *Mechan*, 1 Grat. 292; *Lyon* vs. *Magagnos*, 7 Grat. 879. The personal representative should have invested it in some interest-bearing fund or have paid the same into court to be so invested; and failing to do so retaining the fund he should account for the interest. *Ibid.*

'hether interest ought to be charged in an administration ac-
it is a question the decision of which may be affected by ex-
ieous testimony, and the Court of Appeals therefore refused (no
>ption having been taken to the report on that ground in the
·t below) to allow the exception to be taken in the appellate
·t. *White's ex'ors* vs. *Johnson & als,* 2 Munf. 285.

ı *Strother* vs. *Hull,* 23 Grat. 652, an administrator with the
annexed was charged with the furniture of the decedent,
ıgh he occupied the house which the decedent had occupied
decedent's children lived with him.

ı *Strother* vs. *Hull,* 23 Grat. 652, the testator died in 1851,
ing infant children : by his will he directed a division of his
te to be made in 1861, January 1; meanwhile he directed his
utor to "manage the estate"; the executor was charged with
pound interest as in *Garrett* vs. *Carr.*

testator "desired that no interest shall be demanded on a
cy, but that the executor pay it off as soon as money can be
:d, by selling certain property," no interest was demandable
l a reasonable time for raising the money had elapsed: after
:h, if the executor improperly withheld payment, he was
geable with interest. *Patton* vs. *Williams, &c.,* 3 Munf. 59.

n executor ought not to be charged with interest on small an-
balances, when it appears that he was in no fault in not pay-
:hem over to legatees, and never applied the money to his own
Wood's ex'ors vs. *Garnett,* 6 Leigh 271.

ı *Dunbar* vs. *Woodcock,* 10 Leigh 629, a cause decided in
ch, 1840, a decree for interest upon a balance, consisting en-
y of interest, found due in settlement at the close of the ac-
ıts in 1816, was reversed, and the court below directed to enter
cree allowing interest from the final decree.

n executor is entitled to interest on a balance due him from
estate of his testator, *Jones's ex'or* vs. *Williams,* 2 Call 102.

'here the failure to bring an executor to a settlement appears
ive proceeded from neglect of the residuary legatees, without
wilful default upon his part, interest ought not to be charged
ıe balance due from him to the estate, except from the date of
lecree; neither in such case, ought interest to be allowed him
ayments to the legatees before the decree, though made in bonds
:h carried interest. *Fitzgerald, ex'or* vs. *Jones,* 1 Munf. 150.

he principle established in *Garrett, &c.* vs. *Carr, &c.,* 3 Leigh
applied where the estate is to be put out at interest. The
utor not choosing to do so is to be considered as a borrower,
annually charged with interest, and such interest, not the
:ipal, is to be applied to the disbursements. *Handly* vs. *Snod-*
;, 9 Leigh 484.

ı administrator takes bonds for purchases made at a sale by

himself of testator's personal property, and it does not appear when these bonds were paid off; he will be charged with the principal of the bonds in the year when they fell due, but with interest thereon from the end of the year only. *Rosser* vs. *Depriest*, 5 Grat. 6.

In *Peale* vs. *Hickle*, 9 Grat. 437, a balance was found in the executor's hands in 1826 when his account was settled. The family ceased to live together in 1846. The executor was charged with interest from the last date on the whole balance, principal and interest: but was not charged with interest from 1826 to 1846.

A commissioner having made a special statement at the instance of the administrator, he cannot object that it is not stated on the basis of an executorial account. *Kelly* vs. *Love*, 20 Grat. 124. Interest charged against an executor during the war. *Ibid.*

Executorial accounts should always be brought to a close as soon as the debts are paid and the transactions will permit. Payments to legatees and advances to children should never enter into the general account, both to prevent confusion and because the accounts with them are not to be adjusted upon the principle of the general account. For after the balance of the general account is struck and the portion of the several legatees or distributees ascertained, the account between them and the executor is strictly an account between debtor and creditor. When such balance is struck, the portion of each should be carried to a separate account with him individually. Tucker, P. in *Garrett, ex'or* vs. *Carr, &c.*, 3 Leigh 416.

ACCOUNTS OF GUARDIANS.

Form of guardian's account. The form of guardian's account in Sands's Forms, pp. 192–195, conforms with the principles settled in *Garrett* vs. *Carr*, 1 Rob. R. 196.

A second guardian of an infant has no authority to file a bill in his own name against a former guardian, for an account of his transactions in relation to the ward's estate. *Lemon, guardian*, vs. *Hansbarger*, 6 Grat. 301. But an infant may by his next friend call the acting guardian, or any preceding guardian to account by a bill in chancery; in such case, the bill must be in his own name by his next friend. Ibid. (See *Sillings et als.* vs. *Bumgardner, guardian*, 9 Grat. 273).

A guardian of infants is entitled to compensation for their support, though he may have promised their friends that he would not make any charge for it, and has kept no account against them. *Armstrong's heirs* vs. *Walkup and others*, 9 Grat. 372.

A payment made to the husband of one of those who had been wards, and who is the guardian of another of them, though intended to be a payment to all, is not to be credited against the third ward, who is then an adult, she not having authorized him to receive it; but is to be credited against the husband and wife, and his ward. Ibid.

The accounts of the three wards should be stated separately from the commencement, or at least from the, time when their expenses differ in amount. Ibid.

One of the wards being still an infant, there should not be a joint decree in their favor though made with the consent of the next friend of the infant. Ibid.

The principle on which interest should be charged to guardians in their account, as settled in *Garret, ex'or, &c.* vs. *Carr and ux.*, 1 Rob. 196, has been incorporated into the Code of 1873, chap. 123, §§ 10, 11, 12.

When the property of the infants consists of a single claim and the amount received upon it by the guardian is ascertained, and there is no doubt as to the amount due from the guardian to the wards, the court may decree against him for the amount though no account has been taken. *Sage & als* vs. *Hammonds*, 27 Grat. 651.

From the termination of the guardianship, the accounts between guardian and ward will be stated as between debtor and creditor; sums paid after that time by the guardian to the ward will be credited at the respective dates of such payments, so as to stop interest *pro tanto* from those dates. *Garrett, ex'or* vs. *Carr*, 1 Rob. R. 196; *Cunningham* vs. *Cunningham*, 4 Grat. 43; *Armstrong* vs. *Walkup*, 12 Grat. 608.

A reasonable time ought to be allowed a guardian to put out the ward's money at interest; in this case six months was thought to be such time. *Hooper & als.* vs. *Royster & wife*, 1 Munf. 119; *Armstrong* vs. *Walkup*, 12 Grat. 608. See Code, chap. 123, sec. 12.

A guardian unnecessarily selling bank stock; he and his sureties held liable for its present value and all dividends accruing thereon, *Bank of Virginia* vs. *Craig*, 6 Leigh 399, and no commissions allowed him on the value of the stock. *Ibid.*

In *Griffith & als.* vs. *Bird & als.*, 22 Grat. 73, G. was the guardian of his two children, maintained and educated them at his own expense, and made no charge against them. He died in February, 1861, up to which time his estate was amply able to pay his debts, but by losses incurred since his death it became insufficient. In a question between creditors of G. his two children for whom he was guardian are not to be charged in the guardian account with the expense of their maintenance or education.

When a guardian justified in applying part of the principal of a ward's estate to permanent improvements. *Jackson* vs. *Jackson*, 1 Grat. 143.

A guardian paying sums of money to a mother for the support of a ward but in such a way that it is impossible to say how much should be allowed for a reasonable annual support to the ward. *Cunningham* vs. *Cunningham*, 4 Grat. 43.

It is error to decree against a guardian for a gross sum, consisting of principal and interest, with interest upon such sum from the date of the decree. *Cunningham* vs. *Cunningham*, 4 Grat. 43.

. A guardian, though he may have promised the friends of infants that he would make no charge, and in fact kept no accounts against them, is entitled to compensation for their support. *Armstrong* vs. *Walkup*, 9 Grat. 372.

The accounts of the three wards in this case should be stated separately from the commencement, or at least from the time their expenses differed in amount. *Armstrong* vs. *Walkup*, 9 Grat. 372.

A guardian has his female wards in his family and treats them as his children, but they are required to work as children might be: guardian allowed for their support, and they allowed nothing for their services. *Armstrong* vs. *Walkup*, 12 Grat. 608.

Suit maintained against a guardian and his sureties, though guardian lives out of the State and has no property in it. *Pratt* vs. *Wright*, 13 Grat. 175.

A creditor for the support of the ward, though he has taken the bond of the guardian, may proceed in equity against the guardian and his sureties for the payment of his debt. *Barnum* vs. *Frost*, 17 Grat. 398.

A guardian is not authorized to use the principal of the ward's real estate for the support and education of the ward, and when such use is made of the principal of the ward's realty without first getting the order of the court to authorize its being so used, the Chancery Court is not authorized by the statute, Code 1873, ch. 123, § 13, to sanction such an application. *Rinker, &c.* vs. *Streit*, 33 Grat. 663. The expenditure of a ward's personalty for his support may be sanctioned after it has been made. *Ibid.* See *Hooper, &c.* vs. *Royster, &c.*, 1 Munf. 119; *Barton* vs. *Bowen, &c.*, 27 Grat. 849.

A decree treating L. as guardian without proof of his legal appointment and due qualification as such held erroneous. *Lincoln's adm'ors* vs. *Stern, &c.*, 23 Grat. 816.

A decree was entered against administrators of L. who was alleged to be a guardian; the decree was a personal decree against the administrators; it was error to enter a personal decree against them without having first ordered an account of their testator's estate. *Ibid.*

A ward's estate is not relieved from liability for his support by the undertaking of his guardian to pay it: the creditor may proceed to subject the ward's estate to the payment of her expenses. *Barnum* vs. *Frost*, 17 Grat. 398.

A ward soon after coming of age filed a bill against the administratrix of her guardian for an account. The suit lingered for twenty-four years, and then there was a decree in favor of the ward.

The ward not being able to obtain satisfaction of the decree filed a bill against the surety of the guardian. It was held that the statute of limitations did not bar the claim, that the lapse of time during which the ward was prosecuting her suit against the administratrix of the guardian furnished no ground for the exoneration of the surety. *Roberts* vs. *Colvin*, 3 Grat. 358.

The sureties of the guardian and the guardian himself may be jointly sued. *Magruder* vs. *Goodwyn's adm'or & als.*, 2 P. & H. 561.

Interest was not allowed against the guardian in the case of *Tabb* vs. *Boyd*, 4 Call 453.

In *Cunningham* vs. *Cunningham*, 4 Grat. 43, two months were allowed the guardian to collect and invest the annual proceeds of the ward's estate. See *Hooper, &c.* vs. *Royster*, 1 Munf. 119. In *Armstrong* vs. *Walkup*, 12 Grat. 608, the guardian was allowed six months. But now by statute thirty days allowed to invest moneys received for the ward. See Code 1873, ch. 123, sec. 12.

A guardian who receives the money of his wards and does not invest it, but retains it in his own hands, is to be charged interest thereon from the date of its receipt, and not from the end of the thirty days allowed by the statute to the guardian for making investments. *Snavely* vs. *Harkrader & als.*, 29 Grat. 113.

In *Sayers* vs. *Cassell & als.*, 23 Grat. 525, the guardian not having been allowed anything for the board, clothing and schooling of his ward, under the circumstances of the case should not be charged with interest upon the small amount of the money of his ward in his hands.

A guardian who received money for his wards in 1857 and instead of investing it for his wards purchased a slave for himself and afterwards on being removed as guardian paid his successor in Confederate money, was charged with what he received, with compound interest, and was refused compensation for his services as guardian. *Jennings* vs. *Jennings*, 22 Grat. 313.

Guardian held liable for an uncollected debt due ward. *Ergenbright & als.* vs. *Ammon's adm'or & als.*, 26 Grat. 490.

The guardian of minor children was the acting administrator de bonis non with the will annexed of the testator; and the commissioner who took his account blended his receipts and payments as administrator with his receipts and payments under an agreement between himself as guardian and the widow and daughter, who was of age: *held*, this was error. The account as administrator should embrace only his receipts and disbursements as such. His receipts and disbursements under the agreement not being made as administrator but as guardian of the minor children and agent of the widow and daughter are to be stated on different principles. *Hannah, adm'or*, vs. *Boyd & als.*, 25 Grat. 692.

In *Harvey* vs. *Steptoe*, 17 Grat. 290, the court held that whilst the execution of a continuing trust is in progress the account of the trustee should be stated on the principle of executors' accounts; but when it is substantially closed, it should be stated on the principle of debtor and creditor, the interest to be charged upon each sum received from the end of six months after its receipt, and disbursements first applied to interest whilst there is any due. In *Coltrane* vs. *Worrell*, 30 Grat. 434, the account adopted was settled on the principle of debtor and creditor.

A trustee is liable to pay interest for the trust money in his hands unless he can show that it was necessarily kept in hand for the purposes of the trust; and this he may do upon oath, subject to be controlled by other testimony and the circumstances of the case. *Chancellor Taylor* in *Miller* vs. *Beverleys*, 4 H. & M. 417. Afterwards, interest was charged against the trustee by Chancellor Nelson, and the case went up to the Court of Appeals on appeal from his decision. The Court of Appeals held that under the circumstances of the case no interest should be charged against the trustee but that interest should be allowed him on the balance in his favour. *Beverleys* vs. *Miller*, 6 Munf. 99.

When the trust is not a continuing trust, the account is stated on the principle of debtor and creditor. That is, the disbursements of the trustee are first applied to the interest when there is any due, after that to the principal. See *Pleasants* vs. *Ross*, Wythe's Rep. 10, and note on page 431 of Wythe's Reports by Mr. Wm. Green.

COMMISSIONER'S REPORT.

A decree confirming a report of a commissioner may be reversed where under a general order of reference of all accounts, he states an account as to one subject only, omitting others which ought to have been settled. *Harris* vs. *Magee*, 3 Call 502.

On the motion of a defendant to recommit report of commissioner, the motion as far as it goes to open the accounts anew is overruled on account of defendant's neglect or contumacy; but he may show himself entitled to credits not considered by the commissioner, it appearing from the evidence in support of his motion, that he is entitled to such credits. *Snickers* vs. *Dorsey*, 2 Munf. 505.

On bill of injunction to stay proceedings on a judgment at law, if it appear from commissioner's report, not excepted to by defendant, that the complainant is entitled to a credit which the defendant failed to give, the court ought not to set aside the order for account, and dismiss the bill, on the ground that the complainant had neglected to carry into effect a previous order, referring, by consent of parties, the accounts between them to different commissioners; but the last order having been made on the defendant's motion, the report being excepted to for want of notice to the complainant of the time and place of taking the account, and such exception appearing well founded, a new account ought to be directed to be taken. *Roberts* vs. *Jordan*, 3 Munf. 488.

An error appearing upon the face of the commissioner's report, which is the basis of the decree, and not being susceptible of being repelled by extrinsic evidence, will be corrected in the appellate court, though not excepted to in the court below. *Wills's adm'or* vs. *Dunn's adm'or*, 5 Grat. 384.

It appearing on the face of the report that the commissioner fixed the value of certain property by guess work, yet it appearing not to be unreasonable either way, and no exception being taken in the court below, the appellate court will not notice the objection. *Beckwith* vs. *Butler*, 1 Wash. 224.

An error on the face of a commissioner's account, though not excepted to in court below, ground of reversal of decree. *Walker's ex'ors* vs. *Walke*, 2 Wash. 195; *White's ex'ors* vs. *Johnson & als.*, 2 Munf. 285.

But if the report of the commissioner be impeached on grounds and in relation to subjects which may be affected by extraneous testimony, the exception must be taken in the court below. *White's ex'ors* vs. *Johnson & als.*, 2 Munf. 285.

An error in charging 6 per cent., when it should have been 5, appearing on the face of the report, was corrected in the appellate court, though not excepted to in the court below. *Wills's adm'or* vs. *Dunn's adm'or*, 5 Grat. 384.

Though no order for an account appear in the record, the appellate court will presume that the report was made by proper authority, it not being questioned in the court below. *Ibid.*

Want of notice of the time and place of a commissioner's taking an account and of the court's acting on the report too soon, are not sufficient reasons for a bill of review. *Winston* vs. *Johnson's ex'ors*, 2 Munf. 305.

Exceptions taken to a report; the report recommitted without passing on the exceptions. The recommitted report is not excepted to. The exceptions to the first report are thereby waived. *Kee's ex'or* vs. *Kee & als.*, 2 Grat. 116.

Depositions taken by a commissioner who has given notice to the parties of the proceedings before him are sufficiently taken without a special notice of the taking of the depositions. *McCandlish & als.* vs. *Edloe & als.*, 3 Grat. 330.

When commissioner notified by publication in a newspaper, a party excepting for want of notice should show by affidavit or otherwise that he had not such information of the taking of the accounts as would have enabled him to attend. *McCandlish, adm'or, &c.* vs. *Edloe & als.*, 3 Grat. 330.

A cause is heard upon the report of a commissioner which had not been returned for the legal period, the decree being interlocutory, the error should be corrected by the court upon application of the party aggrieved. *Armstrong's adm'or* vs. *Pitts & als.*, 13 Grat. 235.

Errors in the details of a decree for an account are not a proper subject for appeal and correction in the appellate court; but they may be corrected by exceptions to the commissioner's report. *Humphrey* vs. *Foster & als.*, 13 Grat. 653.

An account of an administrator of a decedent settled under a decree of court in a suit in which the heirs at law were not parties nor in privity with any party thereto is not prima facie evidence against the heirs at law. *Robertson & als.* vs. *Wright & als.*, 17 Grat. 534.

A commissioner's report is based upon papers filed in the cause and there is no exception to the report. The papers not being competent evidence of the facts recited in them, the court may disregard the report and decide the case upon the competent evidence and against the report. *James R. & K. Co.* vs. *Littlejohn*, 18 Grat. 53.

It is no valid objection by a party upon whom process has been served in the suit, that he did not see or hear of the notice by publication (ordered under the provision in the Code of 1860, ch. 175, § 5, Code 1873, ch. 171, sec. 5,) of the taking an account by a commissioner under the order of the court. *Hill & als.* vs. *Bowyer & als.* 18 Grat. 364.

Cases in which it is proper to refer to a commissioner. By Moncure, P., in *Kraker* vs. *Shields*, 20 Grat. 392.

It is not necessary for the court before directing a trustee to proceed to sell, first to refer to a commissioner to report how much and what part of the trust subject shall be sold. It is the duty of the trustee to determine that question and if he finds difficulty in doing so, a reference to a commissioner may be made. *Michie* vs. *Jeffries*, 21 Grat. 334.

What accounts and proceedings should be directed in a suit by donee in a fraudulent deed brought after a decree setting the deed aside at the suit of one creditor of the donor. *Pratt & als.* vs. *Cox & als.*, 22 Grat. 330.

Though a bill does not surcharge and falsify the accounts of the executors settled before the commissioners, yet as there were errors on the face of these accounts and they did not purport to be final or to embrace all the transactions of the executor, it was proper to refer the accounts to a commissioner to be settled and adjusted. *Chapman's adm'ors* vs. *Shepherd's adm'or & als.*, 24 Grat. 377.

An administrator having waived his exceptions to a commissioner's report under the erroneous impression that the report would be sustained and the case finally disposed of, may withdraw his waiver

69

and renew his exceptions. *Hannah's adm'or* vs. *Boyd & als.*, 25 Grat. 692.

Where a commissioner in settling an account of a committee of a lunatic makes two statements, the only difference being that in one he gives the committee a credit of $1,000 which is omitted in the other, and he refers the question to the court; the court adopts the statement giving the credit. On appeal it was held that an exception was not necessary, and the appellate court might correct the decree. *Cole's committee* vs. *Cole's adm'or*, 28 Grat. 365.

When error to decree a sale without referring cause to commissioner to ascertain liens, &c. *Kendricks & als.* vs. *Whitney & als.*, 28 Grat. 646; *Horton & als.* vs. *Bond*, 28 Grat. 815.

The only issue in a cause being whether a gift by a father to his daughter was intended to be absolute or an advancement, and all the evidence having been taken with reference to that issue, it was proper for the court to decide it without a reference to a commissioner to inquire and report upon the question. *Watkins & als.* vs. *Young & als.*, 31 Grat. 84.

An account of purchase money and rents directed in a case in which specific execution of a contract refused. *Stearns & als.* vs. *Beckham & als.*, 31 Grat. 379.

The answer of a defendant in which no reference is made to a commissioner's report will not be regarded as an exception to said report; and where there are no errors on the face of the report, and no exceptions taken thereto, in the court below, they cannot be taken for the first time in the appellate court. *Simmons* vs. *Simmons's adm'r*, 33 Grat. 451.

The commissioner was directed to take an account of the debts of S. (a grantor in a deed to L., a trustee for certain creditors) and of their priorities and of the lands of S., and to whom and when aliened; after stating certain judgments and debts secured by specific liens, he reports that the debts secured by the deed to L. were not presented before him, and he does not report them; held, the report should be recommitted to the commissioner to take an account of said debts, and it was error to make a decree for the sale of the lands of S. before this account was taken. *Shultz & als.* vs. *Hansborough & als.*, 33 Grat. 567.

A cause having been referred to a commissioner and ample opportunity offered both parties to introduce their witnesses, and the commissioner having made his report and the cause being ready for hearing, depositions taken afterwards by one of the parties as to a controverted matter in the report, was under the circumstances properly disregarded by the court in deciding the cause. The statute (Code of 1873, ch. 172, § 36) as to reading depositions taken after an interlocutory decree in reference to any matter thereby adjudicated, is not mandatory, but permissive. *Richardson* vs. *Duble & als.*, 33 Grat. 730.

COMMISSIONS OF FIDUCIARIES.

Five per cent. the usual commission. *Triplett* vs. *Jameson*, 2 M. 242; *Sheppard* vs. *Starke*, 3 M. 29; *Granberry* vs. *Granberry*, 1 Wash. 249; *Hopkins* vs. *Bernard*, 2 H. & M. 21; *Taliaferro* vs. *Minor*, 2 Call 190; *Ferneyhough* vs. *Dickinson*, 2 Rob. R. 582; *Boyd* vs. *Oglesby*, 23 Grat. 688, 689, and this though the testator directs that his executor should be handsomely paid, *Waddy* vs. *Hawkins*, 4 Leigh 458.

More than five per cent. allowed in *Fitzgerald* vs. *Jones*, 1 Mun. 150; *Cavendish* vs. *Fleming*, 3 M. 198; *McCall* vs. *Peachy*, 3 M. 297, 306: *Boyd* vs. *Oglesby*, 23 Grat. 688-9.

A second commission on the same capital not allowed, *McCall* vs. *Peachy*, 3 M. 297, 306.

Sometimes a commission allowed an agent of the executor as well as to the executor himself; *Carter* vs. *Cutting*, 5 Mun. 223, 22 Grat. 649.

Commissions disallowed because legacy deemed in lieu of them. *Jones* vs. *Williams*, 2 Call. 102.

When committee of lunatic not entitled to commission. 33 Grat. 674.

Commissions forfeited under act Feb. 16, 1825, § 8, Supp. R. C. 217, because account not returned in time. *Chapman's adm'ors* vs. *Shepherd's adm'ors & als.*, 24 Grat. 377. See *Boyd* vs. *Boyd*, 3 Grat. 113.

Commissions disallowed in *Strother & als* vs. *Hull & als.*, 23 Grat. 652 because of failure to settle accounts.

Commissions forfeited by one administrator but not by the other. *Turner* vs. *Turner*, 1 Grat. 10; *Boyd* vs. *Boyd*, 3 Grat. 109.

Full commissions allowed in a case though executor guilty of misconduct. *Kee* vs. *Kee*, 2 Grat. 116. An administrator not settling his accounts not entitled to commissions. *Morris* vs. *Morris*, 4 Grat. 293.

Payments to legatees does not take the demand for commissions out of the statute. *Nelson* vs. *Page*, 7 Grat. 160.

Commissions not allowed executor on appraised value of slaves,[73] but allowed on the appraised value of grain and other perishable property divided in kind among the legatees. *Claycomb* vs. *Claycomb*, 10 Grat. 589. See also *Granberry* vs. *Granberry*, 1 Wash. 249; *Hopkins* vs. *Bernard*, 4 Mun. 92; *Ferneyhough* vs. *Dickenson*, 2 Rob. R. 582.

In *Jones* vs. *Lackland*, 2 Grat. 81, under the circumstances of the case, the trustee was allowed a commission upon the amount of the debt secured by the trust deed, but not allowed commissions upon the proceeds of sale beyond the amount of the debt.

---

[73] Slaves were by the statute not to be sold save for payment of debts; and the condition of the estate did not require it.

COMPUTING LIFE ESTATES.

To compute the value of a life estate for an Annuity, see Sess. Acts, 1877–8, pp. 245–7.

DECREES FOR SALE OF LANDS OF INFANTS, &C.

[To illustrate these decrees, it will be better to accompany them by the pleadings, &c., in the suit:

Bill.—To the honorable R. M., judge of the Circuit Court of the county of ——— :

Complaining showeth unto the court, your complainant, James S., guardian of Robert P., that the said Robert P. is under the age of fourteen years, [or, over the age of fourteen years and under the age of twenty-one years], that the said Robert P. is the owner in fee of a tract of land lying in this county, containing 643 acres, bounded as follows: [here give the boundaries]; that he inherited the same from his mother, Agnes P., who recently departed this life, intestate, leaving no other child or heir than the said R. P.; that this is all the property the said Robert P. owns beside a few articles of furniture of little or no value, they would not command if sold more than fifty dollars; that the said tract of land is, as your complainant believes, in great demand at this time, and if sold would command a handsome price, say from fifteen to twenty dollars per acre, and the amount realized from it, if safely invested, would yield a much larger annual return than is now obtained in gross for its renting; for though the land is valuable, your complainant has not been able to get more than two hundred dollars annual rent for it. It is easy to see that if the land brings at public sale even ten dollars per acre (a very low estimate), the nett proceeds of sale properly invested would ensure a much larger annual return to the said Robert P. than is now realized. Your complainant believes and charges, therefore, that it will be greatly to the interest of the said Robert P. to sell the said land and invest the proceeds of sale in some interest-paying stock or other property.

Should the said Robert P. depart this life, his aunts, Jane L. and Virginia M., would be his sole heirs at law.

In the progress of this suit, the court will be asked to decree that proper counsel fees be allowed and paid for the preparation of this bill and the conduct of the proceedings.

In tender consideration whereof, your complainant prays that Robert P., an infant under the age of twenty-one years, the said Jane L., and the said Virginia M., be made parties defendant to this bill, and required to answer the several statements thereof; that a guardian ad litem be assigned to the said infant defendant Robert P. to defend his interests in this suit, who shall also answer this bill; that the said land be decreed to be sold and the proceeds invested as the court shall direct; that all proper allowances of counsel fees may be made in this suit; that proper process issue and all proper orders and decrees may be made and enquiries may be directed; and that all such other, farther and general relief may be afforded your complainant as the nature of his case may require or to equity shall seem meet. And your complainant will ever pray, &c.

WM. W., p. q.

County of ———, to-wit:

This day personally appeared before me the undersigned, a justice of the peace for the said county, James S., guardian of Robert P., and made oath that he believes the several statements made in the foregoing bill to be true.   Given under my hand this ——— day of ———.

GEORGE R., j. p.

Answer of guardian ad litem to bill.   The answer of John H., guardian ad litem to the infant defendant Robert P., and the answer of the said infant defendant Robert P. by the said John H., his guardian ad litem, to the bill in equity exhibited against the said Robert P. and others in the ——— Court of ——— county by James S., guardian of the said Robert P.

For answer to the said bill the said guardian ad litem answers and says that he does not know whether the interests of the infant defendant would be promoted by the sale of the property as prayed for in the said bill or not: and the said infant defendant, by his said guardian ad litem, answers and says that being an infant of tender years he knows nothing of the matters mentioned in the bill, and commits the protection of his interests to the court.   And now having answered, they pray, &c.

JOHN H.,

Guardian ad litem to Robert P., and the said Robert P., an infant defendant, by the said John H., his guardian ad litem.

County of ———, to-wit:

This day personally appeared before me, the undersigned, a justice of the peace for the said county, John H., guardian ad litem of Robert P., and made oath that he believes the several statements made in the foregoing answer to be true.

Given under my hand this ——— day of ———.

GEORGE R., j. p.

Note.—[It is error to decree the sale of infants' lands without the answer of a guardian ad litem. *Ewing's adm'or & als.* vs. *Ferguson's adm'or & als.*, 33 Grat. 548.]

Answer of Robert P., an infant over the age of fourteen years.   The answer of Robert P., an infant defendant over the age of fourteen years, to a bill in equity exhibited against him and others in the Circuit Court of ——— county by James S., guardian of the said Robert P.

For answer to the said bill the said Robert P. answers and says that although under full age he believes he knows what are his interests in the matters referred to in the bill; he believes the statements in said bill are true and that it will be to his advantage to sell the land as therein prayed for and invest the proceeds of sale in other property. And now having fully answered, he prays hence to be dismissed, &c.

ROBERT P.

Add affidavit.

Answer of adult defendants.

The joint and separate answer of Jane L. and Virginia M. to a bill in equity exhibited against them and another in the Circuit Court of ——— county by James S., guardian of Robert P.

These respondents, saving and reserving, &c., for answer to the said bill answer and say that they believe the statements made in the said bill are true. These respondents do not object to the sale of the land as prayed for in the said bill. And now having fully answered, they pray hence to be dismissed with their costs, &c.

JANE L.,
VIRGINIA M.

Affidavit to foregoing answer waived.

WM. W., p. q.

[Or affidavit may be made as on page 549.]

First entry in court on the filing of foregoing bill and answers.

James S., guardian of Robert P.,   Plaintiff.
  against
Robert P., an infant under the age of twenty-one
 years, and Jane L. and Virginia M.,   Defendants.

This day came the plaintiff and filed his bill and John H. is assigned guardian ad litem to the infant defendant Robert P., to defend his interests in this suit, and thereupon the said guardian ad litem filed the answer of the said infant defendant and his own answer to the bill of the plaintiff, duly sworn to [and the said Robert P. being over fourteen years of age filed his own answer duly sworn to, to the said bill], and the adult defendants filed their answer, to which several answers the plaintiff by counsel replied generally, and the cause was docketed by consent, and coming on to be heard, by like consent, upon the bill, answers and replications, was argued by counsel: On consideration whereof, the court doth adjudge, order and decree, that the papers in the cause be referred to one of the commissioners of this court who is directed to inquire into and report to the court,

1. Whether the interest of the infant defendant will be promoted by the sale of the property in the bill mentioned or of any part thereof and the investment of the proceeds of sale in other property;

2. Whether the rights of any person will be violated by such sale;

which enquiries the said commissioner shall make and report to
the court together with any matters specially stated deemed pertinent by himself or required by any of the parties to be specially
stated.

[Usually when there is a reference to a commissioner, the commissioner gives notice in writing to the parties of the time and place of
executing the decree. This notice can, of course, be dispensed with
by consent; in other words, the notice may be waived or the parties
may appear before commissioner without notice.]

Form of Notice.

Commissioner's Office, Hanover C. H., June —, 18—.

To James S., guardian of Robert P.,   Plaintiff,
   and
The said Robert P., an infant under the age of twenty-one
   years by John H., his guardian ad litem and Jane L. and
   Virginia M.,   Defendants.

By a decree made in the above-named suit on the —— day of ——,
18—, by the Circuit Court of the county of Hanover it was adjudged
and decreed that "the papers in the cause be referred to one of the
commissioners of the court," &c. (here copy the terms of the decree):
Take notice, that I shall, as one of the commissioners of said court,
proceed, at my office on the —— day of ——, 18—, at the hour of
10 o'clock A. M., to perform the duties required of me by the said
decree; when and where you may appear if you think proper to
do so.
        Yours respectfully,
                Alex. Stuart, Comm'r.

We acknowledge service of the foregoing notice.

                William W.,
        Counsel for plt'ff and adult defendants.
                John H.,
      Guardian ad litem, to infant deft. Robert P.

Commissioner's Report.

Commissioner's Office, Hanover C. H., June —, 18—.

P.'s guardian
   vs.
P. and others.

Your commissioner (the parties duly acknowledging service of notice
of the time and place of executing the decree made in above entitled
cause on the ——day of ——, 18—) proceeded at this office on the ——
day of ——, 18—, to perform the duties required of him by said de-

cree. In making the enquiries therein directed he took the examinations of Wellington G. and A. D. W. on interrogatories agreed on by John H., guardian ad litem of the infant defendant Robert P. Your commissioner also took the examination of James M. T. At the examination of Mr. T., John H., guardian ad litem was present in person. These examinations of witnesses and the notice aforementioned are returned with this report. And from the evidence thus furnished your commissioner, he now reports,

1. That the interest of the infant defendant Robert P. will be promoted by the sale of the property mentioned in the bill, and the investment of the proceeds of sale in other property.

2. The rights of no person will be violated by the sale.

Respectfully submitted,

ALEX. STUART, Comm'r.

Depositions returned with foregoing report.

COMMISSIONER'S OFFICE, HANOVER C. H., June ——, 18—.

P.'s guardian
vs.
P. and others.

Depositions of Wellington G. and others taken before me the under-signed Commissioner:

Wellington G., being duly sworn, deposeth and saith as follows, in answer to the annexed interrogatories, which are as follows:

Interrogatories to be propounded to the witnesses in P.'s guardian vs. P. and others:

1st *Interrogatory.* Do you or not know the land in the bill mentioned of which Mrs. Agnes P. lately died seized? What is its present rental value?

2nd *Interrogatory.* Is it or not to the interest of the infant defendant Robert P. to sell the said land and invest the proceeds of sale in other property? If yea, state your reasons for thinking so.

3rd *Interrogatory.* Would or not the rights of any person be violated by such sale?

It is agreed that the foregoing interrogatories may be propounded to the witnesses in the above mentioned case by the Commissioner.

WM. W., counsel for adult parties;
JOHN H., guardian ad litem for Robert P.

To 1st *interrogatory* witness answers: I have known this land many years. It is a tract of 640 acres. It contains some fine arable land and portions of it are well wooded. I am informed that it rents for $200 per annum.

To 2nd *interrogatory:* I think it decidedly to the interest of the infant, Robert P., to have the land sold. It would bring a good price.

Land adjoining this, not of better quality or more desirable in any way, has recently been sold at $15 per acre; and I believe this land would sell for that. If it did command that price or as much as $12 per acre the income derived from a proper investment of the proceeds of sale would largely exceed the present income. That is to say, 600 acres at $12 per acre would amount to $7,200. If this sum netted 5 per cent. of income it would amount to $360. At $15 per acre the 600 acres would command $9,000; and if 5 per cent. were netted on that, the income would be $450.

To 3rd interrogatory: I do not know that the rights of any person would be violated by the sale. I suppose not.

And further this deponent saith not.

WELLINGTON G.

A. D. W. being duly sworn, deposeth and saith as follows:

Ans. to 1st Int. I do know the land. I do not positively know what it rents for. The tenant informed me that he was renting it at $200 per annum.

Ans. to 2d Int. Yes, it would be to the interest of the infant defendant to sell. The tract of 600 acres would certainly bring between $7,000 and $9,000, if not more; and even the lowest of these sums would, if properly invested, secure a much larger annual return than is now realized.

Ans. to 3d Int. I have heard of no one whose right would be violated by this sale.

And further this deponent saith not.

A. D. W.

COMMISSIONER'S OFFICE, June ——, 188—.

Present:—*Wm. W.*, counsel for adult parties, plaintiff and defendant.
John H., guardian ad litem to infant defendant Robert P.

James M. T., being duly sworn, deposeth and saith as follows:

1st question by Wm. W. counsel for adult parties. Do you or not know the land in the bill mentioned?

Answer. I do.

2d question by same. Would or not the interest of the infant defendant be promoted by a sale of the land and the investment of the proceeds in other property?

Answer. I think a sale would secure from $7,000 to $9,000, perhaps more; and the income derived from either of those sums would be largely more than is now obtained or can probably be obtained in the shape of rent. I think the sale would promote the interest of the infant defendant.

3d question by same. Would or not the rights of any party be violated by the sale?

Answer. Not so far as I know or believe.

And further this deponent saith not.

J. M. T.

The foregoing examinations of witnesses duly taken, sworn to and subscribed by the witnesses at the times and place mentioned therein.

ALEX. STUART, Comm'r.

Decree confirming report and directing sale.

Names of parties.

This cause came on this day to be again heard on the papers formerly read and on the report of Commissioner Alexander Stuart filed since the last hearing, to which report there is no exception, and on the examinations of witnesses returned with the said report, and was argued by counsel: on consideration whereof the court doth approve and confirm the said report, and doth adjudge, order and decree that William W., who is hereby appointed a special commissioner for the purpose,[74] do, after having advertised the time, place and terms of sale once a week for ———— successive weeks in one or more of the newspapers published in the city of ————, and posting notice of the same in one or more of the public places in this county, proceed to sell at public auction [75] on the premises [or at the front door of the court-house of this county] the tract of land in the bill and proceedings mentioned, in one or more parcels as to the commissioner shall seem fit, upon the following terms, to-wit: one-third cash, and the residue in three equal instalments, payable respectively at one, two and three years from the day of sale, the credit instalments carrying interest from the day of sale and the purchaser or purchasers executing bonds therefor payable at said respective dates, and the title of the property retained until the whole purchase money is paid and a conveyance directed by the court. If the commissioner deem it best to sell in parcels he may employ a surveyor to lay off the same in one or more parcels, making a plat of the same. And the said commissioner is directed to deposit the cash instalment, deducting therefrom the expenses of sale, including his commissions, the fees of

---

[74] If sale be ordered to be made by two commissioners, sale by one is irregular. *Gross* vs. *Pearcy & als.*, 2 P. & H. 483.

[75] See *Cooper* vs. *Hepburn*, 15 Grat. 551, as to sale of infants' land at private sale under decree; and as to the effect of sale, six months after date of decree.

The sale of infants' land was held valid in *Durrett* vs. *Davis, guardian,* 24 Grat. 302.

The errors for which such a sale will be set aside; and the duties and liability of a purchaser were considered in *Zirkle* vs. *McOue & als.,* 26 Grat. 517.

the surveyor (if one be employed), and a fee of $——— to the counsel who instituted this suit, in one of the banks in the city of ——— to the credit of the court in this suit, and to report his proceedings hereunder to the court, returning therewith a certificate of such deposit and the bonds given for the credit instalments. But the said commissioner, William W., shall receive no money under this decree until he shall enter into bond with sufficient security in the clerk's office of this court, payable to the Commonwealth of Virginia, in the penalty of $———, and conditioned for the faithful discharge of his duties hereunder.

Advertisement of Sale.

In pursuance of a decree in P.'s guardian vs. P. & als. made by the Circuit Court of Hanover county on the —— day of ——, I shall, as commissioner appointed thereby, proceed to sell at public auction on the premises [or, at the front door of the court-house of H. county] on the —— day of —— the tract of land containing 643 acres of which Mrs. P. lately died seized. The land lies on the ——— road, distant about —— miles from the court-house. It is very valuable. It will be sold in one or more parcels to suit purchasers. Terms of sale: one-third cash, balance at one, two and three years from day of sale with interest from day of sale, for credit instalments, bonds to be given by the purchaser or purchasers, and title retained until full purchase money is paid and conveyance directed by the court.

WILLIAM W., Comm'r.

Report of Sale.

To the Honorable Judge of the Circuit Court of Hanover county.

P.'s guard'n vs. P. & als.

The undersigned commissioner appointed by the decree made in the above cause, proceeded to execute the duties thereby enjoined upon him. Believing it would enhance the price obtained for the land, your commissioner directed the surveyor, Mr. Henry P., to lay off the land into three tracts as nearly equal as possible. He did so, and made a plat and survey of the land: tract A., embracing the dwelling house containing 186 acres, tract B. containing 216 acres, and tract C. containing —— acres. After advertising the time, place and terms of sale in the ———, a newspaper published in ——— once a week for —— weeks and posting notice of the sale at the front door of the court-house, and at —— and —— in this county, your commissioner proceeded to sell at public auction, to the highest bidder, on the premises [or, at the front door of the court-house of this county] on the —— day of ——, the said land in three parcels:

For tract A., containing 186 acres, Lewis M. made the highest bid and hecame the purchaser at $3,200.

For tract B., containing 216 acres, James G. made the highest bid and became the purchaser at $3,240; and

For tract C., containing —— acres, Richard R., having made the highest bid became the purchaser at $———.

The purchasers, Lewis M. and James G., have complied with their purchases by paying the cash instalment and giving bonds for the credit instalments.

Mr. Richard R. has failed thus far to comply. He claims that the title to the land purchased by him is not a good title and alleges other objections to the sale. He requests your commissioner to return with this report his letter containing the objections he makes to the title. He states that when these objections are removed, he will comply with his purchase. Your commissioner reports the facts to the court for its action in the premises.

Deducting from the cash instalments, amounting to .   . $———
The fee of surveyor, ... $———
The fee of counsel, ... $———
Costs of advertising, ... $———
Costs of posting notices, ... $———
Commissions of commissioner on the $6,440, . $——— $———

your commissioner has deposited the residue of the cash instalments, $———, in the ——— Bank, to the credit of the court in this cause and returns herewith a certificate of such deposit. He also returns the bonds of the purchasers given for the credit instalments.

Your commissioner has given the bond required by the decree directing the sale.[76]

Respectfully submitted,

ALEX'R STUART, Com'r.

Certificate of deposit.

CITY BANK OF ———,

July ——, 18—.

P.'s guardian
    vs.
    P. & als.

William W., commissioner, has deposited to the credit of the Circuit Court of Hanover county in the above entitled cause, the sum of

---

[76] The court should require this statement in every case. Sometimes payments made a commissioner are valid though he has not given bond (the decree did not direct bond to be given, though it should have done so). *Dixon & als.* vs. *McCue,* 21 Grat. 373. At others, if the commissioner has not given bond, it has been held that both the land and the purchaser are liable though the commissioner has received the purchase money from the purchaser. *Hess & als.* vs. *Reeder & als.,* 26 Grat. 746; *Lloyd* vs. *Erwin's adm'or,* 29 Grat. 598. And where two commissioners are appointed, one cannot be the only surety for the other; some other person than the commissioners must be on the bond or bonds as surety. *Tyler* vs. *Thoms,* Va. Law J. 1881, p. 621.

—— dollars, payable to the order of said court without return of this certificate.

$——
W. R. T., Cashier.

Bonds of purchasers.

One year after date I promise to pay to William W., Commissioner of the Circuit Court of the county of Hanover in the suit therein pending known by the short title P.'s guardian vs. P. & als., the sum of $—— with interest thereon from the date hereof; to the payment whereof, well and truly to be made, I bind myself, my heirs, executors and administrators firmly by these presents. Witness my hand and seal this —— day of ——.

LEWIS M. [Seal]

And so as to the other bonds.

Letter of Richard R. to Commissioner returned with the report.

Mr. William W——, Commissioner in P.'s guardian vs. P. & als.

Sir: Since bidding for the land which was knocked off to me at the public sale you made on the —— day of ——, I have had the title examined. There are objections to it which, if not removed, will prevent my complying with the terms of sale. My counsel reports that in the year 18—, while 100 acres of this land were assessed in the name of Junius P., the former husband of Mrs. P., they were returned delinquent for taxes, and at a tax sale made subsequently by the sheriff under the tax law on the —— day of —— one Reverdy Robinson became the purchaser, and he has obtained from the clerk of the County Court of Hanover a deed under which he claims the said land. I am informed that the said 100 acres constitute a part of the land knocked down to me, and I am unwilling to comply until this cloud is removed. My counsel informs me, also, that the answer of —— —— was not sworn to, in the proceedings instituted, and that therefore the sale was irregular. Until these objections are removed I decline to comply with the purchase. Please return this letter with your report of sale.

Yours respectfully,

RICHARD R.

Decree of court confirming sales to Lewis M. and James G., and directing deeds to them when full purchase money paid (authorizing them to anticipate payments).

Names of parties as before.

This cause came on this day to be again heard on the papers formerly read and on the report of sale made by commissioner William W. to which report no exceptions have been filed so far as the sales therein reported to have been made to Lewis M. and

James G. are concerned and on the papers returned and filed with said report and was argued by counsel: On consideration whereof, the court doth approve and confirm the said report so far as the sales made to Lewis M. and James G. are concerned, and doth confirm the sales made respectively to the said Lewis M. and James G. And the court doth adjudge, order and decree that, when and as soon as the said Lewis M. and James G. shall respectively pay and discharge their bonds given for the credit instalments of their respective purchases, by depositing the amounts thereof with interest up to the time of deposit in the City Bank of Richmond to the credit of the court in this cause; (the said Lewis M. and James G. are permitted thus to anticipate at any time the periods of paying the said credit instalments) and shall produce certificates of such deposits to William W. the commissioner who made the sale, then that said William W., special commissioner, shall convey by good and sufficient deed, with special warranty, unto the said Lewis M., on the production of such certificate, all that tract of land lying in the county of Hanover containing 186 acres being the tract A in the plan of survey made by surveyor Henry P. and returned with the report of said commissioner, bounded as follows: (here describe the boundaries); and upon the production of such certificate of deposit by the said James G., the said William W., special commissioner as aforesaid, shall convey by good and sufficient deed, with special warranty, unto the said James G. all that tract of land lying in the county of Hanover containing 216 acres being the tract B in the plan of survey made by surveyor Henry P. and bounded as follows: (here describe the boundaries.) And upon the execution of each of the said deeds and cotemporaneously therewith, the said commissioner William W. shall withdraw from the papers in the cause the bonds given respectively by the said Lewis M. and James G. for the credit instalments and deliver them to the said Lewis M. and James G. And the said commissioner William W. is directed to report his proceedings hereunder to the court.

Entry of rule against the purchaser Richard R. for not complying with his purchase.

Names of parties.
This cause came on this day to be again heard on the papers for-

merly read and was argued by counsel: On consideration whereof the court doth adjudge, order and decree that Richard R. being served with a copy of this order ten days before the ——— day of ———, do on that day show cause to the court why an attachment should not issue against him for his failure to comply with the terms of his purchase of ——— acres of land reported as sold to him by commissioner William W."[77]

Entry of answer to the rule to show cause and time taken to consider.

Names of parties.

This day appeared Richard R. and filed a return and answer to the rule to show cause entered herein on the ——— instant, and an affidavit of Telemachus M., and also filed exceptions to the report of commissioner William W. and the plaintiff filed the affidavits of Xenophon X. and William W. and the said exceptions and motion for a rule to show cause, being argued, the court takes time to consider of its decree.

Entry of order overruling exceptions of Richard R. to commissioner's report and decreeing that he comply with the terms of his purchase.

Names of parties.

This cause came on this day to be heard upon the papers formerly read, on the return and answer of Richard R. to the rule to show cause entered herein on the ——— day of ——— and on the documents and evidence filed therewith in support thereof and on the affidavits of Xenophon X. and William W. and on the report of commissioner William W. and exceptions thereto, and the court now being fully advised of its judgment doth adjudge, order

---

[77] Or " to show cause why he should not be compelled to comply with his purchase of the ——— acres of land from William W., special commissioner, and upon his failure to do so, why the said land should not be resold at his risk and costs."

Purchasers at a judicial sale must resist confirmation of sale to get relief for defects of title. *Threlkelds* vs. *Campbell*, 2 Grat. 198.

Ordinarily objection after confirmation comes too late. *Young's adm'or, &c.* vs. *McClung & als.*, 9 Grat. 336, *Daniel & als.* vs. *Leitch*, 13 Grat. 195, *Watson* vs. *Hey & als.*, Va. Law. Jour., Aug. 1877, p. 473, 28 Grat. 698.

and decree that the exceptions of the said Richard R. to the report
of the said commissioner William W. be overruled and that the
said report be approved and confirmed. And the court doth
farther adjudge, order and decree that the purchaser Richard R. do
comply with the terms of his purchase of the tract of land sold to
him by the said commissioner, William W.; and that the said Richard R. pay to the said William W., commissioner as aforesaid, within
———— days from the entry of this decree,[78] the sum of ————,
that being the cash instalment of his said purchase, and execute to
the said William W., commissioner, his three bonds to be dated as
of the day of sale, to-wit: on the —— day of ——— for the sums
of $———, each, with interest payable from their date, payable
at 1, 2 and 3 years respectively from their date; and unless the
said Richard R. shall within the time aforesaid make the said payment and execute his bonds as aforesaid, *then a peremptory attachment shall be issued by the clerk of this court directing the sheriff of
this county to attach the body of the said Richard R.————, and
hold the same until the further order of the court, which peremptory
attachment shall be returnable to the first day of the next term of
this court.*

[Instead of an attachment as directed above, the court may decree, and
usually decrees, a resale at the risk of the purchaser. In that case, in lieu of
the italics in the preceding form, the decree will be as follows; "then that the
said William W. special commissioner, do after advertising the time, place
and terms of sale, once a week for four successive weeks, in one of the newspapers published in the city of ————, and after posting notices of the sale
in one or more of the public places in this county, proceed to sell, at public
auction, at the risk and costs of the said Richard R.,[79] on the premises [or, at

---

[78] The decree should ascertain how much of the purchase money is due and
should give the purchaser a day in which to pay it; and if not paid in that
time direct the commissioner to sell. *Long & als.* vs. *Weller's ex'or & als.*, 29
Grat. 347. But in this case the decree requiring the payment of "all the
purchase money now due upon their (the appellants') purchase of said property, and all costs at law and in this proceeding" was sufficiently precise:
id certum est quod certum reddi potest.

[79] The point suggested by the Special Court of Appeals in *Gross* vs. *Pearcy*,
2 P. & H. 483, questioning the propriety of ordering a resale for credit payments in a case in which the purchaser has paid the cash instalment and
given his bonds for the credit instalments, (the sale being confirmed and the
purchaser put into possession) has been settled in *Clarkson* vs. *Read & als.*, 15
Grat. 297. In *Clarkson* vs. *Read*, there was a judicial sale of land, partly on a
credit, and the purchaser paid the cash payment and executed his bonds with

the front door of the court-house of this county] the tract of land so pur-chased by said Richard R. to-wit: (here describe it); on the following terms, to-wit[80]: And the said commissioner is directed to deposit the cash instalment in one of the banks of the city of ———— to the credit of the court in this cause and to return a certificate of such deposit, and the bonds given for the credit instalments with his report of sale to the court. But the said William W., commissioner as aforesaid, shall receive no money under this decree until he shall enter into bond, &c., (as on page 555 to the end)].

And the said Richard R. signifying his intention to appeal from this decree, it is ordered that the same be suspended for a period of sixty days from the date hereof, provided the said Richard R. shall, within five days from the entry of this decree, enter into bond, with sufficient security, in the clerk's office of this court, in

---

security for the deferred instalments and the sale was confirmed by the court When the bonds became due, the purchaser failed to pay them. The Court of Appeals held that the purchaser might be proceeded against by a rule to show cause why the land should not be sold for the payment of the purchase money and upon that proceeding a decree might be made for the sale of the land.

[80] The terms of credit ought, of course, to be such as to correspond with the terms of payment under the first sale. Suppose the original sale took place October 1st, 1882, and was for $1,000, cash as to one-fourth and the balance on credits of 1, 2 and 3 years, and the resale was ordered November 2nd, 1883; the terms of the decree so as to meet the original terms of payment would be thus: "for cash as to so much as will satisfy and pay the expenses of sale and $500, with interest at six per centum per annum on $250, part thereof, from the 1st November, 1882, and with like interest on $250, the other part thereof, from the 1st November, 1883, and on a credit as to $250, until the 1st November, 1884, and on a credit as to $250, until the 1st November, 1885 and on a credit of ———— years as to the residue of the purchase money, the purchaser executing his bonds for the credit instalments payable to the said William W., commissioner as aforesaid, and the title retained until the full purchase money is paid and a conveyance directed by the court."

The matter is discretionary with the court to give more liberal terms of credit, and of this, certainly the defaulting purchaser could not complain, and often by giving longer terms of credit the interests of all parties would be promoted. See *Michie* vs. *Jeffries & als.*, 21 Grat. 334.

Whether the whole or only a part of the land should be sold, or whether as a whole or in parcels, must be referred to the discretion of the court and the act of the court will not be disturbed unless plainly erroneous. *Long & als.* vs. *Weller's ex'or & als.*, 29 Grat. 347.

As to the duties and liabilities of a purchaser at a judicial sale, see *Durrett* vs. *Davis, guardian*, 24 Grat. 302.

the penalty of two hundred dollars, payable to the Commonwealth. of Virginia and conditioned to pay all such damages as any person may sustain by reason of said suspension in case a supersedeas to this decree should not be allowed and be effectual within the time so specified.

Exceptions to the Report of Commissioner William W. by Richard R.

In the Circuit Court of the county of Hanover.

P.'s guardian vs. P. & als.

Exceptions of Richard R. to the report of Commissioner William W.

1. The said Richard R. excepts to the said report of sale to him and objects to its confirmation by the court, because in the ——— acres bid for by him, the said Richard R., are embraced 100 acres of land as to which the title is imperfect if not a wholly bad title. The said 100 acres of land were in 18— assessed to Junius P., the former husband of Agnes P., the mother of the plaintiff, from whom he is asserted to have inherited the real estate in the proceedings mentioned; and the taxes on the said 100 acres for that year amounted to 63 cents. The same not being paid, the said 100 acres were sold by the sheriff of this county on the ——— day of ———, and ——— became the purchaser at such sale for delinquent taxes; and on the ——— day of ———, he obtained a deed from the clerk of the County Court of Hanover for the said land. Copies of said deed and of the return of the land as delinquent and of the sheriff's receipt are herewith filed and prayed to be taken as part of this exception.

2. The said Richard R. excepts to the said report of sale and objects to its confirmation, because the said commissioner did not comply with the order of court in making said sale. The sale was ordered to be made on the premises; but when the commissioner made sale, he was nearly four hundred yards distant from any part of the premises purchased by the said Richard R. For this defect in the sale, the same should be set aside. See *Talley & als.* vs. *Starke's adm'x & als.,* 6 Grat. 339.

3. The said Richard R. excepts to the said report of sale and objects to its confirmation, because the proceedings in the said suit did not authorize a decree for sale. To a proper decree for the sale of the lands of infants all the answers in the suit should have been sworn to; and the answers of two of the adult defendants in the suit ——— and ———, were not sworn to   18— July ———.

RICHARD R., by counsel.

Answer and Return of Richard R. to Rule on him to show cause.

The answer and return of Richard R. to the rule entered in the suit of P.'s guard'n vs. P. & als. in the Circuit Court of Hanover to show cause, &c.

The said Richard R. answers and says, that he intended no disrespect whatever to the mandate of the court in the said cause : That he attended the sale of Commissioner William W. and bid for the property knocked down to him in good faith : That it was announced at the sale, that, after the sale was made but before it was reported to the court, the purchasers should have time to examine the title and no purchaser would be required to comply with the terms of sale if the title was not a good one : That he employed a competent person to examine into the title, and it was reported to him that as to 100 acres of his purchase there was a serious defect of title : That the said 100 acres were assessed in the year 18— in the name of Junius P., the husband of Agnes P., who died seized of the said property, that the same was returned delinquent for taxes, that afterwards they were sold for delinquent taxes and ——— became the purchaser; and the said ——— has since obtained a deed from the clerk of Hanover County Court and claims the said land thereunder. It is said that the said Junius P. had only a life estate, as tenant by the curtesy, and that he departed this life before the said year 18— began; while that may be true the taxes for that year 18— on the said 100 acres should have been paid, but were not paid, by the said Mrs. Agnes P. though she was specially applied to by the deputy sheriff and requested to pay the same. See the affidavit of the deputy sheriff, Telemachus M., to that effect.

Under these circumstances, the said Richard R. does not regard the title to the said 100 acres as good. He bought the tract of ——— acres as a whole; and he does not believe he ought to be compelled to take any part of it.

There are other objections to the title and the sale which he has embodied in his exceptions to the report; and he prays to refer to the same as a part of this return and answer. The said Richard R. prays that the said rule be discharged, and that he be relieved and discharged from all responsibility in reference to said alleged purchase.

RICHARD R.

Affidavit should be made to it.

Affidavits taken, on notice to Richard R., in answer to his return.

RICHARD R., ESQ.:

Dear Sir,—Take notice, that on the ——— day of ——— at the hour of — o'clock A. M. at the court-house of the county of Hanover, I will take the affidavit of Xenophon X., to be read as evidence on the rule against you to comply with your purchase made of Wm. W., commissioner, in P.'s guardian vs. P. & als., a suit depending in the Circuit Court of Hanover.

Yours, &c.,

JAMES S.,
G'dn of P., plt'ff in said suit.

Service acknowledged.

RICHARD R.

County of Hanover, Hanover Courthouse, to wit :

P.'s gd'n vs. P. & als.

This day, personally appeared before me, the undersigned, a justice of the peace for the county of Hanover, Xenophon X., and made oath that he was well acquainted with Junius P., that he departed this life in the year 18—, and that affiant believes the said Junius P. had only a life estate as tenant by the curtesy in the 100 acres of land mentioned in the answer and return of Richard R., and that the same expired before the year 18—, at which it is said the 100 acres of land were assessed in the name of said P. and returned delinquent for taxes: this affidavit being taken in pursuance of notice hereto annexed.

Given under my hand, this —— day of ——, 18—.

A. W., j. p.

Affidavit of Wm. W. as to Place of Sale.

County of Hanover,—Hanover C. H,. to wit:

P.'s guardian vs. P. & als.

This day, personally appeared before me, the undersigned, a justice of the peace for the said county, William W., and made oath that he was the commissioner who made sale of the land decreed to be sold by the Hanover Circuit Court in above named suit; that when lot C. was sold, of which Richard R. became the purchaser, he, the commissioner, and the crier who cried the property at auction, and the company gathered at the sale, including the said Richard R., were standing on a corner of the tract of 646 acres, and though not immediately on the lot C. (part of said tract of 646 acres) they were, all of them, in full view of lot C.: this affidavit taken in pursuance of the notice hereto annexed.

Witness my hand, this —— day of ——— 18—.

A. W., j, p.

Affidavit in Behalf of Purchaser.

County of Hanover, to wit:

P.'s guardian vs. P. & als.

This day, personally appeared before me, the undersigned, a justice of the peace for the county of Hanover, Telemachus M., and made oath that he was deputy sheriff for the county of Hanover for the year 18—; that he distinctly remembers that during that year he had a number of tax bills against Mrs. Agnes P., the mother of Robert P., the infant defendant in this suit; that he applied to her for their payment, and Mrs. P. paid them; that then affiant produced the tax bill on the 100 acres which affiant knows constituted a part of the — acres on which Mrs. P. was living then with her child Robert and asked her to pay that; that she had only paid taxes in her own name on — acres and this tract of 100 acres was her property and she should pay the taxes on it. She looked at the bill and seeing that it was made out in the name of ——— and not in hers, she refused to pay it. The bill was returned "no effects."

Given under my hand this —— day of ——— 18—.

A. W., j. p.

The foregoing affidavit taken by consent without notice.

WILLIAM W.,
Counsel for adults.
JOHN H.,
Guardian ad litem to infant def't.

Decree of Court of Appeals affirming decree of Circuit Court.

Virginia : In the Supreme Court of Appeals of Virginia held at the State Court-house in Richmond city on Monday, November ——, 18—

Richard R.,   Appellant,
  against
James S., guardian of Robert P., an infant under the age
  of twenty-one years; the said Robert P., infant as
  aforesaid ; John H., guardian ad litem to the said infant defendant Robert P.; Jane L. and Virginia M., Appellees.

Upon an appeal from a decree made by the Circuit Court of Hanover on the ——— day of ——— in a suit therein pending in which James S., guardian of Robert P., was plaintiff and the said Robert P., an infant, by his guardian ad litem, John H., and Jane L. and Virginia M. were defendants.

This day came the parties by their counsel, and the cause having been fully argued by counsel, the court on consideration of the transcript of the record and the arguments of counsel is of opinion for reasons stated in writing and made a part of this decree that there is no error in the said decree of the Circuit Court of the county of Hanover ; and the court doth adjudge, order and decree that the said decree of the Circuit Court of the county of Hanover be affirmed ; and that the appellant pay to the appellees $——— damages [81] and their costs by them about their defence in this appeal expended. And it is ordered that this decree be certified to the Circuit Court of the county of Hanover.

Entry in the Circuit Court on receiving decree of the Court of Appeals.

James S., guardian of Robert P.,   Plaintiff,
   against
Robert P., an infant under the age of twenty-one
  years, by John H., his guardian ad litem, and Jane
  L. and Lavinia M.,   Defendants.

The following decree of the Supreme Court of Appeals of Vir-

---

[81] It depends upon the construction of the statute, Code, ch. 178, § 24, whether specific damages should be given or not.

ginia was received : (here copy decree). Therefore the court, in conformity with said decree of the said Supreme Court of Appeals, doth decree and order that the said Richard R., the appellant on said appeal, do within twenty days from the entry of this decree deposit in the City Bank of Richmond, to the credit of the court in this cause, the sum of $——— with interest thereon at the rate of six per centum per annum from the ——— day of ———, 18—, and the further sum of $———, with like interest thereon from the ——— day of ———, 18—, that being the cash instalment and the first credit instalment of his purchase of lot C in the proceedings mentioned, and that the said Richard R. do also execute to William W., special commissioner of this court, his two bonds payable respectively at two and three years from the ——— day of ———, 18—, the day of sale, for $——— each with interest from the day of sale, and deliver them to the said commissioner, who is directed to file them in the papers in this cause; and the court doth farther adjudge that the said Richard R. do also pay unto the parties plaintiff and defendant in this suit, the appellees in the Court of Appeals, the sum of $———, their costs by them about their defence on said appeal expended, and $——— damages awarded them by the said decree of the Court of Appeals of Virginia, and also the costs of the rule against the said Richard R. in this court (not including an attorney's fee). And it is farther adjudged, ordered and decreed that when and as soon as the said Richard R. shall make such deposit in the City Bank of Richmond, that William W., special commissioner, shall check on the said bank on an attested extract of this decree for the sum of $———, his commissions, and that B. C., the clerk of this court, do check on the said bank on a like extract of this decree for the sum of $———, his fees in this cause. And it is farther adjudged, ordered and decreed that unless the said Richard R. shall, &c. (following the form on pp. 560, 561, ante).

Petition of guardian to permit him to expend part of principal derived from realty of infant, in support and education of the infant.[82]

To the honorable judge of the Circuit Court of the county of Hanover:

The petition of ———, guardian of P., respectfully represents to the court that your petitioner finds it impossible to meet all the expenses of his

---

[82] On the filing of the petition, the court may decree the money to be expended as prayed for.

ward's education and support from the income of the said ward; that his ward is now in his final year at the University of Virginia, and it is specially important to him that his education should not now be stopped. Your petitioner believes that with the expenditure of $—— his education can be completed; and it is highly judicious that that expenditure should be made. There are funds under the control of the court, in this cause, the proceeds of the realty of the said ward. Your petitioner prays that he may be permitted to expend of those funds the said sum of $—— in the education and support of his said ward. And your petitioner will ever pray, &c.

Order to permit guardian to expend $—— of the principal, and to lend out money.

Names of parties as before.

This cause came on this day to be farther heard on the papers formerly read and on the petition of James S. guardian of Robert P. and was argued by counsel. On consideration whereof the court doth adjudge, order and decree that the said James S. guardian as aforesaid have leave to expend in the support, maintenance and education of the said Robert P. $240 of the principal of his estate and the court doth adjudge, order and decree that the said James S. guardian as aforesaid do check on an attested extract of this decree on the City Bank of Richmond for the sum of $240 to be expended as aforesaid. And it being represented to the court that a safe loan on sufficient security can be effected of $3,200, at 6 per cent., and the said money only realizing five per cent., and the commissioner who effects the loan agreeing to act for one half the usual commissions, and the borrower agreeing to pay the fees for drawing the bonds and deed of trust, attending the said loan, the court doth adjudge, order and decree that William W., who is hereby appointed a special commissioner for the purpose, do lend out on good real and personal security to one or more borrowers the sum of $3,200, deducting a commission of one per cent. therefrom for effecting the loan, the real and personal security to be approved by the commissioner and the real security to be worth at the least twice the amount loaned; if the real security offered be worth three times the amount of the sum loaned, no personal security to be required: the terms of the loan or loans to be as follows: the borrower or borrowers to give bond in a penalty equal to double the amount loaned, payable to the said William W. commissioner as aforesaid, and conditioned to pay interest at the rate of six per centum per annum on the money borrowed, quarterly, in advance, and to pay the principal sum borrowed within sixty days after being required to do so by a decree of the court in this cause made after three years from the date of such loan; such bond or bonds to be secured by a trust deed or trust deeds conveying real property; if the real property conveyed be worth three times the amount loaned there need be no personal security in the bond or bonds, if the real property be not worth three times the sum loaned the court orders and decrees that there shall be also personal security in the bond or bonds. And the said commissioner William W. shall on the execution of such bond or bonds and deed or deeds of trust as aforesaid check on an attested copy of this decree, on the City Bank of Richmond, on the fund standing therein to the credit of the court in this cause, in favour of the borrower or borrowers, for the sum or sums of money so loaned, and in his own favour for his commissions in effecting said loan, said commissions not to exceed — per centum on the amount loaned. And the said commissioner is directed to report his proceedings hereunder to the court.

Report of commissioner of loans effected.

To the honorable judge of the circuit court of the county of Hanover:

P.'s guardian
vs.
P. & als.

Your commissioner reports, that in obedience to the decree made in said suit he has loaned to Ebenezer Elliott the sum of $1,800, and to George G. the sum of $1,368.32 on the terms prescribed by the decree. In each case the real security offered, exceeded in value, in the opinion of your commissioner, three times the amount borrowed; and, therefore, no personal security was demanded. Your commissioner checked on the City Bank of Richmond in favour of the borrowers for the respective amounts loaned to them and in his own favour for the amount of his commissions. The costs of preparing the bonds and trust deeds and of recording the trust deeds were borne by the borrowers. The bonds and trust deeds are returned herewith.

Respectfully submitted, WM. W., Comm'r.

Bond of borrower.

Know all men by these presents, that I, Ebenezer Elliott, am held and firmly bound unto William W., commissioner of the Circuit Court of the county of Hanover, in the suit pending therein known by the short title of *P.'s g'd'n* vs. *P. & als.*, in the just and full sum of thirty-six hundred dollars; to the payment whereof, well and truly to be made to the said William W., commissioner as aforesaid, his executors, administrators or assigns, I bind myself, and my heirs, executors and administrators, firmly by these presents. Sealed with my seal and dated the —— day of July, 18—.

The condition of the above obligation is such, that whereas, in pursuance of a decree made by the said Circuit Court of the county of Hanover on the —— day of ——, 18—, in the said suit of P.'s gd'n vs. P. & als. the said William W., who was thereby appointed a commissioner for the purpose, was directed to lend out certain moneys upon the terms set forth in said decree to which decree special reference is hereby made; and whereas the said William W., commissioner as aforesaid, has loaned to me, the said Ebenezer Elliott, the sum of $1,800, part of the said moneys, upon the terms set forth in said decree: Now, therefore, if the above bound Ebenezer Elliott shall pay to the said commissioner interest at the rate of six per centum per annum on the said $1,800, quarterly, in advance, such payments to be made on the —— days of July, October, January and April in each year, and shall also pay the said principal sum borrowed, to-wit: $1,800, within sixty days after being required so to do by a decree of the said court in the said suit made after three years from the date of this bond, then the above obligation shall be void, otherwise to remain in full force and virtue.

EBENEZER ELLIOTT. [Seal.]

Trust deed to secure bond.

This deed made this —— day of July, 18—, between Ebenezer Elliott and Mary his wife, parties of the first part, and C. R. S., trustee, party of the second part: Whereas by decree made by the Circuit Court of the county of Hanover in the suit of P.'s guardian vs. P. & als., William W., who was thereby appointed a commissioner for the purpose, was directed to lend out certain moneys, to which decree special reference is hereby made, and the said commissioner having loaned the sum of $1,800, upon the terms of the said decree, to Ebenezer Elliott, and the said Ebenezer Elliott having executed his penal bond to the said commissioner as required by said decree, which bond and the condition thereunder written are in the words and figures following, to-wit: (here copy bond and condition) now desires to secure the payment of the sums of money mentioned therein and a compliance with the condition of the said bond by a trust deed on the property hereinafter mentioned: Now therefore this deed witnesseth, that the said Ebenezer Elliott and Mary his wife, in consideration of the premises and of the sum of five dollars, do grant and convey unto the said C. R. S. the following property, to-wit: (here describe the property) in trust to secure the payment of the several instalments of interest and of the principal sum of money at the several and respective periods mentioned in the condition of the said bond and to secure a compliance in every respect with the condition of the said bond to the said William W., commissioner as aforesaid of the said Circuit Court of the county of Hanover in the said suit of P.'s guardian vs. P. & als., and to secure to the said Circuit Court of the said county of Hanover in the said suit a compliance with the condition of the said bond.

In the event there should be default in the payment of any instalment of interest mentioned in the condition of the said bond or in the payment of the principal sum as provided for in said condition sale may be made.

In the event of a sale, the same shall be made after first advertising the time, place and terms thereof, in some newspaper published in the city of —— for —— days, said sale to be made at public auction, on the premises, to the highest bidder, and upon the following terms, to wit: for cash as to so much of the proceeds as may be necessary to defray the expenses of executing this trust, the fees for drawing and recording this deed, if then unpaid, and to discharge the amount of money then payable according to the condition of the said bond; and if at the time of such sale either instalment of interest or the principal be not due then on a credit or credits as to such sums as will meet and discharge such remaining instalments of interest and the

72

principal when they shall respectively mature and become payable according to the condition of the said bond, the payment of which credit instalments shall be properly secured; and if there be any residue of said purchase money, the same shall be made payable at such time, and be secured in such manner, as the said Ebenezer Elliot, his executors, administrators or assigns shall prescribe and direct; or in case of his or their failure to give such direction, at such time and in such manner as the said C. R. S. shall think fit. The said Ebenezer Elliot covenants to pay all taxes, assessments, dues and charges upon the said property hereby conveyed, so long as he or his heirs or assigns shall hold the same.

Witness the following signatures and seals.

——— ———, [Seal.]
——— ———, [Seal.]

The infant coming of age order to transfer the bonds to him.

P.'s guardian vs. P. & als.

It appearing to the court that ——— P. has attained his full age of twenty-one years, it is ordered that this cause henceforth proceed against him as such; and on the motion of the said ——— P., who has now arrived at age and is entitled to the moneys loaned out in this suit to Ebenezer Elliott and George G., it is ordered, adjudged and decreed that William W., commissioner of this court, do withdraw from the papers in this cause the bond of Ebenezer Elliott and the bond of George G. on file among the same, and assign the said bonds without recourse to him the said commissioner, and all securities for the payment of the same to the said ———P.; and leave is reserved to the said ——— P. to apply to the court for such relief on the said bonds or order in reference to enforcing the payment of the same and the securities given for the same as may be requisite.

Report of Commissioner William W.

To the Honorable Judge, &c.:

P.'s guardian *vs.* P. & als.

Your commissioner reports that the purchasers of the several pieces of property sold in this suit have paid their full purchase money and their bonds have been delivered to them, and your commissioner, in obedience to decrees made in the cause, has executed to the several purchasers deeds of conveyance with special warranty for the lands respectively purchased by them. The deposits made by them in the City Bank of Richmond in discharge of their bonds appear from the certificates of deposit on file in the papers. The amount now on deposit in the said bank to the credit of the court in this case is $———. Your commissioner has not been paid his commissions on the sale to Richard R., amounting to $———. He requests that he be authorized to check for that sum.

Respectfully submitted,

WILLIAM W., Comm'r.

Final Decree.

Names of parties.

This cause came on this day to be finally heard on the papers formerly read and on the report of Commissioner William W., filed since the last hearing, to which report there is no exception, and was argued by counsel: On consideration whereof the court doth approve and confirm the said report, and there being now in the City Bank of Richmond to the credit of the court in this cause the sum of $———, to which the defendant, Robert P., is entitled, after paying the fees of the clerk and the commissions of the commissioner, William W., the court doth adjudge, order and decree that B. C., the clerk of this court, do check on an attested extract of this decree on the said City Bank of Richmond for $———, his fees in this suit; that William W. do check in like manner on said bank for $———, the amount of his commissions on the sale to Richard R., and that Robert P. do check on the said City Bank of Richmond, on an atttested extract of this decree, for $———.

And there being nothing farther to dispose of in this suit it is ordered that it be struck from the docket, with leave to any party to have the same reinstated on motion, without notice, should it hereafter become necessary.

DECREES CONCERNING PARTITION.

Decree directing commissioners to allot and apportion shares.

(Names of parties.)

This cause came on this day to be heard upon the bill taken for confessed as to the adult defendants, the answer of the infant

defendants by their guardian ad litem, B. R., and of the said'
guardian ad litem, with replications thereto, and was argued by
counsel. On consideration whereof the court doth adjudge, order
and decree that M. M., N. N., O. O., P. P. and Q. Q., who are
hereby appointed commissioners for the purpose, any three or
more of whom may act, having been first duly sworn, do proceed
to lay off and divide the real estate of which S. S. died seized and
possessed, in the bill mentioned, into five equal parts, having
regard to quality and quantity, and assign one of said five parts
to each of the heirs of said S. S., deceased, namely, to W. J. S.,
one-fifth part, to L. S. one-fifth part, to F. S. one-fifth part,
to M. S. one-fifth part, and to A. E. S. one-fifth part. But if
the said commissioners should find it impracticable to divide said
land among the aforesaid parties, or should be of opinion that
the interest of the said parties would be more promoted by a sale
of the same, in such case they are required to report the facts upon
which their opinion is based, to the court, and also what, in their
opinion, is the fee simple value of the whole of the real estate of
which S. S. died seized and possessed; and in either case they
are required to report their proceedings under this order to the
court.

*Commissioners having reported land indivisible in kind—report con-
firmed and sale ordered.*

(Names of parties.)

This cause came on again this day, to be again heard on the
papers formerly read, and upon the report of I. M. M., W. B. M.
and T. R. B. W., three of the commissioners, under the decree of
the —— day of ——, 187—, to which report there is no exception, and was argued by the counsel for the plaintiff; on consideration whereof, the court doth approve and confirm the said report,
and doth adjudge, order and decree, that G. G., who is hereby appointed a commissioner for the purpose, do proceed, after having
advertised the time, place, and terms of sale, in one or more of the
newspapers published in the —— once a week for twenty-five
days, and also posted notice thereof at the door of the court-house
of —— county, on some court day previous to the day of sale, to
sell the real estate in the bill and proceedings mentioned, of which

S. S. died seized and possessed, consisting of a tract of land of about —— acres, near ————, one other tract of about —— acres, near ————, in the county of ————, at public auction, in front of the court-house, of the county of ————, on some court day, upon the following terms, to-wit; one-third cash, one-third on a credit of twelve months, and the residue on a credit of two years from the day of sale, the credit installments to bear interest from the day of sale; taking from the purchaser bonds with good personal security for the deferred payments, and the title to be retained until the further order of the court. And the said commissioner is directed to report his proceedings hereunder to the court. But the said commissioner, &c., (as on page 555 to the end).

Commissioners having reported a partition, decree confirming commissioners' report (and directing conveyances).

(Names of parties.)

This cause came on this day to be heard upon the papers formerly read, and the report of A. B., C. D. and E. F., three of the commissioners appointed by the decree entered herein, on the —— day of ————, of the partition of the land in proceedings mentioned among the several parties entitled thereto, agreeably to the terms of the said decree, and was argued by counsel. On consideration whereof, it appearing to the court that in the partition made by the said commissioners, lot No. 1, embracing, &c. (here describe it), fell to the share of plaintiff, R. M.; lot No. 2, embracing, &c. (here describe it), fell to the share of the defendant, C. M., and lot No. 3, embracing, &c. (here describe), fell to the share of the defendant, L. B., it is adjudged, ordered and decreed that the said report of the said commissioners be confirmed, and that the partition, in manner and form aforesaid made, be held firm and stable.[83] And the court doth further adjudge, order and decree that the plaintiff, R. M., do pay unto the defendant, C. M., the sum of thirty-five dollars, and unto the defendant, L. B., the sum of forty-two dollars; these sums being respectively due from the said plaintiff to the said

---

[83] In the decrees in the English courts there is here inserted a clause directing mutual conveyances. See *Whaley* vs. *Dawson*, 2 Sch. and Lef. 372; *Miller* vs. *Wormington*, 1 J. and W. 493. See what is said in the note 26 to p. 64, *ante.*

C. M. and L. B., as *owelty* of partition on the division of the afore-mentioned land. And it is ordered that the costs of this suit be proportionally borne by the parties thereto and that the parties to this suit, plaintiff and defendant, do pay to A. B., C. D. and E. F. the commissioners aforesaid, each, the sum of five dollars for their services in making the partition aforesaid.[84]

[Instead of referring the cause to five commissioners to partition and divide in kind, when it is believed that a partition in kind cannot be conveniently made, it is most usual to enter an order like the following:

Order referring cause to one of the commissioners of the court to as-certain whether the property can be divided in kind, &c.

[*] This cause came on, &c., and was argued by counsel: on consideration whereof the court doth adjudge, order and decree that the papers in the cause be referred to one of the commissioners of this court who is directed to enquire into and report to the court—

1. Whether the real property in the bill mentioned can be conveniently divided in kind between the several parties entitled to share therein.

2. If the same cannot be conveniently divided in kind whether any party will take the entire property and pay therefor to the other parties such sums of money as their interest therein may entitle them to.

3. And, if the same cannot be conveniently divided in kind and if no party will take the entire property and pay the others for their shares, whether the interests of those who are entitled to the said property or its proceeds will be promoted by a sale of the entire property or by the allotment of part and sale of the residue.

Which several inquiries the said commissioner shall make and to the court report together with any matter specially stated deemed pertinent by himself or required by any party to be so stated.

[After this decree of reference, it is usually reported that the land is indivisible. A sale then is ordered, and this decree of sale and the subsequent proceedings are very similar to those had on a proceeding for a sale of infants' lands. See pp. 554–8 *ante.*]

---

[84] *Cabell* vs. *Cabell & als.*, 1 H. and M. 436.

PRACTICAL NOTES TO DECREES FOR PARTITION.

See pp. 61–71, *ante*.

The practical notes to bills for partition, *ante*, pp. 61–71, give references to the Code [of 1860.] The provisions in the Code of 1873 are the same, though the numbering of the chapters differs. Chap. 124, in Code of 1860, is chap. 120 in Code of 1873; chap. 123, in the Code of 1860, is chap. 119 in Code of 1873; and chap. 163, in the Code of 1860, is chap. 159 in the Code of 1873.

Before a sale is made, enquiry must be had to show that partition cannot be made according to sections 2 and 3 of chap. 120, Code of 1873. (Ch. 124 of Code of 1860.) *Howery* vs. *Helms*, 20 Grat. 8.

Each party is entitled to his share in kind. *Cox* vs. *McMullen*, 14 Grat. 82.

Partition of dower lands cannot be made till the death of the dowress. *Parker* vs. *McCoy*, 22 Grat. 502.

Reference may be had to 2 White and Tuder's Leading Cases in Eq., edi. 1859, pp. 625 (top); and to the case of *Butler* vs. *Roys*, 12 Amer. Rep. 288.

DECREES CONCERNING WILLS.

Decree Construing Will.

[The form of decree in the first edition of Suit in Equity, pp. 469–471, has been copied in Matthews's Forms, pp. 239–241.]

Decree directing issue devisavit vel non.[85]

This cause came on this day to be heard, &c. On consideration whereof the court doth adjudge, order and decree that an issue be

---

[85] The form of the bill in such a case is as follows:

Bill contesting a will which has been admitted to probat.

To the honorable judge of the Circuit Court of Henrico county:

Complaining, sheweth unto the court your complainant, J. B., that he is one of the children and heirs at law and distributees of Robert B., who recently departed this life possessed of real and personal property. The other children and heirs at law and distributees of Robert B. are Anna B., Thomas B. and William B. Your complainant believes that the said Robert B. died intestate. Since his death a paper writing purporting to be his last will and testament has been admitted to probat in this court, whereby he gives the chief part of his property to one Susan S., and after that the residue of his property to his children; the order admitting the said paper to probat was made on the —— day of ——. An attested copy of the said paper is herewith filed marked exhibit A. Marcellus M., named as executor by the said

made up and tried at the bar of this court, to ascertain and try whether or not any of the paper writing in the proceedings mentioned admitted to probat as the last will and testament of Robert B., deceased, be the true last will and testament of the said Robert B., and if any part, how much of such paper writing is the true will of the said Robert B.; and on the trial of the said issue, the said defendants, Susan S., [Anna B., Thomas B., and William B.[86]] are to maintain the affirmative and the said plaintiff, J. B., the negative.

Practical notes to decrees concerning wills.

See section 378, pp. 419, 420, *post. Malone's adm'or & als.* vs. *Hobbs & als.*, 1 Rob. R. 346; *Kincheloe* vs. *Kincheloe*, 11 Leigh 402. Code 1873, ch. 118, § 34.

A party acting as executor, is not to be made a party in his own right to a bill filed to contest the validity of the will under which he is acting. *Coalter's ex'ors* vs. *Bryan & als.*, 1 Grat. 18.

---

paper writing, has declined to qualify as such executor. Your complainant alleges and charges that the paper writing aforesaid of which probat has been received is not the will of the decedent, Robert B. In tender consideration whereof and forasmuch, &c., your complainant prays that the said Susan S., Anna B., Thomas B. and William B. may be made parties to this bill and required to answer the same; and this merely as a step or part of this proceeding to obtain a trial before a jury; that proper process issue; that an issue devisavit vel non be made up and tried by a jury at the bar of this court to ascertain and try whether the said paper writing admitted to probat as aforesaid is or is not the true last will and testament of the said Robert B., that the said probat be set aside, that the said paper writing be declared and decreed not to be the last will and testament of the said Robert B., and that all such other farther and general relief may be afforded your complainant as the nature of his case may demand or to equity shall seem meet. And your complainant will ever pray, &c.

J. L., p. q.

See section 378, pp. 419, 420 *ante. Coalter's ex'ors* vs. *Bryan & als.*, 1 Grat. 18; *Malone's adm'or* vs. *Hobbs & als.*, 1 Rob. R. 346; *Kincheloe* vs. *Kincheloe*, 11 Leigh 402; Code 1873, ch. 118, sec. 34; *Ballow & als.* vs. *Hudson & als.*, 13 Grat. 672; *Bagwell* vs. *Elliott*, 2 Rand. 190; *West* vs. *West*, 3 Ran. 373; *Nalle* vs. *Fenwick*, 4 Rand. 485; *Vaughan* vs. *Green*, 1 Leigh 287; *Street* vs. *Street*, 11 Leigh 498; *Parker's ex'or* vs. *Brown & als.*, 6 Grat. 554.

[86] Or, instead of putting Anna B., Thomas B., and William B. in this place in the decree, the court may say at the conclusion of the decree : "And on the trial of the said issue, the said defendants, Anna B., Thomas B., and William B., are given their option whether they shall maintain the affirmative or the negative thereof."

Wills vs. *Spraggins*, 3 Grat. 555, and *Schultz* vs. *Schultz*, 10 Grat. 358, have reference to the former law; the present provision of the statute, Code, 1873, ch. 118, § 34, authorizes a party to proceed by bill in equity to establish a will in which he is interested

In *Ballow & als.* vs. *Hudson & als*, 13 Grat. 672, though the bill prayed for an issue *devisavit vel non*, it appearing that the probat was a nullity, the court under the prayer for general relief, without directing an issue, declared the probat void.

See *Bagwell* vs. *Elliott*. 2 Rand. 190; *West* vs. *West*, 3 Ran. 373; *Nalle* vs. *Fenwick*, 4 Rand. 535; *Vaughan* vs. *Green*, 1 Leigh 287; *Street* vs. *Street*, 11 Leigh 498; *Parker's ex'ors* vs. *Brown & als.*, 6 Grat. 554.

DECREES CONCERNING DOWER.

Decree to assign dower.

This cause came on this day to be heard, &c. On consideration whereof the court doth adjudge, order and decree that A. B., C. D., E. F., G. H. and L. M., who are hereby appointed commissioners for the purpose, any three or more of whom may act, do go upon the land in the proceedings mentioned, of which the late N. N. was seized of an estate of inheritance during his marriage with the said Mary N., and assign and allot to the said Mary N., widow of the said N. N., by metes and bounds, one equal third part in value of the said land as her dower therein, and if for the proper performance of duties under this decree it become necessary, in the opinion of the said commissioners who shall act hereunder, they are authorized and directed to employ a competent surveyor, who shall lay off the said land, or such part thereof as may be necessary, and make a plat thereof. And the said commissioners are directed to report their proceedings hereunder to the court.

Decree commuting dower.[87]

(Names of parties.)

This cause came on this day to be farther heard on the papers formerly read, and was argued by counsel. On consideration whereof, the several parties hereto assenting to the commutation of the dower of Mary N. in the real estate of her late husband, N. N., in the proceedings mentioned, the court doth adjudge, order and decree that the said Mary N., in lieu of her dower aforesaid, is entitled to receive at once the gross sum of $650, and the court doth farther adjudge, order and decree that the said Mary N. do check on an attested extract of this decree on the fund standing to the credit of

---

[87] Sess. Acts 1877–8, pp. 245–247.

this cause in the Planters National Bank of Richmond, the proceeds of the real property of N. N. sold under proceedings in this cause, for the sum of six hundred and fifty dollars; which sum is hereby declared to be in full of her dower in the real property aforesaid as widow of the said N. N.

Practical notes to decrees concerning dower.

See Practical notes, on pp. 41–55 *ante.*

Commuting dower. Sess. Acts 1877–8, ch. 263, pp. 245–247 establish a rule and table for computing the value of a life estate for annuity, whether of tenant for life, or tenant by the curtesy, or tenant in dower. The table is as follows:

TABLE

Showing the present value, on the basis of six per centum interest, of an annuity of one dollar, payable at the end of every year that a person of a given age may be living, for the ages therein stated.

AGE.	PRESENT VALUE.	AGE.	PRESENT VALUE.	AGE.	PRESENT VALUE.	AGE.	PRESENT VALUE.
0	$10,439	26	$13,368	52	$10,208	78	$4,238
1	12,078	27	13,275	53	9,988	79	4,040
2	12,925	28	13,182	54	9,761	80	3,858
3	13,652	29	13,096	55	9,524	81	3,656
4	14,042	30	13,020	56	9,280	82	3,474
5	14,325	31	12,942	57	9,027	83	3,286
6	14,460	32	12,860	58	8,772	84	3,102
7	14,518	33	12,771	59	8,529	85	2,909
8	14,526	34	12,675	60	8,304	86	2,739
9	14,500	35	12,573	61	8,108	87	2,599
10	14,448	36	12,465	62	7,913	88	2,515
11	14,384	37	12,354	63	7,714	89	2,417
12	14,321	38	12,239	64	7,502	90	2,266
13	14,257	39	12,120	65	7,281	91	2,248
14	14,191	40	12,002	66	7,049	92	2,337
15	14,126	41	11,890	67	6,803	93	2,440
16	14,067	42	11,779	68	6,546	94	2,492
17	14,012	43	11,668	69	6,277	95	2,522
18	13,956	44	11,551	70	5,998	96	2,486
19	13,897	45	11,428	71	5,704	97	2,368
20	13,835	46	11,296	72	5,424	98	2,227
21	13,769	47	11,154	73	5,170	99	2,004
22	13,697	48	10,998	74	4,944	100	1,596
23	13,621	49	10,823	75	4,760	101	1,175
24	13,541	50	10,631	76	4,579	102	0,744
25	13,456	51	10,422	77	4,410	103	0,314

Suppose a widow 42 years of age, and that the estate in which the widow has dower is worth $10,500, the interest on $10,500 at 6 per cent. is $630 ; one-third thereof is $210. The widow would be thus entitled to an annuity of $210. Commuted by the table above, the commuted value is, 11,779×210, or $2,473.59 cents.

On assignment of dower, it is the duty of clerks to transmit a copy of the assignment with order confirming the same to the clerk of the court of the county or corporation where the land is, and along therewith such description of the land' as may appear in the papers of the cause, for record in the county or corporation. Code 1873, ch. 159, sec. 15, p. 1069.

Though claiming under a deed declared fraudulent, yet held entitled to dower.—A husband makes a fraudulent conveyance of real estate to the use of himself and children, and contingently to the use of his wife, who does not execute the conveyance; after the death of her husband a creditor exhibits his bill against the children and widow to avoid the deed as fraudulent and void; the widow claims under the conveyance; it is declared fraudulent and void. *Held*, the widow is entitled to dower in the estate. *Blow* v. *Maynard*, 2 Leigh, 30.

A husband dies entitled to remainder in fee of real estate, expectant on an estate of freehold therein; his widow is not entitled to dower of the land when the remainder falls in. *Cocke's ex'or., &c.* vs. *Philips*, 12 Leigh, 248.

In *Jones* vs. *Hughes*, 27 Grat., 560, the right of dower was not barred by the Code 1873, ch. 106, § 4.

In *Medley* vs. *Medley*, 27 Grat. 568, a devisee's widow was held entitled to dower.

Mansion house.—The mansion house is not necessarily included in the assignment of dower as matter of right. *Devaughn* vs. *Devaughn*, 19 Grat. 556.

DECREES FOR FORECLOSURE OF MORTGAGE.

Decree for foreclosure of mortgage and sale of property.

(Names of parties.)

This cause came on this day to be heard, &c. On consideration whereof the court doth adjudge, order and decree that the defendant, R. M., do within six months from the date hereof pay to the said plaintiff, X. X., the sum of $300, with interest thereon at the rate of six per centum per annum from the 1st day of February, 18—, until paid; and it is further ordered, that if the said defendant shall, within the period aforesaid, pay to the said plaintiff the said sum of money with interest as aforesaid, that then the said plaintiff do reconvey the mortgaged premises in the bill and proceedings mentioned to the said defendant, free and clear of all encumbrances done by him, or any claiming by, from, or under him, the said plaintiff. And the court doth further adjudge, order and decree that unless the defendant do within six months, from the date hereof, pay the said sum of money with interest as aforesaid to the said plaintiff, then that A. B., who is hereby appointed a special commissioner for that purpose, do after having advertised the time, place and terms of sale for ———, in one of the newspapers published in the city of R———, expose to sale, at public anction, to the highest bidder, &c., (as on p. 522, *ante*, to the end.)

NOTE.

The practice in Virginia differs from the English practice. In Virginia (and in most of the other States of the Union, 4 Kent's Com. 174), the court orders a sale of the mortgaged premises. In England, the decree is that the mortgagor be forever barred and foreclosed of his equity of redemption, and that the mortgagee have the absolute right of property. *Seton on Decrees* (old) 139, *et seq.*

In some cases, however, the courts of England have not adhered to the practice of simple foreclosure. (See 1 Lom. R. P. 401, *et seq.*)

1. Where the estate is deficient to pay the incumbrance.
2. Where the mortgagor is dead, and there is a deficiency of personal assets.
3. Where the mortgage is of a dry reversion.
4. Where the mortgagor dies and the estate descends to an infant.
5. Where the mortgage is of an advowson.
6. Where the mortgagor becomes bankrupt, and the mortgagee prays a sale.
7. Where the mortgage is of land in Ireland, which is, by the local law, subject, of course, to a sale.

Commissioner appointed by foregoing order, reports sale ; sale confirmed, and decree for conveyance.

(Names of parties.)

This cause came on this day to be further heard upon the papers formerly read, and the report of the sale made by the commissioner, pursuant to the decretal order of the 17th day of January last, to which there is no exception, and was argued by counsel.

On consideration whereof, the court approving and confirming the said report, doth adjudge, order and decree, that upon the payment by J. B., Jr., of his two bonds in the report mentioned, as executed by him, for the purchase of the land and premises directed to be sold by said decretal order, the said commissioner do convey to the said J. B., Jr., with special warranty, the said land; and it is further ordered, that when the said commissioner shall have received payment of the bonds for $1,587.73, mentioned in the said report, he shall forthwith deposit the same in the Planters National Bank, of Richmond, to the credit of the court, in this cause, and file among the papers of this court a certificate of such deposit.

Decree for payment to plaintiff of proceeds of sale in satisfaction of his debt, and directing the defendant to check for the residue.

(Names of parties.)

This cause came on, &c. On consideration whereof, it appearing to the court, by the certificate of deposit filed by A. B., (the special commissioner appointed to sell the mortgaged property in the proceedings mentioned,) among the papers in this suit, that there is on deposit in the ——— bank ——— to the credit of this suit, the sum of $———, the proceeds of said mortgaged property; and it further appearing that the plaintiff is entitled to the sum of $———, that being the amount of the debt secured by his mortgage, with interest thereon, and of the costs by him about his suit in this behalf expended, the court doth adjudge, order and decree, that the said plaintiff, (or his counsel, N. O.,) do check on an attested copy of this decree on the said bank, for the said sum of $———. And it is further ordered, that the defendant do check on the said bank on an attested copy of this decree, for the sum of $———, being the balance standing in the said bank to the credit of the court in this cause, after the said plaintiff has checked as aforesaid. [And leave is given the parties, or either of them, to procure attested copies of this decree from the clerk, forthwith.]

Decree for account under bill for equity of redemption.

(Names of parties.)

This cause came on, &c. On consideration whereof, the court doth adjudge, order and decree that the papers in the cause be referred to one of the commissioners of this court who is directed to take an account of what is due the defendant C. R. for principal and interest on the mortgage in the bill mentioned after deducting whatever amount of the rents and profits of the said mortgaged premises the said defendant C. R. may have received or which may have come to the hands of any other person or persons by his order or for his use, or which he without his wilful default might have received.   And the said commissioner is directed to examine, state and settle the said account and report the same to the court with any matter specially stated deemed pertinent by himself or required by any of the parties to be so stated.

Decree requiring plaintiff to pay amount found due by commissioner's report, and in default, a sale of mortgaged premises directed.

(Names of parties.)

This cause came on this day to be farther heard upon the papers formerly read and on the report of commissioner J. J. filed since last hearing, to which report there is no exception, and was argued by counsel.   On consideration whereof the court doth adjudge, order and decree that the plaintiff do pay unto the defendant C. R., within six months after the date of this decree, the sum of $—— with interest &c., that being the balance found due from the said plaintiff to the said defendant C. R. by the report of the said commissioner [and the costs of the defendant expended in his defence in this suit],[88] and that upon the payment of the said principal, interest [and costs] to the said C. R. that the said defendant do re-surrender the mortgaged premises in the bill mentioned to the said plaintiff, or to such person or persons as he shall direct, free and clear of all incumbrances done by him or any person claiming by, through, or under him.   And it is further ordered, adjudged and decreed that if the said plaintiff shall fail within six months after the date of this decree to pay unto the said defendant C. R. the said principal, interest and costs as aforesaid, it is ordered that the said plaintiff be foreclosed of all equity of redemption in the said land and

---

[88] Defendant mortgagee, guilty of no wrong, should have costs.   See *Turner* vs. *Turner*, 3 Munf. 66.

the court doth further adjudge, order and decree that in case of such default in the payment of said principal, interest and costs then that A. B., who is hereby appointed a commissioner for the the purpose, do expose to sale at public auction, to the highest bid-der on the premises, the land mortgaged by the plaintiff, as in his bill mentioned, on the following terms, to-wit: (here prescribe terms, &c.) and the said commissioner is directed to report his pro-ceedings under this decree to this court. But the said commis-sioner shall not receive any money under this decree until he shall &c., (follow form on p. 555 *ante* to conclusion).

NOTES.

The foregoing form has been drawn in conformity with the de-cision in *Turner* vs. *Turner*, 3 Munf. 66.

See following notes on foreclosure, &c., as to sales by commis-sioners and purchaser's rights and liabilities, &c.

Practical notes to decrees for foreclosure of mortgages.

See ante pp. 193–196, 2 Rob. Pr. (old) 50–70 ; 1 Wallace's S. C. R. VII ; Wythe's Rep. 404–430 ; 2 Min. Inst. 278–285, 296–319, 319–330.

As to rights and liabilities of purchasers under sales by the court see *Lovell* vs. *Arnold*, 2 Munf. 167 ; *Anderson* vs. *Davies*, 6 Munf. 484 ; *Heywood* vs. *Covington*, 4 Leigh 373 ; *Taylor* vs. *Cooper*, 10 Leigh 317 ; *Newman* vs. *Chapman*, 2 Rand. 93 ; *Commonwealth* vs. *Ragsdale*, 2 H. & M. 8.

As to when such sales will not be set aside, *Fairfax* vs. *Muse's* ex'ors, 4 Munf. 124 ; *Forde* vs. *Heron*, 4 Munf. 316.

As to when such sales will be set aside, *Quarles* vs. *Lacy*, 4 Munf. 251 ; *Wood's* ex'or, *&c.* vs. *Hudson*, 5 Munf. 423 ; *Tennant's* heirs vs *Pattons*, 6 Leigh 196.

As to other matters connected with mortgages, *Taylor* vs. *Cole*, 4 Munf. 351 ; *Beverley* vs. *Brooke & als.*, 2 Leigh 426 ; *Haskins* vs. *Forsyth & als.*, 11 Leigh 294 ; *Davison* vs. *Waite*, 2 Munf. 527 ; *Ross* vs. *Norvell*, 1 Wash. 14.

As to equity of redemption, *Floyd* vs. *Harrison*, *&c.*, 2 Rob. 161 ; *Turner* vs. *Turner*, 3 Munf. 66 ; *Pennington* vs. *Hanly*, 1 Munf. 140.

In *Brien* vs. *Pitman & Co.*, 12 Leigh 383, a proceeding against an absent defendant's property by foreign attachment, the court after establishing the debt decreed a sale of the lands for cash and in the same decree directed the payment of the money to the cred-itor and a conveyance to the purchaser : held to be error to direct payment and conveyance before the sale was reported and confirmed.

For full discussion of mortgages see 2 Robinson's Pr. (old), and Lomax's Digest of Real Property, and the note of Mr. Green in the Appendix to Wythe's Rep. 404–430.

The 96th Rule of U. S. Sup. Court, 1 Wall. VII provides, that "In suits in equity for the foreclosure of mortgages in the Circuit Courts of the United States, or in any of the courts of the territories having jurisdiction of the same, a decree may be rendered for any balance that may be found due to the complainant over and above the proceeds of the sale or sales, and execution may issue for the collection of the same, as is provided in the eighth rule of this Court regulating the equity practice, where the decree is solely for the payment of money."

DECREES FOR DIVORCE.[89]

Decree for divorce a mensa et toro, for abandonment two years.

(Names of parties.)

This cause came on this day to be heard on the bill, answer and examinations of witnesses, and was argued by counsel. On consideration whereof the court doth adjudge, order and decree that the plaintiff, Lucy L., be divorced *a mensa et toro* from her husband, the said Robert L.

[Clauses may be added concerning alimony and costs, as in next form.]

Decree for divorce and alimony.

(Names of parties.)

This cause came on, &c.; on consideration whereof the court doth adjudge, order and decree, that the marriage heretofore had and solemnized between the defendant, Robert L., and the plaintiff, Lucy L., (formerly Lucy M.,) shall be, and the same is, hereby dissolved ; and that the said Lucy L. be forever divorced from the said Robert L.; and the court doth further adjudge, order and decree, that the defendant do pay annually, unto the said plaintiff, the sum of $———, in quarterly installments, on the first days of January, &c., in each year, that sum being, in the opinion of the court, a sufficient maintenance and support for the said Lucy L.

---

[89] See Practical Notes on pp. 98–100, *ante.*

And the court doth further adjudge, order and decree that the said Robert L. do pay unto the plaintiff her costs expended in the prosecution of this suit.

Decree for divorce, a vinculo matrimonii, on account of abandonment five years.

(Names of parties.)

This cause came on this day to be heard, &c. On consideration whereof, the court being of opinion, from the evidence furnished in the cause, that the defendant has abandoned the plaintiff for a period of five years, doth adjudge, order and decree that the marriage heretofore had and solemnized, &c., &c., (as in last form to end.)

Decree for divorce a vinculo for abandonment for five years, there having been a previous decree of divorce, a mensa et toro.

(Names of parties.)

This cause came on this day to be heard on the papers formerly read, the said cause having been reinstated on the docket on motion of the plaintiff, and was argued by counsel: On consideration whereof, it appearing to the court, as established by the decree heretofore rendered, that the defendant had abandoned the said plaintiff, and a period of five years having now elapsed since the said abandonment, the court doth adjudge, order and decree that the marriage heretofore had and solemnized, &c., (as in last form to end.)

Order for payment to plaintiff pending suit.

(Names of parties.)

On motion of the plaintiff by counsel, and it appearing to the court from the pleadings and proofs in the cause that the plaintiff has no means of support during the pending of this suit, or of prosecuting the same, it is ordered that the said Robert L. do pay unto the said Lucy L. annually the sum of $———, in quarter yearly installments, on the first days of April, &c., in each year, that sum being, in the opinion of the court, a reasonable allowance to the said plaintiff, taking into consideration the value of the defendant's estate.

74

DECREES CONCERNING INJUNCTIONS.

Order of injunction restraining waste.

On motion of the plaintiffs, by counsel, and for good cause shown, an injunction is awarded them to injoin and restrain the defendant R. B., his agents, attorneys and all others, from committing waste upon the tract of land in the bill mentioned, whereof J. W. died seized, lying in the county of Henrico, and containing about ninety acres, and from cutting and removing anything from it until the further order of the court. But the plaintiffs are not to have the benefit of this order until the adult plaintiff shall enter into bond, with sufficient security, in the penalty of two hundred dollars, payable to the defendant, and conditioned to pay all such costs and damages as he may sustain in consequence of the said injunction, in case the same shall be dissolved.[90]

Order of injunction to judgment.

On motion of the plaintiff, by counsel, and for good cause shown, an injunction is awarded him to injoin and restrain the defendant S. L., his agents, attorneys and all others, from further proceeding on a judgment recovered by the said defendant against the plaintiff in the Circuit Court of the county of Powhatan, until the further order of the court. But the plaintiff is not to have the benefit of this order until he shall enter into bond,[91] with sufficient security, in the clerk's office of the said Circuit Court of Powhatan county, payable to said S. L., in a penalty equal to double the amount of the said judgment, conditioned, &c.;[92] *and until he shall*

---

[90] This bond must be given within sixty days from the date of the order of injunction. Session Acts 1874-5, p. 33.

[91] This bond must be given within sixty days from the date of the order of injunction. Session Acts, 1874-5, p. 33.

[92] The condition of the bond to be prescribed in the order of injunction, (See Session Acts, 1874-5, p. 33), either thus: "to pay the said judgment and all such costs as may be awarded against him, and all such damages as shall be incurred in case this injunction shall be dissolved."

Or, "to pay the value of the property levied on under execution on the said judgment by X. X., sheriff, &c., or to have the said property forthcoming

also file with the clerk of the said Circuit Court of Powhatan county a release of all errors at law in the said judgment and proceedings.[93]

Order dissolving injunction on motion.

The defendant this day, in pursuance of notice duly given the plaintiff, moved the court to dissolve the injunction awarded the plaintiff in this cause on the ———— day of ————, [and the said defendant filed his answer[94] and the plaintiff replied generally thereto] and the said motion coming on to be heard on the bill [and on the said answer with general replication thereto] and on the affidavits of R. R., J. J. and L. L., this day filed in behalf of the defendant, and on the affidavits of A. A. and B. B., this day filed in behalf of the plaintiff, was argued by counsel : On consideration whereof, the court doth sustain the said motion, and doth adjudge, order and decree that the said injunction awarded the said plaintiff in this cause be dissolved.

Order dissolving injunction and dismissing bill, on the hearing.

This cause came on this day to be heard on the bill, the answer of the defendant with replication thereto, and on the exhibits and examinations of witnesses, and was argued by counsel : On consideration whereof, the court doth adjudge, order and decree that the injunction awarded the plaintiff in this cause be dissolved, and that the bill of the plaintiff be dismissed, and that he pay to the defendant his costs by him about his defence in this behalf expended.

---

to abide the future order of this court, and to pay all such costs as may be awarded against him, the said plaintiff, and all such damages as may be incurred, in case this injunction shall be dissolved."

Or, if a forthcoming bond has been given under the judgment, with a farther condition in each of the above cases, "to indemnify and save harmless B. B. and A. A., the sureties in the forthcoming bond executed by the said plaintiff and their representatives against all loss or damage in consequence of said suretyship."

[93] See p. 589 post.

[94] See *Goddin* vs. *Vaughan's ex'x and als*, 14 Grat., 115, and sec. 72, p. 112 ante.

Order continuing injunction on terms.

[As in *Ross* vs. *Pleasants, &c.,* 1 H. & M. 1, where the surety being insufficient, the court directed that unless unexceptionable security be given by a specified time, the injunction should stand dissolved *as an act of the day on which the order was made :* or, in *Harrison* vs. *Morton,* 4 H. & M. 483, in which the court being satisfied that a particular individual was interested in the judgment at law, said it would order the injunction to stand dissolved, unless the plaintiff would amend his bill, and make that individual a party; or, in the cases in which a party, plaintiff or defendant, has died, and the injunction is ordered to stand dissolved unless there be a revival of the suit. See "Practical notes to decrees concerning injunctions," *post.* Sometimes before dissolution, unless there be a revival of the suit, a rule is necessary. See *Jackson* vs. *Arnold,* 4 Rand. 195.]

Order continuing injunction, without adjudicating the principles of the cause.

[Such an order in *Balt. & O. R. R. Co.* vs. *The City of Wheeling,* 13 Grat. 40.]

Injunction perpetuated.

This cause, in which the bill has been taken for confessed against the defendant, came on this day to be heard on the bill and exhibits filed, and was argued by counsel: On consideration whereof, the court doth adjudge, order and decree that the injunction awarded the plaintiff in this cause, on the ——— day of ———, to injoin, &c., [here set forth the injunction,] be made perpetual, and that the defendant do pay to the plaintiff his costs by him about his suit in this behalf expended.

Order on injunction to a judgment, decreeing against a plaintiff a sum of money in addition to the judgment.

[Such an order in *Todd* vs. *Bowyer,* 1 Munf. 447.]

Dismission of bill after dissolution of injunction.[95]

The injunction awarded the plaintiff in this cause having been wholly dissolved at the *October* term of this court, and no cause being shown against the dismission of the bill in this suit, it is ordered that the same be dismissed, and that the plaintiff pay to the defendant his costs by him about his defence in this behalf expended.

Order of injunction at suit of husband, parent, or householder or head of a family, or a laboring man, to prevent levy of execution, &c., on property exempted.

[Such an injunction provided for in Sess. Acts 1877-8, chap. 264, p. 247, amending Code 1873, chap. 175, § 1.]

PRACTICAL NOTES TO DECREES CONCERNING INJUNCTIONS.

See "Practical Notes" on pp. 92-95 ante.

The rule requiring a release of errors at law mentioned in *Warwick & als.* vs. *Norvell*, 1 Leigh 96, referred to on p. 92 *ante*, has been greatly modified, if not wholly changed by *Warwick, &c.* vs. *Norvell*, 1 Rob. R. 308, *Great Falls Manfg. Co.* vs. *Henry's adm'or*, 25 Grat. 577, and *Staples* vs. *Turner, adm'or, & als.*, 29 Grat. 830. In *Warwick, &c.* vs. *Norvell*, 1 Rob. R. 308, the syllabus of the reporter is this : "A defendant at law having a legal defence to the action, and a distinct ground for equitable relief against the plaintiff's claim, may bring his suit in equity without waiting for the determination of the action at law, and may, without being compelled to waive his legal defence by confessing a judgment, have a hearing in the court of chancery on the merits of his case, and a decree for the proper relief." This syllabus is cited with approbation by Judge Bouldin in *Great Falls Manfg. Co.* vs. *Henry's adm'or*, 25 Grat. 580, and is followed in that case; and both are cited and followed in the case of *Staples* vs. *Turner, adm'or, & als.*,

---

[95] It is the clerk's duty to enter this dismission on the last day of the term next after the dissolution of an injunction, if in a Circuit Court; if in an inferior court, on the last day of the second term after the dissolution. See Code 1873, ch. 175, sec. 14.

29 Grat. 330. They were all declared to be cases in which it was not proper to require the confession of a judgment in the suits at law as a condition upon which the injunction should be awarded.

DECREES FOR SPECIFIC PERFORMANCE.

Decree for specific performance in suit by vendee against vendor.

(Names of parties.)

This cause came on, &c. On consideration whereof the court doth adjudge, order and decree, that upon the payment of the sum of five hundred dollars by the said A. M., plaintiff (with interest &c.), to the said C. D., defendant, the said C. D. do execute a good and sufficient grant and conveyance to the said A. M., with general warranty and the usual covenants of title; granting and conveying to the said A. M. the land in the bill mentioned according to the metes and bounds laid down in the agreement in writing between the said A. M. and C. D., bearing date on the —— day of ——, and filed as an exhibit with the plaintiff's bill. And it is ordered that the said defendant do pay unto the plaintiff his costs by him about his suit in this behalf expended, and leave is given the said plaintiff to apply to this court for such other relief in the premises as may be necessary.

Decree in a case in which assignee for value of note given for purchase of land brought suit against his assignor, the vendor, and the vendee for specific performance. Hanna vs. Wilson, 3 Grat. 246.

(Names of parties.)

This cause came on, &c. On consideration whereof the court doth adjudge, order and decree, that the plaintiff recover of the said Q. B. W. the sum of $154.34, with interest thereon, from the 5th day of November, 1838, until paid, and his costs by him about the prosecution of his suit in this behalf expended, and upon the payment of said debt, interest and costs, it is further ordered that the clerk do deliver to the said Q. B. W. the original deed filed as an exhibit with the bill, retaining a certified copy thereof, to be filed with the papers in the cause. And it is further adjudged, ordered and decreed, that unless the said Q. B. W. shall pay to the plaintiff the debt, interest and costs aforesaid, within sixty days after the entering of this decree, the sheriff of G——— county, after advertising the time and place of sale by advertisement published, &c., and posted, &c., for four weeks successively, do proceed before the courthouse of said county, on some court day, to sell said land in said deed described, upon a credit of six and twelve months, taking from the purchaser bond and security, and retaining a lien on the land for the security of the purchase money, and report his proceedings in order to a final decree.

PRACTICAL NOTES TO DECREES FOR SPECIFIC PERFORMANCE.

See as to *parties to bills* pp. 209–211, 213, *ante;* Hoover *vs.* Donally, &c:, 3 H. and M. 316; 2 Lom. Dig. 69.

When specific performance refused : Ward *vs.* Webber & als., 1 Wash. 279; Smallwood *vs.* Mercer, &c., 1 Wash. 290; Graham *vs.* Call., 5 Munf. 396; Graham *vs.* Hendren, 5 Munf. 185; Harvie & als. *vs.* Banks, 1 Rand. 408; Darlington *vs.* McCoole, 1 Leigh 36; Reed's heirs *vs.* Vannorsdale & ux., 2 Leigh 569; Watts & als. *vs.* Kinney, &c., 3 Leigh 272; Payne *vs.* Graves, 5 Leigh 561; Moore's adm'r *vs.* Fitz Randolph & als., 6 Leigh 175; Pigg *vs.* Corder, 12 Leigh 69; McCann *vs.* James, 1 Rob. 256; Bowles *vs.* Woodson, 6 Grat. 78; Griffin *vs.* Cunningham, 19 Grat. 571; McComas *vs.* Easley, 21 Grat. 23; Booten *vs.* Schaffer, 21 Grat. 474; Carrington *vs.* Otis, 4 Grat. 235; Clarke *vs.* Reins, 12 Grat. 98; Hoover *vs.* Calhoun, 16 Grat. 109; Pierce's heirs *vs.* Catron's heirs, 23 Grat. 588; Wright *vs.* Pickett, 22 Grat. 370; Christian *vs.* Cabell & als., 22 Grat. 82; Hendricks *vs.* Gillespie, 25 Grat. 181; Kemper *vs.* Ewing, 25 Grat. 427; Cox *vs.* Cox, 26 Grat. 305; Sprinkle *vs.* Hayworth & als., 26 Grat. 384; Stearns & als. *vs.* Beckham & als., 31 Grat. 379; Kenny *vs.* Hoffman & als., 31 Grat. 442.

When specific performance decreed : White *vs.* Atkinson, 2 Wash. 94 : Long *vs.* Colston, 1 H. & M. 111; Hook *vs.* Ross, 4 Munf. 97; Beverley *vs.* Lawson's heirs, 3 Munf. 317; Birchett & als. *vs.* Bolling, 5 Munf. 442; Wilde, &c. *vs.* Fox, &c., 1 Rand. 164; Evans *vs.* Kingsberry, &c., 2 Rand. 120; Anthony *vs.* Leftwich, 3 Rand. 238; Tapp *vs.* Beverley, 1 Leigh 80; Edwards *vs.* Van Bibber, 1 Leigh 231; Foley *vs.* McKeown, 4 Leigh 627; Williams *vs.* Lewis, 5 Leigh 686; Smith *vs.* Jones, 7 Leigh 165; Clarke & als. *vs.* Curtis, 11 Leigh 559; Hanna *vs.* Wilson, 3 Grat. 243; Mays *vs.* Swope, 8 Grat. 46; Parrill *vs.* McKinley, 9 Grat. 1; McKee *vs.* Bailey, 11 Grat. 340; Bailey *vs.* James, 11 Grat. 468; Summers *vs.* Bean, 13 Grat. 404; Goddin *vs.* Vaughan, 14 Grat. 102; White *vs.* Dobson, 17 Grat. 262; Hale *vs.* Wilkinson, 21 Grat. 75; Moss, &c. *vs.* Moorman's adm'or, 24 Grat. 97; Ambrouse's heirs *vs.* Keller, 22 Grat. 769; Talley *vs.* Robinson, 22 Grat. 888; Stimson *vs.* Thorn, 25 Grat. 278; Kemper *vs.* Ewing & als., 25 Grat. 427; Rhea *vs.* Jordan, 28 Grat. 678; Lester *vs.* Lester & als., 28 Grat. 737; White, &c. *vs.* McGannon & als., 29 Grat. 511; Wyeth *vs.* Mahoney & als., 32 Grat. 645.

There should not be a decree to pay money absolutely on bill for specific performance, but the court may give defendant election either to pay the money or to perform the agreement specifically. Hook *vs.* Ross, 1 H. & M., 310.

In a case in which specific performance was decreed against the vendee, he insisted that he should be compensated for injuries to which he had been subjected by the failure of the vendor to comply with his contract, and by the intermeddling of the vendor and his agents with the vendee's possession of the land; compensation for the damages was decreed the vendee, and the damages could be ascertained either by a commissioner or by an issue *quantum damnificatus*. Nagle *vs.* Newton, 22 Grat., 814.

When deficiency in land sold.

See Jolliffe *vs.* Hite, 1 Call, 301; Anthony *vs.* Oldacre, 4 Call, 489; Quesnel *vs.* Woodlief, 6 Call, 218; Nelson *vs.* Matthews, 2 H. & M., 164; Hull *vs.* Cunningham's ex'or, 1 Munf., 330; Humphrey's adm'r *vs.* McClenahan's adm'r and heirs, 1 Munf., 493; Grantland *vs.* Wight, 2 Munf., 179; Nelson *vs.* Carrington's ex'ors, 4 Munf., 332; Fleet *vs.* Hawkins, 6 Munf., 188; Tucker *vs.* Cocke, 2 Rand., 51; Castleman and als *vs.* Veitch and als, 3 Rand., 598; Bedford *vs.* Hickman, 5 Call, 236; Koger and als *vs.* Kane's adm'r and heirs, 5 Leigh, 606; Keytons *vs.* Brawfords, 5 Leigh, 39; Neal *vs.* Logan, 1 Grat., 14.

MISCELLANEOUS ORDERS AND DECREES.

Order for removal from one court to another.[96]

(Names of parties.)

On motion of the defendant, O. D., the plaintiff, A. B., having had due notice of this motion, it is ordered that this suit be removed to the Circuit Court of the county of ———, [or, the judge of this

---

[96] May be made when cause is at rules, *Muller, &c.*, vs. *Bayley and als.*, 21 Grat., 521. See Sess. Acts, 1878-9, p. 24.

court being so situated as to render it improper in his judgment for him to decide this suit, it is ordered, &c., as before.]

Order changing plaintiffs to make them witnesses.[97]

(Names of parties.)   In order to make L. M. a witness in this case, the powers of L. M., as trustee in a deed, &c., having been revoked, and M. N. having been substituted in his stead as such trustee, it is ordered that this suit be discontinued in the name of the said L. M. and be continued in the name of the said M. N. as one of the plaintiffs therein, and the said M. N. and the plaintiff, A. B., are required to pay into court the costs which have been incurred by the defendant, C. D., about his defence to this suit, and to enter into bond with sufficient security, payable to the said defendant, conditioned to pay him all costs which may hereafter accrue to the said defendant.

Defendant's death suggested and rule to speed.

(Names of parties.)

On the motion of the defendant, H. K., late sheriff of the county of Hanover, and as such administrator of W. J., deceased, by counsel, the deaths of the defendants, T. G., administrator of J. M. S., deceased, and B. B., executor of B. O., deceased, are suggested; and on the farther motion of the said defendant by counsel, it is ordered that unless the plaintiffs proceed by proper process to revive and mature this cause for hearing at or before the term next after they shall have been served with a copy of this order, the bill of the plaintiffs be dismissed at their costs.

Order dismissing bill, plaintiff failing to mature suit for a hearing.

(Names of parties.)

The plaintiff in this suit having been duly served with a copy of the order entered herein on the ——— day of ———, he still failing to mature this suit for a hearing against the defendants, R. K., and others, on the motion of defendant, C. D., by counsel, it is

---

[97] Necessary in some cases, now, though the statutes cited on pp. 446, 447, 448, 449 ante, have greatly extended the competency of witnesses.

ordered that the same be dismissed, and that the plaintiff pay unto
the defendant, C. D., his costs by him about his defence in this
behalf expended.

*An order directing pending case to be struck from the docket; no
order in it for seven years but to continue it.*

See Code 1873, ch. 169, sec. 8.

Order appointing guardian ad litem to infant or insane defendants.

Code 1873, ch. 167, sec. 17.

(Names of parties.)

On the motion of ———, D. L. is assigned guardian *ad litem* to
the infant [*or* insane] defendant, N. O., to defend his interests in
this suit.

The court may compel the guardian *ad litem* to act.   Code 1873,
ch. 167, sec. 17.

Rule to speed.

(Names of parties.)

The plaintiff in this cause having failed to prosecute his suit by
maturing his cause for a hearing as against the defendants, R. K.
and L. L., on the motion of the defendant, C. D., by counsel, it is
ordered that unless the plaintiff proceed by proper process to
mature this cause for a hearing at or before the term next after he
shall have been served with a copy of this order, the bill of the
said plaintiff be dismissed at his costs.

Rule for security for costs by clerk.

(Names of parties.)

The plaintiff in this suit not being an inhabitant of this State, the
clerk of this court demands of her security for the payment of the
costs which may be incurred in the prosecution of the same.   And
the court doth order that unless such security be given within sixty
days from the date hereof, that the bill of the plaintiff be dismissed
at her costs.

Order removing a cause to the Circuit Court of the United States.

(Names of parties.)

The defendant, P. B., having this day entered his appearance at the suit of the plaintiff and filed a petition for the removal of this cause into the Circuit Court of the United States for the Fourth Circuit and Eastern District of Virginia, and having also given bond with good and sufficient security for his entering into such court on the first day of the next session, copies, &c., of the proceedings and pleadings in this suit, and the court being of opinion that the said defendant is entitled to have this suit removed to the said court, it is ordered that the same be removed to the said Circuit Court of the United States, &c., and this court will proceed no farther in the cause.

Order allowing creditor to be admitted a party plaintiff.

(Names of parties.)

This day C. N. presented his petition to the court, praying to be admitted a party plaintiff in this suit, and agreeing to contribute to the costs thereof, and it is ordered that the said C. N. be admitted as a party plaintiff with the other plaintiffs in the record, and that he contribute towards defraying the costs and expenses attending the prosecution of this suit.

Order changing next friend to make him a witness.[98]

(Names of parties.)

The defendants desiring to examine as a witness in this cause on their behalf, the said M. N., who is the next friend of the infant plaintiff, and it appearing by an affidavit filed by the said defendants, that the testimony of the said M. N. is material to their defence in this suit, it is ordered that the name of the said M. N. be struck out of the record as next friend, and that J. B. be substituted as the next friend of the said infant, to prosecute the suit in his behalf.

---

[98] See note to form on p. 593, *ante.*

Order for party to pay money into court.

[There are many cases in which such an order should be made. When defendant, in his answer, admits a sum of money to be in his hands belonging to plaintiff, 3 Bro. C. C., 365; 1 New Ch., 202. The purchaser of an estate, when he has, under an agreement, taken possession of the estate without any engagement on the part of the vendor that he should not be called on to pay the purchase-money until a good title can be made, will be ordered to pay the purchase money into court, 15 Ves., 317; 1 New Ch. Pr., 203. And in many other cases a like order will be made. See 1 New. Ch. Pr., 203.]

ORDERS RELATING TO ANSWERS.

Answer referred to commissioner to expunge scandalous matter.

(Names of parties.)
The court doth refer the answer put in by the defendant R. B. to the bill of the plaintiffs to one of its commissioners, for the purpose of expunging the impertinent and scandalous matter therein contained, and order the said defendant to pay the costs of executing this order.

Last order set aside, and commissioner to report scandalous matter.

(Names of parties.)
For reasons appearing to the court, the order made in this cause on Tuesday last is set aside, and the court doth order, on motion of the plaintiffs, by counsel, that the answer put in to the bill of the plaintiffs by the defendant R. B. be referred to commissioner G. for him forthwith to report to the court such matters contained in the said answer as shall be deemed by him impertinent and scandalous.

Exceptions to answer sustained.

(Names of parties.)
The exceptions to the answer being argued, and the said answer being adjudged insufficient, it is ordered that the defendant answer the plaintiff's bill more fully and sufficiently; and that he pay to the plaintiff his costs occasioned by such insufficient answer.

Answer and exceptions referred to a commissioner.

The court doth order that commissioner L. do look into the plaintiff's bill, the defendant's answer and the plaintiff's exceptions taken thereunto, and report forthwith whether the defendant's answer be sufficient in the points excepted to or not.

Report of commissioner confirmed and answer adjudged insufficient.

The court taking into consideration the report of commissioner L., made in pursuance of the order of the 17th day of the present month, doth confirm the said report, and doth adjudge the answer of the defendant, so far as it is reported not to be responsive to the bill, to be insufficient. And it is further ordered that the defendant answer again as to those matters, and pay to the plaintiffs all the costs by them expended about their said exceptions.

Defendant ordered to be brought into court to answer interrogatories.
Code 1873, chap. 167, sec. 47.

On motion of the plaintiff, by counsel, and for reasons appearing to the court, it is ordered that the defendant, H. L., Jr., be brought into court by ———, a messenger for that purpose, to answer interrogatories upon oath, because the said H. L., Jr., hath failed to file his answer in the time prescribed by law, although duly served with process for that purpose.

PROCESS OF CONTEMPT TO COMPEL AN ANSWER.

Order for attachment.[99]

The writ of summons having been duly served on the defendant, J. J., and the said defendant still failing to appear and plead an-

---

[99] The practice in Virginia is before issuing a peremptory attachment to compel a purchaser to comply with the terms of his purchase, to give a rule to show cause why an attachment should not issue. This practice could be conveniently adapted to the case of compelling an answer, and in that event, after the issuing and service of such a rule, in the above form after the word "plaintiff" on third line might be inserted; "and the said defendant failing to show cause why an attachment should not issue."

swer or demur to the bill of the plaintiff, on the motion of the
plaintiff, by counsel, it is ordered that an attachment be issued
against the said defendant for his contempt in failing to answer the
bill of the plaintiff in this cause.[100]

Attachment with proclamation awarded.

The attachment sued forth against the defendant, J. J., for his
contempt in not filing an answer (or a sufficient answer) to the bill
of plaintiff being returned not found, on the motion of the plaintiff,
by counsel, an attachment, with proclamation, is awarded against
the defendant, returnable here, &c.

Commission of rebellion awarded.

The sheriff of the county of H. having returned the attachment with proclamation, sued forth against the said J. J. the 4th
day of October last, that he had caused proclamation to be made
as commanded by the said writ, and that the said J. J. is not to be
found within his bailiwick, on motion of the plaintiffs by counsel, a
commission of rebellion is awarded against the said J. J.

Writ of sequestration nisi.

In appearing to the satisfaction of the court, that J. J., who was
committed to the jail of the county of G. by virtue of a writ of
attachment sued forth against him for his contempt in not answering the bill of plaintiff in this cause, has made his escape from the
said jail and is now going at large, on motion of W. R. by counsel, the court doth award a writ of sequestration against the said
J. J., and appoint B. B., C. C., and D. D., any two or more of whom
may act, commissioners to execute the said writ, unless the said J.
J. on the first day of the ——— term next after he shall have
been served with a copy of this order, show cause to the contrary.

---

[100] If the defendant is brought in under attachment, he will be compelled to
answer. If the attachment is returned "not found," the subsequent steps in
the process of contempt are taken.

Writ of sequestration awarded absolutely.

This day came the plaintiff, W. R., by counsel, and it appearing by the affidavit of J. C. L. that J. J. hath been duly served with a copy of the rule entered against him in this cause, the 23d day of June last, and he failing to appear and show cause against it, on motion of the plaintiff, W. R., by counsel, the said rule is made absolute; and the court doth appoint B. B., C. C., and D. D., or any two of them, commissioners to execute the writ of sequestration awarded·by the said rule.

Order for commissioners named in writ of sequestration to sell goods and rent out lands.

B. B., C. C., and D. D., three of the commissioners named in the writ of sequestration, heretofore issued in this cause, having made return thereof that they have entered upon all the real estate whereof the said J. J. was seized and possessed; and also that they have taken into their hands all his personal goods and chattels whereof he was found in possession, subject, as they suppose, to the incumbrances annexed to their said return, but which they hold ready for the further order of the court: On the motion of the plaintiff by counsel, it is ordered that the said commissioners who made the return aforesaid, or any two of them, after giving reasonable public notice thereof, do sell, at public auction, all the goods taken by them as aforesaid for·ready money, and that they pay the proceeds thereof into the Bank of Virginia to the credit of —————— subject to the future order of the court; and that they, or any two of them, do henceforth proceed to rent out such of the lands stated in their said return as are not already rented; and that they, or any one of them, do proceed to the collection of the rents that are or may become due for any of the said lands rented, or to be rented, and pay the amount thereof into the said bank to the credit of —————— subject to the future order of the court, unless the mortgagees, whose deeds are annexed to the said return, being severally served with a copy of this order, can show cause to the contrary on or before the first day of the next term after such service.

PROCESS OF CONTEMPT TO COMPEL OBEDIENCE TO DECREES.

Rule for attachment against purchaser.

A. B., plaintiff, against C. D., defendant.

It appearing to the court, from the report of P. H., of the sale made by him as commissioner of this court under the decree entered herein on the eleventh day of February, eighteen hundred and forty-nine, that J. R. C. became the purchaser of the property sold under the said decree, and that he hath failed to comply with the terms of his said purchase. On the motion of the plaintiffs, by counsel, the court doth order that an attachment be sued forth against the said J. R. C. for his contempt in failing to pay into the Planters National Bank, of Richmond, the sum of six hundred and seventy dollars and thirty-one cents, on the eighteenth day of May, 18—, that being the amount of the note executed by him for a portion of the said purchase-money, and negotiable and payable at said bank at the date aforesaid, and taken under and in pursuance of the directions of the said decree of sale, unless the said J. R. C. having been previously served with a copy of this order, shew cause to this court to the contrary on Saturday, the twenty-fourth day of the present month.

Attachment made absolute.

On motion of the plaintiff, by counsel, and for good cause shown, the court doth order that an attachment be sued forth against J. R. C., the purchaser of the property sold under the decree entered in this cause on the 11th day of February, 18—, for his contempt in failing to comply with the terms of his said purchase in failing to pay into the Planters National Bank, of Richmond, Virginia, the sum of $670.31 cents, on the 18th day of May, 18—.

If purchaser "not found" proceed as in ' process of contempt to compel an answer." See pp. 598, 599.

OTHER ORDERS.

Order granting leave to re-examine witnesses.

The plaintiff, by his counsel, this day moved the court for an order allowing·him to re-examine and retake the depositions of S. G. and R. H. D., whose depositions have been heretofore taken in this cause, of which motion the plaintiff produced a notice, with evidence of due service thereof upon the defendant W. J. C., and the said plaintiff also filed his own affidavit in support of the said motion : On consideration whereof the court doth grant to the said plaintiff leave to re-examine and retake the depositions of the said S. G. and R. H. D., to be read as evidence in behalf of the said plaintiff in this cause, giving to the defendants reasonable notice of the time and place of retaking the said depositions, and reserving to the said defendants all just and legal exceptions to the reading of the same when retaken.

Demurrer to bill adjudged good and bill dismissed.

This day, &c., and thereupon the demurrer of the defendant to the plaintiff's bill being argued, it is the opinion of the court that the said demurrer is good : Therefore it is decreed and ordered that the said demurrer be sustained and the bill of the plaintiff be dismissed, and that the plaintiff pay to the defendant his costs by him about his defence sustained.

Leave granted to amend bill.

On motion of the plaintiff, by counsel, leave is granted him to amend his bill and to make new parties. And the cause is sent to the rules for that purpose.

Motion to file a bill of review overruled.

This day the plaintiff, by counsel, moved the court for leave to file a bill of review to the decree of this court made on the ——. day of ——, and the said plaintiff tendered in court his said bill, and the said motion being argued, on consideration thereof, the court is of opinion that there is no error in the said decree, and doth reject the said motion.

76

Cause revived by consent.

The defendant B. L. having departed this life, by consent as well of the plaintiffs as of H. T., executor of the said B. L., deceased, it is ordered that this suit stand revived against the said executor.

CHAPTER XII.

Execution of decree.

506. In the United States Circuit Courts, as in the Virginia State courts, decrees or orders in equity for the payment of money, are enforced in the same way as judgments at common law; other decrees or orders may be enforced by the process of contempt or its equivalent, and in special cases, the party may proceed by writ of assistance.

507. In the United States Circuit Courts, if the decree be for the performance of any specific act, as, for example, for the execution of a conveyance of land, or the delivering up of deeds, or other documents, it is required by the eighth rule of practice, that the decree shall, in all such cases, prescribe the time within which the act shall be done, of which the defendant will be bound, without further service, to take notice; and upon affidavit of the plaintiff, filed in the clerk's office, that the decree has not been complied with within the prescribed time, the clerk will issue a writ of attachment against the delinquent party, from which, if attached thereon, he shall not

be discharged, unless upon a full compliance with the decree and the payment of all costs, or upon a special order of the court or of a judge thereof, upon motion and affidavit, enlarging the time for the performance thereof; and if the delinquent party cannot be found, a writ of sequestration will issue against his estate, upon the return of non est inventus, to compel obedience to the decree.[1]

508. In the Virginia State courts, in `the cases mentioned in the last section, the ordinary course pursued is this: the party is, in the first instance, served with a copy of the decree or order requiring him to do the specific act by a day which is usually mentioned in the decree or order; if he fail to comply, a rule is then made upon him to show cause why an attachment should not issue against him for his contempt in not obeying the decree or order of the court, and a copy of this is likewise served upon him; if he fail to appear to this rule an attachment will be issued against him; if he appear and show no sufficient cause, he will be, in some cases, imprisoned or fined, beside being required, before his release, to comply with the former order or decree of the court. In case an attachment issues, and it is not served upon him, the process of contempt may be regularly pursued to the sequestration.

509. *Writ of assistance.* The writ of assistance is a process to put a party in possession of an estate which has been ordered by a decree or order to be

---

[1] Reference has been already made to the 96th rule, concerning decrees in foreclosure suits and the manner of executing the same. See p. 584 *ante.*

delivered. 2 Dan. Ch. Pr. (old) 723. Under the old
practice of the Court of Chancery in England, this
writ could not be obtained without previously suing
out and serving what was termed a "writ of injunction" to deliver possession, which could only be procured upon the issuing of an attachment or other
process of contempt against the parties for not obeying the writ of execution, which attachment or process was not, however, required to be executed. 2
Dan. Ch. Pr. (old) 724. Subsequently, the writ of
injunction was omitted, and by special statute it was
provided that where any party obstinately retained
possession of land or other real property, after a
writ of execution of a decree, or an order for delivery of possession has been duly served, and
demand of possession made, upon an affidavit of
such service of the writ of execution, and of such
demand made thereunder, and a refusal to comply
therewith, on the part of the person against whom
the writ issued, the party issuing it should be at liberty to obtain the usual order of course for the writ
of assistance to issue, and that the intermediate writs
of attachment and injunction, further commanding
the party to deliver possession, on any other writ,
should be unnecessary. 2 Dan. Ch. Pr. (old) 724.

510. This writ is rarely, if ever, used in the Virginia State Courts. The usual course adopted in
these courts in cases in which, according to the practice just mentioned, this writ might issue, is the one
recited in section 508 ante.

511. In the United States Circuit Courts, by the

9th Rule of Practice, when any decree or order is for the delivery of possession, upon proof made by affidavit of a demand and refusal to obey the decree or order, the party prosecuting the same will be entitled to a writ of assistance from the clerk of the court.

512. The forms of several writs of execution of decrees to enforce decrees or orders for the payment of money, are similar to those at common law. Forms of these writs, and of the writ of assistance here follow :

FORMS OF FINAL PROCESS IN UNITED STATES CIRCUIT COURTS.

Fierifacias.

The President of the United States of America to the Marshal of the Eastern District of Virginia, Greeting :

You are hereby commanded that of the goods and chattels of A. B., you cause to be made the sum of $500, with interest thereon at the rate of six per centum per annum from the —— day of ——, 18—, until paid, which J. W., late in the Circuit Court of the United States for the Fourth Circuit and Eastern District of Virginia, hath recovered against the said A. B., by a decree in chancery made on the —— day of ——, whereof the said A. B. is convict, as appears to us of record : And that you have the said sum of money and interest before the judges of the said court at Richmond city, State of Virginia, on the —— Monday of —— next, to render to the said J. W. the sum of money and interest as aforesaid, and have then there this writ.

Witness, R. B. T., Chief Justice of the Supreme Court of the United States, at Richmond, this —— day of ——, and in the —— year of the Independence of the United States of America.

A. A., Clerk.

Writ of assistance.

The President of the United States of America to the Marshal of the —— District of ———, Greeting:

Whereas, by a certain decree (*or* order) made in our Circuit Court of the United States for the —— circuit, &c., in a certain cause therein depending between A. B., complainant, and C. D., defendant, on the —— day of ———, it was [among other things therein contained] ordered, adjudged and decreed by the said court that the said defendant, C. D., should deliver into the possession of the said A. B. a certain lot of land (here describe land); and whereas a proper affidavit has been made before the clerk of our said court that the said A. B. did, on the —— day of ———, make a demand on the said C. D. for the delivery of the said land into his, the said A. B.'s possession, according to the tenor and true intent of the said decree (*or* order,) and that the said C. D. did thereupon refuse to make such delivery and to obey the said decree (*or* order;) therefore we command you that immediately after receiving this writ you go to and enter upon the said land, &c., and that you eject and remove therefrom all and every person or persons holding and detaining the same, or any part thereof, against the said complainant; and that you put and place the said complainant or his assigns in the full, quiet and peaceable possession of the said land, &c., without delay; and him, the said complainant, in such possession thereof from time to time maintain, keep and defend, or cause to be kept, maintained and defended, according to the tenor and true intent of the said decree (*or* order) of our said court.

Witness, R. B. T., Chief Justice of the Supreme Court of the United States, at Richmond, this —— day of ———, and in the —— year of the Independence of the United States of America.

P. M., Clerk.

Process of contempt in United States courts.

See *ante,* pp. 153, 154.

FORMS OF FINAL PROCESS IN VIRGINIA STATE COURTS.

Fierifacias.

THE COMMONWEALTH OF VIRGINIA, *To the* —— *of* —— *County,* *Greeting* :

We command you that of the goods and chattels of A. B., late in your bailiwick, you cause to be made the sum of —— dollars, with interest thereon, &c., which C. D., lately in our Circuit Court for the county of ——, recovered against him by a decree in chancery rendered by the said court; also the sum of —— dollars, which to the said C. D., in the same court, were adjudged for his costs in that suit expended; whereof the said A. B. is convict, as appears to us of record, *and that you have the said sums of money before the judge of our said Circuit Court, at the Court-house in the county of* ——, *on the first day of the next term,*[2] *to render to the said C. D. of the principal money, interest and costs aforesaid.* And have then there this writ.

Witness, J. E., clerk of our said court, this —— day of ——, A. D. 185—, and in the —— year of the Commonwealth of Virginia.

J. E., *Clerk.*

Venditioni exponas.

THE COMMONWEALTH, &c., *Greeting* :

We command you that you expose to sale those goods and chattels of A. B., to the value of ——, which, according to our command, you have taken, and which remain in your hands unsold, as you have certified to our judge of our —— court, to satisfy C. D. the sum of ——, whereof, in our said court, he hath recovered execution against the said A. B. by virtue of a decree in the said court, and that you have, &c. Witness, &c., &c.

---

[2] If returnable to rules, omitting italics, say : "And how you shall have executed this writ make known at the clerk's office of our said Circuit Court at the rules to be held for the said court, on the first Monday in —— next."

Writ of elegit.

The writ of elegit has been abolished. See Code 1873, ch. 183, sec. 26.

Process of contempt.

See pp. 118–125, *ante.*

513. In the United States Circuit courts, by. the 10th Rule of Practice, every person, not being a party in any cause, who has obtained an order, or in whose favor an order has been made, will be enabled to enforce obedience to such order by the same process as if he were a party to the cause; and every person, not being a party in any cause, against whom obedience to any order of the court may be enforced, will be liable to the same process for enforcing obedience to such order, as if he were a party in the cause.

PART II.

BOOK II.

CHAPTER I.

Issues out of Chancery.

514. " Feigned issues," as they are termed, were the means adopted by the English courts to try questions of fact in equity causes. As juries could not be summoned to attend the court of chancery, the fact was usually ordered to be tried at the bar of one of the courts of common law or at the assizes; and to do this effectually, so that the point in dispute, and that only, should be put in issue, an action was *feigned* to be brought, wherein the pretended plaintiff declares that he laid a wager of five pounds with the defendant that a particular thing was true; as, for instance, that A. was heir-at-law to B., and then avers that it is so, and brings his action for the five pounds. The defendant admits the wager, but avers that A. is not the heir-at-law to B., and thereupon that issue is joined, which is directed out of Chancery to be tried. And until this feigned issue was tried, no final decree could be pronounced in the cause. 2. Dan. Ch. Pr. (old), 631.

515. Issues out of chancery are uniformly, in England, directed to be tried before the courts of common law. This is the practice in the United States Circuit courts, these courts sitting as courts of common law when such issues are tried. The Virginia State courts, however, sitting as courts of equity, may direct such issues to be tried at their own bar, or before a common law court. Code 1873, ch. 173, sec. 4. A circuit court will not be compelled to try an issue ordered by a county or corporation court. Code 1873, ch. 173, sec. 4.

516. Feigned issues, strictly so called, are not directed in any case; they have been abolished in England, 8 & 9 Vict., ch. 109, § 19. They are not used in the Virginia State courts or in the United States Circuit courts. The questions at issue are now referred to the jury in a direct form.

517. The course of proceeding upon the trial of an issue is generally the same as that adopted in ordinary trials at law, except where the court directing the issue has given any special directions upon the subject. 2 Dan. Ch. Pr. (old), 742.

The court of chancery usually provides that on the trial of the issue, copies of the bill, answers, exhibits and depositions of such of the witnesses as are dead, or whose attendance cannot be had, may be read in evidence. Roane, J., in *Burwell, &c.* vs. *Corbin, &c.*, 1 Rand., 154. See 2 Dan. Ch. Pr. (old), 744. And the court will impose such restrictions upon the parties as will prevent all fraud and surprise at the trial. *Apthorp, &c.* vs. *Comstock, &c.*, 2 Paige, 484. See *Ford* vs. *Gardner & als.*, 1 H. & M., 72.

In *Steptoe* vs. *Flood*, 31 Grat. 323, the plaintiff in an issue relied upon a receipt to which there was an attesting witness, but both the witness and the principal were dead. The plaintiff having proved the handwriting of the witness, the defendant was permitted to introduce witnesses to prove that the name of the principal was not in his handwriting. There being great conflict of opinion among the witnesses as to the genuineness of the handwriting, the verdict against it, it was held, should not be disturbed.

518. The trial of an issue is usually had by *viva voce* testimony. *Paul* vs. *Paul*, 2 H. & M. 525.[1] The court at whose bar it is tried prevents the introduction of improper testimony. See *Pleasants, &c.,* vs. *Ross*, 1 Wash., 156.

519. After the trial has been had, the court before which the issue is tried certifies to the court directing the issue how the verdict was found; and if any special circumstances occur at the trial which the court may think it right to report, they may be thus certified to the court directing the issue. 2 Dan. Ch. Pr. (old) 746. *Watkins, &c.* vs. *Carlton*, 10 Leigh 560.

[When a verdict is found on an issue directed out of chancery, it is certainly proper that the court in which the issue was tried should certify its opinion of the verdict. *Pendleton*, P., in *Ross* vs. *Pynes*, 3 Call 573. If a party apply for such certificate, and the court refuse it, such application and refusal may be spread upon the record by bill of exceptions. *Stanard* vs. *Graves, &c.*, 2 Call 369.

If the court before which the issue is tried should be of opinion that the verdict is against evidence and certify its opinion upon the record, the chancellor will not generally be satisfied with the verdict. *Stanard* vs. *Graves, &c.*, 2 Call 369; *Pleasants, &c.* vs. *Ross*, 1 Wash. 156. But if the certificate be merely "that the weight of testimony was against the verdict, and therefore that the verdict was not satisfactory," a court of equity will not on this certificate grant a new trial of the issue. *Ross* vs. *Pynes*, 3 Call 568.

Though there be no certificate that the verdict is against evidence, still the chancellor will in some instances direct a new trial

---

[1] If a verdict be found and certified to the court of chancery, and there be nothing in the record showing that the answer and depositions filed in chancery were the only evidence exhibited on the trial of the issue, it cannot be inferred that such was the fact. *Paul, &c.* vs. *Paul*, 2 H. & M. 525. A court before whom the issue was tried being satisfied with the verdict, and overruling a motion for a new trial, to this opinion no exception was taken; held that the verdict should remain undisturbed. *Ibid.*

on affidavits proving misbehaviour in the jury, afterwards discovered. *Pleasants, &c.* vs. *Ross*, 1 Wash. 156.

Where, after a verdict upon an issue directed to be tried on the common law side of a county court, the defendant moved the court . to certify that the evidence was in his favour, on which motion the court was divided, and at a succeeding term a motion was made to the court sitting in chancery for a new trial which was overruled, and a bill of exceptions filed, containing, as the grounds of the motion, allegations of what passed at the trial, but not containing any proof of those allegations, such allegations were regarded merely as the suggestions of the counsel who drew the exceptions, and the truth of them was not considered as admitted by the court's signing and sealing the exceptions. *Ford* vs. *Gardner, &c.*, 1 H. & M. 72.

If the finding of a jury on an issue in equity is not consistent with an admission in the answer, it must be rejected, but both must stand if reconcilable. *McFerran* vs. *Taylor, &c.*, 3 Cr. 270.

520. On the trial of an issue a bill of exceptions for an alleged misdirection of the judge, will not lie. The regular course is, to apply to the court directing the issue for a new trial.   2 Dan. Ch. Pr. (old), 746.[2]

[But in *Stanard* vs. *Graves, &c.*, 2 Call, 369, when the court in which the issue was tried refused to certify its opinion of the verdict, it was held that if a party apply for such certificate and the court refuse it, such application and refusal may be spread upon the record by bill of exceptions. And in *Watkins, &c.* vs. *Carlton*, 10 Leigh, 560, in which bills of exception were taken on the trial of an issue before a common law court, the appellate court, on an appeal from the decree in the chancery cause, looked to the bills of exceptions filed at the common law trial. And in *Fitzhugh* vs. *Fitzhugh*, 11 Grat. 210, where there was no exception spreading the facts on the record, the verdict was held conclusive. See also *Lee's ex'or* vs. *Bock*, 11 Grat. 182.

---

[2] In *Leavell* vs. *Gold's adm'or*, 25 Grat., 473, the question was considered how verdicts on issues should be set aside.

In *McLaughlin* vs. *Bank of Potomac*, 7 How. 220, exceptions were not taken on the trial of an issue and passed on by the Circuit Court sitting in equity; the Supreme Court held, on appeal, that for these reasons it could not notice the points involved. In *Brockett* vs. *Brockett*, 3 How. 691, though exceptions were taken on the trial of the issue, as they were not adjudicated upon by the Circuit Court, the Supreme Court would not pass upon them.]

521. It was a question much discussed in *Powell* vs. *Manson*, 22 Grat. 177, whether on the trial of an issue, the rule in reference to the weight of responsive allegations in the answer was the same as at the hearing. The court held that it was; and that, on the trial of such an issue, all the allegations of an answer responsive to the bill must be taken as true unless contradicted by two witnesses, or one witness and corroborating circumstances.[3]

---

[3] Attention has already been directed to this case in section 375 and note. Here follows a synopsis of the case:

1. Upon the trial of an issue out of chancery, depositions taken in the cause in the chancery court are not to be read to the jury, unless proof be given that the witnesses are dead, or abroad, or otherwise unable to attend the trial.

2. The positive denials or statements of an answer, responsive to the bill, cannot be overthrown by the admissions, evasions and contradictions, if any, which may be found in the answer.

3. The plaintiff cannot destroy the weight of the whole answer by proving that the defendant is unworthy of credit; nor can he do so by proving, directly or indirectly, that the answer is false in one respect, or several respects. The only effect of such proof being to destroy the weight of the answer to the extent to which it is disapproved by that amount of evidence which is required by the rule in chancery.

4. Upon the trial of an issue out of chancery, the bill is not proof of its allegations, except so far as these allegations are admitted to be true by the answer. And the answer is not proof of the allegations therein contained, unless the allegations in the answer, as to facts, be positive, and responsive to

522. The plaintiff in an issue may suffer a non-suit, and if he does so advisedly in consequence of any unforeseen occurrence at the trial which would have rendered further proceeding with it unsafe, the court which directed the issue will grant him a new trial, notwithstanding the nonsuit. 2 Dan. Ch. Pr. (old) 747.

523. If either party is dissatisfied with the verdict, he may apply for a new trial to the court directing the issue, 2 Dan. Ch. Pr. (old) 747, and that court may direct a second or even a third trial of the issue, the object of the trial being to satisfy the conscience of the court. 2 Dan. Ch. Prac. (old) 748.

[The verdict upon the issue is merely advisory to the Court of Chancery: a motion for a new trial can be made only to that court, and the party submitting it must procure for the use of the Chancellor notes of the proceedings at the trial and of the evidence there given, *Watt* vs. *Starke*, 11 Otto 247; the evidence and proceedings then become a part of the record, and are subject to review by the appellate court, should an appeal from the decree be taken. *Ibid.*

---

some allegation of the bill. And to be responsive, such allegations of the answer must not be either evasive or contradictory.

5. On the trial of an issue out of chancery, the rule of evidence is the same as on the hearing in the chancery court, and the allegations of the answer responsive to the bill must be taken as true, unless contradicted by two witnesses, or one witness and corroborating circumstances.

6. Upon ᴀ motion for ᴀ new trial of an issue out of chancery, on the ground that the verdict is contrary to law and the evidence, the judge, overruling the motion, refuses to certify the facts proved, because the testimony was conflicting, but all the oral testimony is certified. The court will consider not merely whether the evidence adduced before the jury warrants the verdict, but also whether, having regard to the whole case, further investigation is necessary to attain the ends of justice.

7. In such a case, although there may have been a misdirection by the court, or evidence may have been improperly rejected, a new trial will not be granted, if the verdict appears to be right upon a consideration of all the evidence, including that which *was* rejected. *Powell* vs. *Manson*, 22 Grat. 177.

In Montana territory, law and equity jurisdiction is exercised by the same court, the distinctions between pleadings and modes of procedure in common law actions and in equity suits are abolished ; yet, says the United States Supreme Court, the distinction between law and equity is not changed, and while the Montana statute declares "that an issue in fact shall be tried by a jury, unless a jury trial is waived " the court in an equity case is not required to regard the findings of a jury called in the case as conclusive, if, in the judgment of the court, the findings are not supported by the evidence. *Basey & als.* vs. *Gallagher*, 20 Wal., 670.

After three verdicts to the same effect, courts of equity will do right in decreeing according to the opinions of juries, *Stanard* vs. *Graves*, 2 Call, 369; and after two concurring verdicts for the same party, the court of chancery is not bound to direct a new trial, though both verdicts are in opposition to the opinions of the judges before whom the issues were tried, and a verdict had originally been rendered in favour of the other party. *McRae's ex'or* vs. *Wood's ex'or*, 1 H. & M. 548. See also *Ross* vs. *Pines*, 3 Call, 568.][4]

524. The court may, even after ordering an issue, proceed to a final hearing without trying the issue, or setting aside the order, *Field* vs. *Holland*, 6 Cr. 8; the decree is an implied discharge of the order directing the issue, and is equivalent to such discharge. *Ibid.*

---

[4] But in *Ruffners* vs. *Barrett*, 6 Munf. 207, upon an injunction to a judgment, a new trial was directed at the bar of the common law court, and a verdict found in favour of the plaintiff. The court certified that the weight of evidence was in favour of the other party, and the chancellor directed another trial. The jury again found for the plaintiff; and the court certified with the verdict, all the evidence given before the jury, from which it appeared that the merits were clearly *against the plaintiff*, and in favour of the complainant at law. The court of appeals determined that the injunction should be dissolved, and the bill dismissed with costs.

Though in *Grigsby* vs. *Weaver*, 5 Leigh 197, the judge before whom the issue was tried certified, that in his opinion the verdict was contrary to the evidence, yet the evidence being also certified, the Chancellor was satisfied with the verdict, and refused to set it aside and to order a new trial, but dismissed the bill. The appellate court held, that the Chancellor was not bound in deference to the judge of the court of law to set the verdict aside, and affirmed the dismission of the case. In *Paul* vs. *Paul*, 2 H. & M. 525, before referred to, p. 613, n. 1, the evidence was not certified.

525. Sometimes the court, instead of directing an issue, directs the institution of an action at law, and, in that case, the motion for a new trial (if verdict be not satisfactory) should be made in the court in which the action is brought. An action at law, instead of an issue, is usually directed whenever the foundation of the claim is a legal demand, and the question whether a new trial should be had can be discussed with more satisfaction in a court of law than in a court of equity. 2 Dan. Ch. Pr. (old) 763, 764.

526. *How venue may be changed.* A chancellor after directing an issue to be tried in the court of one county, may change the venue and direct it to be tried in another county if he find it necessary, *Foushee* vs. *Leg*, 4 Call, 279; and this though *by consent of parties*, the issue was directed before the bar of the first mentioned county. *Ibid.*

527. Issues out of chancery have been directed in the following cases:

Whether claim fair or fraudulent. An issue was directed to ascertain "whether the claim of the appellees, J. H. D. and C. W. D., in the character of creditors of the said T. E. D. was fair and *bona fide*, or fictitious and fraudulent." *Beale* vs. *Diggs & als.*, 6 Grat., 591.

Whether timber taken or not. An issue directed "to ascertain and try whether any timber not accounted for by the appellant in his accounts rendered was taken by him from the lands of the ward and sold or converted to his own use, and what sum would be a proper charge against the guardian for such timber so taken and sold or converted to his own use." *Isler, &c.*, vs. *Grove*, 8 Grat., 259.[5]

To try validity of the will. By the statute, the issue to be made up and tried is " whether the writing be the will of the testatrix or

---

[5] In this case witness impeached, and the nature of the subject unliquidated damages, and for these reasons, an issue properly directed.

not;" yet, if the issue directed be to try the *validity* of the will, and the jury find that it is valid, the issue and verdict will be sufficient, *Ford* vs. *Gardner*, 1 H. & M., 72, and after a verdict against the validity of the will, if the court of chancery *adjudge* that the writing purporting to be the will of the testator, is not his will, but invalid, this in substance is a decree vacating the will, and is sufficient to set aside the will. Roane, J., in *Paul, &c.* vs. *Paul*, 2 H. & M., 534.

Lamberts vs *Cooper*, 29 Grat., 61, was an issue *devisavit vel non*. It was there held that if one be offered as a witness, and he is objected to, and the objection be overruled and the overruling is not excepted to, the party making the objection is deemed to have waived it. The same rule applies on the trial of such an issue as applies on trials at common law.

Whether deed genuine or not.[6] An issue directed to try "whether a certain bill penal, purporting to be executed by the plaintiff's testator, was the deed of the said testator or not; and further to ascertain, if it should be found to be his deed, what was the consideration on which it was founded."

Whether deed procured by fraud; and if so, whether afterwards confirmed without coercion or constraint. The evidence touching M.'s incompetency being contradictory, and there being some proof that M. had confirmed the deed after its execution, the appellate court directed an issue to ascertain—1st. Whether the deed had been procured by fraud; and 2nd. Whether, if procured by fraud, it had afterwards been confirmed by M. without coercion or restraint, when he was competent to act. *Mettert* vs. *Hagan*, 18 Grat., 231.

Whether a bond was obtained by fraud. A bill was filed to set aside the bond of the plaintiff on the ground of fraud in its procurement, the evidence being conflicting, and the appellant, who was the plaintiff in the court below, having asked for an issue in the lower court, the appellate court directed an issue to ascertain the fact. *Magill* vs. *Manson*, 20 Gratt., 527.

Fraud.[7] An issue directed to try whether a paper purporting

---

[6] Peculiarly proper for the decision of a jury, when doubt of its genuineness. *Apthorp* vs. *Comstock*, 2 Page, 482.

[7] In *Doss* vs. *Tyack*, 14 How. 297, the court held that the facts and circumstances necessary to constitute fraud being admitted in the answer, it was wholly unnecessary to direct an issue to try the question of fraud: and an issue having been directed and tried in the case and the jury in their verdict having found the transaction fraudulent, though the verdict was given under a misconstruction and misunderstanding of the charge of the court, the court properly refused to set it aside.

It is not improper to direct an issue on a question of fraud in fact though it also involves matter of law. *McLaughlin* vs. *Bank of Potomac*, 7 How. 220.

to be a gift of property was fraudulently obtained from the plaintiff by the defendant. *Johnson* vs. *Hendley*, 5 Munf. 219. See *Marshall* vs. *Thompson*, 2 Munf. 412.

Whether an absolute deed designed to defraud creditors. An issue was directed, on a bill charging that a conveyance was made without adequate consideration to defraud creditors, to "ascertain what was the amount of the consideration which passed from the grantee to the maker of the deed for the land mentioned in it and whether there was any secret agreement or understanding between the parties that the land was to be holden by the former for the use or benefit of the latter." *Bullock* vs. *Irvine's adm'rs*, 4 Munf. 450.

Whether an alleged sale of a horse was a shift to evade the statute against usury. Douglass vs. *McChesney*, 2 Rand. 109.

Whether a bill of sale was absolute or a security for money. Knibbs ex'or vs. *Dixon's ex'or*, 1 Rand. 249.

Issues directed involving the possession of personal slave property for five years. Galt, &c. vs. *Carter*, 6 Munf. 245 ; *Hudson* vs. *Hudson's adm'r, &c.*, 6 Munf. 357.

Whether a defendant a secret partner. Cocke vs. *Upshaw, &c.*, 6 Munf. 464.

Whether a patent covered certain land. Boyd vs. *Hamilton's heirs*, 6 Munf. 459.

To ascertain damages. An issue quantum damnificatus, when a party applies for relief against a penalty, "to ascertain the damages for which the plaintiff is responsible and which he is bound to pay as the condition of the relief sought." Green, J., in *Meze* vs. *Mayse*, 6 Rand. 660.

And so, an issue was directed to ascertain "the damages sustained by the failure of a party, who had promised another, to pay a debt for him, and who by his promise prevented the other from discharging his debt by other convenient means. *Braxton* vs. *Willing*, 4 Call, 301.

And so, an issue quantum damnificatus was ordered in *Nagle* vs. *Newton*, 22 Grat. 814 to ascertain the damages which a vendee had sustained by the improper acts of the vendor and his agents in a case in which the vendor enforced specific execution by the vendee.

To ascertain whether debt be a gaming debt, and, if so, whether the transferee of it was induced to take it by the concealment or misrepresentation of the debtor. Nelson's adm'r vs. *Armstrong & als.*, 5 Grat. 354.

528. *When the court not bound to direct an issue.*— Issues are usually directed where the testimony is conflicting. The court is not always bound to direct

an issue when the evidence before it is contradictory. In many cases it will judge of the weight of the evidence, and if its conscience be satisfied will decide without a jury. *Nice* vs. *Purcell*, 1 H. & M. 372. See also *Love* vs. *Braxton, &c.*, 5 Call, 537, *Rowton* vs. *Rowton*, 1 H. & M. 93, *Samuel* vs. *Marshall, &c.*, 3 Leigh, 567, *Townsend, &c.* vs. *Graves, &c.*, 3 Paige 453.

Harding vs. *Handy*, 11 Wheat 103, was a case in which it was held that an issue was unnecessary. The bill was filed by some of the heirs of a deceased person to set aside deeds obtained from the ancestor by fraud. The question of fraud largely depended upon the mental weakness of the grantor in the deeds. The court said, "An issue indeed might have been directed, but we do not think it a case in which this course ought to have been pursued. The degree of weakness or of imposition which ought to induce a court of chancery to set aside a conveyance is proper for the consideration of the court itself, and there seems to be no reason for the intervention of a jury, unless the case be one, in which the court would be satisfied with the verdict, however it might be found. A verdict affirming the capacity of the grantor in this case "could not, we think, have been satisfactory to the court; and it was consequently not necessary to refer the question of competency to a jury." The deeds were set aside without an issue.

529. *When the court ought not to direct an issue.*— The court ought not to direct an issue to try a claim unsupported by testimony. When the court directed an issue in a case in which there was no conflict of testimony, though the verdict was found in favour of the party requesting the issue, the appellate court set aside the order directing the issue, and dismissed the bill. *Smith* vs. *Boyce*, 9 Grat. 294. See *Wise* vs. *Lamb*, 11 Grat. 752. See also *Pryor* vs. *Adams*, 1 Call, 382.

In *Paynes* vs. *Coles*, 1 Munf. 373 the court held though infants were interested as complainants, that an issue should not have been directed to try the claim of the complainants, it being altogether unsupported by testimony, or to try a title not alleged in the bill, but suggested in the answer without proof. But in *Watkins* vs. *Carlton*, 10 Leigh 560, though the evidence was not regular, yet if it had been it would have rendered the order for the issue proper, and the court held that if the issue should be set aside as improperly ordered, the cause should be remanded to the court of chancery, where the evidence might be properly taken, and the issue ordered anew.

530. *Other cases in which issues should not be directed.* *Read* vs. *Cline*, 9 Grat., 136, was a case in which there should have been no issue. There was no conflict between different portions of the evidence, no ambiguity or uncertainty in it, but a simple failure to prove material facts.

So also in *Beverley* vs. *Walden*, 20 Grat., 147, where the allegations in the bill were positively denied by the answer, and the plaintiff failed to produce two witnesses, or one witness with strong corroborating circumstances in support of the bill, the court held that it was error to direct an issue; and in *Kraker* vs. *Shields*, 20 Grat., 377, where the question was, whether the contract was made with reference to Confederate currency, as the standard of value, or whether the notes were to be paid in the currency of the time they fell due, the court held that the cause was properly referred to a commissioner, and that it was not a case in which the court should direct an issue.

In *Anthony* vs. *Oldacre*, 4 Call, 489, it was held unnecessary to direct an issue to ascertain deficiency in the land; and so in *Rowton* vs. *Rowton*, 1 H. & M., 92; *Nice* vs. *Purcell*, 1 H. & M., 372; *Samuel* vs. *Marshall*, 3 Leigh, 567; and *Hord* vs. *Colbert*, 28 Grat.,

49, it was held that the court was not bound to direct an issue, but might decide without a jury; and so in *Watkins* vs. *Young*, 31 Grat., 84, it was held, that instead of directing an issue, the cause might be referred to a commissioner.

FORM OF ORDERS DIRECTING AN ISSUE OUT OF CHANCERY.

Issue of devisavit vel non.

See pp. 575–576, ante.

Order directing issue in other cases.

This cause came on this day to be heard upon, &c. On consideration whereof, the court doth adjudge, order and decree that an issue be made up and tried at the bar of this court [or, at the bar of the ——— court of ——— county,] to ascertain and try *whether the claim of the plaintiffs, J. H. D. and C. W. D., in the character of creditors of T. E. D. is fair and bona fide or fictitious and fraudulent* [or, as the case may be.][8] And it is ordered, that on the trial of the said issue, the plaintiffs shall maintain the affirmative and the defendant the negative, and on the trial of said issue, the bill, answers, exhibits and the depositions of such of the witnesses as are dead, or where attendance cannot be secured, may be read in evidence, and such other evidence may be introduced by either plaintiffs or defendant, as may be legal and proper. [*If the trial is directed at the bar of another court,* add " And the said ——— court of ——— county is requested to send and certify the verdict of the jury on such issue to this court, together with any special circumstances which may occur at the trial, and the said ——— court of ——— may think it right to report.]

---

[8] See section 527, p. 618, ante, for other issues.

CHAPTER II.

Proceedings before Masters or Commissioners.

531. The duties of masters or commissioners are so various that we shall not attempt here to detail them all. We propose to treat of the manner in which accounts and enquiries are taken and proceeded in before these officers.

532. On furnishing the master or commissioner a copy of the decree directing an account, he appoints a day to execute it and notifies the parties of the day and place. This notice is given by advertisement, when directed by the court,[1] or when any of the parties reside beyond the State.[2] In other cases, personal service of the notice is required in the Virginia State courts. In the United States Circuit Courts personal service on the parties or their solicitors is required in all cases.[3]

A settlement of an administration account, in a chancery suit, without notice to the legatees or distributees, parties interested, will be set aside if excepted to by them on that ground, and a new account will be directed between the parties upon due notice. Ch. *Taylor* in *Campbell, &c.* vs. *Winston, &c.*, 2 H. & M. 10. See *Roberts* vs. *Jordans,* 3 Munf. 488. But an appellate court will not reverse a decree based upon a commissioner's report merely because the commissioner has failed to set forth in his report that notice was given to the parties. The objection for want of notice should be made in the court below. *White's ex'ors* vs. *Johnson, &c.*, 2 Munf. 285, *Winston* vs. *Johnson's ex'ors*, 2 Munf. 305. See pp. 544, 545, *ante.*

Want of notice of the time and place of taking an account, or

---

[1] Code 1873, ch. 171, § 5.   [2] Code 1873, ch. 163, § 2.
[3] 75 Rule U. S. Sup. Ct.

the court's acting upon it too soon after the report is returned, are not sufficient reasons for a bill of review, such objections not having been taken as they ought to have been, before the rendition of the decree. *Winston* vs. *Johnson's ex'ors,* 2 Munf. 305.

When the commissioner gives notice to the parties by publication in a newspaper, an exception by a party for want of personal notice where that was practicable, ought not to be entertained unless he shows by his own affidavit, or otherwise, that he had no such information of the contemplated proceedings of the commissioner as would have enabled him to attend. *McCandlish's adm'or* vs. *Edloe & als.,* 3 Grat. 330.

And it seems that if process in the suit has been served upon a party, if the court direct that notice may be given by publication, it is no valid objection on his part that he did not see or hear of the notice by publication of the taking an account by a commissioner under the order of the court. *Hill* vs. *Boyer,* 18 Grat. 364.

In *Miller* vs. *Holcombe,* 9 Grat. 665, an exception for want of notice was taken six years after the report was returned, after the argument of the cause, and after the opinion of the court was pronounced. The court disregarded the exception.

533. In the United States Circuit Courts, the party at whose instance or for whose benefit the reference is made must cause the same to be presented to the master for a hearing on or before the next rule day succeeding the same when the reference is made and if he omit to do so the adverse party will be at liberty forthwith to cause proceedings to be had before the master, at the costs of the party procuring the reference.[4] In the Virginia State courts there is no such statute or rule of practice.[5] To effect this object the party desiring greater speed may resort to the rule to speed, if it be a plaintiff who is negligent,

---

[4] 74th Rule U. S. Sup. Court.

[5] There was formerly a rule in the Superior Court of Chancery for the Richmond District to the effect that an order of account would become inoperative (unless for good cause shown to the contrary) if its execution be not begun within twelve months from its date, but there is no rule to that effect now in any of the equity courts of Virginia so far as known to the writer. See *Anonymous,* 4 H. & M. 410.

or if it be a defendant, may obtain from the court an order for a hearing without the account or inquiry directed, if the defendant should fail to prosecute the account or inquiry before the commissioner by a certain date, or, in a proper case, may obtain an order requiring the defendant peremptorily to proceed with the account or inquiry before the commissioner by a day to be named by the court.

534. The master or commissioner is authorized to proceed after the notice mentioned in sec 532, though any party should fail to attend[6] and a party failing to attend subjects himself to the process of contempt.[7] On a report of the commissioner stating that the party ordered to do so has failed to render the account ordered, a rule will be made upon him to show cause why an attachment should not be issued against him for his contempt; and if no such cause be shown the rule will be made absolute and the attachment ordered.[8]

A party may incur other loss by failing to attend before the commissioner. In *Snickers* vs. *Dorsey*, 2 Munf. 505, a motion to

---

[6] See 75th Rule U. S. Sup. Court.

[7] 2 Rob. Pr. (old) 363, *Lane* vs. *Lane*, 4 H. & M. 437. The case in Hening & Munford was a decision of Chancellor Taylor. In that case the party was under process of attachment and the court entered the following order: "that if the said executor do, on or before the 10th August, comply with the terms of the decretal order made in September, 1805, to the satisfaction of the commissioners therein named, to be certified to this court, the attachment is to be discharged as an act of this day; but if these commissioners certify that he had failed to comply with the said order, then it is ordered, that the sheriff of Loudon commit him to the jail of that county, till the judge of this court, in court or out of court, is satisfied that the said executor has fully complied with the said decretal order, and shall order him to be discharged." See Code of 1873, chap 190, sec. 27, 28, 29. Sess. Acts, 1877–8, pp. 298, 299.

[8] Ibid.

recommit the report of a commissioner was made by a party who had refused to attend, though duly notified; and in support of the motion his own affidavit and the affidavit of two witnesses were filed, going to show that less was due from him than the sum reported against him, and that he was prevented from offering his testimony before the commissioner by a belief that he was not interested in the suit. The Court of Chancery overruled the motion. Upon appeal, the Court of Appeals, considering it better to permit individual suitors to abide by the effects of their own negligence than to prostrate those rules which have been established for the furtherance of proceedings in equity, approved the decision of the chancellor so far as it *refused to open the accounts anew;* but the court departed from the decree of the chancellor, so far as to let in the appellant to show himself entitled, if he could, to credits claimed by him upon certain accounts in relation to which the commissioner had no evidence before him.

An order of account, not stating by whom to be taken, must be taken by a commissioner of the court. *Anderson* vs. *Gest,* 2 H. & M. 10.

The court cannot, without the consent of the parties, appoint commissioners beyond the State to take the account. *Ibid.*

535. In the Virginia State Courts, the master or commissioner may adjourn his proceedings from time to time after the notice is given (without a new notice) until his report is completed. When completed he returns his report, with any depositions of witnesses, or examinations of the parties, which may have been taken, and any exceptions which may have been filed, and the decrees, orders and notices under which he acted, and such documents and papers exhibited as the parties require to be returned with the report.

536. Under the general notice given by the master or commissioner when the order or decree is first placed in his hands, the master or commissioner may take the depositions of witnesses without giving special notice to the parties of their being taken.[9]

---

[9] *McCandlish* vs. *Edloe & als.*, 3 Grat. 330. See p. 544; *ante.*

537. To obtain the attendance of witnesses, the master is empowered, in the Virginia State Courts, to issue a summons[10]; in the United States Circuit Courts, he is authorized to obtain a blank subpœna from the clerk, and signed by the clerk, which may be filled up either by the master or by the party praying the same.[11]

538. In the United States Circuit Courts, if the witness, after being duly summoned, fail to attend, or if he attend and refuse to testify, the fact may be reported to the court, and in the one case his attendance will be enforced by the court, and in the other the witness will be compelled to testify by process of contempt, in like manner as if the contempt were for not attending, or for refusing to give testimony in court.[12]

539 In the Virginia State Courts, the witness is compelled to attend by the commissioner in the manner set forth in sections 447–449, pp. 475, 476 *ante.* And should the witness attend and refuse to be sworn or to give evidence, &c., the manner of compelling him to do so is as set forth in section 450, pp. 476, 477 *ante.*

540. In the United States Circuit Courts, it is specially required that "All parties accounting before a master shall bring in their respective accounts in the form of debtor and creditor; and any of the other parties who shall not be satisfied with the ac-

---

[10] Code 1873, ch. 172, sec. 26. See pp. 472, 475, 476.

[11] 78th Rule U. S. Sup. Court.

[12] 78th Rule U. S. Sup. Court.

counts so brought in shall be at liberty to examine the accounting party *viva voce*, or upon interrogatories in the master's office, or by deposition, as the master shall direct"[13]; and "All affidavits, depositions, and documents which have been previously made, read or used in the court, upon any proceeding in any cause or matter, may be used before the master."[14] "The master will be at liberty to examine any creditor or other person coming in to claim before him, either upon written interrogatories, or *viva voce*, or in both modes, as the nature of the case may appear to him to require. The evidence upon such examination shall be taken down by the master, or by some other person by his order and in his presence, if either party requires it, in order that the same may be used by the court, if necessary."[15]

The account may be brought down to the date of hearing before the master. He is not limited to the date of entering the decree. *Rubber Co.* vs. *Goodyear*, 9 Wal. 788.

541. *Examination of party.* When a party is examined before a commissioner in relation to his own rights and the rights of his adversary, the examination is in the nature of a supplemental bill of discovery. If he be called upon to answer specifically as to particular items of charge, he is to give the best answers that he can from his recollection and information aided by a reference to the books and papers immediately within his control and possession; with such explanations, fairly responsive

---

[13] 79th Rule U. S. Supreme Court.
[14] 80th Rule U. S. Supreme Court.
[15] 81st Rule U. S. Supreme Court.

to the questions put, as he may be advised to make for the purpose of excluding any improper conclusion to be drawn from these answers. Walworth, Ch., in *Peck* vs. *Hamlin*, 1 Paige 247. So far as the answers of the party examined are responsive to the questions put by the opposite party, such answers are evidence in his favor, on the same principle that the answer of a defendant responsive to the bill is evidence against the complainant. Walworth, Ch., in *Benson, &c.* vs. *LeRoy, &c.*, 1 Paige, 122. There can be no cross-examination by the counsel of the party examined. Ibid. Nor can such party give testimony in his own favor upon other subjects in reference distinct from those on which he has been examined by the adverse party. *Armsby* vs. *Wood*, 1 Hopkins's Ch. Rep. 229.

How far the doctrines announced in this section have been modified by the recent statutes compelling a party, or permitting him, to testify has not yet been determined by the courts. See sections 409, 410, 418, 419 *ante*.

In *Templeman* vs. *Fauntleroy*, 3 Rand. 434, there was an answer filed which purported to be the joint answer of Templeman and Yeatman as administrators; but it was sworn to by Templeman alone. It acknowledged assets, a willingness to pay the debt really due and a readiness to account. An order was subsequently made directing a commissioner to ascertain the sum due from the administrators and authorizing the plaintiff to examine them on oath. Templeman would never attend, but Yeatman was examined. In his answers to the interrogatories put to him, he stated the amount due from his intestate, that the funds of the estate had been turned over to his co-administrator, and he had none in his hands; that the answer purporting to be joint was filed by Templeman alone and had not been seen by him. *Held*, that the court was to conclude from these facts that the answer was the sole answer of Templeman, and that Yeatman had none of the assets and the decree was rightly against Templeman alone.

542. In the Virginia State· Courts, the commis-

sioner is required to return with his report all the decrees, orders and notices under which he acted. He should not copy in his account or his report any paper; and if there has been a previous account, he should not copy it into his; but taking it as the basis of his, correct the errors and supply the defects thereof by an additional statement. Everything improperly copied into a commissioner's account will be expunged at his costs, on the application of either party; and if on account of his negligence or misconduct, a report be recommitted, he will bear the costs occasioned thereby.[16] A commissioner who doubts as to any point which arises before him, in taking an account to be returned to a Circuit Court may, in writing, submit the point to such court, or the judge thereof, who may instruct him thereon.[17]

543. In the United States Circuit Courts, "in the reports made by the masters to the court, no part of any state of facts, charge, affidavit, deposition, examination, or answer, brought in or used before them shall be stated or recited. But such state of facts, charge, affidavit, deposition, examination, or answer, shall be identified, specified and referred to, so as to inform the court what state of facts, charge, affidavit, deposition, examination or answer were so brought in or used."[18]

544. In the Virginia State Courts, exceptions may be taken to the report either in the commissioner's office or in the court after the report is returned;

---

[16] Code 1873, ch. 171, sec. 9.   [17] Code 1873, ch. 181, sec. 7.
[18] 76th Rule U. S. Sup. Court.

and to afford opportunity for exceptions, the court cannot hear the cause on the report until it has been returned ten days.[19]   The report does not stand confirmed as a matter of course; it is confirmed only by special direction of the court.

545. In the United States Circuit Courts, "The master, as soon as his report is ready, shall return the same into the clerk's office, and the day of the return shall be entered by the clerk in the order book. The parties shall have one month from the time of filing the report to file exceptions thereto; and if no exceptions are within that period filed by either party the report shall stand confirmed on the next rule day after the month has expired. If exceptions are filed they shall stand for hearing before the court, if the court is then in session, or if not, then at the next sitting of the court which shall be held thereafter, by adjournment or otherwise."[20]

546. "In order to prevent the filing of exceptions to reports for frivolous causes, or for mere delay," it is provided, in the United States Circuit Courts, that "the party whose exceptions are overruled shall, for every exception overruled, pay costs to the other party, and for every exception allowed shall be entitled to costs; the costs to be fixed in each case by the court, by a standing rule of the Circuit Court."[21]

---

[19] Code 1873, ch. 171, sec. 10. The statute requiring the report to lie ten days for exceptions in the clerk's office does not apply to recommitted reports. Code 1873, ch. 171, sec. 10.

[20] 83rd Rule U. S. Supreme Court.

[21] 84th Rule U. S. Supreme Court.

547. Exceptions are said, in some authorities, to be of the nature of a special demurrer.[22] The United States Supreme Court says they are not. *Foster* vs. *Goddard*, 1 Black 506. They should set forth with sufficient particularity the thing or matter objected to. 1 Barb. Ch. Pr. 191, 2 Rob. Pr. (old) 383.[23] All parties to the record who are interested in the matter in question may take exceptions to the report. 2 Dan. Ch. Pr. (old) 558.

It was said by Chancellor Taylor in *Read's ex'or* vs. *Winston & als.*, 4 H. & M. 450, that objections for want of proof of any voucher on which a commissioner finds an item in his account must generally be made before the commissioner himself; in which case, if such proof be not supplied, it may be called for at the hearing, but in no other instance unless for good cause shown and upon one month's previous notice." It is doubted whether this rule would now be adopted.

548. The exceptions should state the points of the report excepted to. *Story* vs. *Livingston*, 13 Pet. 359. It is not the province of the court to investigate items of an account. The report of the master is received as true, when no exception is taken; and the exceptions are to be regarded so far only as they are supported by the special statements of the master or

---

[22] 1 Barb. Ch. Pr. 191. 2 Rob. Pr. (old) 383.

[23] Said Spencer, J., in *Wilkes, &c.* vs. *Rogers, &c.*, 6 John. Rep. 591, "the party excepting must put his finger on the error. When he does so, the parts not excepted to are admitted to be correct, not only as regards the principles but as relates to the evidence on which they are founded." In *Foster* vs. *Goddard*, 1 Black 506, the United States Supreme Court said that an exception to a master's report was not in the nature of a special demurrer and was not required to be so full and specific, that it was only necessary in it to point out the finding and conclusion of the master which it seeks to reverse. In the same case, it was held that the exception brought up for examination all questions of fact and law arising upon the report of the master relative to that subject.

by evidence, which ought to be brought before the court by a reference to the particular testimony on which the exception relies. Marshall, C. J., in *Harding* vs. *Handy*, 11 Wheat 126.

549. Reports which are erroneous upon the face of them though not specially excepted to prior to the hearing may perhaps be objected to at the hearing or in the appellate court. But it is clear that reports not excepted to cannot be impeached before an appellate court—in relation to matter which may be affected by extraneous testimony. *White's ex'ors* vs. *Johnson, &c.*, 2 Munf. 285, *Brown* vs. *Hastie & Co.*, 3 Call, 22, *Jones's ex'ors* vs. *Watson*, 3 Call, 253, *Perkins* vs. *Saunders, &c.*, 2 H. & M. 420, *Simmons* vs. *Simmons, adm'or*, 33 Grat. 451.

In *French* vs. *Townes*, 10 Grat. 384, the questions were raised by the pleadings and proofs, and it was held unnecessary to raise them by an exception to the commissioner's report.

In *Williams* vs. *Donaghe's ex'ors*, 1 Rand. 300, there was an exception to the report of a commissioner allowing a charge for a quantity of iron; and the chancellor sustained, the exception and pronounced a decree accordingly. The Court of Appeals was of opinion that there was no sufficient evidence in the record to show that the iron was delivered; and that, in consequence of the absence of such testimony, the exception was correctly sustained. But as there was strong reason to believe that the iron, or a part of it, was delivered, and as the commissioner's having allowed a credit therefor on the evidence exhibited, might have prevented the party claiming the credit from producing other evidence in his power on the subject; the court was further of opinion that under these circumstances the chancellor erred in pronouncing a final decree, and that he ought to have recommitted the account to a commissioner for further evidence and enquiry whether any iron, and if any how much, was delivered. On this ground the decree was reversed, and the cause remanded for further proceedings.

In the *Ship Potomac*, 2 Black 581, the master found the amount due, but stated no account, and his report was excepted to as being excessive, not sufficiently proved, erroneous under the pleadings and founded on illegal evidence; the Supreme Court of the United States held that such exceptions might justly be treated as frivolous, and if overruled, and the case be brought up on appeal, the appellate court could not say that particular charges were wrongly admitted, or particular credits wrongly thrown out.

If the master fail to report all the evidence upon the matter of an exception properly taken, the party excepting should apply to the court, specifying what is omitted, verify his statement, and the court will require a further report. *Story* vs. *Livingston*, 13 Pet. 359.

550. In the United States Courts, no objections to a master's report can be made which were not taken before the master. *Story* vs *Livingston*, 13 Pet. 359, *McMicken* vs. *Perrin*, 18 How. 510. In *McMicken* vs. *Perrin*, the United States Supreme Court cited with approval *Heyn* vs. *Heyn*, 4 Jacob 47, deciding that after a decree *pro confesso* the defendant was not at liberty to go before the master without a special order, but the accounts were to be taken *ex parte*.

551. *Recommitment of report.* There was a suit by distributees against an administrator. The accounts were referred, and a report was returned before the defendant's evidence was filed. He excepted to the report and filed an affidavit showing a sufficient excuse for not sooner taking his evidence, and asked for a recommitment of the report. After the report was returned and before the recommitment, depositions supporting the defence were filed; the defendant upon his affidavit and those depositions asked the recommitment. Under these circumstances it was proper to recommit the report, but it would not have been proper, even though the testimony might sustain the defendant as to the subject of controversy, to dismiss the bill; the plaintiff

should have an opportunity to disprove the testimony, and was also entitled to an account of administration. *Thomas* vs. *Dawson*, 9 Grat. 531.

552. *On appeal how exceptions regarded in United States Courts.* Exceptions cannot be taken on appeal. *New Orleans* vs. *Gaines*, 15 Wal. 632. They must be taken in the court below. *Hudgins & als.* vs. *Kemp*, 20 How. 45, 54; *Canal Co.* vs. *Gordon*, 6 Wal. 561; *Kinsman & als.* vs. *Parkhurst*, 18 How. 289; *Ransom* vs. *Davis's adm'or*, 18 How. 295. In *Oliver* vs. *Piatt*, 3 How. 333, 412, although the exceptions to the master's report were not formally overruled or allowed in the court below, yet it was plain that in the final decree they were all disposed of, some being allowed and some disallowed. The decree was affirmed.

When a chancery suit involves matters of account the action of a master should be had in the inferior court, and the items admitted or rejected should be stated, so that exception may be taken to the particular items or class of items, and such a case should be brought before the Supreme Court on the rulings of the exceptions by the Circuit Court. McLean, J., in *Ransom* vs. *Davis's adm'or*, 18 How. 296.

See pp. 543–546 under title "commissioner's report," a collection of Virginia cases concerning commissioner's reports. See also "Practical notes to decrees for account," pp. 528–543.

CHAPTER III.

Of Injunctions.

553. As to injunctions to judgments, see pages ·86–95, *ante.*

554. Injunctions are granted to restrain waste, to ·enjoin the erection of a nuisance, to prevent the collection of purchase money on account of defective title in land or on account of deficiency in the quantity of land sold, and for other purposes.

WHEN INJUNCTION GRANTED.

Injunction granted—on account of *defective title, Keytons* vs. *Brawfords,* 5 Leigh 39, *Koger & als.* vs. *Kane's adm'or & als.,* 5 Leigh 606, *Miller* vs. *Argyle's ex'or & als.,* 5 Leigh 460: [It is said in *Ross* vs. *Woodville & als.,* 4 Munf. 324, that a purchaser even after suing may waive the defect of title, and the surety in the bond given for the purchase money will not be permitted to insist upon it. *Sed quaere.*]; but in *Long's ex'or* vs. *Israel,* 9 Leigh 556, under the circumstances of the case, the defect of title was not sufficient ground for injoining the collection of the purchase money.

Injunction granted on account *of deficiency in quantity* of land, *Keytons* vs. *Brawfords,* 5 Leigh 39, *Clarke* vs. *Hardgrove,* 7 Grat. 399, *Triplett* vs. *Allen,* 26 Grat. 721, *Koger & als.* vs. *Kane's adm'or & als.,* 5 Leigh 606.

Injunction granted when *title is in dispute. Lane* vs. *Tidball,* Gilm. 130. See *Duncan* vs. *Fisher &c.,* 2 Desau. 369, 2 Rob. Pr. (old) 63.

Injunction granted to protect *vendor's lien* on land and chattels sold for *a sum in gross. Clarke & als.* vs. *Curtis,* 11 Leigh 559.

Injunction granted to prevent a *premature suit* on a bond given for purchase money. *Bullitt's ex'ors* vs. *Songster's adm'or,* 3 Munf. 54.

Injunction granted—in cases of slaves. See note below.[1]

---

[1] *Randolph* vs. *Randolph,* 3 Munf. 99, 2 Rob Pr. (old) 224; *Wilson, &c.* vs. *Butler, &c.,* 3 Munf. 559, 2 Rob. Pr. (old) 224; *Allen* vs. *Freeland,* 3 Rand.

Injunction granted—to prevent the sale of B.'s property under an execution against A.; there being the *pretium affectionis*. *Randolph* vs. *Randolph*, 3 Munf. 99, *Wilson, &c.* vs. *Butler, &c.*, 3 Munf. 559, *Allen* vs. *Freeland*, 3 Rand. 175.

Injunction granted—in cases in which debt secured by deed is regarded in equity as a *penalty*. *Mayo* vs. *Judah*, 5 Munf. 495.

Injunction granted—to prevent, during the pendency of a suit to subject the land, *the cutting and selling timber from it* in a manner calculated to render the land insufficient security for the purchase money. (Ch. Taylor), *Scott* vs. *Wharton*, 2 H. & M. 25. See Code 1873, chap. 133, sec. 5.

Injunction granted—in cases of *usury*. *Marks* vs. *Morris*, 2 Munf., 407; *Stone* vs. *Ware*, 6 Munf., 541; *McPherrin, &c.*, vs. *King*, 1 Rand., 172; *Young* vs. *Scott*, 4 Rand., 415; *Fitzhugh* vs. *Gordon*, 2 Leigh, 629. [See what is said of these cases in 2 Rob. Pr. (old) 63–64.] *Clarkson* vs. *Garland*, 1 Leigh, 147; *Brown* vs. *Toell's adm'r*, 5 Rand., 545; *Fulcher* vs. *Baker & als.*, 1 Leigh, 453; *Cabaniss* vs. *Matthews & als.*, 2 Grat., 325.

Injunction granted—in cases of *gaming*. *Woodson, &c.*, vs. *Barrett & Co.*, 2 H. & M., 80; *Skipwith* vs. *Strother, &c.*, 3 Rand., 214; *Watson* vs. *Fletcher, &c.*, 7 Grat., 1.

Injunction granted—in cases of *nuisance*. Depriving plaintiff of the use of a water-course. *Coalter* vs. *Hunter, &c.*, 4 Rand., 58; *Stokes, &c.*, vs. *Upper Appomattox Co.*, 3 Leigh, 318.

Injunction granted—in cases of *nuisance*. Erecting a dam so as to injure plaintiff's mill, 2 Rob. Pr., (old) 232–233, citing *Arthur, &c.*, vs. *Case, &c.*, 1 Paige's Ch. Rep., 447; *S. C.* on appeal, 3 Wend., 632.

Injunction granted—in cases of *nuisance*, causing irreparable mischief, though nuisance under colour of a statute. *Crenshaw* vs. *The Slate River Co.*, 6 Rand., 245. See *Stokes, &c.*, vs. *Upper Appomattox Co.*, 3 Leigh, 318.

Injunction granted—in cases in which *irreparable damage* would ensue if the aid of equity were denied. See 4 Min. Ins., 109, *Bowyer* vs. *Creigh*, 3 Rand., 32; *Poage* vs. *Bell*, 3 Rand., 583; 4 Min. Ins. 7 and 8, 473; *Beveridge* vs. *Lacey*, 3 Rand., 63. See *Miller* vs. *Trueheart, &c.*, 4 Leigh, 569.

175, 2 Rob. Pr. (old) 225; *Harrison* vs. *Sims*, 6 Rand, 506, 2 Rob. Pr. (old) 225; *Hughes* vs. *Pledge & als.*, 1 Leigh 443, 2 Rob. Pr. (old) 225; *Chapman* vs. *Washington*, 4 Call 327, 2 Rob. Pr. (old) 225; *Sampson* vs. *Mitchell's ex'or*, 5 Munf. 175, 2 Rob Pr. (old) 225, 226; *Scott, &c.* vs. *Halliday, &c.*, 5 Munf. 103, 2 Rob. Pr. (old) 225; *Dunn* vs. *Amey & als.*, 1 Leigh 465, 2 Rob. Pr. (old) 226; *Holliday* vs. *Coleman*, 2 Munf. 162, 2 Rob. Pr. (old) 227; *Mortimer* vs. *Moffatt, &c.*, 4 H. & M. 503, 2 Rob. Pr. (old) 227; *Whitton's admo'r* vs. *Terry*, 6 Leigh 189; *Anderson's ex'ors* vs. *Anderson*, 11 Leigh 616, [the last case concerning prospective right to freedom.]

Injunction granted—in cases of *nuisance*, threatening the health of an individual or his family, 4 Min. Ins. 7. *Miller* vs. *Trueheart*, 4 Leigh 569.

Injunction granted—to restrain *waste*, *Findley* vs. *Smith*, *&c.*, 6 Munf. 142 (see *Crouch* vs. *Puryear*, *&c.*, 1 Rand. 258) 2 Rob Pr. (old) 228–231. Notice differences between Ch. Kent in *Kane* vs. *Vanderburgh*, *&c.* 1 John. Ch. Rep. 11, and Ch. Taylor in *Cutting* vs. *Carter*, *&c.*, 4 H. & M. 424; in the latter, the chancellor refused the injunction there appearing no impediment to the action of waste at law. Chancellor Kent, in *Kane* vs. *Vanderburgh*, granted the injunction saying that it was a wholesome jurisdiction to be liberally exercised in the prevention of irreparable injury and depended on much latitude of discretion in the court. But in *Storm* vs. *Mann*, 4 John. Ch. R. 21 the defendant claiming under a title adverse to the plaintiff, the chancellor refused the injunction. See also *Pillsworth* vs. *Hopton*, 6 Ves. 51 and *Higgins & als.* vs. *Woodard*, *&c.*, 1 Hop. Ch. Rep. 342. See *Garrison* vs. *Hall & als.*, Va. L. Jour. 1881, p. 127.

Injunction granted—at the suit of the owner to prevent one who claimed the land from taking iron ore from it. *Anderson* vs. *Harvey*, 10 Grat. 386.

Injunction granted—to prevent the enclosure of streets covenanted by vendor to be kept open for vendee's free use, *Brooke* vs. *Barton*, 6 Munf. 306; 2 Rob. Pr. (old) 191; and to prevent the closing up of an alley, the vendor assuring the vendee (though not in writing) that it would always be kept open. *Trueheart* vs. *Price*, 2 Munf. 468.

Injunction granted—to relieve against vindictive damages in an action of trespass against a sheriff who had levied on property in possession of a defendant legatee (who had the *beneficial* interest, though the *legal* interest was in the executors of the testator) *Lewis's adm'or* vs. *Wyatt*, 2 Rand. 114.

Injunction granted—to relieve against a decree obtained by surprise. See *Calloway* vs. *Alexander*, *&c.*, 8 Leigh 114. Against a judgment obtained by surprise. *Mason* vs. *Nelson*, 11 Leigh 227.

Injunction granted—in *Hickerson's adm'or* vs. *Helm*, 2 Rob. 628 approving the rule in *Pulliam* vs. *Winston*, *&c.*, 5 Leigh 324, but establishing an exception. The effect of the two decisions is this; that while the general rule denies to a creditor or distributee the aid of a court of equity to intercept by injunction the collection of assets by the executor or administrator, especially those arising from the sales of the executor or administrator, until the administration accounts are adjusted, with the view that the debt or distributee's share may be set off; yet where the title to the set off is founded on the express agreement of the executor or administrator, and this is coupled with long continued delinquency on the part of the executor and, his representative to settle the administration accounts, the injunction should be granted.

Injunction granted—to judgments, when defence though known at the trial could only be made in equity. *Royall's adm'or* vs. *Royall's adm'or*, 5 Munf. 82; *Pendleton's adm'or* vs. *Stuart, &c.*, 6 Munf. 377; *Pickett, &c.* vs. *Stewart, &c.*, 1 Rand. 478.

Injunction granted—to judgments, when matter arising after the judgments make their enforcement improper. *Royall's adm'ors* vs. *Johnson & als.*, 1 Rand. 421; *Miller's ex'ors* vs. *Rice & als.*, 1 Rand. 438; *Crawford* vs. *Thurmond & als.*, 3 Leigh 85.

Injunction granted—to judgment on the ground of the loss of an instrument, without which defendant could not defend himself at law. *Vathir* vs. *Zane*, 6 Grat. 246.

Injunction granted—to judgments at law, in other cases. See pp. 92–94.

Injunction granted—to a judgment in case of slander, on the ground of the insanity of the person uttering the words. *Horner* vs. *Marshall's adm'ix*, 5 Munf. 466.

Injunction granted—to a judgment on a forthcoming bond, at the instance of a surety of the defendant therein on the ground that he is a creditor of the judgment creditor to a larger extent than the judgment and the judgment creditor is insolvent. *McClellan* vs. *Kinnaird*, 6 Grat. 352.

Injunction granted—in case of a discharged bankrupt as to judgment recovered before his discharge. *Peatross* vs. *McLaughlin*, 6 Grat. 64.

Injunction granted—to restrain a sale of land under a trust deed, there being a cloud upon the title. *Faulkner* vs. *Davis*, 18 Grat., 651.

Injunction granted—to restrain a sale under a trust deed, the amount due being uncertain. *Hogan* vs. *Duke*, 20 Grat., 244.

Injunction granted—a temporary injunction. *Goodwyn* vs. *McCluer*, 3 Grat., 278.

Injunction granted—to restrain an administrator from selling land until the matters in controversy between him and the devisee are decided. *Watson* vs. *Fletcher*, 7 Grat., 1.

Injunction granted—to plaintiff in equity attachment to stop sale under subsequent attachments at law. *Moore & als.*, vs. *Holt*, 10 Grat., 284.

Injunction granted—to a judgment, grounds of stated in *Holland, &c.*, vs. *Trotter*, 22 Grat., 136, 140–1. See 1 P. & H., 43.

Injunction granted—to restrain proceeding at law, the plaintiff in equity having the equitable right to the land. *Stafford* vs. *Carter*, 4 Grat., 63.

Injunction granted—to perpetually enjoin a part of a judgment at law on the ground that the plaintiff, who had satisfied the remainder of the judgment, was under his contract, bound for no more. *Booth* vs. *Kesler*, 6 Grat., 350. [*Sed quaere:* for there is nothing in the report of the case to show that the defence was equitable, or that it could not have been made at law.]

Injunction granted—to a surety to enjoin sale under an execution. *Meade* vs. *Grigsby's adm'rs*, 26 Grat., 612.

If a defendant in an execution file a bill to enjoin the execution on the ground that a previous execution sued out on the same judgment had been levied by the sheriff on the property of another defendant in the execution sufficient to discharge it, the bill to enjoin execution must be filed in the county in which the judgment was obtained. *Beckley* vs. *Palmer & als.*, 11 Grat., 625.

Injunction granted—to sureties released by contract for forbearance to principal. *Armistead & als.*, vs. *Ward & als.*, 2 P. & H., 504; *Great Falls Manufacturing Co.* vs. *Henry's adm'or*, 25 Grat., 579.

Injunction granted—to prevent the building of a dike along a stream, on one side of it, the effect of which is to destroy a dike on the other side and injure the land of the proprietor on that side. *Burwell* vs. *Hobson*, 12 Grat., 322.

Injunction granted—to restrain a town from removing buildings said to be in a street. *Manchester Cotton Mills* vs. *Town of Manchester*, 25 Grat., 825. See *Poe* vs. *City of Richmond*, 24 Grat., 149.

WHEN INJUNCTION REFUSED.

Injunction refused—because to grant it would be an improper interference with the discretion reposed in an executor by his testator. *Dixon* vs. *McCue*, 14 Grat. 540.

Injunction refused—to a surety, who alleged his principal obligor obtained his signature by fraud and misrepresentation, but who did not farther allege that the payee was party to the fraud. *Griffith* vs. *Reynolds*, 4 Grat. 46.

Injunction refused—to a judgment at the instance of a surety who pleaded usury at law and was defeated; his alleged after discovered evidence being merely cumulative. *Harnsbarger* vs. *Kinney*, 13 Grat. 311.

Injunction refused—to one who had defended himself at law and failed, alleging that he is now able to prove his defence—but not alleging that he was prevented by fraud, accident, mistake, &c., from establishing his defence at law. *Norris* vs. *Hume*, 2 Leigh 334.

Injunction refused—to a judgment on the ground that as to one of the defences the after discovered evidence was merely cumulative, and as to the other that the defence might have been made at law. *Harnsbarger's adm'or* vs. *Kinney*, 13 Grat. 511. See 1 P. & H. 141.

Injunction refused—because of neglect to defend at law. *Griffith* vs. *Thompson*, 4 Grat. 147; *George* vs. *Strange*, 10 Grat. 499; *Meem* vs. *Rucken*, 10 Grat. 506.

Injunction refused—to a judgment entered by consent under a mutual mistake of law as to right of appeal. *R. & P. R. R. Co.* vs. *Shippen*, 2 P. & H. 327.

Injunction refused—to prevent a joint devisee of land from entering on it, at the suit of one claiming under his joint devisees. *Baldwin* vs. *Darst*, 3 Grat. 126.

Injunction refused—to enjoin directors of a railroad company from doing any act as such, though case made sufficient for the appointment of a receiver of the road. *Stevens* vs. *Davison*, 18 Grat. 819.

Injunction refused—to an execution, the plaintiff in the bill tendering the amount of the judgment after the execution had issued, there being no allegation nor proof that the money was kept on hand for the discharge of the judgment. *Shumaker* vs. *Nichols*, 6 Grat. 592.

Injunction refused—to a judgment on *scirefacias* against a bail though he had surrendered his principal, the bail having failed to defend the *scirefacias*. *Allen* vs. *Hamilton*, 9 Grat. 255.

Injunction refused—to a party claiming additional credits on an execution; his remedy is by application to the court whence the execution issued. *Morrison* vs. *Speer*, 10 Grat. 228.

Injunction refused—to a debtor in an execution who claims that under a prior execution sufficient property had been levied on and its proceeds misapplied; he should apply for redress to the court whence the execution issued. *Beckley* vs. *Palmer*, 11 Grat. 625.

Injunction refused—to a surety, his principal not appealing from an order dissolving an injunction, the injunction being granted on the ground of want of title; the principal may waive a good title, and his waiver binds his surety. *Ross* vs. *Woodville & als.*, 4 Munf. 324.

Injunction refused—to enjoin the sale of personal property; complete remedy at law. *Poage* vs. *Bell & als.*, 3 Rand. 586.

Injunction refused—to a judgment, on application of a person not a party to it. *Jordan's adm'ix* vs. *Williams*, 3 Rand. 501. He may obtain an injunction to the levy of the execution. Ibid.

Injunction refused—in *Rhodes* vs. *Cousins*, 6 Rand. 188; but see Code 1873, ch. 175, § 2, as to rights of creditors before obtaining judgments.

Injunction refused—to enjoin a proceeding under an execution and upon a forthcoming bond, there being a plain remedy at law, *Miller* vs. *Crews*, 2 Leigh 576.

Injunction refused—in the case of Glebe lands. *Overseers of the Poor* vs. *Hart*, 3 Leigh 1.

Injunction refused—under the circumstances of this case in which plaintiff claimed there was defect of title; there was no eviction nor disturbance, and the deed of conveyance was only with general warranty. *Long's ex'or, &c.* vs. *Israel & als.*, 9 Leigh 556.

Injunction refused—to restrain the proceedings of the James River and Kanawha Company: to justify an injunction against the company, it must appear *both* that it is transcending the powers granted by the charter and that the injury sought to be prevented, cannot be adequately compensated by damages. *Jas. R. & K. Co.* vs. *Anderson, &c.*, 12 Leigh 278.

Injunction refused—to a judgment, to permit a defendant in the judgment to establish offsets he was prevented by unavoidable accident from proving in the action at law, the offsets not being connected with the debts sued on; and he having a plain remedy at law for the recovery of his claims. *Hudson* vs. *Kline*, 9 Grat. 379.

555. The method of dissolving injunctions and the consequences of dissolution, and the damages awarded in cases of dissolution appear in the subsection.

ON MOTION TO DISSOLVE INJUNCTION BEFORE REGULAR HEARING. If on motion to dissolve, previous to regular hearing, the court dismisses the bill, it is error. *Blow, adm'or,* vs. *Taylor*, 4 H. & M., 159. See *Rowton* vs. *Rowton*, 1 H. & M., 110; *Wise* vs. *Lamb*, 9 Grat., 294.

On motion to dissolve, it is not required of the defendant to invalidate by full proof the allegations of the bill; the burden is on the plaintiff to sustain them. *North's exo'r* vs. *Perrow*, 4 Rand., 1. See *Randolph* vs. *Randolph*, 6 Rand., 194.

On motion to dissolve, objection that the bill is multifarious, will not avail. *Shirley* vs. *Long*, 6 Rand., 764.

On motion to dissolve before answer filed, the allegations of the bill are taken to be true. *Peatross* vs. *McLaughlin*, 6 Grat., 64. See *Balt. & O. R. R. Co.* vs. *City of Wheeling*, 13 Grat., 40, as to motion after answer filed, and §§ 365–366, pp. 411–412, *ante*.

An administrator enjoining a judgment against himself as administrator on the ground that he is a creditor, to sustain the injunction on a motion to dissolve, must show by his accounts that he is a creditor. *Deloney* vs. *Hutcheson*, 2 Rand., 183.

The court never continues a motion to dissolve unless from some very great necessity. (Ch. Taylor), *Radford's ex'ors* vs. *Innes's ex'ors*, 1 H. & M., 7; *West's ex'or* vs. *Logwood*, 6 Munf., 497, 2 Rob. Pr., (old), 243, When a motion to dissolve should be continued. *Tiffany* vs. *Kent, &c.*, 2 Grat., 231.

When error to dissolve before final hearing. *Gray* vs. *Over-street*, 7 Grat. 346.

DISSOLUTION OF INJUNCTION.—*Death of parties; need of revival.*
When injunction dissolved on death of defendant unless suit revived, *Ross* vs. *Pleasants*, 1 H. & M. 1; *Kenner* vs. *Hord*, 1 H. &
M. 204; and on death of plaintiff, *Carter* vs. *Washington*, 1 H. &
M. 263; *Jackson* vs. *Arnold*, 4 Rand. 195. There is need of a
rule in such cases, *Jackson* vs. *Arnold*, 4 Rand. 195. The court
should not impose unreasonable terms, 2 Rob. Pr. (old) 242. In
Mackays vs. *Hite & als.*, 2 Leigh 145, four plaintiffs in equity
united in the same bill praying, on grounds of equity common to
all, an injunction to stay proceedings on four several judgments
against them respectively. The bill was exhibited against five defendants. The injunction was awarded, and, pending the suit, two
of the plaintiffs and three of the defendants died. The chancellor
ordered that unless the living plaintiffs and the representatives of
the deceased plaintiffs revived the injunction at or before a given
day the injunction should stand dissolved. Held, this order was
irregular and erroneous. See the argument of Wyndham Robertson.

OTHER MATTERS CONCERNING DISSOLUTION. Dissolution unless
new party made. *Harrison* vs. *Martin*, (Ch. Taylor), 4 H. & M.
485.

In *Beale* vs. *Gibson*, 4 H. & M. 481, the injunction was awarded
until the coming in of the answer, and Ch. Taylor held that the
injunction was of course dissolved on the coming in of the answer;
but the Court of Appeals, in *Turner* vs. *Scott*, 5 Rand. 332, overruled *Beale* vs. *Gibson* in this particular.

After bill of injunction has been taken for confessed, a motion
to dissolve the injunction as improvidently granted will not be received. (Ch. Taylor), *Turpin, adm'or* vs. *Jefferson*, 4 H. & H. 483.

In *Todd* vs. *Bowyer*, 1 Munf. 447, the court not only dissolved
the injunction to the judgment at law, but decreed that the plaintiff in equity should pay an additional sum.

An injunction to a judgment for purchase money should not be
dissolved until the vendor tender a good deed. *Grantland* vs.
Wight, 2 Munf. 179.

An injunction dissolved because not supported by evidence.
Greenhow's adm'ix vs. *Harris*, 6 Munf. 472.

If after injunction dissolved, the defendant have the cause set
for hearing on his motion, he cannot claim that the bill should
have been dismissed under the statute.[2] *Franklin* vs. *Wilkinson*,
3 Munf. 112.

---

[2] 1 R. C. p 208, § 60. Sess. Acts 1830-1, p. 56, ch. 11, § 42. Code 1873,
chap. 175, § 14.

The dismission of the bill after two terms[3] does not apply if bill seeks other relief. *Pulliam* vs. *Winston & als.*, 5 Leigh 324.

When the Circuit Court simply dissolves the injunction, the Court of Appeals affirming the order of dissolution will, in a proper case,[4] go on and dismiss the bill. *Heffner* vs. *Miller, &c.*, 2 Munf. 43.

Though an injunction be dissolved as to an assignee, it may be retained to relieve the obligor against the assignor. *Ruffners* vs. *Barret*, 6 Munf. 207; 2 Rob. Pr. (old) 250.

When dissolution of injunction on tendering or filing a deed is 'proper, without requiring the deed to be approved by the court. *McMahon* vs. *Spangler*, 4 Rand. 51.

A dissolved injunction is revived by an appeal. *Turner* vs. *Scott*, 5 Rand. 332.

· When execution may issue on a judgment before the entering of the decree of the Court of Appeals affirming the order which dissolved an injunction to the judgment. *Eppes's adm'or* vs. *Dudley*, 4 Leigh 145.

It was error (when the circuit courts had no power to dissolve an injunction in vacation) to dissolve an injunction in court with direction that the order should not go out; and then in vacation to direct it to go out, *Randolph* vs. *Randolph*, 6 Rand. 194; but quære as to effect of statute authorizing the dissolution of an injunction in vacation. Code 1873, ch. 175, sec. 12. An injunction granted on a pure bill of discovery should be dissolved, when the defendant by his answer makes no discovery but on the contrary negatives the allegations of the bill. *Webster* vs. *Couch*, 6 Rand. 519.[5]

When a judgment creditor dies pending the injunction to the judgment, and a revival is had of the injunction suit, on dissolving the injunction a decree should not go in equity for the money which will be payable to the creditor on the dissolution; the judgment should be revived. *Medley* vs. *Pannill's adm'or*, 1 Rob., 63.

An injunction to judgment dissolved, because the plaintiff should have made his defence at law. *Hendricks, &c.* vs. *Compton's ex'ors*, 2 Rob. 192.

An injunction dissolved after answer, on the hearing, the plaintiffs having in support of their bill only one witness, and no corroborating circumstances. *Thornton* vs. *Gordon, &c.*, 2 Rob. 719.

---

[3] See statutes cited in last note.

[4] In this case the Circuit Court had affirmed the order of dissolution by a county court.

[5] The apparent conflict of this case with *Gilliam* vs. *Allen*, 1 Rand. 414, on a point different from the above, discussed by Mr. Robinson in the first edition of his Practice, vol. 2, pp. 246, 247, has ceased to be of any practical importance.

An injunction dissolved, the bill not showing any equity on its face. *Slack* vs. *Wood*, 9 Grat. 40.

An injunction dissolved, the vendor having removed incumbrances, and obtained title before the decree. *Young* vs. *McClung*, 9 Grat. 336, *Reevis* vs. *Dickey*, 10 Grat. 138, *Jaynes & als.* vs. *Brock*, 10 Grat. 211.

The absence of a foreign corporation, defendant, not a ground for refusing to dissolve the injunction in *Balto. & O. R. R. Co.* vs. *The City of Wheeling*, 13 Grat. 40.

When a judge may dissolve an injunction in a cause removed from one court to another. *Muller* vs. *Bayly*, 21 Grat. 521.

An injunction to a sale under a trust deed should not be dissolved until the amount of the debt is ascertained. *White* vs. *Mech. Building F. Association*, 22 Grat. 233.

An award held invalid, and an injunction depending upon it dissolved. *Tate* vs. *Vance*, 27 Grat. 571.

When the answer denies all the statements of the bill, the court will, on the hearing, dissolve the injunction and dismiss the bill, or will order a sale. *Hogan* vs. *Duke*, 20 Grat. 244.

DAMAGES ON DISSOLUTION OF INJUNCTION. Damages on the dissolution of an injunction to a judgment, computed on the aggregate of the principal, interest and costs due on the judgment at the date of the injunction. *Washington's ex'or* vs. *Parks*, 6 Leigh, 581. See *Jeter* vs. *Langhorne*, 5 Grat., 193.

The damages on dissolution of injunction to a judgment form part of the judgment, and are embraced in the lien of it. *Michaux's adm'or* vs. *Brown & als.*, 10 Grat., 612.

Damages awarded on dissolution of an injunction to a judgment against a person, who, though not a party, enjoins its execution. *Claytor* vs. *Anthony*, 15 Grat., 518. See *Claytor* vs. *Anthony*, also, as to recovery of damages, if injunction bond is too small.

Relief against damages accrued on dissolution of a former injunction. *Crawford & als.* vs. *McDaniel*, 1 Rob., 448.

556. The following forms of bills, and of prayers in bills, of injunction should be referred to:

Bill to cancel a deed obtained by fraud.

[Bill alleges that plaintiff was aged and infirm, unable to read and write, and unaccustomed to the transaction of business, that the defendant, his brother-in-law, obtained from him authority to collect his rents and take charge of his property; and sometime afterwards, with intention to defraud the plaintiff, plied him with intoxicating liquors, and brought him, while thus intoxicated, a document to sign, fraudulently representing it to be a power to collect rents and manage his property ; that this document was not read to the plaintiff, nor was he informed of its true contents, and that he signed it with his mark, relying entirely upon said representation ; that he is now informed that it was a deed of conveyance of his whole estate to the defendant, for the nominal consideration of one hundred dollars; that the consideration was entirely nominal, that nothing was ever paid or agreed to be paid by the defendant for the land, and that the defendant never agreed to buy, and the plaintiff never agreed to sell or convey the land to him, or had any consideration or thought about such a sale; that the defendant now assumed to own the entire estate conveyed in said deed, and had encumbered it with two mortgages [described in the bill] entirely without the consent, knowledge or acquiescence of the plaintiff, and was about to convey away the whole estate, as the plaintiff feared or had reason to believe.]

The bill prayed that the defendant might be restrained from further mortgaging, encumbering or conveying the land, or exercising any act of ownership over it : that the deed to the defendant might be given up and cancelled, and for further relief. _Dodd_ vs. _Cook_, 11 Gray, 495; 3 Dan. Ch. Pr. (Perk.) 1987.

Bill to annul a contract for fraud.

That on the ——— day of ————, 18—, the plaintiff was the owner of a tract of land containing ——— acres, lying in H——— county ; that the plaintiff being then old, infirm and blind, and by reason thereof, incapacitated from attending properly to business, the defendants, on that day, fraudulently taking advantage of the plaintiff's said incapacity, procured him to sign a certain writing without paying him any consideration therefor, and which writing they falsely and fraudulently represented to be a mere matter of form; that the plaintiff has since, on the ——— day of ————, 18—, applied to the said defendants for said writing, or for information as to the contents thereof, but the defendants refused to allow him to see said writing or to give him any information concerning the same ; that, as the plaintiff is informed and believes the said writing is under seal and is a deed of said premises, and conveys the same or some interest therein to the defendants, and that they intend to use the same for their own benefit and to the prejudice of the plaintiff;[6] that plaintiff fears the said defendants will convey in trust, mortgage or sell and convey the said property, which will be greatly to his prejudice.

[Pray that the court declare the conveyance void, and decree that defendants produce said writing and deliver it up to be can-

[6] 3 Dan. Ch. Pr. (Perk.), 1988.

celled; and that meanwhile defendants may be injoined and restrained from conveying in trust, mortgaging or selling and conveying the property, or any part of it, and for general relief.]

Modern English form of prayer in a bill seeking an account of partnership dealings, receiver and injunction.

1. That an account may be taken by and under the decree and direction of this honorable court, of all the said partnership dealings and transactions between the plaintiff and the defendant, and that what shall appear thereon from the defendant may be decreed to be paid by him.

2. That a proper person may be appointed to receive, collect and get in all the outstanding debts and moneys due to or on account of the said partnership business or concern, and also to take possession of all the effects and property of or belonging to the said partnership.

3. That the defendant may be ordered to deliver up to such person all the effects and property of or belonging to the said partnership in his possession or power, and also all books of account, accounts, receipts, vouchers and papers of or belonging to the said partnership; and that the defendant may be restrained, by the order and injunction of this honorable court, from demanding, receiving, or obtaining possession of any debts, moneys or property due or belonging to the said partnership; and also from in any manner intermeddling with the books, papers, bills, or accounts of the said partnership; and that the said effects and property of or belonging to the said partnership may be sold and converted into money by and under the direction of this honorable court.

4. That out of the share of the defendant in the produce thereof, what shall be found due to the plaintiff in respect of the moneys of the partnership so improperly applied by the defendant as aforesaid, may be made good to the plaintiff.

5. That all such farther directions as may be necessary may be given.

Modern English form of bill by creditor against devisees in trust and executors of testator.

TITLE OF CAUSE.

To, &c., Humbly complaining, showeth unto his Lordship, J. S., &c., of, &c., the above-named plaintiff on behalf, &c.:

1. That the said W. W., deceased, was on, &c., indebted to the plaintiff in the sum of two hundred and eighty pounds upon the

balance of accounts then settled by and between the plaintiff and the said W. W., deceased.

2. The said W. W., deceased, by his promissory note, dated, &c., two months after date, promised to pay the plaintiff the sum of two hundred and eighty pounds.

3. The said last-mentioned promissory note was given to secure the amount due to the plaintiff as mentioned in the first paragraph of this bill.

4. The said sum of £————, &c., remained justly due and payable to the plaintiff from the said W. W., deceased, at the time of his decease.

5. The said W. W., deceased, made his will, dated, &c. (and which was dully executed and attested), and the said testator thereby devised all his real estate and personal estate to the defendants, J. A. and E. B., their heirs, executors, administrators, and assigns, upon trust to sell and collect and get in the same. [The trusts of the money arising from such sale being declared for the benefit of the defendant, W. B., if he should die before twenty-five years without leaving issue.]

6. The testator, W. W., died in, &c., without having altered or revoked his said will, leaving the several persons named in his said will him surviving.

7. The said will of the testator was duly proved, &c., by the defendants, J. A. and E. B., who thereby became, and now are, his sole legal personal representatives.

8. The testator was, at the time of his death, indebted to several persons other than the plaintiff.

9. The testator was, at the time of his death, possessed or entitled of or to personal estate of considerable value.

10. The testator also died seized or entitled of or to divers lands, messuages, and other real estate, situate in the county of Gloucester, and elsewhere in England.

11. The defendants, J. A. and E. B., have, since the death of the said testator, possessed themselves of the whole of the personal estate of the said testator, and, as the devisees in trust or trustees of said will, they entered into and are now in the possession or receipt of the rents and profits of his real estate, and they have received a large sum of money in respect of the real and personal estate of the testator.

82

12. The plaintiff has, by himself and his solicitor, made divers applications to the defendants, J. A. and E. B., and requested them to pay what is due to him for principal and interest in respect of his said claim, but they have refused so to do.

13. The said last-named defendants, however, allege that the personal estate of the said testator is insufficient to pay his debts, whereas the plaintiff insists that if such allegation be true, yet that the personal estate of the testator, together with his real estate, is more than sufficient for payment of all his debts and funeral and testamentary expenses.

14. The said defendants also allege that the real estate of the testator is subject to certain mortgages or incumbrances, and that they have been unable to sell the said real estate or any part thereof.

15. The defendant, W. B., has attained the age of twenty-five years.

16. The defendant, W. B., claims to be interested in the matters in question in this suit, and insists that he is a necessary party thereto.

PRAYER.

The plaintiff prays as follows:

1. That an account may be taken of what is due to the plaintiff in respect of his said debt so due and owing to him from the said testator, W. W., as aforesaid, and of all other debts which were owing by the testator at the time of his death, and which still remain unpaid.

2. That the trusts of the said testator's will may be carried into execution by and under the direction and decree of this honorable court.

3. That an account may be taken of the personal estate and effects of the testator received by the said defendants, J. A. and E. B., or either of. them, or by any other person or persons, by their or either of their order, or for their or either of their use, and that the said estate may be applied in payment of the testator's debts and funeral expenses, and that the following further accounts and inquiries may be taken and made (that is to say)—

4. An inquiry of or to what real estate the testator was seized

or entitled at the respective times of the date of his will and of his death.

5. An inquiry whether any and what incumbrances affect the said testator's real estate.

6. An account of the rents and profits of the said testator's real estate received by the defendants, J. A. and E. B., or either of them, or by any person by their or either of their order, or for their or either of their use.

7. That the real estate of the said testator, or a sufficient part thereof, may be sold, and that the rents and produce thereof may be applied in payment of the testator's debts.

8. That the defendants, J. A. and E. B., may, if necessary, be restrained by the injunction of this honorable court from retaining, receiving, or collecting any of the moneys, debts, or other outstanding personal estate of the testator, and from receiving the rents and profits of the real estate of the testator, and that some proper person may be appointed to receive all the outstanding personal estate and effects of the testator, and to collect and get in the debts owing him.

CHAPTER IV.

Of amended bills, supplemental bills and bills of revivor.

557. This chapter will be devoted to the consideration of amended bills, supplemental bills, bills of revivor and to the defences to the same.

Amended bills.

558. When a plaintiff has filed his bill and is advised that the same does not contain such material facts, or make all such persons parties as are necessary to enable the court to grant him the required relief, he may change the bill by inserting new mat-

ter or by adding such persons as shall be deemed
necessary as parties; or, in case the original bill
shall be found to contain matter not relevant or no
longer necessary for plaintiff's case, or parties which
may be dispensed with, the same may be struck out,
and the original bill thus changed is termed an
amended bill. 1 Dan. Ch. Pr. (Perk.) 402.

The proper functions of an amended bill are to bring before the
court other parties and to explain and set forth more fully the
matters of the original bill or matters connected with the original
bill which should be brought into the litigation. An amended bill
is not to be filed if it shows that the original bill is groundless or
presents new and distinct matters of controversy. *Lambert & als.
vs. Jones & als.,* 2 P. & H. 144.

" As a general rule, the court will at any time before the hearing grant leave to amend where the bill is defective as to parties or
in the mistake or omission of any fact or circumstance connected
with the substance of the bill " [but not forming the substance
itself], " or not repugnant thereto. This amendment may be made
by common order before answer or demurrer, and afterwards by
leave of the court." Christian, J., in *Holland, &c.,* vs. *Trotter,* 22
Grat. 136. See *Mason* vs. *Nelson,* 11 Leigh 227; *Parrill* vs. *Mc-
Kinley,* 9 Grat. 1; *Stevenson* vs. *Taverners,* 9 Grat. 398; Id. 372;
Smith vs. *Smith,* 4 Rand. 95; *Boykin's devisees* vs. *Smith,* 3 Munf.
102; *Sutton* vs. *Gatewood, &c.,* 6 Munf. 398.

But where a motion was made to amend in a case in which the
matters sought to be inserted were known to the plaintiff at the
time he commenced his suit, and no excuse was given for not inserting them then, and the answer in which they were stated had
been long since filed, and no cause was shown for not having applied sooner, the application to amend was refused. *Whitmarsh*
vs. *Campbell, &c.,* 2 Paige, 67. Mr. Robinson adds: " in this case
it is proper to remark the amendments were also refused upon the
merits." 2 Rob. Pr. (old), 294. See likewise *Kirby, &c.,* vs.
Thompson, &c., 6 John. Ch. R., 79. as to unreasonable delay.[1] When

---

[1] Mr. Robinson states farther rules in relation to amendments of bill: " After
the answer has been replied to, the motion will be to withdraw the replication and amend the bill. *Matteux* vs. *MacKreath,* 1 Ves., Jr., 142. And then
the plaintiff should satisfy the court of the materiality of the amendments,
and show why the matter introduced was not stated before. *Longman, &c.,*
vs. *Calleford,* 3 Austr. 807. If the replication has been filed several months,
the motion will be denied unless these things are shown. *Brown* vs. *Ricketts,*

the plaintiff has an interest in the subject matter of the suit, the bil may be amended, and other persons having the same interest may be joined as coplaintiffs. *Coffman* vs. *Sangston*, 21 Grat., 263. *A* plaintiff, who was a guardian, filed a bill in his own name, he should have filed it in the name of the ward by his next friend, to obtain possession of the ward's estate; there were other defects in the bill. He was permitted to amend. *Sillings* vs. *Bumgardner*, ' Grat., 273.

559. In the Virginia State courts, before answer the face of the original bill is sometimes altered or added to; after answer always, and sometimes before answer, the new matter is introduced in a separate paper styled an amended bill. See 28th Rule U. S Supreme Court. The amendments are considered as incorporated in and forming part of the original bill *Hurd, &c.*, vs. *Everett*, 1 Paige 124.

560. Matters occurring subsequently to the origi nal bill are, in strict practice, not usually introduced

---

&c., 2 John. Ch. R., 425. In *Thorn, &c.*, vs. *Germand*, 4 John. Ch. Rep., 36* the plaintiffs, before filing the original bill, knew the existence of the matte sought to be introduced into the amended bill, and before the motion wa made a commission had issued to take depositions, and one witness was ex amined. The motion was denied." And he continues: "Greater strictnes is required as to amending injunction bills. The ordinary rules as to amend ing bills do not apply to injunction bills, or other bills which are sworn to *Parker, &c.*, vs. *Grant, &c.*, 1 John. Ch. R., 434; *Renwick* vs. *Wilson, &c.*, John. Ch. R., 81. When the complainant in an injunction bill applies t amend without prejudice to the injunction, he must state the proposed amend ments distinctly, so that the court may see that they are merely in additio to the original bill and not inconsistent therewith, he must render a valid ex cuse for not incorporating them in the original bill; it must appear that th application to amend is made as soon as the necessity of such amendment i discovered; and the complainant must swear to the truth of the several mat ters proposed to be inserted as amendments. *Rodgers, &c.*, vs. *Rodgers, &c.* 1 Paige, 424."

Whether these strict rules would be applied in the Virginia courts may b seriously doubted. The practice in allowing amendments in them is exceed ingly liberal.

into the cause by an amended but by a supplemental
bill; yet there are cases in which such amendments
are allowed, e. g., when the plaintiff, having an inchoate right at the time of exhibiting the original
bill merely requiring a formal act to perfect it, is
permitted by amendment to introduce the fact that
it has been perfected.

A plaintiff sued for the specific performance of a contract for the
exchange of lands. It appeared in the progress of the cause that
the defendant could not specifically perform the contract. It was
held that the plaintiff might amend his bill and ask a rescission of
the contract, and for such other relief as under the circumstances
he was entitled to. *Parrill* vs. *McKinley*, 9 Grat. 1.

A party having an interest in the subject of a suit sues in a
wrong character; his bill should not be dismissed, but he should
have leave to amend and make the proper parties. *Sillings & als.*
vs. *Bumgardner*, g'd'n, 9 Grat. 273. In this case a husband of
one distributee, who was also one of the personal representatives,
and guardian of the other distributee, filed a bill in his own name
as guardian of the infant distributee against the other personal
representative and the sureties, charging that the personal representative was indebted to the estate and insolvent; and asking
a decree against the sureties. There was a decree accordingly
in the lower court. Upon appeal the decree was reversed for
want of proper parties; but the husband having an interest in
right of his wife, the suit was not dismissed, but was sent back
that he might amend his bill and make other partise. *Ibid.*

561. A plaintiff may, in the Virginia State courts,
of right amend his bill before the defendant's appearance, and notwithstanding such appearance may,
at any time in the vacation of the court wherein the
suit is pending, file in the clerk's office an amended
or supplemental bill, or bill of revivor. Code 1873,
ch. 167, § 15. On filing the bill, in vacation, such
proceedings may be had as if leave to file it had been
previously obtained in court, but the court, on the
motion of a defendant, made at the term to which

process to answer the same is returned executed c
him, or if it be returnable to rules, at the first ter:
after it is so returned, may dismiss such amended (
supplemental bill, or bill of revivor. *Ibid.* In th
United States Circuit Courts, the practice is regulate
by the 28th, 29th and 46th rules of practice. The:
rules are as follows:

28. "The plaintiff shall be at liberty as matter of course and witho
payment of costs, to amend his bill in any matters whatsoever, befo
any copy has been taken out of the clerk's office, and in any sme
matters afterwards, such as filling blanks, correcting errors of date
misnomer of parties, misdescription of premises, clerical erroı
and generally in matters of form. But if he amend in a materi
point (as he may do of course), after a copy has been so take
before any answer or plea, or demurrer to the bill, he shall pay
the defendant the costs occasioned thereby, and shall witho
delay furnish him a fair copy thereof, free of expense, with suitab
references to the places where the same are to be inserted, and
the amendments are numerous, he shall furnish in like manner
the defendants a copy of the whole bill as amended, and if the
be more than one defendant, a copy shall be furnished to eac
defendant affected thereby."

29. "After an answer or plea or demurrer is put in, and befo
replication, the defendant may, upon motion or petition, withol
notice, obtain an order from any judge of the court, to amend b
bill on or before the next succeeding rule day, upon payment
costs, or without payment of costs, as the court or a judge there
may in his discretion direct. But after replication filed, the plainti
shall not be permitted to withdraw it and to amend his bill, excel
upon a special order of a judge of the court, upon motion or pet
tion, after due notice to the other party, and upon proof by affidavi
that the same is not made for the purpose of vexation or delay, (
that the matter of the proposed amendment is material and coul
not with reasonable diligence have been sooner introduced into th
bill, and upon the plaintiff's submitting to such other terms as me
be imposed by the judge for speeding the cause."

46. "In every case where an amendment shall be made aft
answer filed, the defendant shall put in a new or supplement;
answer, on or before the next succeeding rule day after that (
which the amendment or amended bill is filed, unless the tin
therefor is enlarged or otherwise ordered by a judge of the couri
and upon his default the like proceedings may be had as in cases
an omission to put in an answer."

After the cause is regularly set for hearing, a plaintiff could not by amendment introduce new charges or put a material fact in issue which was not in issue before: this should be done by a supplemental bill. Ch. Taylor in *Pleasants* vs. *Logan*, 4 H. & M. 489.

In *Baker* vs. *Baker & als.*, 3 Munf. 222, leave given an executor who, in a bill against his co-executors and the legatees, had failed to state his claim with reasonable certainty against his testator's estate, to amend his bill and make a fuller statement of his claim.

A cause was ready for a decision as to substantial parties at a regular term of the court. At a following intermediate term, the plaintiff amended his bill to make a formal party, who came in and filed his answer at the same term and consented that the cause might come on to be heard. The court, it was held, might hear the cause at the intermediate term, though it was objected to by the substantial defendant, as to whom it was ready at the preceding regular term. *Robinson* vs. *Day*, 5 Grat. 55.

In *Jamison's adm'ors* vs. *Deshields*, 3 Grat., 4, the plaintiff had shown a right to relief against parties before the court, but had omitted to make other necessary parties. The appellate court would not dismiss the bill, but sent the cause back with leave to amend the bill and add the necessary parties.

562. The rule as to amending bills in equity in the Circuit Courts of the United States was examined in *Shields* vs. *Barrow*, 17 How., 130. The court held that under the privilege of amending, the plaintiff should not be permitted to make a new and wholly different case from that made in the bill.

Granting leave to amend is a matter of discretion with the Circuit Court, and is not open to examination on appeal. *Sheets* vs. *Selden*, 7 Wal., 416. After demurrer sustained to the bill, the plaintiff is not entitled as of right to amend the bill, it is in the discretion of the court to grant or to refuse him leave to do so. *National Bank* vs. *Carpenter*, 11 Otto., 567.[2]

After a final decree, amendments which changed the character of the bill were allowed, the circumstances being peculiar and the cause having been in fact tried exactly as it would have been if the bill had originally been in the amended form. *The Tremolo Patent*, 23 Wal. 518.

---

[2]And the decision will not be reviewed in the appellate court if the record does not show what amendment was proposed. *Nat. B'k* vs. *Carpenter*, 11 Otto., 567.

Sometimes a case is remanded from the Supreme Court with the direction to amend the bill and bring in proper parties. *Lewis* vs. *Darling*, 16 How. 1.

Eight years after a bill had been filed, and on the day it was dismissed on a final hearing upon the pleadings and proofs, an amended bill was filed without leave. The Supreme Court held that it must be disregarded in the consideration of the case by that court. *Terry* vs. *McLure*, 13 Otto, 442.

After a cause has been heard and a case for relief made out, but not the case disclosed by the bill, the court has the power to allow an amendment of the pleadings on terms that the party not in fault has no reasonable ground to object to. *Neale* vs. *Neales*, 9 Wal. 1.

The objection that all the parties to a supplemental bill were necessary parties to an amended bill, cannot be made for the first time in the United States Supreme Court. *McBurney* vs. *Curson*, 9 Otto, 567.

563. An amendment to a bill authorizes a defendant, though not required to answer, to put in an answer making an entirely new defence and contradicting his former answer. Dan. Ch. Pr. (Perk.) 411; *Trust & F. Ins. Co.* vs. *Jenkins*, 8 Paige 589.

564. By an amended bill persons not before parties to the suit were made defendants. The suit was brought in 1808, the amended bill was filed in 1815. The new defendants alleged an adverse possession of the land for more than twenty years. That possession was proved to have been taken in 1788 or 1789. It was insisted that the amended bill had relation to the commencement of the suit and consequently that the statute could not bar. But the Supreme Court was of opinion that until the defendants in possession were made parties to the suit it could not be considered as having been commenced against them. *Miller's heirs* vs. *McIntyres*, 6 Pet. 61; 2 Rob. Pr. (old) 253, 254.

565. When there is a bill or cross-bill, and the plaintiff ·in the original suit amends his bill before answer, he will lose his priority of suit and his right to have an answer before he is called upon to answer the cross bill. 1 Dan. Ch. Pr. (old) 509. See Code 1873, ch. 167, sec. 16; *McConnico* vs. *Moseley*, 4 Call, 360; *Hudson & als.* vs. *Hudson's ex'or*, 3 Rand. 117.[3]

---

[3] Although in part a repetition of some things already said, the following valuable note in 1 Dan. Ch. Pr. (Perk.) 402 is printed here. The rules announced are taken from reports of cases decided in other States than Virginia; yet they may afford assistance in ascertaining when, and what, amendments may be made in the Virginia courts:

" Amendments being regarded only with reference to the furtherance of justice, as a general rule, are in the discretion of the court, especially in matters of mere form. *Smith* vs. *Babcock*, 3 Sumn., 410; *Garlick* vs. *Strong*, 3 Paige, 440; *McElwain* vs. *Willis*, 3 Paige, 505. Amendments are therefore always allowed with great liberality until the proofs are closed, *Cock* vs. *Evans*, 9· Yerger, 287, except where the bill is upon oath. *Cock* vs. *Evans*, 9 Yerger, 287; *Cunningham* vs. *Pell*, 6 Paige, 655. In case the bill is upon oath, there· is greater caution exercised in reference to amendments. *Ib.*, *Verplanck* vs.. *Mer. Ins. Co.*, 1 Edw., 46, *Swift* vs. *Eckford*, 6 Paige 22; *Lloyd* vs. *Brewster*, 4 Paige, 538; *Parker* vs. *Grant*, 1 John. Ch., 434; *Rogers* vs. *Rogers*, 1 Paige, 424; *Whitmarsh* vs. *Campbell*, 2 Paige, 67. So where the object of the amendment is to let in new facts or defences, there is greater reluctance on the part of the court to allow the amendment where it depends upon parol proof than where it depends on written instruments omitted by accident or mistake.. *Smith* vs. *Babcock*, 3 Sumner, 410; *Calloway* vs. *Dobson*, 1 Brock., 119. And the court will not allow amendments by inserting facts known to the plaintiff at the time of filing his bill, unless some excuse is given for the omission. *Whitmarsh* vs. *Campbell*, 2 Paige, 67; *Prescott* vs. *Hubbell*, 1 Hill Ch., 217.. Nor where the matter of the proposed amendment might with reasonable diligence have been inserted in the original bill. *North Amer. Coal· Co.* vs.. *Dyett*, 2 Edw. Ch. 115."

" When a plaintiff wishes to amend a sworn bill, he must state the proposed amendments distinctly, so that the court can see that they are merely in addition to the original bill and not inconsistent therewith. He must also· swear to the truth of the proposed amendments, and render a valid excuse for not incorporating them in the original bill; and the application to amend must be made as soon as the necessity for such amendment is discovered. *Rogers* vs. *Rogers*, 1 Paige, 424; *Whitmarsh* vs. *Campbell*, 2 Paige, 67; *Verplanck* vs. *Merc. Ins. Co.*, 1 Edw., 46; *Altree* vs. *Horden*, 3 Lond. Jur., 81."

Supplemental bills.

566. Supplemental bills are used to remedy defects existing at the time of filing the original bill, and it is too late to correct them by amendment, or when they have occurred since the filing of the original bill.   3 Dan. Ch. Pr. (old) 150.

A plaintiff cannot, however, support a bad title by acquiring another after the filing of the original bill and then bringing it forward by a supplemental bill. 3 Dan. Ch. Pr. (old) 153.

567. Supplemental bills will not be allowed for the purpose of introducing a completely new case; they must be in aid of that which the court has already done; still less can they be maintained for the purpose of adding to the decree, what, upon the hearing, the court has excluded from it.   3 Dan. Ch. Pr. (old), 159.

In *Belton* vs. *Apperson*, 26 Grat. 207, the original bill was 'filed by Belton to enjoin a sale of real estate by Apperson, the trustee in a deed given to secure the payment of a negotiable note for $1,300. The plaintiff stated in his bill that he supposed Campbell was the owner of the note and charged usury in it and set it out. Apperson and Campbell were made defendants; and they were called upon to answer on oath, and disclose who was the holder; there was a prayer for injunction and that the note should be delivered up and cancelled and Apperson required to reconvey the property to the trustee to whom the estate was conveyed for the benefit of Belton's wife and children. The injunction was granted, and in June, 1869, Apperson and Campbell answered. Campbell said he was a broker and the note was put in his hands for sale and he sold it to Shriver, and he had no interest in it. Both Campbell and Apperson said they did not believe there was usury in the transaction; it was a sale not a loan. In December, 1871, Belton and his wife and infant children, by Belton their next friend, asked leave to file an amended and supplemental bill.' In this bill they are plaintiffs, and Shriver is made a defendant with Campbell and Apperson; they set out the bills and answers, state a conveyance of the property by Belton to a trustee for Belton's wife for life, remainder to the children, they charge usury in the note, *disclaim any discovery from the defendants* and ask for an issue, and if they prove the usury that the note may be declared void, the injunction perpetuated, and for general relief. The amended and supplemental bill was most evidently drawn with reference to the 10th section of the act, Code 1849, chap. 141; it was contended that the original bill was under the 7th section. The court held that the amended and supplemental bill was properly filed, that while a' plaintiff was not permitted to make a new case by an amended bill he might by his amendments so alter the frame and structure of the bill as to obtain an entirely different relief from that asked for originally; that as Shriver was not a party to the original bill, and as the plaintiffs might at once file a new bill against him, the delay in tendering the amended bill could not prejudice his interests; that Campbell and Apperson having no interest in the note the case was virtually ended as to them, and Houston not being a party to the original bill the answer of Campbell and Apperson could not be read for him either under the original or amended bill, and the amended bill under the 10th section of the act might be filed.

In *Linn & als.* vs. *Carson's adm'or & als.*, 32 Grat. 170, the amended bill was held not to be repugnant to the original bill but as auxiliary to it in the presentation of the case more fully and accurately with additional averments, and the amended bill was sustained.

In *McComb* vs. *Lobdell & als.*, 32 Grat. 185, the supplemental bill set up a new contract of partnership entirely different from that set up in the original bill. The supplemental bill was demurrable. Mr. Barton thinks this case confirms *Lambert* vs. *Jones*, 2 P. & H. 163.

In *Ewing's admor* vs. *Ferguson's adm'or & als.*, 33 Grat. 548, the bill having been dismissed on demurrer, leave was given to file an amended bill. Some of the original plaintiffs did not unite in the amended bill. This was held not to be a departure from the original bill. And the amended bill being filed in the name of some of the original parties and of creditors who had come in by petition and only setting out more fully the nature of their claims and the character of the bill as a creditors' bill, this was not a departure from the original bill, but was held to be a valid amended bill.

In *Smith, &c.*, vs. *Smith, &c.*, 4 Rand., 95, certain legatees signed an agreement to submit to an award, others did not; there was an award by the arbitrators awarding the title to the slaves in question to "the heirs of Thomas Smith, deceased." The plaintiffs claimed under this award their proportion of the slaves. They set forth the facts in their bill, but prayed no relief either general or special. The defendants answered, resisting the award on the grounds—1st. That all parties in interest had not signed the submission. 2nd. That the award was contrary to law. The Chancery Court dismissed the bill. On appeal, the Supreme Court of Appeals held that the award was binding as to those who signed, that a court of equity was the proper *forum* for a partition of the property under the circumstances, and reversed the decree, dismissing the bill with direction to the Chancery Court to permit the plaintiffs to amend their bill, setting out their case by showing how many of the representatives of Thomas Smith would have been entitled under this award, had they signed the submission, and thereby established the extent of their own interest in the subject, under the award.

567*a*. It is not every fact occurring subsequent to the filing of the original bill which renders a supplemental bill necessary; such facts only as are mate-rial, *e. g.*, such as alter the interests of the parties or necessitate farther discovery, require the filing of a supplemental bill.[4] If a supplemental bill be filed without necessity, it may be demurred to. See 3 Dan. Ch. Pr. (old) 160.

The court held in *Beckwith* vs. *Avery's adm'or, &c.*, 31 Grat., 533, that it was a case for a supplemental bill.

568. A sole plaintiff, assigning his whole interest, or being deprived of it by an event subsequent to the institution of the suit, the alienee or party claiming his title must proceed not by a supplemental bill, *but by an original bill in the nature of a supplemental bill.* 3 Dan. Ch. Pr. (old) 164. An important dis-

[4] If a plaintiff, when his cause is in such a state that he cannot amend his bill, discovers new matter which may tend to show that he is entitled to the relief prayed by his bill, he may file a supplemental bill for the purpose of putting the new matter in issue. *Crompton* vs. *Wombwell*, 4 Sim., 628; 6 Eng. Cond. Ch. Rep., 286.

tinction, because new defences may be made to the new suit, and the depositions taken and proceedings had in the former suit cannot be used in the new. See *Ibid*.

569. A supplemental bill usually states, in the Virginia State courts, the filing of the original bill and the proceedings thereon. Neither in the Virginia State courts nor in the United States Circuit Courts, is it necessary to set forth in the supplemental bill any of the statements in the original bill, unless the special circumstances of the case require it.[5] If the supplemental bill is occasioned by an event subsequent to the original bill, it states that event and the consequent alteration of parties therein, and it prays that the defendants may appear and answer its charges. 3 Dan. Ch. Pr. (old), 178.

If the supplemental bill has been rendered necessary by the alteration or acquisition of interest happening to a defendant, or a person comes into *esse*, who is necessary to be made a defendant, the supplemental bill may be exhibited by the plaintiff in the original suit against such person alone, and may pray a decree upon the particular supplemental matter alleged against that person only, unless, which is frequently the case, the interests of the other defendants may be affected by that decree, in which case such other defendants may be made parties. 3 Dan. Ch. Pr. (old), 179. When a supplemental bill is used merely for bringing a formal party before the court as a defendant, the defendants to the original bill need not be made parties. *Ensworth* vs. *Lambert*, 4 John. Ch., 605. See also *McGown* vs. *Yorks*, 6 John. Ch., 450.

570. A supplemental bill generally calls upon the defendant to answer the supplemental matter only; if, however, it is occasioned by the transmission of the interest of a defendant who has not answered the

---

[5] See 58th Rule U. S. Sup. C't.

original bill, and it is necessary to have a discovery from the new defendant of the matters in the original bill, it may pray that the defendant may answer the original bill. 3 Dan. Ch. Pr. (old), 181.

Mr. Justice Story states, in his Pleadings in Eq., § 337e, that a supplemental bill may be brought on behalf of the defendant in the suit—that the defendant may, when the matter is newly discovered evidence on the part of the defendant, after the cause is at issue, or after publication passed, or even after a hearing or decree, by a petition to file a supplemental bill obtain relief. See *Baker, &c.* vs. *Whiting*, 1 Story, 218; *Barrington* vs. *O'Brien*, 2 Ball & Beat., 140; *Standish* vs. *Radley*, 2 Atk., 177; *Gould* vs. *Tancred*, 2 Atk., 533.

571. The practice in the United States Circuit Courts in relation to supplemental bills is regulated by the 57th and 58th rule of the United States Supreme Court. As to the practice in the Virginia State courts, see Code of 1873, ch. 167, sec. 15, cited in section 561, p. 654, *ante*.

The 57th and 58th rules of practice in the United States Courts are as follows:·

"57. Whenever any suit in equity shall become defective from any event happening after the filing of the bill (as, for example, by a change of interest in the parties), or for any other reason, a supplemental bill, or a bill in the nature of a supplemental bill, may be necessary to be filed in the cause, leave to file the same may be granted by any judge of the court on any rule day, upon proper cause shown, and due notice to the other party. And if leave is granted to file such supplemental bill, the defendant shall demur, plead or answer thereto, on the next succeeding rule day after the supplemental bill is filed in the clerk's office, unless some other time shall be assigned by a judge of the court."

"58. It shall not be necessary in any bill of revivor, or supplemental bill to set forth any of the statements in the original suit unless the special circumstances of the case may require it."

Bills of revivor.

572. When a suit, perfect in its original formation,

afterwárds becomes discontinued or imperfect by abatement, the general method of continuing it or of remedying the defects in the English courts and in the United States Circuit Courts is by bill of revivor.[6] As we have séen in the Virginia State courts, the writ of *scirefacias* is, in many cases, a sufficient substitute for the bill of revivor.[7]

573. It is not every death of a party to a suit which occasions such abatement as will suspend the proceedings; if the interest of the party dying so determines that it can no longer affect the suit and no person becomes entitled thereupon to the same interest, or if the whole interest of the party dying survives to another party, the suit may go on without revivor. 3 Dan. Ch. Pr. (old), 202.

574. If a bill of revivor seeks merely to revive the suit, it prays simply for a subpœna to revive; if it requires an answer, as in the case of a bill against an executor requiring him to admit assets, it should be to revive and answer. 3 Dan. Ch. Pr. (old), 215. See 56 Rule U. S. Supreme Court.

See Calvert on Parties, 104 *et seq.*, *Metcalfe* vs. *Metcalfe*, 1 Kean, 79.

Bills of revivor and supplement.

575. These are bills combining the characteristics of bills of revivor with those of supplemental bills.

Defences to amended bills, &c.

576. To these several bills the defendant may, as

---

[6] 56th rule U. S. Sup. Ct.   [7] Sec. 87, pp. 125, 126, *ante.*

in the case of original bills, plead, answer or demur;[8] and while many of the causes of demurrer or plea which apply to an original bill will apply to these bills, there are grounds of defence solely applicable to such bills. Thus, if the plaintiff files a supplemental bill [or an amended and supplemental bill] claiming the same matter as in an original bill, but upon a title totally distinct, the defendant may demur. 3 Dan. Ch. Pr. (old) 183. See section 565, *ante.*

Where a plaintiff had in the first instance sued without good title, which he afterwards acquired and endeavored to make effective by amending his bill, it was held liable to demurrer, and he was required to pay full costs. *Pilkington* vs. *Wignall,* 2 Madd. 244.

577. A bill of revivor also is liable to demurrer or plea for reasons peculiar to its character. If it does not shew sufficient ground to revive the suit or any part of it, it is demurrable: if there is not sufficient ground to revive and the fact is not apparent on the bill, the defendant may raise the defence by plea. 3 Dan. Ch. Pr. (old), 218.

The defence that the plaintiff is not entitled to revive should be raised by demurrer or plea; it cannot be made by answer. Yet, if at the hearing, it appears that the plaintiff has no title to revive, the suit will be dismissed. *Harris* vs. *Pollard,* 3 P. Wms., 348.

578. An answer, whether required by the plaintiff or not, may be filed to a bill of revivor. 3 Dan. Ch. Pr. (old), 220. An answer to a bill of revivor is not impertinent, if it states matters of defence which

---

[8] See sec. 571 ante, p. 663, as to time of demurring, &c., to these bills in the United States Circuit Courts.

have occurred since the answer to the original bill was filed, although such matters do not affect the title of the plaintiff to revive. 3 Dan. Ch. Pr. (old) 220.

578a. These several bills, pleas, answers and demurrers have the same general form with that already pointed out in regard to original bills and the defences thereto, and should be accompanied by the same formalities in reference to signing, filing, &c. The following are forms of an amended bill, and of a bill of revivor:

Form of amended bill.

To the honourable judge, &c.

The amended bill of your complainant R. B., respectfully represents that he heretofore exhibited in this court his original bill of complaint against B. [setting forth the original bill, after which state the matter of amendment, &c.] To the end therefore that the said M. M. and L. L. may severally answer all and every the matters and things herein charged by way of amendment, and that they may discover and set forth, &c., [here add interrogatories]. And that your complainant may have full and general relief in the premises such as the nature of his case may require. And your complainant will ever pray, &c.

A. M., p. q.

Form of bill of revivor.[9]

To the honorable judge of the ——— court of ———. Complaining, sheweth unto the court your complainant, I. B., that your complainant heretofore exhibited in this court a bill of complaint against E. J., George R., and Mary his wife, and L. C. and Jane C., his wife, praying that (here state prayer of bill); and your complainant farther sheweth that the said defendants to the said bill afterwards appeared and put in their answers thereto and your

---

[9] See 57th Rule U. S. Sup. Court.

·complainant thereafter by leave of court amended his bill. And your complainant farther sheweth unto the court that before any answer was put in by the defendants to the said amended bill or any farther proceedings had in the cause the said Mary, the wife of George R., died leaving three children her.surviving, her only heirs at law, to-wit: James R., Robert R. and Virginia R., and by the death of the said Mary the said suit ·became abated, and your ·complainant is advised that the said suit and proceedings should ·stand revived against the said James R., Robert R. and Virginia R., and be in the same plight and condition as they were in at the death of the said Mary R., deceased. To the end, therefore, that the said suit and proceedings as abated as aforesaid may stand and be revived against the said James R., Robert R. and Virginia R., and be in the same plight and condition as the same were in at the time of the abatement thereof or that the defendants may show good cause to the contrary. May it please the court to grant unto your complainant* *a writ of summons commanding the said James R., Robert R. and Virginia R. at a certain day personally to be and appear before this court, then and there to answer and show cause if they can why the said suit and the proceedings therein had should not stand and be revived against them and be in the same plight and condition as the same were in at the time of the abatement thereof, and further to stand to and abide such order and decree in the premises as to the court shall seem meet. And your complainant will ever pray, &c.*

Form of amended and supplemental bill.

See p. 102, *ante*: also section 571, *ante* p. 663.

---

* If in the United States Circuit Courts say, after star, in lieu of italics: " a writ of summons directed to the said James R., Robert R. and Virginia R. commanding them at a certain day personally to be and appear," &c., &c. (to the end.)

CHAPTER V.

Bills of interpleader, bills in the nature of a bill of interpleader, bills to perpetuate testimony, bills to examine witnesses de bene esse, bills of discovery.

Bills of interpleader.

579. The object of the bill of interpleader is to protect a complainant standing in the nature of an innocent stakeholder, 2 Barb. Ch. Pr., 117–118; it will not lie if the plaintiff himself claims any interest in the property in dispute, *Ibid;* nor will it lie if the complainant is obliged to admit, that as to either of the defendants he is a wrong doer. 2 Barb. Ch. Pr., 117–118. *Shaw* vs. *Coster*, 8 Paige, 339. Nor where it appears that the double claim has been caused by his own act or conduct. *Crawshay* vs. *Thornton*, 2 M. & Cr., 1; *Disbero* vs. *Harris*, 5 DeG. M. & G., 439. To maintain the bill, the plaintiff must be uncertain to whom the right belongs; and if he shows no right to compel the defendants to interplead, whatever rights they may claim, each may demur. Welf. Eq. Pl., 152, 153; Mitf. Pl., 48–49.

" The definition of interpleader is not and cannot now be disputed. It is where the plaintiff says, I have a fund in my possession in which I claim no personal interest, and to which you, the defendants, set up conflicting claims; pay me my costs and I will bring the fund into court, and you shall contest it between yourselves. The case must be one in which the fund is matter of contest between two parties, and in which the litigation between these parties will decide all their respective rights with regard to the fund." *Lord Cottenham* in *Hoggart* vs. *Cutts*, 1 Cr. & Phil., 204.

580. The bill should show that the plaintiff is a

stakeholder, having no personal interest in the controversy between the parties claiming the funds in his hands, and that their respective claims against him are of the same nature and character; that there is some doubt, in point of fact, to which claimant the debt or duty belongs, so that he cannot safely pay or render it to one without risk of being liable for the same debt or duty to the other. 2 Barb. Ch. Pr. 120.

The bill must relate to a thing in action and not yet passed *in rem adjudicatam*. See *Cornish* vs. *Tanner*, 1 Young & Jer., 333; *Union B. R.* vs. *Kew*, 2 Md. Ch. Decis, 460.

Where an attaching creditor and an assignee both recovered judgments against a debtor of an absent defendant, without objection on his part, although he had notice of the assignment before the judgment in the attachment suit, he could not, after the judgments were obtained, file a bill of interpleader against them to require them to litigate their respective rights to the fund, but was held liable to pay both judgments. *Haseltine* vs. *Brickey*, 16 Grat., 116.

When a sheriff has levied on property on which there are conflicting claims, he may file a bill of interpleader to settle them. *Storrs* vs. *Payne*, 4 H. & M, 506.

581. The bill may be filed when there is danger of injury to the plaintiff from the doubtful and conflicting claims of several defendants, *Mohawk & H. R. R. Co.* vs. *Clute*, 4 Paige 392, Mitf. Eq. 49, though no legal proceedings have been actually commenced, *Langston* vs. *Boylston*, 2 Ves. 101, 107, note (1) *George* vs. *Pilcher*, 28 Grat. 305; and though the claim of one of the defendants is actionable at law and that of the other in equity, *Richards* vs. *Salter*, 6 John. Ch. 445; and it is no objection to the bill, that a suit is pending between the several parties commenced by one of the claimants of the fund. *Warrington* vs. *Wheatstone*, 1 Jac. 202; 2 Dan. Ch. Pr. (Perk.) 1660.

582. To the bill there should be an affidavit that there is no collusion between the plaintiff and any of the other parties. 2 Barb. Ch. Pr., 120 See p. 102, *ante.* The absence of this affidavit is a cause of demurrer. Story's Eq. Pl., § 297; 2 Dan. Ch. Pr. (Perk.) 1671; Mitf. Pl. 143. When in behalf of a company, the affidavit should be that to the best of affiant's belief the company does not collude with the defendants. *Bignold* vs. *Audland,* 11 Sim. 23.

583. The bill prays conformably with the objects for which it is instituted, that the defendants may interplead, that the court will adjudge the questions in dispute between them, and that the plaintiff may be protected. If any suits at law are instituted against the plaintiff, it prays that such suits may be enjoined, but in general the money must be brought into court before the court will grant the injunction. See Story's Eq. Pl. § 297.

584. The defendants may demur if the plaintiff shows no right to compel them to interplead, or if the bill be without affidavit. They may also answer, admitting or denying the statements of the bill. 2 Barb. Ch. Pr. 123, 136; 2 Dan. Ch. Pr. (Perk.) 1674, 1675.

The form of demurrer as given in Willis's Chancery Pleading, pp. 440, 441, is as follows: " That although the said complainant's bill is on the face thereof a bill of interpleader and prays that this defendant and the other defendants may interplead together concerning the matters therein mentioned, and may be restrained by the order and injunction of this honorable court from proceeding at law against the said complainant, touching such matters, yet the said complainant has not annexed an affidavit to his said bill, that he does not collude concerning such matters or any of them with this defendant and the other defendants thereto, or any or either of them, which affidavit ought, as this defendant is advised, according to the rules of this honorable court, to have been made by the said plaintiff and annexed to his said bill. Wherefore this defendant demands the judgment of this honorable court whether he shall be compelled to make any further or other answer to the said bill or any of the matters and things therein contained, and prays to be hence dismissed with his reasonable costs in this behalf sustained."

585. A decree in an interpleading suit may terminate the case as to the plaintiff though the litigation may continue between the defendants by interpleader, and in that case the cause may proceed without revivor notwithstanding the death of the plaintiff. Mitf. Pl. 60, 49, n; 2 Dan. Ch. Pr. (Perk.) 1676.

Where one of the defendants in a bill of interpleader, in his answer, makes a claim against the plaintiff beyond the amount admitted to be due and paid into court, and which is not claimed by the other defendants, he will be permitted to proceed at law to establish his right to that part of the demand which is not in controversy with the other defendants. *Houghton* vs. *Kendall*, 7 Allen 72, cited 2 Dan. Ch. Pr. (Perk.) 1680.

586. An interpleading bill puts the defendants to contest their respective claims. If at the hearing the question between the defendants is ripe for a decision, the court will decide it and make a final decree. If it is not ripe for a decision, as between the defendants, the court merely decides that the bill is properly filed, and dismisses the plaintiff with his costs up to that time, and directs an action or an issue, or a reference to a master, to ascertain contested facts as may be best suited to the nature of the case. 2 Dan. Ch. Pr. (Perk.) 1676, *Angill* vs. *Haddin*, 16 Ves. 202. Story's Eq. Jur., § 822.

587. There are statutes in Virginia providing for

an interpleader at law : Code 1873, chap. 149, §§ 1,
2, 3. An officer required to levy an execution or
warrant of distress or to attach money or property,
if a doubt arise whether the money or property is
liable to levy or attachment, may require an indemnifying bond before levying or attaching, and the
proceedings are as provided by Code 1873, chap.
149, §§ 4–8. The remedies provided by these
statutes obviate the necessity of filing bills of interpleader in many cases.

588. *Bill in the nature of a bill of interpleader.*
Although a bill of interpleader, strictly so called,
lies only where the party claims no interest in the
subject-matter; yet there are many cases where a
bill in the nature of a bill of interpleader will lie by
a party in interest to ascertain and establish his own
rights, where there are other conflicting rights between third persons. Thus, if a plaintiff is entitled
to equitable relief against the owner of property, and
the legal title thereto is in dispute between two or
more persons, so that he cannot ascertain to which it
actually belongs, he may file a bill against the several claimants in the nature of a bill of interpleader
for relief. *Mohawk & Hud. R. R. Co.* vs. *Clute*, 4
Paige 384; *Mitchell* vs. *Hayne*, 1 Sim. & Stu. 63, and
other cases cited; 2 Dan. Ch. Pr. (Perk.) 1680. And
so it was held in *Darden* vs. *Burns*, 6 Ala. 362, that
a vendee of personal property might file a bill in the
nature of an interpleader against his vendor and a
third person who claimed the property, and pray
a decree upon their claims, that he might be secure
in the payment of the purchase money.

Bills to perpetuate testimony.

589. See as to bills to perpetuate testimony 2 Barb. Ch. Pr., 137–142. Such bills accomplish their purpose when the testimony is taken and preserved; the bills are not brought to a hearing. 2 Barb. Ch. Pr., 143.

590. In the Virginia State courts, there is ample provision made for the preservation of testimony without filing such bills. See Code 1873, chap. 172, sec. 40.

Bill to examine witnesses de bene esse.

591. The bill is only sustainable when there is a suit already depending in which the evidence may be used. Its object is to take the testimony of witnesses which otherwise may be lost; e. g., when the witnesses are aged or infirm or about to depart from the State. See 2 Barb. Ch. Pr., 144, 145.

592. The necessity for filing a bill of this kind is obviated by the statutes of Virginia and by the Act of Congress and by the seventieth rule of the United States Supreme Court. See Code 1873, ch. 172, sec. 34, 35, 36, 37. See 70th rule U. S. Sup. Court and Act of Congress, cited in sections 434, 435, pp. 465, 467, ante.

Bills of discovery.

592a. These bills have been already referred to on pages 83, 86 ante.

CHAPTER VI.

Cross bills.

593. If a defendant has any relief to pray other than the dismission of the bill, or discovery to seek, he does so by a bill of his own, called a cross bill.

594. A cross bill may be brought either to obtain a discovery of facts in aid of the defence to the original bill, or to obtain some relief founded on the collateral claims of the party filing it. 2 Barb. Ch. Pr. 127; Story's Eq. Pl., § 389.

> *Camochie* vs. *Christie*, 11 Wheat 446, has been cited to sustain the doctrine that where a bill is filed to set aside an agreement or conveyance, the conveyance cannot be confirmed and established without a cross bill by the defendant. The doctrine may be true, but the case cited does not establish it.
>
> A defendant is not bound to exhibit a cross bill to get relief, even though the relief is properly the subject of a cross bill, when the matters in controversy are substantially presented by the pleadings as they are. *Taylor* vs. *Beale*, 4 Grat. 93.
>
> A decree dismissing a bill in equity was entered; the defendant filed a bill of review. The Special Court of Appeals of Virginia held that the decision to dismiss the bill was in the defendant's favour, and he could not contest it by bill of review or appeal; that if he desired relief he should have filed a cross bill. *Hopkins* vs. *Baker's adm'or & als.*, 2 P. & H. 110.

595. The cross bill afforded a perfect reciprocity of proof to each party derived from the answers of each, when the rule in equity was that a complainant could not be examined as a witness in the suit. See Story's Eq. Pl. 390.

596. Sometimes a cross bill is used by a defendant to avail himself of a defence he could not otherwise

make. Thus, if the defence has arisen after the
cause is at issue, or there has been an award made
on a reference after issue joined, a defendant could
bring them before the court on a cross bill, Cooper's
Eq. Pl. 86, 87 ; Mitf. Pl. 82. And, in most cases, a
cross bill is necessary to enable a defendant to have
a decree against a co-defendant. See Mitf. Pl. 81.

There cannot be a decree between co-defendants in a cause wher
there is no decree in favour of the plaintiff. *Ould, &c.* vs. *Myer.*
& als., 23 Grat. 334. In this case there was no cross bill.

It was not determined in *Kelsey* vs. *Hobby*, 16 Pet. 269, whether
a defendant, to avail himself of a release pending a suit in equity
should file a cross bill, but it was determined in that case that
where a release by the complainant executed pending a suit in
equity was filed in the cause, and the parties proceeded to take
evidence in support and impeachment of it, it was too late to objec·
in the appellate court that a cross bill should have been filed.

Moorman vs. *Smoot & als.*, 28 Grat. 80, was a suit by S., one
tenant in common of slaves subject to the life estate of his mother
against another tenant in common, one M., who had sold the slaves
To this suit N. and Y., two other tenants in common, were made
co-defendants with M. There was a recovery against M. by the
plaintiff, and by the defendants N. and Y. The court held that in
order to set up their claims against M., it was not necessary for N
and Y. to file a cross bill.

597. In *Tarr* vs. *Ravenscroft & als.*, 12 Grat. 642
the Court of Appeals held that a cross bill was
properly filed, and having been filed without objec·
tion and being answered, and the cause coming on to
be heard on the merits, the objection afterwards
taken not having been made in due time and in the
proper form should be disregarded.

An answer was treated as a cross bill in *Mettert* vs. *Hagan*, 18
Grat., 231, to enable the court to do complete justice in the case.

And, in *Sayres* vs. *Wall*, 26 Grat., 354, in which there was a
petition by the children of Mrs. Sayres, setting out a deed from
their father, Reuben Sayres, to his wife and their rights under it

and asking that they might be made defendants in the suit and permitted to defend their rights under the deed, and they were permitted to file their answers without objection by the plaintiffs; it was held that the plaintiffs could not, afterwards, object, that they were made parties, and that, if it would have been more proper to assert their rights by a cross bill, their petition might be treated as such.

But in *Washington R. R.* vs. *Bradleys*, 10 Wallace, 299, a petition filed by "way of a cross bill," which made nobody defendant, which prayed for no process and under which no process issued, was treated as a nullity by the United States Supreme Court.

In *Ayres* vs. *Carver*, 17 How., 591, a cross bill was filed by a part of the defendants after answer filed. The United States Supreme Court said, that the matters sought to be brought into controversy between the complainants in the cross bill and their co-defendants in the original bill, did not seem to have any connection with the matters in controversy with the complainant in the original bill; and that a cross bill should not introduce new and distinct matters not embraced in the original bill, as they cannot be properly examined in that suit, but constitute the subject matter of an original, independent suit. In this case the court refer to *Shields* vs. *Barrow*, 17 How., 130. See sec. 601.

598. The connection of the matter of a cross bill (in itself either legal or equitable)[1] with the subject matter of the original bill gives the court jurisdiction of the cross bill, 2 Barb. Ch. Pr., 128, and the jurisdiction of the cross bill is not ousted by the dismission of the original bill. *Ibid.*, *Wickliffe* vs. *Clay*, 1 Dana, 589; *Ragland* vs. *Broadnax and als*, 29 Grat., 401.

In *Ragland* vs. *Broadnax and als*, 29 Grat., 401, all the parties to the original bill were made defendants to the cross bill. The causes were heard together and the original bill dismissed. It was held, 1. That the second bill asking for relief against the city of Petersburg, which could not be given on the pleadings and proceedings in the original bill, but which was based upon grounds involved in that case, it was the proper subject of a cross bill; but the relief sought by it being outside the original bill, the dismissal of the

---

[1] As to relying upon matters purely legal, see *Hume* vs. *Long*, 6 Monroe, 119.

original bill did not involve the dismissal of the cross bill. 2. Tha:
if the cross bill be treated as an original bill in the nature of a
cross bill, all the parties being before the court, and the case having
been matured, it was proper to proceed to decide it upon the
merits. And certainly the plaintiff in the cross bill is not to be
heard to question the jurisdiction of the court after having had the
determination of the question brought by him into the case.

A cross bill being an auxiliary bill simply, must be a bill touching matters in question in the original bill. If its purpose be
different from that of the original bill it is not a cross bill, ever
though the matters presented in it have a connection with the same
general subject. In the United States courts while as an origina
bill it will not attach to the controversy unless it be filed under
such circumstances of citizenship, &c., as give jurisdiction to origi
nal bills, yet a cross bill may sometimes so attach. *Cross* vs
De Valle, 1 Wal., S. C., 5.

599. A cross bill should state the original bill and
proceedings thereon, and the rights of the party ex
hibiting the bill which are necessary to be made the
subject of cross litigation, or the ground on which he
resists the claims of the plaintiff in the original bill
if that is the object of the new bill. Mitf. Pl., 81.

It should be confined to the subject matter of the original bill
and cannot introduce new and distinct matters not embraced in the
original suit. Story's Eq. Pl., § 401. See *Cross* vs. *De Valle*, :
Wal. S. C., 5.

It may perhaps set up additional facts as constituting part of the
same defence relative to the same subject matter. But it ough:
not to contain new matter not set up as a defence in the origina
cause, unless it be matter which has arisen subsequently. Ken:
Ch., in *Underhill* vs. *Van Cortlandt, &c.*, 2 John. Ch. Rep., 355
Brown, &c., vs. *Story*, 2 Paige, 594; *Galatian, &c., Erwin*, 1 Hop
kins Ch. Rep., 58, 59, 2 Rob. Pr. (old) 318.

A cross bill filed in *Bronson and als* vs. *LaCrosse and M. R. C*
and als, 2 Wal., S. C., 283, without leave, was set aside.

600. In a cross bill a party cannot question wha
he has admitted in his answer to the original bill
Carr, J., in *Hudson, &c.*, vs. *Hudson's ex'ors*, :
Rand. 117.

601. A complainant in the original bill, as well as other parties to the cross bill, may plead, answer or demur to the cross bill; but a plea to the person of the plaintiff in a cross bill (unless exhibited by a person incapable alone to institute a suit), and a demurrer for want of equity in such bill, will not lie. Mitf. Eq. Pl. 81, 82, 291. Nor will a plea to the jurisdiction lie. *Ibid.*

New parties cannot be introduced into a cause by a cross bill, *Shields* vs. *Barrow*, 17 How. 130, nor can a Circuit Court of the United States compel defendants to file a cross bill and bring in new parties whom these defendants are, but the complainants are not, competent to sue in the United States courts. *Ibid.*

602. A complainant in the original bill has the priority and will not be compelled to answer the cross bill until the defendant has put in his answer to the original bill; [2] Lube's Eq. Pl. 143, Code 1873, ch. 167, sec. 16, 72nd Rule U. S. Supreme Court; but if the plaintiff in the original cause amends his bill in material[3] points, subsequent to the filing of the cross bill, the amended bill will be considered as constituting with the original bill a new bill, and he thereby loses his priority (Lube's Eq. Pl. 143) and his right to have an answer before he is called upon to answer the cross bill. Dan. Ch. Pr. (old) 509. See *Steward* vs. *Roe*, 2 P. Wms. 434; *Long* vs. *Burton*, 2 Atk. 218.

---

[2] This right of priority is the plaintiffs' as against those who claim as representatives of the complainants, or one of them, in the cross cause. *Child* vs. *Frederick*, 1 P. Wms. 266.

[3] And, in two cases, it was held to be so, if the amendment was in matter immaterial. *Johnson* vs. *Freer*, 2 Cox 371; *Noel* vs. *King*, 2 Madd. 394. *Sed quære.*

If an original bill is abated by the marriage of a plaintiff, and not revived until after a cross bill is filed, the priority of the original bill is said to be lost. *Smart* vs. *Floyer*, Dick. 260.

603. If a cross bill be taken as confessed, it may be used as evidence against the complainant in the original suit, on the hearing, and will have the same effect as if he had admitted the same facts in an answer. *White* vs. *Buloid*, 2 Paige 164.

604. After both causes are at issue, the complainant in the cross suit may have an order that they be heard together, but it is not indispensable that they be heard together. *Coleman* vs. *Moore*, 3 Little 355.

605. The court will not suspend the hearing of the original cause on account of a cross bill, when the cross bill has been filed at an unreasonably late period, or when the plaintiff in the cross bill has practiced delay in preparing it for a hearing. *Sterry, &c.*, vs. *Arden, &c.*, 1 John. Ch. R. 62; *Governeur, &c.*, vs. *Elmendorf*, 4 John. Ch. R. 357; *White* vs. *Buloid*, 2 Paige 164; *McConnico* vs. *Moseley*, 4 Call 360; 2 Rob. Pr. (old) 319.

Nor is it a matter of course for the court to stay the proceedings in the original suit in any case, except where the defendant in the cross suit (the plaintiff in the original) is in contempt for not answering. *White* vs. *Buloid*, 2 Paige 164, *Williams* vs. *Carle*, 2 Stockt. (N. J.) 545.

606. Sometimes at the hearing of an original cause, a cross bill is directed to be filed ; and even after an interlocutory decree, such direction has been given. Mitf. Pl., 83; *Brown* vs. *Story*, 2 Paige, 594.[4]

[4] In *Brown, &c.*, vs. *Story*, 2 Paige, 594, three persons sued at-law as joint debtors, filed a bill for an account and obtained an injunction to stay pro-

CHAPTER VII.

Of motions and petitions.

607. An interlocutory application is a request made to the court for its aid in a matter arising in the course of the cause. It may either relate to the process of the court, or to the protection of the property in litigation *pendente lite*, or to any other matter upon which the interference of the court is required at any time. Applications of this kind are either made orally or in writing—in the former case they are called *motions*, in the latter *petitions*. 1 Barb. Ch. Pr. 565.

Motions.

608. There are motions of course and special motions. The former may be made without notice to the opposite party; the latter can only be made after reasonable notice.

609. Motions may be made by or on behalf of any of the parties, or by a *quasi* party (as in the case of a purchaser under a decree), but strangers to the

---

ceedings at law. After an order of account, one of the complainants died. By that death all remedy at law against his estate was lost, and there would have been no necessity for proceeding against his personal representative in equity, if the surviving complainants had been solvent. But they were alleged to be insolvent. The defendant was therefore permitted to file a cross bill in the nature of an original bill against the surviving complainants and the personal representative of the decedent, setting forth his joint demand and alleging the insolvency of the survivors by which he was compelled to resort to the estate of the decedent. If the defendant filed such cross bill within one month, and prosecuted with due diligence, the proceedings under the order of account were to be stayed until farther order, so that there should be only one accounting between the parties.

record may not apply to the court by motion; they should file a petition.

610. The essential differences between motions of course and special motions seem not to be very well settled; the former, however, is said to be such as it is a matter of course to grant, while the latter need some ground to be laid for them, either by the previous orders, or by the pleadings in the cause, or by affidavits.

610a. In the sub-section are cases in which relief was granted on motion.

There was a motion, after notice, in *Kenduck & als.* vs. *Whitney & als.*, 28 Grat. 646, under chapter 177, sec. 7, of the Code of 1873, to amend and rehear an interlocutory decree pronounced and entered more than five years before the motion was made. The court of appeals held, that, by that section a motion could not be made after five years had elapsed. But the motion being founded on a notice setting forth the grounds for rehearing and being signed by the counsel and served on the parties, the court treated the notice as a petition for rehearing, and granted the relief sought; the court holding that there is no statutory bar to the time within which a petition for rehearing may be filed to correct an error in an interlocutory decree. See also *Barger* vs. *Buckland & als.*, 28 Grat. 850, in which a notice signed by counsel and setting out the grounds for setting aside a decree was treated as a petition for rehearing.

Decree, containing a reservation, amended on motion in a summary way. In *Sheppard's ex'or* vs. *Starke & ux.*, 3 Munf. 29, it was held that a decree which is final in all respects except that "liberty is reserved to the parties or either of them to resort to the court for its further interposition, if it should be found necessary," may be amended on motion in a summary way, or by bill of review.

Motion, on reservation in a decree. Under a reservation in the decree, a party may be proceeded against by motion. In *Jones* vs. *Hobson*, 2 Rand., 483, the bill was for a legacy, and was brought against the executors and their sureties; and upon the executors confessing that sufficient assets had come to their hands, a decree was pronounced against them, reserving liberty to the plaintiff to apply to the court for further relief against the sureties, if it should become necessary. Execution was issued against the executors and returned *nulla bona;* and then the plaintiff gave notice to the sureties, that under the reservation in the decree, he would apply to the court to decree the legacy against them. The sureties objected, that they could not be liable upon motion, but only by bill. It seemed to the Court of Appeals, that when the executors confessed assets, it was beneficial to the sureties that the decree should be immediately pronounced against the executors, instead of proceeding in the cause so as to subject the sureties jointly with the executors, since there was a better chance of indemnifying them by compelling payment from the executors than if the decree had been delayed. While the course thus taken was obviously beneficial to the sureties, they could suffer no possible injury by being proceeded against by motion. On such motion, the court would proceed against the sureties, if there were already enough in the record to justify a decree, or if there were not, it would order the necessary accounts to ascertain the extent of their liability.

Whether a wife can assert her right to survivorship or to a provision by motion. It was queried in *Sherrard & als.* vs. *Carlisle,* 1 P. & H., 12, whether a wife could, by motion, assert her right to survivorship or to a provision.

Motion to recover money paid under a decree, afterwards reversed. When money is paid under a decree, which has been subsequently reversed by the Court of Appeals, it may be recovered by motion to the lower court after notice. *Flemings* vs. *Riddick,* 5 Grat. 272.

Motion, after notice, for introduction of evidence not offered at the hearing. In *Moore* vs. *Hilton,* 12 Leigh 1, cited before sec. 443, p. 472, it was held that the introduction of the evidence offered depended on the sound discretion of the court and its judgment on the sufficiency of the excuse offered for the failure to have it before the court when the cause was heard, and the interlocutory decree pronounced, and that such excuse might be offered, *either on motion after notice,* or upon a petition for a rehearing of the cause. See p. 500, note to sec. 443.

Motion for time to put in defence. There was a motion for time to put in a defence where some of the defendants were not served with process in *Poultney* vs. *The City of LaFayette,* 12 Pet. 472.

Motion, when required, by a defendant in contempt. From a defendant in contempt no plea or demurrer will be received but upon motion in open court. Ch. Taylor in *Lane* vs. *Ellzey,* 4 H. & M. 504.

Motion to introduce viva voce testimony. *Viva voce* testimony is not, as already seen, allowed as a matter of course. To obtain permission to introduce it, on the hearing, previous notice of the intention to introduce it must be given. Tucker, J., in *Chandler's ex'x* vs. *Neale's executors,* 2 H. & M. 124. And sometimes both notice and an affidavit are necessary as the foundation of a motion to hear it. *Emerson vs. Berkeley, &c.,* 4 H. & M. 441.

Motion by sureties. Session Acts 1877–8, p. 220, §§ 6, 8, give the right to sureties to recover by motion for the amount paid and damages of the principal, and to recover of a co-surety the share he ought to pay. There is nothing in the statute restricting this right to common law courts. No reason is perceived why the motion may not be made in the equity court when the money is paid under decrees.

Motion for injunction, and reference. In *Pennsylvania vs. Wheeling & B. Bridge Co.,* 9 How. 647, there was a motion for an injunction. The court on hearing the motion referred the cause to a commissioner to take proofs upon the questions stated, and to report on these questions, together with the proofs allowing him to employ an expert to aid him and make a report to be annexed to his.

Motion for rule refused: party required to file a supplemental bill. In *Beckwith vs. Avery's adm'or, &c.,* 31 Grat. 533, the suit was instituted by the administrator in 1849, and he was authorized to pay money to M. and N., legatees for life, upon their giving security for its return at their death. This was done. M. died, and by another decree in 1853 the money paid her was collected and paid to N., upon her husband and herself giving like bond. This bond was given. In June, 1874, the remaindermen who were not parties to the record moved for a rule on the legatees for life to give additional security, alleging that the securities were insolvent. The Court of Appeals said that as this proceeding was had *by strangers to the record,* after a long lapse of time, and after the object of the suit by the administrator had been accomplished so far as he was concerned, it was improper to proceed by rule, but that the remaindermen should file a supplemental bill.

The following are cases in which orders have been entered on motion :

Removal of causes from one court to another. Sess. Acts 1878–9, p. 24. This act, which went into force 14th January, 1879, is as follows:

§ 1. On the motion of any party to a suit, motion or other proceeding in a County or Corporation Court, who desires to remove the same to the Circuit Court having jurisdiction over said county or corporation, or to any other County, Circuit or Corporation Court, the Court may, after twenty days' notice to the adverse party, order such removal ; or whenever, in the opinion of the County or Corporation Court, or the judge thereof, it is improper for said judge to try the same, the said County or Corporation Court may order such removal; or upon like motion, the said Circuit Court, or the judge thereof in vacation, "after twenty days' notice to the adverse party, may order such removal to the said Circuit Court.

§ 2. On the motion of any party to a suit in the Circuit Court, the said Circuit Court may order it to be removed to any other Circuit or Corporation Court. The judge of said court, in vacation, may make such order after reasonable notice to the adverse party. The order of removal may be made by the court or judge, without motion or notice, when the judge is so situated as to render it improper, in his judgment, for him to decide or preside at the trial of the cause.

Order changing plaintiffs to make them witnesses. See pp. 593, 595, *ante.*

Order changing a next friend to make him a witness. See p. 595 *ante.*

Order compelling plaintiff to make his election to proceed at law or in equity. Under the statutes, Sess. Acts 1825–6, p. 18, sec. 13 and Sess. Acts 1827–8, p. 21, ch. 26, sec. 1, Supp. Rev. Code, p. 133 and p. 178, cited 2 Rob. Pr. (old), 316, if four months had elapsed after the filing of the answer of the defendant he was entitled to a dismission of the bill, unless the plaintiff should diligently pursue the necessary measures to mature the cause for hearing as to the other defendants; (he is now entitled either to a hearing or to a dismission of the bill as to him, Code 1873, ch. 167, sec. 51;) or if his interests were not so connected with the interests of the other defendants as that it would be improper to decide upon those interests separately, he was entitled to an immediate hearing as to himself. (This latter provision is in the present statutes, Code 1873, ch. 167, sec. 49 and sec. 51.)

Order for payment to plaintiff pending the suit. Code 1873, ch. 105, sec. 10; 2 Rob. Pr. (old), 346; *Meth. Ch.* vs. *Jaques, &c.,* 3 John. Ch. Rep. 1; *Clarkson* vs. *DePeyster,* 1 Hopk. Ch. R. 274, 507. From these cases it appears that such an order may be made when a portion of the claim was admitted to be clear by the answer itself, but in *Cook* vs. *Barker,* 1 Hopk. Ch. R., 117, such an order was refused; the whole subject being in controversy, it would have been prejudging the case to order payment of any part.

Order for party to pay money into court. See p. 596, *ante.*

Order to lend out money, entered on motion. See p. 567, *ante.*

Order allowing creditor to prove his claim. See *Anderson* vs. *Anderson, &c.,* 4 H & M., 475, hereafter cited, p. 689.

Petitions.

611. Petitions are applications in writing for an order of court, stating the circumstances upon which they are founded, and are duly entitled of the cause and court in which they are to be filed. They are usually resorted to when the nature of the application to the court requires a fuller statement than can be conveniently made in a notice of motion. 1 Barb. Ch. Pr., 578. Strangers to the record are, as we have seen, required to file a petition when those who are parties may obtain the relief by motion.

612. It may be difficult to draw a precise line between cases in which a party may be relieved upon petition, and cases in which he must apply more formally by bill. Petitions are generally for things which are matters of course, or upon some collateral matter which has reference to a suit in court. Kent, C. J., in *Codwise, &c.,* vs. *Gelston,* 10 John. Rep , 521.

The case of *Cook, &c.,* vs. *Mancius, &c.,* 5 Johns. Ch. Rep., 89, furnishes an instance in which a petition might have been proper. There a suit had been brought to foreclose a mortgage, a decree was made for the sale of the premises, and the proceeds being more than sufficient to satisfy the mortgage, the surplus was payable to the mortgagor or to his assignee. Pending this suit a judgment was obtained against the mortgagor, and the judgment creditor was, of course, entitled to have his debt satisfied out of the residuary interest in the land after the mortgage debt and costs were paid. If the judgment had been obtained before the commencement of the suit to foreclose, the mortgagee would have been bound to make the judgment creditor a party, or else the decree and sale would not have taken away his right to redeem. But as the incumbrance created by the judgment was *pendente lite,* the mortgagee was not bound to take notice of it. In such a case, it would seem, the judgment creditor must have a right to come in and be made a party, so as to secure his claim to the surplus. 2 Rob. Pr. (old) 348.

In *Sherrard & als.* vs. *Carlisle*, 1 P. & H. 12, A. assigned to B., for value, choses in action claimed by him in right of his wife, but no farther reduced into possession than by the assignment. A suit in chancery was instituted involving those interests to which A. and his wife and B. were made parties. While the suit was pending, A.'s wife filed a petition therein, alleging a divorce from A., and claiming the whole fund in court as a *feme sole*. About five years after the filing of this petition, A. died, and some years thereafter, the court made an order directing a commissioner to report what would be a reasonable provision for the wife of A. out of the fund under its control. The commissioner reported that the fund in court was small ($422), and that the whole of it would be a very inadequate provision for her. A.'s wife then dies, and the suit was revived in the name of her only child C. as her administrator, who also filed a bill supplemental to her petition, and prayed that the whole sum might be decreed to him, in right of his mother, who, he insisted, was entitled, either by survivorship to the whole, or to a settlement by way of provision out of it; and that the whole fund would have been a very insufficient settlement. Held, 1, that the wife was clearly entitled by way of *provision* against the assignee, whether the marriage was ended or not by divorce, or by death, and whether or not she was entitled to the whole by way of survivorship against an assignee for value; and the fund under the control of the court not being more than sufficient for the purpose, the whole should be decreed to her by way of provision or settlement: 2, that the wife might assert her right by survivorship, or to a provision by petition or by bill, (*quære*: Can she do so by motion? Thompson, J.) and though she claimed in her petition or bill only by way of survivorship, yet she might be held entitled by way of provision to a part or the whole, according to the circumstances of the case; 3, that an order having been made before the death of the wife, for a report by a commissioner as to what would be an adequate provision for her, her child surviving is entitled, in her right, to whatever would have been decreed to her, and might assert his right to it by a supplemental bill:[1] 4, that even if the proceedings in the Circuit Court were irregular, (the petition and the supplemental bill), no objection could be taken to them in an appellate court, if not taken in the court below.

Creditors let in by petition or by motion. In the case of *Angell* vs. *Hadden*, hereafter cited, sec. 620, the creditor was admitted *on motion.* A petition was not required.

613. Brevity and form are the two things to be

---

[1] 1 Bright's Hus. and Wife, p. 243, § 6, 1 Dan. Ch. Pr. (old) 138-9.

chiefly observed in drawing petitions; to which may be added care to avoid scandàl and impertinence, for which a petition may be refused. 1 Barb. Ch. Pr., 580.

614. Petitions should be signed by the petitioner and his counsel, and to some petitions an affidavit is necessary.

615. Petitions are, in the Virginia State courts, sometimes treated as cross bills, and sometimes as bills of review.

See *Sayers* vs. *Wall*, 26 Grat. 354, cited *ante* p. 675, as to their being regarded as cross bills.

In *Orickard's ex'or* vs. *Orickard & als.*, 25 Grat. 410, an executor claimed to have made investments in Confederate bonds under the act of March 5, 1863. The court held that not one of the conditions authorizing such investments was found in the case, and that the executor was liable in gold or its equivalent. The legatees had filed a petition to the court to set aside the order authorizing the investment in Confederate bonds and to compel the executors to pay their legacies. On this petition a rule was made upon the executor to show cause against the prayer of the petition. The appellate court treated the petition as a petition to review, and set aside the order, and granted its prayer.

616. *Sale of infants' lands.* Proceedings for the sale of infants' lands may be instituted by petition. *Parker and als* vs. *McCoy and als*, 10 Grat., 594.

617. *Creditors intervening.* Creditors may intervene by petition in a suit of legatees surcharging administration account, *Smith's ex'or* vs. *Britton, &c.,* 2 P. & H., 124, and it makes no difference that their claims will absorb the whole balance fund due by the executor. *Ibid.*

618. *Creditors coming in by petition to a suit attack-*

ing a deed on ground of fraud. Creditors may come
in by petition to a suit attacking a deed on the
ground of fraud, and their priority will be determined by the date of filing their petition—unless
they have other ground of priority. See *Wallace's
adm'or & als* vs. *Treakle. & als,* 27 Grat., 479.[2]

618 *a. Claims against the Commonwealth.* Claims
against the Commonwealth rejected by the auditor
are asserted by a petition to the Circuit Court
of Richmond, other claims against the Commonwealth by petition, or by a bill in chancery, according
to the nature of the case. Code 1873, chap. 44, sec. 1.
See *Arents* vs. *The Commonwealth,* 18 Grat., 764;
Com. vs. *Chalkley,* 20 Grat., 404; *Attorney Gen.* vs.
Turpin, 3 H. & M., 548. See chap. 44, Code 1873,
and Sess. Acts, 1874–5, p. 253, as to mode of recov-

---

[2] In *Wallace's adm'or & als* vs. *Treakle & als,* 27 Grat., 479, it was held
(1.) That creditors at large who file a bill to set aside a deed of their debtor conveying land as fraudulent, and succeed, have a lien on the land for their debts
from the filing of their bill; (2.) the deed of H. for land is set aside as fraudulent at the suit of some of his creditors and there is a decree after the death
of H. for the sale of the land and for account of the debts of H. and their
priorities. The report shows that there was one judgment against H. before
the deed was made. Some of the plaintiffs in the bill were creditors by
judgment, one a creditor at large; *a number came in by petition before the
decree,* and a number came in before the commissioner, and *by petition after
the decree.* In distributing the fund, it is to be applied, 1st, to pay the judgment recovered before the deed was made; 2d, to the judgments recovered
before the bill was filed; 3d, to the creditors at large who joined in the bill;
4th, to the creditors by petition before the death of H., in the order in which
their petitions were filed; 5th, to all the other creditors *pro rata.* It was
farther held, (3.) that though there was in the case a decree for the sale of the
land and a sale before an account of the debts was taken, the sale of the land
will not be set aside upon the objection of some of the creditors who came in
after the decree, made years after the sale, when it is obvious the land would
not sell for as much as it had sold for before, and which was more than some
of these creditors had expressed their willingness to take for it.

ering claims against the Commonwealth or against corporations composed of officers of government.

619. By petition to the Circuit Court of the county in which the land lies one may claim an escheated land, or interest therein. Code 1873, ch. 109, §§ 8, 9, 10. After sale, if he has not asserted a claim before sale or decree, he may claim the proceeds paid into the treasury by presenting it to the auditor of public accounts, and if rejected by him, by petition to the Circuit Court of Richmond city. Code 1873, chap. 109, § 33; chap. 44, § 9.

620. *Petition in creditor's suit.* In creditor's suit by a creditor suing on behalf of himself and others, the court will let in creditors at any time while the fund is in court. Lord Eldon in *Lashley* vs. *Hogg*, 11 Ves., 602. In *Angell* vs. *Hadden*, 1 Madd. Ch. R., 529, the creditor coming in after an account taken upon the usual direction to advertise for creditors, was allowed, on motion, to prove his debt, but upon condition of his paying the costs of the application and the expense of reapportioning the fund amongst the creditors. In that case there was a deficiency of assets. Such applications are usually made by petition. Such petitions are allowed upon the creditor's agreeing to contribute to the expense of the suit. See *Anderson* vs. *Anderson, &c.*, 4 H. & M., 475.

It was held in *Hopkins* vs. *Baker's adm'or & als.*, 2 P. & H. 110, that an assignee of an interest by filing a petition in a suit in the name of his assignor and asking that he may be made a party does not make the assignee a party to the suit.

621. *Order of publication.* There may be an order

87

of publication in a proceeding by petition. Code 1873, ch. 166, § 10.

Petition for rehearing.

622. An interlocutory order or decree may be set aside or otherwise corrected by the court which made it upon motion or petition, Ch. Taylor in *Banks* vs. *Anderson, &c.*, 2 H. & M., 20; by motion, if the erroneous proceeding be a mere order, *Fanning* vs. *Dunham*, 4 John. C. R., 35, by petition for a rehearing, if there has been a regular decree upon the merits. *Radley, &c.*, vs. *Shaver, &c.*, 1 John Ch. R., 200.

623. Until the term is ended at which a final decree is entered, the proper method for correcting error in it is by petition for a rehearing and not by bill of review. See *Hodges* vs. *Davis*, 4 H. & M., 400.

624. Whether a rehearing shall be granted or not is a matter resting on sound discretion. If the chancellor is satisfied that the cause has been exhausted by argument, if he has given to the case the best examination in his power, and has arrived at a conclusion which satisfies his judgment, and the petition for a rehearing rests solely upon the merits of the cause as they stood at the previous hearing, there can be no propriety nor use in granting the rehearing. *Field* vs. *Schiefflen, &c.*, 7 John. C. R., 256. But if one chancellor has pronounced a decree which has been reversed by his successor in office, a third chancellor may very properly review these conflicting decisions of his predecessors. *Land* vs. *Wickham*, 1 Paige, 256; 2 Rob. Pr. (old), 389.

625. Upon the rehearing, the cause, with respect to the party who petitioned to rehear, is open only as to those parts of it which are complained of in the petition. *Consequa* vs. *Fanning,* 3 John. C. R., 594.

626. In Virginia, the Court of Appeals has determined, that after an interlocutory decree has been pronounced, if a party discover new and important testimony of which he had no knowledge when the decree was rendered, he may petition for a rehearing; and if his petition be sustained by the affidavits of witnesses, the court will open the decree so as to allow him the benefit of the newly-discovered facts. *Robert's adm'or* vs. *Cocke,* 1 Rand., 121.

In *Purdie, &c.,* vs. *Jones & als,* 32 Grat. 327, the court held the decrees to be interlocutory, and that they might be reheard on petition. So in the case of *Summers* vs. *Darne & als,* 31 Grat. 805.

An absent debtor who was not served with process, and did not appear in the case before the date of the decree to obtain relief against the decree, must appear and file a petition for a rehearing. *Platt* vs. *Howland,* 10 Leigh, 507. He cannot obtain relief by appealing from the decree. *Ibid.* See Code 1873, ch. 166, § 16.

In a suit, in which there was an absent defendant, there was a decree against the home defendant; from which he appealed. Pending the appeal, the absent defendant, it was held, might file his petition in the court below to be permitted to appear and file his answer in the cause and have the decree reheard and set aside. *Jas. R. & K. Co.* vs. *Littlejohn,* 18 Grat. 53.

There is no statutory bar to the time in which a petition may be filed to correct an error in *an interlocutory decree;* and where there was a notice of a motion to rehear a decree, the notice having been signed by counsel, and specifying with sufficient minuteness the grounds upon which the party relied for reversing the decree, the notice was treated as a petition for a rehearing. *Kendrick & als* vs. *Whitney & als,* 28 Grat. 648. See also *Barger* vs. *Buckland & als,* 28 Grat. 850.

A bill of review was treated as a petition for rehearing in *Ambrouse's heirs* vs. *Keller,* 22 Grat. 769. See 27 Grat. 291.

627. The manner of correcting decrees and the right to have decrees reheard by infant defendants or by parties proceeded against as absent or unknown defendants have been discussed in previous sections.³ And in section 443, p. 471, and the note thereto on p. 500, the reader will find the doctrines laid down in *Summers* vs. *Darne & als.*, 31 Grat., 805, and *Richardson* vs. *Duble & als.*, 33 Grat., 730, as to the introduction of evidence as a foundation for a motion or petition to rehear the decree.

628. *Petition to rehear final decree in United States courts.* A final decree in the United States Circuit Courts, if it be in a case in which there is no appeal to the Supreme Court, may be corrected on a petition for rehearing, provided the petition to rehear is admitted, in the discretion of the court, before the end of the term of the court next after the final decree is made. See 88th Rule of Practice, cited in section 502, p. 516, *ante*.

CHAPTER VIII.

Bills of review.

629. *A bill of review only lies to a final decree.* A bill of review is in the nature of a writ of error, and its object is to obtain an examination and alteration or reversal of a final decree made upon a former bill; 2 Barb. Ch. Pr., 90, and this, after the term has expired at which the final decree was rendered; for,

³ §§ 499–503, pp. 514–517.

during the term, the decree may be reheard on petition for rehearing. *Hodges* vs. *Davis*, 4 H. & M., 400.

A bill of review forms no part of the proceedings in the original cause, but is offered after the suit is completely ended. See *Bowyer* vs. *Lewis*, 1 H. & M., 554.

To authorize a bill of review, the decree sought to be reviewed and reversed must be final and the parties out of court, *Ellzey* vs. *Lane's ex'x*, 2 H. & M., 589, and if it be received before such final decree it should be dismissed at the costs of the party filing it. *Mackey* vs. *Bell*, 2 Munf., 523.

After a final decree has been rendered against a plaintiff, or against a defendant who has answered, and the term has passed in which the decree was pronounced, the cause cannot be reheard in the same court except upon a bill of review. Ch. Taylor in *Hodges* vs. *Davis*, 4 H. & M., 400.

Though the cause had been heard only as to a particular defendant, yet if a final decree has been pronounced as to him, the case will not as to that defendant be within the power of the court after that term, except by bill of review. *Royall's adm'rs* vs. *Johnson, &c.*, 1 Rand., 421; 2 Rob. Pr. (old), 389. And if a *scirefacias* be issued against his executors, it will be considered as improvidently awarded, and may be dismissed at the costs of the plaintiffs. *Ibid.*

A party against whom an interlocutory decree had been rendered, filed a bill which he styled, and which was in form, a bill of review, alleging errors on the face of the decree as well as new facts in relation to the matter in controversy, and praying that the decree be reviewed and reversed; the bill was taken as a supplemental bill in the nature of a bill of review and petition for a rehearing. *Laidley* vs. *Merrifield*, 7 Leigh, 346. Carr, J. dissented. The bill was doubtless rightly treated as a petition for rehearing.[1]

630. *By whom bill may be filed.* The bill may be filed by either plaintiff or defendant. *Osborne* vs. *Usher*, 6 Bro. P. C., 20; 2 Barb. Ch. Pr., 96; *Thornton* vs. *Stewart*, 7 Leigh, 128. It cannot be filed by

---

[1] In the practice which prevails in the Virginia State courts, a bill of review to an interlocutory decree is treated as a petition for rehearing, *Laidley* vs. *Merrifield*, 7 Leigh, 346; *Ambrouse's heirs* vs. *Keller*, 22 Grat., 769, and a petition for rehearing of final decrees, if it conforms to the ordinary requirements of a bill of review, is treated as a bill of review. *Crickard* vs. *Crickard*, 25 Grat., 410; *Kendrick & als* vs. *Whitney and als*, 28 Grat. 654.

a person who has no interest in the question intended to be presented by the bill, and who cannot be benefitted by the reversal or modification of the former decree. *Webb, &c.,* vs. *Pell, &c.,* 3 Paige, 368; *Dyckman, &c.,* vs. *Kernochan, &c.,* 2 Paige, 26; *Wiser* vs. *Blachly, &c.,* 2 John. Ch. R., 492. Even persons having an interest in the cause, if not aggrieved by the particular errors assigned in the decree, cannot maintain a bill of review, however injuriously the decree may affect the rights of third persons. *Thomas* vs. *Harvie,* 10 Wheat, 146; Mitf. Pl., 205. With this exception it may be stated generally, that all the parties to the original bill ought to join in a bill of review. *B'k U. S.* vs. *White,* 8 Pet., 252.

A bill which stated that the complainant had an interest in the subject matter of a former suit in equity, applied to be admitted a party, was refused, and a decree made in fraud of his rights, and praying to have that decree set aside, &c., *is an original bill,* and not a bill of review; and, in the United States courts, the complainant must be competent to sue all the defendants. *Wickliffe* vs. *Eve,* 17 How. 468.

In *Buffington* vs. *Harvey,* 5 Otto, 99, the court approved the ruling in *Whiting & als* vs. *B'k U. S.,* 13 Pet. 6, and *Putnam* vs. *Day,* 22 Wal. 60, that the only questions open in a bill of review, except when it is filed on the ground of newly-discovered evidence, or contains new matter, are such as arise upon the pleadings, proceedings and decree; and that should such a bill set forth the evidence in the original cause, a demurrer specially assigning that error alone should be sustained, or the evidence might, on motion, be struck out; but a general demurrer must be overruled if the bill showed any substantial error in the record.

In *Thompson* vs. *Maxwell,* 5 Otto, 391, the court cites and approves *Buffington* vs. *Harvey, ubi sup.* In *Thompson* vs. *Maxwell,* it was also held that none but parties and privies can have a bill of review, and it will not lie when the decree in question was passed by consent.

631. *When bill of review may be maintained.* The

causes for which a bill of review may be maintained are limited to these: 1. There must be error in law apparent upon the face of the decree,[2] or 2, the party seeking to review the decree must allege and prove the discovery of new matter which could not have been used at the time of making the decree in consequence of the party's ignorance that such matters existed.[3]

In *Clarke* vs. *Kellian*, 13 Otto, 766, a bill of review was proper. It was filed for the purpose of correcting errors apparent on the face of the record, and less than two years had elapsed since the date of the decree before its being filed. See *Thomas* vs. *Harvie*, 10 Wheat, 146.

In *Craig* vs. *Smith*, 10 Otto, 227, it was held that the introduction of newly-discovered evidence, under a bill of review, to prove facts in issue on the former hearing rested in the sound discretion of the court, to be exercised cautiously and sparingly, and only under circumstances which render it indispensable to the merits and justice of the case.

632. *Leave to file bill to be obtained before filing it.* When a bill of review is not founded on error apparent on the decree, according to the english practice, leave should be first obtained to file it; and this leave is obtained on petition. This is the practice in the United States Circuit Courts. See *Dexter* vs. *Arnold*, 5 Mason's C. C., 303. In the Virginia State

---

[2]See sec. 632 *a*, and 633 *post.*

[3] 2 Rob. Pr. (old), 414; *Triplett* vs. *Wilson*, &c., 6 Call, 47; Ch. Taylor in *McCall* vs. *Graham*, &c., 1 H. & M. 13; *Winston* vs. *Johnson's ex'ors*, 2 Munf. 305; Fleming, J. in *Ellzey* vs. *Lane's ex'x*, 2 H. & M. 593; *Wiser* vs. *Blachly*, &c., 2 John Ch. R. 491; *Lansing* vs. *Alb. Ins. Co.*, 1 Hopk. Ch. R. 102.

In *Carter* vs. *Allan*, 21 Grat., 241, the bill was held fatally defective as a bill of review, because it failed to shew defect in the proceedings in the cause it sought to review, and to allege that the plaintiff had discovered evidence since the decree which she could not, by reasonable diligence, have ascertained before.

courts leave is obtained to file the bill on motion.. *Lee's infants* vs. *Braxton*, 5 Call, 459; *Williamson* vs. *Leadbetter, &c.*, 2 Munf., 521; *Quarrier* vs. *Carter's representatives*, 4 H. & M., 243. But a bill of review cannot be filed without leave of the court.[4] See *Hill* vs. *Bowyer*, 18 Grat., 364.

It is not true that errors in a final decree can only be reached by a bill of review. *Hill* vs. *Bowyer*, 18 Grat., 364. A party against whom a decree has been rendered without his appearance may apply to have the decree opened either by petition or by original bill. In either form it is an original proceeding and may be commenced without previous leave of the court. *Ibid.* And if in such case he apply by petition to open the decree and the application is refused, he may nevertheless file his original bill to have the decree opened. *Ibid.*

In *Erwin* vs. *Vint*, 6 Munf. 267, a decree by default was set aside on motion, after the term had expired. In that case, a decree for a conveyance had been obtained by default. It was shown that the party against whom the decree was rendered had been prevented from filing his answer, at one time by a *mistake* as to the day for the session of the court, and at another by a personal disability produced by *accident;* and the party asking the decree to be opened stated farther that he was prepared to show that his title to the land was good, and paramount to the claim of the plaintiff or any other defendant. The Court of Appeals was of opinion, under the circumstances of the case, and on the authority of *Kemp* vs. *Squire*, 1 Ves. Sen., 205, that the decree ought to be set aside, and the party permitted, on payment of costs, to file his answer in order to a trial of the cause upon its merits. 2 Rob. Pr. (old), 406.

---

[4] There is no case in Virginia known to the writer, in which it was held unnecessary to obtain leave of the court to file the bill when it was founded simply on error apparent on the decree. Prof. Minor states the rule of practice to be, following in this Mitford's Pl., p. 84, that no previous leave of court is requisite in order to file a bill of review for error of law apparent on the face of the proceedings; but when it is desired to file such bill by reason of new matter, such previous leave is indispensable. 4 Min. Ins., 1253. Mr. Robinson states the rule as follows: "In Virginia the practice is to apply in the first instance for leave to file a bill of review, whether it is for error apparent on the body of the decree, or upon discovery of new matter since the decree was pronounced. See 2 H. & M., 591, *note*, and Roane, J., in *Quarrier* vs. *Carter's representaties*, 4 H. & M., 243." 2 Rob. Pr. (old), 418.

633. *What is error apparent on face of decree.* It was held in *Quarrier* vs. *Carter's rep.*, 4 H. & M., 242, that an omission to take the preliminary measures necessary to prepare a cause for hearing, should not be regarded as error apparent on the face of the decree; but in *Braxton* vs. *Lee's Heirs*, 4 H. & M., 376, where some of the defendants were infants, and a decree was rendered against them without any answer being filed on their part, and without even taking the bill for confessed as to them, this was considered an error apparent on the face of the decree, and all the proceedings in the cause subsequent to the amended bill, by which the infants were made defendants, were set aside, so far as related to these defendants, and the cause was directed to be regularly matured for a hearing, in order to a just decision upon the merits.

In *Goolsby* vs. *St. John*, 25 Grat. 163, in September, 1871, the court made a decree perpetuating the injunction, setting aside a judgment and remanding the cause to the rules. In March, 1872, St. John by leave of the court filed a bill of review for errors apparent in the decree; and on the 2d September, 1872, the court made a decree in the bill of review case, reversing and annulling the decree of September, 1871, and directing the cause to stand upon the docket as it did before said decree. And on the same day the original case of Goolsby & Rector against St. John was reinstated on the docket, and, on the motion of St. John, it was decreed that the injunction be dissolved. The appellate court held: 1. That it was a proper case for a bill of review. 2. That the court should not only have dissolved the injunction, but should have dismissed the original bill. 3. That the bill of review was a continuation of the original suit, and there should not have been two decrees, but the whole should have been embraced in one decree, and the appellate court will so regard them. 4. That if the case had not been a proper one for a bill of review, still an appeal from that decree brings up the whole case, and the appellate court will go back to the first error and reverse the decree of September, 1871.

633 a. Not sufficient grounds for bill of review.
There were not sufficient grounds for a bill of review
in the case of *Winston* vs. *Johnston's Executors,* and
other cases mentioned in the subsection.

In *Winston* vs. *Johnson's ex'ors,* 2 Munf. 305, the report of the
commissioner on which the decree was founded was made without
due notice, and the report did not lie long enough in the court before the rendition of the decree. Such objections, it was held,
ought to have been taken before the decree was rendered, and were
not grounds for a bill of review.

A fact was stated in the decree as proved, when, in truth, there
was no proof to establish that fact. This was not error for which a
bill of review would lie. The error apparent upon the decree must
be an error in point of law, arising out of facts admitted by the
pleadings or recited by the decree itself. *Webb, &c.,* vs. *Pell, &c.,*
3 Paige, 368; *Barrett & Co.* vs. *Smith & Co.,* 5 Call, 102.

A cause was taken up and decided in the absence of counsel;
this was not ground for a bill of review, *Quarrier* vs. *Carter's rep.,*
4 H. & M., 242; *Wiser* vs. *Blachly, &c.,* 2 John. Ch. R., 409, though
the counsel was unavoidably absent, and the fact of his absence
was unknown to the party until after the decree. *Franklin* vs.
Wilkinson, 3 Munf., 112.

In *Putnam* vs. *Day,* 22 Wal., 60, the court held that on a bill
of review nothing could be examined but the pleadings, proceedings and decree which, in this country, constitute what is called the
record of the case; that the proofs could not be looked into as they
could on an appeal: that on such a bill filed by a defendant to set
aside the decree he is bound by the answer filed in his behalf by
his solicitor though he did not himself read it, unless he can show
mistake or fraud in filing it; that the answers of other defendants could not be read in his favor; and that when a defendant
admitted, by his answer, the claim to be due and prayed contribution from the other defendants, without setting up any defence to
the demand, he could not, after a decree and on a bill of review,
ask to have the decree set aside on the ground of laches on the
part of the complainant in bringing the suit.

In *Mosby* vs. *Mosby,* 9 Grat., 554, it was held, that a bill of review would not lie for error in a commissioner's report to which
there was no exception, and the correctness of which might be
affected by extraneous proof.

In *Niday* vs. *Harvey,* 9 Grat., 454, it was held to be no ground
for a bill of review, that a justice of the peace failed to forward a
deposition taken by him to the clerk of the court in which the

cause was pending, and that the cause had been heard and decided without it.

634. *Other insufficient grounds for bill of review.* There were not sufficient grounds to sustain the bill in *Ellzey* vs. *Lane's ex'ix,* and in *Triplet* vs. *Wilson.* In *Ellzey* vs. *Lane's ex'ix,* 2 H. & M. 593, *Fleming,* J., said, the forgetfulness or negligence of parties who are under no incapacity is no foundation for a bill of review by them. In *Triplet* vs. *Wilson, &c.,* 6 Call, 47, the original bill was to foreclose a mortgage; the accounts were referred to commissioners, and after their report there was a decree. A bill was afterwards filed by the debtor, stating that by mistake his counsel omitted to claim an abatement of interest during the war, and praying that the same might be credited. *Held,* that the rules allowing bills of review would not apply to the case; not the first, because no error in law appeared in the body of the decree, for as no discount of the interest during the war was claimed in the court of chancery, nor any exceptions filed to the commissioners' report upon that ground, the chancellor was under no obligation to allow the defendant what he did not ask for; not the second, because no new fact was alleged to have been discovered, for the interest during the war was a question with which the plaintiff in the bill of review was fully acquainted at the time of the original decree.

It is not a sufficient ground for a bill of review that the documents on which the plaintiff's claims depended, and which were intended to be filed with the original bill, were *lost or mislaid by his counsel,* and not found until after the decree against him, *Jones* vs. *Pilcher's devisees,* 6 Munf., 425, nor that a party was prevented from taking testimony to prove important facts by wrong advice of one of his counsel. *Franklin* vs. *Wilkinson*, 3 Munf., 112. But see *Com.* vs. *Pauly*, 5 Call, 331.

Under a rule of practice, formerly prevailing in the United States Circuit Courts, which ran thus: "If a plea or demurrer be overruled, no other plea or demurrer shall be thereafter received; and the defendant shall proceed to answer the plaintiff's bill; and if he fail to do so within two calendar months, the same, or so much thereof as was covered by the plea or demurrer, may be taken for confessed, and the matter thereof be decreed accordingly,"[5] the United States Supreme Court held that the rule did not require the interlocutory order for taking the bill for confessed to be served before entering the final decree, and consequently the want of such service was not ground for a bill of review. *Bk. U. S.* vs. *White,* 8 Pet., 262.

After a final decree on the merits, a complainant *filed a petition*, supported by his affidavit, asserting that his solicitor had deserted his interests, failed to except to certain reports and improperly consented to the decree. The United States Supreme Court held that it could not consider the alleged errors in the report of the master, or review the action of the court below in refusing to set aside the decree upon an application addressed mainly to its discretion; that if the complainant desired to place the case in a position where the action of the lower court could be reviewed in the appellate court, he should have filed his bill of review and supported it by depositions; that such a bill was the appropriate remedy where the decree was obtained by fraud. *Terry* vs. *Com. Bk. Alex.*, 2 Otto, 454.

635. *Stockton* vs. *Cook.* In *Stockton* vs. *Cook*, 3 Munf. 68, a purchaser of property with a deed warranting the land to be free from all encumbrances sought relief in equity from his bond given for the purchase money, on the ground that the land was under mortgage beyond the full purchase money, although he knew that it was mortgaged when he purchased, and although his bond for the purchase money had been assigned. An injunction was obtained, but afterwards dissolved and the bill dis-

---

[5] The present 34th rule of practice U. S. Supreme Court, is the corresponding rule.

missed. The purchaser filed a bill of review alleging the decree of dismission to be erroneous on its face. The bill of review was dismissed by the Circuit Court and an appeal was taken. The appellate court reversed the decree dismissing the bill of review, reversed likewise the decree sought to be reviewed and perpetuated the injunction with costs.

636. *When bill of review founded on new evidence.* The evidence set forth in the bill of review as new discovered, must appear to be material to the merits of the case, *Ord* vs. *Noel,* 6 Madd. Ch. R., 127; *Livingston* vs. *Hubbs, &c.,* 3 John. Ch. R., 124, and not such evidence as might have been discovered, with ordinary diligence, before the decree, *Livingston* vs. *Hubbs, &c.,* 3 John. Ch. R., 124; *Lansings* vs. *Albany Ins. Co.,* 1 Hopkins's Ch. Rep., 102; *Ord* vs. *Noel,* 6 Madd. Ch. Rep., 127; *Barnett & Co.* vs. *Smith & Co.,* 5 Call, 98; *Winston* vs. *Johnson,* 2 Munf. 305; *Rubber Co.* vs. *Goodyear,* 9 Wal., 805, or before publication, or when, by the rules of the court, it could have been made use of at the hearing. See *Morris* vs. *LeNeve,* 3 Atk., 35; *Standish* vs. *Radley,* 2 Atk., 99; *Lord Portsmouth* vs. *Lord Effingham,* 1 Ves., Sr., 434.[6]

---

[6] If a party were allowed to go to a decree without looking for evidence which might be obtained by a proper search, and afterwards, upon finding the evidence, to file a bill of review, there would be no end to such bills. *Bingham* vs. *Dawson,* Jacob 243; 4 Cond. Eng. Ch. 114; *Pendleton, &c.,* vs. *Fay, &c.,* 3 Paige 206.

In *Suckley* vs. *Robinson,* 12 Grat. 60, a party to a suit claimed to have purchased a part of the real estate of a testator at a sale for taxes, and to have received a conveyance therefor, but such purchase was made before a decree directing the real estate to be sold at a suit of a creditor of the testa-

Evidence, merely impeaching the character of a witness, newly-discovered, is not sufficient to authorize a bill of review. *Southard.* vs. *Russell,* 16 How. 547.

Under a bill of review, to permit the introduction of newly discovered evidence to prove facts in issue on the former hearing rests. in the sound discretion of the court, to be exercised cautiously and sparingly; and only under circumstances which render it indispensable to the merits and justice of the cause. *Craig* vs. *Smith,* 10. Otto, 226.

In *Easley* vs. *Kellam & als.,* 14 Wal. 279, the bill of review was properly entertained on the after discovery of a lost paper and a former decree was, on the new evidence, rightly reversed.

In *State of Pennsylvania* vs. *Wheeling & B. Bridge Co.,* 18 How. 460, there was a motion for a bill of review and for retaxation of costs : both parties had by a written agreement waived all exceptions to the report of costs by the clerk and the report had been confirmed by the court. The counsel for the parties had ample opportunity for examination of the vouchers. The court denied the motion.

637. *Whether after affirmance of a decree by an appellate court a bill of review will be sustained.* After the affirmance of a decree by the Supreme Court of Appeals of Virginia, a bill of review founded merely on error in the decree which is apparent on the face of the record will not be received, *Campbell* vs. *Price, &c.,* 3 Munf., 227; *Campbell's ex'ors* vs. *Campbell's ex'or,* 22 Grat., 649; but there may be a bill of review to correct such a decree on the ground of after discovered evidence, *Ibid;* yet to sustain the bill the greatest caution should be observed, and the new matters to be sufficient ground for the reversal of the decree ought to be very material and newly discovered, and unknown to the party seeking relief at the time the decree was rendered, and such as could not have been discovered by the use of

tor. He set up his purchase by a bill to review the decree on that ground. The court held that as this ground existed, and was known to the party before the decree, the bill of review could not be sustained.

reasonable diligence.   *Campbell's ex'ors* vs. *Campbell's ex'or*, 22 Grat. 649.

After a decree was affirmed by the United States Supreme Court, a bill was filed to review the decree; the ground of review asserted in the bill of review was, that the plaintiff was prevented from appearing and defending the former suit by the fraud and imposition of the prevailing party. The answer denied the fraud and imposition. The bill was wholly unsupported by the proofs. The Supreme Court said the failure to appear and defend his rights in the first suit, for aught that was shown, was attributable to the plaintiff's neglect and inattention, and the bill of review was properly dismissed. *McMicker's ex'ors* vs. *Perin*, 22 How. 282.'

---

¹ From this statement of the case, it appears exceeding strange that it should ever have been presented for adjudication. The plaintiff in the bill of review showed himself persistent enough. But *Purcell* vs. *Minor*, 4 Wallace, 513, presents a case of even greater persistency. Mr. Justice Grier, pronounced the opinion of the court, rejecting the application to allow a bill of review. It here follows:

"We have just decided this case and affirmed the judgment below, because by the complainant's own statement in his bill he has shown no sufficient grounds for a court of equity to grant him the relief sought. We will not repeat the points there decided. The case was too plain to leave any possible doubt respecting the correctness of our decision. Moreover, the record showed an application made in the court below, before the appeal to this court, for a bill of review, which was decided by this court to have been properly refused. But it seems that the appellant is not satisfied with the judgment of the court, and now makes an application to the court to file *another* bill of review in the court below.

"We have no doubt that the complainant honestly believes that he has been greatly wronged by the defendant below, who has taken the liberty of breaking his promise with regard to a parol contract for an exchange of property with the complainant; but we had supposed that in the opinion just delivered, we had shown clearly to the satisfaction of any person who did not suffer under some obliquity of mental vision, that by his own statement of his case, the complainant had mistaken his remedy; and that although he may have suffered a wrong by the defendant's want of good faith, he had not presented a case which required a court of equity to disregard the statute of frauds, because it had been used for the purpose of committing a fraud. As if a party to a contract of exchange had received a deed and kept the land; refusing to give a conveyance for the land given in exchange.

"But in this case there was nothing shown but a breach of promise and a scrambling possession, followed by litigation. The present application shows

638. *Rule in Roemer* vs. *Simon & als.* In *Roemer*
vs. *Simon & als.*, 1 Otto, 149, in the Supreme Court,
a petition and an affidavit of the appellant were presented, stating in substance that new and material
evidence, previously unknown to him, had been discovered since the appeal. The affidavits of other
persons showing the nature of the evidence were attached to the petition, and the court was asked to
enter a rule requiring the appellees to show cause
why the Supreme Court should not remit the record
to the court below for a rehearing of the cause. The
Supreme Court denied the motion ; holding that the
lower court could not, after the term at which the
final decree was made, grant a rehearing, and that
the term had passed ; and that had the term continued the proper practice would be to make application to the court below for a rehearing and have
that court send to the Supreme Court a request for
a return of the record, in order that it might proceed farther with the cause, and that while if such a

---

more perseverance and faith in the applicant than discretion or judgment;
and presents not a single feature of a case proper for a bill of review.

   "By Lord Chancellor Bacon's rules, it was declared: 'No bill of review
shall be admitted except it contain either error in law appearing in the body
of the decree without further examination of matters in fact, or some new
matter which hath arisen in time after the decree ; and not on any new proof
which might have been used when the decree was made. Nevertheless, upon
new proof that is come to light after the decree was made, which could not
possibly have been used at the time when the decree passed, a bill of review
may be granted by the special license of the court, and not otherwise.'

   "We will not put ourselves in the position of seriously noticing the reasons
offered for a review of this case. Suffice it to say that the petitioner has not
presented a single feature of a case within the rules. He offers no new evidence but what he might as well have produced before, and which, if it had
been produced, would not have justified a decree in his favor. Motion denied."

request were made in a proper case and under proper restrictions the Supreme Court might make the necessary order, it could not make it on the application of the parties; that the court below could alone make the request of the Supreme Court and that the application of the parties must be addressed to the lower court.

639. *Affidavit to bill.* A bill of review founded on newly-discovered evidence should be accompanied by an affidavit that such evidence has been discovered since the decree, and could not have been used at the time of the decree in consequence of the party's ignorance that such matter existed. *Barnett & Co.* vs. *Smith & Co.*, 5 Call, 102.

When the bill is filed by infants, such oath by the next friend of the infants is sufficient. *Lee's infants* vs. *Braxton*, 5 Call, 459.

640. *Limitation of bill of review.* In the Virginia State Courts, the bill of review must be exhibited within three years next after the final decree sought to be reversed has been made. Code 1873, ch. 175, sec. 5. An infant, married woman or insane person may exhibit the bill within three years after the removal of his or her disability. *Ibid.*

It ought to appear from the bill of review that the term of limitation has not expired, or that the plaintiffs are protected by some of the savings of the statute. If this do not appear, the bill should be rejected. *Shepherd* vs. *Larue*, 6 Munf., 529. If the fact which is alleged in a bill of review, to bring the plaintiffs within the savings of the statute, be *untruly* stated therein, the answer of the other party may deny it; and on the proofs (if in his favor) the bill will be dismissed. *Ibid.* It is not necessary to plead the statute of limitation to a bill of review. *Ibid.*

In the United States Circuit Courts, by analogy to the time allowed for appealing from a decree, parties are usually allowed five years after the rendition of a final decree in which to file a bill of review, *Thomas* vs. *Harvie's heirs*, 10 Wheat., 150, but it is within the discretion of these courts to permit the filing of a bill of review after this period, if the application be founded on matter discovered since the decree, *Thomas* vs. *Harvie's heirs*, 10 Wheat., 150. Leave to file the bill ought not to be granted in a case where it appears that the plaintiff is not aggrieved by the decree on account of the error assigned; or, that being granted, the court ought to dismiss the bill where no other error is assigned. *Ibid.*

641. *Injunction may be awarded on bill of review.* A court or judge allowing a bill of review may award an injunction to the decree sought to be reviewed. Code 1873, chap. 175, sec. 5.

641 *a*. On a bill of review, the court has power to set aside a conveyance executed under the original decree. *B'k U. S.* vs. *Ritchie*, 8 Pet. 139.

642. *Mandamus to lower court.* When a decree refusing to permit the bill of review to be filed is reversed by the Court of Appeals, and the lower court still refuses, the Court of Appeals will by mandamus compel the lower court to hear the cause. *Kent, Paine & Co.* vs. *Dickinson, Judge*, 25 Grat., 817.

643. *Parties to bill of review.* All the parties to the original bill ought to be parties to the bill of review; it is a principle of natural justice that no one ought to be affected by any decree without first being heard. 2 Barb. Ch. Pr. 94; Cooper's Eq. Pl. 95.

644. *What statements the bill of review should make.* In a bill of review it is necessary to state the former

bill and the proceedings thereon, the decree, and the point in which the complainant deems himself aggrieved by it, and the ground of law, or new matter discovered, upon which he seeks to impeach it. Mitf. Pl. 88.

645. *Prayer of bill of review.* The bill may pray simply that the decree may be reviewed and altered, or reversed in the point complained of, if it has not been carried into execution; but if it has been carried into execution, the bill should also pray the farther decree of the court to put the party complaining of the former decree into the situation in which he would have been, if the decree had not been executed. Mitf. Pl. 89.

646. *Defences to bills of review.* To a bill of review founded upon alleged errors apparent on the decree, the usual mode of defence is to plead the former decree in bar of the suit, and to object by demurrer to its being opened, alleging, as a ground of demurrer, that there is no error. Cooper's Eq. Pl. 96. The defendant may also demur alone or answer. Mitf. Pl. 205.

647. When the bill is founded on the discovery of new matter it is seldom liable to demurrer, for being exhibited only by leave of court, the ground of the bill is generally well considered before it is brought. Mitf. Pl., 205.

648. An answer is rarely filed save when the bill alleges the discovery of new matter. Then, an answer may be put in, controverting the fact that the

matter is newly discovered, and alleging other matter which may rebut the force of such newly discovered matter. In the case of an answer to a bill of review founded on newly discovered facts, there is no farther restriction upon the defendant than there would be if he were answering an original bill: but to a bill of review for errors in law apparent in the proceedings and decree, the defendant in the bill of review cannot in his answer allege any new matter of fact. *Thornton* vs. *Stewart*, 7 Leigh 128.

649. *Bills in the nature of bills of review.* The only difference between bills of review and bills in the nature of bills of review consists in the enrolment or non-enrolment of the decree. In the former case, a bill of review is proper, in the latter a bill in the nature of a bill of review. Story's Eq. Pl., § 421; Mitf. Pl., 90; *Whiting* vs. *B'k U. S.*, 13 Pet., 6, 13; *Bowyer* vs. *Lewis*, 1 H. & M., 553. The true office of such bills is to bring before the court new matter discovered since publication of the testimony in the original cause, when the decree has not been signed and enrolled. The new matter in such case is brought forward by a supplemental bill or a new bill in the nature of a bill of review, and it ought to be accompanied by a petition to rehear the original cause at the same time that it is heard upon the supplemental bill. Mitf. Pl., 91, 92, Story's Eq. Pl., § 422. See farther as to these bills Story's Eq. Pl., §§ 423, 424 and notes.

In *Bowyer, &c.* vs. *Lewis*, 1 H. & M. 553, the distinction drawn between a bill of review and a supplemental bill, in the nature of a bill of review in Mitford's Pleadings, was recognized.

650. If a party proceeds to a decree after a discovery of the facts upon which his new claim is founded, he will not be permitted afterwards to file a supplemental bill in the nature of a bill of review founded on such facts. *Pendleton* vs. *Fay*, 3 Paige 295; Story's Eq. Pl., § 338*a*, 423.

651. *Defences.* The defences to such bills may be by demurrer, plea or answer, as in the case of other bills.

Original bills in the nature of a bill of review.

652. None except parties and their privies in representation, such as heirs, executors, and administrators, can maintain a bill of review strictly so called. Wyatt's Pr. Reg., 95. Other persons in interest, and in privity of title or estate, aggrieved by the decree, such as devisees and remaindermen, obtain relief by an original bill in the nature of a bill of review. Mitf. Eq. Pl., 92, Wyatt's Prac., Reg., 98, 100.

653. *When a petition in the nature of a bill of review does not prevent an appeal from the original decree.* In *O'Hara & als* vs. *McConnell & als*, 3 Otto, 150, the Supreme Court held that a decree in chancery will be reversed if rendered against a woman who is shown by the bill to be both a minor and *a feme covert*, where no appearance by or for her has been entered, and no *guardian ad litem* appointed, and that

the making of a conveyance, as ordered by such a decree, does not deprive the defendant of the right of appeal; and that neither a subsequent petition in the nature of a bill of review, nor anything set up in the answer to such petition on which no action has been had by the lower court, can prevent a party from appealing from the original decree.

654. *Appeal from decree on bill of review.* When a final decree has been pronounced by the Court of Chancery upon a bill of review, it is competent to the party, against whom such decree is pronounced, to appeal therefrom to the Court of Appeals. *Sheppard's ex'or* vs. *Starke, &c.,* 3 Munf., 29. See *Stockton* vs. *Cook*, 3 Munf., 68, cited sec. 635 *ante.*

APPENDIX.

APPENDIX.

I.

Rules of practice in suits in equity adopted by the United States Supreme Court for the use of the United States Circuit Courts, promulgated on March 2, 1842, in force August 1, 1842, with subsequent amendments.

Preliminary Regulations.

I. The Circuit Courts, as courts of equity, shall be deemed always open for the purpose of filing bills, answers, and other pleadings for issuing and returning *mesne* and final process and commissions, and for making and directing all interlocutory motions, orders, rules, and other proceedings, preparatory to the hearing of all causes upon their merits.

II. The clerk's office shall be open, and the clerk shall be in attendance therein, on the first Monday of every month, for the purpose of receiving, entering, entertaining, and disposing of all motions, rules, orders, and other proceedings, which are grantable of course, and applied for or had by the parties, or their solicitors, in all causes pending in equity, in pursuance of the rules hereby prescribed.

III. Any judge of the Circuit Court, as well in vacation as in term, may, at chambers, or on the rule days, at the clerk's office, make and direct all such interlocutory orders, rules, and other proceedings, preparatory to the hearing of all causes upon their merits, in the same manner and with the same effect as the Circuit Court could make and direct the same in term, reasonable notice of the application therefor being first given to the adverse party, or his solicitor, to appear and show cause to the contrary at the next rule day thereafter, unless some other time is assigned by the judge for the hearing.

IV. All motions, rules, orders, and other proceedings made and directed at chambers, or, on rule days, at the clerk's office, whether special or of course, shall be entered by the clerk in an order book to be kept at the clerk's office, on the day when they are made and directed; which book shall be open at all office hours to the free inspection of the parties in any suit in equity, and their solicitors. And, except in cases where personal or other notice is specially required or directed, such entry in the order book shall be deemed sufficient notice to the parties and their solicitors, without further service thereof, of all orders, rules, acts, notices, and other proceedings entered in such order book, touching any and all the matters in the suits, to and in which they are parties and solicitors. And notice to the solicitors shall be deemed notice to the parties for whom they appear, and whom they represent, in all cases where personal notice on the parties is not otherwise specially required. Where the solicitors for all parties in a suit reside in or near the same town or city, the judges of the Circuit Court may, by rule, abridge the time for notice of rules,

90

orders, or other proceedings, not requiring personal service on the parties, in their discretion.

V. All motions and applications in the clerk's office for the issuing of *mesne* process and final process to enforce and execute decrees, for filing bills, answers, pleas, demurrers, and other pleadings; for making amendments to bills and answers; for taking bills *pro confesso;* for filing exceptions, and for other proceedings in the clerk's office which do not, by the rules hereinafter pre- scribed, require any allowance or order of the court, or of any judge thereof, shall be deemed motions and applications, grantable of course by the clerk of the court. But the same may be suspended, or altered, or rescinded by any judge of the court, upon special cause shown.

VI. All motions for rules or orders and other proceedings, which are not grantable of course, or without notice, shall, unless a different time be assigned by a judge of the court, be made on a rule day, and entered in the order book, and shall be heard at the rule day next after that on which the motion is made. And if the adverse party, or his solicitor, shall not then appear, or shall not show good cause against the same, the motion may be heard by any judge of the court *ex-parte,* and granted, as if not objected to, or refused, in his discretion.

Process.

VII. The process of subpœna shall constitute the proper *mesne* process in all suits in equity, in the first instance, to require the defendant to appear and answer the exigency of the bill; and, unless otherwise provided in these rules, or specially ordered by the Circuit Court, a writ of attachment, and if the defendant cannot be found, a writ of sequestration, or a writ of assistance to enforce a delivery of possession, as the case may require, shall be the proper process to issue for the purpose of compelling obedience to any interlocutory or final order or decree of the court.

VIII. Final process to execute any decree may, if the decree be solely for the payment of money, be by a writ of execution, in the form used in the Circuit Court in suits at common law in actions of *assumpsit.* If the decree be for the performance of any specific act, as for example, for the execution of a con- veyance of land, or the delivering up of deeds or other documents, the decree shall, in all cases, prescribe the time within which the act shall be done, of which the defendant shall be bound without further service to take notice; and upon affidavit of the plaintiff, filed in the clerk's office, that the same has not been complied with within the prescribed time, the clerk shall issue a writ of attachment against the delinquent party, from which if attached thereon, he shall not be discharged, unless upon a full compliance with the decree and the payment of all costs, or upon a special order of the court or of a judge thereof, upon motion and affidavit, enlarging the time for the performance thereof. If the delinquent party cannot be found, a writ of sequestration shall issue against his estate upon the return of *non est inventus,* to compel obedience to the decree.

IX. When any decree or order is for the delivery of possession upon proof made by affidavit of a demand, and refusal to obey the decree or order, the party prosecuting the same shall be entitled to a writ of assistance from the clerk of the court.

X. Every person, not being a party in any cause, who has obtained an order, or in whose favor an order shall have been made, shall be enabled to enforce obedience to such order by the same process as if he were a party to the cause; and every person, not being a party in any cause, against whom obedience to any order of the court may be enforced, shall be liable to the same process for enforcing obedience to such order as if he were a party in the cause.

Service of Process.

XI. No process of subpœna shall issue from the clerk's office in any suit in equity, until the bill is filed in the office.

XII. Whenever a bill is filed, the clerk shall issue the process of subpœna thereon, as of course, upon the application of the plaintiff, which shall be returnable into the clerk's office the next rule day, or the next rule day but one, at the election of the plaintiff, occurring after twenty days from the time of the issuing thereof. At the bottom of the subpœna shall be placed a memorandum, that the defendant is to enter his appearance in the suit in the clerk's office, on or before the day at which the writ is returnable; otherwise, the bill may be taken *pro confesso.* When there are more than one defendants, a writ of subpœna may, at the election of the plaintiff, be sued out separately for each defendant, except in the case of husband and wife, defendants, or a joint subpœna against all the defendants.

XIII. (As *amended*) The service of all subpœnas shall be by a delivery of a copy thereof by the officer serving the same to the defendant personally, or by leaving a copy thereof at the dwelling-house or usual place of abode of each defendant, with some adult person who is a member or resident in the family.

XIV Whenever any subpœna shall be returned not executed as to any defendant, the plaintiff shall be entitled to another subpœna, *toties quoties,* against such defendant, if he shall require it, until due service is made.

XV. The service of all process, *mesne* and final, shall be by the marshal of the district, or his deputy, or by some other person specially appointed by the court for that purpose, and not otherwise; in the latter case, the person serving the process shall make affidavit thereof.

XVI. Upon the return of the subpœna, as served and executed upon any defendant, the clerk shall enter the suit upon his docket as pending in the court, and shall state the time of the entry.

Appearance.

XVII. The appearance day of the defendant shall be the rule day, to which the subpœna is made returnable; provided. he has been served with the process twenty days before that day; otherwise, his appearance day shall be the next rule day succeeding the rule day, when the process is returnable.

The appearance of the defendant, either personally or by his solicitor, shall be entered in the order book on the day thereof by the clerk.

Bills taken Pro Confesso.

XVIII. (As *amended.*) It shall be the duty of the defendant, unless the time shall be otherwise enlarged, for cause shown, by a judge of the court, upon motion for that purpose, to file his plea, demurrer, or answer to the bill, in the clerk's office, on the rule day next succeeding that of entering his appearance. In default thereof, the plaintiff may, at his election, enter an order (as of course) in the order book that the bill be taken *pro confesso;* and thereupon the cause shall be proceeded in *ex parte,* and the matter of the bill may be decreed by the court at any time after the expiration of thirty days from and after the entry of said order, if the same can be done without an answer, and is proper to be decreed; or the plaintiff if he requires any discovery or answer to enable him to obtain a proper decree, shall be entitled to process of attachment against the defendant to compel an answer, and the defendant shall not, when arrested upon such process, be discharged therefrom, unless upon filing his answer, or otherwise complying with such order as the court or a judge thereof may direct, as to pleading to or fully answering the bill, within a period to be fixed by the court or judge, and undertaking to speed the cause. [See 7 Otto, viii.]

XIX. (As *amended.*) When the bill is taken *pro confesso*, the court may proceed to a decree at any time after the expiration of thirty days from and after the entry of the order to take the bill *pro confesso*, and such decree rendered shall be deemed absolute, unless the court shall, at the same term, set aside the same, or enlarge the time for filing the answer, upon cause shown, upon motion and affidavit of the defendant. And no such motion shall be granted, unless upon the payment of the costs of the plaintiff in the suit up to that time, or such part thereof as the court shall deem reasonable, and unless the defendant shall undertake to file his answer within such time as the court shall direct, and submit to such other terms as the court shall direct, for the purpose of speeding the cause. [See 7 Otto, viii.]

Frame of Bills. •

XX. Every bill, in the introductory part thereof, shall contain the names, places of abode, and citizenship, of all the parties, plaintiffs and defendants, by and against whom the bill is brought. The form, in substance, shall be as follows: "To the judges of the Circuit Court of the United States for the District of ———. A. B., of ———, and a citizen of the State of ———, brings this, his bill, against C. D., of ———, and a citizen of the State of ———, and E. F., of ———, and a citizen of the State of ———, and thereupon your orator complains and says, that, &c."

XXI. The plaintiff, in his bill, shall be at liberty to omit, at his option, the part which is usually called the common confederacy clause of the bill, averring a confederacy between the defendants to injure or defraud the plaintiff; also what is commonly called the charging part of the bill, setting forth the matters or excuses, which the defendant is supposed to intend to set up by way of defence to the bill; also, what is commonly called the jurisdiction clause of the bill, that the acts complained of are contrary to equity, and that the defendant is without any remedy at law; and the bill shall not be demurrable therefor. And the plaintiff may, in the narrative or stating part of his bill, state and avoid, by counter averments, at his option, any matter or thing, which he supposes will be insisted upon by the defendant, by way of defence or excuse, to the case made by the plaintiff for relief. The prayer of the bill shall ask the special relief, to which the plaintiff supposes himself entitled, and also shall contain a prayer for general relief; and if an injunction or a writ of *ne exeat regno*, or any other special order pending the suit, is required, it shall also be specially asked for.

XXII. If any persons, other than those named as defendants in the bill, shall appear to be necessary or proper parties thereto, the bill shall aver the reason why they are not made parties, by showing them to be without the jurisdiction of the court, or that they cannot be joined without ousting the jurisdiction of the court as to the other parties. And as to persons who are without the jurisdiction, and may properly be made parties, the bill may pray that process may issue to make them parties to the bill, if they should come within the jurisdiction.

XXIII. The prayer for process of subpœna in the bill shall contain the names of the defendants named in the introductory part of the bill, and if any of them are known to be infants under age, or otherwise under guardianship, shall state the fact so that the court may take order thereon as justice may require upon the return of the process. If an injunction, or a writ of *ne exeat regno*, or any other special order pending the suit, is asked for in the prayer for relief, that shall be sufficient, without repeating the same in the prayer for process.

XXIV. Every bill shall contain the signature of counsel annexed to it, which shall be considered as an affirmation on his part, that, upon the instructions given to him and the case laid before him, there is good ground for the suit, in the manner in which it is framed.

XXV. In order to prevent unnecessary costs and expenses, and to promote brevity, succinctness and directness in the allegations of bills and answers, the regular taxable costs for every bill and answer shall in no case exceed the sum which is allowed in the State Court of Chancery in the district, if any there be; but if there be none, then it shall. not exceed the sum of three dollars for every bill or answer.

Scandal and Impertinence in Bills.

XXVI. Every bill shall be expressed in as brief and succinct terms as it reasonably can be, and shall contain no unnecessary recitals of deeds, documents, contracts, or other instruments in *hæc verba*, or any other impertinent matter, or any scandalous matter not relevant to the suit. If it does, it may, on exceptions, be referred to a master by any judge of the court for impertinence or scandal, and if so found by him, the matter shall be expunged at the expense of the plaintiff, and he shall pay to the defendant all his costs in the suit up to that time, unless the court, or a judge thereof, shall otherwise order. If the master shall report that the bill is not scandalous or impertinent, the defendant [plaintiff] shall be entitled to all costs occasioned by the reference.

XXVII. No order shall be made by any judge for referring any bill, answer, or pleading, or other matter or proceeding depending before the court for scandal or impertinence unless exceptions are taken in writing and signed by counsel, describing the particular passages which are considered scandalous or impertinent; nor unless the exceptions shall be filed on or before the next rule day, after the process on the bill shall be returnable, or after the answer or pleading is filed. And such order, when obtained, shall be considered as abandoned, unless the party obtaining the order shall, without any unnecessary delay, procure the master to examine and report for the same on or before the next succeeding rule day, or the Master shall certify that further time is necessary for him to complete the examination.

Amendments of Bills.

XXVIII. See p. 655.
XXIX. See p. 655.
XXX. If the plaintiff, so obtaining any order to amend his bill after answer or plea or demurrer, or after replication, shall not file his amendments or amended bill, as the case may require, in the clerk's office, on or before the next succeeding rule day he shall be considered to have abandoned the same, and the cause shall proceed as if no application for any amendment had been made.

Demurrers and Pleas.

XXXI. See p. 171 *ante*.
XXXII. See p. 171 *ante*.
XXXIII. See p. 171 *ante*.
XXXIV. See p. 171 *ante*.
XXXV. See p. 172 *ante*.
XXXVI. See p. 172 *ante*.
XXXVII. See p. 172 *ante*.
XXXVIII. See p. 172 *ante*.

Answers.

XXXIX. The rule, that if a defendant submits to answer he shall answer fully to all the matters of the bill, shall no longer apply in cases where he might by plea protect himself from such answer and discovery. And the defendant shall be entitled in all cases by answer to insist upon all matters of defence (not being matters of abatement, or to the character of the parties, or matters of form) in bar of or to the merits of the bill of which he may be entitled to avail himself by a plea in bar; and in such answer he shall not be compellable to answer any other matters than he would be compellable to answer and discover upon filing a plea in bar, and an answer in support of such plea, touching the matters set forth in the bill to avoid or repel the bar or defence. Thus, for example, a *bona fide* purchaser for a valuable consideration, without notice, may set up that defence by way of answer instead of plea, and shall be entitled to the same protection, and shall not be compellable to make any further answer or discovery of his title than he would be in any answer in support of such plea.

XL. A defendant shall not be bound to answer any statement or charge in the bill unless specially and particularly interrogated thereto; and a defendant shall not be bound to answer any interrogatory in the bill except those interrogatories which such defendant is required to answer; and where a defendant shall answer any statement or charge in the bill, to which he is not interrogated, only by stating his ignorance of the matter so stated or charged, such answer shall be deemed impertinent. [This rule repealed. See XCIII.]

XLI *Original form.* The interrogatories contained in the interrogating part of the bill shall be divided as conveniently as may be from each other, and numbered consecutively 1, 2, 3, &c.; and the interrogatories which each defendant is required to answer shall be specified in a note at the foot of the bill, in the form or to the effect following, that is to say; "The defendant (A. B.) is required to answer the interrogatories numbered respectively 1, 2, 3, &c."; and the office copy of the bill taken by each defendant shall not contain any interrogatories except those which such defendant is so required to answer, unless such defendant shall require to be furnished with a copy of the whole bill. Amended; see XCVIII.

XLII. The note at the foot of the bill, specifying the interrogatories which each defendant is required to answer, shall be considered and treated as part of the bill, and the addition of any such note to the bill, or any alteration in or addition to such note after the bill is filed shall be considered and treated as an amendment of the bill.

XLIII. Instead of the words of the bill now in use, preceding the interrogating part thereof, and beginning with the words, "To the end therefore," there shall hereafter be used words in the form or to the effect following: "To the end, therefore, that the said defendants may, if they can, show why your orator should not have the relief hereby prayed, and may, upon their several and respective corporal oaths, and according to the best and utmost of their several and respective knowledge, remembrance, information and belief, full, true, direct and perfect answer make to such of the several interrogatories hereinafter numbered and set forth, as by the note hereunder written they are respectively required to answer, that is to say:—

"1. Whether, &c."
"2. Whether, &c."

XLIV. A defendant shall be at liberty, by answer, to decline answering any interrogatory or part of an interrogatory from answering which he might have protected himself by demurrer; and he shall be at liberty so to decline, notwithstanding he shall answer other parts of the bill, from which he might have protected himself by demurrer.

XLV. No special replication to any answer shall be filed. But if any matter alleged in the answer shall make it necessary for the plaintiff to amend his bill, he may have leave to amend the same with or without the payment of costs, as the court, or a judge thereof, may in his discretion direct.

XLVI. See p. 655 *ante*.

Parties to Bills.

XLVII. In all cases where it shall appear to the court that persons, who might otherwise be deemed necessary or proper parties to the suit, cannot be made parties by reason of their being out of the jurisdiction of the court, or incapable otherwise of being made parties, or because their joinder would oust the jurisdiction of the court as to the parties before the court, the court may in their discretion proceed in the cause without making such persons parties; and in such cases the decree shall be without prejudice to the rights of the absent parties.

XLVIII. Where the parties on either side are very numerous, and cannot, without manifest inconvenience and oppressive delays in the suit, be all brought before it, the court, in its discretion, may dispense with making all of them parties, and may proceed in the suit, having sufficient parties before it to represent all the adverse interests of the plaintiffs and the defendants in the suit properly before it. But in such cases the decree shall be without prejudice to the rights and claims of all the absent parties.

XLIX. In all suits concerning real estate which is vested in trustees by devise, and such trustees are competent to sell and give discharges for the proceeds of the sale, and for the rents and profits of the estate, such trustees shall represent the persons beneficially interested in the estate or the proceeds, or the rents and profits, in the same manner and to the same extent as the executors or administrators in suits concerning personal estate represent the persons beneficially interested in such personal estate; and in such cases it shall not be necessary to make the persons beneficially interested in such real estate or rents and profits parties to the suit; but the court may, upon consideration of the matter on the hearing, if it shall so think fit, order such persons to be made parties.

L. In suits to execute the trusts of a bill it shall not be necessary to make the heir-at-law a party; but the plaintiff shall be at liberty to make the heir-at law a party, where he desires to have the will established against him.

LI. In all cases in which the plaintiff has a joint and several demand against several persons, either as principals or sureties, it shall not be necessary to bring before the court, as parties to a suit concerning such demand, all the persons liable thereto; but the plaintiff may proceed against one or more of the persons severally liable.

LII. Where the defendant shall, by his answer, suggest that the bill is defective for want of parties, the plaintiff shall be at liberty, within fourteen days after answer filed, to set down the cause for argument upon that objection only; and the purpose for which the same is so set down shall be notified by an entry, to be made in the clerk's order-book, in the form or to the effect following (that is to say); "Set down upon the defendant's objection for want of parties." And where the plaintiff shall not so set down his cause, but shall proceed therewith to a hearing, notwithstanding an objection for want of parties taken by the answer, he shall not, at the hearing of the cause, if the defendant's objection shall then be allowed, be entitled, as of course, to an order for liberty to amend his bill by adding parties. But the court, if it thinks fit, shall be at liberty to dismiss the bill.

LIII. If a defendant shall, at the hearing of a cause, object that a suit is defective for want of parties, not having by plea or answer taken the objection, and therein specified by name or description the parties to whom the objection applies, the court (if it shall think fit) shall be at liberty to make a decree saving the rights of the absent parties.

Nominal Parties to Bills.

LIV. Where no account, payment, conveyance, or other direct relief is sought against a party to a suit, not being an infant, the party, upon service of the subpœna upon him, need not appear and answer the bill, unless the plaintiff specially requires him so to do by the prayer of his bill; but he may appear and answer at his option; and if he does not appear and answer he shall be bound by all the proceedings in the cause. If the plaintiff shall re- quire him to appear and answer he shall be entitled to the costs of all the proceedings against him, unless the court shall otherwise direct.

LV. Whenever an injunction is asked for by the bill to stay proceedings at law, if the defendant do not enter his appearance and plead, demur, or answer to the same within the time prescribed therefor by these rules, the plaintiff shall be entitled as of course, upon motion without notice, to such injunction. But special injunctions shall be grantable only upon due notice to the other party by the court in term, or by a judge thereof in vacation, after a hearing, which may be *ex parte*, if the adverse party does not appear at the time and place ordered. In every case where an injunction, either the common injunction or a special injunction, is awarded in vacation, it shall, unless previously dissolved by the judge granting the same, continue until the next term of the court, or until it is dissolved by some other order of the court.

Bills of Revivor and Supplemental Bills.

LVI. Whenever a suit in equity shall become abated by the death of either party, or by any other event, the same may be revived by a bill of re- vivor, or a bill in the nature of a bill of revivor, as the circumstances of the case may require, filed by the proper parties entitled to revive the same; which bill may be filed in the clerk's office at any time; and upon suggestion of the facts, the proper process of subpœna shall, as of course, be issued by the clerk, requiring the proper representatives of the other party to appear and show cause, if any they have, why the cause should not be revived. And if no cause shall be shown at the next rule day, which shall occur after fourteen days from the time of the service of the same process, the suit shall stand re- vived, as of course.

LVII. Whenever any suit in equity shall become defective, from any event happening after the filing of the bill (as, for example, by a change of interest in the parties), or for any other reason a supplemental bill, or a bill in the nature of a supplemental bill, may be necessary to be filed in the cause, leave to file the same may be granted by any judge of the court on any rule day, upon proper cause shown, and due notice to the other party. And if leave is granted to file such supplemental bill, the defendant shall demur, plead or answer thereto, on the next succeeding rule day after the supplemental bill is filed in the clerk's office, unless some other time shall be assigned by a judge of the court.

LVIII. It shall not be necessary in any bill of revivor, or supplemental bill, to set forth any of the statements in the original suit, unless the special circumstances of the case may require it.

Answers.

LIX. Every defendant may swear to his answer before any justice or judge of any court of the United States, or before any commissioner appointed by any Circuit Court to take testimony or depositions, or before any Master in chancery appointed by any Circuit Court, or before any judge of any court of a State or Territory.

Amendment of Answers.

LX. After an answer is put in, it may be amended as of course, in any matter of form, or by filling up a blank, or correcting a date, or reference to a document or other small matter, and be resworn, at any time before a replication is put in, or the cause is set down for a hearing upon bill and answer. But after replication, or such setting down for a hearing, it shall not be amended in any material matters, as by adding new facts or defences, or qualifying or altering the original statements, except by special leave of the court or of a judge thereof, upon motion and cause shown after due notice to the adverse party, supported, if required, by affidavit. And in every case where leave is so granted, the court, or the judge granting the same, may, in his discretion, require that the same be separately engrossed and added as a distinct amendment to the original answer, so as to be distinguishable therefrom.

Exceptions to Answers.

LXI. After an answer is filed on any rule day, the plaintiff shall be allowed until the next succeeding rule day to file in the clerk's office exceptions thereto for insufficiency, and no longer, unless a longer time shall be allowed for the purpose, upon cause shown to the court or a judge thereof; and if no exception shall be filed thereto within that period, the answer shall be deemed and taken to be sufficient.

LXII. When the same solicitor is employed for two or more defendants, and separate answers shall be filed, or other proceedings had by two or more of the defendants separately, costs shall not be allowed for such separate answers or other proceedings, unless a master, upon reference to him, shall certify that such separate answers and other proceedings were necessary or proper, and ought not to have been joined together.

LXIII. Where exceptions shall be filed to the answer for insufficiency within the period prescribed by these rules, if the defendant shall not submit to the same, and file an amended answer on the next succeeding rule day, the plaintiff shall forthwith set them down for a hearing on the next succeeding rule day thereafter, before a judge of the court; and shall enter, as of course, in the order book an order for that purpose. And if he shall not so set down the same for a hearing, the exceptions shall be deemed abandoned and the answer shall be deemed sufficient; provided, however, that the court, or any judge thereof, may, for good cause shown, enlarge the time for filing exceptions, or for answering the same, in his discretion, upon such terms as he may deem reasonable.

LXIV. If, at the hearing, the exceptions shall be allowed, the defendant shall be bound to put in a full and complete answer thereto, on the next succeeding rule day; otherwise the plaintiff shall, as of course, be entitled to take the bill, so far as the matter of such exceptions is concerned, as confessed, or, at his election, he may have a writ of attachment to compel the defendant to make a better answer to the matter of the exceptions; and the defendant, when he is in custody upon such writ, shall not be discharged therefrom but by an order of the court, or of a judge thereof, upon his putting in such answer and complying with such other terms as the court or judge may direct.

LXV. If, upon argument, the plaintiff's exceptions to the answer shall be overruled, or the answer shall be adjudged insufficient, the prevailing party shall be entitled to all the costs occasioned thereby, unless otherwise directed by the court, or the judge thereof, at the hearing upon the exceptions.

91

Replication and Issue.

LXVI. Whenever the answer of the defendant shall not be excepted to, or shall be adjudged or deemed sufficient, the plaintiff shall file the general replication thereto on or before the next succeeding rule day thereafter; and in all cases where the general replication is filed, the cause shall be deemed to all intents and purposes at issue, without any rejoinder or other pleading on either side. If the plaintiff shall omit or refuse to file such replication within the prescribed period, the defendant shall be entitled to an order, as of course, for a dismissal of the suit, and the suit shall thereupon stand dismissed, unless the court or a judge thereof shall, upon motion for cause shown, allow a replication to be filed *nunc pro tunc*, the plaintiff submitting to speed the cause, and to such other terms as may be directed.

Testimony, how taken.

LXVII. *Original form:* After the cause is at issue, commissions to take testimony may be taken out in vacation as well as in term, jointly by both parties or severally by either party, upon interrogatories filed by the party, taking out the same in the clerk's office, ten days' notice thereof being given to the adverse party to file cross interrogatories before the issuing of the commission, and if no cross interrogatories are filed at the expiration of the time, the commission may issue *ex parte.* In all cases the commissioner or commissioners shall be named by the court or by a judge thereof. If the parties shall so agree, the testimony may be taken upon oral interrogatories by the parties or their agents, without filing any written interrogatories. [Amended in 1854 and again in 1862. See XCIV and XCV and XCVII, *post.*]

LXVIII. Testimony may also be taken in the cause, after it is at issue, by deposition, according to the acts of Congress. But in such case, if no notice is given to the adverse party of the time and place of taking the deposition, he shall, upon motion and affidavit of the fact, be entitled to a cross-examination of the witness either under a commission or by a new deposition taken under the acts of Congress, if a court or a judge thereof shall, under all the circumstances, deem it reasonable.

LXIX. Three months, and no more, shall be allowed for the taking of testimony after the cause is at issue, unless the court or judge thereof shall, upon special cause shown by either party, enlarge the time, and no testimony taken after such period shall be allowed to be read in evidence at the hearing. Immediately upon the return of the commissions and depositions containing the testimony, into the clerk's office, publication thereof may be ordered in the clerk's office by any judge of the court, upon due notice to the parties or it may be enlarged, as he may deem reasonable under all the circumstances. But by consent of the parties, publication of the testimony may at any time pass in the clerk's office, such consent being in writing, and a copy thereof entered in the order book, or indorsed upon the deposition or testimony. [See XCVII, *post.*]

Testimony De Bene Esse.

LXX. After any bill filed, and before the defendant hath answered, the same, upon affidavit made that any of the plaintiff's witnesses are aged or infirm, or going out of the country, or that any of them is a single witness to a material fact, the clerk of the court shall, as of course, upon the application of the plaintiff, issue a commission to such commissioner or commissioners as a judge of the court may direct, take the examination of such witness or witnesses *de bene esse*, upon giving due notice to the adverse party of the time and place of taking his testimony.

Form of the last Interrogatory.

LXXI. The last interrogatory, in the written interrogatories to take testimony now commonly in use, shall in the future be altered, and stated in substance thus: "Do you know, or can you set forth any other matter or thing which may be a benefit or advantage to the parties at issue in this cause, or either of them, or that may be material to the subject of this your examination or the matters in question in this cause? If yea, set forth the same fully and at large in your answer."

Cross Bill.

LXXII. Where a defendant in equity files a cross bill for discovery only against the plaintiff in the original bill, the defendant to the original bill shall first answer thereto, before the original plaintiff shall be compellable to answer the cross bill. The answer of the original plaintiff to such cross bill may be read and used by the party filing the cross bill, at the hearing, in the same manner and under the same restrictions as the answer, praying relief, may now be read and used.

Reference to and Proceedings before Masters.

LXXIII. Every decree for an account of the personal estate of a testator or intestate shall contain a direction to the master, to whom it is referred to take the same, to inquire and state to the court what parts, if any, of such personal estate are outstanding or undisposed of, unless the court shall otherwise direct.

LXXIV. Whenever any reference of any matter is made to a master to examine and report thereon, the party at whose instance or for whose benefit the reference is made, shall cause the same to be presented to the master for a hearing on or before the next rule day succeeding the time when the reference was made; if he shall omit to do so, the adverse party shall be at liberty forthwith to cause proceedings to be had before the master, at the costs of the party procuring the reference.

LXXV. Upon every such reference it shall be the duty of the master, as soon as he reasonably can after the same is brought before him, to assign a time and place for proceedings in the same, and to give due notice thereof to each of the parties or their solicitors; and if either party shall fail to appear at the time and place appointed, the master shall be at liberty to proceed *ex parte,* or in his discretion to adjourn the examination and proceedings to a future day, giving notice to the absent party or his solicitor, of such adjournment; and it shall be the duty of the master to proceed with all reasonable diligence in every such reference, and with the least practicable delay; and either party shall be at liberty to apply to the court or a judge thereof for an order to the master to speed the proceedings, and to make his report, and to certify to the court or judge the reasons for any delay.

LXXVI. In the reports made by the master to the court, no part of any state of facts, charge, affidavit, deposition, examination or answer, brought in or used before them, shall be stated or recited. But such state of facts, charge, affidavit, deposition, examination, or answer shall be identified, specified, and referred to, so as to inform the court what state of facts, charge, affidavit, deposition, examination, or answer were so brought in or used.

LXXVII. The master shall regulate all the proceedings in every hearing before him, upon every such reference, and he shall have full authority to examine the parties in the cause upon oath, touching all matters contained in the reference; and also to require the production of all books, papers, writings, vouchers, and other documents applicable thereto; and also to examine on oath, *viva voce*, all witnesses produced by the parties before him, and to order the examination of other witnesses to be taken, under a commission to be issued upon his certificate from the clerk's office, or by deposition according to the acts of Congress or otherwise as hereinafter provided; and also to direct the mode in which the matters requiring evidence shall be proved before him; and generally to do all other acts, and direct all other inquiries and proceedings in the matters before him, which he may deem necessary and proper to the justice and merits thereof, and the rights of the parties.

LXXVIII. Witnesses who live within the district may, upon due notice to the opposite party, be summoned to appear before the commissioner appointed to take testimony, or before a master or examiner appointed in any cause, by subpœna in the usual form, which may be issued by the clerk in blank, and filled up by the party praying the same, or by the commissioner, master, or examiner, requiring the attendance of the witnesses at the time and place specified, who shall be allowed for attendance the same compensation as for attendance in court; and if any witness shall refuse to appear, or to give evidence, it shall be deemed a contempt of the court, which being certified to the clerk's office by the commissioner, master, or examiner, an attachment may issue thereupon by order of the court or of any judge thereof, in the same manner as if the contempt were for not attending, or for refusing to give testimony in the court. But nothing herein contained shall prevent the examination of witnesses *viva voce* when produced in open court, if the court shall in its discretion, deem it advisable.

LXXIX. All parties accounting before a master shall bring in their respective accounts in the form of debtor and creditor; and any of the other parties who shall not be satisfied with the accounts so brought in, shall be at liberty to examine the accounting party *viva voce*, or upon interrogatories in the master's office, or by deposition, as the master shall direct.

LXXX. All affidavits, depositions, and documents which have been previously made, read, or used in the court, upon any proceeding in any cause or matter, may be used before the master.

LXXXI. The master shall be at liberty to examine any creditor or other person coming in to claim before him, either upon written interrogatories, or *viva voce*, or in both modes, as the nature of the case may appear to him to require. The evidence upon such examination shall be taken down by the master, or by some other person by his order and in his presence, if either party requires it, in order that the same may be used by the court, if necessary.

LXXXII. The circuit courts may appoint standing masters in chancery in their respective districts, both the judges concurring in the appointment; and they may also appoint a master *pro hac vice* in any particular case. The compensation to be allowed to every master in chancery for his services in any particular case shall be fixed by the Circuit Court in its discretion, having regard to all the circumstances thereof; and the compensation shall be charged upon and borne by such of the parties in the cause as the court shall direct. The master shall not retain his report as security for his compensation; but when the compensation is allowed by the court, he shall be entitled to an attachment for the amount against the party, who is ordered to pay the same, if, upon notice thereof, he does not pay it within the time prescribed by the court.

Exceptions to Report of Master.   •

LXXXIII. The master, as soon as his report is ready, shall return the same into the clerk's office, and the day of the return shall be entered by the clerk in the order book. The parties shall have one month from the time of filing the report to file exceptions thereto; and if no exceptions are within that period filed by either party, the report shall stand confirmed on the next rule day after the month has expired. If exceptions are filed, they shall stand for hearing before the court, if the court is then in session, or if not, then at the next sitting of the court which shall be held thereafter by adjournment or otherwise.

LXXXIV. And in order to prevent exceptions to reports from being filed for frivolous causes, or for mere delay, the party whose exceptions are over-ruled shall, for every exception overruled, pay costs to the other party, and for every exception allowed, shall be entitled to costs,—the costs to be fixed in each case by the court, by a standing rule of the Circuit Court.

Decrees.

LXXXV. Clerical mistakes in decrees, or decretal orders, or errors arising from any accidental slip or omission, may, at any time before an actual enrol-ment thereof, be corrected by order of the court or a judge thereof, upon peti-tion, without the form or expense of a rehearing.

LXXXVI. In drawing up decrees and orders, neither the bill, nor answer, nor other pleadings, nor any part thereof, nor the report of any master, nor any other prior proceeding, shall be recited or stated in the decree or order; but the decree and order shall begin in substance as follows: "This cause came on to be heard (or to be further heard, as the case may be) at this term, and was argued by counsel; and thereupon, upon consideration thereof, it was ordered, adjudged, and decreed as follows, viz.: [Here insert the decree or order.]

Guardians and Prochein Amis.

LXXXVII. Guardians *ad litem,* to defend a suit may be appointed by the court, or by any judge thereof, for infants or other persons, who are under guardianship, or otherwise incapable to sue for themselves; all infants and other persons so incapable may sue by their guardians, if any, or by their *prochein ami,* subject, however, to such orders as the court may direct for the protection of infants and other persons.

LXXXVIII. See p. 516, *ante.*

LXXXIX. The circuit courts (both judges concurring therein) may make any other and further rules and regulations for the practice, proceedings, and process, mesne and final, in their respective districts, not inconsistent with the rules hereby prescribed, in their discretion, and from time to time alter and amend the same.

XC. In all cases where the rules prescribed by this court, or by the Circuit Court, do not apply, the practice of the Circuit Court shall be regulated by the present practice of the High Court of Chancery in England, so far as the same may reasonably be applied consistently with the local circumstances and local convenience of the district where the court is held, not as positive rules, but as furnishing just analogies to regulate the practice.

XCI. Whenever under these rules an oath is or may be required to be taken, the party may, if conscientiously scrupulous of taking an oath, in lieu thereof make solemn affirmation to the truth of the facts stated by him.

XCII. These rules shall take effect, and be of force, in all the circuit courts of the United States, from and after the first day of August next; but they may be previously adopted by any Circuit Court in its discretion; and when and as soon as these rules shall so take effect, and be of force, the Rules of Practice for the Circuit Courts in Equity suits, promulgated and prescribed by this court in March, 1822, shall henceforth cease, and be of no further force or effect. And the clerk of this court is directed to have these rules printed, and to transmit a printed copy thereof, duly certified, to the clerks of the several courts of the United States, and to each of the judges thereof.

XCIII. (December term, 1850.) Ordered that the fortieth rule, heretofore

adopted and promulgated by this court as one of the rules of practice in suits
in equity in the circuit courts, be and the same is hereby repealed and annulled And it shall not hereafter be necessary to interrogate a defendant
specially and particularly upon any statement in the bill, unless the complainant desires to do so to obtain a discovery.

XCIV. (December term, 1854.) *Amendment of the 67th Rule.* See p. 482,
ante.

XCV. (December term, 1861) *Amendment of the 67th Rule.* See pp.
482–483.

XCVI. *April 18th*, 1864. In suits in equity for the foreclosure of mortgages
in the circuit courts of the United States, or in any of the courts of the territories having jurisdiction of the same, a decree may be rendered for any
balance that may be found due to the complainant over and above the proceeds of the sale or sales, and execution may issue for the collection of the
same, as is provided in the eighth rule of this court regulating the equity
practice, where the decree is solely for the payment of money. (See p. 584
ante.)

XCVII. (*December term*, 1869.) [Court may assign the time of taking evidence] Where the evidence to be adduced in a cause is to be taken orally,
as provided in the order passed at the December term, 1861, amending the
67th Gen. Rule, the court may, on motion of either party, assign a time
within which the complainant shall take his evidence in support of the bill,
and a time thereafter within which the defendant shall take his evidence in
defence, and a time thereafter within which the complainant shall take. his
evidence in reply ; and no farther evidence shall be taken in the cause, unless
by agreement of the parties, or by leave of the court first obtained on motion
for cause shewn.

XCVIII. *December term*, 1871. *Amendment of 41st Rule.* 13 *Wal., XI.*
If the complainant, in his bill, shall waive an answer under oath, or shall
only require an answer under oath with regard to certain specified interrogatories, the answer of the defendant, though under oath, except such part
thereof as shall be directly responsive to such interrogatories, shall not be evidence in his favor, unless the cause be set down for hearing on bill and answer only ; but may nevertheless be used as an affidavit, with the same effect
as heretofore, on a motion to grant or dissolve an injunction, or on any other
incidental motion in the cause; but this shall not prevent a defendant from
becoming a witness in his own behalf under section 3 of the act of Congress of
July 2nd, 1864.

XCIX. *January* 13, 1879. Called Rule 93 in 7 Otto., VII. When an appeal from a final decree in an equity suit, granting or dissolving an injunction
is allowed by a justice or judge who took part in the decision of the cause, he
may, in his discretion at the time of such allowance, make an order suspending or modifying the injunction during the pending of the appeal upon such
terms as to bond or otherwise, as he may consider proper for the security of
the rights of the opposite party.

C. [*Called Equity Rule 94, promulgated October term*, 1881.] Every bill
brought by one or more stockholders in a corporation, against the corporation and other parties, founded on rights which may properly be asserted by
the corporation, must be verified by oath, and must contain an allegation
that the plaintiff was a shareholder at the time of the transaction of which he
complains, or that his share had devolved on him since, by operation of law,
and that the suit is not a collusive one to confer on a court of the United
States jurisdiction of a case of which it would not otherwise have cognizance.
It must also set forth with particularity the efforts of the plaintiff to secure
such action as he desires on the part of the managing directors or trustees,
and, if necessary, of the shareholders, and the causes of his failure to obtain
such action.

II.

Doctrine concerning Parties in United States Circuit Courts.

1. *General rule.* The general rule in equity is, that all persons materially interested, either legally or equitably, in the subject matter of a suit, should be made parties to it, either as plaintiffs or defendants, however numerous they may be, so that there may be a complete decree, which shall bind them all. *Caldwell* vs. *Taggart*, 4 Pet. 190, *Whiting* vs. *Bank U. S.*, 13 Pet. 6, *Hopkirk* vs. *Page*, 2 Brock. 20. See *Coy* vs. *Mason*, 17 How. 580.

2. *Dispensing with parties.* If possible, consistently with the merits of the case, the United States Courts dispense with all parties over whom the courts would not possess jurisdiction. *Milligan* vs. *Milledge*, 3 Cran., 220, *Elwendorf* vs. *Taylor*, 10 Wheat. 152, *Vattier* vs. *Hinde*, 7 Pet. 252, *Payne* vs. *Hook*, 7 Wal. 431.

3. *Exceptions to general rule in United States Courts.* In the United States Circuit Courts, the general rule is as stated before. But there are qualifications arising out of public policy and the necessities of particular cases. The true distinction appears to be as follows: First, Where a person will be directly affected by a decree, he is an indispensable party, unless the parties are too numerous to be brought before the court, when the case is subject to a special rule. Secondly, Where a person is interested in the controversy, but will not be directly affected by a decree made in his absence, he is not an indispensable party, but he should be made a party if possible, and the court will not proceed to a decree without him, if he can be reached. Thirdly, Where he is not interested in the controversy between the immediate litigants, but has an interest in the subject matter, which may be settled in the suit, and thereby prevent further litigation. he may be a party or not, at the option of the complainants. *Williams* vs. *Bankhead*, 19 Wal. 563, 571.

4. *Hearing in the absence of parties beyond the jurisdiction.* The act of Congress of February 28, 1839, substantially the same with section 737, Rev. Stat. 1873–4, p. 139, provides that causes may be heard in the United States Courts, though there be defendants beyond their jurisdiction, as to those parties properly before these courts, such hearing to be without prejudice to persons not regularly served with process, and not voluntarily appearing to answer; and the act further provides that the absence of parties not inhabitants, nor found within the district in which the suit is,

shall constitute no abatement or other objection to the suit. This act dispenses with the necessity of making persons parties who have a nominal interest, and are beyond the jurisdiction of the court, and when a decree can be made without prejudicing them, *Union Bk. of Louisiana* vs. *Stafford*, 12 How. 327, but it has been held that neither this act, nor the 47th rule of equity practice of the U. S. Circuit Courts enables a circuit court to make a decree in equity, in the absence of an indispensable party, whose rights must necessarily be affected by such decree. Curtis, J., in *Shields & als.* vs. *Barrow*, 17 How. 139. See *Russell* vs. *Clarke's ex'ors*, 7 Cranch 98. *Mech. Bk. Alex'a* vs. *Seton*, 1 Pet 299, *Conson & als.* vs. *Millandon & als.*, 19 How. 113; see also *McCoy* vs. *Rhodes*, 11 How. 131, as to the effect of 47th and 48th rules of Equity practice of the U. S. Circuit Courts. See also 22nd Rule of practice as to frame of bill in such cases.

5. *When party must be within the jurisdiction, or voluntarily appear, to bind him personally.* To give judicial proceedings any validity, there must be a competent tribunal to pass upon their subject matter; and if that involves merely a determination of the personal liability of the defendant, he must be brought within its jurisdiction by service of process within the State, or by his voluntary appearance. *Pennoyer* vs. *Niff*, 5 Otto. 714.

6. *Formal parties.* As to formal and unnecessary parties, see *Wormley* vs. *Wormley*, 8 Wheat. 451, *Carneal* vs. *Banks*, 10 Wheat. 188, *Vattier* vs. *Hinde*, 7 Pet. 266.

7. *Proper, though not indispensable, parties.* As to parties having a substantial interest, but not so connected with the controversy that their joinder is indispensable, see *Cameron* vs. *McRoberts*, 3 Wheat. 591, *Osborn* vs. *Bk U. States*, 9 Wheat. 733, *Harding* vs. *Handy*, 11 Wheat. 132, *Hogan* vs. *Walker*, 14 How. 36 *Elwendorf* vs. *Taylor*, 10 Wheat. 167, *Union Bank, &c* vs. *Stafford*, 12 How. 327, *N. O. Canal & Banking Co* vs. *Stafford*, 12 How. 343, *Trades Bank* vs *Campbell*, 14 Wal 97, *Payne* vs. *Hook*, 7 Wal. 431, 12 How. 343, 7 Pet. 252, 12 Wheat. 193, *French* vs. *Shoemaker*, 14 Wal. 314.

8. *Indispensable parties* As to parties having an interest inseparable from the interests of those before the court, and who are therefore indispensable parties, *Cameron* vs. *McRoberts* 3 Wheat. 591, *Mallow* vs. *Hinde*, 12 Wheat 197. *Shields* vs. *Barrow*, 17 How. 140, *North Ind R. R Co* vs. *Michigan Cent. R. R. Co.*, 15 How. 233, 19 How. 113, 17 How. 130.

Robertson vs. *Carson*, 19 Wal. 94, presented a case in which the court held that E, one of the trustees, C., the purchaser from the executors, and F., a retiring member of a partnership, were all indispensable parties.

9. *Parties beyond the jurisdiction.* As to persons beyond the jurisdiction of the court who are necessary or proper parties, see

the 22d rule of equity practice for the Circuit Courts U. S., 19 How. 113, 12 How. 327.

The bill may be dismissed as to a party over whom the court has no jurisdiction, and a decree made as to other defendants, if it can be done without affecting his interests. *Vattier* vs. *Hinde*, 7 Pet. 252.

10. *Persons who should not be parties.* No one ought to be made a plaintiff in whom there is no interest, and no one a defendant from whom nothing is demanded. *Kerr* vs. *Watts,* 6 Wheat. 559. *Mech. Bk. Alex'a* vs. *Seton*, 1 Pet. 299. In *French* vs. *Shoemaker*, 14 Wal. 314, A, B, C and D, having a dispute about their rights in a railroad company, entered into a contract of settlement, by which they divide the stock in certain proportions among them. A. refused to carry out the contract. B. filed a bill to compel him to stand to his agreement. A., after answering, filed a cross bill, insisting that B. ought to have made C. and D. parties to his original proceeding. *Held*, that the bill, not seeking any relief against C. and D., it was not necessary that they should be parties.

11. *Numerous parties.* When parties are numerous, and the suit is for a common object, the court entertains jurisdiction at the suit of certain of the parties suing in behalf of themselves and others having a common interest. *Smith & als.* vs. *Swormstedt*, 16 How. 288.

12 *Cause retained in the United States court until the matter is litigated with persons not joined.* In a proper case, the United States Circuit Court will retain the cause while matters are litigated before the State Courts or other tribunals, between the complainant and others, not made parties to the suit, because of the peculiar structure of the limited jurisdiction of the United States Courts over persons. *Mallow* vs. *Hinde*, 12 Wheat. 193.

13. *Who may unite in one bill.* Where one partner dies, a creditor may go at once into equity for an account of his assets, and may and should join the surviving partner, and the representative of another deceased partner: And several distinct creditors may join in such a bill; and where the deceased partner was a member of two firms, the creditors of both firms may join, and may make the surviving partners of both firms, and the representatives of any deceased partner of either firm, parties defendant. *Nelson* vs. *Hill*, 5 How. 127.

14. *What are the rights of alien enemies made parties.* "It is clear that an alien enemy is liable to be sued, and this carries with it the right to use all the means and appliances of defence." *Swayne*, J., in *McVeigh* vs. *United States*, 11 Wal. 267.

15. *Want of proper parties.* Where a bill stated that the complainant had an interest in the subject matter of a former suit in equity, and had applied to be admitted a party, and was refused, and a decree had been made in that suit in fraud of his rights, and

the bill prayed to have that decree set aside, the court held, that the bill was not a bill of review, but an original bill; and so dismissed the bill because both complainant and defendants were citizens of Kentucky, and the court had no jurisdiction for want of proper parties. *Wickliffe* vs. *Eve*, 17 How. 468.

In *Milligan* vs. *Milledge*, 3 Cr. 220, the Court held that the Circuit Court erred in dismissing the bill for want of parties, and erred too in admitting the plea of the want of *proper parties*,[1] the bill suggesting that the parties joined were out of the jurisdiction of the court.[2]

16. *Non-joinder of parties will not oust jurisdiction of United States Courts.* These courts will not suffer their jurisdiction in an equity cause to be ousted by the circumstance of the joinder or non-joinder of merely formal parties, who are not entitled to sue or liable to be sued in the United States Courts, *Wormley* vs. *Wormley*, 8 Wheat., 322, but will rather proceed without them and decide upon the merits of the case between the parties who have the real interests before it, whenever it can be done without prejudice to the rights of others. *Ibid.* And so, in *Elmendorf* vs. *Taylor*, 10 Wheat., 152, it was held that if the cause can be completely decided as between the litigant parties, an interest in some other person who cannot be reached by process should not prevent a decree.

17. *When objection for want of parties may be taken.* See *Story* vs. *Livingston*, 13 Pet., 359; *Livingston* vs. *Woodsworth*, 15 How.; *Connor* vs. *Millaudon*, 19 How., 113; *Lewis* vs. *Darling*, 16 How., 1; *Mech. Bank Alex.* vs. *Seton*, 1 Pet., 299; *Whiting* vs. *B'k U. S.*, 13 Pet., 14, and *Hunt* vs. *Wickliffe*, 8 Pet., 215, as to the period at which objection for want of parties may be taken. See also Story's Eq., Pl., 236.

The 53d rule of the Supreme Court governing the equity practice in the United States Circuit Courts should be specially referred to. See p. 719, ante. See also 47–52d rules and 54th rule, pp. 719, 720, *ante*.

The doctrine of parties has been applied, in United States Courts, to the following special cases:

18. *Absent persons.* See sec. 4, p. 727, *ante*. See sec. 738 Rev. Statutes U. S.

In *Cooper* vs. *Reynolds*, 10 Wal., 318, the court said: "The plaintiff is met at the commencement of his proceedings by the fact that the defendant is not within that territorial jurisdiction, and cannot be served with any process by which he can be brought personally within the power of the court. For this difficulty the statute has provided a remedy. It says that upon affidavit being made of that fact a writ of attachment may be issued and levied

---

[1] See sec. 7, ante.   [2] See sec. 4, ante.

on any of the defendant's property, and a publication may be made warning him to appear, and that thereafter the court may proceed in the case, whether he appears or not. If the defendant appears the cause becomes mainly a suit *in personam*, with the added incident that the property attached remains liable, under the control of the court, to answer to any demand which may be established against the defendant by the final judgment of the court. But, if there is no appearance of the defendant, and no service of process on him, the case becomes in its essential nature a proceeding *in rem*, the only effect of which is to subject the property attached to the payment of the demand which the court may find to be due to the plaintiff."

19. *Administration of estates and disposition of assets.*

See *Harding* vs. *Handy*, 11 Wheat, 103.

An administrator to whom letters of administration were granted before the separation of the District of Columbia from the original State, could not, after that separation, maintain an action in the county of Washington by virtue of those letters of administration; but must take out new letters within the District. *Fenwick* vs. *Sears*, 1 Cranch, 258.

In *Vaughan* vs. *Northup*, 15 Pet., 1, the Supreme Court held that an administrator appointed in a State was not liable to be sued in the District of Columbia in his official capacity for assets lawfully received by him under his letters of administration, that he was only accountable to the proper tribunal of the government from whose laws he derived his authority, not to the tribunals of another State. See also *Peale* vs. *Phipps*, 14 How., 368. An *administrator de bonis non* cannot sue the former administrator or his representative for a *devastavit*, or for delinquencies in office, either at law or in equity; but the former administrator or his representatives are liable directly to creditors and next of kin. *Buall* vs. *New Mexico*, 16 Wal., 535, and cases cited p. 540 of 16 Wal.

A legacy was given jointly to several families, whose individual members were not ascertained by the will. All the legatees were necessary parties to a bill for payment of the legacy. *Perry* vs. *Belt*, 1 Pet., 670–681.

On a bill for payment of a legacy, the answer of the personal representative shewed that another bill had been filed against him by persons claiming as creditors or mortgagees, and a third by persons claiming as heirs at law and distributees; it was held, that the heirs at law and distributees were necessary parties; and the decree was reversed and the suit remanded to enable the plaintiff to amend. *Armstrong* vs. *Lear*, 8 Pet., 51.

In Georgia, under its colonial law, the heirs were not necessary parties to a bill to subject the lands of a decedent to his debts. *Telfair* vs. *Stead's ex'ors*, 2 Cr., 407.

In a bill against an executor to obtain an account and payment of a legacy, it is not necessary to join as a defendant a devisee of a tract of land in another jurisdiction. *West* vs. *Smith*, 8 How., 402.

A creditor, before obtaining judgment, may file a bill against the administrator and the fraudulent grantee of his deceased debtor to subject property fraudulently conveyed, to the payment of the debt. *Hagan* vs. *Walker*, 14 How., 29.

To a bill seeking to charge a legacy on land of a married woman, she is a necessary party. *Lewis* vs. *Darling*, 16 How., 1.

On a bill by one distributee of an intestate's estate against the administrator, the other distributees are not indispensable parties, *Payne* vs. *Hook*, 7 Wal. 425; the sureties of the administrator may be united as defendants in the same suit. *Ibid.*

Heirs at law sought to set aside a sale of their ancestor's realty which had been sold at the instance of a creditor; it was held, that the creditor and all the heirs at law were necessary parties. *Hoe & als.* vs. *Wilson*, 9 Wal. 501.

In *Dandridge* vs. *Custis*, 2 Pet. 377, it was held that in case of a bequest to executors to invest a fund and from the interest pay for the proper education of three nephews, in a suit by one of them against the executors to enforce the execution of the trust, the three should be made parties: but the residuary legatees were not necessary parties.

In a bill by an executor against a devisee of lands, charged with the payment of debts, for an account, &c., the creditors are not indispensable parties. *Potter* vs. *Gardner*, 12 Wheat. 499. In this case, a purchaser from the devisee was charged with what of the purchasee money he had aided the devisee in misapplying. *Ibid.*

In a suit by a distributee to recover a distributive share, the mere fact that the administrator was ordered to account did not make parties all who were entitled to distribution nor authorize a decree in their favour; and if such persons do not appear before the master, no decree could be made for or against them because they would not be bound thereby. *Hook* vs. *Payne*, 14 Wal. 252.

It is not irregular for two mercantile firms to unite as complainants in a creditor's bill, *Nelson* vs. *Hill*, 5 How. 127, and in such a bill against a deceased partner's estate, it is proper to join the surviving partner and the representative of another deceased partner. *Ibid.*

Parties to a bill charging executors with fraud and seeking to reinstate a mortgage, *Robertson* vs. *Carson*, 19 Wal. 94, cited ante p. 728.

See 49th, 50th and 51st rules of Supreme Court, and see Story's Pl. § 150, n. 5, and *Telfair* vs. *Stead's ex'ors*, 2 Cr. 407.

20. *In amended and supplemental bills.* See *Shaw* vs. *Bill*, 5 Otto 14. See pp. 651–663 *ante.*

21. *Appeals.* One defendant, whose interest is separate from that of the others, may appeal. *Forgay* vs. *Conrad*, 6 How. 201.

22. *Assignees and assignors.* An assignor still retaining an interest in the patent, though none in the particular territory, may join as complainant in a bill for an injunction to restrain the violation of the patent in that territory. *Woodworth* vs. *Wilson*, 4 How., 712.

Assignees in bankruptcy are indispensable parties to a bill against the bankrupt and certain parties to whom he had previously conveyed property in trust. *Russell* vs. *Clark's ex'ors*, 7 Cranch, 69.

If the plaintiff's equity depend on the invalidity of an assignment of the equitable title, and the defendant be the sole assignee, his assignor need not be made a party. *Boon's heirs* vs. *Chiles*, 8 Pet., 532.

The rule laid down in Mitford's Pleading, 179, is repeated, with a caveat, in Story's Eq. Pl., § 153. Judge Story states the true principle to be, that in all cases in which the assignment is absolute and unconditional leaving no equitable interest whatever in the assignor, and the extent and validity of the assignment are not doubted or denied, and there is no remaining liability in the assignor to be effected by the decree, it is not necessary to make the latter a party. Story's Eq. Pl., § 153. See *Batesville Institute* vs. *Kauffman*, 18 Wal., 151.

See Story's Eq. Pl., § 216a, as to fraudulent assignments, &c.

See *Fitch* vs. *Creighton*, 24 How., 159; *Gaines* vs. *Hennen*, 24 How., 553.

An objection that the assignor of a patent was improperly joined as coplaintiff with the assignee in the bill was, in *Livingston* vs. *Woodworth*, 15 How., 546, taken for the first time on the appeal in the Supreme Court. The court held that the objection came too late.

In *Fitch* vs. *Creighton*, 24 How., 159, the case was this : The statutes of Ohio gave to the local authorities of cities, &c., power to make various improvements in streets and to assess the proportionate expense thereof upon the lots fronting thereon, which was declared to be a lien upon the property. The City Council of Toledo directed certain improvements to be made, and contracted with two persons (one of whom purchased the right of the other) to do the work, and authorized them to collect the amounts due upon the assessments; the contractor who did the work sued in the United States Court. His suit was maintained, and it was held not necessary to make the contractor who had sold out, a party. The court also held, that the bill was not multifarious, because it claimed to enforce the liens upon several lots.

23. *Banking associations and corporations.* If the members of an unincorporated banking company are numerous and in part unknown, it is not necessary to bring all the stockholders before the

court before a decree can be made; but where such stockholders die after having been regularly served with process, their representatives should be made parties unless some good reason, such as absolute insolvency, should justify their omission. In such a case, it is error to dismiss the bill as to stockholders named in the bill but not served with process; proceedings, in case of their being non-residents, may be had against them by publication under the act of Congress of 1803. *Mandeville* vs. *Riggs*, 2 Pet., 482.

To a bill by the creditors of a corporation against its stockholders to compel payment of the arrears of their subscriptions, all the stockholders need not be made parties. *Ogilvie* vs. *Knox. Ins. Co.*, 22 How., 380. If necessary the court may, at the suggestion of either party that the corporation is insolvent, administer its assets by a receiver, and thus collect all the subscriptions or debts to the corporation. *Ibid.* See *Sawyer* vs. *Hoag*, 17 Wal. 610.

In *Railroad Co.* vs. *Howard* 7 Wal., 392, it was held that a sale by a railroad company, not authorized in its corporate capacity to make it, may be yet validly carried into effect by the consent of all parties interested in the subject matter of it; and that stockholders in a corporation need not be individually made parties in a creditors' suit where their interest is fully represented both by the railroad company and by a committee chosen and appointed by them.

A railroad corporation by mortgage, whose sufficiency to secure what it was given to secure was doubtful, mortgaged all its property directly to its bondholders to secure specifically to each the amount due him. *Held*, that no one even when professing to act in behalf of all who might come in and contribute to the expenses of the suit could proceed alone against the company and ask a sale of the property mortgaged. The other bondholders should be parties. The adequacy of the security being doubtful, each should be present to defend his own, and, if necessary, attack the claims of others. If successful in the latter, his own security is enhanced. All interested having notice could endeavor to have as advantageous a sale as possible. Even in equity, a suit on a written instrument must be brought in the name of all who are formal parties to it and retain an interest in it. *R'l R'd Co.* vs. *Orr*, 18 Wal., 471. In *Terry* vs. *Com. B'k Alex.*, 2 Otto, 454, a suit to wind up an insolvent bank, the stockholders were not parties nor served with process, it was held that so much of a final decree as discharged them from all liability for any debt against the bank was erroneous.

In a suit against a national bank under the National Bank Act of June 3, 1864, sec. 50, it is no objection to the bill properly filed against the stockholders within the jurisdiction of the court, that the stockholders named in the bill and averred in it to be without the jurisdiction, are not made co-defendants. *Kennedy* vs. *Gibson & als*, 8 Wal., 498.

A stockholder has his remedy in chancery against the directors to prevent them from doing acts which would amount to a violation of the charter, as to prevent any misapplication of their capital or profits which might lessen the value of the shares, if the acts intended to be done amount to what is called in law a breach of trust or duty; *Dodge* vs. *Woolsey*, 18 How., 331, but there must be a clear default on their part involving a breach of duty within the rule established in equity. *Memphis City* vs. *Dean*, 8 Wal., 73. A stockholder also has a remedy against individuals, in whatever character they profess to act, if the subject of complaint is an imputed violation of a corporate franchise or the denial of a right growing out of it. *Dodge* vs. *Woolsey*, 18 How. 331.

Although a stockholder in a corporation may bring a suit when the corporation refuses, yet as in such case the suit can be maintained only on the ground that the rights of the corporation are involved, the corporation should be made a party to the suit and a demurrer will lie if it is not so made. *Davenport* vs. *Dows*, 18 Wal., 626.-

See C. Rule of practice (called Eq. Rule 94) p. 726, *ante*.

24. *Bankrupts.* Assignees in bankruptcy are indispensable parties to a bill against the bankrupt and certain persons to whom he conveyed property in trust before he was decreed a bankrupt. *Russell* vs. *Clarke's ex'ors*, 7 Cranch 69.

The proceeds of the sale of a bankrupt's goods being in the hands of one sued as a defendant by a judgment creditor of the bankrupt, another person who had a like judgment and levied on the same goods is not a necessary party, he being without the jurisdiction. *Traders Bank* vs. *Campbell*, 14 Wal. 87.

When the assignee in bankruptcy of a mortgagor is appointed during the pendency of proceedings for the foreclosure and sale of mortgaged premises, he stands as any other purchaser would stand on whom the title had fallen after the commencement of the suit; if there be any reason for interposing, the assignee should have himself substituted for the bankrupt, or be made a defendant on petition. *Eyrster* vs. *Graff & als.*, 1 Otto 521.

25. *Claimants under the same title.* If both the plaintiff and the defendant in a bill to obtain the legal title claim under and assert the validity of a conveyance, it is not necessary to make the parties to that conveyance parties to the bill. *Boon's heirs* vs. *Chiles*, 8 Pet., 532.

26. *Cities, towns, &c.* Though the courts of the United States will not entertain a suit brought against a State by an alien, or the citizen of another State, yet they may, in equity, restrain by injunction a public officer of the State from acting under a void law of the State to destroy a franchise; and as the State cannot be joined as a defendant, its agent may be sued alone; the prohibition to sue a State does not extend to cases in which a State is not

a party on the record, even if the State has the entire ultimate interest in the subject of the suit. *Osborn* vs. *B'k U. S.*, 9 Wheat., 738

27. *Corporations.* See Banking associations, and corporations, *ante*, p. 733.

28 *Creditors' bills.* See *Judgments*, p. 738, *post.*

See *Railroad Co.* vs. *Orr*, 18 Wal., 471, referred to under title ˙*Banking Associations*, p. 734, *post.*

29. *Debts to debtor.* A bill was filed by the United States in the U. S. Circuit Court for the district of Massachusetts, to recover of Howland and Allen a sum of money in their hands alleged to be the money of Shoemaker and Travers, merchants who were stated to be insolvents and to be indebted to the United States. Shoemaker and Travers had made a trust deed assigning all their estate in trust to secure certain enumerated creditors, and first the United States. *Held*, that the United States Court sitting as a court of equity had jurisdiction, and that though there was an act of the Massachusetts Legislature allowing a creditor to sue the debtor of his debtor at law, yet that act did not affect the jurisdiction in equity. *U. S.* vs. *Holland*, 4 Wheat. 108.

Ordinarily, a debtor to the estate is not a proper party to a suit brought by a creditor against a personal representative for payment of his debt out of the assets; because the liability of the debtor is solely to the personal representative; but if a special case is made out, such as collusion between him and the personal representative, or as the insolvency of the personal representatives, the debtor may be made a party as a means of uprooting the fraud or of securing the property. See Story's Eq. Pl. § 227. See *Rhodes* vs. *Warburton*, 6 Sim. 617; Calvert on Parties, 25.

It seems that a *cestui que trust*, or other principal, would not be justified in filing a joint bill for an account against the trustee, and an individual or sub-agent employed by him in the execution of the trust, who had received money belonging to the *cestui que trust*, and dealt with it according to the direction of the trustee. *Lockwood* vs, *Abdy*, 14 Sim. 437.

30. *Disability of parties.* See *O'Hara & als.* vs. *McConnell*, 3 Otto 152 cited sec. 47, p. 740.

31. *Discovery.* After discovery had, a suit for discovery merely cannot be revived. *Horsburg* vs. *Baker*, 1 Pet. 232.

32. *Disposition of a fund.* See "Administration of estates and disposition of assets," p. 731, *ante.*

In *Williams & als.* vs. *Bankhead*, 19 Wal. 563, it was held that where a proceeding in equity concerned the disposal of a specific fund, a person claiming the fund and liable by a decree to have it wholly swept from him was an indispensable party.

33. *Foreclosure.* See Mortgages.

34. *Fraud.* To a suit by some of the heirs of a decedent to set

aside a deed procured from the ancestor by fraud, it was held that all the heirs should be made parties before a sale was ordered to satisfy what was justly due. *Harding* vs. *Handy*, 11 Wheat, 103. It was a case, however, in which the court might have proceeded if all the heirs could not have been made defendants by the service of process. The undivided interest of those who appeared might be sold and the lien of the defendant permitted to remain on the parts unsold, to secure the payment of so much of the money due to the defendant, as those parts might be justly chargeable with. 11 Wheat, 133.

Where a decree set aside certain conveyances as fraudulent as against creditors, but expressly exempted a certain mortgage from the effect of the decree, it was held that the mortgagee was not a necessary party to the bill. *Venable* vs. *Bank U. States*, 2 Pet., 107.

A fraudulent auctioneer, who, without the knowledge of the owner, had, by fictitious bids, obtained $40,000 for property sold at public auction, when $20,000 was the highest real bid, was held not to be a necessary party to a suit by the purchaser against the owner to recover the excess of $20,000 he had paid. *Veazie* vs. *Williams, &c.*, 8 How., 134.

On a bill to set aside a fraudulent conveyance, the alleged fraudulent grantor is a necessary party. *Gaylords* vs *Kelshaw*, 1 Wal., 81.

Where a bill was filed by a third party to set aside, as fraudulent, completed judicial proceedings, regular on their face, the plaintiff in those proceedings should be brought in as a party. *Harwood* vs. *R. R. Co.*, 17 Wal., 78.

See 19 Wal., 94, and *Administration of Estates, &c.*

36. *Husband and wife.* To a bill to charge a legacy on the land of a *feme covert*, she is a necessary party. *Lewis* vs. *Darling*, 16 How., 1.

The husband may join his wife as a complainant in a suit in which he has no interest; in such case he is considered as merely the next friend of the wife. *Bein* vs. *Heath*, 6 How., 228.

A married woman may sue her husband, in equity, by her next friend. *Barber* vs. *Barber*, 21 How., 582.

A married woman may sue, by her next friend, to recover a legacy bequeathed to her, where the husband has transferred all his marital rights in the legacy to his wife. *Gallego* vs. *Gallego*, 2 Brock., 285.

37. *Injunctions.* See *Dodge* vs. *Woolsey*, 18 How., 331, cited, p. 735, *ante*, and *Judgments, post*, p. 738.

38. *Insolvents.* See *Bankrupts*.

There was a bill by the heirs of an insolvent to set aside on the ground of irregularity a sale of mortgaged property in Louisiana. The mortgagees had been paid their share of the purchase

93

money and had an interest in upholding the sale. It was held that the mortgagees were necessary parties, *Coiron & als.* vs. *Millaudon & als.*, 19 How. 113; and the fact that they were beyond the jurisdiction of the court was not a sufficient reason for not making them parties.

39. *Insurance.* Several persons underwriters, who have claims to a return of moneys by them actually paid on account of a loss, cannot unite in one bill. *Yeaton* vs. *Lenox*, 8 Pet. 123. See *contra,* Story's Eq. Pl. § 537; see also Story's Eq. Pl. §§ 161, 286*a*; 286*b* and notes.

40. *Joint interests and obligations.* See *Payne* vs. *Hook*, 7 Wal. 425, cited sec. 7, p. 728.

41. *Judgments.* See *Creditors,* p. 736, *ante,* and *Specific Performance.*

To a bill by purchasers from a judgment debtor to set aside the legal title of a purchaser at sheriff's sale, on the ground that the judgment was satisfied before the levy, both the judgment debtor and creditor are necessary parties. *Field* vs. *Holland*, 6 Cran. 24.

A judgment at law cannot be enjoined without making the judgment creditor a party; it is not enough that the defendant admit himself to be the owner of it, for such admission may be collusive. *Marshall* vs. *Beverley*, 5 Wheat. 313.

A bill to enjoin a judgment at law is not considered as an original bill, and therefore the introduction of parties who would otherwise be necessary may be dispensed with if the jurisdiction might be thereby affected; and the court will decree as to parties properly before it, leaving the rights of others unaffected. *Simons* vs. *Guthrie*, 9 Cranch 19; *Mallow* vs. *Hinde*, 12 Wheat. 194. See *Dunn* vs. *Clarke*, 8 Pet. 1.

To a bill to enjoin a judgment by an endorsee against the endorser of a bill of exchange, on the ground that it had been paid by the drawer, before the judgment, without the complainant's knowledge, the drawer is not a necessary party. *Atkins* vs. *Dick*, 14 Pet. 14.

Different judgment creditors may unite in one bill for discovery and account, the object being to set aside impediments to their remedies at law, created by the fraud of their common debtor. *De Wolf* vs. *Johnson*, 10 Wheat, 367.

42. *Lost deeds.* See *Findlay* vs. *Hinde*, 1 Pet. 241.

43. *Mortgages.* To a bill of foreclosure a prior encumbrancer should be made a party, but if not joined and a decree of sale be executed before the existence of a prior encumbrance becomes known to the court, it is not error to refuse to vacate the decree; the prior encumbrance is not affected by such sale. *Finley* vs. *Bank U. States*, 11 Wheat, 304.

Whenever the first mortgagee is not subject to the jurisdiction of the court and cannot be joined without defeating the jurisdiction, and the validity of his incumbrance is not disputed, he need not be a party to a bill by a second mortgagee. *Hagan* vs. *Walker*, 14 How., 37.

Subsequent lien creditors are not necessary parties to a bill of foreclosure. *Brewster* vs. *Wakefield*, 22 How., 118.

When a sale of mortgaged property was made under proceedings in insolvency, and the heirs of the insolvent filed a bill to set aside the sale for irregularity, the mortgagors, who had received their share of the purchase money, were held to be necessary parties. *Coiron* vs. *Millaudon*, 19 How., 113.

When mortgaged real property is conveyed to a trustee for the benefit of children in being and to be born, the children *in esse* at the time of the filing of the bill of foreclosure should be made parties; if they are not, they do not lose their right to redeem by the decree of foreclosure. *Clark* vs. *Reyburn*, 8 Wal., 318.

When there were several successive mortgages on a railroad, it was held that the suit might be maintained by one suing on behalf of all the holders under the several mortgages. *Galveston R. R.* vs. *Cowdry*, 11 Wal., 478.

When suit is for the purpose of foreclosing a mortgage on part of a railroad, parties to a mortgage on another part are not necessary parties. *Bronson* vs. *Railroad Co.*, 2 Bl., 524.

A majority of the stockholders and creditors of a railroad company which had several mortgages on the road agreed to sell for a price offered, and to divide the proceeds among all the stockholders and creditors in a way settled on by those agreeing to the plan. Other stockholders and creditors refusing to agree, in order to get around their opposition, a sale was effected through the action of the majority by an amicable foreclosure of mortgage, the trustees in one of the mortgages being complainants, and those in the other mortgages, with the corporation whose road was intended to be sold, the defendants. The dissatisfied stockholders and bondholders then filed a bill against the purchaser and the railroad corporation whose road had been sold, *but not making any of the trustees or any of the consenting stockholders parties*, charging collusion in this sale, and praying that it might be set aside, a resale made, and the money arising from the sale be applied primarily to their benefit. *Held*, that the bill was fatally defective for want of proper parties. *Robin* vs. *R. R. Companies*, 16 Wal. 446.

44. *Nuisances.* A public nuisance may be abated on a bill in equity, brought by a private party who has suffered special damage; and it is necessary for the plaintiff in such a bill to show that he has sustained and is still sustaining individual injury by the nuisance. *Miss. & Misso. R. R. Co.* vs. *Ward*, 2 Black 484.[3] If

---

[3] It is not necessary in such case to show that the plaintiff's damage amounts to the sum required to give the United States Court jurisdiction: The jurisdic-

the private party has partners in the particular business affected by the nuisance he need not join them as plaintiffs, any more than he need join other persons who have suffered similar injuries. *Ibid.*

45. *Partition suits.* Part owners or tenants in common in real estate of which partition is asked in equity have an interest in the subject matter of the suit and in the relief sought, so intimately connected with that of their cotenants, that if these cannot be subjected to the jurisdiction of the court, the bill will be dismissed. *Barney* vs. *Baltimore City*, 6 Wal., 280. See *Coy* vs. *Mason*, 17 How., 580, and *Thompson* vs. *Tolmie*, 2 Pet., 157.

46. *Partnership.* See *Nelson* vs. *Hill*, 5 How., 127, cited, *ante*, p. 732; *Bank* vs. *Carrolton R. Road*, 11 Wal., 624. See "Joint interests and obligations."

Where a complainant sued as an administrator of a deceased partner, praying an account of the partnership concerns, alleges in his bill that he is the sole heir of the deceased partner, the fact that he is not so, does not make the bill abate for want of necessary parties, since a decree in his favour as administrator would not interfere with the rights of others who might claim a distribution after the complainant received the money decreed to him. *Moore* vs. *Huntington*, 17 Wal., 417.

See Story's Eq. Pl., §§ 78, 167, 178, 667–669, 673.

Where the surviving partner of an insolvent firm assigned certain lots of ground belonging to the firm for the benefit of its creditors, the heirs of the deceased partner cannot be made parties to a suit involving the title to the lots, on the ground of any relation of trust or confidence subsisting between them and the assignee. *Rothwell* vs. *Dewees*, 2 Black., 613.

47. *Purchaser.* A married woman as trustee conveyed without her husband joining in the deed; a suit was brought against her heirs to quiet the title. It was held that the *cestui que trust* was not a necessary party. *Gridley* vs. *Winant*, 23 How., 500.

When the object is to divest a *feme covert* or minor of an interest in real estate, the title to which is in a trustee for her use, the trust being an active one, it is error to decree against her without making the trustee a party to the suit. *O'Hara & als* vs. *McConnell & als*, 3 Otto, 150.

48. *Purchaser pendente lite.* A court of equity is not bound to take notice of an interest voluntarily acquired in the subject matter of the suit *pendente lite*. *Mech. B'k Alex.* vs. *Seton*, 1 Pet., 299; Story's Eq. Pl. §§ 156, 351. When the assignment is by operation of law, the rule is different. *Ibid*, § 158a. *Lowry* vs. *Morrison*, 11 Paige, 327.

---

tion is tested by the value of the object to be gained by the bill, and that object is the removal of the nuisance. *Miss. & Misso. R. R. Co.* vs. *Ward*, 2 Black, 484.

49. *Petitions for rehearing, bills of review, &c.* See §§ 622–628, 637–638. *ante.* See *Thomas* vs. *Harvie*, 10 Wheat., 146, *Whiting* vs. *B'k U S*, 13 Pet., 6.

50. *Religious associations.* A portion of the members of a voluntary religious association may sue in behalf of themselves and others having the like interests as part of the same society for purposes common to all and beneficial to all. *Beatty* vs. *Kintz*, 2 Pet., 566; *Smith* vs. *Swornstedt* 16 How., 288.

50a. *Specific performance.* In a suit by the vendees for specific performance or indemnification, all the co-heirs of the deceased vendor must be made parties. *Morgan's heirs* vs. *Morgan*, 2 Wheat, 290.

To a bill for specific performance, the vendor is a necessary party, though he has conveyed all his title to the other defendants. *Findlay* vs. *Hinde*, 1 Pet., 241.

Whether a sub-purchaser of part of the land from the vendee be a necessary party or not to a suit against the vendor for specific performance, his joinder, under circumstances, which had no practical effect on the vendor's rights, cannot be objected to by him. *Taylor* vs. *Longworth*, 14 Pet., 172. See Story's Eq. Pl., § 351a.

To a bill by purchasers from a judgment debtor in which they sought to set aside the legal title of a purchaser at a sheriff's sale on the ground that the judgment was satisfied before the levy, both the judgment debtor and creditor are necessary parties. *Field* vs. *Holland*, 6 Cranch, 24.

In general, the original parties to the contract are the proper parties to a suit to compel the specific performance; and the fact that the complainant has made an assignment of a partial interest in the contract (although before filing his bill) to a person who does not join in the suit, is no defence to the bill. *Willard* vs. *Tayloe*, 8 Wal. 557. Mr. Justice Field said in this case; "Except in the case of an assignment of the entire contract there must be some special circumstances to authorize a departure from the rule" [that the parties to the original contract are the only proper parties to the suit for specific performance]. *Ibid.*

Creditors of the vendor who recovered judgments and sold the property, pending a suit for specific performance in which the purchase money had been paid into court, are not necessary parties to the suit, nor are the purchasers at the sheriff's sale under such judgments. *Secombe & als* vs. *Slute*, 20 How. 94.

Parties to a suit to compel specific performance of a contract for the exchange of lands lying in different States In a suit demanding the specific performance of a contract, by conveying lands in the State of Ohio, stipulated to be conveyed as the consideration for other lands sold in the State of Kentucky, or, in lieu thereof, requiring indemnification by the payment of money; it was held that all the co-heirs of the vendor, deceased, ought to be made parties to the bill, and that the death of one of the heirs ought to be proved, in order to excuse his omission as a party to the bill. *Morgan's heirs* vs. *Morgan & als.*, 2 Wh. 290.

51. *Sureties.* Where money was borrowed from a bank upon a promissory note signed by the principal and two sureties, and the principal debtor, by way of counter security, conveyed certain property to a trustee, for the purpose of indemnifying his sureties, it was necessary to make the trustee and the *cestui que trust* parties to a bill filed by the bank, asserting a special lien upon the property thus conveyed. *McRea & als.* vs. *Branch B'k Ala.*, 19 How., 376.

52. *Trusts.* The general rule is, that in suits respecting trust property, brought either by or against the trustees, the *cestuis que trust,* as well as the trustees, are necessary parties. *Swayne,* J., in *Carey & als.* vs. *Brown,* 2 Otto., 172.

When land is conveyed in trust to secure a debt, the trustee and grantor are necessary parties to enforce the trust, but they are not necessary parties to set aside a fraudulent conveyance by the debtor; in such case, a bill against his administrators may be sustained to bring such property into a course of administration. *McRea* vs. *Branch B'k Alex.*, 19 How., 376.

When a suit is brought by a trustee to recover the trust property or reduce it to possession and in no wise affects his relations with his *cestuis que trust,* it is unnecessary to make *cestuis que trust* parties. *Carey & als* vs. *Brown,* 2 Otto, 171 ; see *Story* vs. *Livingston,* 13 Pet., 359.

In suit against a trustee invested with such powers and subjected to such obligations that his beneficiaries are bound by what is done against him or by him, the beneficiaries are not necessary parties. *Kerrison* vs. *Stewart & als,* 3 Otto, 155.

In a bill to divest a *feme covert* or minor of an interest in real estate, the title to which is in a trustee for her use, the trust being an active one, her trustee is a necessary party. *O'Hara & als* vs. *McConnell & als,* 3 Otto, 150.

To a suit to enforce the trusts of a will the residuary legatees are not generally necessary parties ; their interests are represented by the executors. *Danridge* vs. *Custis,* 2 Pet., 370. See *Hopkirk* vs. *Page,* 2 Brock., 20.

A surviving trustee, under a decree of a court of equity, reconveyed the trust property to the heirs of the grantor and died; his representatives were held to be not necessary parties to a suit to enforce a claim upon the trust estate. *McCall* vs. *Harrison,* 1 Brock., 126.

To a bill by a bona fide purchaser from a trustee, who being a *feme covert* had conveyed without her husband joining in the deed, against her heirs to quiet the title, the *cestui que trust* is not a necessary party. *Gridley* vs. *Winant,* 23 How., 500.

See 49th, 50th and 51st Rules Sup. Ct., Story's Eq. Pl., § 150, n. 5.

53. *Vendor's lien.* If the purchaser from a vendee be dead, leaving a widow his executrix, and héirs at law to whom with her his real estate has descended, the heirs ought to be made parties defendant to any bill to foreclose. *Lewis* vs. *Hawkins*, 13 Wal., 119.

III.

Complete Form of Record as made by clerk for appeal to an appellate court.

Virginia: Pleas before the honorable W. S. B., judge of the Circuit Court of the County of Hanover, on the —— day of ——. Be it remembered that heretofore, to-wit: At a Circuit Court of the county of Hanover, held at Hanover Court-house on the—— day of ——. (Here the clerk copies the first entry found on page 550, *ante*.)

Which bill and answers are in the words and figures following, to-wit: (Here the clerk copies the bill and answers on pages 548–550, *ante*.)

And afterwards, to-wit: on the —— day of ——, 18—, the commissioner, Alexander Stuart, filed his report, which report, together, with the depositions and papers therewith returned, is in the words and figures following, to-wit: (Here the clerk copies the notice, commissioner's report and depositions found on pp. 551–553, *ante*.)

And at another day, to-wit: At a Circuit Court of the county of Hanover, held at Hanover Court-house on the—— day of ——, 18—. (Here the clerk copies the decree on p. 554.)

And afterwards, to-wit: On the —— day of ——, 18—, the commissioner, William W., returned and filed his report of sale and other papers, which report and the papers therewith returned are in the words and figures following, to-wit: (Here the clerk copies the report of sale and accompanying papers—pp. 555–557, *ante*.)

And at another day, to-wit: At a Circuit Court of the county of Hanover, held at Hanover Court-house on the —— day of ——, 18—. (Here the clerk copies the decree on pp. 557–558. *ante*.)

And at another day, to wit: At a Circuit Court of the county of Hanover, held at Hanover Court-house on the —— day of ——, 18—. (Here the clerk copies the entry beginning on p. 558.)

And at another day, to-wit: At a Circuit Court of the county of Hanover, held at Hanover Court-house on the —— day of ——, 18—. (Here the clerk copies the entry "taking time to consider" on page 559.)

The following are copies of the return, answer, affidavits and exceptions referred to in the foregoing order: (Here the clerk copies these papers as found on pp. 562–563 and 564, *ante*.)

And now at this day, to wit: At a Circuit Court of the county of Hanover, held at Hanover Court-house on the —— day of ——, 18—. (Here the clerk copies the decree on pp. 559–562, *ante*.)

A true transcript of the record.

Teste:

J. A. B. *Clerk.*

Form of Record, in which Suit Matured by service of Summons, filing Answers at Rules, &c.

Virginia: Pleas before the honorable W. S. B., Judge of the Circuit Court of the county of Hanover, on the —— day of ——, 18—.

Be it remembered that heretofore, to wit: on the —— day of ——, 18—, came J. R. B. and sued out of the clerk's office his writ of summons in equity against L. L. and others, which writ with the returns of service thereon is in the words and figures following, to wit: [here the clerk copies writ and returns.]

And afterwards, to wit: At rules held in the clerk's office of the said court for the month of —— in the year 18—, came the plaintiff and filed his bill which bill and exhibits therewith filed are in the words and figures following, to wit: [here the clerk copies the bill and exhibits.]

And at the same rules, to wit: L. L appeared and filed his answer to the said bill and the plaintiff replied generally to the said answer, and the cause is set for hearing as to the said L. L. on his said answer and replication. The said answer and exhibits therewith filed are in the words and figures following, to wit: [here the clerk copies the answers and exhibits.]

And at the same rules, to wit: At rules held in the clerk's office of the said court for the month of ——, 18—, on motion of the plaintiff D. X., the clerk of this court is assigned guardian *ad litem* to the infant defendant O. P. to defend his interests in this suit, and thereupon the said guardian *ad litem* filed his own answer and the answer of the infant defendant O. P by himself as guardian *ad litem*, and the plaintiff replied generally to the same, and on his motion the cause was set for hearing on the said answer and replication as to the said infant defendant.

And at the same rules, to wit: At rules held in the clerk's office of the said court for the month of ——. 18—, the writ of summons issued in this cause having been duly served on the defendant, Catharine D., and the bill of the plaintiff having been filed, and the said C. D. still failing, &c., (as on p. 128, *ante*.)

And afterwards, to-wit: At rules held in the clerk's office of the said court for the month of ——, 18—, the defendant, Catharine D., not yet having appeared and pleaded, answered or demurred to the plaintiff's bill, the same is taken for confessed as to the said defendant, and the cause is set for hearing as to her.

And afterwards, to-wit: On the —— day of ——, 18—, the following depositions were filed: [Here the clerk copies the depositions.]

And at another day, to wit: At a Circuit Court of the county of Hanover, held at Hanover Courthouse on the —— day of ——. (Names of parties.) This cause came on this day to be heard on the bill taken for confessed as to the defendant Catharine D., and set for hearing as to her on such confession, on the answer of the defendant L. L. and on the answer of the infant defendant by D. X, his guardian *ad litem*, and the answer of the said guardian *ad litem*. and replications to said several answers, and on the exhibits and examinations of witnesses, and was argued by counsel: On consideration whereof, &c., &c (Here follows the order or decree entered).

[The subsequent proceedings may be recited as in previous form of record, p. 743, *ante*, to the last decree appealed from.]

A true transcript of the record.

Teste:

B. H. B., Clerk.

IV.

Amendments to Code of 1873, made in subsequent Session Acts, affecting Equity practice in the Virginia State Courts.

Code 1873, chap. 12, sec. 6, amended by Sess. Acts 1874–5, p. 53.

Code 1873, chap. 76, sec. 13, amended by Sess. Acts 1878–9, pp. 161, 347–8.

Code 1873, chap. 105, sec. 1, amended by Sess. Acts 1878–9, p. 207.

Code 1873, chap, 112, sec. 6, amended by Sess. Acts 1876–7, p, 213. See Sess. Acts 1877–8, p. 239.

Code 1873, chap. 114, sec. 5, amended by Sess. Acts 1876–7, pp. 34, 35, 357.

Code 1873, chap. 115, sec. 4, amended *last* by Sess. Acts 1879–80, p. 38.

Code 1873, chap. 115, sec. 5, amended *last* by Sess. Acts 1874–5, p. 437.

Code 1873, chap. 115, sec. 13, amended by Sess. Acts 1878–9, p. 178.

Code 1873, chap. 118, sec. 37, amended by Sess. Acts 1875–6, p. 109.

Code 1873, chap. 122, sec. 8, amended by Sess. Acts 1875–6, p. 267.

Code 1873, chap. 123, sec. 6, amended by Sess. Acts 1875–6, p. 211.

Code 1873, chap. 123, sec. 7, see in connection Sess. Acts 1877–8, pp. 247, 248.

Code 1873, chap. 123, sec. 13, amended by Sess. Acts 1874, p. 133. See also p. 224.

Code 1873, chap. 155, sec. 6, amended by Sess. Acts 1874, p. 224.

Code 1873, chap. 126, sec. 25, amended by Sess. Acts 1879–80, pp. 146–147.

Code 1873, chap. 128, secs. 11, 12, amended *last* by Sess. Acts 1877–8, pp. 67, 68.

Code 1873, chap. 128, sec. 16, amended *last* by Sess. Acts 1875–6, p. 53.

Code 1873, chap. 128, sec. 18, amended by Sess. Acts 1877–8, p. 157.

Code 1873, chap. 137, secs. 4, 5, 6, 7, 8, amended by Sess. Acts 1874, pp. 134, 135.

Code 1873, chap. 137, sec. 10, repealed by Sess. Acts 1874, p. 135.

Code 1873, chap. 141, sec. 5, amended last by Sess. Acts 1876–7, p. 28.

Code 1873, chap. 141, secs. 7, 8, amended by Sess. Acts 1878–9, pp. 379, 380.

Code 1873, chap. 141, sec. 11, amended by Sess. Acts, 1875–6, p. 263.

Code 1873, chap. 143, amended and re-enacted by Sess. Acts 1877–8, pp. 218–220.

Code 1873, chap. 146, sec. 9, amended by Sess. Acts 1877–8, p. 221.

Code 1873, chap. 146, sec. 20, amended by Sess. Acts, 1874, p. 69.

Code 1873, chap. 148, sec. 5, amended last by Sess. Acts 1877–8, p. 217.

Code 1873, chap. 149, sec. 7, amended by Sess. Acts 1877–8, pp. 185, 186.

Code 1873, chap. 155, sec. 14, amended by Sess. Acts 1874–5, p. 12.

Code 1873, chap. 155, sec. 15, repealed by Sess. Acts 1874, p. 151.

Code 1873, chap. 155, sec. 21, amended by Sess. Acts 1874–5, pp. 8, 9.

Code 1873, chap. 157, sec. 20, added by Sess. Acts 1874–5, pp. 19, 20.

Code 1873, chap. 157, sec. 21, added by Sess. Acts 1874, p. 17.

Code 1873, chap. 166, sec. 10, amended by Sess. Acts 1876–7, p. 274.

Code 1873, chap 167, sec. 33, amended by Sess. Acts 1875–6, p. 209.

Code 1873, chap. 169, sec. 2, amended by Sess. Acts 1875–6, p. 11.

Code 1873, chap. 170, secs. 1, 2, amended last by Sess. Acts 1878–9, p. 24.

Code 1873, chap. 171, sec. 2, amended last by Sess. Acts 1878–9, p. 21.

Code 1873, chap. 172, sec. 5, amended by Sess. Acts 1879–80, p. 185.

Code 1873, chap. 172, sec. 21. See Sess. Acts 1876–7, p. 265.

Code 1873, chap. 172, sec. 22, amended by Sess. Acts 1876–7, pp. 265–6, 184–5.

Code 1873, chap. 172, sec. 36; amended by Sess. Acts 1874–5, p. 139.

Code 1873, chap. 174, sec. 8, amended by Sess. Acts 1874–5, p. 423.

Code 1873, chap. 175, sec. 1, amended by Sess. Acts 1877–8, p. 247.

Code 1873, chap. 175, sec. 10, amended by Sess. Acts 1874–5, p. 33.

Code 1873, chap. 178, sec. 1, amended by Sess. Acts 1878–9, p. 381–2.

Code 1873, chap. 178, sec. 6, amended by Sess. Acts 1876–7, pp 70–71.

Code 1873, chap. 178, sec. 17, amended by Sess. Acts 1876–7, pp. 30–31.

Code 1873, chap. 182, sec. 4, amended last by Sess. Acts 1877–8, pp. 92–94.

Code 1873, chap. 182, sec. 9, amended by Sess. Acts 1877–8, pp. 68–69.

Code 1873, chap. 185, sec. 1, amended by Sess. Acts 1877–8, pp. 211–212.

Here follow these amendments, arranged alphabetically, according to the subjects of the statutes:

APPEALS, when granted, Code 1873, chap. 178, sec. 1, amended by Sess. Acts 1878–9, pp. 381, 382.

———, record exhibited with petition of, Code 1873, chap. 178, sec. 6, amended by Sess. Acts 1876–7, pp. 70–1.

———, limitation of, Code 1873, chap. 178, sec. 17, amended by Sess. Acts 1876–7, pp. 30–31.

APPRENTICES, with form of indenture, Code 1873, chap. 122, sec. 8, amended by Sess. Acts 1875–6, p. 267.

ATTACHMENTS against vessels, Code 1873, chap. 148, sec. 5, amended by Sess. Acts 1877–8, p. 217.

BENEVOLENT ASSOCIATIONS, sale of property, &c., Code 1873, chap. 76, sec. 13, amended by Sess. Acts 1878–9, pp. 161, 347–8.

BILLS AND NOTES, Code 1873, chap. 141, sec. 5, amended by Sess. Acts 1876–7, p. 28.

———, Code 1873, chap. 141, sections 7, 8, amended by Sess. Acts 1878–9, pp. 379, 380.

———, Code 1873, chap. 141, sec. 11, amended by Sess. Acts 1875–6, p. 263.

BONDS, taken by courts, Code 1873, chap. 12, sec. 6, amended by Sess. Acts 1874–5, p. 53.

———, *Forthcoming*, Code 1873, chap. 185, sec. 1, amended by Sess. Acts 1877–8, pp. 211, 212.

———, *Mechanics*, Code 1873, chap. 115, sec. 5, amended last·by Sess. Acts 1874–5, p. 437.

———. See *Judgment Liens.*

LIMITATION OF SUITS, Code 1873, chap. 146,.sec. 20, amended by Sess. Acts 1874, p. 69.

MARRIED WOMEN'S ACTS. Act March 31, 1875, in Sess. Acts 1874–5,. p. 442; act February 10, 1876, in Sess. Acts 1875–6, p. 49; act April 4, 1877, in Sess. Acts 1876–7, p. 333; act March 14, 1878, in Sess. Acts 1877–8, p. 247.

MECHANICS' LIENS. See *Liens of Mechanics.*

MONEY·AND INTEREST. Code 1873, chap. 137, sections 4, 5, 6, 7 and 8,. amended by Sess. Acts 1874, pp. 134, 135.

———. Code 1873, chap. 137, sec. 10, repealed by Sess. Acts 1874, p. 135.

NOTICE, &c., FOR TAKING DEPOSITION. Code 1873, chap. 172, sec. 36, amended by Sess. Acts 1874–5, p. 139.

ORDER OF PUBLICATION. Code 1873, chap. 166, sec. 10' amended by Sess. Acts 1876–7, p. 274.[1]

PARTIES. See *Death or change of parties.*

PERSONAL REPRESENTATIVE. Code 1873, chap. 126, sec. 25, amended by Sess. Acts 1879–80, pp. 146, 147.

POOR DEBTORS' DEEDS. Code 1873, chap. 112, sec 6, amended by Sess. Acts 1876–7, p. 213. See Sess. Acts 1877–8, p. 239.

REMOVAL, *of causes.* Code 1873, chap. 170, secs. 1, 2, amended by Sess. Acts 1878–9, p. 24.

———, *of judges from, &c.* Code 1873, chap. 157, sec. 20, added by Sess. Acts 1874–5, pp. 19, 20.

Notice that to Code, chap. 157, sec. 21 is added in Sess. Acts 1874, p. 17.

STATE. See *Transferring effects out of.*

SURETIES, *relief of,* Code 1873, chap. 143, amended and re-enacted in Sess. Acts 1877–8, pp. 218, 220.

SUSPENDING BONDS. See *bonds.*

TERMS OF COURTS, Code 1873, chap. 155, sec- 14, amended by Sess. Acts 1874–5, p. 12.

———, *Special, causes tried at,* Code 1873, chap. 155, sec. 21, amended by Sess. Acts 1874–5, pp. 8, 9.

TIMES OF HOLDING CIRCUIT COURT. Code 1873, chap. 155, sec. 15,. repealed by Sess. Acts 1874, p. 151.

TRANSFERRING EFFECTS OUT OF STATE. See Code 1873, chap. 125, sec. 3, and Sess. Acts 1874, p. 224.

---

[1] This amendment to the section, as published on pages 115, 116 ante, is as follows:

§ 10. On affidavit that a defendant is not a resident of this State, or that diligence has been used by or on behalf of the plaintiff to ascertain in what county or corporation he is, without effect, or that process directed to the officer of the county or corporation in which he resides, or is, has been twice delivered to such officer more than ten days before the return day, and been returned without being executed; or that the defendant in a suit for a divorce from the bond of matrimony is under sentence to confinement in the penitentiary, an order of publication may be entered against such defendant. And in any suit in equity where the bill states that the names of any person interested in the subject to be divided or disposed of are unknown, and makes such persons defendants by the general description of parties unknown, on affidavit of the fact that the said parties are unknown, an order of publication may be entered against such unknown parties. And in any suit in equity in which the number of defendants, upon whom process has been executed, exceed thirty, in which it appears to the court by the bill or other pleading or exhibits filed, that the parties before the court represent interests like the interests of those not served with process, an order of publication may be entered against such persons. Any order under this section may be entered either in court, or by the clerk of the court, at any time in vacation, except in cases in which the number of parties exceeds the number of thirty as aforesaid. In a proceeding by petition, there may be an order of publication in like manner as in a suit in equity.

USURY. See *Money and Interest.*
WITNESSES, *competency of,* Code 1873, chap. 172, sec. 21. See Sess. Acts 1876-7, p. 265.
————, *competency of,* Code 1873, chap. 172, sec. 22, amended by Sess. Acts 1876-7, pp. 265, 266.
WILLS, Code 1873, chap. 118, sec. 37, amended by Sess. Acts 1875-6, p. 109.

V.

Additional cases on Parties to suits in the Virginia State Courts.

Parties to suits concerning assets and administration of estates. *Wernick* vs. *McMurdo,* 5 Rand., 51; *Heffernan* vs. *Grymes,* 2 Leigh, 512; *Clarke* vs. *Well's adm'r,* 6 Grat., 474; *Morris's adm'r* vs. *Morris's adm'r & als.,* 4 Grat., 294, as to what assets are administered, and whether an administrator *de bonis non* can sue an administrator. Whether curator may be sued by administrator *de bonis non* see *Halsey & als.* vs. *Craig's adm'or & als.,* 23 Grat., 716.

Tunstall vs. *Pollard,* 11 Leigh, 1; *Andrews* vs. *Avory,* 14 Grat., 239; *Powell* vs. *Stratton,* 11 Grat., 792, administrator qualifying in another State bringing assets into this.

Kinker, &c., vs. *Streit,* 33 Grat., 663, foreign guardian coming into this State.

Sheldon vs. *Armistead,* 7 Grat., 264; *Sillings* vs. *Bumgardner,* 9 Grat., 273, suits by legatees or distributees against administrator and other legatees or distributees.

. *Mann* vs. *Flinn,* 10 Leigh, 93, opinion of Stanard, J., creditor suing representative of deceased executor. See *Moore* vs. *George,* 10 Leigh, 228, 244; *Chamberlayne* vs. *Temple,* 2 Rand., 384.

Married woman administratrix, 2 Lom. Ex., p. 815 (marg. 519) should be read in connection with the provision of the statute, Code 1873, ch. 126, § 9.

Parties to suits concerning creditors. Creditors' bill, though not filed as such. *Ewing's adm'or* vs. *Ferguson's adm'or & als.,* 33 Grat., 548.

Simmons vs. *Lyles & als.,* 27 Grat., 928, after a decree for a general account in suit against a decedent's estate, even by a single creditor, all the other creditors may prove their debts before the commissioner, and they are all treated as parties to the suit.

Shand's ex'ix vs. *Grove & als.,* 26 Grat., 229, suit in equity against garnishee on judgment against him without making original debtor a party.

Barger vs. *Buckland & als.,* 28 Grat., 850, trustee not signing, and out of State, not made a party.

Parties to suits concerning assignors and assignees. Whether and
when assignor a necessary party. Corbin vs. *Emerson,* 10 Leigh,
668, explained in *Littlejohn* vs. *Ferguson,* 18 Grat., 83 ; *New-*
man vs. *Chapman,* 2 Rand., 93 ; *Tichenor* vs. *Allen,* 13 Grat., 15 ;
Auditor vs. *Johnston's ex'ors,* 1 H. & M., 541. See Bart. Ch. Pr.,.
164.

See *Jeffress* vs. *Clark & als,* Va. L. J., 1881, p. 521.

Parties to suits concerning bankrupts and assignees. Barger vs.
Buckland, 28 Grat., 862.

Parties to suits concerning corporations. Officers made parties.
B. & O. R. R. Co. vs. *City of Wheeling,* 13 Grat., 61. Officer
suing ; suit by members of a voluntary association ; suit by an un-
chartered banking company. *Coffman* vs. *Sangston & als,* 21
Grat., 263 ; *Berkshire* vs. *Evans & als,* 4 Leigh, 223.

Successor of a corporation sued by one creditor without making
his co-creditors parties ; or making parties the creditors of H, to
whom the successor of the first corporation had contracted to pay
an annual rent. *Barksdale* vs. *Finney,* 14 Grat., 328.

Parties to suits concerning foreclosure of trust or mortgage. Rey-
nolds vs. *Bank of Va.,* 6 Grat., 81 ; *Price* vs. *Thrash,* 30 Grat.,
515 ; *Hortons* vs. *Bond,* 28 Grat., 815 ; *McDearman's ex'ors* vs.
Robinson, Va. L. J., 1879, p. 175.

Heirs as Parties. As to them, what the effect of a judgment or
decree against personal representative. *Street* vs. *Street,* 11 Leigh,
498 ; *Pugh* vs. *Russell,* 27 Grat., 789 ; *Mason's devisees* vs. *Peters'*
adm'r, 1 Munf., 437 ; *Shields's adm'r* vs. *Anderson's adm'r,* 3
Leigh, 729, 736 ; *Foster* vs. *Crenshaw's ex'ors,* 3 Munf. 520 ; *Hud-*
gins vs. *Hudgins,* 6 Grat., 320 ; *Robertson and others* vs. *Wright,*
17 Grat., 534, 540.

Husband and wife as parties.. Harrison vs. *Gibson,* 23 Grat.,
212 ; *Spencer* vs. *Ford,* 1 Rob., 684.

Parties to suits concerning class. Bull vs. *Read.* 13 Grat., 86.
Some inhabitants of a district may file a bill in behalf of themselves and other inhabitants similarly situated seeking any relief
to which they might all in common be justly entitled, although
their individual interests might be several and distinct.

Parties to interpleader suits. How long plaintiff in interpleader
a party to the suit. *George* vs. *Pilcher,* 28 Grat., 305.

Next friend, guardian ad litem, committee, &c., of parties. Wilson, &c. vs. *Smith*, 22 Grat., 494 : whether next friend for the infant in this case.

Beverley vs. *Miller*, 6 Munf., 99 : answer of a mother, who was guardian, and who made full defence to suit, treated as the answer of a regularly appointed guardian *ad litem* to the infant.

Campbells vs. *Bowen's adm'or, &c.*, 1 Rob., 241, as to appointment of guardian *ad litem* to an alleged insane defendant, insanity denied.

Lemon vs. *Hansbarger*, 6 *Grat.*: 301, suit by infants by next friend against former guardian, &c.; present guardian as such no right to sue former guardian.

Durrett vs. *Davis & als.*, 24 Grat., 310 : answer treated as answer of guardian *ad litem* who signed it, though purporting to be the answer of the infant by his guardian *ad litem.*[1]

Cole's Committee vs. *Cole's adm'or*, 28 Grat., 370, treated as a suit by the committee, the bill stating that "the complainant, C, who, being a person of unsound mind, sues by his next friend and committee, A."

Parties in Partition suits. The cases of *McClintic* vs. *Mann*, 4 Munf., 328, and *Custis* vs. *Snead & als.*, 12 Grat. 264, are not in conflict. See those cases cited on pp. 65–66, *ante.*

Parker vs. *McCoy*, 10 Grat., 594, cited p. 687, ante, has reference to the sale of lands of infants in proceedings for partition, under the act 1 R. C., ch. 96, sec. 20, Supp. R. C., ch. 149, sec. 2.

Parties to suits concerning Partnership. Cannon & als. vs. *Welford, Judge*, 22 Grat., 195, as to whether assignee in bankruptcy of firm or assignees of each partner should be the plaintiffs, when both the firm and each partner had been adjudicated bankrupts.

Parties to suits concerning Purchasers. Purchasers of interest pending suit when to file a petition. *Price* vs. *Thrash*, 30 Grat., 515. When assignee in bankruptcy pending the suit to file a petition. *Bar, assignee*, vs. *White & als.*, 30 Grat., 543.

The purchaser in *Chowning* vs. *Cox*, 1 Rand., 148, required to be made a party.[2]

---

[1] In this case the decree reciting that the cause came on to be heard on the answer of the guardian *ad litem*, the court presumed that the answer was sworn to though no evidence of the fact in the record.

[2] In *Chowning* vs. *Cox & als.*, 1 Rand., 306, recognized and followed in *Breckenridge* vs. *Auld & als.*, 1 Rob., 148, and distinguished from *Floyd* vs. *Harrison, &c.*, 2 Rob., 161, the court held that a deed executed by a debtor conveying land to his creditor and purporting to constitute him a trustee for selling the land and applying the proceeds of sale to his debt, was a mortgage to which the right of redemption was incident.

Purchasers at judicial sales. As to purchasers at judicial sales; whether parties. *Londons* vs. *Echols & als,* 17 Grat., 19 ; *Pierce* vs. *Trigg,* 10 Leigh, 406; *Huston* vs. *Cantril,* 11 Leigh, 136; *Parker* vs. *McCoy,* 10 Grat., 594 ; *Buchanan* vs. *Clark,* 10 Grat., 164 ; *Hughes, &c.,* vs. *Johnston,* 12 Grat., 479 ; *Cocke's adm'r* vs. *Gilpin,* 1 Rob. R., 26 ; *Rogers* vs. *McCluer's adm'r,* 4 Grat., 81. What their responsibilities and rights. *Zirkle* vs. *McCue & als,* 26 Grat., 517, cited p. 554 ; *Hess & als* vs. *Rader & als,* 26 Grat., 746, purchaser paying to a commissioner of sale who has not given the bond as such does it at his peril; he must see that the bond has been given before he pays; *Durrett* vs. *Davis,* 24 Grat., 302, cited p. 561; *Cooper* vs. *Hepburn,* 15 Grat., 551, cited p. 554; *Lloyd* vs. *Erwin's adm'r,* 29 Grat, 598, cited p. 556 ; *Tyler* vs. *Thoms,* V. L. J., 1881, p. 621, cited p. 556 ; *Threlkelds* vs. *Campbell,* 2 Grat. 198; *Young* vs. *McClung & als,* 9 Grat., 336 ; *Daniel* vs. *Leitch,* 13 Grat., 195; *Watson* vs. *Hoy & als,*[3] Va. Law J., 1877, p. 473, 28 Grat. 698, cited p. 559; *Long* vs. *Weller's ex'or & als,* 29 Grat., 348, cited pp. 560, 561 ; *Clarkson* vs. *Read & als,* 15 Grat., 297, cited p. 560, and *Michie* vs. *Jeffries & als,* 21 Grat. 334, cited p. 561, and *Thornton* vs. *Fairfax & als,* 29 Grat., 669.

Representation—when persons interested represented sufficiently by others. See *Buck* vs. *Pennybacker's ex'ors,* 4 Leigh, 5.

Parties to suits concerning resulting trusts. Phelps vs. *Seely, &c.,* 22 Grat., 573, to set up resulting trust by parol testimony it must be clear and unquestionable, and *Borst* vs. *Nalle & als,* 28 Grat., 423, a resulting or implied trust may be established by parol evidence.

Parties to suits concerning sureties. Craighton vs. *Duval,* 3 Call, 74, right of sureties to compel payment of bond by principal, and to compel creditor to receive payment.

Parties to suits concerning tenants. Winchester and Strasburg R. R. Co vs. *Colfret & als,* 27 Grat., 777.

Parties to suits concerning trusts. Hogan vs. *Duke & als,* 20 Grat., 244.

Parties to suits concerning wills. Kincheloe vs. *Kincheloe,* 11 Leigh, 400, validity of will not affirmed unless all persons concerned in interest before the court; *Osborne & als* vs. *Taylor's adm'r & als,* 12 Grat., 117, for the construction of a will affecting the residuum of an estate, all persons having an interest or color of interest in the residuum should be parties.

---

[3] But see *Thompson & als* vs. *Brooke & als.,* 6 Va. L. J., 42, when bond is given by one of two commissioners and payment is made to both commissioners.

VI.

Additional cases on Dower.

Of what widow endowed. Medley vs. Medley, Jones vs. Hughes.
Reference has already been made, p. 579, *ante,* to *Medley* vs *Medley,* 27 Grat., 568, and to *Jones* vs. *Hughes,* 27 Grat., 560. In these cases it was held that the widow of one holding an estate in ·fee defeasible upon his dying without issue, though he die without issue, was entitled to dower in the land.

Whether an alienee of the husband and wife, in such case, could claim the dower estate of the wife after the death of the husband. Corr vs. *Porter.* The cases of *Medley* vs. *Medley* and *Jones* vs. *Hughes, ubi supra,* were distinguishable, the court said, from *Corr* vs. *Porter,* 33 Grat., 278. In *Corr* vs. *Porter,* the alienee of the husband and wife, the husband holding such an estate and dying without issue, leaving his wife surviving, claimed that he was entitled to the dower of the wife as established in *Medley* vs. *Medley* and *Jones* vs. *Hughes.* But the court held that the alienee of the husband and wife did not obtain by their conveyance the wife's dower right which she would have enjoyed but for the conveyance, that such conveyance simply relinquished her contingent right of dower, did not create an estate separate and distinct from the hus· band, and that the title acquired by the alienee was not to *two* es· ·tates or interests, that of the husband and wife, but to *one* estate, that of the husband, discharged of the wife's contingent claim of ·dower.

Dower in Beneficial ownership. Wilson vs. *Davison.* "A legal title in the husband is nothing as regards the wife's right of dower, unless accompanied by the beneficial ownership; and the beneficial ownership is everything though separated from the title." *Baldwin, J.,* in *Wilson* vs. *Davison & als.,* 2 Rob. R. 384.

Waller vs. *Waller.* The Court of Appeals had Judge Baldwin's remark in mind, and cited it when deciding *Waller* vs. *Waller's adm'or & als.,* 33 Grat. 83. Waller, in 1853, before his marriage, sold land to Bigler and took a deed of trust to secure what was to be paid of the purchase money. In 1862, *flagrante bello,* while Bigler was a citizen and resident of the North, Saunders, the trus· tee, was required to sell and Waller purchased, and a deed was made to him. Waller married in 1863. The sale to Waller was

95

afterwards set aside by the U. S. Court, and a decree made directing the land to be sold and the purchase money due Waller to be
paid him. Waller's widow claimed dower. It was held that the
sale to Waller by Saunders, the trustee, was a nullity, and that
the widow was not entitled to dower in the land.

*When a wife's contingent right of dower destroyed. Robinson
vs. Shacklett.* In *Robinson* vs. *Shacklett*, 29 Grat., 99, the wife was
a party to the suit in which the sale of the land was decreed, and
it was held that the wife's contingent right of dower was covered
by the decree.

*Wife's right of dower estopped as to a certain fund in a receiver's
hands. Tilson vs. Davis.* Tilson vs. *Davis*, 32 Grat., 92, was a
creditor's suit against the estate of *the administrator* of the husband. In that suit, the widow filed a petition claiming a share in
the estate of her son, whose guardian the administrator had been,
but making no claim of dower. A final decree was rendered, directing a distribution among the creditors of the administrator's estate by the receiver. *Held*, that this decree was a bar to the subsequent bill of the widow to subject a fund in the receiver's hands
to the payment of her dower interest.

*Wife's claim for dower abating ratably with creditors. Miller
vs. Crawford.* In *Miller* vs. *Crawford*, 32 Grat., 277, the contingent right of dower of the wife of A., was, together with indebtedness to B. and C., secured by a deed from A. and wife, in which the
wife, B. and C. were secured as creditors of the first class of the
husband, they to pay off certain judgments and executions paramount to the deed. The property did not sell for enough to pay
the three in full and one D., who had recovered a judgment. *Held*,
that the wife of A. must abate ratably with B. and C. for the payment of said judgments, &c., and their own claims.

*When wife may claim dower, the settlement upon her having been
set aside. Davis vs. Davis.* In *Davis* vs. *Davis*, 25 Grat. 587,
a settlement was made upon the wife, the consideration for which
was that she united with her husband in conveying away her interest in his real estate. The settlement was set aside. *Held*,
that she should be restored to the rights she had before she united
in the deed conveying the property, as far as this could be done
without prejudice to the rights of creditors or of purchasers.

*Dower not commuted at instance of widow without consent of
other parties. Harrison vs. Payne.* In *Harrison* vs. *Payne*, 32
Grat. 387, it was held that commutation of dower would not be
given the widow unless by consent of all the parties interested,
even though the dower could not be assigned in kind, and must be
satisfied out of the proceeds of sale. She is only entitled to the
interest on one-third of the proceeds of sale. This case settles the
doctrine adversely to the view presented by Mr. Green in the note
printed on pp. 55, 56, *ante*, and adversely to the cases of *Cassa-*

more vs. *Brooke*, 3 Bland. 267, and *McCormick* vs. *Gibson*, 3 Bland. 499, 502*n*, therein cited.

How widow's dower assigned, as against lien creditors of her husband created since her marriage. Simmons vs. *Lyle's adm'or.* It was decided in *Simmons* vs. *Lyle's adm'or*, 27 Grat. 922, that as against creditors of the husband by lien created since her marriage the widow was entitled to have her dower assigned without regard to its effect upon the interest of the creditors; that if from the nature of the property or of the husband's interest in it, the dower could not be assigned in kind, the court might sell the whole property and make her a moneyed compensation. It was error in such case to decree a sale of the land until the widow's dower had been assigned her or it was ascertained that it could not be; and, in the latter event, until the money compensation in lieu of her dower had been ascertained.

Simmons vs. *Lyle's adm'or*, 32 Grat. 752. The widow occupied the mansion, having with her her two infant children, whom she supported, and no assignment of dower was made to her. She paid a balance of the purchase money due for the property and secured by the vendor's lien; and she paid the taxes due upon the property. As against the judgment creditors of her late husband it was held—1. That she was entitled to amount of taxes. 2. To so much of the purchase money paid by her as was properly payable by the heirs, and this should be a prior lien to the creditors. 3. Having held the mansion house, and the heirs being infants unable to assign dower, she must be considered as holding as to one-third of the house as dowress and liable to pay one-third of the rest of the purchase money during her life. 4. It becoming necessary to sell the property, and therefore to fix the present amount chargeable to her on account of said interest, the annual rent was to be treated as an annuity, to be computed for so many years as she might be supposed to live, regard being had to her state of health; and the sum so ascertained in gross was to be deducted from the amount of the purchase money paid by her. 5. There being accounts to be taken in the case, so that the property cannot be sold at once, the court should appoint two or more discreet persons to fix a rent upon the house; and if the widow will take it at the rent so fixed, she to pay two-thirds thereof, it should be rented to her; and as the court had funds of hers under its control sufficient to pay the rent, no security should be required of her.

Dower of widow of a vendor assigned in other land in exoneration of land sold. Stimson vs. *Thorn.* In *Stimson* vs. *Thorn*, 25 Grat. 278, it was held that if one who sells land die seized of other real estate on which he in his lifetime, and his widow since his death lived, her dower should be assigned her out of that land in exoneration of the land sold.

When outstanding right of dower should not prevent specific per-formance of a contract of exchange of lands. Stimson vs. Thorn.
T. had contracted with H. for an exchange of land. H. had been in possession of his land for twelve years, and had paid all the purchase money. D. from whom T. had purchased had died, and his widow was entitled to dower in the land proposed by him to be exchanged with H. *Held*, that if the dower estate of D.'s widow were the only defect in the title of H. in the land, such defect was not sufficient to prevent the specific execution of the contract of exchange, but the same might be executed with an allowance of compensation for such defect in the terms prescribed in the Code, ch. 106, § 12, p. 855.

Widow, under a mistake as to her rights under a will, takes land under it and a legacy ; yet, after this permitted to elect and take her dower. Dixon vs. McCue. In *Dixon* vs. *McCue*, 14 Grat., 540, previously cited, p. 51, the widow had taken the whole land under the will for five years, and also a legacy of property to the value of $500, to aid her in carrying on the farm, yet having been under a mistake as to her rights under the will, she was not held to have elected under it, but might still take her dower.

Parties to dower suit : when bill not multifarious. Boyden, &c., vs. *Lancaster.* In *Boyden and wife* vs. *Lancaster,* 2 P. & H. 198, the bill was by a widow to recover lands aliened by the husband during coverture without the relinquishment of the wife. To such a bill the heirs of the husband were not necessary parties, nor any purchasers of the land except the holders when the suit was insti-tuted. In that case the bill was filed against several purchasers of separate and distinct tracts aliened by the husband during the coverture : the bill was not multifarious. The widow might elect to proceed against each separately or all together.

VII.

Additional cases concerning Partition.

See the notes on Partition on pp. 61–71, 575, *ante.*

Commissioner becoming purchaser. Howery vs. Helms. In *How-ery* vs. *Helms,* 20 Grat., 8, cited before, p. 575, the commissioner to sell became the purchaser in fact, though the purchase was nominally by a third person. The court held that the purchase was voidable at the election of any party interested in the land. Some of the parties elected to avoid the sale ; others affirmed it. The entire property was resold (not merely the undivided interests of the parties objecting to the sale), and the court held that the original purchaser was entitled to the shares of the proceeds of the resale, which would otherwise have belonged to those who had elected to affirm the original sale.

Decree in Partition not to be impeached collaterally. Wilson vs. Smith. In *Wilson vs. Smith*, 22 Grat. 493, the court held that a decree under Code of 1860, ch. 124, § 3, (Code 1873, ch. 120, § 3,) could not be impeached in any collateral proceeding except on the ground of fraud or surprise.

Heirs refusing to come in on first division permitted to come in on the second, when the dower property was divided. Persinger vs. Simmons & als. In *Persinger vs. Simmons & als.*, 25 Grat., 238, heirs who had refused to come in on the first division were permitted to come into the partition when land assigned as dower to the widow was divided. In that case it was also held that the surviving husband of one of the heirs was a proper plaintiff in a suit for partition.

After sale made in Partition suit of land in one county, no objection to its sale that if land in another county had been brought in partition in kind could have been made. Frazier vs. Frazier. In *Frazier vs. Frazier*, 26 Grat. 500, the parties to a partition suit owned, besides the land decreed to be sold, other land in another county. It was objected to the sale that if the two tracts were regarded partition in kind could be made and the sale was illegal. The parties did not wish to sell the other tract, which was productive. The court would not sustain the objection after the sale made, and refused to set it aside. In that case the fact that the sale was made for Confederate bonds, which afterwards became worthless, was no ground for setting aside the sale. Nor was it a ground for setting the sale aside that the testimony of the witnesses who testified as to the price offered was confined to the value of the real estate sold and did not embrace certain furniture sold with it, which was not worth more than $2,000 or $2,500 in Confederate money, for this could not have been a material element to charge the estimate of the value of the real property, all agreeing that the purchase money offered was a very high price for the property.

Where a will directed that division of the estate should not be made until certain contingencies had happened, the renunciation of the will by the widow did not authorize the partition before the contingencies occurred. Gregory vs. Gates & als. In *Gregory vs. Gates & als.*, 30 Grat. 83. The testator directed that his estate should be kept together for the support of his wife and children until his widow should marry or die, or until his youngest child should come to the age of twenty-one years. And he directed that a certain sum should be paid to a child who should marry, and thus cease to be supported out of the profits of the estate. The widow renounced the will. *Held*, that this did not authorize a division of the estate, but it was to be kept together until one of the contingencies mentioned in the will occurred.

*What a Partition suit by guardian : right of guardian to institute :
rights of purchaser under a judicial sale. Zirkle vs. McCue.*
In *Zirkle* vs. *McCue & als.*, 26 Grat. 517, the bill was by a widow
against her own infant children and the adult children of her husband by a former wife. The bill stated that the plaintiff was
guardian of her infant children and in her bill the plaintiff set out
her rights and the rights of her children, and prayed for assignment of her dower or commutation, and that the interest of her
infant children should be ascertained and placed under her control
as their guardian, and for full and final adjustment and settlement
of the rights of all parties in the whole estate of the decedent,
real and personal. The court held that the bill was plainly a suit
for assignment of dower and for partition of the realty among the
heirs or a sale, as might be deemed most conducive to the interests
of all; and although the plaintiff did not formally sue as guardian
the averments of the bill were sufficient to bring her before the
court in that character; and that she as guardian had a right to
sue for a partition.

The case is instructive on other points; specially so, as to the
rights of purchasers under judicial sales. The court expressly
waived the decision of the question, whether the title of such
a purchaser is or is not affected by a reversal of the decree
under which the sale is made. That question, say the court,
is still an open question in Virginia. But the court cited with
approval its former decisions, *Parker* vs. *McCoy*, 10 Grat. 594,
605, *Daniel* vs. *Leitch*, 13 Grat. 195, 210, *Walker* vs. *Page*,
21 Grat. 636, 643, in which was manifested a very strong disin-
clination to interfere with the rights of such purchasers, unless
upon palpable and substantial errors in the proceedings and
decrees under which such titles are acquired. And the court held,
that in the case at bar, in which there had been a sale fairly made,
and subsequent confirmation of it, and a conveyance to the purchaser, the purchaser's title should not be disturbed, though the
facts necessary to warrant a sale did not appear from the commissioner's report or by the depositions: it was sufficient that facts
appearing elsewhere in the record warranted the sale.

VIII.

Note on bills of review.

Error on the face of the decree. Whether a bill of review for
error on the face of the decree might be filed without leave of the
court was doubted on page 696, n 4. The question therein mooted
is put at rest by a decision of the Supreme Court of Appeals of
Virginia in the case of *Davis* vs. *Morris's ex'ors*, not yet reported.

In that case the court regard the rule as laid down in *Hilb* vs. *Bowyer*, 18 Grat. 364, 376, cited p. 696 *ante*, that previous leave is necessary to the filing of such a bill. And the court say, whatever may be their conviction of the inconveniences of the rule, they do not feel at liberty now to change it. Burks, J., in *Parker* vs. *Dillard & als.*, 5 Va. L. J., p. 389, defines *error of law apparent on the decree*, as error appearing "in the record, exclusive of the evidence." In *Thompson & als.* vs. *Brooke & als.*, 6 Va. L. J., 42, it was held that on a bill to review a decree on the ground of errors in law, the errors must be such as appear on the face of the decrees, orders and proceedings in the cause, arising on facts either admitted by the pleadings or stated as facts in the decree: and if the errors complained of be errors of judgment in the determination of facts, such errors can only be corrected by appeal.

Bill of review for newly discovered evidence. Upon asking leave to file a petition for a rehearing, or bill of review, on the ground of newly discovered matter, the new matter must be so stated in the bill as to enable the court to see, on inspecting it, that if it had been brought forward it probably would have changed the character of the decree; and it must be so stated that the defendant can answer it understandingly, and thus present a direct issue to the court. It is not sufficient to say that the party asking the leave expects to prove certain facts. He must state the evidence on which he relies distinctly, and file affidavits of witnesses in support of his averments. *Whitten, &c.* vs. *Saunders, &c.*, 6 Va. L. J. 48.

IX.

Note on Interlocutory and final decrees.

On page 506, *ante*, there will be found a collection of cases on this topic. See also *Rawlings's ex'or* vs. *Rawlings & als.*, 5 Virginia L. J., p. 498. In *Ryan's adm'or* vs. *McLeod & others*, 32 Grat., 367, cited *ante*, p. 507, Judge Staples cites and comments on the cases as to interlocutory and final decrees. Judge Baldwin, in *Cocke's adm'or* vs. *Gilpin*, 1 Rob. R., 20, 28, after a review of the cases reaches the conclusion mentioned on p. 505, *ante*. This conclusion was approved by Staples, J., in *Ryan* vs. *McLeod, ubi supra*, and by Burks, J., in *Rawlings's ex'or* vs. *Rawlings & als.*, 5 Va. L. J., pp. 498, 504. See Judge Burks's comment in 5 Va. L. J., p. 507, on Judge Tucker's remark in *Hill's ex'or* vs. *Fox, Adm'or*, 10 Leigh 587, 591, that the decree was interlocutory because an attachment was necessary to enforce it. Such is not understood to be the true criterion of interlocutory decrees. In *Rawlings* vs. *Rawlings* the court held that in a suit for the administration of an estate a decree which settles the principles of the case,

distributes the whole property to the parties entitled, and directs
the payment of the costs, leaving nothing to be done in the cause,
is a final decree, though it may possibly become necessary to resort
to measures to enforce it. See *Thompson & als.* vs. *Brooke & als.,*
6 Va. L. J., 42.

See *Wooding's ex'x* vs. *Bradley's ex'or*, &c., 5 Va. L. J., 765, as
to the power of the court to set aside an interlocutory decree confirming a commissioner's report, when it is clearly shown that the
commissioner's report if carried out would be productive of injustice and wrong.

X.

The doctrine of representation is well illustrated by *Baylor* vs.
Dejarnette, cited on p. 217 ante. *Buck* vs. *Pennybacker*, cited p. 752
ante, illustrates as strongly as any case can, the reluctance of the Court
of Appeals, when a cause has been proceeded in to final decree, to
undo all that has been done, because of a failure to make certain persons defendants, who, strictly speaking, ought to have been parties.
In *Buck* vs. *Pennybacker's ex'ors*, there was an assignment of certain
choses in action to *Buck*, upon trust that he should apply the
moneys collected to the payment of the debts due from *Dickerson*
& Conn, and such debts of *Dickerson & Amis* as *Buck* had in any
way become bound for, and pay the surplus to *Dickerson & Amis,*
or to their order. Afterwards *Dickerson & Amis* drew an order
on *Buck*, requiring him to pay to B. *Pennybacker* $1,533, out of
any moneys that might be in his hands after paying the debt of
Dickerson & Conn and such debts of *Dickerson & Amis* as he was
bound for; and *Buck* accepted this order conditionally. On a bill
by *Pennybacker's ex'ors* against *Buck alone*, an order was made by
consent of the parties referring the accounts to a commissioner.
Dickerson was present at the taking of the accounts in the commissioner's office, and was a witness in the suit. The commissioner's
report shewed that after satisfying all the preferred debts there
was a surplus in *Buck's* hands, applicable to the debt due to
Pennybacker, of $1,060, with interest. Whereupon the court de-
creed that *Buck* should pay that sum to the plaintiffs; and he appealed. In the Court of Appeals the question was whether *Dickerson & Conn* ought not to have been made parties. It was said by
the president, with great force, that if *Dickerson & Conn* should
hereafter sue *Buck*, they might shew that there were yet other
debts due them for which the fund was primarily liable; that in
such case the decree in their favour would be inconsistent with
that in favour of *Pennybacker's ex'ors;* and between the two decrees *Buck* would suffer. But two judges, in a court consisting of
three, affirmed the decree of the court below. They placed their
decision chiefly upon the ground that the *cestuis que trust* provided
for by the assignment, were represented by the trustee.

INDEX.

INDEX.

The References are to the Pages.

B

.C

D

E

(*a*) This form should have a provision for costs similar to that found in the form on p. 598.

F

After the term has expired, the only method of correcting a final

H

(b) See also *Hayes & Wife* vs. *The Mutual Protection Association*, 6 Va. L. J., 152, as to *Husband and Wife; Knick, &c.*, vs. *Knick*, 5 Va. L. J., 579, as to *when party interested, not a party to the contract, a competent* witness; *Kelley* vs. *B'd Pub. Works*, 5 Va. L. J., 279, as to *Corporations.*

Lightning Source UK Ltd.
Milton Keynes UK
UKHW010854060219
336748UK00007B/356/P